AQA Philosophy

Exclusively endorsed by AQA

7/16

Mike Atherton
Chris Cluett
Oliver McAdoo
David Rawlinson
Julian Sidoli
Series editor
Martin Butler

Nelson Thornes

Published in 2008 by:
Nelson Thornes Ltd
Delta Place
27 Bath Road
CHELTENHAM
GL53 7TH
United Kingdom

08 09 10 11 12 / 10 9 8 7 6 5 4 3 2

A catalogue record for this book is available from the British Library

ISBN 978 0 7487 9858 2

Cover photograph/illustration: Getty/Peter Dazeley
Original artworks by Angela Knowles; additional illustrations by Hart McLeod
Page make-up by Hart McLeod, Cambridge

Printed and bound in China by 1010 Printing International Ltd.

The authors and publisher are grateful to the following for permission to reproduce photographs and other copyright material in this book:
p10 ©The New Yorker Collection 1955, Alain, from cartoonbank.com. All rights reserved; p27 ©Ace Stock Limited/Alamy; p75 ©Gianni Dagli Orti/Corbis; p77 ©Photolibrary; p79 ©Mary Evans Picture Library; p90 ©Rex Features; p99 ©Asier Villafranca Velasco/iStockphoto; p100 Hercules and the Centaur Eurytion (bronze) by Giambologna (Giovanni da Bologna, 1529–1608), Museo Nazionale del Bargello, Florence, Italy/The Bridgeman Art Library; p105 The Death of Chatterton, c.1856 (oil on panel), by Henry Wallis (1830–1916), Yale Center fro British Art, Paul Mellon Collection, USA/The Bridgeman Art Library; p109 ©Richard Levine/Alamy; p135–5 extracts from The Republic pp 189–91, 263, translated with an introduction by Desmond Lee (Penguin Classics 1955, 4th edn 2002). Copyright © H. D. P. Lee, 1953, 1974, 1987, 2002; p176 ©Nik Wheeler/Corbis; p186 ©Steve Bell 2006. All rights reserved; p194 ©Jen Sorenson 2006 slowpokecomincs.com; p203 ©Bettmann/Corbis; p207 Sistine Chapel Ceiling, 1508–12: The Creation of Adam, 1511–12 (fresco, post-restoration), by Michelangelo Buonarroti (1475–1564), Vatican Museums and Galleries, Vatican City, Italy/The Bridgeman Art Library; p219 St Jerome Praying (oil on panel) by Hieronymus Bosch (c.1450–1516), Museum voor Schone Kunsten, Ghent, Belgium/The Bridgeman Art Library; p227 (top) ©Rex Features/Paul Brown; p227 (bottom) ©Photoshot/Suzanne Plunkett; p234 (both) by kind permission of N. R. Mann, taken from Glastonbury Tor: A Guide to the History and Legends, Glastonbury, 1993; p252 ©Topfoto/Charles Walker; p268 ©Ronald Grant Archive/Film Four; p269–70 http://news.bbc.co.uk/1/hi/northern_ireland/7029011.stm www.bbc.co.uk, 4 October 2007; p273 © NBC/Photofest; p281 ©Ronald Grant Archive/20th Century Fox; p287 ©Karel Broz/iStockphoto; p354 ©Alamy/Tim Cuff.

Every effort has been made to contact copyright holders and we apologise if any have been overlooked. Should copyright have been unwittingly infringed in this book, the owners should contact the publishers, who will make corrections at reprint.

Contents

AQA introduction

Nelson Thornes and AQA

Nelson Thornes has worked in collaboration with AQA to ensure that this book offers you the best support for your AS or A level course and helps you to prepare for your exams. The partnership means that you can be confident that the range of learning, teaching and assessment practice materials has been checked by the senior examining team at AQA before formal approval, and is closely matched to the requirements of your specification.

Blended learning

Printed and electronic resources are blended: this means that links between topics and activities between the book and the electronic resources help you to work in the way that best suits you, and enable extra support to be provided online. For example, you can test yourself online and feedback from the test will direct you back to the relevant parts of the book.

Electronic resources are available in a simple-to-use online platform called Nelson Thornes learning space. If your school or college has a licence to use the service, you will be given a password through which you can access the materials through any internet connection.

Icons in this book indicate where there is material online related to that topic. The following icons are used:

Learning activity

These resources include a variety of interactive and non-interactive activities to support your learning.

Progress tracking

These resources include a variety of tests that you can use to check your knowledge on particular topics (Test yourself) and a range of resources that enable you to analyse and understand examination questions (On your marks…).

Research support

These resources include WebQuests, in which you are assigned a task and provided with a range of web links to use as source material for research.

When you see an icon, go to Nelson Thornes learning space at www.nelsonthornes.com/aqagce, enter your access details and select your course. The materials are arranged in the same order as the topics in the book, so you can easily find the resources you need.

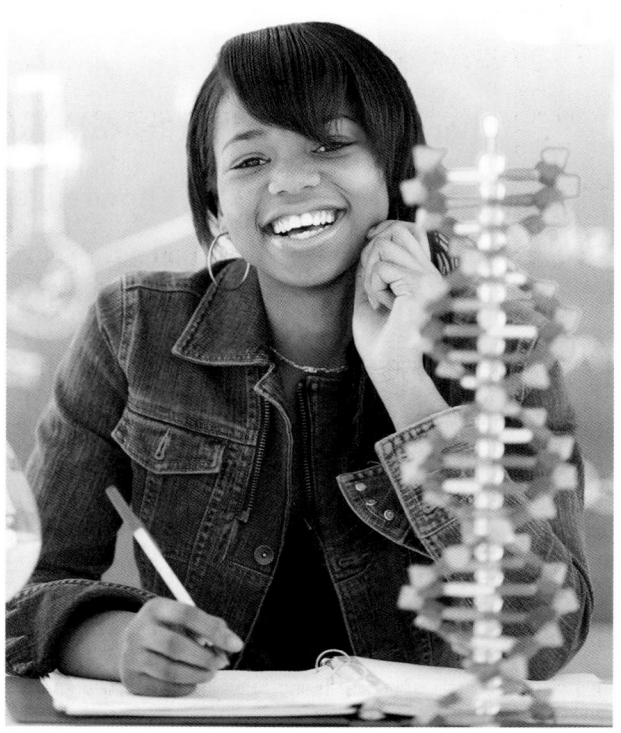

How to use this book

This book covers the specification for your course and is arranged in a sequence approved by AQA.

The book content is divided into five sections – epistemology; questions of value; political philosophy; the philosophy of religion; and mind and metaphysics. The first chapter in each section covers a subject from Unit 1 – An Introduction to Philosophy 1 from the specification. The second chapter in each section covers a subject from Unit 2 – An Introduction to Philosophy 2 from the specification. Each chapter is divided into three topics, which match the divisions in the specification. At the beginning of the book there is a map to specification table so you can see at a glance where to find the information that you need.

The final chapter is an exam skills chapter which talks you through how to use the information that you have learned effectively in the AS examination.

The features in this book include:

Learning objectives

At the beginning of each topic you will find a list of learning objectives that contain targets linked to the requirements of the specification.

▪ Key terms

Terms that you will need to be able to define and understand.

▪ Key philosophers

A short biography of the important people who have contributed to the topic.

▪ Think about

Questions for you to consider, based on what you've just learned.

AQA↗ Examiner's tip

Hints from AQA examiners to help you with your study and to prepare for your exam.

After working through the topic, you should:

At the end of each topic you will find a list of learning outcomes, linked to the learning objectives, which show what you should have learned having worked through the topic.

▪ Summary questions

Short questions that test your understanding of the subject and allow you to apply the skills you have developed.

AQA↗ Examination-style questions

In the exam skills chapter there are questions in the style that you can expect in your AS examination, along with annotated example answers.

AQA examination questions are reproduced by permission of the Assessment and Qualifications Alliance.

▪ Web links in the book

Because Nelson Thornes is not responsible for third party content online, there may be some changes to this material that are beyond our control. In order for us to ensure that the links referred to in the book are as up-to-date and stable as possible, the web sites provided are usually homepages with supporting instructions on how to reach the relevant pages if necessary.

Please let us know at **webadmin@nelsonthornes.com** if you find a link that doesn't work and we will do our best to correct this at reprint, or to list an alternative site.

Map to specification

1 Reason and experience

Mind as a tabula rasa

- to be able to explain Locke's and Hume's accounts of the origin of ideas

- to understand the distinction that Hume makes between 'ideas' and 'impressions'

- to give an account of Hume's method for gaining 'greater clearness and precision in philosophical reasonings'

- to explain the role that 'ideas' play in word meaning, according to Locke and Hume

- to explain how the empiricism of Locke and Hume leads to problems concerning our knowledge of the external world and the use of language as a means of communication

- to be able to articulate arguments for the view that sense impressions are neither necessary nor sufficient for shared ideas.

Key terms

Tabula rasa: this term means 'blank slate' and is used to express the view that at birth the human mind is empty of all ideas and knowledge, and can only be filled through experience.

Where do ideas come from?

Most things that we think about are the everyday objects (e.g. tables and chairs) and events (e.g. having lunch) that make up our daily lives. As our ideas are about such things, it seems reasonable to suppose that our ideas derive from or originate in those things. In fact, is it not because ideas come from these objects and events that our ideas are *about* those specific objects and events and not something else? For instance, the idea of my mother is the idea of *my* mother and not somebody else's, just because the idea originated in my experience of my mother. My mother has left her stamp on my understanding, and my idea of my mother consequently reflects that original experience. Tracing the causal origin of ideas would explain why or how my thoughts and ideas are about the things they are. Where does the causal chain take us if we follow it back? The sense organs are where the world impacts upon our body, presumably causing the processes that lead to our awareness by way of sight, sound, smell, taste and touch. It looks as if our experience of the world is constructed out of the building blocks provided by the senses, presented to us as sensation. So, ideas are constructed from sensation; but presumably they reach further, beyond our awareness or thoughts of these objects and events towards the objects and events themselves.

Locke and Hume on ideas

Let us develop the account that ideas come from sense experience. Locke says:

> Let us then suppose the mind to be, as we say, white paper [**tabula rasa**], void of all characters without any ideas; how comes it to be furnished? Whence comes it by that vast store, which the busy and boundless fancy of man has painted on it with an almost endless variety? Whence has it all the materials of reason and knowledge? To this I answer, in one word, from EXPERIENCE.

Locke (1964, Book 2, chapter 1)

Following Locke, Hume argues that our ideas are *copies* of original sense impressions. My ideas of 'white' and 'cold' are faded copies of sensing white or cold by, for instance, originally seeing and feeling snow. Because my original experience of snow was forceful and vivid, it impressed upon me, like a stamp, a copy of itself. Hume provides a neat argument to show that ideas depend on sense impressions:

> If it happen, from a defect of the organ, that a man is not susceptible of any species of sensation, we always find that he is as little susceptible of the correspondent ideas. A blind man can form no notion of colours; a deaf man of sounds. Restore either of them that sense in which he is deficient; by opening this new inlet for

Key philosophers

John Locke (1632–1704)

One of the most influential English philosophers, who could be described as a founding father of empiricism and also an early psychologist. In *An Essay Concerning Human Understanding* (1690), Locke (1964) grapples with many of the concerns about reason and experience.

David Hume (1711–76)

A Scottish empiricist philosopher and historian best known for his scepticism and atheism. Hume is still very influential in philosophical circles, even amongst those who disagree with him.

> his sensations, you also open an inlet for the ideas; and he finds no difficulty in conceiving these objects.
>
> *Hume (1999, section 2)*

So, based on this view, ideas depend upon sense impressions. Let us interpret this view in the 'strong' sense that *all* ideas depend upon sense impressions, so that I will have an idea *if and only if* I have experienced the corresponding sense impression.

One obvious objection to this strong claim is that, as a counter-example, I have ideas about things I have never experienced. Although it might be true that most of our thinking concerns the everyday objects and events we encounter in our daily lives, this is not always so. For instance, I can imagine a golden mountain, but I have never experienced one. Hume's response is to suggest that because I have experienced gold and I have experienced a mountain, I combine the two simple ideas to form a complex idea – 'a golden mountain'. Unless we can think of ideas that cannot be analysed this way – as either simple or complex – then we should accept the 'strong' claim. Why? Because if you had only experienced gold, but never experienced a mountain, it is not obvious how you could have the idea of 'a golden *mountain*'. We would all have a better idea of 'a golden mountain' if we saw one for ourselves and had the chance to explore it. Hume draws an austere conclusion, that although it appears boundless the imagination:

> is really confined within very narrow limits, and that all this creative power of the mind amounts to no more than the faculty of compounding, transposing, augmenting, or diminishing the materials afforded us by the senses and experience.
>
> *Hume (1999, Section 2)*

Think about

Is Hume right about what can be imagined?

Philosophical method

The implication of Hume's analysis of the idea of a golden mountain is that to really understand 'mountain' I need to have sense impressions of a mountain. Just as the police might construct a profile of a suspect from various eyewitness reports – filling in details here, ignoring this or that feature, stressing prominent characteristics, etc. – so the imagination can build an image of an object or event that we have not yet apprehended in experience, from fragments of evidence. Until the profile has been clarified by encountering the suspect directly, the idea the police have of the suspect might be too elusive for them to fully understand who the criminal is and what happened at the scene of the crime. Likewise, until our ideas are confirmed by sense impressions our apprehension of the reality that our ideas depict will lack the clarity and precision of the sense impressions themselves. So although our cognitive powers are 'confined within very narrow limits' at least we have a method for making exact the content of an idea. Why would we need to do this?

> All ideas, especially abstract ones, are naturally faint and obscure … they are apt to be confounded with other resembling ideas; and when we have often employed any term, though without any distinct meaning, we are apt to imagine it has a determinate idea annexed to it.
>
> *Hume (1999, Section 2)*

This vagueness and confusion is then contrasted with the clarity of sense experience.

On the contrary, all impressions, that is, all sensations … are strong and vivid: the limits between them are more exactly determined: nor is it easy to fall into any error or mistake with regard to them.

Hume (1999, Section 2)

And so we have a method for clarifying ideas: in order to 'reach a greater clearness and precision in philosophical reasonings' all we need do is:

Produce the impressions or original sentiments, from which the ideas are copied. These impressions are all strong and sensible. They admit not of ambiguity. They are not only placed in a full light themselves, but may throw light on their correspondent ideas, which lie in obscurity.

Hume (1999, Section 7, Part 1)

Unless a proposed 'idea' can be tied to experience so that it 'stands for' that experience, then explaining it, or talking about it, produces merely empty words, just as a painting that in no way resembles an object might be dismissed as merely meaningless abstraction. Words without reference to experience are senseless, because they signify no idea. Because, as Locke explains:

words in their primary or immediate signification, stand for nothing but the ideas in the mind of him that uses them

Locke (1964, Book 3, Chapter 11)

Without the required corresponding idea, words would just be meaningless noises, marks on paper or patterns on a screen.

And so when we come across some highly abstract, obscure 'idea' that has no corresponding impression, 'this will serve to confirm our suspicion' that the proposed 'idea' is bogus. A police profile that fails to match any possible suspect is not really a profile of a suspect at all. Hume employs this method when he analyses the idea of 'a time during which nothing happens'. If time is something that is independent of things changing – if time is real or substantial – then this implies there could be a time during which nothing happens. If we can entertain the idea that there could be a time during which nothing happens, we would establish that substantial time is at least a logical possibility, just because it is thinkable. Hume applies his new method of checking ideas against sense impressions and comes to the conclusion that although you might think you are reflecting philosophically about a time during which nothing happens, it turns out upon analysis that because the idea of such a time 'does not arise from an impression of sensation … you may be certain you are mistaken, when you imagine you have any such idea' (Hume, 1969). Hume says that metaphysical 'ideas' that speculate about a reality beyond or behind our experience are 'nothing but sophistry and illusion'.

So far we have focused on the empiricist account of the acquisition of ideas and the implications this account has regarding the limits of thought. Hume sums up what has been described as 'empiricism about ideas' when he says it is:

impossible for us so much as to conceive or form an idea of any thing specifically different from ideas and impressions … we never really advance a step beyond ourselves, nor can conceive of any kind of existence, but those perceptions, which have appeared in that narrow compass.

Hume (1969)

> **Think about**
>
> Does Locke's suggestion seem reasonable? Why?

> **Think about**
>
> Can you think where this method could help?

But at least, more positively, we have identified a method for analysing ideas into their simple constituents, clarifying them and distinguishing between those ideas that have substance or make sense and those that do not. If we could return ideas to their original sense impressions then the disagreements and disputes characteristic of philosophy, but also familiar enough from everyday life, could be dissolved as the 'facts speak for themselves' – just as the police can solve a mystery by matching a suspect's profile to the indisputable facts present at the crime scene.

> If the doors of perception were cleansed, everything would appear to a man as it is

William Blake (1977)

Setting up in business

Locke and Hume are often called empiricists (from the Greek word *empeiria*, meaning 'experience') because they stress that experience is the source, the limit and the benchmark of our ideas. This focus on experience is thus called empiricism.

R. F. Holland characterises empiricism in the following way:

> To set up in business an individual only has to be exposed to the elements with his senses unshuttered. Experience will then print its marks upon his mind as upon 'white paper' ... The imprinted marks or ideas are simple and separate, but operations are performed on them to form complex and abstract ideas. Every mind is a complete and independent factory, where raw materials enter, are processed and emerge cut and dried. And when at the end each mind's eye surveys the products of its own efforts ... the results will be found to coincide with those of the rest, as though by pre-established harmony

Holland (1980)

Think about

Consider what you have read regarding the account of ideas put forward by Locke and Hume.

How convincing is Holland's characterisation? Why?

Examiner's tip

When answering exam questions avoid expressions such as 'Locke claims we are born as blank slates *because* he was an empiricist ...' Remember that Locke and Hume do not argue in the way that they do because they are empiricists. Rather, because they argue as they do, other people have called them empiricists. What matters philosophically are their arguments, not the label, although the label might sometimes be useful shorthand.

Criticisms of Locke and Hume on ideas

We are now going to look at some powerful criticisms of Locke and Hume on ideas. These criticisms lead to the conclusion that, as we have understood it, empiricism fails. It fails because sense impressions cannot be the basis of our understanding of the world. These criticisms have their responses, but they are beyond the scope of this chapter. However, even the critics agree that the following arguments are something to reckon with. Thinking about them will give you an insight into the way philosophy works as much as what philosophers have said.

The external world

Empiricists who hold sense data theories will have difficulty in claiming to have knowledge of the external world when all they are directly of are sense data. However, it should be realised that not all empiricists hold the same sense data theory. Above we supposed that ideas are constructed from sense impressions, but presumably reach further out beyond our awareness or thoughts of these objects and events towards the objects and events themselves. This presumption turns out to be unsupportable according to empiricism itself:

> It is a question of fact, whether the perceptions of the senses be produced by external objects, resembling them: how shall this question be determined? By experience surely; as all other questions

of a like nature. But here experience is, and must be entirely silent. The mind has never anything present to it but the perceptions, and cannot possibly reach any experience of their connexion with objects. The supposition of such a connexion is, therefore, without any foundation in reasoning.

Hume (1999, Section 12, Part 1)

So empiricism leaves us with two unanswerable questions:

- Is there an external world, beyond sense impressions, at all?
- Even if there is, in what way could our ideas be said to reflect that external reality? (This issue is dealt with in detail in chapter 2.)

Communication

Empiricism, or any theory which regards sense data or ideas as the immediate object of perception, will have difficulty in explaining the possibility of sharing ideas.

First, we take it for granted that I cannot have your sense impressions; you cannot have my sense impressions. If I experience a sense impression then it would be, say, how the tree appears to me or how the food tastes to me; it cannot be something that you could have. Second, let us get the order of priority right. Words stand for ideas. Ideas stand for sense impressions. Sense impressions (after scepticism) stand for themselves. Therefore, any meaning words have derived from the sense impression they stand for. Now we have our problem. My words stand for my sense impressions (which you cannot have) and your words stand for your sense impressions (which I cannot have). So, because words track back their meaning to exclusive sense impressions, we never mean the same thing when we think we are communicating – we cannot mean the same thing. This shows that empiricism is absurd.

What do you see?

The German illustrator Ludwig Richter relates how he and his friends, all young art students in the 1820s, visited the famous beauty spot of Tivoli and sat down to draw. They looked with surprise, but hardly with approval, at a group of French artists who approached the place with enormous baggage, carrying large quantities of paint which they applied to the canvas with big, coarse brushes. The Germans, perhaps roused by this self confident artiness, were determined on the opposite approach. They selected the hardest, best-pointed pencils, which could render the motif firmly and minutely to its finest detail, and each bent down over his small piece of paper, trying to transcribe what he saw with the utmost fidelity. 'We fell in love with every blade of grass, every tiny twig, and refused to let anything escape us. Everyone tried to render the motif as objectively as possible'.

Nevertheless, when they compared the fruits of their efforts in the evening, their transcripts differed to a surprising extent. The mood, the colour, even the outline of the motif had undergone a subtle transformation in each of them … these different versions reflected the different dispositions of the four friends, for instance, how the melancholy painter had straightened the exuberant contours and emphasized the blue tinges. We might say he gives an illustration of the famous definition by Emile Zola, who called a work of art 'a corner of nature seen through a temperament'.

Gombrich (2002)

> How did the artists' attitudes impact on what they saw?
>
> How might the artists' equipment impact on the way they *looked at* the beauty spot?
>
> Could the artists have produced a more objective rendering of the motif if they had taken photographs?
>
> Could the artists have rendered their experience of the motif so that it was neutral – as if it were a view 'from nowhere' or 'everywhere', rather than a view from somewhere in particular?
>
> Were the artists transcribing the same scene? Would you know it was 'the same scene' just by looking at the drawings and paintings? What do we mean by 'the same scene'?

Suppose there are five artists. We shall take it for granted that they drew their impressions perfectly, so that any differences between their paintings were not due to a lack of technique. What is the idea of Tivoli? It is a copy, in this case a drawing. But there are five different drawings. The drawing, copy or idea of Tivoli is something different for each artist.

Solipsism

Thinking our ideas are ultimately about the sense impressions from which they derive can lead to the following conclusions:

■ the external world might not exist and even if it did it is unknowable, and

■ I can never share ideas with others, neither can they share with me. I appear to be completely self-contained.

As Milton puts it in *Paradise Lost* 'the mind is its own place and in itself'. So the world I experience and the ideas that I have are dependent upon and inseparable from me – the only world I can know is my world. This position is known as solipsism. F. H. Bradley describes the situation like this:

> My external sensations are no less private to myself than are my thoughts and feelings. In either case my experience falls within my own circle, a circle closed on the outside.

Bradley (2003)

So empiricism can take us a long way from common sense, as the world and its content implodes into me. What I am always really thinking about is me. Certainly there is something preposterous about solipsism and the fact that it is implicit in empiricism counts against the attempt to derive reality from mere sense impressions; this strategy seems to be the root of the problem.

Let us return to the world of mind-independent objects and events where persons communicate with one another, sharing ideas.

Sense impressions are not necessary for ideas

Ideas are supposed to be copies of sense impressions. Without sense impressions there can be no copies of sense impressions. But should we accept that ideas copy sense impressions? Is it helpful to see things this way? We have already seen that thinking of ideas as copies of exclusive sense impressions leads to the conclusion that we never share ideas. That is one strong reason for not accepting the claim that ideas are copies of sense impressions. Let us turn the issue on its head. If we do share ideas then the ideas we share cannot be 'stand ins' for exclusive sense impressions – exclusive sense impressions can play no part in the exchange of ideas.

> Suppose everyone had a box with something in it: we call it a 'beetle'. No one can look into anyone else's box, and everyone says he knows what a beetle is only by looking at his beetle. – Here it would be quite possible for everyone to have something different in his box. One might even imagine such a thing constantly changing. But suppose the word 'beetle' had a use in these people's language? – If so it would not be used as the name of a thing. The thing in the box has no place in the language-game at all; not even as a something: for the box might even be empty. – No, one can 'divide through' by the thing in the box; it cancels out whatever it is.
>
> *Wittgenstein* (1968)

Key philosopher

Ludwig Wittgenstein (1889–1951)

Wittgenstein was a Viennese philosopher who studied under Russell and taught at the University of Cambridge. Widely regarded as one of the most important philosophers of the 20th century, he published only one book during his lifetime: *Tractatus Logico-Philosophicus* (1981). Of the many posthumously published writings, by far the most important is his *Philosophical Investigations* (1968).

Here is a simple test:

Fig. 1.1 *Select the grey patch*

If you understand English you will select the third patch from the left. In fact, this exercise could be used to test your understanding of the word 'grey'. Suppose someone insists that between the incoming patch and the outward expression of the idea – 'that (pointing) patch is grey' – there must be an intermediate sense impression. We have already seen why we do not want to say that this intermediate sense impression is what your idea of grey is about, because it makes communication impossible. Like 'the thing in the box' in Wittgenstein's example, the intermediate sense impression appears to play no role in our shared idea of 'grey'. So what job is this intermediate sense impression supposed to do?

There is a distinction to be made between understanding the meaning of something and the having of mental pictures. It is possible to do the former without the latter. Descartes made this point with his reference to complex geometric figures. We can understand what a chiliagon or myriogon is without being able to form a mental picture of either. Therefore understanding does not consist of having mental pictures. It is possible to lack the facility for forming mental pictures completely and still be able to understand.

> Much to my astonishment, I found that the great majority of men of science to whom I first applied protested that mental imagery was unknown to them ... Men who declare themselves entirely deficient in the power of seeing mental pictures can nevertheless give life-like descriptions of what they have seen, and can otherwise express themselves as if they were gifted with a vivid imagination. They can also become painters of the rank of Royal Academicians.
>
> *Galton* (2000)

And although, in accordance with my custom of always making use of my imagination when I think of corporeal things, it may come about that, in conceiving a chiliagon, I picture confusedly to myself some figure, yet it is very evident that this figure is not a chiliagon, since it differs in no way from the figure which I would picture if I thought of a myriogon or any other many-sided figure, and since it in no way serves for the discovery of the properties which constitute the difference between a chiliagon and other polygons.

Descartes (1968, Meditation 6)

But, in a way, everyone might agree that sense impressions are necessary for ideas, if 'sense impression' is just a way of saying 'experience' as that is commonly understood. Perhaps seeing, hearing, touching, tasting and smelling are like triggers that switch on the mind or its various faculties. So saying that experience is necessary for ideas in this sense does not imply that all ideas are copies of sense impressions. It could be that the person already possesses ideas that are not engaged until the appropriate triggers have been activated. Leibniz says something similar about innate ideas in relation to experience:

I have taken as an illustration a block of veined marble, rather than a wholly uniform block or blank tablets, that is to say what is called *tabula rasa* in the language of the philosophers. For if the soul were like those blank tablets, truths would be in us in the same way as the figure of Hercules is in a block of marble, when the marble is completely indifferent whether it receives this or some other figure. But if there were veins in the stone which marked out the figure of Hercules rather than other figures, this stone would be more determined thereto, and Hercules would be as it were in some manner innate in it, although labour would be needed to uncover the veins, and to clear them by polishing, and by cutting away what prevents them from appearing. It is in this way that ideas and truths are innate in us.

Leibniz (1996a)

Whether the understanding is more like a *blank tablet* or *veined marble* is a central issue in psychology and linguistics and the focus of research. But both sides agree that even if it is true that unless you have activated your senses you cannot have ideas, this is too general a truth to support the empiricist claim that the mind contains no innate ideas.

Here is another argument that sense impressions cannot be necessary for ideas. We understand that amongst all things, some things can be either red or yellow. If it is red then it is not yellow, and if it is either red or yellow then it is coloured. Notions like 'all', 'some', 'if', 'then', 'is', 'is not', 'either', 'or' and 'so' seem essential for formulating ideas, categorising and giving reasons. But these logical connectives do not seem to find a corresponding sense impression. The same applies to numbers.

The role of words

it is plain that every word we speak is in some degree a diminution of our lungs by corrosion, and consequently, contributes to the shortening of our lives. An expedient was therefore offered … that, since words are only names for things, it would be more convenient for all men to carry about them such things as were necessary to express a particular business they are to discourse on. And this invention would certainly have taken place, to the great ease as well as health of the subject, if the women, in conjunction with the vulgar and illiterate, had not threatened to raise a rebellion, unless they might be allowed to speak with their tongues, after the manner of their forefathers; such constant irreconcilable enemies to science are the common people. However, many of the most learned and wise adhere to the new scheme of expressing themselves by things, which only has this inconvenience attending it, that if a man's business be very great, and of various kinds, he must be obliged, in proportion, to carry a greater bundle of things upon his back, unless he can afford one or two strong servants to attend him. I have often beheld two of these sages almost sinking under the weight of their packs, like pedlars among us; who, when they meet in the street, would lay down their loads, open their sacks, and hold conversation for an hour together, then put up their implements, help each other to resume their bundles, and take their leave.

But for short conversations, a man may carry implements in his pockets, and under his arms, enough to supply him: and in his house he cannot be at a loss. Therefore the room where company meet who practise this art is full of all things, ready at hand, requisite to furnish matter for this kind of artificial converse.

Another great advantage proposed by this invention was, that it would serve as a universal language, to be understood in all civilised nations, whose goods and utensils are generally of the same kind, or nearly resembling, so that their uses might easily be comprehended. And thus ambassadors would be qualified to treat with foreign princes, or ministers of state, to whose tongues they were utter strangers.

Swift (2003)

In the above passage Jonathan Swift is ridiculing the assumption that words gain their meaning simply by naming things. We might note that the objects that Swift's characters carry about with them as the bearers of word meaning are at least public and can be apprehended by more than one mind, unlike the 'ideas' that Locke claims as the 'signification' of words.

The assumption that *all* words act simply as labels for things, whether they are public or private things, has been rejected by most modern philosophers. Instead, the notion of a 'concept' is used. Rather than being private mental entities, concepts can be regarded more like sets of abilities that allow language users to employ relevant words correctly. Having the concept of grey, for example, means being able to pick out grey items and correctly apply the term 'grey'.

Think about

Read the quote from Wittgenstein about the beetle in the box on p7. Why does 'the thing in the box' cancel out?

Listen to someone speaking for a minute. Note down any images that are set off in your mind while you listen. Do you think you could have understood the speaker without these images? Did the images help or hinder your understanding?

Identify evidence for the view that experience merely acts as a 'trigger' which activates an innate capacity to speak language, as opposed to the claim that we are linguistic 'blank slates' when born. (By 'language' we do not mean a specific language like English or French but any language.)

What is the difference between an innate capacity and an innate idea?

Sense impressions are not sufficient for ideas

Fig. 1.2 *What everyone sees?*

According to Holland, empiricists maintain that experience alone can produce ideas. Hume's example of the person whose restored sight causes him to acquire colour ideas would seem to confirm Holland's interpretation. Here are some reasons for thinking that merely experiencing sense impressions is not sufficient for acquiring ideas.

First, consider what we all know about learning. It seems to involve more than just having experiences. Most learning involves teachers – not only school teachers, but family, friends, role models and so on. These teachers, more or less explicitly, pose questions, draw attention, make distinctions, offer analogies and follow connections, show, demonstrate, describe and define, explain, interpret, evaluate, drill, guide, etc. Teachers are people whose judgement we trust, all things being equal. That human learning involves so much teaching is surely a remarkable fact about human beings. The suggestion that teaching is surplus to requirements because sense impressions alone could have done the work goes against what we all know about learning.

Wittgenstein says:

> Isn't it experience that teaches us to judge like this, that it is correct to judge like this? But how does experience teach us, then? We may derive it from experience, but experience does not direct us to derive anything from experience.

Wittgenstein (1977, paragraph 130)

Suppose someone said 'This is tove' whilst holding up a pencil. If sense impressions are sufficient for acquiring ideas you should acquire the idea of tove from your sense impression of the pencil. But the sense impressions are not sufficient because 'This is tove' could mean any one of the following:

Think about

What could you learn on your own?

'This is a pencil'
'This is round'
'This is wood'
'This is one'
'This is hard'

Wittgenstein (1958, p2)

Nothing about the experience itself teaches us how we should judge it. Wittgenstein makes the point that sense impressions cannot determine how we ought to interpret them. If we think of sense impressions as images then it is tempting to think that the correct interpretation is somehow compelled by the image itself:

> I see a picture; it represents an old man walking up a steep path leaning on a stick. – How? Might it not have looked just the same if he had been sliding downhill in that position? Perhaps a Martian would describe the picture so.

Wittgenstein (1968)

Why would a Martian describe it differently? Understanding an idea, interpreting an experience, drawing conclusions, etc. does not, as the empiricist picture implies, occur in a social vacuum. Rather, learning presupposes a 'stage setting' or context. This stage setting could include all sorts of local social conventions, but it might also point to typical innate learning strategies employed by humans:

> Experiments show that one-and-a-half-year-old babies are not associationists who connect overlapping events indiscriminately. They are intuitive psychologists who psych out other people's intentions before copying what they do. When an adult first exposes a baby to a word, as in 'That's a toma,' the baby will remember it as the name of the toy the adult was looking at at the time, not as the name of the toy the baby herself was looking at. If an adult fiddles with a gadget but indicates that the action was an accident (by saying 'Whoops'), a baby will not even bother trying to imitate him. But if the adult does the same thing but indicates that he intended the action, the baby will imitate him. And when an adult tries and fails to accomplish something (like trying to press the button on a buzzer, or trying to string a loop around a peg), the baby will imitate what the adult tried to do, not what he did do.

Pinker (2002)

So ideas are not acquired by merely opening 'an inlet for … sensation' as Hume suggests. We learn from others who we *see as* thinkers like us. Descartes says:

> If I chance to look out of a window on to men passing in the street, I do not fail to say, on seeing them, that I see men … and yet, what do I see from this window, other than hats and cloaks, which can cover ghosts or dummies who move only by means of springs? But I judge them to be really men, and thus I understand, by the sole power of judgement which resides in my mind, what I believe I saw with my eyes.

Descartes (1968, Meditation 2)

We shall come back to what we can know and understand 'by the sole power of judgement that resides in my mind' when we discuss innate knowledge.

Think about

There are two issues: (a) whether all ideas ultimately derive from sense experience and (b) whether knowledge requires more than the inputting of sense impressions. Which one do you think that Wittgenstein is talking about?

Think about

What is the stage setting for learning to play the guitar?

Think about

Do you think that Descartes has downplayed the role of the senses? He 'judges' people to be under the hats and coats but he could only know that there are such things in the first place from sensory information. His 'judgements' relate to past *experiences*.

The empiricist method

The recommended method of returning ideas back to their original sense impressions appeared straightforward: like the familiar practice of using an example to clarify or display our understanding; where we learn through, and show our grasp of ideas by, selecting samples. For instance, suppose you have just begun working on a building site. The foreman calls out 'Fetch the pick axe'. You have a faint and obscure idea that a pick axe is something like a hammer, but you do not know precisely what a pick axe is. How would you find out? You would ask the foreman and he would select an example – 'This is a pick axe' – draw attention to its characteristic features and explain what it does and so on. Then you would understand what a pick axe is, and you could show this by picking another pick axe out as an example, or by explaining what jobs a pick axe could be used for. The foreman would then confirm your understanding or correct it. But this is not like the situation that Hume describes where the sample you are going to use to exemplify the idea is an inner object of attention, accessible only to you; a sense impression. There, you must ask the questions, select the samples, provide explanations and correct and confirm your understanding alone. But if you are the learner and the teacher then does the idea of 'getting it right' have any application?

As sense impressions are neither necessary nor sufficient for having an idea, then it is difficult to see what role they could play in clarifying faint or obscure ideas. Whether the third patch from the left really is grey is not something I can establish by attending to my exclusive sense impressions. We saw that, if exclusive sense impressions were the source from which ideas derived their content, we could never share ideas. But we do share ideas; and so exclusive sense impressions cannot be the source from which ideas derive their content. Sense impressions cannot themselves guide judgement or determine how we take them. Rather, what an idea is about can only be understood in the context of the social practices (formal and informal) of teaching and learning, where my understanding of an idea can be fostered, assessed and modified. If I am going to clarify whether the third patch from the left really is grey, I need to ask you. So the nature of teaching and the matter being learned can only be understood in the broader context of a shared way of life.

> What determines our judgement, our concepts and reactions, is not what one man is doing now, an individual action, but the whole hurly-burly of human actions, the background against which we see any action.

Wittgenstein (1967, paragraph 567)

> Knowing is a kind of being which belongs to being-in-the-world.

Heidegger (1978, p88)

As ideas are shared and passed on by a community of thinkers, ideas can only be exemplified and acquired, our grasp assessed and our understanding corrected if, in principle, those ideas are about a world accessible to that community. By thinking of ideas as copies of exclusive sense impressions Locke and Hume missed this point. That there are other thinkers who experience objects and events as I do appears to be a precondition of having ideas at all; that is, not something I might or might not learn through merely opening up an inlet to sensation.

Think about

What does learning by doing mean?

After working through this topic, you should:

- understand that, according to the early empiricists, all of our ideas originate in experience
- comprehend how Hume's 'copy principle' allows him to check the validity of philosophical ideas
- know how the assumptions made by the early empiricists about the nature of experience seem to cut us off from knowledge of the external world and threaten solipsism
- realise how assumptions about the private nature of our ideas made by the early empiricists fail to explain our ability to communicate through language
- understand that sense impressions are neither necessary nor sufficient for the acquisition of ideas.

 Examiner's tip

Remember that in an exam, criticisms of one philosophical position can sometimes be used to support an opposing one. Therefore, some of the criticisms of the view that we are born as blank slates and ideas arise merely from the exposure to sense impressions, could be used to support the opposite view, i.e. that the mind is active from the beginning, or must at least have some innate ideas that allow it to make sense of experience.

Innate knowledge

Learning objectives:

- to understand the role that the intellect plays in allowing the mind to make sense of experience
- to understand how the rationalist's approach to knowledge was shaped by the role that mathematics plays in scientific explanations of the world
- to understand the central place that rationalism gives to a priori knowledge and our innate rational capacities
- to understand Descartes' conception of the role of God as guaranteeing the correctness of our innate understanding of the world

Introduction

So, sense impressions are not sufficient for the acquisition of ideas. Rather, in order to learn from what I see, taste, touch, hear or smell, I must draw on what is already understood by me or by others. But what if 'what is already understood' distorts my ideas or misleads me in some way? For instance, a detective trying to solve a crime has to have a clear idea about all of the events leading up to the crime and how they are related. If the detective gets the wrong idea – perhaps because false assumptions distort their view of things – then the detective will be misled about what really occurred. Conversely, if they have a clear idea about all of the events leading up to the crime and how they are related then they will discover the truth. Perhaps, like the detective, if we can get a clear idea about objects and events and how they relate then we will also know the truth. But what does getting a clear idea about something involve? (This might also depend on what it is a clear idea of.) As we have argued, it can never be just a matter of experiencing sense impressions. Consider an artist who has a similar problem: the artist wants to represent things as they are, but how? Jonathan Richardson responds:

> no man sees what things are, that knows not what they ought to be. That this maxim is true, will appear by an academy figure drawn by one ignorant in the structure, and knitting of the bones, and anatomy, compared with another who understands these thoroughly ... Both see the same life, but with different eyes.

Gombrich (2002)

- to recognise that rationalism underplays the role of experimentation in our knowledge of the world

- to recognise that both Hume and the rationalists understood that general laws of nature could not be justified by experience alone

- to gain an understanding of Hume's Fork and his attack on the view that a priori knowledge of the world is possible

- to understand Hume's psychological account of the feeling of necessity that we have when we observe events linked by the cause/effect relationship.

So seeing what things are depends on knowing about 'the structure, the knitting of the bones, and anatomy', and on knowing how things 'ought to be'.

If this is right then it is not surprising that students of life drawing will often study anatomy. In order to gain an accurate representation of the human form they use their *understanding* as well as their eyes.

Rationalism: the primacy of reason

Suppose it is the late 1630s and you start to think about the sun: what is it? Like the detective you need a clear idea of the sun if you are going to understand it. Perhaps most people's idea of the sun is something 'extremely small' that passes across the sky every day. But if you have been educated you will have a more sophisticated idea. You will have learned that the sun is a heavenly body that orbits the earth above the sphere of the moon. We now know that both of these ideas were misleading. Such ideas 'based on such insecure principles could only be most doubtful and uncertain' (Descartes, 1968). Descartes was in this position in the late 1630s, thinking about the sun. Descartes was certain that the sun was not extremely small, but 'several times larger than the whole earth'. Nor was it a heavenly body orbiting the earth above the sphere of the moon, as his 'former opinions' led him to believe. Descartes had a better idea of the sun 'based upon the reasons of astronomy'. Unlike the confused ideas that had so far misled Descartes, the ideas grasped through 'the reasons of astronomy' were perfectly rational.

According to Descartes' contemporary, the scientist and astronomer, Galileo:

> The real world is the world of bodies in mathematically reducible motions, and this means that the real world is a world of bodies moving in space and time.

Trusted (1994)

And so the only way to read nature and penetrate the phenomena is through 'the language in which it is written – the language of mathematics'. The idea that there is a deep relationship between reality and mathematics is an old one. For instance, the medieval philosopher Roger Bacon claimed:

> Mathematics is the door and the key to the sciences … For the things of this world cannot be made known without a knowledge of mathematics.

Bacon (2002)

But Galileo reveals the details of this deep relationship as he uses it to illuminate the world around him. In a famous experiment using an inclined plane consisting of 'a wooden moulding' with a specially polished channel, Galileo demonstrates that the velocity of a falling body – in this case 'a hard, smooth, and very round bronze ball' – is proportionate to the time it has been falling, measured by a water clock. The experimenter carefully records time and distance before concluding:

> we always found that the spaces traversed were to each other as the squares of the times, and this was true for all inclinations of the plane.

Galileo (1967)

The experiment is organised to capture any changes that occur to the ball's spatial and temporal location; so what matters is 'mathematically reducible motion'. The experiment shows that in order to calculate distance, 'time taken' is the only relevant variable; weight of ball and degree of incline have no effect. Organising the experiment like this subtracts from the measurement any effects caused by the kind of friction a ball would typically encounter if it rolled down a slope in normal circumstances. The ball comes to represent a universal abstraction, a falling body, the behaviour of which, on the incline, can be expressed in a simple formula:

$$d \propto t^2$$

The world discovered by mathematically reducible motions is not the disjointed and transient world of particular sense impressions described by Hume:

> where several perceptions successively make their appearance; pass, re-pass, glide away, and mingle in an infinite variety of postures and situations.

Hume (1969)

Rather, the real world is the world of moving bodies expressed mathematically. Descartes claims he knows this **a priori** and shows it by considering his idea of a stone. He classes the variable properties of 'hardness', 'colour', 'heaviness' and 'heat' as merely accidental properties belonging to the idea of a stone. The essence of an idea of a stone is nothing more than 'something extended in length, breadth and depth' (Descartes, 1985). The essence of a stone is identical to the essence of a falling body. The essence of physical things is being a mathematically conceivable object extended in space. So Descartes thinks he knows, simply by thinking about it, the essence of bodies, the behaviour of which is described by Galileo using the language of mathematics: the exercise of pure reason.

Descartes reinforced the point with his consideration of the wax, e.g. in *Meditations II*. Here he appeals to a transformation which involves a change in *all* the sense given qualities. A piece of wax is removed from the hive and is melted and becomes liquid. We would still say this was the same wax even though all the sense-given properties have changed. The only property that remains the same is that of extension in space. Descartes concludes that extension in space is the essential nature of the wax. Given that the property of extension is studied by geometry and geometry is purely a priori, it follows that we can have a priori knowledge of the wax. This applies to all physical objects and is rationalism in its most extreme form. Descartes also said that the melted wax can adopt an infinite amount of different shapes. As the concept of infinity is grasped by the mind not the senses, he claimed that we could know the wax through an intuition of the mind.

So Descartes regards the new science as exhibiting a method for truth rooted in mathematics and a priori reflection and abstraction. Descartes' analysis of the idea of a chiliagon showed him that he could conceive of objects independently of being able to sense or imagine them. Unlike the intermingled and confused ideas delivered by the senses and imagination, innate ideas are clear and distinct and present the idea of a chiliagon precisely. Just as the detective needs a clear idea about the events leading up to a crime, Descartes is seeking ideas so 'transparently clear and at the same time so simple that we cannot ever think of them without believing them to be true' (Descartes, 1968). What is it like to just 'see' purely intellectually that something must be true? Spinoza sets the following exercise, finding the 'fourth proportional'. Take three numbers:

1, 2, 3

and complete the following:

1 is to 2 as 3 is to …

💡 Key terms

A priori: knowledge that is known independently of experience. For example, once I understand the statement 'no object can be red and green all over at the same time', I recognise that it *must* be true. There is no need to check through observation or experimentation. Innate knowledge will be known a priori.

■ Think about

Think back to the earlier quote regarding Descartes looking at people out of the window and ask yourself whether the wax example makes the same mistake?

■ Think about

Can you think of examples where you just know something immediately?

Spinoza comments that:

> given the numbers 1, 2, and 3 no one fails to see that the proportional number is 6 – and we see this … clearly because we derive the fourth number from the very ratio which we see at one glance obtains between the first and the second.

Spinoza (1985)

And this innate rational capacity to grasp ideas purely intellectually and work with them is crucial in science. As Leibniz explains:

> a corpuscle hundreds of thousands times smaller than any bit of dust which flies through the air, together with other corpuscles of the same subtlety, can be dealt with by reason as easily as can a ball by the hand of a player.

Leibniz (1996a)

To really understand the essence of a thing, free from confusion, I have to conceive it using my intellect alone; just like a mathematical idea. So:

> bodies are not really perceived by the senses or the imaginative faculty, but only by the intellect; that they are perceived, not by being touched or seen, but by being understood.

Descartes (1968, Meditation 2)

Returning to the late 1630s, Descartes reflects on his idea of the sun, or rather two ideas of the sun. There is the misleading idea of the sun as he has experienced it – as something 'extremely small' – and there is his mathematical idea of the sun which is:

> drawn … from certain notions born with me … Certainly these two ideas which I conceive the sun cannot both resemble the same sun, and reason makes me believe that the idea which derives immediately from its appearance is the one which is most dissimilar.

Descartes (1968, Meditation 3)

Why prefer the idea conceived intellectually? The physicist, Paul Dirac says:

> It is more important to have beauty in one's equations than to have them fit experiment … because the discrepancy may be due to minor features that are not properly taken into account and that will get cleared up with further developments of the theory … It seems that if one is working from the point of view of getting beauty in one's equations, and if one has really a sound insight, one is on a sure line of progress.

Dirac (1963)

But how do you know if you have sound insight? You might argue that because the universe is by its very nature essentially expressible in beautiful equations, your theory is approximating to a true description of reality as it also exhibits a similar beauty.

> The beauty in the laws of physics is the fantastic simplicity that they have … What is the ultimate machinery behind it all? That's surely the most beautiful of all

Wheeler (1979)

But although deep, as it stands, this conviction that the universe is intrinsically intelligible to reason is only an assumption. In contrast, Descartes is certain there is a necessary symmetry between his innate understanding and the real structure of the universe – so that he is able to understand how the universe ought to be:

> I noticed certain laws which God has so established in nature, and of which he has implanted such notions in our minds, that after adequate reflection we cannot doubt that they are exactly observed in everything which exists or occurs in the world.

Descartes (1968)

And Leibniz said:

> The beauty of the universe could be learnt in each soul, could one unravel all its folds … Each soul knows the infinite, but confusedly. Just as when I walk along the shore of the sea, and hear the great noise it makes … so our confused perceptions are the result of the impressions which the whole universe makes on us.

Leibniz (1996b)

How do we know God sustains this symmetry? According to Descartes:

> Every clear and distinct perception is undoubtedly something real and positive, and hence cannot come from nothing, but must necessarily have God for its author. Its author, I say, is God, who is supremely perfect, and who cannot be a deceiver on pain of contradiction; hence the perception is undoubtedly something true.

Descartes (1968, Meditation 4)

Spinoza is more radical. The order we read in nature is an attribute of an immanent God, for 'whatever is, is in God'. So everything, including ourselves, is an aspect, or 'part of the infinite intellect of God' (1985); everything is an all-embracing oneness, exhibited through different aspects.

Think about

Why do you think that a scientific description of the world can be expressed so neatly and elegantly using mathematical formulae? Is mathematics 'imposed' on nature by us or is it just 'in' the nature of things?

Try to describe what it would be like if the motion of everyday objects could not be reduced to a set of fixed laws.

Which of the following statements can be known as a priori?

■ Parallel lines can never meet.
■ All sounds have a pitch.
■ All swans are white.
■ Every event has a cause.
■ People need water to live.
■ Space has three dimensions.
■ Time moves forward.
■ 2 is to 4 as 4 is to 8.

Criticisms of rationalism

Necessity and the a priori

Descartes' ambition to develop, through the exercise of reason, a mathematical a priori description of the universe by drawing on God-guaranteed self-evident innate ideas exemplifies a tendency in philosophy described as rationalism. There are two stands to rationalism; (a) innate ideas/knowledge and (b) whether the use of reason alone can provide knowledge of the world. Whether the philosophers who are usually described as rationalists thought they could attain such all embracing a priori knowledge in practice is debatable. Although Descartes, Spinoza and Leibniz share a common estimation of the primacy of reason in uncovering the rational order of the universe, as a matter of fact they were all heavily involved in the business of experimental science. Perhaps the idea of an a priori science was merely an ideal to which they aspired; but only an omniscient God could ever fully comprehend such a system. For the imperfect investigator, a compromise of reasoning and experimentation seems inevitable.

> To ask for geometrical demonstrations in a field within the range of physics is impossible.

Descartes (1985)

Perhaps what strikes us now about Galileo's experiment with the inclined plane is that Galileo is performing an *experiment*. We might say that observation should guide and correct the theory, and Galileo appears to agree that asking for experimental confirmation is a reasonable request:

> for this is the custom – and properly so – in those sciences where mathematical demonstrations are applied to natural phenomena

Galileo (1967)

Nevertheless, as we have seen, reason and intuition have a role to play in the construction and expression of a theory, and also in the interpretation of the observations.

> Noting and reporting readings of dials ... is nothing. Another kind of observation is what counts: the uncanny ability to pick out what is odd, wrong, instructive or distorted in the antics of one's equipment.

Hacking (1983)

Descartes was trying to formulate a method for attaining truth that reflected his understanding of the practices employed in what we later see as science. This reminds us that from the outset, science is an abstract, idealised and profoundly theoretical way of knowing about the world. Even if rationalism over-emphasises the role of reason in science, it is an equally misleading caricature of science to see it as merely the careful amassing of observational data.

And rationalism is right to insist that observation is not sufficient to justify the generalisations characteristic of scientific theories. Hume saw this as well, arguing that any 'universal law of nature' supposedly justified by what can only be a restricted sample (what has been observed so far) is bound to be logically defective because it commits the fallacy of generalising from the particular. Scientific generalisations, which are based on **inductive arguments**, are never logically justified by the evidence given their universal character. This logical discovery might

Think about

What does Galileo mean by 'custom'?

Key terms

Inductive arguments: arguments that move from premises about particular observations to a conclusion which is a general principle. For example, we might conclude that night will always be followed by day given the fact that every night so far experienced has been followed by day. Inductive arguments are normally assumed to produce a conclusion which is merely probable.

lead us to doubt the rationality of performing experiments at all, because a limited sample plus one is still too limited to support a universal generalisation. Only if we know that nature must behave in a uniform way – at all times and all places – can particular experiences, observations or experiment be seen as revealing instances or tell-tale symptoms of a deeper order. But equally, the principle of the uniformity of nature itself cannot be justified by a restricted sample of 'uniform behaviour so far observed', however uniform that behaviour has so far been. So if we are going to provide a rationale for observation and experiment it might be that only a principle grasped a priori – that nature is uniform – can bypass the obstacle of limited experience. On the other hand, we could just admit scepticism and acknowledge that 'for all we know, everything is entirely loose and separate' (Hume, 1999). As we cannot justify our conviction that what lies beyond our experience *must* resemble what lies within our experience, the idea of a comprehensive necessity in nature appears to dissolve.

Nevertheless, even if we cannot establish **necessary truths** in nature from our limited perspective, the appearance that all is **contingent truths**, where everything is entirely loose and separate, might be misleading (from God's perspective):

> A thing is contingent only because of a defect in our knowledge … when we can affirm nothing certainly about the necessity or impossibility of its existence, because the order of causes is hidden from us

> *Spinoza (1985)*

Spinoza wants to claim that if our knowledge was complete and perfect, as God's is, then what appears to be merely contingent would reveal itself to be necessary.

Scepticism appears the only option for Hume, because his analysis of a priori truth reduces necessity to merely grasping *relations* of ideas – self-evident necessity is a function of the structure and not the content of the propositions which we grasp a priori. For instance, you know that if a thwack is a zak and all zaks are daks, then this thwack is a dak. 'This thwack is a dak' must be true. This truth is grasped just by thinking about the structure of this **deductive argument**. But it seems a hollow truth: you still do not know what a 'thwak', or a 'zak' or a 'dak' *is*. Empiricism's stress on the need to refer ideas to experience seems right here, as long as we avoid treating the terms as names standing for exclusive sense impressions.

Hume's distinction between ideas and fact

Hume criticised rationalism by claming that the a priori knowledge that Descartes sets so much store by cannot be substantive knowledge of the world, it will only tell us about the connections between *ideas* – what he calls 'relations of ideas'. Such knowledge turns out to be concerned with definitions, and logical and mathematical relations. Matters of fact, on the other hand, are substantial truths about the world but can only be obtained through experience. Hume also denied Descartes' doctrine of innate ideas and insisted all ideas were based on sense impressions.

Fig. 1.3 is a diagram that presents Hume's distinction between relations of ideas and matters of fact. This distinction is often called Hume's Fork. We can regard the fork as a kind of machine that processes anything that purports to be knowledge. Once all the possibilities have been considered, the purported knowledge will either gain a full bill of health as genuine knowledge or be discarded as mere 'sophistry and illusion'.

■ Think about

Is Galileo's custom rational?

💡 Key terms

Neccessary truths: a necessary truth is such that its denial will involve a self-contradiction. In other words, it is inconceivable that it is not true. 'All red things are coloured' is an example of a necessary truth. There is a close link to a priori knowledge. Necessary truths are normally regarded as being known a priori – although there are exceptions.

Contingent truths: a contingent truth is one that could have been otherwise. 'London buses are red' is a contingent truth as they could have been some other colour. Although false, it would not be contradictory to claim that they are green. Contingent truths are known as a posteriori.

Deductive argument: an argument in which the truth of the premises will guarantee a true conclusion. For example, if it is true that 'all cats are mammals' and 'Timmy is a cat' then the conclusion that 'Timmy is a mammal' must also be true. So, unlike inductive arguments, deduction can produce certainty.

According to Hume, a proposition either expresses relations of ideas or matters of fact. Hume says there is no third option.

⬇

'All the objects of human reason or enquiry may naturally be divided into two kinds, to wit, Relations of Ideas, and Matters of Fact'.

⬇ | ⬇

Relations of Ideas
Relations of ideas are 'discoverable by the mere operation of thought without dependence on what is anywhere existent in the universe'. As such, we come to know relations of ideas a priori.

Matters of Fact
Matters of fact 'are not ascertained in the same manner' as relations of ideas, but rather arise 'entirely from experience' through the impressions we receive. As such, we come to know matters of fact a posteriori.

⬇ | ⬇

How are these ideas presented to us? | *How are these ideas presented to us?*

⬇ | ⬇ | ⬇ | ⬇

A by *intuition* – where we just see the truth of the proposition. For instance, we can know by intuition that 'where there is no property there can be no injustice' once we have defined 'the terms, and explain injustice to be a violation of property'.

B *demonstration* – which involves using knowledge provided by intuition to demonstrate something that 'cannot be known, let the terms be ever so exactly defined, without a train of reasoning and enquiry'. For instance, I can demonstrate that 'the square of the hypotenuse is equal to the square of the other two sides' even if I do not have the intellectual capacity to simply 'see' the truth of this.

A by an *outward sense* – where an impression made upon the outward senses causes us to have a corresponding idea. This explains why 'a Laplander or Negro has no notion of the relish of wine' – they have no experience of tasting it.

B by an *inward sentiment* – where an impression made on our internal senses causes us to have a corresponding idea. This explains why a person with 'a selfish heart' cannot easily conceive the heights of generosity of friendship' – they lack the internal constitution that would allow them to become sensitive to such things.

⬇ | ⬇

Hume believes that the propositions of 'Geometry, Algebra, and Arithmetic and in short, every affirmation which is either intuitively or demonstratively certain' express relation of ideas.

Hume believes that apart from 'the sciences of quantity and number' all the 'other enquiries of men regard only matter of fact and existence, and these are evidently incapable of demonstration'.

⬇ | ⬇

What is it about relations of ideas that allows us to know them with certainty? | *What is it about matters of fact that stops us from knowing them with certainty?*

⬇ | ⬇

The *truth* of the proposition 'a triangle is a figure composed of three straight lines meeting the others at different points' is *necessary* given the definition of the term 'triangle'. Indeed, we cannot imagine, or think of, a triangle without at the same time thinking of such a figure because to do so 'would imply a contraction, and could never be distinctly conceived by the mind'. Philosophers have called such propositions **analytic** because we know they are true simply by analysing the terms contained in the proposition. We do not need to refer to anything outside the proposition to test whether it is true. Propositions with these features can be known with certainty.

The proposition 'I will pass my A-level philosophy exam' might turn out to be true, but it could turn out to be false. As such, its truth is contingent. Indeed, supposing you do pass your exam, it is clear that you can imagine failing 'with the same facility and distinctness, as if ever so conformable to reality'. As Hume says, 'the contrary of every matter of fact is still possible'. From this Hume concludes 'Whatever is may not be'. Philosophers have called propositions expressing matters of fact **synthetic** because they are composed out of – they synthesise – distinct ideas. Because the ideas that make up synthetic propositions are distinct, any connections between ideas they propose must be validated by experience. As such, their truth is not known with certainty; we have to make an observation before we know whether they are true.

⬇

'When we run over libraries, persuaded of these principles, what havoc must we make? If we take in our hand any volume; of divinity or school metaphysics, for instance, let us ask, does it contain any abstract reasoning concerning quantity or number? No. Does it contain any experimental reasoning concerning matter of fact and existence? No. Commit it to the flames: for it can contain nothing but sophistry and illusion.'

Fig. 1.3 *Hume's Fork*

According to Hume, a proposition *either* expresses relations of ideas *or* matters of fact. Hume says there is no third option.

> All the objects of human reason or enquiry may naturally be divided into two kinds, to wit, *Relations of Ideas*, and *Matters of Fact*.
>
> *Hume (1999)*

Hume has in mind here many of the claims made by the rationalist philosophers. For example, Spinoza says:

> The more we understand individual things the more we understand God.
>
> *Spinoza (1985)*

In terms of Hume's Fork this claim does not do well. Firstly, is it a matter of fact? If so then the ideas it expresses should be knowable either through 'outward sense' or 'inner sentiment'. This is clearly not so, for what sense impressions or inner feelings could possibly lead us to accept its truth? Secondly, does the statement express a relation of ideas? If so then it will be possible to either demonstrate its truth, as, for example, we can demonstrate Pythagoras' theorem, or its truth will be evident through intuition, i.e. we will just be able to 'see' immediately that it must be true as is the case with 'All aunts are female'.

Neither of these options seems to apply. As a result Hume would condemn such a claim as mere 'sophistry and illusion'. We should be clear here that Hume is not just saying that Spinoza's statement is not true; he is saying it does not express any coherent idea.

Think about

Using Hume's Fork, analyse the following statements:

- Triangles have 3 sides.
- God is love.
- 457 + 398 = 855.
- Sitting on a drawing pin is painful.
- A penny and a book will hit the ground together if dropped together from the same height.
- Everything is entirely loose and separate.
- 'All the objects of human reason or enquiry may naturally be divided into two kinds, to wit, relations of ideas and matters of fact.'

The feeling of necessity

If all necessity is only to be found in relations of ideas, how does Hume explain the feeling that there is necessity in sequences of natural events? Our feeling of necessity at work in nature is ultimately illusory according to Hume. Because ideas are copies of impressions, the force and frequency of similar impressions determines how vividly the resulting ideas are imprinted on the mind. Repeated experience ingrains ideas and triggers feelings of expectation, which we mistake for necessity. For instance, the belief that flames cause snow to turn to water consists in the combination of distinct ideas, 'flame', 'snow', 'water' (each one being

Key terms

Analytic: although there are a number of definitions, an analytic statement is essentially one that is true by definition. 'All aunts are female' is analytic because 'being female' is part of the definition of 'aunt'. Analytic statements can be known a priori. Once they are understood their truth will be evident. They carry no information about the world.

Synthetic: a synthetic statement is one that is not analytic; it is not true by definition. They do contain a descriptive load in regard to the world.

AQA Examiner's tip

Just stating a point will not earn as many marks in an exam as stating it and showing you can illustrate it. Illustrating how Hume's Fork works, for example, is evidence that you can *apply* your knowledge.

knowable in sense experience without necessarily involving the thought of any other) with a habituated feeling of expectation that flames *must* cause snow to turn to water. Habit has triggered the feeling of expectation that, when flame and snow are combined, water will follow, just because whenever I have experienced the combination of flame and ice, as a matter of fact, water has followed. Nevertheless, in the imagination, you are free to combine what you will (see the idea of a golden mountain above) and so you can think of water being poured on ice, which then turns to flames. Whether flames cause snow to turn to water or water causes ice to turn to flames is something you can only settle by reference to experience. The 'must' you thought you perceived in nature is merely a projection:

> Tis a common observation, that the mind has a great propensity to spread itself on external objects, and to conjoin with them any internal impressions, which they occasion, and which always make their appearance at the same time that these objects discover themselves to the senses.

Hume (1969)

After working through this topic, you should:

- know the value of the intellect when learning from experience
- understand the rationale behind the view that primacy should be given to reason and a priori knowledge in any attempt to understand the world
- recognise how the role of mathematics in science influenced rationalist thought
- understand the role that God plays in securing our knowledge of the world
- realise that rationalists underestimated the role of experimentation in their account of knowledge – if not in their practice
- understand the different responses to the problem of induction adopted by Hume, on the one hand, and rationalism on the other
- know how Hume characterises all knowledge in terms of the distinction between *relations of ideas* and *matters of fact*
- know how Hume accounted for the fact that we appear to 'see' necessity in nature.

Think about

Can you think of an exception to Hume's repetition thesis?

Think about

Can you think of other things that we project onto the world?

Conceptual schemes

Learning objectives:

- to understand how basic assumptions made by both the rationalists and empiricists meant that they failed to provide an adequate account of our knowledge of the world

- to understand how Kant's insight that objects must conform to our knowledge allows him to synthesise rationalism and empiricism

- to grasp the distinction between scheme and content

- to understand and exemplify the claim that different groups of individuals may conceptualise the world differently

- to understand why it is impossible to assess whether a conceptual scheme accurately corresponds to reality

- to begin to grasp what is meant by the claim that knowledge and justification occur in 'the logical space of reasons'.

Introduction

We said that our ideas are *about* the world. At least that is their character when what we think is also true. But often our ideas about the world turn out to be false or misleading – they fail to deal with the objects and events themselves. Just as we might wonder if there is a way of painting an accurate picture, we can ask if there is a way of making sure that our thought accurately captures reality. The empiricism of Locke and Hume recommends that only ideas that precisely copy what we see, hear, taste, touch and smell will avoid the ambiguities, illusions and sophistry that typically distort a less careful rendering of reality; just as an artist who fails to pay attention to what is *here*, *now*, will be liable to paint inaccurately. In contrast, rationalism recommends that it is only by getting behind the appearances of things, and understanding their underlying nature, that we will be able to see reality for what it is; like an artist needs to understand 'the structure, the knitting of the bones, and anatomy', or how things 'ought to be', to capture the reality of the object they are trying to paint. In both the empiricist and rationalist account, how the idea comes to be possessed is taken as a mark of its truthfulness. Empiricism assumes that ideas originate in our encounters with particular objects and events in the world, and so ideas most like the originals will be most truthful. The rationalists doubt the truthfulness of ideas drawn from the senses. Instead, the truths of reason are grounded in innate ideas, ultimately planted in us by God. But neither empiricism nor rationalism can take the ultimate origins of their ideas for granted:

> Of course, we can't get outside our skins to find out what is causing the internal happenings of which we are aware.

Davidson (1986)

Empiricism, which endorses the sense data theory, makes the mind-independent world unknowable. Descartes also doubts whether he can trust a priori judgement if his stock of ideas originate in 'some evil demon, no less cunning and deceiving than powerful' so 'that I should be deceived every time I add two or three or count the sides of a square, or form some judgement even simpler' (Descartes, 1968). So both empiricism and rationalism look for conclusive signs of truth from the inside. Hume focuses on force and vivacity whilst Descartes stresses clear and distinct self-evidence as marks that distinguish ideas that are more or less truthful. But introspection is inconclusive. Hume's forceful and vivid sense impressions seem hopelessly intermingled and confused to Descartes, obscuring our intellectual contemplation, whereas Descartes' transparent truths of reason appear 'abstruse' or empty to Hume. Without establishing a footing in the world, empiricism dissolves into mere sense impressions, where even the self disappears into:

> a bundle or collection of different perceptions, which succeed each other with an inconceivable rapidity, and are in perpetual flux and movement.

Hume (1969)

Think about

Is solipsism inevitable?

Likewise, Descartes is trapped in a vicious circle where only a benevolent God can guarantee the truth of his innate self-evident ideas and only innate self-evident ideas can guarantee the existence of a benevolent God. So it is:

> as though I had suddenly fallen into very deep water, I am so taken unawares that I can neither put my feet firmly down upon the bottom nor swim to keep myself on the surface.

Descartes (1968, Meditation 2)

Kant's synthesis

> Hitherto it has been assumed that all our knowledge must conform to objects. But all attempts have, on this assumption, ended in failure. We must therefore make trial whether we may not have more success in the tasks of metaphysics, if we suppose that objects conform to our knowledge.

Kant (1934)

What is involved in experiencing something? You are presently reading these words in this book, here and now. It is impossible to think of this experience without thinking of it in terms of space and time. The Kantian categories are supposed to be necessary forms of experience which render experience possible. What could it be like to subtract space and time from your experience; can you experience an object not occupying a space or persisting through time? But if space and time are necessary dimensions for experience, the ideas of space and time cannot be derived from experience. You cannot split experience in two by analysis, which you would need to do in order to show that one element (space and time) derives from another (the supposed primordial experiential soup out of which the ideas of space and time are supposed to have emerged). Our ideas of space and time are a priori because they are not derived from experience. But the a priori truth that objects must be experienced in space and time is not a self-contained analytic truth. Rather, what justifies our judgement that objects must be experienced in space and time is the a priori knowledge that this is how we must *experience* objects. So taken altogether, our knowledge that objects must be experienced in space and time is **synthetic a priori knowledge**. In a deep way, 'we can know a priori of things only what we ourselves put into them' (Kant, 1934). Kant's two other categories of great importance for the possibility of experience are causality and number.

Kant's analysis led him to suppose that the mind had three characteristic powers:

- *sensibility*: the mind has the power to be receptive to particular objects and events in experience (which he calls intuitions)
- *understanding*: the mind has the power to think, imagine, and judge (so it has concepts)
- *reason*: the mind has the power to make logical inferences.

Unless these powers have something to work on then they are idle. Unless these powers are activated, raw sensation remains unintelligible. How are all of these powers integrated to form a unified experience? Kant argues that we have a body of a priori rules for synthesising experience into an integrated whole. So in this way objects must conform to our knowledge. Kant argues that a self-conscious subject of experience is a necessary condition for the possibility of experience at all. What is a self-

Key terms

Synthetic a priori knowledge: knowledge that can be known independently of experience but it is nevertheless not analytically true. 'Every event has a cause' is an example of synthetic a priori knowledge endorsed by Kant. Hume does not accept that synthetic a priori knowledge is possible. According to his Fork, all knowledge that is a priori must be analytic.

conscious subject of experience? It is that which thinks about the world in the structured way that Kant indicates.

> Our knowledge springs from two fundamental sources of the mind; the first is the capacity of receiving representations … the second is the power of knowing an object through these representations … Intuition and concepts constitute, therefore, the elements of all our knowledge, so that neither concepts without an intuition in some way corresponding to them, nor intuition without concepts, can yield knowledge … Thoughts without content are empty, intuitions without concepts are blind.

Kant (1934)

So Kant thought he had reconciled empiricism and rationalism with a new synthesis. Empiricism was right to insist that ideas must be somehow grounded in sense experience otherwise they were empty and merely reflected the a priori structure of thought. However, rationalism was right to insist that a priori knowledge is possible, but what they were revealing a priori was not the structure of things, the knitting of the bones, and anatomy of the world itself (**noumenon**), but the structure their experience of things must have (**phenomenon**).

Scheme and content

Kant's revolution – making the world conform to our idea of the world – appeared to stress the mind's *active* power in experience. This could be contrasted with Hume's passive model, human knowledge being explained in terms of the mechancial operation of principles of association. Even if Kant's proposed schema was not the actual schema to which objects must conform, at least there must be a schema actively organising the content of thought, our intuitions. It should, however, be realized that Kant intended his categories to be absolutely fundamental to the possibility of experience and human knowledge. There may be other schemes for viewing the world but it isn't clear that a consideration of these would in any way undermine Kant's position. The example of the duck/rabbit, whichever way it is seen, is still seen as spatial. Perhaps there are numerous different schemas. Look at Fig. 1.4.

Fig. 1.4 *Duck*

Fig. 1.5 *Rabbit*

Then look at Fig. 1.5.

First you see a duck and then you see a rabbit; so you see two different things. The only thing that has changed is the idea or schema – either duck or rabbit. So ideas or schemas are active in experience.

We cannot see the drawing without seeing it as something. Even if we reduce that something to mere squiggles, squiggles are still *kinds* of things. So there must be a schema organising content. But the schema can be different: in this case duck or rabbit.

So perhaps different people or groups apply different schema to their intuitions or content, and because schema structure experience, different schemas produce different experiences. Because objects must conform to our knowledge, what one group knows by its schema cannot be what we know by our schema. So what is true for them is true for them and what is true for us is true for us and that is all there is to it. Different schemas amount to different worlds.

According to Sapir:

> The 'real world' is to a large extent unconsciously built up on the language habits of the group … We see and hear and otherwise experience very largely as we do because the language habits of our community predispose certain choices of interpretation.

Quoted in **Whorf** *(1956)*

Think about

What is the evidence for unconscious build ups? Is there a circularity problem here?

The linguist, Whorf, provides examples which he thinks illustrate and support this claim. In the Native American language Nootka, the language does not allow us to think 'a house' when viewing what we would call a house. Rather, in Nootka we would think something like 'house occurs' or 'it houses' when viewing something we would see as a house. Another group, the Hopi, make no distinction between insects, aeroplanes and aviators, classing them all by the same word *masa'ytaka*. However, the Hopi do have a distinct word for birds. So Whorf concludes that given their linguistic schema, the Hopi experience a world in which there is a distinctive kind of thing that we would experience as birds, and there is another distinctive kind of thing – roughly whatever flies – that we do not experience because our language carves up reality differently.

According to Whorf:

> This fact is very significant for modern science, for it means that no individual is free to describe nature with absolute impartiality but is constrained to certain modes of interpretation even while he thinks himself most free … We are thus introduced to a new principle of relativity, which holds that all observers are not led by the same physical evidence to the same picture of the universe, unless their linguistic backgrounds are similar, or in some way calibrated.

Whorf (1956)

Think about

Does this assume that there is a reality to carve up?

If Sapir is right, then the way the world *is* is not something to be explained by referring to the way the world impresses itself on us. Rather, the way the world is to us is explained by the 'language habits of our community' which 'predispose certain choices of interpretation'. According to Whorf, we cannot get outside our different conceptual schemes to check which one best matches 'the same physical evidence' as there is no experience without schema:

> to talk about the world we must already impose upon the world some conceptual scheme peculiar to our own special language.

Quine (1980)

However, the principle of relativity referred to by Wharf would also apply to himself. This is part of a more general problem of trying to revitalise conceptual schemes via an *absolute* judgement regarding such schemes. We should note that there is a sense in which this vision of language users being inducted into a set of language habits, which predispose them to certain ways of thinking, has an empiricist dimension. Unlike Kant, who believed that all of humanity structures experience in essentially the same way, the Sapir–Whorf view involves the belief that at birth no particular scheme takes precedence. We are 'blank slates'. The scheme is learnt from experience, but here experience is not understood in terms of the occurrence of sense impressions, but rather in terms of exposure to the language habits of the host community.

Political thought control

The idea that the structure of language determines the structure of thought has political implications. George Orwell in his novel *Nineteen Eighty-Four* envisages a totalitarian society in which the government controls the thoughts of the populace by inventing a language (Newspeak) that makes unacceptable modes of thought impossible:

> It was intended that when Newspeak had been adopted once and for all and Oldspeak forgotten, a heretical thought … should be literally unthinkable, at least so far as thought is dependent on words.

Orwell (1954, p241)

The adoption of so-called 'politically correct' language has the laudable aim of attempting to change prejudiced modes of thought and getting us to think in a more enlightened way. Whether language can have this kind of power to mould patterns of thought is contentious. Certainly language is constantly changing and language users always seem to have the power to subvert any 'correct' usage.

Competing conceptual schemes

And so, how can we recommend one conceptual scheme over and above any other? Let us suppose that my conceptual scheme is inherited from my host community. Through the lenses of my particular conceptual scheme the world will present itself in a particular way, because conceptual schemes:

> are ways of organizing experience; they are systems of categories that give form to the data of sensation; they are points of view from which individuals, cultures, or periods survey the passing scene.

Davidson (2006)

But through the lenses of another conceptual scheme, the world will present itself in its own peculiar way. Which lens captures it right? There is no way of seeing the world itself, except through some conceptual lens, and so there is no neutral viewpoint from which an impartial assessment of different conceptual schemes could be made. On this view, we must give up the hope that an idea can approximate to pure sense impressions – **the given**. Likewise, we should reject the view that what is rational for us is universally rational. Our way of carving up experience accords with our norms and reasons. But these norms and reasons are just our lenses. There are different lenses, none of which more or less 'penetrate the phenomena'.

Can we recommend one conceptual scheme over and above any other? According to Quine, any justification for preferring one conceptual scheme over another must be decided on the grounds of usefulness:

> Concepts are language, and the purpose of concepts and of language is efficacy in communication and prediction. Such is the ultimate duty of language, science and philosophy, and it is in relation to that duty that a conceptual scheme has finally to be appraised.

Quine (1980)

For instance, whereas the rationalists believed they could justify their beautiful mathematical models of the universe by appealing to the God-

Key terms

The given: this expression is used to refer to the raw, unstructured, unconceptualised content of experience which should provide the foundation for our knowledge of the world according to empiricism. If all experience is conceptualised then it is not clear how we could ever come to know 'the given'. To this extent the given is a purely hypothetical notion.

Think about

Do different groups see different worlds?

Fig. 1.6 *Subject and object*

Think about

Should we prefer some theories over others on practical grounds?

decreed order of nature, Quine recommends elegance in theories on different grounds:

> Elegance can make the difference between a psychologically manageable conceptual scheme and one that is too unwieldly for our poor minds to cope with effectively.

Quine (1980)

Ultimately, according to Quine, the justification takes us back to the sense organs where we took it for granted that the world impacts upon our body, presumably causing the processes that lead to our awareness of sights, sounds, smells, tastes and feels.

> Our talk of external things, our very notion of things, is just a conceptual apparatus that helps us to forsee and control the triggering of our sensory receptors. The triggering, first and last, is all we have to go on.

Quine (1986)

The claim that all we have to go on is the triggering of our sensory receptors marks Quine's position as a modern form of empiricism. But just as we asked with sense impressions, what are these triggerings of our sensory receptors supposed to be, and what role could they play in justifying the ideas we have? Sellars argues that merely having a sensation is nothing like grasping a fact:

> instead of coming to have a concept of something because we have noticed that sort of thing, to have the ability to notice a sort of thing is already to have the ability to have the concept of that sort of thing, and cannot account for it.

Sellars (1997)

In other words, it is the conceptual apparatus, whether it is innate or learned, which characterises the experience rather than the experience characterising the idea as Locke and Hume thought.

According to Sellars:

> In characterising an episode or a state as that of knowing, we are not giving an empirical description of that episode or state; we are placing it in the logical space of reasons, of justifying and being able to justify what one says.

Sellars (1997)

Accepting that knowledge and justification occur in the *logical space of reasons* can lead us to the view that:

> Instead of seeking 'vertical' relationships between language, or ourselves and language users, and the world, we must concentrate upon 'horizontal' or inferential processes, whereby we advance and accept reasons from each other. Justification becomes a 'social phenomenon' rather than a transaction between a 'knowing subject' and 'reality'.

Rorty (1981)

We might illustrate this with the issue of inductive arguments discussed above. Giving a justification for the general principle that dry wood will burn, for example, cannot be deduced directly from experience as Hume showed. Past experience is entirely separate from future experience unless we assume, a priori, some underlying principle of uniformity. However, referring to past experience of burning dry wood provides a legitimising reason why we take as warranted the belief that the dry wood which is about to be placed on the fire will burn. This is not because sensory receptors have been triggered in the right way and sense impressions have occurred, although this might be true, it is because such a reason is legitimated by a norm of what counts as a good reason in these circumstances, it occupies a legitimate place within 'the space of reasons'. The idea of a norm turns out to be crucial for this approach to the theory of knowledge and norms are a 'social phenomenon'.

Rorty recommends that we drop the model of a vertical relationship between knowing subject and reality, just because the 'something waiting to be organised' (Davidson, 2006) has no role to play in the space of reasons. What are the consequences? According to Davidson, 'If we give [that] up it is not clear there is anything left to call empiricism'.

After working through this topic, you should:

- realise how Kant's account of knowledge allows him to synthesise rationalism and empiricism and thus overcome the drawbacks of both of these views

- be able to distinguish between scheme and content when understanding how we represent the world

- be able to consider the possibility that different groups may conceptualise the world differently according to the structure of their language

- realise that conceptual schemes cannot be assessed in terms of how well they correspond to reality

- understand that knowledge and justification may be understood in terms of the 'logical space of reasons'.

Further reading

The following primary texts are referred to in the chapter. They should be accessible and reading them ought to give you a sense of what philosophising involves.

Descartes, R. *Discourse on Method and the Meditations*, trans. F. E. Sutcliffe, Penguin, 1968.

Hume, D. *Enquiry Concerning Human Understanding*, T. L. Beauchamp (ed.), Oxford University Press, 1999.

Locke, J. *An Essay Concerning Human Understanding*, A. D. Woozley (ed.), Fontana/Collins, 1964.

Wittgenstein, L. *The Blue and Brown Books*, Blackwell, 1958.

These secondary texts are clear and should help put specific arguments addressed in the chapter in context:

Hospers, J. *An Introduction to Philosophical Analysis*, Routledge, 4th revised edition 1997

Bennett, J. *Locke, Berkeley, Hume: Central Themes*, Oxford University Press, 1971

Cottingham, J. *The Rationalists*, Oxford Paperbacks, 1988

Dancy, J. *A Companion to Epistemology*, Blackwell, 1993

Two texts, not explicitly philosophy but certainly full of philosophical material, used in the chapter are worth reading

Gombrich, E. H. *Art and Illusion*, Phaidon, 2002

Pinker, S. *The Blank Slate*, BCA, 2002.

Summary questions

1. List the reasons identified in the 'Mind as a *tabula rasa*' topic for the view that sense impressions are not sufficient for ideas.

2. Explain why science is not concerned merely with the amassing of observational data.

3. 'Observation is not sufficient to justify the generalisations characteristic of scientific theories.' What are the implications of this statement according to the rationalists? How does their response differ from Hume's?

4. Explain clearly how Kant synthesises the empiricist's and rationalist's conceptions of knowledge.

5. Explain what is meant by the claim that 'every event has a cause' is a synthetic a priori proposition.

6. Explain why it is impossible to justify the adoption of a conceptual scheme on the grounds that it corresponds to the facts.

7. If we justify the adoption of a conceptual scheme on the basis of its usefulness, as Quine does, does this mean that whatever scheme we find useful must be correct?

8. Suppose you were an explorer watching a mother teaching her child 'this is tove'. What would you need to know in order to understand what she meant? What could she mean by 'tove'? Why prefer one translation over another?

9. Assess whether we could take Galileo's claim that 'the real world is the world of bodies in mathematically reducible motions' as simply illustrating the adoption of a particular conceptual scheme.

10. To what extent do conceptual schemes threaten to cut the link between knowledge and reality?

Knowledge of the external world

Realism

Key terms

Sense data: (from the Latin *datum* meaning 'what is given'); these are said to be the empirical mind-dependent ingredients of perception. They are the colours, sounds, smells, tastes and textures out of which all experience is built.

■ Introduction

If a tree were to fall in a forest where there was no one around to hear it, would it still make a sound? This question, perhaps the oldest and most quoted in philosophy, can only be addressed within the context of perceptual theory. Your immediate response might be, of course, yes; the existence of a sound is no more dependent upon someone to hear it than the existence of the tree is reliant upon there being someone around to perceive it. However, what such a response fails to take into account is the *nature* of perception. Many would argue that a sound can no more exist without a hearer than a thought could exist without a thinker. Of course we could still maintain that there exists a bunch of particles vibrating in space – is this physical description not what sound ultimately reduces to? No. Such a response fails to take into account the distinction between the object of perception (in this case the falling tree) and the act of perception (somebody hearing the tree fall). When described like this, it seems that such an act makes little sense considered independently of an actor (in this case a 'someone' who hears).

So if we accept that sound requires a hearer, then it is no less true that taste requires a taster; smell a smeller; texture a feeler; and colour a viewer. Following this line of reasoning to its logical finale we are left with the disconcerting possibility that it is my perception of the world that floods it with all the colours, textures, sounds, smells and tastes found therein. We must now ask what reality would be like beyond my perception of it. For the sake of consistency, perhaps we should say that reality exists as a collection of colourless, odourless objects situated in time and space – but this presents us with the question of how we can know this. On the other hand, perhaps all we have direct access to is our own immediate perception and never the world that exists behind such a 'veil'. If this is the case, is the inference from **sense data** to object a valid one? Does it even make sense to talk of a world existing beyond my perceptions of it? Given that we can never 'step outside our minds' to ensure what we perceive is an accurate representation of what is, in the same way that we can compare a photograph of an object with the original object itself, then perhaps talk of a reality beyond our experience of it is nonsensical. Or maybe we should remain philosophically agnostic with regard to the existence of such a reality. Issues such as these require us to reflect on **ontological** questions concerning the nature of reality and **epistemological** ones relating to the extent of our knowledge of it.

This chapter considers a number of philosophical theories about the nature of the external world (if, indeed, there is one). The one thing that they all have in common is their empirical nature. Empiricists claim that knowledge of matters of fact is based upon experience, which is to say that we learn new things a posteriori. The mind is a 'blank slate' which fills up over time by means of perception and **introspection**. So the empirical method is one of developing theories in the light of what we perceive in the external world. The most well-known use of the empirical method is that of testing scientific hypotheses by means of experiments. It may be helpful to consider the arguments in this chapter in this light as you work through them.

What is realism?

Would the world be any different were we not here to perceive it? Would all the sounds, colours, tastes and smells that excite the senses still remain to be perceived in our absence? As we have seen, the obvious, non-philosophical answer to this question is 'yes'. The world is in no way dependent upon human experience of it for it to exist as it does; experience merely reveals that which is already there to be perceived. This position is known as direct realism and its account of reality is such that the world exists with all of its properties intact outside of the mind. Subsequently, on the direct realists' account, what we perceive is not an image of the world in our own private cinema in our heads, but rather the material objects themselves.

Common-sense/naive realism

Often referred to as 'the man in the street view' for its failure to take philosophical considerations seriously, common-sense realism is regarded as being 'naive' because of its connections with uneducated, everyday intuitions. It asserts that what we are aware of in experience is the world itself and not a mental representation of it. Common-sense realists operate with a 'what you see is what you get' policy, believing that the way the world is, is identical to the way we perceive it and the reason we perceive it as we do is because of the way that it is. For the common-sense realist, all of the qualities of an object (its colour, sound, smell, taste and texture) alongside its size and extension, exist within the object itself and our perception of these qualities is **unmediated**.

Properties of colour, taste, texture, dimension and weight

Perceiver

Fig. 2.1 *Common-sense view of realism – all properties are external to the perceiver*

Think about

Summarise in your own words the relationship between acts and objects of perception according to common-sense realism.

Pick an object and explain how the common-sense realist would describe/illustrate our experience of it.

Why might common-sense realism be seen as an attractive theory of perception? Can you see any problems with it?

Think about

Try to provide your own example of a time when your senses have deceived you. What does this tell us about experience?

Why does the second option above appear more viable? What premises are we making about the external world and the way we perceive it when we dismiss the idea of the stick changing its state when immersed in water?

Consider an apple. Its reddish-green colour, glossy texture, the crisp sound that it makes when bitten into, its acidic taste and particular smell; these, for the common-sense realist, are all qualities that somehow exist within the apple itself. Were there no one around to perceive the apple, all of these qualities would continue to be, as their existence is not dependent upon human experience for sustenance. Not only this, its size, shape, extension in space and time and all of the aspects of it that are measurable, such as weight and diameter, also exist within the object and all of these qualities are perceived directly by me as I apprehend them in experience. On this account, there is no mediation between the world and my experience of it; my awareness of the apple (my perception) and the apple itself (the object of my perception) are identical.

Can we trust our senses?

The most obvious problem to arise out of common-sense realism is the question as to whether our senses are completely reliable. Clearly, if they are not then common-sense realism runs into difficulties as we cannot then claim that our perceptions of objects are always identical to the objects themselves. In fact, perceptual error is a fairly common occurrence in our everyday lives, and this is precisely what the argument from illusion demonstrates.

The argument from illusion

Cases of perceptual illusion or error occur when one's experience misrepresents reality. Imaginative examples include 'impossible' M. C. Escher-type illustrations: forward-moving car wheels that appear to be moving backwards; touching the tips of your index fingers together, holding them a few inches away from your eyes and letting your gaze lose focus (if done correctly, an 'extra' finger emerges – see!). The standard case is of the straight stick that appears bent in water. This example is often used to set up a dilemma whereby if we accept, as the common-sense realist suggests, our experience is of reality itself, we are also forced into accepting that either:

- the stick itself does actually bend when immersed in water and straightens again when removed, or
- the common-sense realist is wrong and our perception of an object is not always identical to that object.

Given that the second point appears to be the only viable option here, we automatically inherit the view that distortion occurs at the perceptual rather than objective level. A partition seems to have been drawn between reality and our experience of it.

Perhaps the examples given here are slightly contrived; illusion only occurs under exceptional circumstances. While not 'prudent', to use the words of the philosopher Descartes, to trust completely in something which had previously deceived, nevertheless:

> although the senses sometimes deceive us, concerning things that are barely perceptible or at great distance, there are perhaps many other things about which one cannot reasonably doubt, although we know them through the medium of the senses, for example, that I am here, sitting by the fire, wearing a dressing-gown, with this paper in my hands, and other things of this nature.

Descartes (2007)

Descartes used the example of the phantom limb to illustrate sensory deception. People report experiencing pain in limbs that have been amputated.

Here Descartes maintains that singular occurrences of perceptual error are not yet enough to establish a thoroughgoing scepticism (doubt) of the senses. However, such a response is misguided. The necessary occurrence of at least one instance of perceptual error is all it takes to sufficiently refute the general rule of perceptual reliability and thus common-sense realism. The technical term for this is **refutation by counter-example**. Moreover, the notion of circumstances under which 'doubt is quite impossible' is precisely what is being called into question here. When do we perceive an object 'correctly'? When viewed under a bright light? When close to it? When there are no extenuating circumstances that might call our perception into question? When the perceiver has twenty-twenty vision, the nose of a connoisseur and taste buds of a gourmet? An appeal to the general reliability of the senses or of the particular nature of illusions is too ad hoc here for the notion of perceptual accuracy is already built in.

Still, most people would like to believe such a view and philosophers themselves are no exception. Its simplicity when placed alongside the more abstract accounts of perception that we are about to consider make it an attractive option. Moreover, there does seem to be something intuitively right about such an approach. Common sense, often cited as the enemy of philosophy, is often overlooked by philosophers at their peril. The robust account of reality and our subsequent experience of it is seen by many to be direct realism's greatest virtue and has prompted some philosophers to offer a more sophisticated direct realism which exploits the advantages, whilst avoiding the inadequacies of its naive predecessor.

Philosophical direct realism

Just because we know of an object through its appearance in no way necessitates the view that what we are aware of in experience is not the object itself. The more sophisticated realist could appeal to science, notably physics, to demonstrate that illusion does not have to occur internally at the level of perception but can be accounted for externally, at the level of objects themselves. The stick appearing to bend when placed in water is due to a physical fact about refraction rather than a mental episode of human error; it is this process of refraction that I directly observe when perceiving such events. The following example from J. L. Austin should help clarify this point. There is also the point of how it is *possible* for us to recognise illusions.

> If, to take a rather different case, a church were cunningly camouflaged so that it looked like a barn, how could any serious question be raised about what we see when we look at it? We see, of course, a church that now looks like a barn. We do not see an immaterial barn, an immaterial church, or an immaterial anything else. And what in this case could seriously tempt us to say we do?

Austin (1962)

In other words, our perception still matches the object and an illusion is not so much a failure of my senses as a property of the object and the world around it and we come to know the object as it is (in this case, a camouflaged church), not simply as it appears (a barn).

Key terms

Refutation by counter-example: a method of dismissing a general, or universal, proposition by pointing to a single exception to that proposition, e.g. the universal proposition 'all swans are white' may be refuted if we can point to the existence of a black swan.

Key philosopher

J. L. Austin (1911–60)

English philosopher of language best known for his speech act theory as laid out in *How to do Things with Words* (1962).

Given that it is not just the sense of sight that can be deceived, create a list of illusions that involve each one of your five senses. How might you recognise and subsequently correct such examples when they occur?

Describe how a more philosophical realist might counter the argument from illusion. Do you think he is successful? Why?

Remember that when discussing objects in the external world, direct realism is not committed to saying that they remain in the same state, simply that changes in appearance imply real, physical, changes.

Hallucination

It should now be clear how the more sophisticated realists might go about handling cases of illusion; it is not yet clear how they might handle cases of hallucination. Here we discover objects of perception that lack correspondent articles in the world and thus cannot be explained away by appealing to circumstances external to us. Consider the plight of Macbeth, plagued by the prospect of murder:

Is this a dagger which I see before me,
The handle toward my hand? Come, let me clutch thee.
I have thee not, and yet I see thee still.
Art thou not, fatal vision, sensible
To feeling as to sight? or art thou but
A dagger of the mind, a false creation,
Proceeding from the heat-oppressed brain?
I see thee yet, in form as palpable
As this which now I draw.

Shakespeare (2007)

Key terms

Veridical: a veridical experience is a non-illusory experience which accurately captures reality. This is contrasted with a non-veridical experience (e.g. those that occur in dreams and illusions) which fails to either accurately resemble reality or has no corresponding object in reality (e.g. hallucination).

Phenomenologically: phenomenological (aspect) is the qualitative feel of experience. This point is often appealed to in order to distinguish between physical processes, which do not feel like anything, and conscious/mental ones, which do.

In the case of hallucinations, what we are acquainted with in **veridical** experience can be **phenomenologically** identical to that of non-veridical experience, meaning we experience the two in the same manner as they have the same 'feel'. So Macbeth has no method of visually distinguishing between the dagger produced by his 'heat oppressed brain' and one which really does exist externally to him. It is true that Macbeth is able to recognise the dagger as hallucinatory when he attempts to grasp it and is unable to do so. However, it is not simply sight which is capable of being deceived by hallucination; auditory hallucinations are equally common. Experiments with isolation tanks have shown that subjects placed therein sometimes imagine people with whom they hold conversations. The key point is that if this is demonstrable in an isolation tank, how can we know that the same thing is not happening on an everyday basis? This poses a significant problem for the direct realist because, while we accept that there must be a difference – hallucinations are purely internal phenomena whereas objects are external – nevertheless we have no method of 'stepping outside' of experience in order to establish this. Subsequently, if we have no means of establishing that it is the external world that is the cause of our perceptions and accordingly, in its dependence upon such a hypothesis, any form of realism fails.

It seems odd that the rare but potential occurrences of hallucination present such a stumbling block for our enquiry into the external world. Some philosophers have set aside such cases as scarcely worth observing. J. L. Austin, in *Sense and Sensibilia* (1962), dismissed them on these grounds. Nevertheless, they do appear to present a problem. It might be argued by the more sophisticated realist that, since hallucination also provides a problem for other theories of perception, then it is unfair to shelve direct realism in light of a criticism that no perceptual theory adequately deals with. Another line of reasoning could query the move from the epistemological problem of perception to the ontological problem of the world. Such a move, on this account, confuses two distinct lines of enquiry which ought to be kept separate. The problem here is that if we hold to the empiricist view that our understanding of the external world can only be accessed via our perception of it, and it is perception itself that is being called into question, then any attempt at dealing with the ontology of the world outside of perception would be futile. Our account of the latter will always be restricted by the limitations of the former, and empiricism collapses. Consequently, we need to consider counter-arguments to the claim that hallucinations are indistinguishable from veridical experience.

Counter-arguments

Hallucinations are a rare occurrence; most people go throughout life without ever having experienced one. Therefore we need not concern ourselves about them.

A common-sense counter-argument and Austin's claim, noted above. This response is problematic for two reasons:

- it fails to grasp a crucial aspect of the argument. Regardless of whether or not a person has undergone such an experience, it is the possibility rather than the actuality of delusion that is required for the argument to work

- if we accept that lucid hallucinations are a possibility (which this counter-argument does, in fact, do) then we are also forced into accepting that there is no way of telling whether or not such an event has occurred to begin with. Given that this is a necessary requirement for the argument to succeed, the criticism falls short. Perhaps more disconcertingly, it also implies that we have no means of telling that we are not hallucinating now though some would argue that hallucinatory experiences are corrected by other senses.

There are physical or psychological features (psychosis, drunkenness, etc.) at play which lead to one hallucinating. Where these factors are not present, we need not concern ourselves with such possibilities.

A slightly more nuanced version of the common-sense argument above, which is equally as weak. The use of hallucinations is put forward as a thought experiment; a method for seeing whether we can establish the existence of the external world and our subsequent knowledge of it by appeal to experience alone. For thought experiments to work, all that is required is a possibility. The fact that the majority of standard examples of hallucinations might be explained away by appeal to the psychological state of the perceiver fails to affect the argument in any way. However, we need something with which to contrast the hallucination in order for us to recognise hallucinations. The concept of an hallucination is an essentially parasitic concept. Once again, all that is needed is the potential for hallucinations to occur with no corresponding psychological abnormality for the argument to succeed in order to generate scepticism with regard to the possibility of identifying veridical experience.

Hallucinations and perceptions are distinct; the former would be better categorised alongside the objects of memory and the imagination.

This is a more philosophical counter-argument. In order to distinguish between perceptual activity and the introspective processes of memory and the imagination, we have to appeal to some form of categorical distinction between the two. It was argued by David Hume that objects of introspection (he calls them 'ideas') strike us with less force and vivacity than our individual perceptions (Hume calls these 'impressions'). You will have already come across this distinction in Chapter 1 and will learn more about the details of Hume's theory in the A2 course. For our present purpose it is enough to consider an actual example – contrast my memory of Paris in the springtime with my actual *experience* of this event. Plainly the latter is easily distinguishable from the former. However, the argument from hallucination is founded upon the premise that, on some level, hallucinations have the *potential* to feel as real as veridical experience. Consequently, if there is a distinction between perceptions and hallucinations, it is not to be found at this level.

Hallucinatory perceptions are distinct from veridical ones. If they were not, we would not be able to recognise them as hallucinatory in the first place.

This is where the argument from hallucination falls down, because it does not take into account a basic feature of how we make sense of experience. The easiest way to understand this is with an example. Consider Descartes on the hallucination of a phantom limb:

> for is there anything more intimate or internal than pain? And yet I have sometimes heard people say, who have lost arms or legs, that they still sometimes seemed to feel pain in the limb which had been amputated; and this caused me to think that I too could not be quite certain that any one of my limbs was really affected, although I felt pain in it.

> **Descartes** *(2007, 'Meditations on First Philosophy', Meditation 6)*

Here we have Descartes' version of the argument from hallucination. The possibility that one may feel pain in a missing limb leads him to doubt his perception of his own limbs. The key point here is that his doubt arises because he has heard of others who have felt pain in phantom limbs. It arises in the context of the experience of others who have suffered this particular hallucination and then gone on to recognise it for what it was. How have they recognised it? By reference to their prior knowledge that the limb in question has been amputated; when rationally considered in the light of what they have previously learnt about their bodies, the pain is obviously hallucinatory. The fact of the matter is that we do distinguish hallucinations from reality (though not necessarily immediately) and we have no evidence to suppose otherwise. If this were not the case, we would not recognise a hallucination as such in the first place. The thought experiment is flawed because, while it is not contradictory to posit total lucid hallucinations which we could never recognise, there are no empirical grounds for supposing that such hallucinations actually occur.

Let us return to Macbeth: he sees a dagger floating in front of him and doubts the evidence of his eyes because, in his experience, daggers do not float. Consequently, he reaches out to touch it and, when he finds he cannot, he recognises it as a hallucination. Now consider what would be involved in him not being able to distinguish hallucination from reality: he would have seen the dagger, seized it, stabbed Duncan, Duncan would have appeared to die, and everyone Macbeth apparently then encounters would think that Duncan had died. This is so counter-intuitive as to seem absurd, and so direct realists are able to rebut arguments from hallucination. The phantom limb case, alluded to earlier, does not support a general scepticism. In fact, the opposite is the case. In order to recognise the illusion, we have to know that the limb is not present and/or that others are providing us with testimony. These considerations imply that my senses are reliable on at least these occasions.

Think about

Why is the argument from hallucination a stronger argument than that of illusion?

Note that, unlike the preceding ones, this final counter-argument does not accept the possibility of permanently undetectable, fully lucid hallucinations. Do you think this is justifiable?

There is a sceptical argument with regard to hallucination which still has force despite the final counter-argument above. Can you work out what it is? We will come back to this later in the chapter.

Given all that has been said about illusion, hallucination and perceptual variability, can we really trust our senses to deliver veridical experience?

Perceptual variation

Perceptual variation, or relativity, is a more serious problem for the direct realist, focusing as it does on the perceiver-dependent nature of perception. Standard examples tend to borrow from cases of:

- spherical objects appearing circular when viewed from above, but elliptical when viewed from the side
- white pieces of paper appearing blue under a blue light and blue pieces appearing white under white light (appeal to colour-blindness achieves a similar result)
- train-tracks appearing to converge in the distance, etc.

Whilst similar, examples such as these are distinct from the examples of perceptual error because, in the former cases we would be loath to admit that our perceptions inaccurately represented reality. Rather our experience of reality is situated, it takes place from within a position in time and space and under certain conditions and is, therefore, **perspectival**. On this account, the notion of seeing the world 'correctly' becomes problematical. Bertrand Russell gives us the following example to help clarify this position.

> To make our difficulties plain, let us concentrate attention on the table. To the eye it is oblong, brown and shiny, to the touch it is smooth and cool and hard; when I tap it, it gives out a wooden sound. Any one else who sees and feels and hears the table will agree with this description, so that it might seem as if no difficulty would arise; but as soon as we try to be more precise our troubles begin. Although I believe that the table is 'really' of the same colour all over, the parts that reflect the light look much brighter than the other parts, and some parts look white because of reflected light. I know that, if I move, the parts that reflect the light will be different, so that the apparent distribution of colours on the table will change.

Key terms

Perspectival: something may be said to be perspectival if it appears to differ when experienced from different positions or under different conditions.

Key philosopher

Bertrand Russell (1872–1970)

An English empiricist philosopher particularly noted for his work in logic and the philosophy of mathematics. Russell is regarded as one of the founders of analytic philosophy and was also a prominent political activist and pacifist. Russell was an extremely prolific writer. Two books of his that are of particular relevance are *The Problems of Philosophy* (1980), and his *History of Western Philosophy* (1979).

> It follows that if several people are looking at the table at the same moment, no two of them will see exactly the same distribution of colours, because no two can see it from exactly the same point of view, and any change in the point of view makes some change in the way the light is reflected

Russell (1980, p2)

Such an example shows the notion of no absolute vantage point. That we perceive the same object differently depending on where we stand in relation to it, and that the same object yields different perceptions to different people perceiving it at the same time, is enough to establish this point. Consider my current experience as I observe a penny placed upon a glass table. When I reposition myself around the penny, my perception changes: once spherical, now elliptical; its colour changes in relation to the light; its very size appears to alter as I move myself away from and towards it and, were I to look at it under a microscope, the surfaces that once appeared smooth would look as rugged as a landscape. Nevertheless, the penny *itself* does not change. Russell's argument is: what I see changes; the object itself can't be supposed to change; therefore what I see is not the object.

- my perception of the penny changes in relation to the conditions of my perception of it
- the penny itself remains constant
- conclusion: my perception of the penny, what I perceive, and the penny itself must be distinct.

Such an argument can be developed further by showing that perceptual relativity is not restricted to cases of the same person perceiving the same object differently at different times, nor different people perceiving the same object differently at the same time, but also to incorporate the possibility of the same person perceiving the same object at the same time in different ways.

A counter-argument

While such an argument may well refute naive realism, a more sophisticated realist could respond in kind by showing that just because we come to know of objects through their appearance that in no way necessitates that what we directly apprehend in experience is an appearance and not the object itself (see the comment from Austin about the camouflaged church quoted on p33). Such a move is no more valid than the claim that, because there are five people perceiving the same object, there are five further existent objects generated by the act of perception itself! Thus analysed, appearance is defined as being a direct experience of an object from a specific position in time and space; different positions yield different perceptions. Perspectival distortion is as much a physical fact of the world as the penny's roundness. The **reification** of a separate realm of perception is both unwieldy and unnecessary, and it fails to establish the falsity of the direct realist's claims. Consider the argument from double vision: when you see a penny that looks double you're not seeing two of something called sense data, you simply see one penny which *looks* double. There are not two *things* in the world called sense data.

Key terms

Reification: to reify means to bring something into existence. Reification is thus the process of bringing something into existence which might not have been held to exist otherwise.

Furthermore, perceptual variation does not occur randomly. Scientific disciplines such as optics can not only explain why such variations occur, they can also successfully predict them. This means that when we consider his table, Russell is not only able to say why some parts will look white, he can also pinpoint the exact position that an observer would need to be in order to see these parts looking white. As our empirically based scientific method teaches us to expect perceptual variation, the fact that such variation then occurs serves to confirm the realist worldview rather than cast doubt upon the object of perception.

Think about

When I perceive a coin as elliptical, is there any difference between this type of experience and an experience which involves illusion (for example, a stick appearing to be bent when placed in water)? Give one reason to think there is and one reason to think there is not.

Write down or draw on paper three examples of a perceptually relative experience. Do you think these show there is a difference between what you perceive and what exists in the world? Why? Give reasons for your answer.

After working through this topic, you should:

- be able to distinguish between naive and philosophical direct realism
- know about the problems posed for direct realism by examples of perceptual error such as illusion and hallucination
- understand what is meant by perceptual variation and how it may be accommodated into a realist epistemology.

Representative realism

Learning objectives:

- to understand what is meant by the expression 'representative/indirect' realism

- to be able to give an account of what sense data are

- to understand how science-inspired arguments affect the claims of the sense-data theorist

- to understand Locke's ontological position, and how he argues for it

- to be able to define and illustrate the primary/secondary quality thesis

- to demonstrate an appreciation of the arguments for and against the primary/secondary quality thesis.

Key philosopher

A. J. Ayer (1910–89)

English philosopher best known for his verification principle, by which he claimed to be able to separate meaningful sentences from meaningless ones; leading to a form of analytical philosophy known as logical positivism. Ayer's foremost work is *Language, Truth and Logic* (1936).

If we were to take the criticisms laid against common-sense realism seriously and leave aside, for the moment, sophisticated responses to such censure, could an alternative account of perception be offered that might evade such problems? If so, what would such an account look like? The following explanation of the external world and our perception of it seeks to address some of the problems laid against common-sense realism whilst at the same time preserving some of its strengths.

Sense data

The criticisms we looked at above have prompted some philosophers to argue that, contrary to direct realism, the immediate objects of awareness are not physical objects but sense data. Sense data are the subjective, mind-dependent intermediaries of perception that supposedly provide us with knowledge of a mind-independent, physical world. They are the empirical atoms of colour, sound, smell, taste and texture out of which experience is composed. The term 'sense data' gained popularity within the works of the 20th-century philosophers G. E. Moore and Bertrand Russell and came to fruition within the works of A. J. Ayer and his theory of 'phenomenalism' (Ayer used the term 'sense contents'). All three employed this concept to address the problems of illusion, hallucination and perceptual relativity outlined previously; cases where it would seem that what we are confronted with in experience is not the external world but rather an appearance of it. Developing this point in line with the above four arguments, sense data can accommodate cases of perceptual relativity, for sense data themselves, unlike the objects of the external world, are perceptually relative and perceiver dependent. In relation to perceptual error, it is argued that distortion takes place, not at the level of the external world, but rather at the level of our perception of it: illusion is simply a particular sense datum failing to accurately match up with an external object. Hallucinatory experiences are instances of sense data without any correspondent object in the world. We might distinguish between sense data and objects as shown in Table 2.1.

Thus, on this account, when I view an object such as Russell's table, what I am directly aware of is a series of sense data which give rise to my perception (Russell uses the term 'sensation') of the table. These data vary as my perspective changes in the manner that Russell outlines in the quote we considered earlier. A sense datum, as opposed to the table itself, depends for its existence upon my perceiving it; it exists, unlike the table itself, exactly *as* I perceive it, and when I cease perceiving it, it ceases to be. It is:

- subjective – determined by my experience of it

- mental, it exists in the mind; relative to me – the sense datum, unlike the table itself, will change in accordance with my perceptual position

- infallible – whereas the table might not exist, I cannot doubt the existence of the table-like datum

- private – only I can perceive it, and subject to illusion; whereas the table beyond my perception of it may well be brown, this in no way guarantees that I will see it as such.

Table 2.1 *The differences between objects and sense data*

Objects	Sense data
Mind independent	Mind dependent
Have an existence distinct from our apprehension of them in experience (are permanent)	Exist as they are perceived (are transient)
Exist regardless of whether or not they are perceived	Exist only when perceived (*esse est percipi*)
Objective	Subjective
Physical	Mental (or possibly neutral)
Not relative to the perceiver	Relative to the perceiver
Can be subjected to doubt (are fallible)	Are not subject to doubt (are infallible)
Are public (accessible to all perceivers)	Are private (accessible only to the perceiver)
Not subject to illusion/error	Subject to illusion/error

■ Think about

Consider Table 2.1. Given the claims made about sense data, where do you think they exist?

How do you think a realist can use sense-data theory to say anything about the external world?

Sense data and the external world

According to representative realism, sense data mediate between the perceiver and the external world. While the real table is distinct from sense data relating to it, the sense data all represent the table in some way as they allow me to manipulate it (by moving it into the light, for example) and make accurate predictions about it (if Russell knocks over his ink, the table will stain). Furthermore, while the sense data are private, the fact that we can have meaningful discussions about the objects of the sense data (we could both count the legs on the table and come to agreement) seems to imply that the sense data do relate to a real public object somehow. Again, the fact that we could sit at the table playing cards until the sun goes down and it is too dark to see implies that the object in question is permanent. This is in distinct contrast to Macbeth's dagger which is completely private to him and apparently winks in and out of existence, so it would seem justifiable to label it a hallucination.

So the version of representative realism that Russell adheres to in *The Problems of Philosophy* (he changes his position later, but that need not concern us here) claims an apparent correspondence between sense data and objects. These data represent objects to me but, unlike in direct realism, there is no guarantee that they are identical with the objects in question (Russell doesn't claim that they are). Rather the relationship could be thought of as being like a map to a territory: reading a map can tell us things about the territory that it represents without necessarily resembling it. Contour lines, for example, are simply flat irregular circles on the paper, but they allow me to infer the presence of mountains in the Lake District National Park even if I never go there. Similarly, Russell claims that sense data allow us to infer the existence of the objects they supposedly represent and, in so doing, make a further inference as to the existence of an external world. The crucial point to understand here is that he is in no way claiming that the perception of sense data *proves* the existence of an external world. Rather, the external world has the status of a working hypothesis which seems the best fit for the facts as we know them. To return to our map analogy, while I could conceivably visit the Lake District to check on the accuracy of my map, representative realism holds that all experience of the external world is necessarily mediated and so the working hypothesis is the best result we can come up with. For Russell the existence of the external world is the most economic and systematic hypothesis for explaining the occurrence of the sense data.

Think about

How would you assess the strength of the proposition that the most we can say about the external world is that it is a hypothesis that fits the facts? If you feel it is rather weak, consider that the bulk, if not all, of our science is based upon hypotheses. How strong a proposition do you think it is now?

On one definition, science proceeds via falsification, and a hypothesis cannot be defined as such unless it can be falsified (disproved) in principle. Can you think of a way in which Russell's hypothetical external world could be subject to falsification?

Key terms

Material substance: the doctrine that the sense-given qualities of an object must be bound together by an underlying substance, e.g. the sweetness, colour, texture of an apple require a substance to bind them together. They can't simply exist on their own.

Berkeley's 'scepticism' was primarily directed at Locke's idea of **material substance**.

Some problems with sense data

In recent years, sense-data theories have gone out of fashion amongst realists. This is because they arguably generate more questions than they manage to answer. We will now briefly examine some of these questions.

The ontological question

If sense data sustain no physical existence, then the question of their location becomes problematic. Earlier sense-data theorists, such as Russell, argued that they are mental phenomena, occurring within the mind, but few modern philosophers would be happy to accept such a view. One reason for this is that if, as we have seen, Russell thinks that both sensation and sense data belong to the mental realm, quite how sense data are supposed to provide a mechanism that mediates between the apparently ontologically separate mental and physical realms is not really explained.

Two sceptical questions

The first of these depends upon how satisfied we are with Russell's hypothesis of an external world. If the hypothesis is not legitimate because it can neither be tested nor falsified, sense-data theorists are left vulnerable to a radical scepticism of the external world of the type we find in Berkeley's idealism (discussed below).

Following on from this, sense-data theorists inherit a scepticism of other minds: if my sense data are private and accessible only to me, then I have no way of establishing that they are anything like yours. It may be true that we can both look at the table and agree that it is brown, but neither of us have any way of knowing if what one means by 'brown' is the same as the other (see Chapter 1). This makes it very difficult to demonstrate that we really have genuine knowledge of what colour the table is.

The question of representation

There are really two of these questions as well, but as the first question is tied to the fact that we can never really know what sense data represent, it is really covered by the sceptical questions above. The second question is rather more telling and that is: 'How can we know that sense data are representations in the first place?' Let us return to the example of the map: how do I know that the contour lines represent mountains? Because I can map read. This could have come about in one of two ways:

- I have a key to the map (or a teacher who acts as a key)
- I have compared at least one previous map to its territory and noted how they coincide.

Now consider what happens if I encounter a box full of maps for the first time but have no key or access to any of the territories they cover. How could I possibly recognise that they represented anything, let alone that they were maps? And yet this situation is analogous to the way in which we are supposed to initially encounter sense data: they are completely private so I can have no outside help in interpreting them, and I have no direct access to the objects that they are supposed to represent.

Science-inspired arguments for sense data

As mentioned above, empiricism leads to science as a method of investigating the physical world. Whereas sceptical arguments for the existence of sense data deal with epistemological issues concerning the extent of our knowledge of the external world, science-inspired arguments deal with ontology. Scientists claim to give an objective account of how the world is and argue that their success is demonstrated by their abilities to make accurate predictions on all sorts of scales, and to carry out incredibly complicated procedures such as sending men to the moon. However, when we look at what science tells us about the world, we seem to run into problems for the common-sense realist which are then exploited by the representative realists to argue in favour of sense data.

The argument from physics

Physicists make some very counterintuitive claims about the world which do not seem to match up to our perceptions of it at all. Physics tells us that Russell's apparently solid table is reducible to a collection of colourless, odourless atoms, the varying combinations of which produce within us the visual, auditory, gustatory, olfactory and tactile building blocks of experience. These atoms themselves are further reducible to the quantum level where discrete quanta appear to share properties of particles and waves. So at this level the table is not solid at all, but rather a lattice of energy. Clearly if we accept the physicists' account, then what the common-sense realist asserts is wrong: reality as is and reality as perceived are two separate things. Were common-sense realism correct in its assumptions, i.e. were we to apprehend reality directly, then it would follow that the objects of our experience would present themselves to us as lattices of energy and not, as is the case, the colourful objects of experience. Common-sense realism fails.

The representative realist approach is to argue that just because the world can be reduced to smaller physical constituents in no way entails that it has to be. That the table is reducible to a collection of measurable quanta no more entails that the quanta constitute its being than that, because my everyday experience of it is reducible to 'oblong, brown and shiny, smooth and cool and hard' these are discrete properties of the table rather than sense data. What I am directly confronted with in experience are these data themselves and not the table. Likewise when I observe its atomic structure and then go further down to the quantum level I am again confronted with sense data. Or, to give another example, I can look along a beach, or I can sit down and count the grains of sand. Once again, as with perceptual relativity, there are different levels of analysis and explanation.

Think about

One possible way to account for how we could recognise sense data as representations is if we possess an innate idea of what a sense datum is. Why is this option not available to an empiricist such as Russell?

Think about

Why, if at all, should philosophers of perception care about what science has to tell us about the world? Are our concerns about the nature of the world philosophical or scientific? Would it be possible to mix the two?

Moreover, a separate strain of argument could be developed: the more sophisticated representative realist could claim that it is the perceiver-dependent nature of language that leads us astray. Our mental vocabulary of sounds and colours brings into play a secondary realm of sense data, detached from the articles that occupy the external world. Were we to construct a perceiver-independent language of objects that reduced the language of perception to its correspondent physical processes (which is, arguably, physics' ultimate goal), we might be able to circumvent such a problem. Thus analysed, the claim: 'I am currently experiencing a sensation of brownness' would be translatable into/shorthand for: 'I am currently experiencing a frequency and amplitude of photons of light x received by colour receptors y'. Russell draws an analogy between catalogues and the objects depicted in the catalogues. The pictures *represent* the objects.

Time-lag arguments

Time-lag arguments draw our attention to the time difference between an event's occurrence and our subsequent experience of it, claiming that if an object ceases to exist but a time-lag occurs so that we continue to view it as existing, then we cannot be directly viewing that object. If this sounds initially rather far fetched, this example from Russell should clarify things:

> It takes eight minutes for the sun's light to reach us; thus, when we see the sun we are seeing the sun of eight minutes ago. So far as our sense data afford evidence as to the physical sun they afford evidence as to the physical sun of eight minutes ago; if the physical sun had ceased to exist within the last eight minutes, that would make no difference to the sense data we call 'seeing the sun'. This affords a fresh illustration of the necessity of distinguishing between sense data and physical objects.

Russell (1980, pp16–17)

As we shall see below, this argument suffers from the same fundamental flaw as the other arguments in this section. However, even if it did not, it is far from clear that it undermines direct realism in the way that Russell thinks it does. While it would be naive to suppose that what we perceive directly we also perceive instantaneously, this is not being claimed by the more sophisticated realist. Time-lag arguments only refute the realist who claims that direct perception is synonymous with immediate perception. This is a misconception. Accepting the truth of time-lags merely requires a caveat to be added to the direct realists' claims: what we are directly aware of in perception is an object as it *was*. For the majority of cases this temporal gap is so minimal it is scarcely worth observing. For instances of objects of a greater distance, including those objects that have ceased to be, we are directly aware of the object as it was at the time that light waves first reflected off it.

The argument from causal dependency

Like time-lag arguments, the argument from causal dependency attempts to open up a gap between the object and act of perception which the representative realist hopes to bridge with sense data. It does this by an appeal to the physics and physiology of perception in general. Science tells us that perception is one end of a causal chain dependent on a number of physical processes. Sight, for example, depends upon light reflected from the object bouncing off the retina and sending an electric signal down the optic nerve to be ultimately decoded in the brain. If this is the case, all we are actually aware of is the final sensation in the brain

Think about

How convinced are you by the direct realists' claims here? Consider them in the light of a comment made by A. J. Ayer: which is more paradoxical, to say that we do not perceive physical objects or that we can see into the past?

Think about

Illustrate the argument from causal dependency for a sense other than sight.

so we cannot be certain that there is an external world at the other end of the chain; it must remain a hypothesis at best.

Counter-argument

There is a single counter-argument which deals with all three of these science-inspired arguments for sense data. Each time, the representative realist's case hinges upon the dubitability of the external world and puts forward the argument that because of this dubitability, all we can be certain that we are perceiving are sense data. Unfortunately all three arguments start from the premise that there is an external world in order to promote the argument for sense data and so cannot then use sense data to cast doubt upon that world, i.e. claim that the world is a hypothesis that we can never know. This becomes obvious if we summarise the three arguments, italicising the relevant claims.

The argument from physics

Physics gives us *objective truths about the world*, but in so doing demonstrates that the world is not as we immediately perceive it. Therefore, what we perceive are variable sense data rather than the world itself. Scientific arguments frequently make the point that the scientist is providing an objective account of what the world is *really* like. Such an account would not include references to colours, tastes, smells, etc. Therefore we do not perceive the world as it really is given that we do perceive colour, taste and smell.

Time-lag arguments

Physics tells us that *there is a sun*, the light from which takes eight minutes to reach us. The sun could have *ceased to exist* within the last eight minutes, but we would still see it shining. Therefore, what we perceive are sense data rather than the sun itself.

The argument from causal dependency

Physics gives us *objective truths about the world* and tells us that perception *is caused by something*. As we are only aware of the sense data at our end of this causal chain, we can have no option but to doubt the existence of the thing at the other end. These arguments use premises about physical objects to get started and conclude that we do not know there are such objects, or at least directly know that there are. They are open to the charge of self contradiction.

▦ Primary and secondary qualities

We are now in a position to say that the science-inspired arguments that we considered above fail to support sense-data theory because it is dependent upon the separation of world and perception in such a manner that all we can know is sense data and not the world itself, but science takes the world and our ability to investigate it as a given. However, if we discard sense-data theory, we are still left with the puzzling question of how sensations like taste and smell can be wholly present in a physical object. It is here that science may be able to help us by providing evidence in support of the thesis of primary and secondary qualities originally propounded by Locke.

Locke's concept of ideas

Although it has its roots in the philosophy of Descartes and the mechanical science of Isaac Newton, an earlier version of Locke's general

▦ Think about

If we have already granted the existence of the external world, do we still need sense-data theory?

Key philosopher

Democritus
(c.460–c.370 BC)

He was an Ancient Greek philosopher and early atomist, i.e. he believed that matter is composed of atoms. What is known about him is mostly second-hand as only a few fragments of his own writings survive.

Key terms

Materialist: someone who believes that the ultimate nature of reality is material and all explanations will ultimately be in terms of matter and its motions.

Substance: this is a technical philosophical term ultimately deriving from the Ancient Greeks and which has been the subject of disputes ever since. The finer details of these arguments need not concern us. A substance may be defined as an ontological class which has independent existence.

AQA Examiner's tip

Locke does not have recourse to modern physics and optics to help substantiate his claims; you are in a position to bolster (or, perhaps, undermine) his argument by this means if asked to assess them in the exam.

thesis can be traced back to Democritus whose work on '*atoma*' bears a striking resemblance, as we shall see, to Locke's realism:

> Sweet exists by convention, bitter by convention, colour by convention. Atoms and void alone exist in reality

Democritus, in **Freeman** *(1948, p93)*

That the material world has a physical existence external to my perception of it – the central tenet of realism – Locke accepts. That such a world constitutes the *direct* object of perception he rejects, not least of all because of the sceptical arguments generated by common-sense realism outlined above. So he is a representative realist of sorts, but not in the same way that Russell is, as we shall see.

In defending his position, Locke exploits a distinction between ontology and epistemology. Ontologically, he advances a series of arguments to show that reality, as it exists external to us, is distinct from our apprehension of it in experience and epistemologically; what is directly *known* in experience are 'ideas' (perceptions/sensations/impressions) and not the physical objects that cause them (note that Locke does not distinguish between idea and impressions as Hume did). While it is not necessary to get too bogged down in the detail of Locke's arguments, we need to sketch in some of the debate in order to understand why such a move is valid. Then we will be in a much better position to see how such an account resolves the problems that confront common-sense realism. Locke's argument is essentially the argument from causal dependency that we considered above: objects in the external world are constituted in such a way that they affect our senses which then cause a simple idea within the mind. So ideas are the simple objects of sensation; sounds, colours, textures, tastes and smells that are 'excited in us' by the objects of the external world. Where Locke parts company with the argument from causal dependency is that, rather than doubting the existence of the beginning of the causal chain, he is a thoroughgoing **materialist** who believes that science demonstrates the existence of a single material **substance** that constitutes the external world. While we cannot know substance directly, primary qualities are demonstrable properties of material substance and this substance is the 'glue' that binds together all qualities.

While Locke is plainly using a version of the causal argument, note how he is bringing in elements of the argument from physics in order to strengthen his claims. This recourse to scientific evidence is a key feature (and, arguably, a major strength) of Locke's empiricism.

The primary/secondary quality thesis

In order to separate ideas from the external 'bodies' that produce them, Locke distinguishes between the qualities of an object which belong to the object itself:

> These I call original or primary qualities of body, which I think we may observe to produce simple ideas in us, viz., solidity, extension, figure, motion or rest, and number

Locke (1690, Book II, Chapter VIII, paragraph 9)

and those that are found in perception:

> such qualities which in truth are nothing in the objects themselves but power to produce various sensations in us by their primary qualities,

i.e., by the bulk, figure, texture, and motion of their insensible parts, as colours, sounds, tastes, etc. These I call secondary qualities

Locke (1690, Book II, Chapter VIII, paragraph 10)

An exhaustive list of the former qualities (Locke is not consistent in his applications) gives us 'solidity', 'extension', 'figure', 'mobility', 'motion or rest', 'number', 'bulk', 'motion', 'size', and 'situation'. These in turn have the 'power' to produce within us the qualities of colour, sound, taste and odour. Finally Locke explains the process that bonds the two:

If then external objects be not united to our minds when they produce ideas therein; and yet we perceive these original qualities in such of them as singly fall under our senses, it is evident that some motion must be thence continued by our nerves, or animal spirits, by some parts of our bodies, to the brains or the seat of sensation, there to produce in our minds the particular ideas we have of them. And since the extension, figure, number, and motion of bodies of an observable bigness, may be perceived at a distance by the sight, it is evident some singly imperceptible bodies must come from them to the eyes, and thereby convey to the brain some motion; which produces these ideas which we have of them in us

Locke (1690, Book II, Chapter VIII, paragraph 12)

Here we find a fairly sophisticated scientific analysis of perception; Locke was a great defender of the ideas being presented in the physical sciences of his day, most importantly Newton's account of the 'mechanical' nature of perception. The atomic ingredients of reality 'convey' to the brain via the causal process of perception, the qualities of experience that 'fall under the senses'. Thus, the lines between appearance and reality are drawn. As with sense-data theory, the type of relation Locke is referring to here is one of representation rather than resemblance:

that the ideas of primary qualities of bodies are resemblances of them, and their patterns do really exist in the bodies themselves, but the ideas produced in us by these secondary qualities have no resemblance of them at all. There is nothing like our ideas, existing in the bodies themselves. They are, in the bodies we denominate from them, only a power to produce those sensations in us

Locke (1690, Book II, Chapter VIII, paragraph 15)

This point is important as it allows Locke to deal with cases of illusion, i.e. where perception and reality conflict. Thus, while the primary qualities of objects are accurate semblances of the objects themselves, our subsequent experience of them shares no such relation. It is here that we can begin summarising Locke's division.

The divisions outlined in Table 2.2 overleaf allows us to explore in greater detail the epistemological implications of Locke's account and, of course, the problems it generates. Before we do so, we need to address the question of why such a division was of importance to begin with. Whilst it should be clear from our initial objections to common-sense realism that there are good, independent reasons for distinguishing between reality and our subsequent experience of it, we have already seen with Locke's earlier example of water that 'heat' cannot be 'in' the water in the same way that the molecules of hydrogen and oxygen are – were this so, then everybody would experience the water in the same way. Nevertheless, we do not need to appeal to examples of perceptual relativity and error to see why Locke's account is compelling:

Think about

Explain in your own words what Locke understands by the term 'idea'. List three examples.

Can you identify any problems with Locke's terminology? Why might the concept of an 'idea' mislead us? (Hint: is there a difference between what is perceived by the memory and imagination and what we perceive in experience?)

Table 2.2 *The ontology of primary and secondary qualities*

The nature (ontology) of primary qualities: solidity, extension, figure, motion or rest, and number	The nature (ontology) of secondary qualities: colour, sound, taste and odour
Exist within the object (perceiver-independent)	Are sensations within the mind of the perceiver (perceiver-dependent) Do not exist within the object but are caused within us by the primary qualities of the object
Accurately resemble the object	Represent, but do not resemble, the object
Are measurable	Are non-measurable
Are physical	Are experienced mentally
Are often accessible via more than one sense (for example, seeing and feeling)	Are always accessible via only one sense (colour (by vision); texture (by feeling), etc.)
Cause secondary qualities	Are caused by the powers of primary qualities
Constitute reality	Constitute experience

Think about

Are primary qualities subject to perceptual variation? Think back to our earlier discussion of Russell's table.

The particular bulk, number, figure, and motion of the parts of fire or snow are really in them – whether any one's senses perceive them or no: and therefore they may be called real qualities, because they really exist in those bodies. But light, heat, whiteness, or coldness, are no more really in them than sickness or pain is in manna. Take away the sensation of them; let not the eyes see light or colours, nor the ears hear sounds; let the palate not taste, nor the nose smell, and all colours, tastes, odours, and sounds, as they are such particular ideas, vanish and cease, and are reduced to their causes, i.e., bulk, figure, and motion of parts

Locke (1690, Book II, Chapter VIII, paragraph 17)

Primary qualities embody the essential nature of objects and do not, contrary to secondary ones, require a perceiver for their existence. If we return to our initial example of what the world would be like were there no one around to perceive it, we can see that on Locke's account, as in that of the argument from physics, such a world would be devoid of sound, colour, taste and odour (it is interesting that he avoids the example of texture; conveyable as a secondary quality when felt, or a primary one when measured. Locke actually categorises texture as a primary quality although this was perhaps a luxury he could not afford – a point borne out by the subsequent criticism it generated). Although this is a strange idea, we can perhaps understand Locke's intentions. Philosophically speaking, the notion of an 'unheard sound' or an 'un-smelt odour' sounds rather bizarre. While we might happily concede to the existence of a 'vibrating column of air' that gets converted one way or another when it comes into contact with one of the senses, nevertheless the thought that, for example, an apple could taste like something even if it had never been bitten into sounds implausible. Likewise, if we accept what physics tells us of the world, then we inherit the view that reality is nothing over and above an abundance of particles vibrating in time and space. Particles themselves are without odour, resonance, taste and

Think about

In a couple of paragraphs, describe and illustrate Locke's primary and secondary quality distinction.

colour and only acquire such properties when they come into contact with humans. Even the observation of such particles under a microscope requires us to access them via the secondary properties of experience, and as such, misrepresents the actual nature of the particles themselves. To this extent, Locke has science on his side.

There is much to be said for Locke's account. Before moving on, a summary of the epistemological implications of the primary/secondary quality distinction would be helpful. Fig. 2.2 ilustrates this.

Fig. 2.2 *Locke's concept of ideas, showing the relative positions of primary and secondary qualities*

Evaluation of the primary/secondary quality thesis

A major strength of the primary/secondary quality thesis is that it manages to encompass:

- the common-sense view that there is an external world in which objects possess properties which we perceive
- the sense-data theorist's representative view, bolstered by science, that the world may not be as we perceive it and that there are qualities of sensation that are dependent upon us rather than the object.

It manages this by avoiding the claim that the two are mutually exclusive, but rather combining them. This is an attractive option because it allows us to give a sophisticated account of perception that seems to gel with our experience of it. To return to the falling tree example at the beginning of the chapter, we can see how the primary/secondary quality thesis will allow us to say that there is no sound (secondary quality) if there is nobody to hear it fall, without having to doubt that the solid object that is the tree actually falls (primary qualities). Not only does this appeal to common sense, it also accords with what physics tells us.

However, problems start to arise if we look closer at Locke's classification of primary and secondary qualities. To demonstrate let us look at an example.

Solidity

We have seen that Locke regards solidity as a primary quality; the solidity of an object is a property of that object. This is not to say that the object must remain inert and its solidity never change (the standard example is that used by Descartes of a piece wax being heated and going from solid to liquid, yet remaining wax), rather that at any given point in time, the relative solidity of an object is a given. Yet when we considered Russell's table, which was apparently hard to the touch, from a physicist's point of view we saw that ultimately it broke down to a latticework of indeterminate waves or particles. The question is whether, at this level, the concept of relative solidity makes any sense. We would either have to redefine what we mean by solidity in the light of quantum mechanics, or admit that we attribute solidity to the table in the same way that we do colour. Either way, Locke's definition of solidity as a primary quality fails.

Of course, given the advances in physics, it might be possible to come up with a much more satisfactory classification of primary and secondary qualities than Locke's. However, there is a more serious criticism of Locke which remains unaffected no matter how you reclassify them. This is considered in the next topic.

After working through this topic, you should:

- be able to demonstrate an understanding of the philosophical arguments for sense data: what they solve and what problems they generate

- be able to offer a sophisticated account of the implications of the claim that sense data represent objects

- be able to demonstrate knowledge of and illustrate criticisms of how representative realism cannot adequately account for the existence of the world beyond our perception of it

- be able to demonstrate knowledge of science-inspired arguments against common-sense realism in favour of representative realism

- clearly understand what is meant by the terms primary and secondary qualities

- be able to demonstrate knowledge of the ontological implications of the primary/secondary quality thesis and how it accords with modern science

- be able to offer illustrative examples for all of the above points.

> **■ Think about**
>
> Do you think that it is possible to provide a non-contentious division of primary and secondary qualities?
>
> If yes, what would it look like? If no, why not?

Idealism

Learning objectives:

- to understand Berkeley's critique of Locke

- to understand how Berkeley's idealism works, and to appreciate the role of God within it

- to be able to argue for and against Berkeley's idealism

- to understand what solipsism is

- to be able to illustrate and critically assess the argument for brain stimulation.

Key philosopher

George Berkeley (1685–1753)

He was an Irish empiricist philosopher and priest, and Bishop of Cloyne from 1734. Berkeley is best known for his idealism and this is explored here.

Key terms

Esse est percipi: 'to be is to be perceived'. This is the ontological foundation of Berkeley's idealism. Any form of existence is dependent upon an act of perception. If something is not being perceived, it does not exist.

💡 Berkeley's critique of Locke

Berkeley presents a critique of Locke in both the *Principles of Human Knowledge* (1710) and *Three Dialogues Between Hylas and Philonous in opposition to Sceptics and Atheists* (1713). The main thrust of this critique is found in the first of the *Dialogues* where he presents the view that it is not just secondary qualities that are mind dependent, but primary ones too. This established, the ground becomes fertile for the introduction of a new set of ideas on perception; immaterialism or idealism, the view that reality is mind dependent.

The perceiver-dependent nature of secondary qualities

The first section of the *Dialogues* (1713) deals with 'sensible things', i.e. those qualities that are immediately perceived. Berkeley shows that for each quality, or 'combination of qualities', each depends 'for its reality' upon experience – most famously summarised in part one of the *Principles* (1710) by the slogan '***esse est percipi***'. The first stage of the argument relates to tactile experience: the feeling of pain induced by the pricking of a pin must lie in the mind of the perceiver for it would be absurd to attribute such pain to a material object. But what about the *cause* of pain, surely that must lie in the object? Hylas, the Lockean protagonist who argues against Philonous representing Berkeley, argues that this must be so of the intense heat which might bring about such pain. Philonous argues against this by pointing out the inseparability of the experience of heat and its accompanying pain when holding one's hand to a flame; tactile qualities (those of touch) cannot exist in the object. A similar line of reasoning shows that the same is true of all sensible qualities. The perceptual pleasure and pain accompanying the 'sweetness of sugar' and the 'bitterness of wormwood' show us that gustatory properties (those of taste) must be separated from their original bodies. 'That which at other times seems sweet, shall, to a distempered palate, appear bitter' (Berkeley, 1713) further embellishes this point. That the odours of 'filth and ordure' appear agreeable to 'brute animals' yet unpleasing to man serves to show that olfactory properties (those of smell) cannot be qualities of objects; were this so, humans and brutes would have to experience them in the same way. The same is true of auditory qualities (those of sound), at first rationalised by Hylas to be vibrations 'in the external air'. Philonous points out that 'motions' are not the object of hearing but rather of sight, and thus the qualities of sound and motion are distinct; the former auditory and perceiver dependent, the latter visual. Finally we come to the visual properties themselves. Hylas' last line of defence is to ask 'can anything be plainer than that we see them on the objects?' To this Philonous responds: 'are then the beautiful red and purple we see on yonder clouds really in them?' (Berkeley, 1713). Hylas, realising the foolishness of such a claim argues that the colours which adhere to objects are only grasped correctly when viewed up close. That the 'nearest and exactest survey' is given by a microscope and not the naked eye serves to refute this position. Hylas concedes to this and thus to the perceptually relative and perceiver-dependent nature of all sensible things.

> **Think about**
>
> While by no means hostile to science, Berkeley's philosophy is explicitly motivated by a desire to combat materialism in order to maintain the importance of God. It will be helpful to keep these points in mind as you work through this topic.

> **Think about**
>
> For each one of the senses, explain and illustrate Berkeley's argument that the secondary qualities of experience exist in the mind of the perceiver alone.

Berkeley's arguments for the perceiver-dependent nature of primary qualities

You should have recognised the above argument – it is fundamentally the same as Locke's. Berkeley does not stop there though. He goes on to apply the same arguments about perceptual variability levied against secondary qualities to the primary qualities that supposedly adhere to matter:

> Philonous: You are still then of opinion that extension and figures are inherent in external unthinking substances?
>
> Hylas: I am.
>
> Philonous: But what if the same arguments which are brought against Secondary Qualities will hold good against these also?
>
> Hylas: Why then I shall be obliged to think, they too exist only in the mind.

Berkeley (1713)

A 'mite' (tiny insect) would see its foot as 'a body of some considerable dimension', while for a smaller creature we could imagine it taking on mountainous proportions. For us, such an object would be deemed minute. If extension were really a feature of the object and not perception, we would be forced to accept that the same object could entertain different dimensions at the same time. The variable presentation of dimension leads Berkeley to conclude that extension itself is not 'inherent within the object' as Locke believes. The property of figure is similarly dealt with as when one eye perceives an object through a microscope and the other without, the same object appears to the latter as 'smooth and round' while the former perceives it as 'great, uneven and regular'. Thus figure cannot belong to an object, but rather our perception of it. Extension and figure dispatched, Philonous turns his attention to motion. He asks: 'Can a real motion in any external body be at the same time very swift and very slow?' (Berkeley, 1713). Hylas responds in the negative. To this Philonous responds that motion is nothing over and above the 'succession of ideas' in the mind of the perceiver, and, given that it is possible that the succession of ideas moves more rapidly for one individual than it does for another, then motion too is relative to the perceiver. Of course, one could respond to this by claiming that speed is determinate regardless of our perception of it. That a car appears to move more quickly when viewed up close than when viewed from afar, but it will still be travelling at a determinate speed (say 70 mph) independent of our perception of it, in no way affects Berkeley's argument here for such a measurement itself can only be gauged in terms of our perception. How fast *is* 70 mph? What would it be like to perceive or even imagine such a speed correctly? For Berkeley, we could never come to such an understanding. Motion, as with all the other supposed primary qualities of bodies, is perceptually dependent and thus not objective/determinate. Finally he deals with solidity, defined as either 'hardness or resistance'. Such a quality is not difficult to dismiss as 'relative to the senses' for it is 'evident that what seems hard to one animal may appear soft to another, who hath greater force and firmness of limbs'. Thus the qualities that Locke sees as belonging to objects themselves, collapse, upon analysis, into the secondary qualities of perception. The former cannot be conceived of as existing without the latter.

Fig. 2.3 *Idealism: all properties are internal to the perceiver*

Berkeley's denial of material substance

Again, you should recognise the position we are now in, as Berkeley has basically collapsed primary and secondary qualities into sense data. For Berkeley, what we call sense data and what we call actual objects are referred to as *ideas*. However, it is at this point that he makes the really radical move: he attacks Locke's argument for a material substance and he does this from two directions:

- You will remember Locke's claim that primary qualities are properties of substance; Berkeley argues that his demonstration that primary qualities are no different from secondary qualities and that they are mind dependent shows that there is no necessity for material substance. Consequently we lose nothing by denying it.

- He accepts Locke's empiricism and pushes it to its logical conclusion: if everything we can know we know by experience, and Locke claims that we can never know material substance directly but only via the ideas generated by primary qualities, then from an empirical point of view we can never know material substance at all. If this is the case, then any arguments about material substance are completely vacuous as, on Locke's account, we are discussing something for which there is no corresponding idea.

So all that Berkeley has left are ideas, and he claims that the objects of perception are collections of ideas. His radical empiricism leads him to make the ontological claim that existence depends upon perception (*esse est percipi*) and when things are not perceived, they cease to exist. Berkeley thought it absurd to suppose that you could have ideas without a perceiving mind. It is at this point that Berkeley believes he has successfully refuted materialism and paved the way for his own idealism (also referred to as immaterialism or anti-realism). Everything, on this account, is mind dependent.

A naive criticism

The world appears, to all intents and purposes, to have an existence beyond my perception of it. Furthermore, it has a regularity about it that allows me to predict things that happen outside of my perception. Therefore idealism fails.

Think about

Explain how Berkeley shows that primary qualities are perceiver dependent. How convincing do you find his argument? Why?

Think about

Can you see how Berkeley has not only rejected Locke's material substance, but also effectively shut off Russell's 'external world as hypothesis'?

We have mentioned that Berkeley is not hostile to science. How do you think that he can account for it?

Think about

There is an obvious, but mistaken, criticism of idealism that is often raised at this point in the argument. Can you work out what it is?

We can clarify this with another example from Russell. Here he is arguing for the existence of the external world apart from sense data, but the illustration is equally applicable to Berkeley's ideas (although, for reasons you will shortly come to appreciate, Russell would never use it this way himself):

> If the cat appears at one moment in one part of the room, and at another in another part, it is natural to suppose that it has moved from the one to the other, passing over a series of intermediate positions. But if it is merely a set of sense data, it cannot have ever been in any place where I did not see it; thus we shall have to suppose that it did not exist at all while I was not looking, but suddenly sprang into being in a new place. If the cat exists whether I see it or not, we can understand from our own experience how it gets hungry between one meal and the next; but if it does not exist when I am not seeing it, it seems odd that appetite should grow during non-existence as fast as during existence.

Russell (1980, p10)

This argument would count against any version of idealism which held that the existence of physical objects was dependent on our perceptions of them. However, this is an absurd theory and was certainly not held by Berkeley. We shall now turn to Berkeley's explanation.

Berkeley's response

We have seen that idealism argues that all that exists are 'minds and their ideas' and that, on this account, it is not just the case that the external world cannot be thought of outside of a mind, but rather that such a world ceases to exist when unperceived. In order to avoid the charge of absurdity at the non-existence of unperceived objects, Berkeley puts forward an argument to show that all objects and all minds (for if the mind itself ceases to perceive, then so too it ceases to exist) continue, perceived in the mind of a greater being: God:

> Some truths there are so near and obvious to the mind that a man need only open his eyes to see them. Such I take this important one to be, viz., that all the choir of heaven and furniture of the earth, in a word all those bodies which compose the mighty frame of the world, have not any subsistence without a mind, that their being is to be perceived or known; that consequently so long as they are not actually perceived by me, or do not exist in my mind or that of any other created spirit, they must either have no existence at all, or else subsist in the mind of some Eternal Spirit

Berkeley (1710, Part 1, para. 6)

In choosing between objects 'having no existence at all' outside of perception or their being perceived by 'some Eternal Spirit', Berkeley opts for the latter. His idealism commits him to ideas being dependent upon mind; it does not commit him to them being dependent upon a human mind or minds. This is Berkeley's key principle. No human mind could create nor sustain such perfection as we find in the cosmos so, Berkeley reasons, we require a greater and eternal mind as the perceiver of all things. Such a mind is identified as God. God perceives all things at all times and thus guarantees that the universe continues to be when unperceived by lesser beings such as ourselves. Idealism is saved.

AQA Examiner's tip

If you are asked to critically assess idealism in the exam, it is vitally important that you do not present this criticism as a serious blow against it.

The role of God in Berkeley's idealism

Before offering an analysis of Berkeley's position, we need to briefly comment on the role that God plays in Berkeley's idealism. Many have argued that this role is simply to rescue Berkeley from the absurdity detailed in the naive criticism. However, such an understanding is misconceived and can be accused of putting the cart before the horse. As we noted at the beginning of this topic, Berkeley's philosophical agenda is to combat the Locke-influenced materialism popular amongst his contemporaries. So, far from God rescuing Berkeley's idealism, it is Berkeley's idealism that rescues God. Berkeley, concerned at the growing atheism of his day, saw science and philosophy (particularly the empirical philosophy of which he was a proponent) as contributing to such atheism. His idealism was an attempt to rescue empiricism from materialism, thereby preserving what he recognised as the benefits of empirical/scientific methods, without falling into atheism. God is therefore the cause rather than a symptom of Berkeley's philosophy. However, what we are concerned with is whether the appeal to God is philosophically justifiable. It is crucial that our understanding of Berkeley takes such a point into account.

Think about

How convincing do you find Berkeley's idealism? What reasons might there be for rejecting it?

Why might the introduction of God be problematic here? Think about whether or not God could be perceived as an idea to inform your answer.

Evaluation of idealism

The strengths of idealism lie with its simplicity: only one type of quality is posited in comparison with the dual account of qualities presented in representative realism, for example, so no questions arise with regard to how different qualities relate to each other. Furthermore, whereas the external world can be called into doubt, the same is not true of our perceptions of it (although perhaps the 'it' is inappropriate here). Developing this latter point further, in eliminating the external world from our enquiries, we do away with the very thing that allows the sceptic a foothold. Sceptical doubts surrounding perception are generated by inconsistencies between the world and our experience of it. If we do away with the former, then the latter develops sceptical immunity; the seeming absurdity of idealism is matched only by its irrefutability. A certain strong point of idealism is that it avoids the linking problem which is characteristic of representative realism. One does not have to explain how the sense data link to anything as objects simply are collections of sense data (ideas).

Criticisms of Berkeley's idealism

Consider this:

> No one has refuted Berkeley, even though most people insist that his view is false.

Priest (1990, p113)

If Priest is correct here, does this mean that Berkeley's idealism wins the day and the nature of reality is mental? Not necessarily. The aspect of Berkeley's argument Priest is referring to is the proof that we cannot know that physical objects exist because Berkeley has successfully destroyed the difference between primary and secondary qualities. So how do we criticise Berkeley? One way is to focus upon his notion and use of God:

All of Berkeley's empiricism gives him is a series of perceptions. He then uses the *esse est percipi* principle to posit these perceptions as evidence for an ideal (i.e. 'mind-dependent') world.

■ However, these perceptions change state in a predictable manner when he is not perceiving them (Russell's cat), so this ideal world is apparently regular and intransient.

■ Such a world requires a permanent perceiver. This perceiver is God, in whose mind everything subsists.

This is a circular argument as the existence of God guarantees the principle and the principle demonstrates the necessity of God. What Berkeley requires at this point is an independent proof for God in order to break the circle and provide a proper guarantee for the principle.

Unhappily for Berkeley, it is hard to see how he can come up with an independent proof of God: as an empiricist, Berkeley is committed to the view that all we can know is ultimately derived from our senses and God, at least as Berkeley conceives of him, is not reducible to such atoms – it would be absurd to claim God smelt like something or was of a particular colour – so Berkeley has no grounds whatsoever for insisting upon his existence. God cannot be perceived in the same way that objects can, so, appealing to Berkeley's *esse est percipi* principle, any appeal to a divine presence will lack foundations. Berkeley's God suffers from the same criticisms as Locke's material substance. This would also apply to any appeal to *mental* substance.

Is Berkeley's idealism indistinguishable from direct realism?

A final issue with Berkeley's philosophy comes about when we take a step back and ask ourselves just what has Berkeley established? Well, first, if correct, he has shown that reality has an existence independent of being perceived by a human mind. Second, he has shown that such objects continue to exist with all properties untouched, within the mind of God. Finally, he has shown that when we come into contact with such objects, we perceive them directly, with all of their properties intact. But now we can ask just how is such a position distinct from the direct realism that we encountered in the first section of this chapter? Such a theory of perception was developed as the philosophical antithesis to idealism. We perceive a material reality directly and objects support all of the properties that experience reveals in them independent of human perception. But is this not precisely what Berkeley is saying? Of course Berkeley could respond by pointing out that his reality is a purely mental construct. But here we can ask just what role we can accord to the concept 'mental'. The ideal objects that exist in God's mind are phenomenologically identical to the objects that are perceived in the material universe of direct realism. The cerebral nature of Berkeley's objects fails to distinguish them in any way from the material objects of common sense. Here the word 'mental' becomes empty of content – we could substitute the concept 'God' for the idea of a 'material universe' without loss of meaning. From an epistemological point of view, such an exchange would not affect Berkeley's position. The key distinction between realism (of whatever kind) and idealism is on the ontological level where the two camps will want to offer conflicting accounts of the nature of reality and have opposing opinions as to the existence of an external world.

However, Berkeley thought that because there was no difference to items of common sense of his scheme of things, that this was a strong point of his theory. Clearly Dr Johnson was in error in thinking he could refute Berkeley by kicking a stone. The appeal to phenomenological differences is not likely to advance matters as there are no such differences between *any* theories of perception. The fact that there is no phenomenological difference between Berkeley's idealism and direct realism does not entail that there are no ontological differences. Whether an argument in favour

Think about

■ Why is God's existence incompatible with Berkeley's principle that *esse est percipi*?

■ Can the principle be rescued if there is no God to guarantee it?

Explain and illustrate one criticism of idealism.

Think about

How can it be argued that Berkeley's idealism is compatible with direct realism? How convincing do you find this argument? Give one reason to support this claim and one reason to oppose it.

The similarity sometimes found between realist and idealist epistemologies, coupled with their fundamental ontological difference, has led to much debate in philosophical circles about whether epistemology or ontology is the more primary, or important, discipline. Which do you think, and why?

of the mental nature of reality can be established ultimately depends on the consistency of the argument advanced. It is unlikely to be settled decisively by appealing to the way things feel.

An important criticism of Berkeley has been made by Russell. Berkeley tends to exploit an ambiguity in his use of the term 'idea'. Berkeley uses the term idea to refer to sense data, objects and thoughts. The word 'idea' has obvious mentalist connotations, i.e. when we think of ideas we naturally think of them belonging to some mind or other. If we are thinking about a tree then we have an idea of a tree in mind. This, however, needs to be distinguished from the claim that the tree itself is in the mind. Berkeley tends to conflate these different meanings and this opens up the road to idealism. You cannot establish idealism by simply calling objects collections of ideas.

Solipsism and the problem of other minds

Solipsism is the belief that the only thing I can be absolutely certain of is my own mind. So, while my immediate perceptions cannot be doubted, any inferences that I make with regard to an external source for those perceptions can be. Taken to its logical extreme, this leads to the conclusion that the only thing that exists is me, and everything else is a product of my own mind. Not only are ideas the immediate objects of knowledge, they necessarily become the sole source of knowledge for the empiricist. It then follows that all other minds must also be products of my mind and so other people become reduced to the status of mental objects.

So why is this a problem? Firstly, as we shall see below, the question of whether we can be aware of anything outside our own minds can be asked in such a way that it presents serious difficulties for indirect realism, in that it is the ultimate sceptical argument with regards to the existence of an external world. If all I can be certain of is my own mind, it is illegitimate for the sense-data theorist to talk about anything but sense data, and the primary/secondary quality theorist is left with nothing but secondary qualities. On the other side of the coin, if solipsism is correct, it does not refute idealism; if anything, it does the opposite. However, the certainty achieved by such a commitment is made at the expense of just about every common-sense view that we hold about the world and our place in it. Could you really accept that you inhabit a world in which all the other occupants (including myself) may well be no more than the products of your own mind? Does it seem likely that everything than you have learnt on this course has come from within yourself rather than coming from an external world in which there reside different people who have different experiences and so can impart knowledge of them to each other? Bertrand Russell once described solipsism as being more redolent of a psychological disease than a serious philosophical position. While it is beyond the scope of this chapter to deal with this concern – some of the greatest philosophical minds of the past four centuries have devoted the majority of their attention to it – it is enough that the need for a solution is highlighted. Wittgenstein once remarked in relation to this point that:

> a man will be imprisoned in a room with a door that's unlocked and opens inwards; as long as it does not occur to him to pull rather than push

Wittgenstein (1980, p42)

Think about

Is solipsism a problem for direct realism? Give your reasons.

The argument for brain stimulation

This argument has its roots in Descartes (2007), where he considers the possibility that he is being universally deceived by an evil demon, but a more contemporary version is the 'brain in a vat' thought experiment:

> You do not know that you are not a brain, suspended in a vat full of liquid in a laboratory, and wired to a computer which is feeding you your current experiences under the control of some ingenious technician scientist (benevolent or malevolent according to taste). For if you were such a brain, then, provided that the scientist is successful, nothing in your experience could possibly reveal that you were; for your experience is *ex hypothesi* identical with that of something which is not a brain in a vat. Since you have only your own experience to appeal to, and that experience is the same in either situation, nothing can reveal to you which situation is the actual one.
>
> *Dancy (1985, p10)*

So it is logically possible, however unlikely, that all my experience is not produced by the external world, but rather the electrical stimulation of part of my brain by a neuroscientist. This could be done in such a way so as to deceive each of my five senses into thinking the object of my perception existed when in fact it did not. There would be nothing present in my experience that would allow me to set apart this non-veridical experience from a veridical one, so we could not know whether such an object existed to begin with in order for me to have a direct perception of it. This is the stronger version of the argument from hallucination alluded to earlier in the chapter. Its strength lies in the fact that it posits sensory deception with no possibility of any other form of experience to compare it against; the situation is akin to the map analogy that we considered above.

Key terms

Ex hypothesi: according to this hypothesis, i.e. something has already been assumed. In this case, that there is no phenomenological difference between the two situations posited.

Think about

'The claim that currently I could be a brain in a vat, reality being "fed into me" by some maniacal scientist is so absurd that it is not worthy of consideration.' How convincing do you find such a response? Why?

Is there any way that you could establish that right now you are *not* a brain in a vat? Is there anything available to your current experience that could establish this? Why/why not?

If you could not know either way, is there anything you *could* know? What might this tell us about experience?

Key philosopher

John Stuart Mill (1806–73)

An English empiricist philosopher best known for his utilitarianism and political philosophy. Mill's *On Liberty* (1985) is his most famous work.

Think about

Is the argument about contextualisation as forceful here as it was against hallucination?

Does this counter-argument actually refute solipsism?

A counter-argument

Contextualisation – this is the same argument as we put forward with regard to hallucination. The question arises as to how I could advance the possibility that I was a brain in a vat in the first place, particularly if empiricism is correct. The only way seems to be via contextualisation, in that I perceive something similar in my experience and then analogously apply the same possibility to myself, or there is something about my everyday experience of the world at times which does not quite feel right. If this is the case, as it must be in order for me to come up with the hypothesis, then I have to concede that not only is the scientist completely deceiving me, he is also supplying the seeds of doubt within me. This seems a very strange thing to do, but perhaps we should not try to second-guess someone with so much power over us.

Conclusion

We have assessed three differing fundamental theories about the existence of, and our relation to, the external world in this chapter:

- direct realism – naive and sophisticated versions
- indirect realism – sense-data theory and the primary/secondary qualities thesis
- idealism.

We have seen that they all seem to contain strengths and weaknesses. As we come to a close, you would be forgiven for wondering what the point of all this is if philosophers have been arguing over the external world for centuries and failed to come to agreement. However, consider this: you may recognise the brain in a vat scenario as being fundamentally similar to that of the recent *Matrix* films. In the films, the Matrix is a virtual reality environment manufactured by machines to engage and divert human beings' consciousnesses whilst the machines use their bodies as a power source. All but a few humans are completely unaware of this. Cypher, one of the humans who is aware, delivers the following speech when negotiating the price for betraying his comrades whilst 'sitting in a restaurant' inside the Matrix:

> You know, I know this steak doesn't exist. I know that when I put it in my mouth, the Matrix is telling my brain that it is juicy and delicious. After nine years, you know what I realise? [*Takes a bite of steak*] Ignorance is bliss.
>
> I don't want to remember nothing. Nothing. You understand?

The Matrix (1999)

Cypher's point is that as long as he is not aware that he is a brain in a vat, if you will, he is perfectly happy to be one. However, the film starts out with Neo, the lead character, beset by a nagging doubt that reality is not as he perceives it and, when given the chance, he chooses to try to resolve that doubt. It is this doubt that drives philosophers to pose epistemological and ontological questions even if the answers that they come up with are not always entirely satisfactory.

Those in the Matrix cannot make a reality/appearance distinction. Their ability to distinguish illusions will not suffice as that too is part of the Matrix. However, this leads to **infinite regress**. How do those that control the Matrix make the distinction? How would they know they are not being deceived by a team of gods and how would that team know it was not being deceived by Descartes' demon? In order to set up an example like the Matrix, there must be *some* criterion for distinguishing what is real from what is not. When that criterion is started we can then ask the reasonable question why it is that we can't satisfy it. The only way you block the infinite regress is by stating what such a criterion might be.

AQA Examiner's tips

- It is not enough to critically analyse a particular theory, you also need to assess and evaluate it. In order to do this, you need to answer the question, 'Is a particular theory valid, and if so, why?' If a particular theory is not valid, you need to address the questions of: 'If not, why not?' and, 'Could there be an alternative theory on offer which addresses the problems of perception in a more satisfactory manner?' and, 'If so, how/why?' It is not enough, for a top-level response, merely to 'juxtapose' two theories against each other and leave evaluation implicit.

- Following on from this, in order to gain top marks in the exam, it is important that you are aware of at least one strength as well as at least two or three criticisms of a particular theory for essay-based questions; more so now that assessment will focus heavily upon interpretation, analysis and application as well as evaluation.

Key terms

Infinite regress: a series of questions that only lead to more questions rather than answers. It is unsatisfactory because no explanation is sufficient or complete. There is no foundation for our beliefs.

Summary questions

1 Given the nature of the empirical method, summarise why questions about the external world are crucial to empiricism.

2 Provide examples of objects of perception and objects of introspection. Explain how you would differentiate between the two.

3 Describe and illustrate what is meant by the term 'sense data'. Try to list three ways in which sense data differ from physical objects.

4 Say whether the following are examples of primary qualities, secondary qualities, both, or neither. Ensure you give reasons for your answer:

Heat	Velocity	Pleasure
Pain	Circularity	Colour
Existence	Mass	Atoms

5 Describe and illustrate one epistemological distinction between primary and secondary qualities and one ontological one.

6 Does Berkeley use God to save idealism or is idealism used to save God? If God's existence was questioned, what effect would this have on Berkeley's account of the existence of the world?

7 What do the arguments from hallucination and brain stimulation share in common? Do these arguments refute realism's claim that we can know of the world beyond our perception of it? Why?

8 Is solipsism a help or a hindrance to an idealist?

After working through this topic, you should:

■ understand Berkeley's critique of Locke

■ be able to demonstrate knowledge of and illustrate Berkeley's arguments for the perceiver-dependent nature of secondary *and* primary qualities

■ understand Berkeley's idealism, in particular the role of God in Berkeley's arguments

■ understand the problems posed for realism and idealism by solipsism

■ be able to outline, illustrate and assess the argument for brain stimulation.

Further reading

Austin, J. L. *Sense and Sensibilia*, Oxford University Press, 1962. This offers an excellent explanation and critique of the notion of sense data.

Bennett, J. *Locke, Berkeley, Hume: central themes*, Oxford University Press, 1984. An accessible, if controversial, introduction to two key philosophers of this chapter.

Berkeley, G. *A Treatise Concerning the Principles of Human Knowledge*, 1710, may be found at http://18th.eserver.org/berkeley.html. This is a detailed analysis of Berkeley's idealism.

Berkeley, G. *Three Dialogues Between Hylas and Philonous in opposition to Sceptics and Atheists*, 1713, may be found at http://www.bartleby.com/37/2/. See particularly the first Dialogue. Using Philonous as a mouthpiece, Berkeley lays out his critique of Lockean realism in order to present his own idealism in the strongest possible light.

Descartes, R. *Discourse on Method and the Meditations*, trans. F. E. Sutcliffe, Penguin Classics, 2007. Meditation 1 contains some classic sceptical arguments.

Locke, J. *An Essay Concerning Human Understanding*, 1690, may be found at http://arts.cuhk.edu.hk/Philosophy/Locke/echu/. In particular Book II, vol. 1. Chapter 8 offers an excellent treatment of the primary and secondary qualities debate and a sophisticated critique of direct realism.

Pinchin, C. *Issues in Philosophy: an introduction*, 2nd edn, Palgrave, 2004. Chapter 1 offers a clear and concise account of the major issues surrounding this topic. Chapter 2 situates some of these issues in a wider framework and contains a useful account of scepticism.

Priest, S. *The British Empiricists: Hobbes to Ayer*, Penguin, 1990. Provides overviews of Russell, Locke and Berkeley.

Russell, B. *A History of Western Philosophy*, Unwin, 1979. A very readable but idiosyncratic account. Gives Russell's take on many of the thinkers covered in this course. Chapters XV to XVII are of particualar relevance to our present concerns.

Russell, B. *The Problems of Philosophy*, Oxford University Press, 1980. An excellent introduction to the issues surrounding the philosophy of perception.

3 Why should I be moral?

Morality as a social contract

Learning objectives:

- to understand the problems in deciding whether to act morally

- to explore what egoism says about decision making and investigate the problems

- to explain why an egoist would make a contract with others

- to describe what kind of contract a self-interested person would make

- to evaluate whether moral principles can be justified through a contract.

Key philosophers

Plato (427–347 BC)

Plato was the first great systematic philosopher of the Western tradition. He often wrote in dramatic dialogue, with Socrates as his mouthpiece and other characters expressing contrary opinions. One of his major works is *The Republic*.

Jean-Paul Sartre (1905–80)

Sartre was a French existentialist philosopher. In an early lecture, *Existentialism and Humanism*, he explored the implications for freedom and morality of being an atheist.

💡 Introduction

Why be moral? At times it seems useless to do good. Any student will have encountered situations where others ignore conventional standards of morality and not only get away with it, but seem to profit! In the wider society, unscrupulous people can flourish, become wealthy and enjoy a prosperous life, while others who appear to be virtuous do not.

This is clearly portrayed in the novel *Lord of the Flies* (Golding, 1954), where a group of young boys are stranded on a tropical island without any adult authority. Ralph, the initial leader, tries to instil in the boys normal civilised behaviour such as tolerance, care for others, and duties such as keeping a fire going, etc.; but he is undermined by Jack. Physically as strong, and more charismatic, Jack uses his power to take control and dominate the boys. When Ralph pleads 'stick to the rules', Jack's reply is, 'Bollocks to the rules … they don't count any more'. This violent dictatorship is thwarted only by the arrival of adult authority. Without the navy, Jack would have benefited from the consequences of behaving badly. Jack's position is strengthened in philosophy by various attacks on conventional morality. In Plato's *Republic*, one character, Thrasymachus, claims that justice (morality) is simply 'the interests of the stronger'. In other words, our moral values have been imposed on us by those who have had the power throughout history to control our moral beliefs. The implication is that they lack legitimacy, since they are simply the values that the strong have desired, usually to maintain their own position of strength. For example, Marx suggests that the middle class promote the value of individual freedom (as in the right to own property) because they are in a position to exploit the benefits. The poor working class would probably prefer less freedom and more social support. So if values simply reflect social or cultural bias, why be moral?

A belief in some kind of valid morality may not necessarily be supported by appeals to religion. Apart from atheistic denials of the existence of God, even if there was a God we would still have to interpret His commands, and every religious text has a varied account of what God wishes. Sartre (1948), in his lecture *Existentialism and Humanism*, claims as much and approvingly quotes Dostoevsky: 'If God did not exist, everything would be permitted', and this is exactly the position that underpins his existentialism. We are in the position of having to create our own morality or at least promote our own interpretation of sacred texts.

Indeed, in Dostoevsky's novel *Crime and Punishment* (1866) which takes place in the slums of St Petersburg, the central character, Raskalnikov, is a penniless student who is led to commit a savage murder. His female acquaintance, Sonja, who is also very poor, uses prostitution to help support her parents and family. In a strange way, the reader condones both 'crimes' and supports the actions of the two characters.

Think about

If you can find the video or the novel of *Crime and Punishment*, look at the first part and see if you could also justify murder and prostitution!

Think about

There have been many attempts to design a **Utopia**. Plato's *Republic* is one example. Imagine being stranded on a tropical island, or at least imagine living in a student house, where a new society with new rules needs to be established. As there is no other authority, what basic rules would you want to lay down, and how would you justify them?

Key terms

Utopia: a society with ideal laws and an ideal way of life. The term derives from Thomas More (1516) who set out his version of the ideal community.

Egoism: this was first proposed by Epicurus (341–270 BC) who believed that pleasure alone was good. The view that pleasure is the highest goal is called hedonism.

In the face of difficult questions about how to behave, we might well conclude that we should just act in our own self-interest. Since no moral belief is true or false in itself, and morality like beauty 'is in the eye of the beholder', I may as well act to further my own well-being. This is the theory of egoism, which has a long and respectable history. It is in essence what Jack is doing on the island. He decides to spend his time hunting pigs, having feasts and ruling over his followers.

So, in answer to the question 'Why should I be moral?', we shall consider the following responses:

- We should act morally because it is in our self-interest to do so: egoism.
- As part of our self-interest, we will need to make a contract with others. So acting morally is justified by the contract we have made: contractarianism.

Egoism

Although the theory of **egoism** can be traced back to Greek philosophy, it still has a very contemporary feel, that we need only desire things for our own self-interest rather than for their own sake and because they are right. We should act in order to further our own happiness or for our own good. The opposite is altruism, where we act for the good of others, regardless of our own good.

There are generally two versions of egoism:

- ethical egoism, which is a statement of value: that we ought to maximise our own good
- psychological egoism, which is a statement of fact about human motives and human nature, that we cannot do anything other than act in our own self-interest.

Ethical egoism

At first sight, ethical egoism appears to recommend extreme selfishness, but that is not so. It does not necessarily propose a life of short-term pleasure, although it might!

Consider these positions. Could an egoist do the following?

- give blood
- stop taking foreign holidays to reduce global warming
- contribute to a charity for children in a foreign country

From such considerations, it can be seen that egoists do not necessarily lead a hedonistic life of sex, drugs and rock and roll. Longer-term pleasures such as health and lasting relationships yield more satisfaction and could possibly even accommodate actions to help others for the pleasure of seeing others happy. The philosopher Hume seeks to base moral behaviour on our human 'sympathy', the degree to which we are all affected by other people's happiness or suffering. For example, a mother who makes her child happy will, as a result, make herself happier. So, part of our own good might extend to helping others.

This sympathy is not for Hume a virtue, but explains the humanity that we feel, say when someone else is in distress. However, it is only exercised because it brings happiness to its owner:

> Sympathy, we shall allow, is much fainter than our concern for ourselves.

Hume (1969)

However, this implies that we could be affected in different ways and that our behaviour towards others remains precarious. Supposing that I do not feel sympathy in a particular case, or have mixed feelings. Hume rather assumes that our concern for others is universal and that we cannot be indifferent, while the above quotation suggests we can.

Yet, charitable or selfless acts could be described as 'enlightened egoism', where we seek a long-term self-interest. Thus we study hard for several years, denying short-term pleasures for the goal of more lasting satisfaction. So in answer to the question 'Why be moral?', the egoist may reply that, 'I stay loyal to my friends' or, 'I don't lie, cheat or steal'; in other words, 'I do my "duties" because it enables me to maximise my happiness'.

However, some people may feel dissatisfied with this reply, and one way to illustrate this is to play the following game.

Think about

Could an egoist explain altruistic acts such as a soldier in battle giving his life to save his comrades?

Think about

Prisoner's dilemma

Two guilty suspects, Tom and Dick, have been arrested. The police keep them in separate cells and there is no chance of communication. But the police know it will be hard to get a conviction, so separately they offer Tom and Dick the following deal:

'Tom [or Dick], if you confess, but Dick [or Tom] stays silent, you will go free and Dick [or Tom] will get 10 years' imprisonment.

However, if you both confess, you will both get a moderate sentence of about five years in prison.

If you both continue to remain silent, we cannot charge you, but we will give you a minimum sentence for wasting our time of one year in prison.'

The offer can be summarised as:

	Tom	Dick
Both confess	5 years	5 years
Both stay silent (trust card)	1 year	1 year
Tom confesses and Dick stays silent	0	10 years
Dick confesses and Tom stays silent	10 years	0

The sentences above are the scores that you use in the game.

To play the game, you need two cards each, one with C (cooperate/confess) on it and one with S (silence) on it. You play in pairs and it is suggested you play several pairs. With each pair, you take five turns and score for each turn.

At each turn, both players select a card in secret and place it face down on the table. The choice is whether to confess or to stay silent. You cannot discuss card selection with anyone! The cards are then revealed and the scores noted. For each of the five turns, players can make different choices and perhaps develop a strategy.

When you have played five different partners five times, add up your total prison sentence. A score card is suggested below:

	Opponent 1	Opponent 2	Opponent 3	Opponent 4	Opponent 5	Opponent 6
Turn 1						
Turn 2						
Turn 3						
Turn 4						
Turn 5						
Total						
Final score:						

The teaching point of the exercise is that if players pursue their crude self-interest (play the 'S' card), they will cease to be trusted and eventually they will lose out. However, the dilemma is that if you seek cooperation (the 'C' card) you are always open to exploitation.

Discussion issues

- Is human nature self-interested?
- Simple ethical egoism or cooperation (enlightened egoism) – which is more profitable?
- Contract theory – should ethical egoists make a contract?
- What is ethical? Do we need to establish principles?

In the game, cunning players may have played the 'C' card until the final turn and then played the 'S' card. This illustrates the instability of the egoist's position. While they might stay loyal when it is in their own interests, there is always the possibility that they will deceive or double cross if they can get away with it. Moral action is still a matter of calculation rather than doing things because they are right. Indeed, the egoist argument may be rational: 'I consider other people's interests only in so far as they further my interest'; but is this a sufficient account of moral duty? Is there more to morality than simply pursuing your own advantage? Moral duties are more than just guides to increasing pleasure, and some commonly recognised duties may not give any pleasure at all.

An illustration of this moral attitude is provided by Machiavelli in *The Prince*. He debates whether for a prince (or anyone else) it is better to be loved or to be feared. He grants that it is praiseworthy to be loved, but recognises that respect and obedience are often given to those who are feared. He concludes that an effective prince will do well to be caring, compassionate and kind but:

> I would go so far as to say that if he has these qualities and always behaves accordingly, he will find them ruinous ... his disposition should be such, that if he needs to be the opposite he knows how. He should not deviate from what is good, if that is possible, but he should know how to do evil, if that is necessary.

see Palmer (1991)

In this sense, morality is whatever is advantageous, but is this a satisfactory account? Surely we would expect a prince to fulfil his moral duty at all times.

Think about

Would an egoist steal from a large supermarket retailer if he could escape detection and punishment? Would we condemn this behaviour?

Think about

Would you recommend this moral position to your teachers to make them more effective in the classroom? They should appear to do good, but to be effective they must be prepared to do evil!

One final problem with ethical egoism, although not insurmountable, is generally regarded as crucial. It would seem that an egoist would not want other people to be self-interested egoists, rather he/she would prefer them to be genuinely altruistic. It would make the egoist very uneasy to know that his/her friend is loyal only while it serves the friend's purpose. So the egoist cannot recommend egoism to anyone else – in other words, he/she cannot universalise egoism. More will be said about universalisation in the third topic but, for the moment, it seems inconsistent that the egoist denies to others what he/she wants for himself. Surely by choosing the egoist philosophy, he/she is setting an example that others can also choose to follow.

🔲 Psychological egoism

If you are not yet persuaded that egoism gives a plausible account of moral duty, then there is one more weapon in its defence. Psychological egoism claims that human nature is such that we cannot help but pursue our self-interest. We are biologically and psychologically disposed to behave this way. It is a fact that we automatically act to promote our own interest and we cannot do otherwise. This theory highlights a strength of egoism, that it explains ethical motivation. I act morally because it benefits me, it furthers my own life. It places human action firmly and consistently within the natural world: like all plants and creatures we seek our own good, and that is a convincing answer to the question: 'Why be moral?'

An illustration of such a view is provided by an interpretation of Nietzsche (1998) in *Beyond Good and Evil*. The foundational concept for Nietzsche is the will to power. 'Life itself is the will to power' and every living thing acts 'to release its strength', to further its own sake. Everything from 'alimentation' and physical action to morality and philosophy is simply a means to create ourselves, to impose ourselves upon the world. In this version of psychological egoism, it is a natural fact about man that the 'innermost drives of his nature' are to 'subdue' others. Philosophers are 'commanders and lawgivers' who strive to impose their values on others. For Nietzsche, the most 'world affirming human' is so satisfied with his life that he 'wants to have it over again' and subscribes to the doctrine of eternal recurrence: he loves his life so much that he would gladly live it over and over again. In another memorable simile, he compares a healthy human being to the plant called a sipo matador, which will exploit others in order to climb to the top of the jungle, to produce an exquisitely beautiful flower and 'make a show of [its] happiness'. For Nietzsche this will to express our power is the physiological and psychological phenomenon behind all of our moral dispositions.

According to this view, even the selfless life of Mother Theresa dedicated to ministering to the poor would ultimately be interpreted as exercising the will to power. Even if we disregard an undue emphasis on power, it would still be argued that she furthered her own interest by satisfying her own instincts for care and compassion. Ultimately the case for psychological egoism comes down to peace of mind. A story about Abraham Lincoln quoted in *Moral Problems* (Palmer, 1991) illustrates the point. Lincoln apparently claimed that all men were motivated by selfishness, yet he himself was seen to jump from a coach and go to considerable trouble to rescue pigs from a swamp. When a companion queried how compatible this was with his claim about human nature, Lincoln replied that his actions were 'the very essence of selfishness', because if he had not saved the pigs, he would have lost 'peace of mind'.

Key philosopher

Machiavelli (1469–1527)

Machiavelli was an Italian political thinker who condoned the use of fraud and immoral actions to preserve the order of the state.

Think about

Try to collect criticisms for each theory in order to develop them in the exam. Three criticisms of ethical egoism have been mentioned here:

1 Egoism does not account for the importance of moral duty.

2 You can never trust an egoist.

3 Egoists will not recommend their theory to anyone else.

Key philosopher

Friedrich Nietzsche (1844–1900)

He was a German philosopher known as a radical critic of Western philosophy, famous for his claim, 'God is dead'. He claimed that all of life seeks to enhance its power and even religion is a camouflage for self-interest.

So the psychological egoist is able to argue that every action, however altruistic, is really performed for selfish motives – to gain power or to gain peace of mind.

However, theories that give non-moral accounts of why we should be moral run into several problems:

1 Is the factual account correct? We could deny the facts that are presented about people and their motivations.

2 Even if the facts are correct, these will not justify a morality, because they simply tell us how people actually behave. It does not inform us whether we ought to do something.

3 Nietzsche and Machiavelli draw moral conclusions from their theories that few would recognise and which are seriously at odds with conventional notions of right and wrong.

There is something very unsatisfactory about theories that claim to know the *real* motivation behind human action. Put simply: how do you know? What tests have been done? Has everyone been checked out? Is this an empirical generalisation that is scientific or just an interpretation which can be rejected as just one perspective of many? Nietzsche's will to power seems to be presented as a foundational premise, which offers a way of seeing the world, rather than a discovery about human nature which is supported by evidence.

Also, more seriously, this final support of the egoist's case leaves it empty. If absolutely every action is performed to gain peace of mind or to release one's energy, then it leaves completely open the moral debate on the best way to gain such satisfaction. An assassin carries out a job efficiently and an old lady gives to charity. Both actions produce peace of mind, but we would not say that this establishes something common to both and certainly not from a *moral* point of view. The whole discussion is thrown wide open and thus the claim is empty. Is the best way to gain peace of mind to be ambitious, unscrupulous or to work for the good of others? What is the most fulfilling way to exercise one's will? Granted that any kind of action may be considered, then the egoist is no further forward in answering the question 'Why be moral?'. The question of what to do in order to maximise self-satisfaction is still left unanswered and will be down to the individual. All that has changed is the language. Instead of asking what is the right action, the egoist will ask what will deliver peace of mind, but in neither case do we have a clear answer. All that the psychological egoist has shown is that whatever we choose it will give us peace of mind, whether it be vindictive or charitable. There are different varieties of peace of mind that can be distinguished.

Finally, psychological egoism wavers between making empirical claims and claiming an a priori necessity about its status. Are counter-examples, at least in principle, possible? If not, then it appears not to be an empirically-based theory. We might well ask how the theory accommodates the sacrifice of ones' own life for others.

So psychological egoism will not help us answer the question 'Why be moral?'. It simply informs us that whatever we choose will, due to our human nature, be in our self-interest.

Contractarianism

Sooner or later the rational, enlightened egoist will realise that he or she needs to make a contract with others. It will be in his/her self-interest to limit any threat that others may pose and to see if alliances with others bring additional benefits, e.g. the gain that comes from being a member of a team. In this sense, morality is 'a convention' – an agreement on a set of rules to our mutual advantage which is often referred to as a **social contract**.

An early version of this contract, explained in more detail with Hobbes below, stems from the egoist position: that it is in my self-interest to ensure peace, security and stability; and so rationally we will mutually agree on a set of values that will deliver this. This agreement is the contract or 'covenant'.

Although some might object that we have never *actually* made such a contract with others, we can argue *hypothetically* that we would agree to accept moral conventions because they maximise our satisfaction. This hypothetical contract can also be used as a device to reconsider current moral rules to check whether they are still mutually acceptable, and if not, we can change them. Thus, for example, if parties to the contract decide that it is now in their interest to treat animals well, and animal suffering detracts from personal happiness, then changes can be made to the contract. It is important to note that such a theory does not suggest that contracts and obedience to contracts are a good thing in themselves, but simply that this is the best way to achieve all of our interests. But remember the exercise of the prisoner's dilemma. Would an egoist give in to the temptation to cheat on the contract if they could get away with it?

Furthermore, making a contract assumes that we have common interests, that despite our various conceptions of what benefits us, we also share ideas about what the good life entails.

A modern example of the contract is offered by Rawls, where it is employed as a fictional device for revealing agreed, moral principles.

He invites 'rational and mutually self-interested' parties to consider what principles they would accept if they were *impartially* committing themselves *in advance* to a set of rules. The condition is that we are behind 'a veil of ignorance'. We are asked to imagine that we have no idea what will happen in the future and what our position will be. Imagine that you are sitting down to a game of cards with friends and family. Before you start you will agree the rules together and that certain practices are unfair and will be regarded as cheating. You do this before you know how the game will unfold and what your situation will be.

As we are hidden behind this 'veil' and cannot know the outcome of our decisions, Rawls contends that the rational, self-interested person will choose impartial, fair principles, which are stripped of prejudice and selfishness in case, as the future unfolds, we become a victim of such unjust rules. He suggests that we would ban free riders, people who take benefits and give nothing in return (such as scroungers, tax dodgers, social security fraudsters, etc.), because although we might be tempted on occasions to do this, we know these practices would be detrimental to 'the game'. Thus he establishes the moral principle of fair play, that taking advantage of people in an underhand way, contrary to the spirit of cooperation, is wrong.

It is easy to see how an egoist would support this to ensure security, peace of mind and advantage for the future. Thus 'the veil of ignorance' converts selfish self-interest into a more universal concern. The egoist learns that the general interest of society is their personal concern and will join the covenant to promote agreed rules.

However, these values and rules are justified *only* by the convention of a contract. For example, it will only be right to treat animals well because

Key terms

Social contract theory: this seeks to base agreement on moral principles through the device of a contract which free individuals have consented to. Once we are part of the contract, we are obliged to obey the agreed moral rules. This is just, as we accepted the conditions when we entered the contract.

Key philosopher

John Rawls (1921–2002)

In *A Theory of Justice* (1971), John Rawls argued a contractarian defence of liberal principles of justice. He maintained that this conception of justice is most likely to gain an 'overlapping consensus' in modern **pluralist societies**.

Key terms

Pluralist societies: societies that allow individuals to choose their own values and permit a diversity of answers to what is the good life.

that was what was agreed and not by appeal to any more fundamental moral belief. Contract theory reduces moral obligations to legal ones: 'You cannot make me do it if it is not in the contract!' Would you stop and help someone in a car crash, even if it was not a legal duty? (This will be explored in the two topics below.)

The difficulty with this position is whether we would really call it moral. If people are still acting from motives which maximise their own advantage, would we want to praise them or blame them? We generally recognise individuals as meriting praise when they perform an act 'because it is right' (regardless of self-interest), because it has moral worth or because it is done from a sense of duty. This is a distinction that will be developed in the next topic with Kant's deontological ethics.

Impartiality

A problem with values decided behind the veil of ignorance is that they are not really impartial. A definition of impartiality could be: 'not unduly favouring anyone's interests, including one's own'. It is likely that whatever is chosen will fail this test, because Rawls recognises that people are self-interested. Consequently they will choose what suits them, and this will reflect their background beliefs. Rawls himself offers three principles, which are clearly inherited from a Western, **liberal** tradition:

- The liberty principle: everyone ought to have an equal right to the most extensive liberty, compatible with a similar liberty for others.
- An equal opportunities liberty: inequalities are unjust unless they are attached to offices open to all, under conditions of equal opportunity.
- A difference principle: inequalities must be to the advantage of everyone in society (the bottom class must benefit from the inequalities).

> ### Key terms
>
> **Liberal:** with a small 'l', relates to a political ideology, opposed to conservatism in that it is centered on the freedom of the individual as possessing rights and liberties that should not be constrained by government, including rights of equality and respect.

Think about

Match these three examples to the three principles put forward by Rawls:

- In school we will create a special top set and bottom set, so that we can give each set specialised teaching to suit their needs.
- Everyone should be allowed to say what they think (free speech) as long as they do not bully anyone else.
- The benefits of going to university are fair because anyone is free to apply and take the exams.

To consider whether you would support these principles, imagine that you are 18 years old and just about to leave home. You are behind the 'veil of ignorance' in the sense that you do not know how your life is going to turn out. What kind of society would you like to join? Would you accept these suggestions?

- If you work hard, you deserve a greater reward.
- The richer you are, the more tax should be taken from you to help those in need.
- Children should not be allowed to inherit vast sums of money from their parents.
- There is nothing wrong with especially talented individuals (such as footballers) earning in a week more than most people earn in a year.

- You should be allowed to spend your money as you wish, e.g. on a second home, flying off on frequent foreign holidays, extra tuition to pass exams.
- There is nothing objectionable about the vast amounts of private property in the ownership of the few. In Britain, approximately 10 per of the population own 90 per cent of the land.

Rawls can be criticised for promoting the values of a Western, liberal tradition that favours the freedom and rights of the individual as well as a strong socialist ethic. Furthermore, it could be argued that the liberty principle, and the equal opportunity and difference principles are in direct conflict. If we are going to give extra support to the least advantaged in society, we will have to remove resources from the most favoured. This contravenes their liberty.

The problems for social contract theories multiply when we examine the variety of contracts proposed. Two classical contracts will be used as examples, those of Hobbes and Locke. They illustrate that often contracts are based on preconceived values and background beliefs. Both Hobbes and Locke ground their theories in assumptions about human nature.

Hobbes lived through the violence of the English Civil War and witnessed the worst excesses of what he considered to be human nature. Hobbes' egoism is reflected in Jack in *Lord of the Flies*, that people are motivated by self-preservation, power and selfish self-interest. Both Hobbes and Locke refer to 'man in a state of Nature'. This is meant to describe what a human being would be like, prior to the civilising effect of civil society and government. Whether man ever lived in a state of nature is questionable, but a modern version would be an account of the basic psychology of a human being, our strongest drives. According to Hobbes, human beings will do anything, even take another's life, if it helps them to survive. Fundamentally we are 'nasty' and 'brutish', mistrustful and competitive, and self-glorifying. Without social control, life would be 'the war of all against all'. This inevitable conflict is exacerbated by the scarcity of the earth's resources that will intensify the fight for survival.

In order to escape from such destructive chaos, we make a contract with others in order to gain stability, security and protection of life. These values, for Hobbes, clearly underpin any other values that might be added to the contract, although any other moral laws are dependent on the all powerful sovereign, the '**leviathan**', that maintains order. If one has experienced the horrors of civil war, then it would be easy to agree with Hobbes that stability at any cost, the chance to live a settled life and plan for a future has priority over other values and is the foundation of any contract.

Nevertheless, this is to agree to life under a Jack, a strong dictator and sovereign power who, as long as he maintains order and security, can do as he wishes. Hobbes accepted this, that the leviathan needs to be as strong as possible in order to protect us from returning to a state of nature. This sovereign could employ the methods of Machiavelli and, in short, do anything necessary, short of threatening life, in order to retain power. In these circumstances, it would not be surprising if some chose to fight for what they perceive as a more just society at the risk of descending back into chaos. We see such demonstrations today against capitalism, nuclear weapons and carbon emissions. Also, although political considerations are not relevant here, it is possible that Hobbes has misrepresented strength. It is claimed that 'the strong are never

Key philosopher

Thomas Hobbes (1588–1679)

His most famous work is *Leviathan* in which he argues that all human beings pursue 'felicity' – the continual satisfaction of desire or appetite. Problems arise when greedy individuals want the same things and resources are scarce.

Key terms

Leviathan: a legendary sea monster with terrifying power. Hobbes believed a sovereign needed power to maintain order.

AQA Examiner's tip

There are two valid criticisms of Hobbes here. Firstly, the sovereign may be able to maintain order, but might be brutal. Secondly, surely someone is stronger if they have not only physical strength but moral strength too.

strong enough, until they convert might into right'. Moral strength is more durable than physical force.

To be fair to Hobbes, he maintains that the sovereign has to fulfil his part of the bargain, which demands the protection of those who make the contract (which Jack does not do in *Lord of the Flies*). But is a sovereign who is also an egoist necessarily going to do this, unless his power is threatened? In the novel, Jack victimises the twins because he can get away with it as his control over the tribe is secure. A contract based on self-interest would not automatically guarantee that everyone will be treated the same.

It is also inherently unstable, for if the sovereign does not maintain peace and security, a stronger faction can then (legitimately) overthrow him. A rebellion is justified, but only if it is strong enough to succeed. An unsuccessful attempt only undermines stability. So we have a moral position that an act is right if it succeeds! This will not satisfy those who seek clear rules on right and wrong.

Locke, writing approximately 50 years later, starts with very different assumptions. Locke makes use of **natural law** (discussed below). This implies that the state of nature is a state of perfect freedom, in which human beings can order their actions and dispose of their possessions as they think fit. This natural condition is governed by reason, where one shows respect for the freedom and property of others. These are all natural rights: the right to life, liberty and property. The reason for making a contract is to protect these rights and freedoms, and to have an authority to settle any disputes that may occur. Thus, government becomes a referee, and as Locke assumed there was a natural abundance of resources on the planet, such disputes will be relatively few.

The language of rights that Locke employs barely disguises the moral principles that are to be regarded as universal, inviolable and owed to every human being in virtue of being human. They are justifiably part of the contract since we are born with these rights, we all 'possess' them and they are rational. In the words of the American Constitution, men are 'created equal' and 'endowed by their Creator' with these rights, which are 'self-evident'. For Locke, such principles included the importance of individual freedoms, for example the right to own any property that we have worked for. Some 150 years later, the philosopher, Mill, outlined in detail what these basic freedoms should entail (though Mill was not particularly concerned with natural rights as such):

- liberty of thought and feeling on all subjects (e.g. being allowed to question everything you hear and develop your own views)
- liberty of expressing opinions on all subjects (freedom of speech and freedom to publish opinions)
- liberty to do what we want as long as we do not harm others (e.g. taking drugs, making money)
- liberty to meet people as long as it does not harm others (friendship groups, societies, trade unions, etc.).

These freedoms, for Locke, are moral rights, to which we are entitled, even if the law does not recognise them. They protect what is fundamental and integral to being human.

While we may wish to agree with many of these values, one obvious criticism of these contracts is the assumption on which they are based. As in the criticism of Nietzsche, no real empirical and scientific evidence is forthcoming on whether their theories of human nature are correct, and in the cases of Hobbes and Locke they conflict! Far from demonstrating universal truths on which to base a contract, they

Key terms

Natural law: those rights allegedly conferred on us by nature or derived from our status as human beings. They are rights we all share and do not depend on government.

Think about

Can you think of any reason for limiting these freedoms?

betray the cultural background and normative values of their time. It demonstrates the problem with contract theory that participants will come to the contract not to create a set of values through agreement, but with a set of values already in mind. In the cases of Hobbes and Locke, it is encapsulated in their description of the state of nature. Hence any social contract is merely a convention and relativistic, just preferences and recommendations of a particular culture with no other justification. Therefore, the moral duties outlined in any contract will not be impartial, and are open to challenge. If you wish to find out more on social contracts, look at Chapter 5: Why should I be governed?

Think about

Equality and justice

After a catastrophe, there are only four people left in the village. There is only one food parcel left. Help is on its way, but no one knows when it will arrive. The four people are:

What one deserves	What one needs
1 A successful businessman	He is unharmed and overweight
2 A caring housewife	She can survive on little food
3 An intellectual philosophy teacher	He is fainting from lack of food
4 An idle student	She is dying of starvation

Who gets the food parcel?

How would you divide up the shares of the parcel?

How useful are the following maxims?

'First come, first served'	(equality of opportunity)
'Those who work more deserve more'	(equality of desert)
'Those in need shall receive more'	(equality of need)
'Equal shares for all'	(equality of outcome)

Useful quotes:

- 'Justice is having and doing of one's own' (Plato): one should receive according to desert.
- 'Justice is the interests of the stronger' (Thrasymachus and Hobbes)
- 'Justice consists not only in treating equals equally, but in treating unequals unequally' (Aristotle)
- 'From each according to his ability, to each according to his need' (Marx)
- 'Treat people as Ends' (Kant)
- 'All animals are equal, but some animals are more equal than others' (Orwell, 1945)

Which of these principles would you choose to base your contract on? How would you wish people to treat you and vice versa?

AQA Examiner's tip

There are various views on what is fair and just and about the way we should treat people equally. Try to divide the pros and cons of dealing with people on what they deserve, or treating them according to their needs.

A more fundamental criticism of Hobbes, Locke and similar social contracts is that even if scientific agreement was reached on human nature, it would not validate a moral contract. For example Dawkins

The fact–value distinction is a major point of contention among moral philosophers. It is worthwhile researching the topic further, and it is also developed in the third topic in this chapter.

Think about

If genes do not have a conception of self or of others then in what sense is their behaviour 'selfish'? Is the term selfish being used in the same way as when we describe each other as selfish? Think about cases where you might describe your friends as selfish. What reasons could you have? Could they possibly be extended to genes?

Key philosopher

Peter Singer (1946–)

In his own self-portrait, Peter Singer maintained that the key question of ethics is 'How are we to live?' He is famous for his stance on animal welfare, that it is speciesist not to consider the happiness of animals when deciding the right action to take. He proposed a form of preference utilitarianism, where the preferences of animals are given 'equal consideration'.

Think about

Assuming that animals (like children) could be represented by an intelligent adult, would you want to enter into a contract to ban animal suffering? Consider, animal experiments, factory farming and meat eating? Is it in your self-interest to include animals and vulnerable people in a contract?

claims that our genes are engaged in a selfish competition to replicate themselves and fight off opposition from other genetic pools to ensure their survival. But even if we assume that our DNA is programmed to ensure it is passed on, we can nevertheless question whether this is good or right, which is a question of *value*. Even if something is factually correct, that does not entail that we should endorse and recommend it. It is a fact that I like chocolate, but that does not mean I ought to eat it. Similarly, I may be genetically disposed to be selfish, but I still have the ability to consider whether selfish actions are right or wrong and to compensate in my behaviour. No desire needs to be satisfied, no disposition needs to be enacted unless we endorse it. For example, men apparently have an Oedipus complex – a desire to sleep with their mother – but are usually able to repress this. No *fact* necessarily leads to any value, and we can choose to endorse and promote aspects of our nature or not. If we accept that the survival of DNA is the basis of our action, how we choose to survive is still an open question. Dawkins admits, for example, that genes may maximise their welfare by 'unselfish co-operation' (Palmer, 2001). Similarly, Hobbes' and Locke's accounts of human nature do not entail that we should incorporate their points in any contract.

A final limitation of the contractarian approach to morality is highlighted by Peter Singer in *Practical Ethics* (1993). In the introduction to this topic it was claimed that a contract could provide an *explanation* and *justification* for moral rules. But does it do both?

Contract with animals?

Singer argues that only the former is accounted for, and this can be highlighted in our regard for animals. A contract is an exclusively human device and since animals are not party to any covenant, this would justify their exclusion from any concerns about their welfare. Animals obviously cannot reciprocate and offer duties in return. When we promise to take good care of our pets, we do not expect them to promise to behave well in return. So would this mean that we can choose to treat animals however we wish? Of course that does not mean we would necessarily mistreat animals, but does the absence of a contract remove the obligation to treat animals well?

This problem has wider implications in that it might also absolve us of any responsibility to other human beings who cannot make the contract. There are vulnerable people with whom it might not be in my self-interest to have such a convention, as I am unlikely to be a net gainer; and certainly as far as animal rights are concerned, unless I am extremely sensitive to animal suffering, need I bother with the demands of a contract?

Explanation or justification?

Singer distinguishes between an explanation of the origins of ethical judgements and the justification. The contract theory explains how we arrived at certain laws, and why a self-interested individual could subscribe even to animal welfare, but a justification requires a stronger foundation for moral values than just one of consent.

Just as early cultures in history only felt it necessary to treat other members of the tribe properly and believed they could do what they liked with their enemies, so a merely contractual convention would not necessarily protect other cultures from enslavement or worse. It would not necessarily protect animals or severely intellectually disabled human beings. In order to bring all living creatures into the ethical community, we cannot rely on a contract but must look to a further, more fundamental justification. We cannot underpin moral values simply by enquiring what is to our advantage and what is not if we believe that moral behaviour dictates that we treat all living creatures ethically. Therefore, in conclusion, if we wish to protect some of our most cherished values, that everyone should be treated with respect whether it is to our advantage or not; and that we have a duty of care to other creatures and the environment whether it benefits us or not, then we have to search beyond egoism to defend these moral ideals.

After working through this topic, you should:

- know that the answer to the question 'Why be moral?' is that it is to my advantage, it is in my self-interest
- understand that one advantage of egoism is that it gives me a motive to be moral
- know that egoism either advocates pursuing our self-interest, which may be enlightened rather than immediate or superficial; or claims that all human beings cannot do otherwise but pursue their own welfare
- understand that problems with egoism are that it could be a recipe for selfishness and deceitfulness, and not a theory that we could recommend to everyone. The psychological theory may leave us empty, in trying to establish moral principles and behaviour, and so might not be helpful
- understand that an egoist will make a contract to ensure long-term benefits, such as safety and security
- understand that a self-interested person might accept duties and concern for others in return for freedom, justice and rights
- consider whether the social contract can be fair and impartial if people choose laws behind 'a veil of ignorance'
- understand that the contract explains rather than justifies moral rules and might discriminate against the vulnerable.

Morality as a constitutive of self-interest

Learning objectives:

- to explore how self-interest can be realised within a moral life
- to understand the relevant aspects of virtue ethics
- to investigate what are the essential qualities of a healthy life

The myth of Gyges

In Plato's *Republic*, the challenge to the position adopted by Thrasymachus and developed by later philosophers such as Machiavelli – that being moral is simply pursuing self-interest – begins with a story called 'The ring of Gyges'.

In this myth, we are asked to imagine the following scenario: that Gyges, a poor shepherd boy, after a terrific storm and an earthquake, finds a strange dead body with a magnificent gold ring on one of its fingers. He takes the ring and as he plays with it, he finds it has a special magic power – to make him invisible whenever he wishes. With this incredible power, he goes to the Royal Court where he turns himself invisible and

■ to consider whether altruistic acts are part of a flourishing human life.

■ Key terms

Instrumental: something is useful to achieve a further end.

Intrinsic: belonging to the nature or essence of something.

seduces the queen. Then he kills the king and takes his place. So, he can gain whatever he wants and avoid any serious reprisals by becoming invisible whenever he chooses!

We are invited to imagine that we have now found an identical ring. Would we not similarly take advantage of everyone, cheat, steal and seduce whenever we wished? The conclusion of the myth is that 'Man is just, not *willingly*, or because he thinks that justice is any good to him, but of *necessity* … for all Men believe in their hearts that injustice is far more profitable than justice' [author emphasis].

The conclusion to the last question could be that we follow an enlightened egoist's path, exploit situations where we can, but make contracts where necessary.

But this is not what Plato proposes. Instead, he argues that 'the healthy option' is not to exploit the possibilities of the ring. The genuinely rewarding life cannot be one which exploits others and uses people as a means to satisfy desires. This would rob life of all meaning and the possibilities of fulfilment.

In contrast to the preceding topic, doing good is not a matter of calculation, where right actions are **instrumental** to achieving self-interest, a tool in order to achieve the egoist's objectives. Instead good actions are *constitutive* of self-interest, they are in themselves the most rewarding life, virtue is **intrinsic** to human fulfilment. A comparison could be made, for example, with athletics, which could be regarded either solely as a means to win medals or as an intrinsically fulfilling activity.) To sum up, virtue brings its own reward. For the egoist, doing what makes me happy is right, whereas it is doing what is right that really makes me happy.

As an egoist, I could reject virtuous acts if they did not lead to my long-term interest (as in making a contract with vulnerable people) but in the topic we will explore the theory that the good life and self-interest are in harmony. This is the theory of virtue ethics, as proposed by Plato and Artistotle.

■ The healthy personality

Plato believes that the human personality has three parts: reason, spirit and desire. Desire accounts for the more physical appetites for sex, food and power. An assumption is made that these are lower pleasures, common to all human beings and many animals. Spirit consists of emotional capacities, strength of will, and encompasses courage, anger, guilt, loyalty, etc. Reason is an exclusively human capability which separates us from animals and enables us to make judgements. Reason gives us the ability to harmonise our personality, to control desire and spirit to the maximum benefit of the individual. Thus reason teaches us to avoid becoming obsessive, reckless or addicted to bad habits. Plato uses the analogy of a charioteer with two wild, headstrong horses. The horses of Spirit and Desire threaten to break loose and destroy the chariot. They fight and there is a 'war' between them. So Reason (the charioteer) is necessary to subordinate the horses in order to achieve health, beauty and fitness and reach the destination.

There is a clear comparison with physical health and with the contemporary debate about a balanced diet. This discussion incorporates at least three principles adopted by Plato:

■ we are *aiming at* a particular *goal*, where all our organs, muscles and glands are working efficiently and *harmoniously*

Fig. 3.1 *Reason controls Spirit and Desire*

- *discipline* is necessary to repress desires for unhealthy food
- *good habits* need to be fostered over the *long term* and short-term remedies and diets are unsuccessful.

The same is required for mental health according to virtue ethics. In the situation of the ring of Gyges, to maximise self-interest by cheating, deceiving and exploiting others will not deliver a flourishing and fulfilling life. Who could live with themselves if they habitually used and violated others? This is not to claim that the egoist would feel a sense of guilt. The egoist does not recognise traditional moral values and would not feel any guilt when breaking them. However, if you continue to treat others without respect, surely you will start to lose respect for yourself. Eventually all sense of self-worth, self-esteem and respect would also vanish if we treated others in such a way. Behaving virtuously, therefore, becomes the key to a happy and healthy lifestyle.

Think about

Can we agree on what makes for a healthy life and a fully functioning human personality? Compile your own list of what you require for a fulfilling life, then compare it with the following:

- genuine, supportive friendships
- the satisfaction of working for something and achieving it
- physical health and a long life
- the influence over others through their respect
- a supportive and mutually loving family
- a certain amount of excitement and risk
- enough money (not too much or too little) to live comfortably.

Could any of these be obtained by abusing the ring of Gyges?

And finally, real happiness comes with the *conviction* that we are contributing to positive relationships and a flourishing community. Are we not happier when all around us are positive and supportive? Would an egoist ever be able to gain the satisfaction that comes from genuine concern for others and genuine moral conviction?

So Plato rejects the assertion of Thrasymachus that justice simply serves the interests of the strong. Firstly, the powerful can be wrong and can act and make laws which are not in their interest. It is possible for anyone

Think about

How can we describe this satisfaction: togetherness? Team loyalty? 'All for one and one for all'?

to be mistaken. Therefore, it is possible not to do what a powerful ruler wants and yet be right, because it really is in their interest.

Secondly, Plato argues that only a 'skilled' person really understands someone's interest, e.g. a doctor truly understands the welfare of his patient. By introducing the need to be skilled, Plato opens the way to argue that the good life (the happiest and most worthwhile life), understood by the expert, is the life of virtue and justice.

This raises the question of whether such moral experts exist.

Mental health – extension

In his excellent book, *The Moral Philosophers*, Richards (1998) provides a fascinating comparison of Plato and Freud and their similarities on mental health and the dangers of the obsessive, insecure and egocentric nature. In *Practical Ethics*, Singer (1993) describes the psychopath as antisocial, impulsive, unemotional, lacking in empathy and remorse and unable to form enduring relationships. He concludes that while short-term pleasures are available to the psychopath, longer, deeper happiness that comes from having meaningful purposes and achieving goals will be lacking. And all of us, no doubt, will have our own views on the celebrities who indulge in an excess of hedonistic pleasure, followed by prolonged treatment in rehabilitation clinics.

Nevertheless, it may be argued that Plato's account of psychic harmony is not only questionable in terms of psychology, but also conceals value judgements which ought to be questioned. Consider who you might propose as a good example of a healthy, harmonious, fulfilled individual.

Is the sophisticated, balanced, prosperous pillar of society healthier than the creative, tortured soul or the ascetic, unworldly life of meditation?

The Forms

Underpinning Plato's world view is his theory of **the Forms**.

The theory of the Forms is discussed more fully in *Issues in Philosophy* (Pinchin, 2004) and here we are only concerned with ethical implications. In our day-to-day, physical world, examples of goodness are imperfect, incomplete, changeable and relative. Thus, donating money to a children's charity is never wholly adequate, certain to help or even desirable. Particular acts of goodness are always a matter of opinion. Plato contends that in order for us to understand real goodness, there must be a realm where true goodness is knowable, where an absolute, universal form of goodness exists. We come to access this perfection through rational thought and how we do this is described in his allegory of the cave, the similes of the sun and the divided line. It is recommended that these analogies are studied in order to understand how an individual can free themselves from this world (the cave) and discover the Form of the Good (the sun). By this Plato means the supreme Form. It is the Form from which all the other Forms derive their being.

Here we will only concern ourselves with Plato's contention that the good for something is closely related to its *function*. Just as we can specify what a good kidney or heart is, through its role in our physical well-being, so a psychologically healthy person can be described in terms of their function as a human being. Plato uses comparisons with our wider roles in society as examples. Each person has roles in society, e.g. mother, teacher, voter, and a good person performs their tasks well.

Think about

Can you name your role model, past or present, who embodies as near as possible your view of 'the healthy personality'?

Key terms

The Forms: Plato argued that what we see around us on an everyday basis is not 'real' but a mere imitation of true reality which consists in 'the Forms'. These Forms are eternal and non-physical and, for Plato, more important than the sensory impressions that we usually receive of them.

Think about

Can you list your roles? Would you be happy to be judged according to the criteria for that role, for example a good son will be dutiful, hard working, kind, etc.?

The ideal

While Plato grants every person a role in society – slave, carpenter, civil servant, etc. – the ideal character (truthful, honest, wise, brave, beautiful, etc.) is achieved by the philosopher, who excels in the life of the mind, is devoted to rational thought, and therefore will begin to understand the Forms. While ordinary people will live a life preoccupied with desire (e.g. artist, musician) or spirit (e.g. soldier), and will consequently be limited and never satisfied, the philosophical nature will be balanced and harmonious.

The philosopher achieves a harmony of the soul that is reflected in a society where all classes combine together for maximum benefit. Reason will rule, spirit will provide courage and self-control, and desire will be regulated to the satisfaction of essential needs.

To obtain this life requires rigorous education and training to control desire and spirit and develop virtuous and rational habits, guided by knowledge of the Form of the Good. So the philosopher will be physically fit and healthy, but above all will be a lover of knowledge, particularly mathematics where certainty is demonstrated, and a seeker of truth in all things. The ultimate happiness will be found in the life of the mind – contemplation – and physical pleasure will seem trivial and unsatisfying and a distraction from the highest forms of life.

So platonic love is non-physical, avoiding lust, sex and longing (desire) and is not even to be found in devotion (spirit) but is a spiritual, selfless, benevolence towards someone, with an intellectual appreciation of the beauty of their personality. The God of Eros is transformed from erotic love, which is relative and changeable in its pleasure, to a pure, timeless affection and respect.

Fig. 3.2 *Rodin's* The Thinker

John Stuart Mill – an alternative view

Alternative theories of 'the healthy ideal' abound in philosophy, and a brief juxtaposition is provided here.

In Chapter 3 of *On Liberty*, Mill (1985) argues that mankind is not infallible. The truth is complex and certainty is unlikely. We all only arrive at a portion of the truth. In these circumstances, there should be 'different experiments in living', so that 'individuality should assert itself'. Spontaneity, eccentricity and diversity should be fostered so that each individual develops in his/her own way to 'the highest and most harmonious development of his powers'. The emphasis is not on training, but on strong impulses and personal energy, leading to creativity and originality. Mill employs a comparison between 'trees' and 'trains' which is illustrated below. It should be noted that trains have a function and are organised to achieve a destination, whereas trees are regarded as existing only for themselves.

Key philosopher
J. S. Mill (1806–73)

Educated by the philosopher Jeremy Bentham, a famous utilitarian, Mill set about reconciling the utilitarian aims of maximising happiness with the importance of liberty and aesthetic pleasure. His essay *On Liberty* (1859) emphasised the importance of freedom of the individual from coercion and restraint in order to achieve well-being.

AQA Examiner's tip

When two theories are juxtaposed, as they are here, try to pinpoint the exact differences between them, e.g. Plato (reason), Mill (energy).

Think about

Is this convincing? Is there a comparable purpose for human beings? Which account of the harmonious, ideal personality do you prefer?

Growing	Training
Every individual is in themselves 'beautiful'	People are only 'successful' if they achieve a 'destination'
More vital/alive because it grows out of deep roots, instincts and convictions	Soulless, lacking in character, dead, a copy or a clone
More genuine and true to its own nature	Forced, fashioned into an identical copy of a blueprint
A fully rounded individual who can develop in many directions	Suppressed, made to conform to tracks – one-sided development
Organic, balanced, self-disciplined and responsible	Only has one function, and is otherwise useless, not suited for anything else

Mill clearly favours 'the tree' simile. But could you make a case for 'the train' analogy of mental health? What might an international footballer, a talented musician or a priest say?

Underlying these images of psychic health is a stark difference on moral absolutes. Mill emphasises our fallibility while Plato asserts that true virtue and real flourishing is knowable. Moreover, the essential difference for Plato is that knowledge cannot be found in this physical world. Mill's requirements for 'experiments in living' – an empirical enquiry – will only yield more muddle and uncertainty about the good life. Judgements about lifestyles are notoriously difficult to make so Plato invites us to access a quite independent world where the pure essence of morality and justice and beauty can be found. These essences are not just ideas, but can be discovered by reason and intellectual intuition.

As you drew nearer to complete knowledge, you would gain an understanding of the ultimate purpose and harmony of the whole of society and the human race; and how your own life contributed to the good of the whole. The nearest that Plato comes to explaining this is the Form of the Good, which is compared to the sun. The sun not only sustains growth and life, but is itself wonderful to behold as it is the source of life. Similarly the Form of the Good enables us to understand the perfections of justice and beauty, and is the embodiment of goodness and excellence itself.

The price that Plato might pay for this mystical vision of the Forms is that it is completely theoretical and impractical. There are numerous problems with the Forms and just a few are mentioned here.

Think about

Using beauty as your example, is it possible to conceive of perfect symmetry and proportion? It may help to consider principles of design and mathematical perfection in a building. Can we not rank human faces on a scale of ugliness to beauty and arrive at a perfectly proportioned face?

AQA Examiner's tip

In a lengthy discussion, relate the debate back to the main argument. Here it is maintained that a virtuous life is a healthy life, so morality constitutes self-interest.

The virtuous, healthy life is known through the exercise of reason

Firstly, how do we know when someone has achieved this knowledge? How will we distinguish the true philosopher from the fake? Presumably such knowledge is self-evident, self-authenticating, but can this be demonstrated to the rest of society? In the case of mathematics, self-evident truths are possible because of the logical, coherent nature of the subject; but ethics is very different from logic. Why could the meaning of life not be discoverable instead through refined emotional sensitivity or practical, empirical enquiry?

Secondly, why should there be one single Form of the Good rather than lots of different goods, and why should goodness be related to function (rather than need or desire) even if we accept that the human race as a whole has a function? These points will be considered further in the critique of Aristotle.

One final point refers specifically to Plato, and it concerns weakness of the will. Anyone who has ever tried to diet will be aware that knowledge does not necessarily lead to self-control. Plato argues that if we *know* what is right, then we will *act* morally. If we act wrongly, he must claim that we do not really have knowledge, but are ignorant. In his account of the ideal, the philosopher's knowledge will necessarily entail the noble character (unless his education is faulty). However, everyday experience teaches us that we can know what is right for us, we can be fully aware of our duties, obligations and consequences, and yet we still succumb to temptation or weakness of the will. So, eating a second piece of chocolate cake is not something you are compelled to do, it is not irresistible and you know exactly why you should not – but you do it. Such examples raise difficult questions about the relation between thought and action and Plato's account is not convincing. How can a highly abstract, theoretical concept of the good motivate someone to act.

Plato is, firstly, assuming that we can reason our way to our ultimate aims in life. This is a particular use of the faculty of reason, and many doubt that using reason, you can prove what 'good' is. One notable critic, the philosopher Hume, claims, 'since we cannot by reason alone discover how we should act, any values are as good as any others'. It is emotion that causes us to desire particular goals in life, and Hume continues with a memorable illustration:

> where a passion is neither founded on false suppositions, nor chooses means insufficient for the end, the understanding can neither justify it or condemn it. It is not contrary to reason to prefer the destruction of the whole world to the scratching of my finger.

Hume (1969)

Secondly, we may use reason to justify or to find reasons why we should act in a certain way, but reason alone cannot find 'the ends' or goal of moral action. To some extent, Plato's comparison of the balanced soul to society is misleading. In a society with competing interests, some balance which is rationally justified is necessary to accommodate all people, e.g. the equal consideration of interests. But the individual soul is not like a

Fig. 3.5 *This picture of the cave analogy shows the ascent from darkness and ignorance to knowledge of moral goodness*

society. Fulfilment and purpose could be formed in excess or self-denial, or the narrow pursuit of a goal, rather than psychic harmony and balance.

Thirdly, Plato seems to believe that reason has its own desires, that the motive of a desire for truth and the harmony of a healthy mind will overcome the weak will in the philosopher. In a memorable simile, Plato describes the pleasures of those who have no wisdom as 'like sheep, they stuff themselves and copulate … and kill each other because they are *not* satisfied' (Plato, 1955); whereas the philosopher has 'the most pleasant of lives … infinitely greater in terms of grace and beauty' (Plato, 1955). This would be a most satisfactory answer to the question 'Why be moral?', but is it convincing?

Aristotle

For Aristotle ethical knowledge guides our action. Therefore, he rejects that abstract knowledge, only obtainable in another realm (the world of the Forms), can be a necessary precondition of moral behaviour. Moral dilemmas are about particular situations, so any useful knowledge needs to be a generalisation about experience.

Despite this, Aristotle's foundations bear a striking resemblance to Plato. In the *Nichomachean Ethics* (1953), he lays out his premises, as follows:

1   Everything tends to its own good: every action is aimed at some positive end or ideal situation, a **teleological** approach.
2   This ultimate end or purpose for human beings is happiness (Greek term – *eudaimonia*). This is not to be thought of as pleasure only, or a narrow conception of happiness, but as well-being, flourishing or fulfilment.
3   Happiness is achieved by exercising the unique human faculty, which separates us from other living creatures.
4   This unique human faculty is reason.

Conclusion: the flourishing human being achieves the good life by exercising reason, which is our chief function.

Thus in answer to the question 'Why be moral?', Aristotle will reply that through exercising the virtues we will achieve happiness. He argues that happiness is the ultimate end because it is the only end which is desired for its own sake. While we may ask: 'Why do you seek friendship (or power or prosperity, etc.)?', the answer will be: 'Because it makes me happy'. But if we ask: 'Why do you want to be happy?' there is no possible further reply. Happiness is not a means to anything else, it is the final goal of human activity. It is desired in itself.

As with Plato, self-interest is fulfilled in that a virtuous life is a constituent of the happy, good life: 'For even if the good of the community coincides with that of the individual, the good of the community is clearly a greater and more perfect good both to get and to keep' (Plato, 1955).

Before we consider Aristotle's description of the good life, it must be acknowledged that each of the four steps above is open to question.

To some, a teleological view of human existence is implausible. Granted that each, individual human action may have a purpose, it does not mean that human life as a whole has a purpose. The reason for a particular action can be simply ascertained by asking 'Why did you do that?'. But the question, 'What is the meaning of life?', (or 'Why bother to get up every morning?'), is a completely different order of questioning and will

Key philosopher

Aristotle (384–322 BC)

While a student of Plato, he nevertheless opposed the theory of Forms. For Aristotle, ultimate realities were concrete things. So the basis of his ethics was an account of human nature.

Key terms

Teleological: everthing has a telos or purpose. Thus, in ethics, both individual actions have a purpose, and also inherent in human nature is a function or purpose.

not have such a simple answer, or indeed any answer at all. Russell's analogy illustrates this well: that every individual has a mother, does not imply that the human race *as a whole* has a mother. Thus it is questionable whether human life has any purpose. Everything just is. A rose just exists, it is not aiming at anything, and the same could be said of the human race.

Secondly, the identification of human flourishing as our goal conceals a massive assumption. While it is clear that a carpenter or a flautist has a purpose, that is because it has been assigned to them in their job description. But who assigned the purpose to the human race? Sartre in *Existentialism and Humanism* (1948/1974) clarifies this point with his example of the paper knife. The essence and the purpose of the knife is determined prior to its existence. There is a blueprint, a plan for the perfect knife which guides its production. But where is the blueprint for the human race? Only a god could decide this, and Aristotle's theory is not meant to depend on the existence of a divine designer. In the absence of a divine purpose for man, then any account of the ideal end or function will be a matter of opinion. For example, the survival of the planet might be preferred as an alternative to human flourishing and happiness.

This is further illustrated when Aristotle identifies reason and language (logos) as the unique, special quality of human beings, which we should develop. Incidentally, this allows him to relegate women, children and slaves in the hierarchy of human existence; and this is exactly the kind of fascist doctrine which Sartre condemns. Once you cite an ideal, human purpose, then every human being can be ranked in value according to how they measure up. There are three points for concern in Aristotle's reasoning:

- Is reason a unique human faculty? Recent research shows some animals capable of reason. Aristotle does not appear to offer scientific data in support of his claim.
- If another unique feature is found, would this also be part of our function? Some emotions such as compassion appear exclusive to people.
- Why should exercising our unique feature be a precondition of happiness?

There is no clear link between something being unique and it being a constituent of well-being. A unique quality could just as well be the downfall of a particular species, as the dinosaurs probably show.

Nevertheless, despite these objections, many people might accept that the flourishing of human beings does provide a persuasive end and goal for our activity. If morality is not so concerned, it is difficult to see the motivation for being moral unless virtue brings its own reward, benefiting not only the individual, moral agent but also the community, and generally making life as agreeable as possible. Indeed, Aristotle underlines that a person cannot flourish unless they are part of a successful and flourishing community. It is in everybody's self-interest, therefore, to work for the good of society as a whole. On this basis, we can still engage in virtuous behaviour even if we are sceptical that human life has a purpose.

However, even if we accept that the capacity to reason and use language are the distinctive mark of a human being, and do enable us to empathise, and reason about moral health, there will still be disagreements as to what constitutes social goods. Aristotle's answer is below, together with others for comparison.

The virtues

Aristotle's emphasis on reason leads to his famous doctrine of 'the mean': that excess is to be avoided and that human beings should moderate their behaviour in order to flourish. Virtues are those excellent traits of character and skills which enable us to act 'for the right reasons, with the right feelings, to the right degree, towards the right person' – in other words, the perfect response. Aristotle uses the analogy of an archer able to hit a target. The moral virtues (as well as intellectual virtues) guided by reason enable us to hit the target, to avoid destructive extremes by choosing 'the mean', a moderate course of action which will be wise, prudent and just. Vices, on the other hand are excessive, either through lacking or over-indulging a particular trait. For example:

Deficiency	*Virtuous mean*	*Excess*
cowardice	courage	recklessness
humbleness	pride	arrogance
meanness	generosity	extravagance

Unlike Plato, Aristotle does not suggest that knowledge alone can make us virtuous. He stresses that we must practise the virtues and acquire them through following role models of virtuous people. Just as young people become builders or lyre players, etc. by instruction from wise experts and by practising until they develop the skill to a degree of excellence, so virtues will eventually become our habit and, like good music, will flow naturally.

Another difference is that while Plato advocates that reason should *rule* the emotions and suppress 'the Beast' within us, for Aristotle, reason *guides* our feelings to an appropriate degree, suitable to the situation. Norman suggests that Aristotle resolves an awkward 'antagonism between Reason and feeling'. It is not that desire is disgusting and degrading, but we can express it in a moderate and fitting way. Thus anger can be appropriate to a certain extent depending on the situation. This may seem preferable to Plato's concept of the 'healthy option'.

But can we determine a sufficiently clear and specific set of virtues? Besides Aristotle, different cultures, religions and philosophers have all compiled their own list. Is this a weakness or a strength of the theory?

> ### Think about
>
> Can you apply Aristotle's doctrine of the mean to modern-day behaviour? In what context can people today be advised to be moderate or proportionate in their response?

Think about

Here are some contrasting lists. Which would you advocate or criticise? Are there any missing, which you regard as essential for a flourishing life in the 21st century?

Aristotle	Christian	Hume	Modern suggestions
Friendliness	Selfless love	Benevolence	Honesty
Courage	Justice	Hard work	Strength of mind
Pride	Humility	Cheerfulness	Trustworthiness
Just anger	Hope	Modesty	Loyalty
Self-discipline	Mercy	Humaneness	Self-respect
Prudence	Temperance	Politeness	Wise judgement
Practical wisdom	Charity	Decency	Altruism

One further aspect of virtue ethics needs to be highlighted. In contrast to other theories such as deontology (discussed in the next topic), Aristotle places the emphasis on *character* rather than a particular *action* in the context of a person's *whole life*. So, when faced with a moral problem, we should enquire how a virtuous character would respond. This allows the action to be 'situation sensitive', applicable to the individual, sensitive to their emotions and their life circumstances. Surely this is preferable to a hard-and-fast rule where all people could be required to perform a ready-made solution, e.g. stealing is wrong, when a Robin Hood scenario might be more virtuous.

Furthermore, virtuous behaviour enables the community as well as the agent to flourish. We should recognise that we as individuals cannot have a positive future unless the welfare of the community is part of the consideration. The more flourishing the society, the more opportunity and support there is for individual fulfilment. The educational aspects of virtue ethics demonstrate this. We learn from wise role models.

And finally, the theory offers the possibility of moral progress and learning from one's mistakes. Practical wisdom is developed over a lifetime of practising virtues and thus moral development is not oversimplified.

Nevertheless, there are reservations about the doctrine of the mean. Here are a few to consider:

▪ There appears to be a circularity in the reasoning. If we ask what the virtuous mean consists of, we are told that it is the right action, at the right time, to the right degree, for the right motive that leads to human flourishing. When we enquire what flourishing consists of, we are referred to the virtuous mean.

▪ The virtues appear extremely cautious and dull. It begs the question, what is a fulfilling life; and passion, desire and risk taking are just as plausible.

▪ It ignores the fact that good can come out of immoderation. Jesus Christ and other hold teachers reached enlightenment through extreme behaviour.

▪ Abortion

As we examined animal welfare with egoism, so we can consider how virtue theory would cope with a practical issue. To thoroughly test the theory, note down several different situations in which a woman might consider terminating a pregnancy; for example, a woman who already has three children feels the family could not cope with another.

Now instead of looking for her duty, or as an egoist calculating self-advantage, the virtuous woman will act according to the virtues to achieve the most flourishing result in the context of her whole life, consistent with right motives and right feelings to the right degree. She will ask: 'What sort of person do I want to be?'

Think about

What are the relevant virtues? To start with, love, compassion, justice. What else?

How might they be applied? For example, if the foetus is likely to be severely handicapped, compassion might suggest a termination, especially if the family is struggling to care for three other children. However, if the pregnancy was planned, justice might demand that the potential baby is given a chance of life. Relevant to the decision is the maturity of the mother and how this child will affect her life and the character she wishes to be; and how such abortions might affect the community (for example, is there community support?).

Can you suggest a relevant virtue and how it will affect the decision.

Obviously the woman must avoid vices such as cruelty, selfishness and cowardice. Have you been able to reach decisions for the particular situations that you specified at the beginning of the exercise?

Critics of virtue ethics point out that it does not offer clear enough guidance that enables real people to make actual decisions. It offers relevant consideration and we all recognise the importance of virtuous motives, but it does not give practical solutions. This point is strengthened if you believe that we need a law on abortion, and that we cannot leave virtuous people to arrive at very different answers to their dilemmas. If, for example, you believe that the foetus has a right to life, which should be enshrined in law, then a theory which is 'situation sensitive' will make it very difficult to apply a law. However, it should be noted that virtue theory is not **relativistic**. The virtues are universal, moral guidelines on how to behave, and supporters will argue that it is an advantage not to oversimplify situations, and reduce all cases of abortion to one simple law. The balance is not easy to find, but you should consider which way you would argue.

A further difficulty for virtue ethics is, as we have seen, the different virtues inherent in different cultures; and unless some measure of agreement is reached, then the theory could slide into moral relativism. This point is well illustrated by Hamilton in *Understanding Philosophy for AS Level* where he quotes Aristotle's version of the virtuous 'great-souled' man. Extracts from Chapter 3 of Book 4 of the *Nichomachean Ethics* (Aristotle, 1953) are as follows:

> the superior man has the right attitude to honours and dishonours … greatness in all the virtues stamps him for what he is … it would be totally out of character for such a man to run away … or be guilty of cheating … It is also part of his character to confer benefits, but he hates receiving them, because the former implies superiority, the latter inferiority. When he meets with ordinary people, he is moderate, since superiority over them is easy and he is not a gushing person because nothing strikes him as a subject of mighty admiration … moreover he is concerned for the truth more than for people's opinion. He is open in his speech … since his disdain makes him speak freely. He cannot let anyone else … determine his life. For that would be slavish.

Aristotle (1953, Book 4, Chapter 3)

It is perhaps difficult for a modern audience to accept these virtues as a healthy ideal, especially the pride and sense of superiority. His sense of self-worth does not fit easily, for example, with the Christian virtue of modesty. And yet, surely, self-esteem is important for psychological health, and false modesty is hypocrisy and pretence, pandering to common jealousy. The more one considers the virtues in practice, the less straightforward they appear.

Key terms

Relativistic: ethical relativism holds that there are no absolute moral values, and point to different cultures holding widely different beliefs about right and wrong. Some philosophers regard this as a problem, for how then can we condemn incest, torture and tyranny, etc.?

Think about

Try to summarise arguments for and against Aristotle's account of the virtuous life.

A common core

However, perhaps some measure of agreement on core virtues might be possible. Hamilton cites Nussbaum – that there are features of life, to which we all have to respond, such as our own self-worth, how we would wish others to treat us and the importance of positive, trustworthy relationships. In *Moral Beliefs* (reprinted in Foot, 1967*)*, Foot argues that for 'good' to be meaningful, it must apply to demonstrable benefits and that 'the happy *unjust* man' will not gain real advantages in the long run. He will continually have to be on his guard, in case he is found out and then loses everyone's trust. History shows that most evil dictators have found that out to their cost. Just as in the ring of Gyges, only a *consistently* virtuous person will live the life of *eudaimonia*. So trustworthiness, loyalty, and genuineness would seem to be essential.

Virtue theory and self-interest

Does virtue theory give an adequate explanation of self-interest? It claims that the ultimate end for the individual is his/her own happiness, which is only achieved through the virtuous life. Norman contrasts Aristotle's version of true happiness which stems from 'an activity of the soul', with the egoist position where virtuous behaviour is like a 'mutual insurance policy'. For the egoist, there is an '**external**' relationship between virtue and benefit – virtue is used as a means to happiness (instrumental), but for virtue theory, the relationship is '**internal**'. The life of *eudaimonia* entails virtue, and virtue is a necessary condition of well-being. Indeed these two positions would necessitate a very different psychological state: a 'healthy' state where I genuinely rejoice in the success of others, because their happiness constitutes my happiness; and an 'unhealthy' state where others are used, and I rejoice in their success only if it benefits me.

Nevertheless, some may feel that virtue theory does not go far enough. It attempts to reconcile virtue and self-interest, whereas self-interest should not even be a consideration in moral action. Surely when we ask questions such as 'Why be moral?' or 'Why care for others?', we do not expect an answer of the type 'Because it enables me and others to flourish' but more of the type 'Because it is the right thing to do'.

This is a weakness in the position above. If one asks, 'why behave morally?' the answer is because it will benefit me and the community. This is unsatisfactory because the emphasis is on my well-being. In the case of abortion, many would argue that the foetus deserves rights and respect and protection, because of the sanctity of life, regardless of whether those involved will flourish.

Think about

> You should think about whether morality can rest on the *contingent* fact that you *might* be found out.

Key terms

> **External:** in this context it means not valuable for its own sake, but leads to happiness, instrumental.
>
> **Internal:** in this sense it means integral, an essential part, intrinsic.

Think about

This can be illustrated by asking yourself why you give presents to parents. You might answer:

1. I give presents to my parents to encourage them to buy me presents.
2. I give presents to my parents because it makes me happy to see them happy.
3. I give presents to my parents because it is right to show gratitude for what they have done.

Which is the most praiseworthy reason?

In point 3 above you would feel obligated to give presents, even if it gave you no personal satisfaction at all. So it may be argued that there are some duties we ought to perform because independent of benefits to yourself, they can be established as the right course of action. The important focus now shifts away from *you* and *your well-being* and onto the act itself. It is the act which is important, and this is the essential characteristic of altruism. When a soldier gives up his life for his comrades, it is not for personal fulfilment (such as a lasting reputation). The only consideration is the rightness of the act itself. The value of this ultimate sacrifice is evident in the act, we do not need to appeal to the goal or purpose of *eudaimonia*. A further illustration of this would be the son or daughter who looks after an ailing parent. In such circumstances, there is little chance of this bringing much happiness, and indeed will probably restrict their chances of a fulfilling life in other ways. Doing what is right may not lead to *eudaimonia*, but many people would feel it their duty to look after an ill parent.

This also provides an explanation of our concerns about the great-souled man. Our reservation lies in that he cultivates the virtues *for himself*. He is still, ultimately, self-centred even self-obsessed, and this is not true morality. In the next topic, we will now consider that the true moral agent, like the soldier, *overcomes* self-interest rather than viewing virtue as constituent of self-interest or instrumental to achieving it (as in the first topic above).

After working through this topic, you should:

- understand why self-interest could be a constituent of a happy, flourishing life, rather than a means to it
- be able to explain how virtue ethics reconciles self-interest and the virtues, through its concepts of function and the healthy soul
- know how the essential qualities of the healthy life focus on the relationship between reason, spirit and desire
- be able to evaluate virtue ethics, in the light of topic 3 which is about overcoming self-interest.

Morality as overcoming self-interest

Learning objectives:

- to consider whether actions are right, regardless of self-interest
- to understand how deontological ethics establishes universal moral duties

Doing your duty

Whether we like it or not, some actions are self-evidently right and some are just plain wrong. Even Homer and Bart Simpson recognise this. In the excellent book *The Simpsons and Philosophy*, James Lawler (2001) charts the struggles that Homer and Bart have with their consciences. In one episode, 'War of the Simpsons', he discusses how Homer has to decide between his duty as a husband to Marge when he is expected to attend a marriage counselling session, and his personal desire to go fishing for a legendary, monster catfish. The usual hilarious plot develops, but by the end Homer 'recognises his dutiful sacrifice: "I gave up fame and breakfast for our marriage"'. This particular chapter goes on to contrast Lisa and Flanders as interesting and different conceptions of conscience and duty.

So, in this topic, we consider that the answer to 'Why be moral?' is that it is your *duty* to do the right thing. This is regardless of your self-interest, and self-interest may have to be overcome in order to fulfil your duty. This is the philosophy of Kant, and he illustrates this point in the example of the honest shopkeeper. The honest shopkeeper charges fair prices for his goods and Kant reviews the reasons why he does not overcharge:

1   because it is sensible for a successful business not to cheat customers

2   out of love and care for his customers

3   because he recognises the principle of fair dealing.

Kant rejects points 1 and 2 as unsatisfactory because if the shopkeeper ceased to gain benefit or pleasure from fair dealing, he would cease to be honest. The only motive for the moral act is therefore point 3, the intention to do the right thing – 'duty for duty's sake'. The importance of the right motive is central to the concept of duty. We should not act because we want to do it, are inclined to do it our even out of love. These are personal desires and only remain as long as the person enjoys what they do. The real test is that you perform your duty even if you are not inclined to do it. Kant also referred to the *consequences* of overcharging but this seems to be inconsistent with the duty for duty's sake claim.

The categorical imperative

According to Kant, real duties contain an 'intrinsic dignity' and 'command' which means you must do them regardless of how you feel. These principles hold good everywhere and are often referred to as laws. The use of the word 'law' emphasises the command or imperative implicit in them. You *must* do it if it is your duty. Kant refers to these moral commands as the 'categorical imperative'.

Moreover, as these laws are universal and absolute, and apply to all human beings everywhere regardless of culture or historical period, they cannot depend on consequences or particular situations, they are **deontological**.

Duties do not depend on consequences

This can be illustrated with the following episode which occurred during the troubles in Northern Ireland. One day, a car thief broke into the boot of a parked car and to his amazement found a cache of IRA weapons and bombs. He was so concerned he went to the police, admitted the burglary and gave in the weapons. Nevertheless, he was still convicted and punished for car theft because his original act and motive was wrong, regardless of the fact that it led to the favourable consequences of making the armaments safe. However, the judge was lenient when he gave the sentence! But in deontological ethics, the action itself is right or wrong regardless of the results. A good example is presented in the classic film 'The Maltese Falcon' where Sam Spade turns over the woman he loves to the police, 'regardless of consequences' because it is his duty.

to explore the problems of duty ethics

to explain why we should be moral.

Key philosopher
Immanuel Kant (1724–1804)

Kant was one of the most influential philosophers. In the *Critique of Practical Reason* (1788), he emphasises that it is man's reason that enables him to discover duties which all mankind should accept.

Think about

Which of these duties would you perform even if you did not wish to do so?

- Write a thank you letter to an aunt for the birthday present she sent you.
- Stand up and give your seat to a pregnant woman on a bus or train.
- Get to work or lessons on time.
- Buy a poppy for charities that look after ex-soldiers.
- Take part in a minute's silence, as a mark of respect, when someone has died in tragic circumstances.
- Allow everyone the right to say what they think.

Key terms

Deontological: deontological ethics considers the rightness or wrongness of the act itself. It refers to moral duties that we ought to perform regardless of the consequences. They are usually justified on religious or rational grounds. The opposite is teleological, where one acts for a purpose or to achieve favourable consequences.

The importance of reason

How are we to arrive at these laws that everyone should obey? How can we tell what is intrinsically good? Kant's reply is that we use our uniquely human and universal power of reason.

Reason dictates that everyone should obey laws, for if something is right for me, then others should also act accordingly in the same situation; and vice versa, if I expect others to act in a certain way, it must also apply to me in the situation. There does seem to be something fundamental to human consciousness in this expectation. It is implicit in the young child's complaint about favouritism: 'It is always him and never me', or the discipline of parent and teacher, 'What if everyone did that?'. Kant has discovered a basic foundation to morality – it contains a universalised command. When something is right, then everybody ought to do it. So if we lay down a ground rule in the classroom, for example that we respect each other, this must apply all of the time, to everyone. It is rational to claim that moral laws express unconditional commands applicable to all. This is the 'categorical imperative'. This fundamental aspect of morality brings out the fairness, the sense of equality and respect for all human life that is integral to moral behaviour. This is captured by Kant in two versions of the categorical imperative, summarised as:

1 I should universalise my motives and only act in a way that I would want to be a law for all people to follow.
2 I should treat people as 'ends' rather than 'means' – I should treat all people as valuable, with respect and dignity, counting each one equally and never exploiting or using people.

Reason informs us that if we are going to have any moral system at all, we cannot favour certain groups or allow prejudiced interests, it must be the same principles, laws and treatment for everyone. In *The Moral Philosophers*, Richard Norman (1998) states, 'persons are what gives value to things. Persons themselves, therefore as the source of value, must have … an intrinsic worth, that is *dignity*. Persons are … irreplaceable.'

How to use the categorical imperative

So Kant sets out to discover which duties can be universalised and will respect the dignity of each individual. Something will be wrong if it cannot be universalised, it contains a contradiction or is self-defeating. Take the example of queuing (for a bus). Once someone tries to jump a queue, the whole system of queuing is destroyed. The rush to get on the bus becomes a free for all and this situation does not help anyone. So it is contradictory to consider jumping a queue. Again, imagine I see no problem in conning people – if they are so stupid and gullible as to believe me then they deserve to be defrauded. But now I must universalise my motives and allow others to do the same. They can similarly take the same attitude, so I must agree to a law saying conning is all right. Yet under this law, the very trust that I need in order to deceive people will disappear. With widespread fraud nobody will be trustful of anybody. Thus it would be contradictory and self-defeating for me to make this law. Therefore, it is wrong for me to have this motive and carry out an action – I cannot be an exception to the moral rule.

Think about

Contrary to Kant, can you think of a situation where it might be justifiable to sacrifice some people for a greater good?

Think about

Is there an implicit appeal to consequences?

Think about

Kant provides examples of how this would operate. In each case, can you explain how there would be a contradiction when you ask: 'What if everyone did that?'

- A person desperately wants the latest … (you decide on the article). One day, he/she sees the very thing lying around in school. The opportunity to steal someone else's private property presents itself. Should he/she take it?
- A person needs to borrow money. He/she manages to secure a loan from a friend and promises to repay it at a certain date. His/her affairs go from bad to worse. He/she considers whether to break the promise to return the money. Should he/she break the promise?
- A person is inclined to be lazy. Rather than work for a living, he/she prefers to lie on the beach and listen to the sea, or sit in a café and watch the world go by. He/she considers living on handouts from the state and living a life of idleness. Should he/she?

You will notice that the device of universalising removes self-interest from the consideration and renders our justifications impersonal, universal and rational. The concern is much more about the consistency of our behaviour. This is yet another interpretation of the power of reason. In contrast to Plato, who saw reason as capable of determining goals and intrinsic goods, for Kant reason is employed as a test of consistency. Wrongness is identified with contradiction, inconsistency and self-defeating motives. So Kant is emphasising the form that morality must take. Duties take the form of universal rules, applicable to all in the same situation.

However, it may be that this emphasis on consistency will not deliver all of the duties that Kant would wish. He concedes that some acts are not contradictory in themselves, but that a moral person could not wish to have them universalised. The contradiction is that rational people would not universalise a rule that later would be used against them. So Kant contends that 'flourishing' people will support people in distress, even though it is not contradictory in itself to lack charity. He believes that a rational person will not want a lack of charity to become a law of nature, because 'a situation might arise in which a man needed love … and he would rob himself of all hope of the help he wants for himself'. So it could be possible to say 'I won't help others', but this would deprive us of charity if we fall on hard times. Is this convincing? Surely it would be possible to consistently say 'I don't expect any charity if I get into trouble', and avoid a contradiction. Furthermore, the whole thrust of the argument is in danger of looking like enlightened self-interest – I will help others in case I need help myself. The categorical imperative is supposed to overcome self-interest.

In addition, the argument appears to appeal to consequences, depending on a situation I might find in the future. Yet the rightness of an action is deontological; which stresses the motive for the action, so duties are imperative regardless of the consequences.

Suicide

More difficulties appear when Kant argues that suicide is contradictory. He argues that there is a natural law of self-love among human beings which stimulates self-preservation and self-improvement. He proposes that suicide is also a form of self-love, and therefore to destroy oneself out of self-love contradicts the law of self-preservation and is consequently wrong: 'it is then seen at once that a system of nature … whose function is to stimulate the furtherance of life should actually destroy life and contradict itself'.

Is there a real contradiction here? Surely it could be argued that the principle of self-love is not only about self-preservation but also about the quality of life. Is it contradictory to consider mercy killing or **euthanasia** to alleviate irreversible pain and terminal decline?

Of more concern is the appeal to the 'system of nature' and 'universal law of nature'. The concerns with this have been mentioned in the topics above and are summarised below under 'The naturalistic fallacy'.

Euthanasia

The issues surrounding deontological ethics can be illustrated in practical examples. In the case of Diane Pretty who died in 2002, there was widespread debate about her appeal to the European Court of Human Rights for the right to die at the time of her choosing. She was suffering from motor neurone disease and she was paralysed from the neck down. She could not end her own life, so she wanted her husband to be granted permission to help her to die when her distress became unbearable. However, assisted suicide is against the law.

Diane argued that her death was imminent and her illness was incurable. Also, she should have the right to determine what happened to her own life. There is also a human right not to be subjected to inhuman and degrading treatment.

Nevertheless, the European Court of Human Rights rejected her right-to-die challenge, and her husband would have been prosecuted if he had aided her death. Sadly, she suffered for a number of weeks before she eventually died on 2 May 2002.

While there are other issues here, such as the inherent dangers of framing an adequate law, and possible abuse, the key issue is whether treating people as valuable in themselves extends to keeping them alive at any cost.

Key terms

Euthanasia: this translates literally as 'a good death'. It usually refers to mercy killing, ending someone's life to alleviate pain and suffering.

Fig. 3.6 *Diane Pretty*

Think about

The principle we are considering is whether voluntary euthanasia or mercy killing should become a universal law. What arguments can you suggest for and against? Try to support your points with principles that you would want to universalise into laws, e.g. **the right to self-determination**. The following points might help:

- Diane Pretty voluntarily and clearly requested euthanasia, leaving no doubt of her desire to die, and without any pressure from others.
- She had an irreversible medical condition, causing long-term physical and mental suffering.
- Doctors take an oath that they will always try to save life and alleviate suffering.

Key terms

The right to self-determination: the freedom to decide how you live your life, provided you do not harm others.

■ Many people gained strength and inspiration from her dignified courage in the face of death.

Can you make a list of 'duties' that are relevant to euthanasia?

Are there any problems? For example, more and more exceptions can be added to your universalisation 'only allow mercy killings if … and under these circumstances … provided that …' and so on.

Kant proposes that human life is sacred and that this should be universalised. Yet you may have found that alternative laws are also non-contradictory. However, he may support his position with the second version of the categorical imperative which is to treat people as ends. All human life is valuable, it has value and dignity, and no one should be exploited.

The difficulty is whether we can clearly discern our duty and whether we can and should overcome self-interest. One could argue that it is not life itself which is valuable, but a quality of life. It is not mere existence which ought to be sacred, but (human) feelings and capacities, and the unique contribution that an individual personality makes. This would entail that we protect those in suffering, while they still feel they can make choices and exercise capacities, but it allows us to recognise the point at which it is impossible to live a dignified and meaningful life.

Conflicting duties

One problem that may occur when we regard human beings as valuable in themselves is that we derive a number of duties which could be mutually incompatible. In the following exercise, our duties are expressed as rights. Firstly consider whether any of these rights do not treat human beings with dignity and therefore should be removed. Then decide which rights are more important and therefore override less important ones. Finally, using the case study below, try to point to where duties conflict.

Think about

Deontological ethics

In matters of life and death, decisions have to be made about the relative importance of principles, values or rights. But which rights are more important? Some rights 'trump' others, but which ones?

Attempt to rank these principles in order:

■ right to follow conscience (e.g. doctor)
■ right to follow religious conviction (e.g. parents)
■ right not to suffer (e.g. patient)
■ right to control over your own body (e.g. mother)
■ right to self-determination (to choose your life) (e.g. parents)
■ right to life (e.g. foetus)
■ right to equal consideration of interests (all)
■ right to justice (a fair public hearing) (e.g. foetus)
■ right to a quality of life (e.g. patient)
■ right to be treated with respect (all)
■ right to freedom of speech (all)

■ right not to suffer (all)

■ right to make decisions for one's children (e.g. parents).

Can you justify your choice?

Which, in your opinion, is more important: a right to life, or a right to a quality of life? Do we ever remove someone's right to life?

Now consider the following true cases:

■ A boy was severely injured in a car crash. He was rushed to hospital and needed a blood transfusion to save his life. However, his parents were Jehovah's Witnesses, and such treatment is contrary to their religious beliefs. They refused permission. What should be done?

■ A mother is informed that she is carrying twins who are joined at the head and other vital organs. If they are born, they could probably survive joined together. Surgery to separate them after birth will be very painful and both might die. What should be done?

Clearly we need a decision procedure for when duties conflict.

As you consider the practical application of Kantian duties, further problems may occur. Here are a few to consider:

■ Who qualifies to be considered as an end? Kant refers to rational human beings, capable of universalising the moral law. This would seem to exclude children, the senile, foetuses and animals. Does this mean we can use them?

■ The process of universalising does not give enough consideration to important emotions, such as love, or special relationships. Can a relative considering euthanasia really act out of impersonal motives? Surely the intensity of feeling for loved ones means the wishes of those closely involved overrides theoretical laws?

■ The two versions of the categorical imperative might conflict. Consider the dropping of a nuclear bomb on Hiroshima to end the Second World War. Some victims were 'used' to bring a speedy end to a war where many more could have died. They were not treated as ends, but it still seems rational and non-contradictory to sacrifice a few to save the many if there is no other alternative. More valuable human beings will flourish. (You might wish to find Bernard Williams' relevant case study of Jim and the Indians, see Smart, 1985.)

■ The previous example also illustrates the importance of consequences. Would we continue to observe a duty that might bring about disastrous consequences? Consider a case for lying.

If we cannot, therefore, provide a case for unassailable duties, and exceptions can be justified, the egoist might well discount overcoming their self-interest. Kant also distinguishes between perfect and imperfect duties. Perfect duties admit of no exception, while imperfect duties can be overridden by perfect ones. To make this distinction, we would need clear criteria on how to distinguish them. Kant's perfect duties are:

1 the duty to refrain from suicide
2 the duty to refrain from making false promises.

And the imperfect are:

3 the duty to develop our talents
4 the duty to help others.

A part from the fact that the first two are negative, and the second pair are positive, can you find a convincing distinction between them? Can you conceive of situations where 1) and 2) could admit exceptions?

However, this might not be the end of the story. It may be felt, by those who have a religious faith, that so far in this chapter all we have demonstrated is the difficulty of finding a satisfactory moral position if you do not believe in God. The quotation from Dostoevsky at the beginning of the chapter is true: 'without God everything is permitted'.

This may have to be the case, but sidestepping the debate about the existence of God, will such a belief solve moral problems? A brief consideration of the theory of natural law will throw light on some of the issues.

Natural justice

The idea of some form of natural justice was implicit in the topic on virtue ethics above – that there is a purpose for human beings, and from that purpose moral virtues can be deduced. The theory is given a Christian dimension if you believe that God is the creator of Nature and therefore the author of natural laws. Aquinas describes natural law as a moral code existing within the purpose of nature. Thus, moral principles are discoverable, either through revelation, as in the form of God's word, e.g. the Bible, or in the use of God-given reason, which will understand partially the divine reason evident in nature and the design of the universe. Through both sources we can discover the natural moral laws which are the same for all mankind. For Christians, these must start with the 10 commandments, and other faiths have their core precepts which will enshrine the will of God or are principles of ultimate wisdom.

This extremely brief summary will be sufficient to highlight difficulties which must be addressed by supporters of the theory:

1 Moral rules will depend on correctly identifying the purpose of human life, which may be open to interpretation. For example, it is argued that the function of sex is reproduction and creation of new life. If so, then contraception and homosexuality are wrong. On the other hand, why can't the function of sex be the fostering of love and pleasure? The difficulty is clearly in discovering the true purpose, and reason may not enable us to decide once and for all. Furthermore, as was suggested above, there may not be a purpose at all. Science is able to hypothesise about how human life began and developed, purely as a matter of fact, without purpose. And scientific laws are very different from moral laws – see below.

2 Real-life moral dilemmas are usually complicated and the application of moral commands will be unclear. Sartre in *Existentialism and Humanism* (1974/1948) demonstrates this with the story of his 'pupil' who during the Second World War in France was torn between joining the Free French Forces or staying at home to care for his mother. The former would enable him to join his compatriots in the fight for freedom and decent moral values; and the latter would protect his mother and save her from despair and loneliness. What should he do? The point is that 'general' laws, however valid, cannot solve particular dilemmas. Christian love would be demonstrated, whichever he chose, and how do you decide between love for your country and love for your mother? Similarly, Kant's 'treating people as ends' will apply in either course of action. He can demonstrate his respect for his mother and support her life or he can value the actions of the resistance fighters and help them. Both could be seen as duties;

Key philosopher

Thomas Aquinas (c.1225–74)

Aquinas was a Dominican friar who studied Aristotle and combined the philosophy of Aristotle and Christianity. He is well known for his 'five ways' to show the existence of God.

Think about

Relate points 1 and 2 to the main topic. Why do they present a problem for those who maintain that we should otherwise overcome our self-interest and do our duty?

the support for a mother or the fight for freedom. The main thrust of Sartre's argument is that we cannot avoid an individual, human interpretation of what the relevant laws are and how we apply them. In most moral situations, we are 'abandoned', we have to create our own ethic: 'Man himself interprets the sign as he chooses' (Sartre, 1974/1948). So moral decisions become subjective – a matter of individual judgement and perspective.

Of course, one might object to Sartre's radical subjectivity. The fact that the pupil has a dilemma at all is surely because he recognises the demands of different moralities. Otherwise he would have acted just as he thought appropriate. Yet he does not deny the importance and responsibility involved in making this choice, he just exposes the difficulty of finding unassailable principles. Elsewhere, Sartre reminds us that our actions are examples to others and we will be judged.

Below are two views about moral principles, one which will support Sartre's position and one against. Can you identify them?

The naturalistic fallacy

One last serious problem has to be raised and it is referred to as the **'naturalistic fallacy'** or the 'fact–value gap' or the 'is–ought gap'.

In the first topic at the beginning of this chapter, we questioned whether the *fact* of psychological egoism could provide us with any *values*. I may be genetically programmed to be self-interested (*fact*), but that does not necessarily lead to any *values*, that it is right and that I *ought* to behave in such a manner. I do not need to endorse selfishness and I can compensate in my behaviour.

In the next topic, we considered that happiness is desired for its own sake, so that is what human beings *ought* to pursue. This does not logically follow. The fact that we desire something does not entail that it is right to pursue that desire. It is conceivable that human desires could be wrong, as from the standpoint of God or for the survival of the planet.

In this current topic, we started from the premise that human beings *are* rational (*fact*), and so our duties (*value*) will be rational laws or commands. Thus contradictory motives are wrong. But even if all human beings are rational, that would not automatically prove that acting rationally is right and good. To select reason as our value and standard is a choice, a recommendation that is open to question. As Nietzsche (1998) emphasises in *Beyond Good and Evil*, 'behind all logic, too, and its apparent tyranny … there are value judgements'. Every great philosophy and every moral code is 'the personal confession of its author'.

We must therefore make a distinction between scientific laws (*fact*) and moral laws (*value*). Scientific laws describe the universe and contain no moral implications. For example, the laws of gravity tell us how objects will behave, but do not tell human beings how they ought to behave in moral dilemmas. You cannot read nature and find conclusive moral principles. There is a gap between *des*criptive scientific laws and *pre*scriptive moral commands, and to try to deduce the latter from the former is to make a jump in reasoning that is not logical. There is a clear difference, it is maintained between, say, wanting pleasure and claiming that it is good to want pleasure.

Key terms

Naturalistic fallacy: a term coined by G. E. Moore to show that 'good' could not be defined in terms of *anything* else. Moore was distinguishing indefinables, not facts and value.

G. E. Moore exposed the difficulty of defining 'good' in terms of a natural property (Moore, 1968). Supposing we define 'good' as 'pleasure'. Then we rob the sentence (a) 'pleasure is good' of any real meaning. It becomes (b) 'pleasure is pleasure', which says nothing. If (a) is to be meaningful, then 'good' must have a meaning over and above 'pleasure', or any other quality that we might substitute, e.g. rationality. So whatever definition of 'good' as a natural property is offered, it is always an 'open question' whether that property really is good. Thus again there is a gap between facts and values. Moore himself goes on to argue that 'good' is an indefinable, non-natural property.

The contrary view will make a case for moral realism and claim that there are moral facts, which are independent of our beliefs and attitudes. Virtue ethics and deontology, respectively, point to facts about wants that all men have, the purpose of life, or qualities such as 'rationality' that are common to all men. One argument in favour is that it does not make sense to value anything we like. Whereas with aesthetic judgements, we could make a case that anything might be beautiful, we cannot make a similar case that any action can be right. Moral goodness must be attached to perceived goods for mankind. So we cannot say that clapping hands three times before breakfast is morally right, because it bears no relation to human flourishing or the formal qualities of moral duties identified by Kant.

Think about

Can you separate facts and values?

Are these statements of fact or statements of value and are some being used in both senses?

- Greenhouse gases are causing rises in world temperature.
- We must do something to stop global warming.
- If the sea level rises, many communities will be threatened.
- We ought to reduce all carbon emissions.
- I desire to leave a small carbon footprint.
- It is desirable that we change our way of life.
- Eating vegetables is a healthy option.
- Talking to strangers is a dangerous thing to do.

Some statements are clearly giving us information and some are recommending values and choices. Some statements do both, and that is often a source of confusion in moral debate.

Nevertheless, deontological ethics, despite its difficulties, has its supporters. In particular, it provides a solid foundation for justice, with its emphasis on the equal value of every individual, and it provides a possible foundation for our belief in human rights – that any human being anywhere in the world can claim basic human rights, e.g. the right not to be tortured.

It also offers an answer to the question, 'Why be moral?' and clearly separates morality from self-interest. There is an issue of whether there is a clear dichotomy between facts and values. There are value judgements which have some descriptive content and there are factual statements which contain concepts that we learn with moral import. There are

Think about

Try to think of your own examples of factual and evaluative statements that cross over.

duties which I have to perform and which can be justified independently of whether it benefits me. Indeed I may have to overcome my self-interest.

Why be moral?

The time has come to make a decision.

In one sense, we cannot avoid being moral, simply because we cannot avoid making choices. This is a condition, a *fact* of life. As our lives develop, we have to make commitments – to study, travel, work, to pursue interests, to marry, to worship; in other words, 'getting up in the morning' is a choice that has to be faced. As Sartre says, 'what is not possible is *not* to choose … even if I do not choose, that is still a choice'!

Furthermore, we do not make our own choices in isolation. It is not simply that my actions affect others and vice versa, but even my self-image, my view of myself, depends on others. I cannot regard myself as intelligent or caring or creative without considering how others see me. I can only relate myself to the opinions and values of those around me. To some extent, I must be recognised by others. I cannot escape the judgement of others and that is why I may feel guilt or pride or embarrassment. Whether we like it or not, our view of ourselves is inextricably linked to the views and judgements of others. Therefore, when we act we consider not only what we want but also how others and ourselves will come to regard our choice: 'the other is indispensable to my existence, and equally so to any knowledge I can have of myself' (Sartre, 1974/1948).

In addition, it is almost impossible to not make some long-term commitments. While we can all live from day to day at times, it is unlikely we can avoid making longer-term plans and eventually undertaking projects and making commitments, for example to stay on in education, to take a gap year, to form relationships, to get a job. We are then on the road to seeing our lives as significant, beyond the day to day, and wanting some meaning to our existence.

It becomes important what projects we undertake for we are creating our lives. Sartre compares moral choices to painting a picture. Just as we compose a picture by choosing one colour or another, so a person's life story unfolds like the painting. When we ask 'Why be moral?', we want some coherence and significance for our story. We look for a purpose.

Whichever of these three theories were chosen as a basis for life, a different self-portrait would be drawn, and we would be able to look at ourselves in the mirror, with the eyes of others, and recognise the purpose we have chosen. The choice presented so far is:

- Theory one – to maximise your own self-interest, which may or may not lead to exploiting and using others, depending on the long-term benefit.
- Theory two – behaving virtuously, because to live in a flourishing society, will mean that you will also have a flourishing life.
- Theory three – to overcome self-interest, to do your duty and, like the soldier, act altruistically because it is the right thing to do.

It is noticeable at the end of *Lord of the Flies* how Jack behaves when the adults finally arrive to rescue the boys. Until that moment, he has been so dominant and ruthless, but under the gaze of the naval officer, he retreats and shrinks back into the group and once more becomes a little boy.

We know at least that our choices and commitments will be seen by us and will be watched by others. Under these conditions, how will you choose?

After working through this topic, you should:

- be able to explain why rational, objective, universal duties overcome considerations of self-interest

- understand that duties are non-contradictory laws, that we can universalise or discover in natural law, that treats every individual as significantly valuable

- be able to explain the problems with determining our duties

- consider that we can't avoid moral choices, seeing ourselves through the eyes of others, and giving meaning to our lives.

Further reading

Golding, W. *Lord of the Flies*, Faber, 1954, but available in several paperbacks. An enjoyable and challenging novel that raises many of the issues referred to in this chapter.

Hamilton, C. *Understanding Philosophy for AS level: AQA*, Nelson Thornes, 2003. A well-researched section on ethics that covers many of the issues raised in this chapter.

MacIntyre, A. *After Virtue: study in moral theory*, 3rd edn, Duckworth, 1981. A comprehensive analysis of virtue ethics and its relevance to modern conceptions of justice.

Norman, R. *The Moral Philosophers – an introduction to ethics*, Oxford University Press, 1998. This has an excellent discussion of egoism, altruism and also contractarian ethics, as well as helpful chapters on virtue ethics.

Palmer, M. *Moral Problems*, Lutterworth Press, 1991. Chapter 2 is a very clear presentation of egoism and Chapter 4 discusses Kant. There are also extracts from Rawls and Machiavelli.

Sartre, J. P. *Existentialism and Humanism*, trans. P. Mairet, Methuen, 1974/1948. This provides a critique of theories of moral objectivity and how to create a subjective morality based on authenticity.

Singer, P. *Practical Ethics*, 2nd edn, Cambridge University Press, 1993. This discusses social contract theory in relation to animals; see Chapters 2 and 3.

Summary questions

1. What is the difference between ethical and psychological egoism?

2. What is altruism? Can appeals to self-interest explain altruistic acts?

3. What are the principal ingredients of a healthy soul?

4. What is the teleological approach to ethics and why are the virtues important?

5. What is the relationship between duty and self-interest?

6. How would deontological ethics approach an issue of life and death such as euthanasia?

7. What is the naturalistic fallacy? Do theories of duty cross the fact–value gap?

4 The value of art

We value art because it informs us

Learning objectives:

- to learn what is meant by the phrase 'art informs us'

- to see a range of examples of what is meant by 'art informs us'

- to consider whether or not this constitutes either the sole value or the primary value of art

- to understand potential problems with this viewpoint.

Key philosopher

Immanuel Kant (1724–1804)

Immanuel Kant was an 18th-century German philosopher and one of the greatest philosophers of all time. Kant's account of what constitutes aesthetic experience remains influential to this day.

Key terms

Universality: whether something is universal or not is an important concept in many branches of philosophy. Universality is identified by Kant as a key feature of aesthetic experience and as something that applies to all people, at all times and all places.

💡 Introduction

The philosophy of art, often called 'aesthetics', seeks to examine philosophically the claims of art, particularly the nature of value judgements that we may make in regards to it. It considers questions such as 'What is art?' and 'What is beauty?'. It considers the relative places of artist and audience and many other issues. It is not the study of the history and development of art but, instead, seeks to address the core questions underlying all art. If the history of art considers and describes the development of a particular style or artistic movement, aesthetics focuses on the meaning of the resulting art at a deeper level. Fundamentally, aesthetics considers the value of art, and this chapter seeks to consider that question.

While 'art' understood in the widest sense goes back to the earliest stages of human development, the philosophy of art is a relatively modern discipline. Its origins as the structured study of art qua art dates back only to the 18th century, and although there are some valuable earlier contributions, notably by Plato and Aristotle, there are some fundamental distinctions between the generic view of 'art' before the 18th century and after it. The most important distinction that emerged during this period was the separation between art and craft. Up until this point it was largely assumed that art and craft were broadly the same thing, hence the man that made wooden trinket boxes and the man that 'made' an oil painting were fundamentally doing the same thing. The same notion extended even as far as composers and poets who were also perceived as craftsmen – individuals who had a particular skill which was developed by practice and frequently by a period of apprenticeship under an acknowledged master. Modern notions of the uniqueness of the artist, his genius and inspiration were largely alien.

The most important contribution to aesthetics is Immanuel Kant's *Critique of Judgement* (1790). In it Kant creates a criterion for recognising and assessing art that remains influential to this day and to which most thinkers owe some reference. Kant describes four stages or 'moments' in the aesthetic judgement of beauty:

1 Firstly, a particular feeling characterised by *disinterestedness*. There should be no feelings of possession of the object or strong emotions aroused. Unlike pornography, for instance, a portrait of a nude woman is there only for contemplation and not to stir certain desires.

2 The second moment conveys a feeling of **universality**. The object should be beautiful to all who behold it; however, this universality is not 'conceptual' as there are no fixed rules by which one can prove that something is beautiful.

3 Thirdly, there is what Kant calls *the form of purposiveness*. Judgements of the beautiful have no end or purpose, unlike moral judgements which do, but there is still some element of directedness.

The mind is encouraged to range with the object or the feelings that emerge.

4 Fourthly, Kant argues that while not everyone will realise the same sense of universality or the other attendant feelings in relation to the same object, they *ought* to feel the same. Thus, for Kant judgements of beauty have an element of *necessity*. As there are no specific rules the link between the object and the subject in terms of aesthetic appreciation is one of a particular form of pleasure felt by the subject for the object in itself.

To give a brief example of this view in practice, albeit heavily simplified, take Michelangelo's *David*. We admire and feel its beauty, the perfection of the body and its overall composition, but we have no sexual feelings towards it nor do we have any strong 'active' emotions aroused by it. We are not jealous or angry because we are less 'perfect' than it, we are not filled with fierce determination to go to the gym or to wear more 'heroic' clothing like the loincloths of the Ancient Greeks! In short, we admire it for itself and from a certain aesthetic 'distance'. We do feel, though, that the beauty is real – that it transcends cultures and times. That it captures something of value that we can partake of. It further encourages us to wider reflection, not – using our example of *David* – of the mechanics of the human body nor of the intellectual concept 'youth' as 'that period following the onset of manhood but prior to its full manifestation' but, instead, of wider-ranging thoughts like, for example, courage, idealism or human fragility. Finally, this experience of beauty is one that should be shared by all who come to contemplate it.

One of the most basic and also most important distinctions in aesthetics is the question of whether aesthetic judgement is objective or subjective. If it is objective this means that the judgement of one person may be absolutely and universally true or false. If it is subjective then there are no universal or absolute judgements but rather a number of competing views to which we may give our support according to various criteria. There is also a 'crude subjectivism' which argues that there are no rules of judgement whatsoever and that 'good' art is just what any particular individual likes or dislikes. Emerging from this is the issue of whether we 'feel' aesthetic pleasures which would mean that they emerge from our senses and are therefore far more likely to be broadly subjective in nature. Or, alternatively, whether we come to 'know' aesthetic judgements which suggests that it is an intellectual matter which would then make it more of an objective affair. These positions are not necessarily mutually exclusive and it is, of course, possible to perceive aesthetic judgement as possessing both elements in varying degrees.

Fig. 4.1 David *by Michelangelo*

David Hume supports the view that aesthetic judgements are subjective. He argues that it is the feeling and not thought that gives us an idea of beauty in a given object. For Hume there is nothing in the object itself that carries any aesthetic property. He states 'The very *feeling* constitutes our praise or admiration' (Hume, 1978, p471). What Hume means by this is that the 'sentiment' or feeling that is experienced by the individual actually is the beauty of the object – any rationale for this feeling comes later. Despite this fundamentally subjective approach Hume nonetheless argues that there are aesthetic sensitivities which he calls 'standards of taste' that are the collective resource of humanity derived from experience resulting in a broad consensus about a common human sentiment. He suggests that the 'test of time' is one way of examining the universal potential of a work of art. If it has been appreciated by many generations who have all felt a great sentiment towards it then it is likely that this is so because of its quality. Hume's other main suggestion in establishing

Think about

How consistent is Hume's account of art appreciation? Is he really saying that some people just have better taste than others? Is this elitist and wrong or is it simply true? Does Hume really try to support an 'objective' view (based on the 'test of time' and knowledgeable and sensitive critics)?

the standard of taste is to follow the collective wisdom of highly competent critics. These critics or judges must have a 'delicacy of taste' – an ability to appreciate the finest details of a work of art. They must have a great deal of practice and must be able to compare various works of art – by doing so they will refine their judgements still further. They must avoid prejudices and use reason to be calm and neutral about the objects themselves. By following this approach Hume believes that a standard of taste can be achieved and it would be confirmed by many others apart from the expert judges which would, in turn, thus confirm the opinions of the judges themselves. To summarise then, Hume supports a strongly subjective view of aesthetic experiences as they are based on sentiment or pleasure and thus can vary markedly between individuals. However, Hume holds that these sentiments can be mistaken and so, in another sense, they can be seen as objective.

What is the purpose of art?

It has often been assumed that art needs to have a purpose. If we are to remove the notion that art 'entertains' or 'diverts' us then many would say that the purpose of art is to inform us – that it allows us to develop a greater understanding of life in all its facets. A principal way that this is thought to be achieved is by valuing art because of its qualities of imitation. By looking at representations of the world – be they vividly realistic or highly idealistic – we can gain a deeper view of existence and possibly share in a particular vision of how life should be. *War and Peace* by Leo Tolstoy is often valued because of its recreation of Russian aristocratic life of the period and its vivid descriptions of high society balls, battles and the landscape. We often admire a painting because of its resemblance to the person it depicts and we admire the sculptures of Auguste Rodin because of the vitality and fluidity of the human forms. If we can recognise a particular character-type, say a joker or bore, in a film or play it increases our sense of engagement with the drama.

Art as imitation

Plato in Book X of *The Republic* offers a very famous account of art as imitation. If we imagine a particular object, let us say a table, for Plato this is a table because it shares in the universal form of a table. Plato believed that there were objective universal forms in our world. These forms were not actually physical but gave an organising principle to everything in the world – or certainly to natural objects such as trees. This form – freed from material constraints which make it susceptible to change and decay and which are not part of the essence of 'table' – is the only 'true' and 'real' table. The actual walnut table in my drawing room is a mere example, a 'particular', which shares some of the 'universal' features of it. Where, then, does Plato place an oil painting of a walnut table? For him, it is a mere copy of a copy and thus one further stage removed from ultimate reality which is the form of the table. This is why Plato had concerns over art and its role. Art had the power to excite strong emotions which could lead individuals to act impetuously without rational control, and it was no more than a limited depiction of a particular object rather than the universal form which was fundamental. For Plato, art was falsehood and a smokescreen that hid real life.

However, even if we accept the Platonic view that there are eternal and unchanging forms to which we should aim in all things, it is possible nonetheless to view art positively. If we were to consider an Ancient Greek statue, say *Leonidas*, or a Renaissance one, say Giambologna's

Fig.4.2 Hercules and the Centaur *by Giambologna*

Hercules and the Centaur, we have, on Plato's terms, a copy of a copy with the real form of 'man' elsewhere. However, in both cases we have, arguably, an attempt to go beyond the physical to an idealised version of mankind that is more akin to Plato's form than any particular human. This view of representation in art is positive. It allows us to go beyond a mere particular example of a certain thing, be it a particular human form or a particular mountain or a particular dramatic crisis, to the universal 'truth' of man or nature or drama. The idea that beauty is inextricably linked to truth has a long history, of course, stretching all the way back to Plato and there is perhaps something intuitive that beauty should equal perfection which in turn should equate to truth. This might be a possible explanation for why art can be thought of as offering truth. Beauty is to be found in a harmony between different parts of nature and these factors are linked to truth which itself has intrinsic aesthetic properties. The individual desires to know and we can know just as much through aesthetic insights as we can through mathematical or logical insights, hence art can give us truth.

Art as representation that conveys 'truth'

This view that art can convey 'truth' and go beyond mere imitation has become the predominant one in Western art. It began with Aristotle in his *Poetics*, directly opposing the views of his former teacher Plato, and he thought that art could convey universal truths and that it was especially adept at doing it in an understandable manner. For example, a story such as that of Shakespeare's *King Lear* can help convey a moral truth in a poignant way that affects the individual much more so than if the same moral insight were merely to placed on a notice board to be read casually by a passer-by. It can be argued that humans have always learnt from stories and images. Aesop's fables have a distinct moral message, and stained glass windows in mediaeval churches had an educational aspect as well as a decorative one. Art, then, can be viewed as a continuation and refinement of this. However, art should seek to go beyond simple articulations of a moral or political message and should allow us to better understand the whole nature of experience, bringing aspects of being to the fore of which we were otherwise unaware. While imitating real life through depictions of character or place or story, art nonetheless does so to bring forth the central truths.

Over the course of art history the vast majority of non-musical art has aimed at representing something. This has often been a naturalistic representation, but it can also include a devotional approach typically evidenced in religious art or a fantastical approach typified in surrealist art or the much earlier work of Hieronymus Bosch. Our typical vocabulary when speaking of art shows this close link. It is natural to commend a painter because of the *likeness* between the subject and the painting. We can speak of a film as being a *realistic* portrayal or a play as accurately capturing the period or recreating the experience of childhood. Indeed, the fact that something is *unrealistic* is usually considered a criticism of representational art. Even music has often attempted to represent moods or activities or natural phenomena, for example the 'Storm Interludes' in Benjamin Britten's *Billy Budd* or Tchaikovsky's *Charge of the Light Brigade*. More recent representational art, for example the works of the impressionists and later the expressionists, moved from a more purely representational style to one which sought to convey a fuller grasp of reality. Impressionism sought to do this through movement and a better understanding of light, expressionism through a greater emotional depth and vigour. Nonetheless they were still engaged

Key philosopher
Plato (427–347 BC)
Plato argued that art was largely representational and as such had limited value as it was one further step away from ultimate reality, namely '**the Forms**'.

Key terms
The Forms: Plato argued that what we see around us on an everyday basis is not 'real' but a mere imitation of true reality which consists in 'the Forms'. These Forms are eternal and non-physical and, for Plato, more important than the sensory impressions that we usually receive of them.

in the process of representing in order to provide a fuller or 'truer' version of life. Thus, it is possible to argue that imitation is central, if not to all art then at least to most of it, and that aesthetic judgements fundamentally remain based – as our usual laudatory language about art proves – on the representation in some way of something or other.

Problems with this view

Forgeries are not art

It is worth considering in a little more detail what we mean by 'representation' and 'imitation' as they are terms that can be used in a number of contexts. Why, then, if art is primarily representation, do we not eulogise the forger? A certain person may be exceptionally talented and be able to recreate a perfect copy, exact in every detail to the original, but why do we value the forgery less and would not count it as 'real' art? The same is true of the look-alike. Just because a certain person looks like a famous person, maybe dresses like them and attempts to speak or act like them, that does not mean that they are artists or that what they are doing has artistic merit. This is probably connected to the fact that mere copying is of limited value artistically. A very accurately drawn picture of a wanted suspect may help the police, but it is not valued artistically. What is required is for the artist to add their own dimensions and uniqueness to the representation. They may emphasise a particular facial feature or they may capture a certain expression in their subject. Their choice of colour may add something and the overall composition will bring fresh insight. This is easily demonstrated by looking at different portraits of a certain figure. They are quite often markedly different because each painter has brought different aspects to the fore and executed them in different ways. Thus, we can dismiss copying as art because it fails to bring anything further out of the subject. It is like a photocopy – no more, no less, even if the level of skill required is high.

Non-representational art has value

There is a further problem with the idea that art involves representation, namely that not all art is representational. Very obviously much 20th-century abstract art in both painting and sculpture is not representational and neither is the vast majority of music. In isolation this may not matter but it surely does matter when we claim that representation or imitation is fundamental to art when there are so many glaring exceptions. It cannot be the case, then, that representation is a necessary element in aesthetic appreciation. Leading on from this, the value of a work of art is usually not judged by its absolute proximity to its subject. A great portrait has those elements of artistic brilliance which we discussed above. The mere similarity is only valuable if it casts a greater light on the subject, not just because it looks the 'spitting image' of him or her.

In what sense does art represent truth?

The idea that art provides us with 'truth' needs further examination. Facts can be communicated in art, for example a painting by Landseer tells us something of the landscape of Scotland. However, these points are usually incidental to the work of art rather than the primary reason why that particular work of art was created. Indeed, we do not use works of art to inform us of basic natural phenomena and to do so would be to trivialise it. In visual art this is even more so the case since the emergence of photography. If we think of truth, it is clear that art does not usually aim to provide us with truth in any normal sense and, for example, it does set out primarily to tell us about a series of facts about the world. Truth, then, in an artistic sense usually means an insight into the way individuals and the world work at some more fundamental level of being. Typically, it involves bringing into sharper focus some idea or notion of which we are already in some way aware. For example, we have some basic grasp of fate and human tragedy but this is brought to the fore in the play of *Oedipus Rex* by Sophocles where Oedipus unwittingly kills his father and marries his mother through no fault of his own. So truth, in an artistic sense, is necessarily an abstract notion, but is saying this any more than conceding that art does *not* give us truth about the world? Indeed, are we not presupposing that there is such a thing as 'truth' as we have not supplied an argument for it? Are these 'truths' really truths at all then? Or are they mere subjective feelings that do not provide us with anything substantial about the way the world actually is? A Greek tragedy might leave us feeling a certain way and help develop a better understanding of human nature, but is this really informing us or is it easier to obtain these insights from other avenues?

Further, Alexander Solzhenitsyn's *The Gulag Archipelago* (1973) is a non-fictional account of life in Soviet camps that were largely for political prisoners. It is factual, informative and deeply moving. It could be classed as a work of art but it is non-fiction and therefore is more properly classified as history or reportage. Surely, a work such as this is of more value as 'truth' than a 'purer' work of art. It is truth in the usual sense we use truth – that of correspondence to the facts – but it also has the ability to convey to us at a universal level the horror of totalitarianism, the individual crushed by the state. If we reflect further on how art may inform us we again can see its limitations. If we take the example of film there are a number of highly acclaimed films set in the Vietnam War such as *Platoon*, *Apocalypse Now* and *We Were Soldiers*. Whilst they convey the horror of war it is worth asking ourselves if this isn't largely obvious. Were we really made aware that war involves killing and death and that notions of glory are usually misplaced? Further, the emphasis on an individual character can blur the factual account by giving greater weight to a particular sequence of facts. There is also the additional and inevitable problem of perspective. That the artist gives us one particular perspective is not a problem unless we wish to press the claim that art gives us truth, whereas what frequently appears to be the case is that the artist gives us a particular slanted account from his or her own perspective. Are we, then, really, informed by art or are we just given a range of views for us to digest ourselves?

Art as an opportunity to reflect

The traditional view of art assumes that the artist has a message that he or she wishes to convey. This is not always the case though. Indeed, it is perfectly possible to argue that each individual responds differently, possibly markedly differently, to each work of art. Is that clear evidence that art does not provide us with truth but, perhaps, instead just encourages us to reflect upon life and existence and to form our own conclusions? On this model which sees the artist as a conveyer of a message, we can still hold that art informs us. However, it informs us not of something specific but, instead, it informs us generally by encouraging us to be reflective individuals. A writer such as Nicholas Mosley in his series of novels entitled *Catastrophe Practice* (1979–90) is not primarily aiming to convey a message so much as encouraging the reader to engage with the material and reflect themselves on it. Also, a great deal of modern art is concerned with the actual act of 'creating' and therefore is concerned with the medium and not the over-arching message or vision. This has been a noticeable feature in both the Modernist and Post-Modernist movements. Further, the more abstract the art (be it experimental visual art or contemporary dance or classical music) then the harder it is to speak of a definite message as opposed to a range of ideas or moods that may be conveyed. Are these difficult and challenging images or sounds there to really inform us or simply to unsettle us and encourage us to probe more deeply for ourselves? However, could this type of intellectual challenge to the individual be sufficient to justify art's role as informing us? Rather than offering us a particular vision of life we instead are responsible for fashioning our own.

Art has an intrinsic value apart from representation

There remains a fundamental problem with this understanding of art. While it appears that art certainly informs us at some level, this surely cannot be the primary reason why we value art. This view can be seen as reductivist. According to this view, art is not something of **intrinsic value** – that is, valuable for its own sake – but it is something that only has **instrumental value** – it is valuable only if it is useful in some way. This narrow approach to art can be condemned as philistinism. If art is merely reduced to a moral or social force then it would appear that something vital is missing from it. There are many examples of this trend throughout history, no more so than the communist regime in the 20th-century USSR. Soviet social realism was the official approved style of artists working in the Soviet Union. Its aim was to convey realism, but a certain type of realism: the content agricultural worker, the happy factory worker, the fecund family with well-fed offspring. All would typically be portrayed gazing into the future, confident of tomorrow and tomorrow's technology, secure in the direction of the country under the Soviet masters. While this is an extreme example it nonetheless demonstrates a problem for this approach to art.

How can you measure the 'truth' of art?

If you were to stand back still further, from a strictly philosophical perspective there is the question of how we can quantify or confirm the truths of art. Usually, for example, with mathematics there are proofs that demonstrate the validity of the proposition. With science there are experiments that give us not truth but, at least, the best current working hypothesis. How can the truths of art, so abstract at the best of times, be compared to these tried and tested methods? It might be argued that the truths that art provides are insights into the human experience and therefore cannot be categorised in the same way as everyday knowledge. Feelings such as love, despondency, anguish, hope and awe cannot be neatly categorised but are real and important. Further, while these feelings can be explained via biology, psychology or neuroscience, these are not the 'real' explanations that people actually understand by these feelings. Does the validity of art depend on how close the work of art comes to providing an accurate account of these deep human psychological or moral truths? D. H. Lawrence, the 20th-century British novelist, has often been criticised for his sometimes one-dimensional portraits of some of his central characters and for a limited grasp of women. Does this mean that the truth value of his work is lessened and therefore that it is less valuable as art than, for example, a novelist with a better overall grasp of characterisation? Alternatively, is Lawrence's particular vision (one that stresses the sensuous and natural) still valid – both as art and truth? We could argue that we do not look at Lawrence, or indeed any artist, for a full account of the ultimate nature of life but for a *particular* perspective. This perspective emphasises certain aspects of human life more than others and draws our attention to things that we do not usually focus on. It is left to us as individuals to integrate the competing visions of differing artists into an overall account of truth.

Anthony Savile in his book *The Test of Time* (1982) argues that great art can be distinguished by its longevity and its ability to speak to people from very different ages and social milieu. This means that the work has broad appeal and approaches or perhaps attains universal value and is not just of value to the people it immediately concerns. Without considering the intricacies of Savile's argument here it is perhaps sufficient to say that art, like law, social relations, food and the like, all benefit from the input of very many people over many years and thus, over time, we are able to arrive at a consensus. This agreement over time may be the closest we can get to finding the truth or the insight of art; perhaps it is all that can be expected, perhaps it is enough.

After working through this topic, you should:

- be able to identify what constitutes the informative element in art

- be aware of the types of viewpoint that often support this view of the value of art

- be able to discuss problems with this approach to art, evaluating their philosophical validity.

We value art because of its expressive qualities

Learning objectives:

- to explore what is meant by the 'expressive' in art

- to consider differing rationales in support of such a view

- to critically examine a range of issues that emerge from this perspective.

Introduction

The 19th-century painting *The Death of Chatterton* by Henry Wallis depicts Thomas Chatterton's death at the age of 17 after drinking arsenic. The painting itself is well known and a work of some merit, but what is

Fig. 4.3 The Death of Chatterton *by Henry Wallis*

more significant for our purposes is the attitude that has been ascribed to the subject of the painting, Thomas Chatterton. He was a poet and forger of prodigious early talent who took his own life rather than die of starvation. He is widely assumed to be the first British Romantic figure, displaying the apparently deep feelings and other-worldliness that we now frequently assume to be the hallmark of the real artist as opposed to the solid, workmanlike but uninspired work of the craftsman. **Romanticism** as an artistic movement emerged at broadly the same time that aesthetics became an academic discipline in the 18th century. This movement was enormously influential and remains seminal in the way that it has shaped our view of art and artists to this day. Romanticism was a reaction against the mechanistic and scientistic view of some enlightenment thinkers who saw humankind as machine-like and hence having very limited, if any, real freedom of action. Instead, they saw humanity as a unique, creative and spiritual force with the artist as the ideal mediator between 'ordinary' life and the transcendent.

Art affects us emotionally

The Romantic artist is someone who experiences great and real emotions. Often part of the challenge for the artist is to control their emotions and channel them towards artistic creation. The second stage is the actual production of the work of art which essentially must carry with it the emotional charge from which the inspiration itself first emerged. Finally, there is the reception of the work of art by the audience – be they the watcher, the listener or the reader. They must also ideally receive the emotional impart of the work of art and be affected by it. This account is fairly straightforward and one that is easy to recognise. We are all familiar with the idea that art can affect us emotionally. The language we naturally use to describe art is filled with terms that recognise this. For example, the film *Schindler's List* can be described as 'moving', Wagner's operas are 'powerful' and Thomas Hardy's *Tess of the D'Urbervilles* is 'tragic'.

Think about

Think about a work of art that you have enjoyed. Make a list of the words that you use to describe the thoughts or feelings that occur to you. Try to classify each word or phrase that you have come up with as either 'emotion' (if the word you have chosen describes an emotion or a feeling), 'form' (if the word describes an aesthetic or artistic quality) or 'inform' (if the word or phrase describes a moral, intellectual or factual quality in the art). Is it the case that most of the words chosen describe 'emotions'? Is this because art is primarily concerned with emotion or are there any other possible reasons?

The earliest account of the view that art can affect us emotionally comes from Aristotle. When discussing Greek tragic drama he outlines what he terms **catharsis**, which literally means a 'purging' or 'cleansing'. Aristotle used the term to describe the feeling that would overcome the audience at the end of a tragic play. They enter into the play with the characters, traverse the events of the drama, and witness their fatal mistakes and the role of fate in the characters' ultimate destinies. At the end, having been through a tumult of emotion – the audience emerges emotionally purged. Aristotle only acknowledges a role for emotion in a fairly narrow context. More recent thinkers, however, have identified the expressive or emotional response as the prime, or indeed, the sole value of art.

💡 There are a number of notable thinkers who have argued that art is essentially emotion. Leo Tolstoy, the great 19th-century Russian novelist published *What is Art?* (1996). In it he puts forward a relatively simple account similar to that described above, where the artist experiences and conveys emotion. The audience receives the same emotional feelings as the artist. What is important for Tolstoy is the quality, or moral worth, of those feelings communicated. So art that produces self-indulgence, arrogance and excessive individuality, for example, is of less worth than art that produces 'higher' feelings of selflessness, charity and love. Clearly, Tolstoy's account introduces a strong degree of moral censure on art and it is right to ask where this comes from. Tolstoy is guilty of confusing moral and aesthetic criteria or, at the very least, of failing to account for their amalgamation. Is Tolstoy guilty of assuming that art should only serve a religious, moral or political purpose irrespective of its value as art *qua* art? Further, on Tolstoy's account many works of art acknowledged to be great would be dismissed in favour of simple folk art. Richard Wagner's operas *Ring of the Niebelungen*, a paradigm of artistic achievement on musical, lyrical and conceptual grounds, is dismissed by Tolstoy because the emotions conveyed are not those of universal benevolence.

The role of conscious expression

More satisfying theories based on expression are offered by the important Italian philosopher Benedetto Croce and R. G. Collingwood. Both philosophers are broadly idealists, that is they see the priority of things in the mind as opposed to material things. The key distinction is between intellectualised, conceptual thought and what Croce terms 'intuition'. (Collingwood uses the term 'imagination' in virtually the same sense.) Croce states:

> Knowledge has two forms: it is either intuitive knowledge or logical knowledge; knowledge obtained through the imagination or knowledge obtained through the intellect; knowledge of the individual or knowledge of the universal; of individual things or the relations between them, it is, in fact, productive either of images or of concepts.

Croce (1909)

This *intuition* allows the mind to grasp the ultimate essence of an object without categorising it in the way that we do when we think, in order that it can be used in a variety of different ways. Thus, artistic *knowing* is quite distinct from intellectual knowing. Both philosophers then proceed to elaborate different types of expression in order to define precisely how they separate expressions and emotions of a peculiar artistic nature from mere physiological or biological unconscious human reactions such as quivering or sweating. Conscious expression is, for both of them, the criterion, the sole criterion, for assessing art. However, it must be a certain type of 'pure' expression separated from any other non-artistic concern. Hence, a piece of music designed to arouse religious sentiment would be condemned for insufficient purity of motive. In this case the artist is not really producing art as he/she is also interested, possibly primarily so, in inducing certain specific religiously motivated emotions. Collingwood argues that this cannot be the case. A truly expressive artist has no other concern but artistic expression itself and for itself; indeed, so moved is the artist that they do not know the outcome of their expression until the work of art is complete. Expression at this level seeks to develop

Key philosophers

Robin George Collingwood (1889–1943)

Collingwood was an important British idealist philosopher. He argued that art's value lies in its emotional engagement.

Benedetto Croce (1866–1952)

Benedetto Croce was a leading 20th-century Italian philosopher and one of the most influential modern aestheticians.

■ Think about

Must the person that made or created the work of art be conscious that they were making 'art' or at least something creatively akin to it? For example, if someone took a holiday photograph of some friends sitting around a table which – by chance – critics then thought to be, say, compositionally brilliant or capturing a certain 'spirit of the age' would this lessen the 'value' of the art or not? Would it really be art at all?

the idea that pure expression in art brings greater clarity and refinement to our emotions; feelings that were confused or unclear are brought into full focus by the depth and power of the expression.

What surely must be important is not merely that emotion is expressed or that a significant quantity of emotion is expressed, but it is the qualitative aspect of the emotion that matters. It is not the poet's love per se nor the fact that he loves a great amount, but that the love he is attempting to convey is in some way noble, selfless, pure or unrequited. It is the quality of the expression that matters, but how are we to be sure that our understanding of the artist's expression is the correct one and, indeed, does it actually matter if it is or not? In essence, does art become art when it is perceived by a certain individual in a certain way or is it art from the moment of creativity? Probably, we would instinctively like to suggest the second option. It is more in keeping with our traditional view of the artist as a paradigm of insight, emotion and creativity. However, this view is not without its problems. For instance, the artist has created an object and it is this object that is supposed to convey the deeply felt expression of the artist. It is not clear either how that emotion is transferred to the object or how that same emotion is transferred to the recipient. It is more straightforward to argue that there is the initial expression of the artist which results in the creation of a work of art. This work of art then becomes the catalyst for feelings of emotion and expression in the individual that views or listens to it. They partake in a work of art and find their own expression within it. Ideally, we would like to see both aspects happening, i.e. the aspect of the individual finding meaning and the aspect of the artist conveying meaning.

Problems with this view

Emotion as irrational

Not everyone views the expressive approach to art in a positive light. This emotional expression can be viewed as anti-rational and therefore dangerous. Plato was concerned with this aspect of art and thought it ought to be controlled and regulated. The German Romantics that we discussed above had an interest in and sympathy for suicide. They saw this as a valid response to an emotional trauma. However, we would usually consider this to be somehow irrational (there is a strong link between suicide and depression and other forms of mental illness) and we would usually caution against this. We also are not keen on people who lose complete control of their emotions thus resulting in argument and conflict for a number of people. It is clear that we do not think in everyday terms that all expression is good.

■ Think about

How far should an artist be allowed to go in his/her search for self-expression? Does an artist have an absolute right of self-expression? If an individual or a group objects to a particular work of art should it be banned? What are the dangers of censorship?

The artist is given a 'special' status

A further problem is that this view can deify a certain type of individual and a certain artistic viewpoint rendering others worthless. Although we need to recognise that art is distinct from craft, the expressive model can fail to value the importance of skill. The artist and his or her life can become the main subject of conversation rather than their actual artistic output. If the artist looks 'like an artist' and lives a certain sort of bohemian life, then they can be considered greater than they actually are. This can be demonstrated at a lower level by the fact that the fame and reputation of an actor like James Dean or a musician like Kurt Cobain is increased by their early death. Thus the excessive emphasis on the artist and their deeply felt creative 'genius' can result in the art itself not being properly considered in its own right.

A great deal of modern art is based on the view that as long as it involves expression then it is also art; for example, conceptual art as exemplified by Damien Hirst. His most famous work is his *Natural History* series, in which a variety of dead animals (including a sheep and a cow) are preserved in formaldehyde. The most famous of this series features a 14-foot shark and is titled *The Physical Impossibility of Death in the Mind of Someone Living*. Usually it is the case that established artistic techniques or skills are absent and, further, that the works are obtuse and difficult. However, most relevant for our discussion here is that a common defence given by this type of artist is that it is *their* expression. Whether or not their expression has any value to anyone other than themselves is not considered relevant, nor is their ability to communicate that expression to others. Some critics object to this approach. For example, the *Daily Standard*'s art critic Brian Sewell is outspoken in his criticism of conceptual art, denying that it is genuine art at all, and part of his reasoning is based on the fact that it is mere untrammelled expression. Simply because someone says they are an artist and then states that this is their expression does not mean it is art in the same way that a child demonstrating their anger by stamping their feet does not constitute art. By doing so they may bring into doubt the whole expression-based approach as they argue not that expression may be an important part of art which might find wide agreement but that it is the only criterion.

Fig. 4.4 The Physical Impossibility of Death in the Mind of Someone Living *by Damien Hirst*

Emotions and the need for them to find expression do appear to be basic to a human being's life. So it may not be surprising that art is interested in this. While it seems unquestionable that art does communicate an individual's expression, it is worth considering whether the fundamental value of art can be ascribed to this. As we all feel emotions on a regular basis, including many deeply felt ones, and express them in our daily lives, we may ask why we need art to do this as well. In fact, if you wish to express love then taking hold of the beloved and kissing them is certainly more direct and probably a more honest thing to do than reading love poems in solitude. If we are angry then stamping our feet and raising our voices is also natural. We understand these emotions either intuitively or through experience, but either way art probably cannot convey anything to us that we have not already come to understand. In that case, art as expression merely reinforces or reminds us of lost innocence, unrequited love, betrayal, despondency or whatever other state of being we may care to imagine. Perhaps, what art aims to do is to provide us with paradigms of these feelings so that it is the rarity, the quality of the emotion that is important in a great work of art and not merely emotion per se. However, there is another potential response, one that denies that there is a problem here. It is perfectly possible to argue that we do appear to be aware of the differences between expressive outbursts such as described above and the expression that is felt and communicated by art. How this is done is not entirely clear. It may be due to the channelling of emotions or something inherent and obvious to the individual. If this is the case then, arguably, this potential problem would not even arise.

Art should take us beyond mundane emotion

There is another possible worry that needs consideration. It is often thought that art conveys something that is ineffable, transcendent and literally beyond any form of description, and therein lies its value. If that is the case then it would seem that art cannot be reduced to a description at all, not even a description of some expression. Indeed, if art came down simply to the expression of this and that feelings, it would be at best trivial. It is precisely because great art takes us beyond that which we feel we can comfortably understand, feel or relate to that it derives its value.

■ Think about

Is it possible for an atheist to fully appreciate religiously inspired works of art? Wittgensteinian thought might suggest that such people aren't able to grasp the 'form of life' out of which a work such as a mediaeval gothic cathedral arose. The inspiration of the artist and his or her motivations in completing the work of art might appear strange or ludicrous. Is this true?

■ Think about

Does some art date more than others? If this is so, why? Are film and photography, because of their visual medium and relatively modern origins, more prone to this effect than, say, classical music which is usually more abstract? Alternatively is it more to do with the quality of the art? Are great films, for example François Truffaut's film *Jules et Jim*, capable of being great art even if the cinematography may be considered old-fashioned?

■ The universality of expression

If we do accept that art can indeed express something of value given the right conditions, there still remains the question of how universal can this expressive approach to art be? The Shakespeare play *Romeo and Juliet* engages us because we are familiar with Western notions of romantic love. To a Muslim fundamentalist both Romeo and Juliet are fundamentally immoral and deserve the consequences. The same can be said of Christian religious art which has been the main inspiration for Western art for most of its history. If we think of a Renaissance Madonna, the inspiration and cultural reference for this work of art is rooted in a particular type of Roman Catholic world view. Is a secular person likely to draw the same expression from this work of art as was intended by the artist over 500 years ago, and even if one can, will those qualities be appreciated? Is even a contemporary Roman Catholic likely to properly grasp, for example, the particular form of piety and particular theological slant of the artist?

This issue, though, could also be looked at as a positive defence of the expressive view of art. The fact that the audience does not have to sympathise with or fully understand a work of art in order to appreciate it lends support to the view that the emotional, expressive element of art is the most important and transcends both our moral and intellectual belief systems and our inevitably limited perspectives. For example, the great Sanskrit epic poem *The Mahabarata* is filled with religious and cultural matter that is difficult for someone without a significant knowledge of classical Hinduism to understand. However, as a work of art the expressive element remains untouched and can therefore be appreciated as art by someone with no knowledge of the cultural milieu which created it. The human dramas and emotions it describes, the empathies it creates in its audience are universal and timeless, and therefore it is a compelling example that art as expression goes beyond our usual criteria of knowledge and provides insight at quite another level. Is this always the case though? Elizabethan humour in the form of the verbal pun is now tedious to most modern audiences. Humour in Ancient Greek comedy would now be thought crude in the extreme. Many films can 'date' fairly quickly despite nonetheless having a 'universal' theme. Does the universality of expression, perhaps, depend on the work of art being reinvented for each succeeding generation? This is certainly the case with theatre where new directors can produce radically different works based on the same scripts.

After working through this topic, you should:

- be able to discuss the nature of the expressive in art
- be able to consider with a range of examples the strengths and weaknesses of such a view
- be able to critically evaluate the various objections to such a view forming value judgements based on reason.

We value art because of its particular 'artistic' qualities

Learning objectives:

- to examine what constitutes the formal aspects of art
- to consider whether these formal aspects are fundamental to art and, if not, whether they are nonetheless valuable
- evaluate the value and significance of art's unique 'artistic' elements.

Key terms

Form: the underlying elements of a work of art that are arranged by the artist to produce the most aesthetic effects.

Aesthetic appreciation: this is the particular way of appreciating the formal elements in art which many argue are different from an intellectual or emotional approach.

💡 Introduction

Imagine a statue of a young British soldier proudly celebrating victory at the end of the Second World War. He strides purposefully forward. His head is raised to the sky, his eyes look out to the distance, one arm is raised out in front of him palm facing upward. The other arm holds a rifle below his hip slightly behind him as if he were about to drop it. When we look at this statue a number of things might occur to us. For example, we might feel a sense of pride in his achievements and bravery, relief that the terrible war is over, sorrow as we reflect upon those that have died, etc. However, as well as considering how this imagined work of art makes us feel or what it makes us think, we can also think in terms of its 'form'.

By **form** we mean the specific 'artistic' qualities present in the work of art itself. These things in everyday language might be called elegance, beauty, grace or the like. Returning to our soldier example above, we might consider that the particular position of the arms presents a 'balance'– one held forward and above the waist, the other somewhat behind him and below the waist. We could note that in the soldier's upturned face there might be a pleasing 'proportion' between his facial features, nothing being too large or small, nothing unduly predominates. Looking at the complete statue there might be a harmony between the various parts which creates a particular sense of 'wholeness'.

These various *formal* qualities of a work of art can give the individual appreciating it a variety of responses quite apart from any feelings they might have. For example, you might look at an oil painting of a political figure and dislike the subject matter and the values that the particular politician stood for. Nonetheless, it is still possible to appreciate the formal elements of the picture, say its beauty or its vividness or its structure. An understanding of these specific features of art is called **aesthetic appreciation**.

What are these formal qualities? How do we identify them? How important are they and how do they relate to each other? This topic explores the concept of form in art. It considers in some detail if form is an essential component of art and looks at what aesthetic experience consists of. It examines whether these formal qualities are objective, universal features (and, if so, where they might come from) or whether, alternatively, they are dependent on subjective factors (and, if so, is this satisfactory). Finally, it will consider whether a formalistic approach to art is valuable or whether the real value of art lies elsewhere.

The variation in formal aspects

We briefly touched upon what constitutes the formal aspects in art above. It is clear that each particular art form has its own unique formal aspects and that it is not possible to provide a short, tidy list of those features of a work of art that are formal. However, it may be sufficient for our purposes to locate the formal aspects in the arrangement or ordering of the features of the particular art form.

> Despite the diversity of what counts as 'formal', there is one thing which all these examples have in common: in every case relationships between features are involved. In visual art the relationships may be between shapes or between colours; in music they may be between notes or between instruments; in literature they may be between metrical units, words, parts of a plot, or presentations of a theme. In every case it is the ordering of the formal features which matters.
>
> *Sheppard* (1987)

While the formal is often thought to be a hallmark of art it is not the case that anything which has formal aspects is art. Cookery, for instance, most notably *haute cuisine* but certainly most food served in a decent restaurant, displays formal traits. There is usually a balance between certain flavours, the chef will attempt to arrange the food on the plate to be pleasing to the eye either by being harmonious or by creating contrasts. There will also often be an attempt to visually stimulate, and complementary wine will be chosen. The same formal principles can also apply to gardening, designing of many kinds and other activities too. There are numerous reasons why these activities are not art, but they are essentially beyond the scope of our discussion. Suffice to say that they are considered primarily crafts and do not meet the standard criteria of universality. Even more fundamental is the fact that the formal in all of these elements cannot be the sole criteria. For example, in the case of food if it looks beautiful but tastes appalling then it is not great food. A fashion designer still has the practical aim that the clothes should be *worn*, unlike, say, a piece of sculpture in which the formal aspects of its composition are paramount.

Think about

The nude human form, both male and female, has a long history and tradition in visual art. It is usually clearly distinguished from pornography. Why is this so? Is this distinction fair and accurate? Might pornography be art or are all nudes pornographic?

The notion of 'form'

There are many reasons why these formal elements have a strong claim to being the essence of art. While many things can engage our emotions (a sporting contest, a love affair or the loss of someone close to us) and many things can stimulate us intellectually (a documentary, a conversation or a newspaper article), it is only in art where this formal element is ever-present and of sustained importance. It does appear then that art is different from other activities in this important respect. Not all art conveys emotion or attempts to engage us cognitively, but all art has a formal element. Further, it is perfectly acceptable for the artist to concern themselves solely with matters of form to the exclusion of all else. Many artists have a reputation for formal mastery without any great concern for other aspects of art, and yet the work they produce is still accepted as art and indeed often great art. However, this is not the case with cognitive or affective approaches to art. If the work is purely cognitive then it is not art at all, and the same can be said of expression. If all we have is something that claims to be informative (say, a council brochure) or a mere expression of emotion (say, a crying girl), then these are not considered as examples of art at all. The best that can be said in these cases is that the objects are interesting intellectually or alternatively passionate and emotive, but they fail to meet the full requirements of art.

Another value to formalism in art is the fact that it allows us to separate the content of the work plus other factors such as the social context and the moral or political views of the author, and focus purely on the art itself. Richard Wagner was widely known as an anti-Semite and most accounts of him describe him as thoroughly unlikeable, but his operas are widely esteemed. Thus, we can ignore other factors of his life and political views and, indeed, even largely ignore the Germanic themes of his operas and, instead, discourse about the actual music itself, for example its use of 'unending melody' as opposed to the usual structure based around aria and chorus. The converse is also the case. In criticism it is perfectly possible, indeed common, for the critic to see value in the themes of the work of art but to believe it to be poorly executed. This sort of language is rife in book reviews and the like with comments like 'ambitious in scope but fails to be thoroughly convincing'.

At the start of this chapter we briefly looked at Kant's account of the aesthetic appreciation of beauty. The characteristic states of mind and attitudes described by Kant and many others since then seem to fit very naturally the concerns of the formal. The states of mind appropriate for *aesthetic experience* such as disinterestedness, a concern for universality, neutrality and distance would appear to be naturally sensitive towards formal concerns. If we were to consider a neo-classical building on the shore of a lake we could see that the contemplative attitude required for this type of experience would naturally value elegant proportions, a setting harmonious with nature, the contrast between the use of materials and the surrounding nature.

Problems with form

Does form exist?

It is possible to take a more critical attitude towards the whole idea of form. Is it largely a philosophical abstraction (i.e. it matters only to philosophers) that actually means little? Is it simply a way of trying to explain why we like something? Is form, for example, any more than 'skill'? We admire a skilful footballer and a skilful driver and we acknowledge that they have talent. Does the formal equate to talent and no more? Do we usually prefer the more talented artists over the less talented ones in the same way that watching a graceful, balanced winger in a rugby match is more pleasurable than watching a leaden-footed one?

Are there formal qualities that apply to all the arts?

There is also the more complex problem of how formal features in different art forms relate to one another if, indeed, they can at all. Each art form utilises a quite distinct method and has its own range of techniques and its own scope of possibilities. Above we talked about how what matters is the 'ordering' of the formal features of the work of art, but it is worth considering whether this account is sufficient. The elements of metre and rhythm in poetry can be seen as having a relationship to various elements in the formal appreciation of music. However, this is not the case for most art forms. Sculpture, for example, will often emphasise the texture of the material used in relation to the final shapes created. Drama might place an emphasis on stage layout and the physical location of the actors. However, these formal elements clearly bear very little if any real relation to one another. It seems then that talk of form fails to identify a particular type of feature that applies across the whole range of art. Does this matter? Or are we possibly approaching form from an overly narrow perspective?

If it is impossible to find a coherent range of things that can be classed as formal features across the whole spectrum of art is it possible to argue that there cannot be a coherent aesthetic response across different art forms? For example, is the sensation of hearing Bach's *Brandenburg Concertos* in any way similar to looking at a Henry Moore sculpture? It seems that while the actual sensation may be different at a very basic level, at the level of aesthetic appreciation there remain the same essential features. There is still the element of studied contemplation, there may be an emotional uplifting of the spirit, there may be feelings of universal worth. The same is true of any art. While we engage at a practical level with different arts in different ways by reading, listening, watching and so on, when we actually engage with them at an intellectual, spiritual or emotional level we do something very similar with all of them.

It could also be argued that these formal elements are universal features in the same way that we can see symmetry in nature; for example, a river running equally between two hills is usually pleasing to the eye. There are many other examples of things in nature that give us aesthetic pleasure and there is a strong argument that when we appreciate nature we are doing something very similar to when we appreciate art. There are certain forms, shapes, colours, harmonies, balances and the like in nature that are universally beautiful, and if they are beautiful in nature then they are beautiful in art. Both nature and art allow us a sense of transcendence and, of course, both allow us to experience beauty. In the same way as we cannot classify all of the different elements of nature and find links between them because, for example, the beauty of a sun-drenched beach bears no relationship to the beauty of an ancient forest, so the beauty of a poem is different at a basic level from the beauty of a sonata – yet both share the universal quality of beauty.

Is form the essence of art?

If you take a strictly formalist approach to art then you are literally *only* considering those formal features. For example, in the case of visual art then you are only concerned with the various shapes, colours or patterns that appear in the painting. We should not be concerned with what shapes they are or what the colours are meant to depict or what the patterns are meant to represent. In poetry, it is only the metre, rhythm, sound and structure that matter. The sentiments of the poem are not to be considered. This formalist purity would appear to be very difficult to achieve in practice. How can you separate, for example, the lines of a painting from what they are supposed to represent? In the case of genuinely abstract art which is not supposed to represent anything this may be possible, but even then there is a distinct tendency to find mental comparisons between the image and things that it reminds us of. Even music, the most abstract art form of all, frequently draws a link between the formal element and a representational element. This is clearly true of opera where the formal elements such as melody and tone are linked to words, drama and characterisation. It is also certain that even in instrumental music the composer often aims at representation. This can be seen from the titles that various pieces of music are given, for example *The Swan of Tuonela* by Sibelius attempts to capture the presence of a mystical swan around Tuonela, the island of the dead. Clearly, the formal elements of the music cannot be separated from the intentions and representations of the composer.

In the 20th century many critics attacked the 'ivory tower' view of art – aestheticians in university departments writing arcane commentary in difficult language about obscure matters of no value to the real world. When thousands of people die in genocidal wars the artist that focuses solely on the 'balance' and 'fusion' of his paintings might seem at least distant and at worse callous and inhumane. Often the formal elements in art, which seem the most removed from ordinary human experience, take the blame for making art irrelevant to the average person in the street. Prior to the separation of art and craft, the role of the artist/craftsman

Think about

Is it possible to compare the artistic merits of different art forms, for example a novel and a symphony and a sculpture? Is there a central element that unifies all art? If so, what do you think this is? Are some art forms more valuable than others? If so, how and in what ways?

was widely acknowledged. They were part of the human community and the artist shared and celebrated that common life. Since that earlier distinction broke down the artist has been divorced from the masses and from everyday life and an excessive concern with form over content has resulted in much art being an irrelevance. For example, it could be argued that with war, poverty, suffering and many other kinds of human misery a focus on composition and technique is misplaced. Art could, and maybe should, have a wider emphasis on concerns that really matter to people in real life. The plays of the Czech Vaclav Havel are not usually considered 'formal' masterpieces, but their value as art emerges from his portrayal of a totalitarian socialist regime under which he suffered political oppression.

Despite these numerous problems it would be a brave person to state that the formal has no place in art. There still remains for most people a sense that if there is no formal element at all then it cannot be 'real' or 'proper' art. There is still a level at which art becomes art and not just craft or imitation or expression because there is something peculiar to art itself which other things do not have. While form might not be the answer to its uniqueness, it still nonetheless makes a very strong case for it.

Conclusion

The philosophy of art is a complex area and there is very little agreement. It is correspondingly difficult to come to any firm conclusions. It is perhaps enough to offer a few broad thoughts.

Aesthetic judgements are often finely distinguished with subtle differences in interpretation that result in quite different conclusions. Aesthetic judgement can also be seen to be influenced by a very wide range of factors. Thus, judgements might be influenced or based on:

> the senses, emotion, intellectual opinions, will, desires, culture, preferences, values, subconscious behaviour, conscious decision, training, instinct, sociological institutions, or some complex combination of these, depending on exactly which theory one employs.

*Based on **Korsmeyer** (1998, see http://en.wikipedia.org/wiki/Aesthetics)*

The same work of art can divide critics strongly dependent usually on what their underlying motivations are. Despite this, there remains a concern that all art appreciation must in some way involve intellectual activity. It could be argued that all talk of competent judges or critical experts is really dependent on a variety of intellectual processes. Further, it could be argued that appreciation of art at any sophisticated level requires learning; for example, it is common for critics to have degrees in their field of expertise often coupled with significant practical experience and training. If this is so then art might not be as universal as some would like to claim. It may be that the masses can gain only a small amount of aesthetic pleasure when compared to the experts. This view though can be considered elitist and divisive and has resulted in a number of Marxist-inspired accounts of aesthetics which are concerned with art being accessible to all and dealing with themes that the 'common man' would understand.

In the discussion above we have separated the value of art into three distinct elements: the moral or intellectual element of art, the expressive and the formal.

Think about

Should we look for 'value' in art at all? Maybe the best that we can hope for is a personal, subjective insight that can't be communicated further and is separate from typical intellectual or moral thoughts. Is the search for 'value' an attempt by philosophers and artists and others to advocate a particular way of looking at the world?

Think about

If we believe that art has no ultimate value what is its role or purpose? Indeed, does it have one at all, even a simple utilitarian one? Consider other reasons why art – in its many various forms – exists.

■ Think about

There has been a longstanding debate about whether popular music – rock, rap, R&B, indie – is art. Many now make claims for this type of music to be placed alongside classical music and to be given serious critical attention. Others think that it is nothing more than light entertainment. Consider if popular music is art. Try to utilise ideas that you have read about in the chapter.

■ Think about

The composer Richard Wagner was anti-Semitic and many Jewish people have over the years refused to listen to his work. There was controversy when his work was first performed live in Israel in 2001 after an informal ban on his work for over 50 years. Does it matter if the artist in question holds moral or political views that you disagree with? Is it important to separate the art from the person that made the art?

AQA Examiner's tip

Try to use examples when you write. Philosophy can often be abstract and difficult to express. By using a relevant example you add originality to your writing while also giving it greater clarity.

AQA Examiner's tip

Make sure you use reasoned arguments (and if the question asks for three reasons make sure you give three different reasons not three versions or examples of the same problem!). It is all too easy when writing about the philosophy of art to let yourself wander off the point and spend time describing rather than arguing.

It is important throughout to bear in mind that we are considering art in terms of its value. That places it alongside ethics, political philosophy and other areas that we normally consider to be involve moral judgements in some way. Many philosophers have tried to draw links between the moral and the aesthetic, but it is not straightforward. This is probably more so because there are a number of ways in which value can be given to art and not because there is no link at all. With all three ways of attaching value to art, it could be argued that there are ways in which links could be made to overtly moral issues, for example, a paternalistic moral position would surely advocate a paternalistic and educative approach to art and to the sorts of thoughts and feelings that art should seek to elicit.

Much of the disagreement outlined above rests on whether you believe that art has intrinsic or extrinsic value. If you believe art has value simply as art then you are unlikely to place too much emphasis on the view that art can inform us. Instead, you would prefer the formal or by the expressive. If on the other hand you think art must have a distinct purpose, you are more likely to see value in art that tells us something about the world. There is no fixed way of looking at this or settling the question without delving deeper into what we place ultimate value on in life as a whole, and that is another question.

After working through this topic, you should:

■ be aware of what constitutes formal elements in art

■ be able to critically engage with a variety of positions concerning the formal value of art

■ be able to put forward considered arguments with suitable support and to argue coherently.

Further reading

Aristotle, *The Poetics*. This is available online: http://ebooks.adelaide.edu.au/a/aristotle/poetics. In this work Aristotle puts forward his view of art as catharsis, looking particularly at Greek tragic drama.

Budd, M. *Values of Art: pictures, poetry and music*, Allen Lane, 1995. This is a thoughtful book by one of Britain's leading aestheticians, formerly professor of philosophy at University College London.

Croce, B. *Aesthetic*, Macmillan, 1909. A very famous work which outlines in detail the author's view of art as expression.

Kant, I. *Critique of Judgement*, trans. P. Guyer and E. Matthews, Cambridge University Press, 2000. Also available online from the University of Adelaide: http://philosophy.eserver.org/kant/critique-of-judgment.txt. Immanuel Kant effectively created the modern discipline of aesthetics with this work. In it he discusses aesthetic experience and the requirements for making aesthetic judgement.

Plato, *The Republic*, Book X, trans. D. Lee, Penguin, Rev. edn 1987. This is Plato's most famous discussion of art as representation and it is a good place to begin any further reading on the subject.

Sewell, B. – various articles are freely available online, e.g. www.thisislondon.co.uk, click on 'Arts and Exhibitions' and 'Brian Sewell Archive'. While these are not concerned with academic matters, they are well written and often humorous and they give an insight into a well-known critic's approach to art generally.

Sheppard, A. *Aesthetics: introduction to the philosophy of art*, Oxford University Press, 1987. An accessible introduction to the subject that covers many of the same issues that are discussed above.

Woolheim, R. *Art and its Objects*, Cambridge University Press, 1980. One of the most influential British aestheticians of the past 50 years, a former professor at London University. This well-known work discusses issues relating to the perspective of both the artist and the audience.

Summary questions

1 Do you think that all art is equally valid? Are some types of art more valid than others?

2 Do you agree that craft is not art, or is this distinction based on prejudices of some kind?

3 Can art really be universal?

4 Is it possible, or even desirable, to separate art from the person or the environment out of which it grew?

5 If art is really about informing us, can music be art at all? If so, what makes it art?

6 Are photography, dance, rock music and landscape gardening art forms? Justify your reasoning.

7 Are there a certain number of features that are required in order for an object to be a 'work of art'?

8 Is there a relationship between art and entertainment?

9 Should there be any limits on artistic expression and freedom?

10 What separates merely copying something from a work of art?

5 Why should I be governed?

The state of nature

Learning objectives:

- to understand what we mean by the state of nature and why it is significant
- to describe the different versions of the state of nature, particularly those of Hobbes and Locke
- to explore the benefits of making a social contract and submitting to some form of authority
- to evaluate the problems with concepts of the state of nature.

💡 Have you ever broken the law?

This is not meant to be a question about those moments of weakness, when you hoped no one saw you, or a request for *factual* information. So to re-phrase the question: 'Would you ever be prepared to break the law?'

This is a question about what you consider to be fair and just and what you believe in. It is a question about *values* and choices.

Throughout history millions have disobeyed the law, because of their principles. They have challenged governments over unfair discrimination, violation of rights, unjust taxes and many other causes. In Britain in 1990, thousands of normally law abiding citizens refused to pay the Poll Tax (a local authority tax) because they considered it morally unfair. Many were sent to prison. In other parts of the world there have been demonstrations about racial segregation, victimisation by governments and inhumane social conditions. There is scarcely a state that does not hold some political prisoners.

There are really two issues here:

1 objections to particular unjust laws that have been passed by the rightful authority, e.g. the Poll Tax

2 objections to the nature of the government itself, and whether it is a legitimate authority.

With regard to the second objection, in the UK we have had a settled democracy for centuries. But other states have had to endure unpleasant and immoral dictatorships, or a sudden seizure of power by a military junta. In these circumstances, you might well ask what right they have to dictate what people should do and to administer punishment.

With regard to issue 1 above, would you be prepared to challenge a law passed by Parliament?

Think about

Consider the following possibilities. Would you be prepared to break the law?

- The government brings in conscription for 18–20-year-olds. As in some other European countries, all young people will be required to serve one year in military service or two years in social services.
- A new law is passed concerning the sale of cigarettes. The legal age for buying tobacco is raised from 16 to 18.
- In a gap year, you start a temporary job to earn some money. The manager offers to pay you cash out of the till so that you avoid paying National Insurance and tax.

■ Permission has been given to build a new motorway in your neighbourhood. The road will pass through a beautiful and sensitive environment and it is near to your house.

Would you consider breaking the law in any of these cases? How would you justify the decision? Are there any other causes where you would challenge the morality of a law?

The discussion that we have started is a debate about political authority. It includes questions like:

■ Who should be the sovereign power (e.g. a hereditary monarch, a counsel of wise men, the people's representatives)?

■ What areas of our life should be subject to law (e.g., should the authorities dictate what we do in our private lives?)

■ What kind of society do we want and should we protect this by law (e.g. should the law enforce certain kinds of moral behaviour)?

For the purposes of this topic, law is defined as a command by the sovereign power, backed by punishment. In considering the commands and the punishments, you will begin to examine your views on freedom, equality and justice.

You might wonder why we have to make laws and form a government. Why is it not possible to just organise ourselves like a group of friends?

This is the view put forward by the **anarchists**. People are quite capable of living in a natural state and organising their own lives.

■ Anarchy

In a natural state, individuals recognise their common interests and will cooperate to build a society of equals. Much will be achieved by the united efforts of individuals. Houses will be built and food produced for all through communal effort. Most resources, except for very private items, are shared, so no one is able to exploit anyone else.

If there are disagreements they can be resolved through rational, open debate and informal, personal approaches. If someone is being selfish, then a caring personal discussion is far more effective than laws and punishments. And because people grow in a supportive atmosphere, there will be far fewer disputes. People will be much more socially minded, they will find fulfilment in group projects and they will be much more ready to compromise.

The reason that people are self-interested and antisocial is that they have been corrupted by:

■ unjust laws

■ a capitalist system that allows exploitation, rich and poor, and private property

■ above all, a government that is oppressive, passing law after law to restrict our freedom; and which uses violent punishment to terrorise opposition.

The result is that citizens are repressed and mediocre specimens, their initiative is stifled, and they are trained to be obedient to a self-serving, bureaucratic government.

If we return to the state of nature and set up anarchic societies, we can banish private property, learn to share, and achieve much more through

■ Think about

Imagine you and your group landed on a wild and deserted island, or even just took over a student house together. Could you live side by side without laws and people in charge? Why have a government?

■ Key terms

Anarchists: anarchy is a political doctrine that states human communities could flourish without a need for government or laws. Government corrupts human nature and our natural sentiments. Anarchist groups are associated with small communes, or traditional tribal communities, which have a unifying set of common values and are self-supporting.

the efforts of willing volunteers cooperating together. Living positively in a group will reduce crime and remove poverty. If there are a few selfish or violent members, we will care for them, support them and heal them rather than punishing and rejecting them.

Those who have read Darwin will have learnt that life is governed by natural selection, the survival of the fittest. We are all apparently in competition with each other. But surely, the fittest will be those who learn to cooperate. Those who are selfishly self-interested will achieve very little in a state of insecurity and war. Those who are more likely to survive are the groups who establish peace and unity, and therefore can devote time and effort to being more creative and mutually supportive.

Here are some quotes from the famous 19th-century anarchist, Kropotkin.

> We are so perverted by an education which from infancy seeks to kill in us the spirit of revolt, and to develop that of submission to authority; we are so perverted by this existence under the ferrule of a law, which regulates every event in life – our birth, our education, our development, our love, our friendship – that, if this state of things continues, we shall lose all initiative, all habit of thinking for ourselves …

> The millions of laws which exist for the regulation of humanity appear upon investigation to be divided into three principal categories: protection of property, protection of persons, protection of government. And by analyzing each of these three categories, we arrive at the same logical and necessary conclusion: the uselessness and hurtfulness of law.

> Socialists know what is meant by protection of property. Laws on property are not made to guarantee either to the individual or society the enjoyment of the produce to their labour. On the contrary, they are made to rob the producer of a part of what he has created, and to secure to certain other people that portion of the produce which they have stolen either from the producer or from society as a whole.

> Peoples without political organization, and therefore less depraved than ourselves, have perfectly understood that the man who is called 'criminal' is simply unfortunate; that the remedy is not to flog him, to chain him up, or to kill him on the scaffold or in prison, but to help him by the most brotherly care, by treatment based on equality, by the usages of life among honest men.

> No more laws! No more judges! Liberty, equality, and practical human sympathy are the only effectual barriers we can oppose to the antisocial instincts of certain among us.

*quoted in **Palmer** (1991, chapter 1)*

Think about

Are you persuaded? Would you rather remain in a 'natural state' than join a conventional society? Do you think an anarchic society could handle the following issues?

■ Multiculturalism – lots of groups having very different values.

■ Rewarding experts – how to encourage someone to do a long and difficult job, e.g. brain surgeon.

- Idleness – how could the group ensure everyone contributes?
- Complex societies – could this system work with large-scale groups? What problems would there be?
- Do people need private property – why?

You may feel that anarchists are too optimistic about human nature. The rational and cooperative aspects of our character have been over-played. For example, personal relationships, love, jealousy and sex, together with the associated problems, will cause conflict and without at least the protection from harm that is provided by the law, such communities will never survive. On the other hand, some communities with a strong, shared morality could resolve such problems, for example religious communities.

Thus the debate about human nature is very relevant to political theory. Whenever you hear a political debate, it is likely that assumptions about human nature, what people are really like and what people really want will underpin the discussion. This is the topic that classical philosophers referred to as 'the state of nature' and is the focus of this topic.

The state of nature

Initially, the state of nature was an account of the nature of mankind before the formation of societies, perhaps around the time that we were hunter-gatherers. This 'noble savage' is supposed to embody what human beings were really like, before civilisation educated and changed us. So our fundamental qualities are revealed in the state of nature.

However, many commentators are doubtful whether such a state ever existed. The idea that barbarians inhabited the planet at some stage in history has declined as we have come to realise that even these primitive groups had a social structure. If that is the case, an actual state of nature, if it ever existed, was far too long ago to be of serious use for modern philosophy.

Nevertheless this thought experiment can be meaningful if it is reworded in hypothetical terms.

What would human beings be like *if* there was no political authority?

Suppose we were all stranded on a tropical island – if you have read *Lord of the Flies* or *Coral Island* or seen recent films based on this scenario, you will appreciate the issues. Reference to this is made in Chapter 3 (see the first topic) and would be useful reading.

For the purposes of political philosophy, we can treat the discussion about the state of nature as:

- A psychological enquiry – a search for the fundamental drives and instincts which move human beings. This assumes that we have universal, innate or inherited tendencies, such as the dispositions which stem from our biology and psychology.
- A moral thesis – a device for deciding on what basis all human beings are equal, so that any political authority must respect these claims to universal and equal treatment.

So instead of entering into an anthropological debate about the existence of pre-social beings, the discussion is about our common human nature, which should be regarded as significant and taken into account when we consider what kind of society we want and who should rule. For example, we would all consider freedom from fear as an essential human need that must be protected, e.g. fear of arbitrary arrest.

Therefore, this enquiry into human nature will start with facts, but in selecting what are relevant facts, the values of different philosophers will appear. In your discussions, try to recognise whether people are presenting facts or trying to persuade you to accept their values. The difficulty of jumping from facts to values will be assessed in the next topic below.

What can we say about human nature?

Think about

What do these facts suggest about the basic human drives?

- There has been a recent spate of teenage gun crime and some cases have been fatal.
- Human beings have landed on the moon and explored the outer reaches of the universe.
- The human race has contributed to global warming.
- We have a UN Charter of Rights that nearly every country in the world subscribes to.
- The gap between rich and poor is widening.
- Whenever a child disappears or there is a natural disaster, people always give generously of their time and money.
- We bury our dead with serious and elaborate rituals.
- Our species working with scientists from all over the world has been very successful at colonising the planet.
- Oil is scarce, and already there is conflict about who owns it.
- In nearly every culture, people treasure their own private property and enjoy expressing themselves through art, music, dancing, etc.

When you have come to your conclusions about human nature, check them against the 10 conclusions from different philosophers.

Hume: 'it is a just political maxim that every man must be supposed to be a knave' (Hume, 1947b). A knave is selfish and untrustworthy.

Bentham: 'Nature has placed mankind under the governance of two sovereign masters, pain and pleasure' (Bentham, 1962). All of our behaviour can be seen as an attempt to avoid pain and maximise pleasure.

Darwin: 'all the corporeal and mental organs ... of all beings have been developed through natural selection and survival of the fittest' (Darwin, 1903). So our basic instinct is self-preservation.

Mill: 'Man is an exerter and enjoyer of his own powers. We are self-developers and growing into individuals is "the leading essential of well being"' (Mill, 1985).

Freud: 'the distinctive and aggressive nature ... our death instinct' (Freud, 1957) is a significant human quality, that makes us destructive, even self-destructive.

Marx: We have a 'species essence' (Marx, 1970b). Human beings need to 'objectify' themselves, to turn their desires into something objective, to transform the world to meet their needs.

Kant: We are moral creatures. We have a moral faculty that enables us to overcome our self-interest and 'treat people as ends, rather than means' (Kant, 1993).

Rousseau: 'men are not naturally enemies' (Rousseau, 1968). We have a natural instinct for compassion and sympathy for others.

Locke: 'the brutes do not share with man the power of deliberate choice … the power of reason' (Locke, 1947). So our essential quality is the god-like ability to reason.

Hobbes: The life of natural man 'is nasty, brutish and short' (Hobbes, 1982). We are self-interested, without any natural morality and so inclined to fight and steal.

The last two philosophers are the main focus for our consideration of the state of nature and the benefits of forming a society. They will be contrasted with the different views of Rousseau. All three theories are referred to as 'social contract theories'. The same basic model is employed: that people in a state of nature will find such a state unsatisfactory, and they will therefore *consent* to form a *contract* with each other, which will limit their freedom but will deliver important *benefits*. The consent and the benefits provide the justification for political authority, they explain why we ought to obey the law.

Hobbes

Hobbes was writing around the time of the English Civil War and will have witnessed the horrors of the inter-fighting. However, he maintains that his views on human nature come from self-analysis.

According to Hobbes, in the state of nature we are equally free, but without any rules of justice, so there are no duties and this freedom is really a licence to do as we please. Human beings are also self-interested and permanently concerned with self-preservation and the selfish satisfaction of needs and wants. We are all egoists (see Chapter 3 'Why should I be moral?' topic 1) and enjoy the exercise of power to dominate and control.

Because of this freedom and self-interest, the state of nature is a state of war, where disputes are frequent. It is survival of the fittest, the law of the jungle and fighting, stealing and rape are commonplace. There is little opportunity to plan a stable life, so there is 'no industry … no culture … and no society'. He sums up such a life as 'the war of all against all'. Remember Hobbes is describing the basic instincts in human nature!

What are the benefits of a social contract?

Hobbes paints such a grim picture of human nature that it is clear why we choose to join a society. The primary motive is fear, because even if you are one of the big fish in the pond, there is always the possibility of an even bigger fish swallowing you up. Thus it is a rational calculation that in a society with the enforcement of laws, you can stop people doing nasty things to you in return for treating them similarly – a sort of mutual insurance policy: 'whatsoever you require that others should do to you, that do ye to them' (Hobbes, 1982).

The benefits of this contract are that with a controlled balance of freedom and power, you and everyone else will gain the benefits of safety, security

> ### Key philosopher
>
> #### Thomas Hobbes (1558–1679)
>
> He was a philosopher who was sceptical and pessimistic about morality. His most famous work is *Leviathan* (1651) in which the terrifying monster is a metaphor for the state, but such a state is necessary to maintain law and order.

and stability. That may not seem like much. There is no promise of morality, social justice or cooperative achievement. But Hobbes has discovered the fundamentals of any form of civilised life. Anyone who has witnessed the insecurity of a civil war knows that personal safety is the first requirement of everyone who is worried about the future. The second desire is for stability – the chance to plan a life, work and raise a family etc. Even under the most unpleasant dictator, if these two requirements are met, then many would endure other more objectionable aspects of a regime. In the past, people have supported immoral governments as long as they maintain law and order and provide the basic necessities of life. Very few ever gain in a time of prolonged conflict.

So entering into a social contract is enlightened self-interest to Hobbes. It is a rational calculation that although I lose the chance to exploit others, I gain the security of not being exploited myself. This is particularly important as he also notes that there is a scarcity of resources to go round, and therefore some kind of sharing and balance of power will be necessary if war is to be avoided. It is in everyone's long-term self-interest to make the contract.

This situation is well illustrated in a game of trust based on a situation called 'The prisoner's dilemma'. It can be represented in a card game, which helps to explore the issues. The situation in the prisoner's dilemma is as follows.

Think about

The prisoner's dilemma

Two guilty suspects, Tom and Dick, have been arrested. The police keep them in separate cells and there is no chance of communication. But the police know it will be hard to get a conviction, so separately they offer Tom and Dick the following deal:

'Tom [or Dick], if you confess, but Dick [or Tom] stays silent, you will go free and Dick [or Tom] will get 10 years' imprisonment.

However, if you both confess, you will both get a moderate sentence of about five years in prison.

If you both continue to remain silent, we cannot charge you, but we will give you a minimum sentence for wasting our time of one year in prison.'

The offer can be summarised as:

	Tom	Dick
Both confess	5 years	5 years
Both stay silent (trust card)	1 year	1 year
Tom confesses and Dick stays silent	0	10 years
Dick confesses and Tom stays silent	10 years	0

The sentences above are the scores that you use in the game.

To play the game, you need two cards each, one with C (cooperate) on it and one with S (silence) on it. You play in pairs and it is suggested you play several pairs. With each pair, you take five turns and score for each turn.

At each turn, both players select a card in secret and place it face down on the table. The choice is whether to confess or to stay silent. You cannot discuss card selection with anyone! The cards are then revealed and the scores noted. For each of the five turns, players can make different choices and perhaps develop a strategy.

When you have played five different partners five times, add up your total prison sentence. A score card is suggested below:

	Opponent 1	Opponent 2	Opponent 3	Opponent 4	Opponent 5	Opponent 6
Turn 1						
Turn 2						
Turn 3						
Turn 4						
Turn 5						
Total						
Final score:						

After the game discuss the following:

- What card would the self-interested Hobbes play?
- What happens if people pursue a narrow, short-term interest?
- What is the 'trust' card? Will it gain the best results for everyone?
- Does it take only one person to destroy the trust between people?

The results of the prisoner's dilemma should show the following:

- that the best case scenario for *everyone* is that everyone trusts each other and stays silent
- that if everyone confesses and is not trustworthy, we all suffer moderately.
- However, the nightmare situation is that those who trust are constantly exploited by those who try to gain at the expense of others. This makes any attempt at a contract inherently unstable.

This last point highlights a problem for Hobbes. Even if we try to form a contract, if he is right about human nature then it only takes a few unenlightened egoists to destroy everyone's trust, and we revert to a state of nature.

So Hobbes proposes that the sovereign must be an all-powerful authority – a leviathan – preferably a dictator, who is needed to maintain order. Even if this is not popular, strength is needed to control the untrustworthy. So the strongest dictator is the ideal sovereign and this is a direct consequence of Hobbes' theory of human nature. Whether this is acceptable will be discussed in the next topic below.

Do we agree with Hobbes?

Think about

Is Hobbes right about human nature? To help you decide, consider what happens in these situations:

- when a large number of tickets for a music festival are suddenly released
- when a lot of people are queuing for a bus
- when a park or play area is constantly vandalised
- when the players in a team play for themselves rather than the team
- when people sharing a house find things start to go missing
- when we all dutifully pay our taxes for the National Health Service.

As with all individuals who wish to live together and who have very different desires, some kind of enforcement of the contract seems inevitable. There must be coordination, even if it is a simple agreement on which side of the road to drive or how to bury the dead. Regardless of whether you agree with the arrangements, some organisation is better than none. But the first criticism of Hobbes is whether people that are as wild as Hobbes describes even conceive of such a contract, let alone be able to keep it. Would warring individuals in his state of nature be rational enough to maintain the agreements? Some degree of rationality must be assumed.

Secondly, Hobbes' leader is simply the strongest individual of a group of self-interested individuals – a bully that is stronger than the rest. But is there more to leadership than simply strength – what about virtue and wisdom? The distinction between being '**in authority**' and '**an authority**' is highly relevant and is also discussed in the next topic. The point here is that because of his theory of human nature, the primary requirement for the leader must be someone who can 'crack the whip' to ensure compliance with any laws they command. So for Hobbes, might is right. Sovereignty is reduced to power and strength, and the leader is 'in authority' and not necessarily 'an authority'.

Key terms

In authority: being 'in authority' is being able to command obedience, in Hobbes' case, because you are the strongest.

An authority: being 'an authority' is having the necessary knowledge, wisdom and expertise to rule. This will include moral wisdom.

Locke

Locke agrees with Hobbes that society is founded on a contract, but Locke's account of human nature is much more positive. His religious beliefs inform his view that this state of natural freedom is one where we respect each other's claim to life, liberty and property. The state of nature is a state of liberty, but not licence. As we are God's creatures, we have a natural understanding that we cannot interfere with another's body, so it is not permissible to attack others. We also have a basic sense of justice, that if someone has worked for something then they deserve to keep it. It is right that we own the product of our labours, so stealing is wrong. Moreover Locke believes that there are plentiful resources and space for everyone, so life is relatively peaceful and contented.

Locke was writing before the American War of Independence, and the subsequent American Constitution expresses similar views on liberty and human nature.

We hold these truths to be self-evident, that all men are created equal and that they are endowed by their creator with certain inalienable rights; these are life, liberty and the pursuit of happiness.

American Constitution

Locke similarly claims that human beings are born with inalienable rights – rights that *should not* be removed. He emphasised our rights to life, liberty and property. Therefore, the state of nature is moral and rational where natural law (God's law) prevails:

reason teaches all mankind ... that being all equal and independent, no one ought to harm another in his life, health, liberty or possession.

Locke (1947)

So why make a contract?

If the basis of human nature is so positive, Locke needs to explain why we need a contract and a sovereign rather than being able to just flourish in an anarchic society. For Hobbes, the motive was fear, but for Locke it is rational and moral. We need to protect our rights, and without any authority at all there will be some disputes, mainly about justice and where our rights may clash. So people might disagree over whether an offence has occurred, or how much property someone deserves, or what the proper punishment is. To see that our rights are not violated and justice prevails, an authority is created. This will have limited powers: just to administer justice and to act as a referee.

The benefits are that we have an agreed process for sorting our disputes, while leaving people as free as possible to carry on with their lives.

While Hobbes' account of human nature seemed overly pessimistic, do you think that Locke is very optimistic?

Much would appear to depend on the religious premise that we are God's creatures and, although flawed, we have a natural capacity for rationality and morality. Some commentators have pointed to a number of assumptions underlying Locke's theory which may be questionable. Do you think he may have confused **facts and values**? Has he assumed that we are all independent individuals, that we are all equal, and that liberty and property are good things?

Individualism

Built into Locke's theory is the primacy of the individual – the importance first and foremost of the single, unique person. For Locke, everyone has intrinsic value and dignity, and deserves respect. Any authority must accommodate these beliefs.

He assumes, moreover, that as individuals we are largely self-sufficient and self-reliant and that we have an identity that is quite separate from any role we acquire in society. We are also autonomous, able to choose our own way of life, and capable of acting on our choices. All of this is achievable prior to entering any social contract and becoming a member of a society! In the last section of this topic we shall consider a contrasting theory; that people are the products of their society, and our sense of identity and what rights we may claim are actually derived from the economic, social and cultural institutions that surround us. Primacy, therefore, should go to a consideration of society and its structure rather than starting with the individual, who is moulded by society.

Think about

If you look back at the 10 quotations from philosophers on pp122–3, who might agree or disagree with Locke?

Key terms

Facts and values: facts provide information about how things *are*; values prescribe and recommend how they *should* be. That people are rational is a fact, that they ought to be treated as equals is a value.

Think about

Look again at the quotation from the American Constitution. Is it expressing facts about people, or values?

Again we see with Locke the influence of the religious belief that it is the individual's conscience and soul which is significant. God created all human beings with natural capacities and this belief led Locke to take a great interest in education and to stress the importance in early years of training the rational faculties so that a child 'may consent to nothing, but what may be suitable to the dignity and excellency of a rational creature'.

Education enhances our natural, individual talent rather than being a moulding process for creating self-sufficient individuals.

Linked to this individualism is his **pluralist** theory about what lives people should pursue.

With his insistence on the power of individual reason, the individual therefore can establish what is best for themselves, and there are many good things in life. No one, no wise philosopher, has a monopoly on wisdom to decide for others. This is challenged at the very end of this topic with the extract from Plato. Locke expressly wrote about the need for religious toleration for Protestants who dissented from the Anglican state Church. The importance for political obligation is that each person must first consent to authority, and then has the right to judge whether authority is acceptable or not. The sovereign is therefore subject to the judgement of the citizens, and should not interfere with their choices unless the fundamental, inalienable rights of an individual are violated.

Equality

In the words of the American Constitution, all men are created free and equal. For Locke the state 'that all men are naturally in' is 'also of equality, where all power is reciprocal, no one having more than another' and 'without subordination or subjection'. There is an absence of natural hierarchy, we all have a universal and common humanity which entails equal rights to justice and freedom. We are all equal in the eyes of God, who loves us all.

However, this equal freedom also allows people to keep what they work for. So if you plant a crop and harvest it, then you are entitled to the profit. Since individuals will differ in how hard they work, some will achieve far more profit than others. So a gap between rich and poor will develop that may not seem very egalitarian. But this is equality of desert – everyone receives a fair amount according to their merits and how hard they have worked. So equality of deserving is bound to lead to differences in what people earn.

Needless to say, Locke's interpretation of equality has been challenged. It is not disputed that we should treat people equally, but the question is, 'Equality of what?'. What are the most important and relevant facts about human nature that make us equal? Locke favours freedom and consequently desert. Others have stressed needs, and equality according to need.

A need might be defined as a necessity that must be satisfied before we can function as human beings. Needs must be fulfilled before we can earn the deserts of our labour. So it is seen as morally more important to satisfy basic needs because otherwise a genuine human existence is impossible. Yet Locke's emphasis on the independence and autonomy of the individual rather assumes that basic needs are catered for. Consequently there is not a role for his minimalist government to ensure that adequate food supplies, health care and welfare are provided. The more needs that are identified, the more extensive the role for a government. Once again, do you think Locke's account of human nature contains some assumptions of value about the nature of equality?

Key terms

Pluralism: there is no way of stating the unique truth about what life to value, so we should tolerate a variety of lifestyles and experiments in living. That does not mean that all cultures are necessarily of equal value, but there are a diversity of 'goods'.

Think about

Which interpretation of the state of nature is employed here: the psychological enquiry or the moral thesis?

Think about

What basic needs do you think a government should provide and ensure for its people?

- the need for food and water
- the need for shelter – a house
- the need for rest and sleep
- the need for health care
- the need to exercise
- the need for companionship
- the need for education
- the need for love and sex
- the need to be free from fear and harm
- the need for respect and self-esteem
- the need for entertainment and a variety of activities
- the need for happiness and fulfilment.

You might like to distinguish between needs and wants. Needs are universal and apply to all human beings, whereas wants are specific to individuals and groups. Are some of the above wants?

Liberty

Locke describes the original condition of human beings as 'a state of perfect freedom, to order their actions, and dispose of their possessions, and persons, as they think fit … without asking leave, or depending upon the will of any other man'.

This is a classic statement of what is termed **negative liberty**. This notion of freedom is freedom from interference, restraint or coercion (contrast this with positive freedom under Rousseau). A person is free when no obstacles are put in their way. Mill defines it as 'doing what one desires'. Hobbes describes it as 'the silence of the laws'. According to Locke, it is our nature to be free and to act as we choose provided we respect the freedom and property of others. So, inevitably, our consent is necessary before an authority can act on our behalf, and the social contract is one we freely enter into without coercion. Moreover, the primary justification for any government is that it protects our freedom, and to do this it must keep its interference and legislation to the minimum. This kind of government was described by the philosopher Nozick as a 'protection agency', and is in stark contrast to Hobbes' dictatorship.

For Locke, 'that government is best, which governs least' (Jefferson, quoted in Gaus, 2000), and the model of society is often referred to as 'atomistic'. It comprises a collection of individuals (atoms) who voluntarily enter into agreements and contracts, or join together in alliances, in order to promote their interests. The benefit, for Locke, of joining a society is individual self-interest, which is the freedom to do as one pleases in conjunction with other free individuals. This is of course possible because it is human nature to desire freedom from restrictions and to acknowledge other people's similar rights.

As we saw with equality, this concept of freedom can be challenged, and will be contrasted next with Rousseau. For the moment, it could

Key terms

Negative liberty: in discussions of liberty, philosophers often use a distinction between negative and positive liberty. The former is 'freedom from' restrictions and the latter is 'freedom to' lead a life of your own choosing. This distinction has been challenged.

be pointed out that without satisfaction of basic needs, people are not free. If we take the example of a beggar, under negative freedom he/she will appear free if no one interferes or hinders them in any way. But is a beggar really free? Surely a minimum amount of social security and education is essential before someone can even begin to think or act as they desire. To be autonomous, to develop independence and to work for your deserts, a certain amount of support is necessary, but that will require more than minimum intervention by society. Taxes and therefore laws will be required. If we therefore modify our conception of liberty, government becomes more than just a necessary evil, and instead is a caring, supportive, paternalistic intervention for our own good.

However, both Hobbes and Locke see law as coercion, in order to restrain individuals from encroaching on one another. But the key distinction is that while Hobbes emphasises the need for security and stability because human nature is selfish and competitive, Locke emphasises our freedom and rights because we are moral and rational beings. Thus they differ about the nature of authority. Hobbes' sovereign needs to be an all powerful organiser (in authority), while Locke requires a government to be wise and just, in order to sort out disputes (an authority). And for Locke, if the government is not up to the job, the people have a right of resistance and may be justified in revolution. For Hobbes, rebellion is just a matter of power, especially if the sovereign can no longer protect lives.

Rousseau

Yet a third version of human nature is offered by Rousseau. His description of the state of nature is summed up in the phrase 'the noble savage'.

Rousseau disagrees with Hobbes. The pre-social human being is innocent, has no pride and limited wants, so disputes are few and far between. Also, we all have a natural sympathy which makes us compassionate towards others in distress. We hate to see others in pain.

He agrees with Locke that we are free, but disagrees about our powers. The savage is 'stupid and unimaginative' and so seeks society. Without society, there is no language (especially of rights), no real family bonds and no opportunity for self-development. He certainly has no conception of morality and justice – this is impossible prior to forming a social contract.

Why make a contract?

For Rousseau, the contract is not made out of fear or a rational decision, but out of weakness. We have natural tendencies to be good, but without society we cannot realise them. Through making a social contract, we can enjoy the benefits of working together, developing common goals and becoming comrades. We are no longer a private, isolated, limited individual, but we can share the achievements of the whole group – the collaborative benefits. Rousseau calls these goods, achieved through cooperation and which we can share – the 'common good' or the 'common interest'. You will also hear modern politicians refer to the 'public interest'. It is encapsulated in the motto of the Three Musketeers: 'All for one and one for all'. As an example, you might consider what benefits you gain from playing in a sports team or joining an A-level class rather than learning on your own.

Think about

Should we sack the referee?

Imagine the referee makes an awful mistake, and awards a crucial penalty for what is clearly a foul outside the penalty area.

Should we crowd the referee and demand he goes?

- Hobbes would say no – why?
- Locke would say yes – why?

Answers are at the end of this topic. Who would you agree with?

Key philosopher

Jean-Jacques Rousseau (1712–78)

A French philosopher famous for his work on early-years education ('Emile' 1762), and in political philosophy his conception of civil society as an organic unity with a single desire for the 'common good'.

Think about

Persuade someone that the good of everyone is also their good.

For example, no one likes paying taxes. We all want tax cuts. But if everyone took a tax cut, we might only gain, say, £10 each. If we gave back the money, we would have millions of pounds to spend on a new hospital, etc.

What would you say to these people?

- I cannot be bothered to recycle.
- I want to fly around the world.
- I do not care about carbon footprints.
- I am short of money. I do not want to donate aid money to the homeless.
- I do not get on with the conductor. I am going to leave the orchestra and go solo.
- I am not going to fight for my country.

Rousseau's notion of liberty clearly contrasts with that of Hobbes and Locke. For Locke, joining a society involves giving up freedom. You can either be free in the state of nature or ruled and accept some limits on that freedom. Liberty is the silence of the laws. However, Rousseau suggests another possibility. People can make a social contract and trade the freedom of the state of nature for the liberty of ruling themselves.

If the people make laws and agree to the laws, then they are simply obeying themselves, and this entails no loss of freedom. All that is necessary is that the laws promote the good of all. Rousseau would agree with Hobbes and Locke that simply being ruled by another person is a loss of freedom, but if the law embodies the common good, which is also your good, then you have not lost anything. Liberty is the rule that you would prescribe to yourself, it is following your own interests.

If, for a moment, you lapse into purely selfish mode and forget that real freedom comes from obeying the common interest and the good of all, then Rousseau explains that you can 'be forced to be free'! Imagine that your little brother or sister is being really annoying and stopping the family from freely enjoying themselves. Then you might explain to them that greater freedom will come from participating in a positive, family atmosphere.

Positive freedom

Rousseau therefore develops a different conception of liberty. The state of nature described by Hobbes and Locke is not real freedom. Instead of 'doing what one desires', Liberty consists in 'choosing what one desires'. Under the condition of negative liberty, we saw that the beggar and also the addict and the ignorant are apparently free. While under positive liberty, one is only free if one can choose one's desires and select the wisest and most liberating opportunities. The addict is not free to give up their addiction, and the beggar has no real opportunities. Real freedom, positive freedom, entails empowerment, the ability to choose what you want (although this does not entail you will get it). When the addict and the beggar take control of their lives rather than simply following their desires, then they are developing positive freedom. This distinction has been characterised as follows:

■ negative freedom allows you to walk towards the door of your choice without hindrance

■ positive freedom gives you the key to open the door or an alternative door.

Liberty and authority

For Rousseau there is no conflict between liberty and authority as long as everyone participates in the common good. The laws actually enable the citizen to become a team player. Cooperating with everyone in our joint interest, playing for the good of the team opens up new horizons and new possibilities. We swap the life of a noble but limited savage for the opportunities of citizenship.

Think about

Look at the list below. Select what you would identify as the best descriptions of freedom. Can you distinguish between negative and positive freedom?

What is liberty?

■ Freedom to do what I want. *

■ The chance to improve myself, become enlightened (education). #

■ Freedom from interference by others (being left alone). *

■ Opportunity to participate in government (voting). #

■ Being able to adopt my own lifestyle/not conform. *

■ Achieving my full potential, developing my talents. #

■ Having my own private space to make 'authentic' decisions (an independent mind). *

■ Opportunities to choose from (e.g. wide range of choices). #

■ Having as few rules to obey as possible. *

■ Access to the benefits of living in a community (health care, education). #

■ Being in control rather than being a victim (not being forced to do something). *

■ Being part of a successful team (e.g. sports team, music group, etc.). #

You will probably have noticed that negative freedom is marked *
and positive freedom is marked #.

The last word

The state of nature described by Hobbes, Locke and Rousseau make three assumptions:

1 There has been a time when human beings lived outside society or we can understand hypothetically what such a condition would be like.

2 There are universal features of human nature which characterise all human beings, regardless of history or culture.

3 Primary importance should be given to individuals, rather than the nature of authority. In other words, the exercise of authority requires consent.

All three of these assumptions need to be considered.

Is the state of nature meaningful?

Can we really conceive of 'natural' human beings who are pre-social? Some philosophers think not. They point to the fact that we begin life in a social family unit which is itself part of a social structure, whether tribe or modern democracy. This is not just a historical point, it is a conceptual point. For social contract theorists, the individual self is prior to any roles or relationships that we might experience. But on the contrary, it could be argued that a sense of self can only be situated within social roles. The very conception of individuals is a product of a particular, cultural view. We could not even develop language unless we had regular social interaction. So consciousness from the beginning develops in a community, and we understand ourselves only from within the values and norms of a particular culture. The philosopher Bradley argues that our identity, our very sense of self 'is penetrated, infected, characterised by the existence of others, its content implies in every fibre, the relations of the community' (Bradley, 1914). If this is true, then a sense of self can only be meaningful in the context of community. The idea of a pre-social self is meaningless.

Common features?

We might still try to identify those universal human qualities around which we should build our society. Thus all three of our theories suggest that we promote people's interests by allowing them to choose the life they want. To be human is to be free to consent.

But suppose that human nature can be moulded, and our identity is constituted by our role in society. Thus, the environment, particularly social institutions, shape our nature – we are members of an occupation, a gender, part of an ethnic group, a class, a football supporter and so on. As Pascal says, 'custom is our nature'. Our 'universal' qualities are not universal at all, our nature depends on historical and economic circumstances, or the spirit of the times. Marx identifies economic and social relations as shaping our nature, and so what we consider to be common human qualities could actually just be relative to those circumstances: 'The nature of individuals thus depends on the material conditions determining their production' and our consciousness, 'is determined by quite definite class relationships'.

So in their accounts of the state of nature, Hobbes, Locke and Rousseau are simply expressing the values of their time and their position in society.

Strength through unity

Finally, we might question whether political philosophy should begin with the individual. For if we cannot understand individuals separately from the society in which they developed, then it is the nature of society that should be the primary focus. We should design society – the ideal first, and the identity of individuals will develop within this social ideal. So some philosophers have begun with a plan for **Utopia**.

Below is Plato's description of how the philosopher (called 'the artist') will design the ideal community. Even if you disagree with Plato's conception of a Utopian community, you might still argue that primary consideration should be given to creating a fair and just society first. If we could develop and perfect social institutions, then individuals would find their rightful place within a just system. This is preferable to building a system based on a fictitious state of nature. These extracts are taken from *The Republic*:

Key terms

Utopia: a society with ideal laws and an ideal way of life. The term derives from Thomas More (1516) who set out his version of the ideal community.

'The first thing our artists must do', I replied, '– and it's not easy – is to wipe the slate of human society and human habits clean. For our philosophic artists differ at once from all others in being unwilling to start work on an individual or a city, or draw out laws, until they are given, or have made themselves, a clean canvas.'

'They are quite right.'

'After that the first step will be to sketch in the outline of the social system.'

'Yes, and then?'

'Our artist will, I suppose, as he works, look frequently in both directions, that is, at justice and beauty and self-discipline and the like in their true nature, and again at the copy of them he is trying to make in human beings, mixing and blending traits to give the colour of manhood, and judging by that quality in men that Homer too called godly and godlike.'

Plato (1955, Book VI)

'In our society of all societies, then, the citizens will agree in their use of that phrase we were talking about just now, and will refer to the successes and misfortunes of an individual fellow-citizen as 'my success' or 'my misfortune'.'

'That is very true,' he agreed.

'And didn't we say that this way of thinking and talking leads to common feelings of pain and pleasure?'

'Yes, and we were quite right.'

'Our citizens, then, are devoted to a common interest, which they call my own; and in consequence entirely share each other's feelings of joy and sorrow.'

'Yes.'

'And the element in our constitution to which this is especially due is the community of women and children in the Guardian class.'

'Yes, that is the chief reason for it.'

'But we agreed that this unanimity was the greatest good a society can enjoy – we compared, you remember, a well-run society to the human body, in which the whole is aware of the pleasure and pain of the part.'

'And we were quite right,' he said.

'And so we may say that the community of women and children among its protectors confers the greatest of all benefits on our state.'

'Yes, we may.'

'And what is more, we are being quite consistent, because we said earlier that our Guardians, if they were to do their job properly, should have no houses or land or any other possessions of their own, but get their daily bread from others in payment for their services, and consume it together in common.'

'Yes, we said that.'

'Then don't you agree that, as I say, these further arrangements will make them even truer Guardians than before? They will prevent the dissension that starts when different people call different things their own, when each carts off to his own private house anything he can lay hands on for himself, and when each has his own wife and children, his own private joys and sorrows; for our citizens, whose interests are identical and whose efforts are all directed so far as is possible towards the same end, feel all their joys and sorrows together.'

'Yes, I entirely agree.'

'And besides, since they have no private property except their own persons (everything else being common), won't litigation virtually disappear? There won't in fact be any of the quarrels which are caused by having money or children or family…'

'But we shall lay it down that older men are to have the authority over all younger men, and power to punish them.'

'Obviously.'

'And that, as is only right, no younger man shall attempt to do violence or strike his elders, unless ordered to do so by the Rulers. Indeed I don't think that the young will behave badly to their elders in any way, because they will be prevented by two effective safeguards, fear and respect. Respect will stop them laying hands on their parents, and they will fear the assistance the victim would get from those who count themselves his sons and brothers and parents…'

Plato (1955, Book V)

'The object of our legislation,' I reminded him again, 'is not the special welfare of any particular class in our society, but of the society as a whole; and it uses the persuasion or compulsion to unite all citizens and make them share together the benefits which each individually can confer on the community; and its purpose in fostering this attitude is not to leave everyone to please himself, but to make each man a link in the unity of the whole.'

'You are right; I had forgotten,' he said.

'You see, then, Glaucon,' I went on, 'we shan't be unfair to our philosophers, but shall be quite fair in what we say when we compel them to have some care and responsibility for others.

We shall say, "we have bred you both for your own sake and that of the whole community to act as leaders and king-bees in a hive; you are better and more fully educated than the rest and better qualified to combine the practice of philosophy and politics".'

Plato (1955, Book VII)

Think about

- Do you like Plato's theory of making people fit the system?
- Is the ideal human society similar to the relationship of bees in a hive?
- Do you agree that people are bred for a particular position in society?

Think about

Answer to 'Should we sack the ref?'

For Hobbes, if you challenge the referee you are in danger of returning the game to a state of nature – chaos. Only if a stronger referee could impose stronger order would you contemplate change.

For Locke, playing in an unjust game is worse than having no referee. If disputes are not fairly dealt with, it would be better for the players to return to the state of nature until a new, just authority can be found.

After working through this topic, you should:

- understand that the state of nature refers to basic human qualities which provide a moral foundation
- know how Hobbes and Locke describe human nature
- be able to explain the benefits of political organisation
- understand the problems of using the state of nature to justify authority.

Political obligation and consent

- to consider whether political obligation is based on consent
- to explore what is meant by the terms power, authority and legitimacy
- to investigate whether legitimacy requires popular approval
- to evaluate the problems of basing political obligation on consent.

Key terms

Political obligation: this is about our rights and duties as citizens. It concerns who should rule us and how they should rule. It is about who should have power and how much power.

When do you feel obliged to do something? Do you feel obliged: to help the family with housework, or to turn up to team practices, or to pay your way when out with friends, or to obey school/college rules?

There may be two senses in which you feel obliged:

- because you are coerced, and if you do not fulfil your obligations something unpleasant will happen
- because you feel a moral duty, it is right to do it and you acknowledge that you ought to do it.

Which of the above do you see as a moral duty?

The contract theory introduced in the first topic is a moral obligation. The contract is firstly with other people – that we feel obliged to regulate our behaviour towards others; and secondly with the sovereign power – that we have a duty to obey in return for benefits. Sometimes the second point may collapse into the first point, but this chapter is concerned to discover whether **political obligation** can be based on a moral duty to comply with the contract. The moral force of this duty will derive from the fact that we consented to be part of the arrangements. Clearly, if we had entered against our will, then the moral argument dissolves.

At least one philosopher, Hume, denies that there was any contract:

> But were you to ask the far greatest part of the nation, whether they had ever consented to the authority of their rulers, or promis'd to obey them, they wou'd be inclin'd to think very strangely of you; and wou'd certainly reply, that the affair depended not on their consent, but that they were born to such obedience.

Hume (1947b)

He mocks the idea of a contract by comparing our situation to that of a sailor who is press-ganged into joining the navy. Halfway across the ocean, he is told that he consented to a contract with the navy, and if he does not like it he can leave. Where is he supposed to go?

> Can we seriously say that a poor peasant or artisan has a free choice to leave his country, when he knows no foreign language or manners, and lives from day to day, by the small wages which he acquires? We may as well assert that a man, by remaining in a vessel, freely consents to the domination of the master; though he was carried on board while asleep and must leap into the ocean and perish the moment he leaves her.

Hume (1947b)

So the notion of consent is a controversial one, leading to a number of distinct questions.

1 When and how did we consent to a contract?
2 What did we actually consent to?
3 Why did we consent? What are the benefits?

In point 1 we are looking for an actual occurrence to validate the contract, while in points 2 and 3 we are searching for justifications as to its legitimacy.

Contracts

Your own experience of a contract may be relatively clear. When you entered college, sixth form or university, you may have signed an agreement. Do you know the answers to the following?

- when the contract actually began
- what you had to do to enter into it
- what you have contracted to do – your duties
- why – what the benefits are and what you can expect from the institution
- what rewards, sanctions and punishments there are, if either party fails in their obligations.

Do you keep the contract for the following reasons?

- because you are coerced
- out of self-interest
- out of moral duty.

The college will probably cite all three reasons for keeping their part of the bargain, but it is the final point that provides the clearest sense of obligation.

The question we now have to address is whether this model provides a satisfactory explanation for political obligation, or whether we agree with Hume.

The quest is to find what makes the exercise of power legitimate. We must bear in mind that while the justification of power requires rational arguments, which can be assessed and evaluated, legitimacy is not always based on reason. People may accept the obligation to obey from emotional and psychological reasons. So we need to have some account of how power is employed before we can subject it to rational scrutiny.

Power

Power is a contested concept. In other words, different interpretations or strands of meaning are applied to the concept.

Hobbes defines power as *power to*, the power to satisfy desires:

> The power of a man ... is his present means to obtain some future or apparent good

Hobbes (1982)

So we have power if we have the means to achieve our self-interest. Power is to be able to do what one desires – such as play the guitar, become a model, assemble flat-pack furniture, etc. This definition coheres with the notion of negative liberty – freedom to act as one desires, and the absence of obstacles: Locke uses this interpretation when he describes our natural right to private property, 'the power to use it, sell it and exclude trespassers'.

Part of power to is *power over*. This is defined as the ability to affect another person's interest or life. Critics of private property point out that excluding others from private property entails considerable power over other people's right to roam, etc. Less obviously, power over may happen through the ethos of an institution or custom and social practice. For example, whether you work in a democratic or authoritarian institution will influence how you think, and affect your wants and needs. You might wish for more consultation or, conversely, stricter discipline. If we accept Rousseau's contract, we could be forced to ignore our personal, selfish desires for the sake of our real interest and the common good. The public ownership of property could empower all individuals and ensure no one has power over another.

'Power over' is further subdivided into 'control theory' and 'effect theory'. The control strand emphasises the intention to overcome resistance. In a basic form it could be bullying; but in a more subtle approach it could be setting the agenda for a meeting or assembly, so that only the issues that the powerful want debated are on the agenda. In other ways, control may be exercised through moral force or sheer charisma. Someone such as Nelson Mandela could be said to have both. Liberals like Locke, who value negative freedom, seek to minimise this form of power in order to protect their concept of liberty, in contrast to Rousseau who advocates mastery and control of desires by each individual, and by the general will, in order to achieve positive liberty.

The 'effect theory' of power is defined as the ability to adversely affect the interests of others without any intention. What powerful people do can affect other people, even though no obvious control is intended. So powerful companies can unknowingly show discrimination, such as institutional racism, or neglect of health and safety, which has major influences on working conditions. Those who criticise negative freedom point out how a free, capitalist economy can adversely affect workers, for example through sudden unemployment, even though this is not intended. It is an effect of the system.

To summarise, it is possible to have 'power to' without having 'power over'. However, 'power to' can become 'power over'; and this in turn can be subdivided into 'control theory' and 'effect theory'. Any exercise of power, therefore, might embrace different forms at the same time. My power to satisfy sexual desire will involve power over and control.

So far we have attempted to define what power is. We can also distinguish what forms the exercise of power may take. Here are different ways in which 'power to' and more especially 'power over' can be manifested:

- charismatic power – the power of personality, enhanced by the media through glamour and sexual attractiveness
- traditional power – the respect for the wisdom of previous generations and the need for stability, such as a hereditary monarch
- legal power – the respect for the rule of law, and the power of legislation to regulate people's lives in a rational way, such as driving laws
- moral power – the appeal to agreed values, such as human rights or religious commands
- persuasive power – the power of communication skills, to lobby and present an attractive or convincing case
- expertise and knowledge – the power of being 'an authority' and possessing the skills to be able to do something
- intimidation – the power to motivate people through fear with the threat of unpleasant consequences.

The issue that needs to be decided is which forms of power should be accepted as legitimate. Legitimate power is called *authority*. While power

Think about

Can you identify these examples of power?

- parental discipline
- being able to sell your own goods
- college policy on equal opportunities
- buying your own house.
- playing the guitar
- deciding who you will marry
- the expectation that MPs in the House of Commons work until 11.00pm
- shop opening times.

Think about

Name two people who have 'power over' you in your daily life. What types of power do they use? In which ways does a modern politician exercise power over the citizens?

gives someone the *ability* to rule, authority confers the *right* to rule. Political obligation is ultimately concerned with authority.

It is possible to have authority without power. A leader may be legitimate, but impotent and unable to gain power over the citizens even though they are the legitimate ruler. Hobbes reminds us of the dangers of a weak leader. But we may not agree with Hobbes that the sovereign is entitled to use any means at their disposal (save killing someone) to ensure order and obedience. In this case, authority seems to dissolve into nothing but power and the use of force, and this is discussed below. Anarchists, on the other hand, maintain that any exercise of political power is illegitimate and unwarranted. Most opinions lie somewhere between these extremes.

> **AQA Examiner's tip**
>
> This is a key distinction that underpins all consideration of political obligation.

Think about

Look at the following list and decide what kind of power each point represents and whether it is legitimate. Then justify your answer.

- police controlling a demonstration
- fashion designer setting trends
- a party political broadcast
- scientists imposing a ban on the movement of livestock
- religious groups influencing the law on abortion
- the mafia collecting protection money
- top bands leading musical tastes
- the Queen speaking to the nation
- kidnapping by a terrorist group
- changing the laws on drugs.

The decline in authority

Some kinds of authority are now in decline. If you look at the list of types of power, which do you think would be less acceptable in a modern society?

It may be hard to believe, but the power of tradition was once a major force. 'We have always done it this way' used to silence critics and reformers. Now, modern organisations are expected to adapt quickly to meet changing demands. Similarly moral authority is challenged in pluralistic societies which may embrace multiculturalism. The UN charter of human rights is nevertheless one of the most powerful attempts to impose a universal set of moral values, although as we shall see, not everyone subscribes to them.

In addition, those who have been regarded as 'an authority' may see their legitimacy ebb away, as modern technology gives ordinary people quick access to knowledge. For example, doctors and teachers often find themselves in a position where a patient or a student knows more than they do on a particular topic.

Therefore, it seems inevitable that in a modern society, the essential condition that legitimises power is *consent* – the consent of the governed. The rest of this topic is therefore devoted to the three questions posed above:

1 When and how did we consent?
2 What did we actually consent to?
3 Why did we consent? What are the benefits?

Consent

When and how

The right to make laws, to require obedience and to punish, may be justified by an appeal to a particular event, e.g. you signed a contract which set out in advance what the duties and benefits on both sides were. Such legal contracts are commonplace. But with regard to political obligation, it is very unlikely that this has ever happened, although new immigrants to this country may have to sign a contract in the future. Legal contracts involve a procedure, of an offer and a clear indication of acceptance. But in political life, the sovereign is already in place, and the citizen is already participating in society. So those who wish to base obligation on consent usually refer to two other kinds of events: tacit consent and voting.

Tacit consent

Tacit consent is 'assumed' or 'implicit' consent and is a concept employed by the 20th-century contract theorist, John Rawls. We will consider his theory of justice in more detail below, but part of his conception of 'fair play' is that if one accepts the advantages of living in a society, then in return one must accept duties and obligations. It is not fair if 'participants who have knowingly accepted the benefits of their common practice … accept the benefits of government but refuse to do their part in maintaining the contract'. Rawls gives the example of a tax dodger, who clearly benefits from social services, but does not contribute as he should to the funding. Such people are often called **free riders**.

If we accept the duty of fair play, then we can assume that everyone who accepts the advantages of society is tacitly (implicitly) consenting to the authority of the state, the constitution and the government. Whether all this is implied by our enjoyment of benefits is considered controversial.

It might firstly be noted that many advantages were gained as a child, when we were completely unaware of the contract and were in no position to accept or deny them. Hume's analogy of the press-ganged sailor makes the point. However, can you name three distinct benefits that you would have accepted in your early years?

Secondly there is a question about the degree of obligation that can be assumed from the gains that you have received. Does the health care you had as a child require you to pay student tuition fees, or fight for your country, or accept the wishes of the majority, or obey an unjust law? Later Rawls argues that the last two in the list are fair obligations that can be expected of you: 'In agreeing to a democratic constitution … one accepts at the same time, the principle of majority rule … there is nothing unusual in our being required to comply with unjust laws' (Rawls, 1999).

Yet many will want to query whether there is any clear way of assessing the benefits of a democratic society in order to ascertain what degree of obedience is fair. Is it even possible to conceive how one might argue for such a balance? Each individual would have to weigh up what they have received, and if some have received very little, what obligations can we expect? The use of tacit consent inevitably leads to a consideration of justice. For example, would 16-year-old boys have received enough benefits to justify conscription in the army? You may feel this kind of calculation is impossible.

One of the most famous accounts of tacit consent comes from Plato's Socrates. Socrates has been imprisoned by the Laws (the authorities)

Key terms

Free riders: people who enjoy the benefits of a society, but refuse to share in the burdens and duties.

Think about

Can you think of any other free riders in society? Do you share Rawl's view that their behaviour is unjust?

for his beliefs. He has been offered the chance to escape, but he actually allows the authorities to keep him in prison and later execute him! He argues that he is obligated to obey the demands of the authorities, including his own death sentence on account of his tacit consent to authority. Here is his argument:

> Socrates: 'Consider, then, Socrates,' the Laws would probably continue. 'whether it is also true for us to say that what you are now trying to do to us is not right. Although we have brought you into the world and reared you and educated you, and given you and all your fellow-citizens a share in all the good things at our disposal, nevertheless by the very fact of granting our permission we openly proclaim this principle: that any Athenian, on attaining to manhood and seeing for himself the political organization of the State and us its Laws, is permitted, if he is not satisfied with us, to take his property and go away wherever he likes…
>
> On the other hand, if any one of you stands his ground when he can see how we administer justice and the rest of our public organization, we hold that by doing so he has in fact undertaken to do anything that we tell him; and we maintain that anyone who disobeys is guilty of doing wrong on three separate counts: first because we are his parents, and secondly because we are his guardians; and thirdly because, after promising obedience, he is neither obeying us nor persuading us to change our decision if we are at fault in any way … These are the charges, Socrates, to which we say that you will be liable if you do what you are contemplating; and you will not be the least culpable of your fellow-countrymen, but one of the most guilty … You have never left the city to attend a festival or for any other purpose, except on some military expedition; you have never travelled abroad as other people do, and you have never felt the impulse to acquaint yourself with another country or constitution; you have been content with us and with our city. You have definitely chosen us, and undertaken to observe us in all your activities as a citizen; and as the crowning proof that you are satisfied with our city, you have begotten children in it.

*Plato's dialogue Crito, quoted in **Palmer** (1991)*

Voting

The act of voting seems the most visible act of showing consent, and it meets the objections that we are unaware of giving consent or that consent by past generations cannot be binding on the present. Nevertheless, we must consider whether a comparatively brief and weak process can carry the serious importance that attaches to it.

When we place our X next to the name of a candidate, we appear to be voting for a representative. Are we not then voting for policies as well? And by participating in the democratic process once every four or five years, are we also endorsing the **constitution**? It would seem that if you use the democratic process to ensure your voice is heard, then at the same time, you support a democratic constitution and the authority of those elected. But does it necessarily entail that? Although you wanted to express your view, the result of the election may be so morally objectionable that you cannot accept the authority of the winning party. Many people in Germany must have felt just that when the Nazi party was elected.

Another problem is that the distribution of votes in any election can affect the results in a way that was not intended.

> **Think about**
>
> What three arguments does Socrates offer to support the case for tacit consent? Would you agree that he must therefore accept his punishment?

> **Key terms**
>
> **Constitution:** the rules which define the power and the limit of government. For example, a government must be elected by a process of 'one man – one vote'.

Think about

Consider the results of the following election. There are two parties: the fascists (F) and the loony left (LL). The state consists of five constituencies. In each constituency, people voted on three issues: war, education and health. The results of the vote were as follows.

Constituency	War	Education	Health
1	F	LL	LL
2	F	F	F
3	LL	F	LL
4	F	F	F
5	LL	LL	F

In each constituency, which party had most votes? So overall, which party won the most constituencies, and should form the next government?

For each of the three policies, which party's policy was more popular?

So based on policies, which party should form the next government?

You might defend your right to vote, but would you accept the authority of the government if your party was not in power?

There are also other problems with voting that call into question just how satisfactory it is as an indication of consent.

In a representative democracy such as that in the UK, we elect our representatives to make political decisions on our behalf. We hope they are expert and reliable and we trust them for up to five years. If the MP truly consults his constituents, then our voices may be heard, but if he does not then it seems more like licensed tyranny. It is quite possible for an MP to vote on his/her own views or to toe the party line, in which case we could even be taken to war without our consent. Again, some liken the voting procedure to a popularity contest rather than a serious register of the people's wishes.

But would our consent be more accurately represented if we voted for policies. The parties do produce a manifesto, but they always reserve the right to modify it in light of changing events. In which case, we are voting for whatever the government might do in advance, and there is no guarantee they will fulfil their election promises. Moreover, it is still the political parties that are setting the agenda and controlling what we assent to. Only the issues that the party want to discuss will be raised.

And yet would we want to consult the people directly on every issue? This would be like having a referendum on every important decision. Oscar Wilde pointed out that such a democracy might sound fine but 'would take up too many evenings'. Many issues are so complex that much of the population might vote in ignorance on trivial concerns. Would we want to consent to the tyranny of the majority?

Plato raises the problems of democracy in his simile of the ship. In this analogy, the ship represents the ship of state.

Examiner's tip

Here we have an example of 'power to' entailing 'power over'.

Examiner's tip

Here is an example of control, which is less obvious.

Suppose the following to be the state of affairs on board a ship or ships. The captain is larger and stronger than any of the crew, but a bit deaf and short-sighted, and similarly limited in seamanship. The crew are all quarrelling with each other about how to navigate the ship, each thinking he ought to be at the helm; they have never learned the art of navigation and cannot say that anyone ever taught it them, or that they spent any time studying it; indeed they say it can't be taught and are ready to murder anyone who says it can. They spend all their time milling round the captain and doing all they can to get him to give them the helm. If one faction is more successful than another, their rivals may kill them and throw them overboard, lay out the honest captain with drugs or drink or in some other way, take control of the ship, help themselves to what's on board, and turn the voyage into the sort of drunken pleasure-cruise you would expect. Finally, they reserve their admiration for the man who knows how to lend a hand in controlling the captain by force or fraud; they praise his seamanship and navigation and knowledge of the sea and condemn everyone else as useless. They have no idea that the true navigator must study the seasons of the year, the sky, the stars, the winds and all the other subjects appropriate to his profession if he is to be really fit to control a ship; and they think that it's quite impossible to acquire the professional skill needed for such control (whether or not they want it exercised) and that there's no such thing as an art of navigation. With all this going on aboard aren't the sailors on any such ship bound to regard the true navigator as a word-spinner and a star-gazer, of no use to them at all?

Plato (1955, Book VI)

> **Think about**
>
> Can you identify the captain, the crew and the navigator?

Plato's point is that in the struggle for power and control of the ship, the person who has wisdom and expertise – 'an authority' – is usually ignored. Here, the navigator's knowledge is dismissed as impractical star gazing. The strongest of the crew will ultimately take charge, based on his popularity with the captain, and he has little knowledge of how to direct the ship. The result is a 'drunken pleasure-cruise'!

Plato is raising the question whether popular approval is the best way to secure legitimacy. Is voting going to lead to the wisest and most just decision? If not, are the results of majority voting nothing more than a tyranny by an ill-informed group, who just happen to have a numerical advantage. This does not appear to be a sound basis for legitimate government.

Think about

In trying to decide whether you agree with Plato or not, you should consider the following issues:

- Are people as ignorant as people suggest and can politicians succeed if they are corrupt?
- Do people learn from their mistakes? If they elect the wrong people, they surely learn from that error.
- Is there a clear 'direction' for a state, like there is a ship? Surely the goal of a state is to satisfy its people.
- Can a philosopher know objective moral values, like a navigator can know the stars?
- What is the value of consent through the ballot box if it is 'manufactured' through bribery, flattery or drugs?

Authority dissolves upon challenge

A frequent criticism of modern democracy is that people are alienated from their real interests because they are 'drugged' into consent. This is a metaphorical use of 'drugged'. The word 'drugged' can of course refer to propaganda, manipulation through the media and restricted access to knowledge. Popular approval is consequently of little worth if consent is achieved or manufactured through indoctrination. Thus Marxists account for the fact that workers still support a capitalist system which oppresses them because the middle class control the 'production of ideas' and successfully create 'a false consciousness' that the economic system is in everyone's interest. Hence, the dominant ideology in a society is the ideology of the dominant class. For example, it is interesting how popular the idea of tax cuts has become. Yet reduced taxation is bound to benefit the wealthy rather than the working class, when higher taxes could actually improve the social services which support the less well off. If consent is not the result of rational and autonomous thought, but 'produced' by the class 'which has the means of material production at its disposal', and thus 'has control over the means of mental production', then it cannot be used to legitimise the exercise of power. Appeals to consent are false and empty if people are duped or brainwashed into agreement. Thus some commentators maintain that this attempt to legitimise power through voting is a bogus sham. There is no such thing as legitimate power, there is just power. Justice is nothing more than the interests of the strongest class or individuals.

Hence the importance of what we mean by a free press, freedom of speech, an independent judiciary, a democratic education system and all the other preconditions of an open society, is underlined if consent is to be regarded as meaningful. Do you think in today's society, people are able to make an informed, genuine, rational choice? And is it possible any more to identify a class interest which predominates?

One final difficulty with voting as an indication of consent is the number of people who do not vote, especially if they are deliberately confronting the system. Some people do not vote because they cannot find anyone who sufficiently represents their views. They are consequently denying legitimacy to the elected government, although preserving the legitimacy of the constitution. Can these people be allowed to opt out of their duties if they do not participate in the act of consent? It seems we may then have to fall back on tacit consent in order to ensure obligation and compliance.

Related to this issue is the fact that very rarely in the UK does a winning party achieve over 50 per cent of the votes in an election. From the point of view of simple statistics, a minority of the population actually support the government. Yet the people generally accept the government's right to rule. This illustrates what Rawls claims, that by voting we are agreeing to a democratic constitution and 'one accepts at the same time the *principle* of majority rule' [author emphasis]. So at the same time as choosing a government, we are also endorsing a principle.

What to and why

It is clear from our considerations of acts of consent that there are issues about what we are consenting to. This becomes more apparent when we consider the differing accounts of the social contract. Because of the various interpretations of human nature, the kind of authority we should accept and the benefits we will gain vary considerably. It is now time to review Hobbes, Locke and Rousseau.

Hobbes

Hobbes maintains that we should consent to an all-powerful sovereign. His notion of consent is controversial. The choice is between the violent chaos of the state of nature or obedience to a dictator. Since life is otherwise a 'war of all against all', consent is little more than conquest. If the most powerful leader says, 'Yield or die', then if you yield, that is consent. Whether such an agreement under extreme duress really constitutes consent is debatable. Hobbes is endorsing the view that whoever is strongest and can demand obedience is the legitimate authority. This is known as 'might is right'. A similar view was offered by the Chinese communist leader, Mao Zedong. Allegedly, when asked to justify his right to rule, he replied, 'Power comes from the barrel of a gun'. He did not distinguish between power and authority!

Hobbes' account of minimal consent raises an issue which we will return to in the last topic. Is it the act of consent which entails obligation or is it pure self-interest? If you look back at the section on contracts, is there a moral duty to obey because we have consented, or is the obligation arising from a natural act of self-interest? Since Hobbes allows that we are entitled to remove the sovereign if we can defeat him and replace him with a stronger power, then the emphasis is clearly one of self-interest.

Since Hobbes bases obligation on power, the leader need only be a coordinator who ensures order and security. He or she is 'in authority' because of his/her strength, but he/she need not be 'an authority', particularly a moral authority. Thus he/she need not demonstrate wisdom, virtue or a respect for rights and moral virtues. He/she could rely on his/her power 'to crack the whip', to command and to punish. Life under such a ruler would be subject to the whim of one person. The only check on his/her power is that he/she would be careful not to stir up rebellion. The popular image of Henry VIII gives us a picture of what such a leader might be like.

Yet although the leader is autocratic and perhaps tyrannous, such a society is always going to be unstable. This is illustrated in the prisoner's dilemma above. The best outcome for everyone is that everyone cooperates and stays silent, but it only takes a breach of trust by a few people confessing for all the order and stability to evaporate and we then return to the state of nature. An important criticism of Hobbes' account of obligation is his limited conception of strength. It is summed up by Rousseau: 'the strong are never strong enough, until they convert might into right'. In other words, power by itself is not enough, it has to be legitimised, and leaders are always stronger if their power is justified – if they have right on their side.

So we might argue that Hobbes is correct to identify power as a precondition of authority, but it is not sufficient. Authority is achieved when that power is perceived to be wise, or moral, or just, or some other justification is offered. This is the key to Plato's dictatorship, the rule of the wise philosopher kings. Their 'strength' derives from their rational knowledge, their understanding of moral excellence, the Form of the Good. This enables them to design the kind of harmonious society described at the end of the first topic above. Consent here would also be a formality, since Utopia, by definition, is what all citizens seek. However, you will already have decided whether a philosopher really can obtain knowledge of objective moral values, and thus a just and successful social structure.

In defence of Hobbes, it must be said that he is not *advocating* a brutal, repressive dictatorship, but only a strong power. The leader must be strong enough to protect the citizens, maintain order and defend any rights that are given to the people. Only the most powerful sovereign can guarantee that. So justice is not entirely what the dictator says it is, for he must achieve these goals and he is not permitted to take life. Hobbes recognises that everyone has a right of self-defence. So in a minimal sense, there are higher standards which the sovereign power must live up to. So there is an ideal form of justice over and above the wishes of the sovereign. Even for Hobbes, might is not always right. Power is only legitimate if life is better under the contract than it is in the state of nature. But if it is, then in a limited sense there is a moral obligation to obey.

But if Hobbes recognises that certain values are universal and in some sense a government must concern itself with justice, then why not adopt Locke's position that a leader is not the sole arbiter of what is right, but is bound to protect some system of natural rights. Being moral as well as powerful is surely stronger than ruling according to mere self-interest.

Morality as weakness!

Machiavelli says no. Morality is a sign of weakness, and a leader will find that some virtues 'can ruin him'. Compassion may be interpreted as a lack of resolve, while cruelty can keep your subjects 'united and loyal'. In *The Prince*, he asks the question 'whether it is better to be loved than feared'. His answer is that while both are preferable, he believes that respect and obedience are more likely to be granted out of fear. While being moral is laudable, it may be seen as a limit on power and an indication of weakness.

Machiavelli concludes that a ruler should *appear* just and moral whenever he can, but behind the appearances he must be prepared to do evil whenever it is necessary. This has been characterised as 'the iron fist in the velvet glove'. This 'flexible disposition' is obviously nothing more than gross deceit. We must therefore ask whether under the social contract we would feel obliged to obey such an authority. While there may be some benefits in terms of a united, loyal disciplined society, what will happen when the citizens find out that they have an unscrupulous leader? Would you want to continue to give allegiance to such a cunning character, and is fear the best way to retain respect?

Locke

For Locke, the contract is a matter of trust – investing and loaning power in return for the protection of our rights. If the government is unworthy we are entitled to withdraw consent, and this justification for rebellion will be discussed in the next topic.

Because 'men being all the workmanship of one omnipotent and infinitely wise maker', natural law dictates that we all possess inalienable rights. 'Natural reason, which tells us that men being born, have a right to their preservation ...'.

His appeal to reason barely disguises that Locke is presenting his own values as though they are facts about the state of nature. This is especially apparent when he is talking about property. He admits that, 'God hath given the world to men in common', which should imply that property is communal as the anarchists claim. However, he then defends the right to private property, arguing that, 'he that hath mixed his labour' with land deserves to own it, and he can 'exclude the common right of other men'. Now this is by no means a fact, and is a questionable value: why should working the land give someone the right to own it? We can

Key philosopher

Machiavelli (1469–1527)

An Italian political thinker. The ends justify the means and, in *The Prince*, he condones the use of fraud, deceit and worse if it is necessary to safeguard security and prosperity.

Think about

Would you recommend Machiavelli's leadership style to your teachers in order to make them more effective in the classroom? Are teachers ever justified in using deception, cunning or telling lies? Can they be cruel in order to be kind, or must they always convert might into right?

concede that they have a claim to what they produce, but why should they gain ownership of the land itself and the right to exclude others. The land could be on loan to anyone who is prepared to work it, but ownership remains in common. So, for example, all local people could put their stock on the land to graze rather than annexing private property. Should property rights imply the right to exclude others?

Practically, there might be the problem of over-use or abuse of common land, and some form of limitation to local farmers will be necessary. But Locke's argument for individual ownership is the basis of a capitalist system that is highly controversial. Does everyone have an equal opportunity and access to land, so that they can work for their produce? Marx highlights the **alienation** felt by the property-less, as they are forced to sell themselves as wage slaves, which is an 'open, clear and absolute negation of humanity'.

A wider issue is whether we *possess* rights at all. It may be argued that rights are not possessions that we acquire at birth and carry around with us, but are freedoms and benefits that we *confer* on each other. My right to walk down the street unmolested is given to me by you and vice versa. If rights are indeed granted to one another, then they are not inalienable because they are subject to agreement rather than determining the agreement. Thus rights are really legal rights, rights that we have all agreed should become law. They probably represent our deepest and strongest moral convictions, such as the right to life (the sanctity of life) and the right to self-determination. But as moral values, they are debatable matters of opinion, not facts about people. Thus the philosopher, Bentham, called *natural* rights 'nonsense on stilts'. In his view, rights were legal creations designed to maximise happiness. So their status becomes social conventions, based on what individuals regard as in their interests, hence the international agreement of the European Convention on Human Rights.

If we agree that rights are not God given or a natural possession, then Locke's reason for making a contract and the nature of that contract is a fiction. If rights are created by societies, then individuals have nothing to trade in and negotiate when they enter the contract. The whole thesis of a demand for minimal government and authority as a trust disappears. The notion of a rational individual voluntarily transferring power also vanishes if there never was such a state of nature.

On the other hand, we could adopt the moral thesis that some rights are so essential to being human that without them humanity vanishes. So although we are not born with them and do not possess them (*facts*), we may argue that certain rights are intrinsic to what we understand to be a genuine human existence. Thus governments could be obligated still to protect these *moral* claims to universal freedoms.

Introduction to human rights

In December 1948 the United Nations produced its Universal Declaration of Human Rights which stated the following.

- All human beings are born free and equal.
- Everyone has the right to life, liberty and freedom from fear and violence.
- Everyone has the right to protection of the law without discrimination.
- No one shall be subjected to arbitrary arrest, detention or exile.
- Everyone has the right to a fair and public trial.

- Everyone charged with a penal offence has the right to be assumed innocent until proved guilty.
- No one shall be subjected to arbitrary interference with his privacy, family, home or correspondence, nor to attacks on his reputation.
- Everyone has the right to a nationality.
- Everyone has the right to freedom of movement within his own country and abroad.
- Adults have the right to marry and found a family regardless of race or religion.
- Both men and women are entitled to equal rights within marriage and in divorce.
- Everyone has the right to own property. No one should be arbitrarily deprived of his property.
- Everyone has the right to freedom of thought, conscience and religion and the right to express their opinion both privately and publicly.
- Everyone has the right to attend meetings and join associations.
- No one should be forced to join an association.
- Everyone has the right to take part in the government of his or her country.
- Everyone has the right to work and to just and favourable conditions of employment.
- Everyone has the right to equal pay for equal work.
- Everyone has the right to fair pay to enable him or his family to live with self-respect.
- Everyone has the right to join a trade union.
- Everyone has the right to rest and leisure, including reasonable working hours and holidays with pay.
- Everyone has the right to a standard of living adequate for their health and well-being including housing, medical care and social security in the event of unemployment, sickness, widowhood and old age.
- Everyone has the right to an education.
- Everyone has the right to enjoy the cultural life of the community and to share in its scientific advancements and benefits.
- Everyone has duties to the community to ensure the full recognition and respect of the rights and freedoms of others.

Christian viewpoint

Each individual is truly a person, with a nature that is endowed with intelligence and free will, and rights and duties … these rights and duties are universal and inviolable.

Think about

- Are there any rights you find strange or controversial? Does this suggest they are legal?
- Are some more moral and basic than others, inalienable?
- Do some conflict? What does this indicate?
- Do some rights conform to negative freedom and some to positive freedom?
- Justify the right to education.

Notice the last bullet point in the Universal Declaration of Human Rights.

- Are these facts or values?
- Can you think of a situation where you would expect people to give up their rights?

How would you convince a regime that violated and completely ignored human rights that they were politically obliged to restore them. Would the terms 'happiness', 'human self-fulfilment', 'flourishing' and 'self-realisation' be more useful than an appeal to a state of nature?

Rousseau

For Rousseau, we agree to become citizens, to exchange a limited freedom for a glorious liberty which offers the opportunity to develop. We bring no rights with us or we surrender any claim to individual preference. Instead, we master and control our self-interest in order that we can participate in the collective enterprise. Examples of such benefits will be efficient transport systems, enhanced food production, a national health service and so on. This increased freedom is achieved through cooperation when our private will coincides with the general will to achieve our common good.

Yet this theory has an enigmatic and perhaps sinister implication. If we do not agree with the general will and assent to the common good, then our belief is regarded as deficient, irrational and not what we really want. And many people might object to being told where their real interest lies. For example, the present UK government believes it is in the real interest of all young people to stay in education until the age of 18, but they have yet to persuade young people themselves. As 'the common good' is crucial to Rousseau's justification of the social contract, it is important to examine it more closely.

Rousseau argues that the good of the community is a higher good and is superior to private, self-interest. To find this common good, each citizen is required to focus on what is good for everyone. If there is a difference of opinion, then debate should take place until there is unanimous agreement on what is in everyone's interest. Because everyone will benefit, this will be voted for by everyone and becomes the general will. This general will then becomes the law. In describing this process, Rousseau makes two assumptions:

1 There is no loss of freedom, as the law enacts what everyone agrees is the right thing to do. So the law only enforces what we all want to do anyway!
2 That focusing on the common good allows us to share in benefits that we can only achieve as a group, and these benefits are superior to what we might achieve as individuals.

Both of these assumptions look very idealistic and perhaps unconvincing.

It is quite likely that not everyone will be able to agree on what is right for the group. The belief that we can discard conflicting opinions and 'distil' a pure consensus could be very unrealistic. Most political debates happen because we do not agree on the public interest. We might all agree that the happiness of the individual is important, but that is a fairly empty piece of common ground. The conflicts will appear as soon as we begin to define happiness and how it can be achieved.

Secondly, there may be confusion over what the concept of the common good actually means and consequently whether it is a higher interest.

Think about

Everyone's a winner?

Let us assume that your college/school is considering whether to attract more students. It will be argued that more students means that there will be more money available to spend on the educational process. Surely this is a public interest, a common good.

But can you think of ways in which the money could be spent?

1 for the good of the institution (school/college)
2 for the good of each individual in the institution
3 for the good of the most involved members of the institution

Point 1 is the good of the whole, 2 is the good of each part in the whole and 3 is the majority of the parts.

Here are three possibilities:

1 using the extra money to revamp the prospectus or organise a series of publicity days
2 replacing the chairs in each classroom with more comfortable seats
3 building a new science laboratory.

All three possibilities might be represented as the common good. Which would you accept? Supposing now you are told that each class will be larger, because of the increased intake of students. Would you still regard it as in the common interest to attract more students? The problem with this concept, therefore, is that there is no way to ensure that the benefits and disadvantages are apportioned equally. Inevitably, what might be represented as a common interest results in winners and losers.

The philosopher Mill was very critical of the concept of the common good and the idea that we would be free because the law only enacts what we all want. He believed that such a public interest would result in a tyranny. He maintained that we are very unlikely to get point 2 above. We are far more likely to get point 1 where our private interests are ignored for the sake of the state. For example, the reputation of the country may be put above the interests of the citizens. Otherwise, we are likely to get point 3 where the majority might benefit but a minority will not. This is part of what he meant by the phrase 'the tyranny of the majority'. Thus an influential group will dominate discussions and will benefit, while others are forced to conform.

Furthermore, there is no guarantee that what we might agree on is also the wisest decision. We might all decide to spend the extra money on a 'drunken pleasure-cruise' (Plato). There is no direct correlation between unanimity and wisdom, as Plato would point out. Rousseau realised this and therefore introduced a role for a 'wise legislator' to guide the people on what to choose. So the people no longer set the agenda, and critics will see this as a real infringement of freedom.

Rousseau maintains 'that of itself, the people always wishes the good; of itself it does not always see it'. Everyone who is familiar with the totalitarian regimes of the 20th century will recognise the danger of this. Giving such power to someone runs the risk of a Machiavellian figure gaining control of the decision-making process. If a clear public interest is not discernible by the people, then surely Locke's minimal government with built-in checks and balances is preferable.

Conversely, we might reason that as globalisation reveals the need for global solutions to global problems, then more than ever we need to agree on common goods. The problems of scarce resources, increasing population and pollution affect us all and, *guided* by experts, we need to find solutions. Thus the debate over Rousseau's account of political obligation is set to continue.

Rawls

Rawls presents a contemporary version of the contract theory, with a presumption of tacit consent. However, his state of nature is not an 'initial position' of equality. In fact it is decidedly unequal because some people have talent, strength and resources, and some do not. People are born with advantages and disadvantages. So Rawls proposes a thought experiment in order to achieve justice between 'rational and mutually self interested parties'.

> no one knows his place in society … nor does anyone know his future … the principles of justice are chosen behind a veil of ignorance.
>
> *Rawls (1999)*

If you set out to play a game with friends, before you start you will clarify or lay down the rules of what is fair and permissible and what is not. This is an important procedure because at this stage, no one knows how the game will unfold and who will benefit. Thus the consent to this social contract is founded on the fact that the game (social structure) will be just. A just set of laws, impartially determined is both rational and self-interested. As we are behind a veil of ignorance, we have no idea whether we will personally benefit from the laws or not. So we give our consent to this fair procedure and continue to give consent by participating in the game and accepting the benefits alongside obligations.

This is the moral thesis in the state of nature and is intended 'to represent equality between human beings as moral persons'. It asks us to set aside our inequalities of privilege, talent, etc. (these are matters of fact), so that we choose impartial laws leading to equal treatment of all (value). It is in our interest to be fair because we do not know whether we will be a winner or a loser in the game. So this veil of ignorance encourages everyone to 'step into each other's shoes'. We will want to improve everyone's access to the good life and to maximise benefits for all. Thus Rawls contends we will 'maximise the minimum', we will ensure that the worst off in society fares better than they might otherwise do. We will choose this in case we should end up as one of the worst off.

Needless to say, the theory becomes controversial as soon as we try to set out exactly what a fair and impartial society will look like. Possible objections to this process are listed below. See if you remember having the same problems when you set up a game.

Key philosopher

John Rawls (1921–2002)

In *A Theory of Justice* (1971), he argued a contractarian defence of liberal principles of justice. He maintains that this conception of justice is most likely to gain an 'overlapping consensus' in modern pluralist societies.

Think about

Which of these 'income parades' will maximise the minimum?

1 A gets 10 slices, B gets five slices, C gets one slice.

2 A gets seven slices, B gets five slices, C gets four slices.

3 A gets seven slices, B gets seven slices, C gets two slices.

What kind of distribution of income would this represent in society?

1 People are never completely unbiased when they choose rules. We bring with us inclinations and beliefs, which means we choose rules to suit ourselves.

   a likes risk

   b likes security

2 We are already in society. The game is already under way. So we do know what privileges we have, and that makes it difficult to be impartial when we need a new rule.

   a knows she is strong and likes competition

   b knows she is vulnerable and seeks support

3 We may not agree to maximise the minimum. Some will argue that natural talent should be rewarded, and that even if you try to balance out inequalities, the talented will always become richer, and the weaker will always become poorer. That is life.

   a likes sudden-death games and winner takes all

   b prefers a limit on how much you can win and lose

If you were behind a veil of ignorance, what kind of economic laws would you choose for your society?

The important question is whether you would feel equally obligated to obey laws in whichever society you found yourself. Or are there laws that you would not be prepared to endure. This is the problem of basing political obligation on justice. We may not ever agree on what constitutes a just society. It will be remembered that Rawls maintains that 'there is nothing unusual in being required to comply with unjust laws', but he also adds, 'provided the injustice does not exceed certain limits'. And that is the crux. Some players may regard a competitive, high-risk economy as perfectly fair and desirable, while others would redistribute wealth from those who have, to those who are in need. If you are not sympathetic to the economic and social system of your society, you might find life intolerable.

One way to alleviate this problem is to ensure there are adequate opportunities in society to show dissent and to effect change. This will be discussed in the next topic.

Does political legitimacy require popular approval?

Think about

Some will argue that an authority only has legitimacy if they have gained approval from the majority of the people. Below are different views on this. Sort them out into those for and those against. Can you develop each of these points into a sustained argument?

Plato: a legitimate ruler has knowledge that is not available to everyone. The people may not realise this. What do philosophers know?	Rousseau: a legitimate rule must be one accepted as the common good, which will be agreed by all. How do we arrive at the common good?
Machiavelli: a legitimate ruler must be feared in order to secure obedience. It may be necessary to be cruel. Why is it better to be feared than to be loved?	Locke: a legitimate government loses its authority when it ceases to protect our human rights. We are then entitled to rebel. How do we justify human rights?

Rawls: we should obey the law because it offers a just society, when we choose behind a veil of ignorance. What does he suggest is a fair society?	Mill: the majority can be a tyranny and it is not legitimate to expect individuals and minorities to conform to the wishes of the majority. How does he criticise the concept of the common good?
How do we accurately assess what is the majority view? Different distributions of votes lead to different interpretations of results. How do we measure popular approval?	The consent of the majority can be manufactured. The people are fickle and easily swayed. Referenda may not deliver wise decisions. Who/what should we vote for?

Is the notion of consent a useful device?

We have seen that contract theorists claim that consent in one way or another justifies political obligation. It legitimises power. Where they differ is how/when we consent and what we agree to and why.

However, some philosophers deny that society is based on consent and some form of contract. Hume enquires whether it is the consent itself which entails obligation or whether it is simply the benefits that persuade people to obey authority. He distinguishes between:

1 an obligation based on consent and keeping our word and
2 an obligation based on self-interest and utility.

> If the reason be asked of that obedience, which we are bound to pay to government, I readily answer, Because society could not otherwise subsist; and this answer is clear and intelligible to all mankind. Your answer is, Because we should keep our word. But besides, that no body, till trained in a philosophical system, can either comprehend or relish this answer; besides this, I say, you find yourself embarrassed when it is asked, Why we are bound to keep our word? Nor can you give any answer but what would, immediately, without any circuit, have accounted for our obligation to allegiance.

Hume (1947a)

His argument is that point 1 actually collapses into point 2 on closer inspection. We only keep our word because it is useful for us to do so. So consent is not by itself a reason for obligation, it is simply useful to us that we keep our word. So it is really self-interest or the benefits (why we consent) that is an explanation of our obedience to authority. The need for a contract is redundant.

Once we separate the importance of consent from obligation, then allegiance to a sovereign is just a matter of evolution. We have come to accept authority over time out of necessity or advantage and more often as a matter of habit. The contract theorists are wrong to dress this up as *moral* obligation:

> when we reflect on the advantage, which results from such human instincts … (to live in society) … we pay them the just tribute of moral approbation.

Hume (1947a)

but in actual fact, obedience is

> performed from a sense of obligation, when we consider the necessities of human society

Hume (1947a)

A contract could only be agreed by people already in a society

This view supports a second criticism. Critics point out that a sense of obligation because we agreed to something, and the very notion of a contract, are in fact moral conventions. Moral conventions only arise from social education. The idea of obligation arises out of and presupposes a social morality where binding agreements between people are understood. So the concept of moral obligation is logically prior to the concept of a binding contract. Therefore contracts cannot be used to derive moral obligations to other citizens and to a sovereign. Contracts are born out of pre-existing social relationships and understanding, so cannot be used to determine those relationships. Only people who are already in society could make a contract. So the need for a contract and consent become redundant.

This leads us to think about an alternative view of political obligation. Society has not been constructed according to people's wishes but has evolved out of necessity. The idea of pre-societal man is a nonsense. We have always lived in society and the nature of obligation has naturally developed as society has developed. The analogy with a family is useful. Obligations and duties within a family change and develop as the family grows up. So as social institutions have developed through history our opinion on the nature of the individual and the need for obedience has also altered. The emphasis on consent is a product of a society that values individual liberty and acquiescence rather than force and imposition. The notion of contracts is the expression of a community that already has a moral code and wishes to bind its citizens further to certain agreements about their rights and duties.

Thus Aristotle claims in Book 1 of his *Politics* that 'the state is both natural and prior to the individual'. Man is by nature a political animal and it is his nature to live in a state. With regard to political obligation, it is a matter of natural superiority that 'every household is ruled by its senior member'. The individual only gains purpose and importance through his or her relationship to the whole. 'For the whole must be prior to the parts. Separate hand or foot from the whole body … and it will have been ruined by such treatment.' If we agree with Aristotle, then the debate about political obligation cannot be about *whether* we are obligated, but about the nature of the relationship between citizens and the state. That is a discussion about what constitutes justice and harmony. It is a debate about values not facts. How should the political 'body' function? What is a healthy and harmonious body politic? So the question of whether we consented or not has disappeared!

In assessing whether political obligation is founded on consent, we need to consider a number of issues:

- When/how did we consent? Is there an act which we can use as evidence?
- What do we consent to? Is it just a government, or a set of policies, or a constitution, or political authority itself?
- If political obligation is legitimised by the benefits we receive, are these benefits clear, coherent and genuine?

- When we examine attempts to *legitimise* power, do they actually dissolve into simply the *exercise* of power?
- Is it consent which is at the heart of political obligation or is it self-interest?
- Is society founded on consent at all? Or is society logically and empirically prior to notions of contracts and agreements that bind individuals?

After working through this topic, you should:

- be able to describe different kinds of consent and contracts
- be able to discuss definitions of power and authority
- understand the difficulties of basing political authority on popular approval
- understand the debate over whether consent justifies political authority

Disobedience and dissent

Learning objectives:

- to explore whether political obligation entails the right to dissent
- to describe different forms of dissent and disobedience and their justification
- to discuss the proper scope of the law
- to evaluate whether violent revolution is ever justified.

Introduction

In the last topic we discussed what made authority legitimate and the role of consent in that process. The alternative possibility is that a government could be illegitimate, and that instead of consent, we dissent. If the individual fails to live up to a contract they can be punished. But what if the government fails the people? What should the people be entitled to do?

In this topic we shall consider what our four contract theorists would say about dissent and disobedience. Initially you might consider that at least two would not view dissent favourably – why? We shall also review the arguments of the philosopher, Mill, who wrote extensively on freedom and the legitimate role of government in *On Liberty*. And finally we will consider the possibility of revolution and the theory of Marx.

There are lots of different ways in which a citizen might protest, from voicing dissent to violent rebellion. In modern Britain we take the former for granted, but there are countries where free speech is not permitted. We shall therefore discuss Mill's famous defence of free speech. At the other extreme is the complete overthrow of a corrupt, political system, 'ridding itself of all the muck of ages' (Marx, 1970b), and the case for revolution will be scrutinised. Some famous figures have advocated non-violent protest and passive resistance, such as boycotts, which operate within the law. Others justify civil disobedience: the deliberate violation of the law in order to draw attention to and rectify an injustice. This must be clearly distinguished from any personal vendetta or self-interest so that it is a public act of breaking the law in order to draw attention to the moral issue.

Below is a list of ways in which you might demonstrate your objection to authority. Do you have any views on what is acceptable and what is not?

- *Voicing dissent* and publishing anti-government material.
- *Marches* to show disagreement and strength of feeling.
- *Boycotts*: not using a product or a service in order to cause difficulties for the authorities.
- *Non-cooperation:* not performing a task, such as completing paperwork, in order to obstruct government.
- *Strikes*: withdrawing labour to disrupt the workplace.
- *Mass demonstration* which defies public order arrangements.
- *Civil disobedience*: breaking the law, such as trespass or damage to property, or not paying taxes.
- *Rebellion*: overthrowing a particular regime while accepting the political system or constitution.
- *Revolution*: overthrowing the whole political organisation in order to achieve a radical, new social structure.

Most campaigns against injustice will of course employ a number of tactics, and different types of protest are not always clear-cut and distinct. Thus, one person deliberately breaking the law is small-scale civil disobedience, but a million people doing so is close to rebellion. Do you find there is a problem reconciling **autonomy** and **social utility**? How would Locke and Rousseau respond?

One important consideration is that the degree of protest should be proportionate to the injustice. Think about a moral cause of your own, or consider the facts about child labour below.

> Child labour has serious consequences that stay with the individual and with society for far longer than the years of childhood. Young workers not only face dangerous working conditions. They face long-term physical, intellectual and emotional stress. They face an adulthood of unemployment and illiteracy.
>
> *United Nations Secretary-General **Kofi Annan***

> We have no time for study and education, no time to play and rest, we are exposed to unsafe working conditions and we are not protected.

Children's Forum Against the Most Intolerable Forms of Child Labour, Bangkok, 1997

How big is the problem?

The International Labour Organization estimates there are 246 million working children aged between five and 17:

- 179 million are estimated to work in the worst forms of child labour – one in every eight of the world's 5–17-year-olds
- 111 million children under 15 are in hazardous work and should be 'immediately withdrawn from this work'
- 8.4 million children are in slavery, trafficking, debt bondage and other forms of forced labour, forced recruitment for armed conflict, prostitution, pornography and other illicit activities

- Some of the cheap goods sold in this country are made by young children in sweat shops.

Before you pursue the arguments in this topic, you might wish to research some of the most famous cases of dissent and disobedience in order to find out exactly what action the protestors took and whether it achieved their ends. For example:

- the suffragettes and the fight for equal rights for women
- the Russian Revolution and the overthrow of Tsar Nicholas II, who believed in his divine right to rule
- Oskar Schindler who subverted Nazi orders about the treatment of Jews in the Second World War
- national liberation movements such as India's struggle for independence, led by Gandhi. Gandhi advocated non-violent protest 'in defence of the truth'
- the civil rights campaigns and anti-apartheid struggles led by Martin Luther King in the US and Nelson Mandela in South Africa
- the CND anti-nuclear campaign against the proliferation of nuclear weapons
- the Animal Liberation Front and their violent action to stop cruelty to animals
- the overthrow of dictators such as Pinochet in Chile or Franco in Spain
- British soldiers who have campaigned against the war in Iraq.

In your research, you might consider whether the reason for the dissent – the injustice, merited the kind of civil disobedience that was taken. Was it reasonable and proportionate?

This topic will address two aspects of dissent and disobedience:

- Are we entitled to protest? What are the arguments for and against?
- What kind of protest is justified?

The second part of the topic will focus on:

- voicing dissent
- civil disobedience
- revolution and violence.

⁊ Are we entitled to show dissent and disobedience?

The moral challenge

Socrates initiated the debate about whether an individual or group is entitled to challenge authority on moral grounds, when considering his own execution. His arguments against disobeying the state take two forms:

- **deontological**
- **teleological**.

1 Deontological ethics: Socrates cites two principles that lie at the heart of any moral society:

   a two wrongs do not make a right: 'so one ought not to return a wrong … whatever the provocation is'

   b 'One ought to fulfil all one's agreements'.

> ### Key terms
>
> **Deontological:** deontological ethics considers the rightness or wrongness of the act itself. It refers to moral duties that we ought to perform regardless of the consequences. They are usually justified on religious or rational grounds. The opposite is teleological, where one acts for a purpose or to achieve favourable consequences.
>
> **Teleological:** everthing has a telos or purpose. Thus, in ethics, both individual actions have a purpose, and also inherent in human nature is a function or purpose.

2 Teleological ethics: Socrates also points out the dire consequences if individuals disregard the laws, whenever they feel wronged: 'Do you imagine that a city can continue to exist and not be turned upside down if the legal judgements … can be nullified and destroyed by private persons?'

Socrates raises an important issue for the would-be dissenter. To live in society is to accept the rule of law and the benefits that order and justice bring. It is therefore right to obey the law. So a protestor has to be sure that the moral case for disobedience outweighs the moral case for obeying the laws. And this is not an easy matter to assess. For example, many people would support the cause of animal welfare, but not acknowledge that breaking the law to cause distress to scientists and farmers is reasonable. Does an injustice ever merit breaches of public order and the violation of individual rights? This will always be a controversial debate, particularly if the law is supported by a majority. The question then becomes an issue of whether the will of the majority takes precedence over the minority, or whether this is a tyranny. A further issue is whether the law has encroached into an area of our lives where it ought not to meddle. This will be discussed later with Mill and the Hart-Devlin debate on homosexuality.

However, the views of Socrates are opposed by some 19th-century thinkers such as Thoreau and Wolff. They argue that individual conscience overrides law: 'I think we should be men first and subjects afterwards. It is not desirable to cultivate a respect for the law, so much as for the right' (from *Civil Disobedience* by Thoreau, in Palmer, 1991).

And Wolff argues that there will always be conflict between the right to rule and the moral autonomy of the individual, and that we must side with the individual for we cannot avoid being moral creatures.

You will remember that Locke argued that:

- the government is only legitimate if it upholds our claim to natural rights
- individuals should have as much moral freedom as is compatible with dispensing justice.

If either was not respected then the contract was under threat. Locke seems to have thought in terms of two agreements: a contract with society and a consensual arrangement with the government based on trust. This agreement with the government is fiduciary, that is, the government is trusted to act for the good of the community, but it has no claim on the people in return. If the obligations of government are not kept, then authority dissolves. Contrary to Hobbes, the people are entitled to rebellion in order to remove an untrustworthy government. However, for Locke this would not return everyone to the state of nature as the contract with the community would remain intact.

A possible criticism of Locke is the notion of a community without a sovereign power: 'when any number of men have so consented to make one community or government, they are so incorporated' (Locke, 1947). Locke's belief that a community can be a voluntary coherence of members is unrealistic. Without a power to enforce coherence, society will return to the uncertain state of nature. For Socrates and Hobbes this means chaos.

Nevertheless we must still consider whether the supremacy of the individual conscience is acceptable. We will sidestep the issue of whether conscience is an 'internal voice' or an aspect of social conditioning, and agree with Thoreau that we cannot expect human beings to obey the law unthinkingly and unquestioningly: 'The mass of men serve the state thus, not as men mainly, but as machines, with their bodies … in most cases, there is no free exercise whatever of the judgement, or the moral sense' (extract in Palmer, 1991).

This seems persuasive. It is surely a denial of the full potential of a human life to expect people to obey the law as if they were robots. Can you think of tragic examples in history?

Nevertheless, one can also require that an individual's moral voice is sufficiently well grounded as to provide a sufficient justification for challenging the law. In other words, is the moral objection genuine and serious enough?

Think about

Consider the following reasons for breaking the law. Do you think they are sufficient?

- The law does not maximise the happiness of the people, e.g. a law that stops people having full access to the internet.
- The law does not respect our basic human rights, e.g. the law that detains terror suspects for long periods of imprisonment without trial.
- The law does not respect religious commandments, e.g. a law that allows abortion of a foetus under 27 weeks.
- The law has an unacceptable understanding of equality, e.g. a law that permits young people to be paid less than the minimum wage.
- The law does not promote social utility, e.g. a law that allows private citizens to own a gun.

In making your decisions, you have begun to weigh up whether moral objections should override respect for the law. A sensitive government would of course take steps to consult, perhaps compromise, and provide avenues for dissent so that protest does not endanger public order yet goes some way towards meeting the moral concern of individuals. But often this is just not possible. The impasse can then only be resolved by an exercise of power. Here the authority has dissolved into a test of strength.

One view of these conflicts is that the law should be obeyed because it is the expression of the legitimate authority, a command by the sovereign power. If the law has been produced in a proper, constitutional manner, for example decided by a parliamentary democracy, then that is sufficient. It is the will of the political leaders, who are entitled to expect obedience. It is not necessary for the law to conform to some higher moral authority. This would be the view of Hobbes, that a law emanating from an appropriate source is a valid law regardless of its moral content. If the sovereign wishes to regulate social behaviour in a particular way he is entitled to do so.

However, this would imply that laws from grossly oppressive but legitimate regimes have to be obeyed, whatever. The well-known example is the election of the Nazi party to power in the 1930s in Germany.

Think about

Who would you side with in these cases?

- nurses and policemen who strike for a fair salary
- a soldier who refuses to fight in a war he considers unjust, and is court-martialled
- pro-life campaigners who break into an abortion clinic and destroy equipment.

There is also a problem for international law. If the law is simply the command of the sovereign power, then how can we judge disputes between nations? At the moment, the UN Charter of Rights provides a moral standard to resolve such disputes, but that is based on a contract between nations who sign up to this higher, moral authority; although, under contract theory, it must be remembered that people consented in order to be liberated from violence, insecurity and instability. So we must conclude that the content of the law is significant, and legitimacy cannot just derive from the process by which it is formulated. Otherwise it becomes merely 'organised force' or 'systematic violence'. The UN rights are not 'a child of the law', but should determine the law.

Finally, it must be stressed that so far we have assumed that the laws are fairly drafted and enacted:

- that a law should make a general pronouncement and not victimise a particular group. It applies to all citizens
- that laws are not the whim of one person, but develop from a proper constitutional process
- that a law is not retrospective and is not used to punish past actions. Everyone must be able to be aware of the law, which is predictable and known in advance.

The wisdom of ages

A different approach to dissent and disobedience emanates from those philosophers who, like Hobbes, fear the random, violent and chaotic state that people degenerate into when they lose their respect for the law. The **conservative** view stresses the need for law and order and, like Plato, would see the law as expressing the wisdom of leaders who have special qualities. Plato argues that wise leaders will necessarily be impartial, far-seeing, courageous, truthful and civilised, and 'best able to guard the laws and customs of society'. This past wisdom has been entrusted to us by previous generations through our laws and customs, and any change that is not carefully considered endangers the state. The state is 'the rule of reason'. It embraces virtue and ensures the moral health of the nation.

Thus, for example, the education system does not just impart knowledge in order to train a workforce. It provides a set of values, a sense of identity and place in society that should be respected as over and above the personal beliefs of individuals. The conservative view is that the whole is more than the sum of its parts. It therefore directly challenges the emphasis on individualism of society. The social fabric (Church, family, state and education system) create, develop and embody a heritage that guides relationships between individuals and is much more than just a collection of individual beliefs. The social structure of our society is fashioned from century-old beliefs and practices that have evolved over time and enshrine knowledge that extends far beyond any individual's comprehension and limited capacity to reason. If we break the law, we damage this cohesion and thus the health of the nation.

So, while individual consciences should contribute to the progress of society and the evolution of beliefs and practices, encouraging gradual change and reform that can be tested by practical application, civil disobedience causes conflict and harm and should be suppressed. In the conservative model, revolutionary change only brings disaster. Attempts to create a new social order, however rational, are doomed to failure because they over-rate any individual's ability to reason.

Key terms

Conservative: with a small 'c', refers to an ideology that wishes to conserve the accumulated wisdom of a heritage, which has stood the test of time. This is embodied in law.

We are afraid to put men to live and trade each upon his own private stock or reason; because we suspect that this stock in each man is small, and that individuals would do better to avail themselves of the general bank and capital of nations, and of ages.

Burke from Reflections on the Revolution in France, *quoted more extensively in* **Gaus** *(2000)*

This challenges the fact that all people are rational and emphasises the emotional, instinctive and irrational aspects of our nature. An individual cannot fully grasp the mysteries of life and can only theorise. It is in society that real experience and knowledge are gained. So we must protect the social structure and develop respect for tradition and the law.

This thesis is famously challenged by the **liberal** philosopher, Mill. He argues in *On Liberty* that because the conservative society is resistant to change, it will not meet the needs of new generations. Then social progress is stifled under the dead weight of custom and tradition. He cites the example of China in the 19th century where 'the despotism of custom' crushed the spirit of liberty. The result is that talented individuals and geniuses cannot thrive and stimulate change and progress. The result is a mediocre, undynamic society that is loath to improve morally and intellectually.

Mill himself, in contrast to the above, emphasises the wisdom of individuals. He argues that individuals know more about their own personal circumstances than anyone else. Traditional wisdom from past generations may be too narrow, wrongly interpreted, or not suitable to new, modern conditions, and will inevitably be generalised. Furthermore, it is the individual who cares more what happens to them, society's interest will only be indirect. And also, individuals can only develop by making their own decisions and following the dictates of their own conscience, rather than from passive obedience. A person 'who chooses his plan for himself employs all his faculties' and grows accordingly. So challenge of accepted ideas and the law is to be encouraged. 'The young should be taught to question'! Here man is depicted as a progressive being, who can learn from his experience, 'and requires to grow and develop itself on all sides, according to the tendency of the inward forces, which make it a living thing' (Mill, 1985).

Underpinning these divergent views on the relationship between the state and the individual is a differing conception of human nature. In trying to decide between the two, you might like to consider the questions that follow.

Key terms

Liberal: with a small 'l', relates to a political ideology, opposed to conservatism in that it is centred on the freedom of the individual as possessing rights and liberties that should not be constrained by government, including rights of equality of respect.

Key philosopher

John Stuart Mill (1806–73)

His moral and political philosophy is based on utilitarianism, but he distinguished between higher and lower pleasures. This he reconciled with a defence of liberty, arguing that equal liberty for all would maximise happiness.

Think about

- Is there such a thing as social and moral progress? Or do we make the same mistakes over and over again?
- Do individuals actually know what is best for themselves? Or are we fallible, even about our own circumstances and relationships?
- Can we reason our way to what is an ideal society or, in Burke's words, is reason 'presumptuous ignorance'?
- Does the law represent 'the wisdom of ages' or the 'prejudice of ages'?

■ Mill contends that 'human nature is not a machine to be built after a model, and set to do exactly the work prescribed for it, but a tree, which requires to grow and develop itself on all sides, according to the tendency of the inward forces, which make it a living thing'.

Do you agree?

How far should the law intrude into our private lives?

The liberal attitude

In *On Liberty*, Mill (1985) professes to be a utilitarian: 'I regard utility as the ultimate appeal on all ethical questions'. But his thesis shows that maximum happiness can only be obtained by granting each citizen the most extensive negative liberty. Thus Mill sets the boundaries for law. His main principle is that 'legal penalties', which interfere with 'the liberty of action' are only justified 'to prevent harm to others'. He cannot 'be rightfully compelled' to act for his own good or because others regard it as wise to do so.

This is a direct attack on Rousseau's conception of the common good. Mill advocates a maximum amount of private ('self-regarding') life, free from interference. This will allow individuals to grow and develop their potential to be original and autonomous and this will result in fulfilment and happiness. Happy, flourishing individuals make up a successful, progressing society – thus the utilitarian ideal. So citizens should fight against nearly all forms of social control: 'all restraint is an evil', and government is only justified in preventing people from encroaching on one another's liberty and harming each other. There are also a few minimum duties that can be demanded for the defence and protection of people. Like Locke, the role for government is minimal otherwise it is a tyranny, and in a democracy it becomes 'the tyranny of the majority'. In a rousing attack on state intervention, Mill concludes: 'a State which dwarfs its men, in order that they may be more docile instruments in its hands even for beneficial purposes – will find that with small men no great thing can really be accomplished.'

The foundation of Mill's argument is our fallibility. There is 'no certain truth', so dissent and individuality must be allowed at all times. The main thrust of his argument is set out below.

Do you accept each stage of Mill's argument or would you challenge his assertions?

■ Fallibility – no certain truth – truth is complex
↓

■ We are experts on our own lives
↓

■ Therefore, no interference with individuals – liberty allows different experiments in living and diversity of values and ideas
↓

■ This will generate individuality, spontaneity and originality
↓

■ Happy, progressive individuals will develop and flourish
↓

- Therefore we will develop a happy, open, progressive society where geniuses can thrive

  ↓

- Utilitarian 'happiness of majority'
- Therefore liberty leads to happiness (it is a necessary but not a sufficient condition).

Think about

What problems can you find with each stage of the argument?

How would you answer the following questions?

- Is 'diversity' of ideas and lifestyles necessarily a good thing? Diversity by itself is a questionable value. We do not want diversity of evil!
- Does not interfering with individuals mean not supporting them, not resolving conflict and not promoting social cohesion?
- Does a collection of happy individuals automatically blend into an integrated and flourishing team? Do we need rules and practices to harmonise the group?
- Does empirical evidence show that geniuses have developed successfully in repressive societies as well as open tolerant ones?

The conclusion that Mill comes to is that we should resist any encroachment of the state into our private lives. Chapter 4 of 'On Liberty' is entitled, 'Of the limits to the authority of society over the individual' and it concludes: 'I am not aware that any community has a right to force another to be civilised'. This invites the crucial question: what should be the limit to the power of the state? And what interference should be resisted? Some may argue that we need a more paternalistic state, that supports and cares for its citizens like a parent.

Think about

Consider the following areas of public life and try to decide when the state is justified in intervening in our lives.

What is the proper role of the state?

What are the limits of sovereignty?

- Social organisation, e.g. should governments run the main transport systems? Should road/rail be privatised?
- Economic management, e.g. should governments control economic systems, restrict monopolies, assist the unemployed, etc.?
- Social justice, e.g. should governments redistribute wealth or maintain some form of equality?
- Moral leadership, e.g. should governments interfere with gambling, prostitution, foxhunting on private land, etc.?
- Education, e.g. should governments control the school curriculum – sex education, religious education, etc.?

The Hart–Devlin debate

A 20th-century debate on how far the law should extend into our private lives was provided by the Hart–Devlin debate in the 1960s over the legalisation of homosexuality. Devlin argued against new permissive legislation on the grounds that the law should enforce morality, even in private life.

If moral behaviour becomes too lax, it threatens the fabric of society. Our private lives can affect attitudes and our respect for one another and authority. So if sexual practices cause revulsion, the moral 'health' of the nation should be protected. For example, we find incest and paedophilia repugnant. They degrade human beings and are a 'moral pollution'. So there is a public duty on the government to forbid such acts. An interesting case is that the generation of disgusting electronic images, which need not involve anyone else, is regarded as morally depraved and punishable. Recently, a judge also sent several men to prison for sadomasochistic acts that were so disgusting as to be unacceptable, even though the men were consenting adults. People should be protected from themselves.

Hart, on the other hand, argued that the morality of sexual behaviour is not the proper concern of the law. Sexual practice among consenting adults is a 'victimless crime', that should be decriminalised. As long as people do not harm each other directly and without consent, then the law should stay out of people's private lives. The proper business of the law should be to ensure that people can live together, not to make them better people.

Homosexuality was decriminalised, but which way would you vote on the justified scope of the law? Should the state concern itself with how citizens behave in their private lives, or should we resist the intrusion?

Think about

- Do we need shared moral bonds to make our social relationships more predictable, easier to develop and cohesive?
- Do we need a shared understanding of how to behave and is there a moral code that we can all agree on?
- Instead of enforcing moral values, is it not better to be tolerant of a variety of lifestyles?
- What we do in our private lives surely does not affect anyone else, does it? Or is no man an island?
- But surely every law has a moral content – can we avoid dictating morality? Even a 30 mph speed limit indicates that the safety of pedestrians is more important than the speed of the motorist.

What kind of dissent and disobedience is permissible?

In this section we consider the case for:

- voicing dissent
- civil disobedience
- revolution.

Dissent and freedom of speech

At the beginning of Chapter 2 in *On Liberty*, Mill states in stark terms his views on allowing freedom of dissent: 'If all mankind minus one were of one opinion, mankind would be no more justified in silencing that one person, than he, if he had the power, would be justified in silencing mankind'.

Mill would have agreed with Voltaire that though I may strongly disagree with what you say, I defend to the death your right to say it.

Mill presents the following defence of free speech:

■ No one is infallible – there is no certain truth – any error may contain a portion of truth. Mill is making a logical point that to suppress opinion *logically* amounts to an assumption of infallibility.

■ Suppression of discussion is an assumption of infallibility and could lead to tyranny/despotism.

■ To fully understand truth, you have to discuss why it is true – the reasons and justifications.

■ If there is free discussion, the truth is more likely to emerge and falsity be discovered.

■ People have to make judgements – but these are usually from one class/prejudice and do not justify suppression of discussion. Discussion discourages elitism.

Socrates and Christ were regarded as dangerous and ignorant in their own time. Now they are respected, which shows how generations think differently.

Aurelius persecuted Christians because he thought they were a danger to the Roman Empire. Truth was persecuted and this hindered the progress of civilisation. Discussion is necessary for society to progress; it enables the human mind to develop and is important for *eudaemonia* (self-fulfilment).

Why allow people to speak falsely or offer bizarre views? Mill argued that:

■ The truth is strengthened if it has to be defended.

■ Discussion improves the human mind; and part of wisdom is knowing why false opinions are false.

■ If truth is not defended against falsity, it can become dogma and may be distorted/undermined.

How does freedom of speech fit with utilitarianism?

■ Discussion leads to truth. Knowing the truth will in the long term bring happiness.

■ Discussion develops the mind and brings fulfilment in a progressive, tolerant society.

Offence

One of the key issues is the problem of 'offence'. Mill would only limit free speech if it directly led to harm. The problem is assessing the harm that offensive views may cause. Vicious invective is clearly a form of abuse and it can be maintained that repetitive, insensitive and biased commentary is a form of discrimination. Yet where is the dividing line between an occasional, well-argued, balanced criticism and a constant, prejudicial, inflammatory campaign against a minority?

Ideally, if we accept people's right to protest and criticise, we should also ensure a duty to be responsible, moderate and sensitive to the views

Examiner's tip

It is worth looking at passages from Chapter 2 of *On Liberty* to see Mill's arguments in detail. See particularly the first part of the chapter.

■ Think about

Do you agree with all of Mill's arguments? Do truth and utility coincide? Can you think of exceptions? In a democracy minorities have the opportunity to be a majority. Can this happen without free speech?

■ Think about

Is it always possible to interpret 'offence' so widely that it will provide a justification for suppressing *any* contrary view?

of others. And absolutely essential, is a clear opportunity for a right of reply. So, for example, minority opinion must be represented fairly in the media. Liberalism is committed to a pluralistic society, where all people are entitled to form their own values and views. It is also vital therefore that the opportunity to express those views is protected.

Further discussion of these issues will be found in Chapter 6 on tolerance.

At the same time, there is a case for censorship where clear proof of harm can be established, for example pornography and terrorist propaganda. The question for this chapter is whether voicing dissent ever causes harm to a government.

Mill's view was that 'law and authority have no business in restraining' verbal attacks because of the difficulty of establishing whether harm to a government has occurred, and because of the strength of a government's resources to defend itself. Nevertheless, a powerful, modern press campaign has led to the demise of some politicians, and it is difficult to defend yourself against innuendo and emotive propaganda. It is naive to believe that freedom of speech ensures reasoned and responsible debate.

Underpinning Mill's arguments is a belief in social progress, where dissent and playing devil's advocate is essential to discovering an improved and clearer conception of the truth. We see these conflicts of ideas played out in courts of law (prosecution and defence) and in the Houses of Parliament. But we also see how destructive oppositions can be, and how dissent can be misused to destroy faith and create mayhem. Shakespeare's Mark Antony demonstrates that well in *Julius Caesar*, and Plato railed against the sophists whom he portrayed as intellectual charlatans. Apparently the sophist Protagorus taught his students to 'make the weaker argument, the stronger' (Norman, 1998), so as to alter people's perception of what was right or wrong. This is clearly always the danger of allowing open dissent in society.

Nevertheless, there is something persuasive about Mill's contention that being able to express and publish your views is 'one of the principal ingredients of human happiness'; and offence can be so widely interpreted, that it can be used as an excuse to suppress any contrary views. The crux of the issue is to demonstrate that the harm caused by the offence outweighs the harm of suppression. Also, in a democracy, where free speech exists, minorities have the opportunity to persuade others of their cause. Surely rational persuasion is better than imposition. You must decide whether the overall benefit that free speech brings outweighs the possible damage to the common good.

Civil disobedience

Civil disobedience is:

- the deliberate violation of a law
- to draw attention to and rectify an injustice.

Although Rawls argues that there is nothing amiss under a democratic constitution, to being required to obey an unjust law, he also lays down the conditions for justifiable civil disobedience. This assumes, nevertheless, that from behind the veil of ignorance the citizens who consented to the contract would have accepted his principles of justice.

Firstly Rawls argues that disobedience must be a public act, so that it should not appear to be a matter of personal gain or revenge. The clear intention must be to draw attention to an unjust law, and the fact that

Examiner's tip

A starting point for assessing Mill is his initial premise that we are all fallible and there is no certain truth. Would you agree that there are no certain moral truths?

breaking the law may benefit the protestor should be irrelevant. So an unpublicised, secret attack on an animal laboratory looks like a personal vendetta rather than a matter of conscience.

Then Rawls states that while breaking a particular law it is important that general support for the rule of law is demonstrated. So protestors do not avoid punishment in order to show that they accept the (democratic) constitution and only wish to reform a particular aspect of the law. So poll tax protestors in 1990, who refused to pay what they considered to be an immoral tax, nevertheless were prepared to go to prison.

Rawls goes on to say that the degree of disobedience should be proportionate to the injustice. Winning hearts and minds is a necessary condition of changing a law in a democracy; and to retain 'the moral high ground', the damage to society must seem a fair response to the problem. This delicate balance is also demonstrated in strike action, where the public expect the degree of inconvenience to reflect the seriousness of the injustice.

The protestors must show that they have a moral sense, and they do not allow their action to degenerate into terror and violence. It would appear that some animal rights protestors have lost public support in their struggle for the welfare of animals as a result of their inhumane intimidation of scientists. Yet they will maintain that their acts are proportionate to the cruelty inflicted on the animals. Thus what is a sense of proportion is a matter of debate. As has already been noted, the issue is more complicated if the existing law is the will of the majority. Then it would seem it is even more important to allow freedom of speech, to give minorities the opportunity to change public opinion, since disobeying a democratically constituted law is very difficult to justify.

It must also be emphasised that the principles of civil disobedience also demand an equally proportionate response from the authorities. They have a duty:

- to genuinely listen and take note of concern, so that a proper debate can happen
- to make a real attempt to consider the grievance and compromise where possible. The power to make a law is not only in the hands of the sovereign, but can be a reflection of the wishes of the people
- to ensure that government action does not deliberately provoke extreme responses or escalate the grievance
- to observe due process of law so that punishment is fairly and independently administered by the justice system: the government should not interfere in the legal process
- to maintain checks and balances of power, so that those who carry out the law are free from political manipulation.

Needless to say, this limited disobedience is not sufficient if you believe that the whole political system is corrupt. It may deliver gradual, measured reform, but it is not going to overturn a morally bankrupt regime. For this, a revolution must be considered.

Reform or revolution?

Those who advocate reform maintain that huge-scale social disruption rarely achieves anything. People revert to a state of nature, with all of their fears and grievances exposed. Conservatives point to the aftermath of revolutions, such as those in France and Russia, as a time of destructive turmoil. It is far better to build on the past, to allow the evolution of the state, so that through natural selection best practice will emerge. The

> ■ **Think about**
>
> From your research into different causes and civil disobedience at the beginning of this topic, what were the moral issues that justified civil disobedience?
>
> Would they have strengthened their moral case if they had shown passive resistance rather than actually breaking the law?

rational abilities of mankind are limited, and attempts to design Utopias remind us of our fallibilities. Think back to your response to Plato's revolutionary social design, modelled on the beehive (see end of topic one).

Those who advocate revolution claim that reform will only mask the corruption in society. Thus Marxists argue that human rights only give the appearance of freedom (political freedom) but do not provide real economic freedom for the working class. What is the good of free speech if you will be sacked for speaking out? So even though a worker has a right in theory, in practice they may not be able to exercise that right. Restrictions of poverty and limited access to education may also diminish the benefits of being accorded rights.

Furthermore, rights separate man from man and hinder progress towards collaboration. People learn to defend their rights against society ('I know my rights!'), and thus everyone else becomes an opposition. The trend is away from the power of united individuals who recognise what they share in common and could achieve together. So for philosophers such as Marx, the revolution is necessary and justified.

Revolution

There are two strands of thought in Marx's case for revolution in *The German Ideology*.

Firstly, he claims to offer a scientific study of society, so the revolution is explained as the inevitable consequence of the crises in capitalism, which sows the seeds of its own downfall. This analysis is presented as *fact*.

Yet at the same time his language suggests that the revolution is desirable because it will restore social justice. These are opinions and matters of *value*. In the course of his treatise, both kinds of arguments become entangled.

This topic concentrates on the second of the two approaches: that the revolution is justifiable. Marx argues that under a capitalist system the alienation of the worker will become intolerable, and this is the first step towards revolution. What does he mean by alienation?

Alienation

Alienation can mean a number of things for Marx. Essentially the word means estrangement or separation, and a worker can be alienated in a number of different ways, for example:

1   The worker is separated from the value of what he produces. He gives what he produces to the owner of the business, who sells it at a profit. The worker does not therefore receive the full reward for his labour. Thus the dangerous and difficult work in a diamond mine, for example, is not rewarded with the value of the diamonds. This profit enables the capitalist to acquire private property, which ensures his power over the life of the worker, who cannot afford private property. So the worker's own labour and produce contribute to his exploitation. He becomes a wage slave.

2   Alienation refers to the lack of control we have over how we work and what we produce. So labour is not a fulfilling activity. We work simply to reach targets and so we are alienated from our true self. The worker is no longer a self-determining being, but is subject to the laws of economics, supply and demand. So for example, at any time we could be made redundant. The economic forces of capitalism are cruel and indifferent. A person is only valued in terms of what they produce and we lose control over how we live.

3 The nature of work in a capitalist society is that people are required to specialise, in order to be more efficient. This division of labour means that workers must perform a limited range of repetitive tasks. At work, they can only function in a limited way and realise a 'one-sided, crippled, development', instead of expressing the whole of their individuality and full self-realisation. They are alienated from the satisfaction of their full potential and self-realisation. They become stunted.

Once this alienation becomes intolerable, workers will see that the state, the laws and the economic conditions are all alien to their interests, and they will develop class consciousness and seek to take responsibility for their own actions and change both themselves and the system. On one level, Marx presents this economic and social analysis as a scientific analysis of the contradictions within capitalism. On this basis, the revolution is as inescapable as global warming.

But it is also clear that he sees the revolution as desirable, because out of it will come a classless society. Then class rule is abolished, the means of production will be held in common, and through this collective control over labour, over how and what we produce, work will once more become a fulfilling activity. People will be able to develop many sides to their character and it will be 'possible for me to do one thing today and another tomorrow, to hunt in the morning, fish in the afternoon, rear cattle in the evening, criticise after dinner, just as I have a mind'.

The revolution is the only way to achieve social justice. The working class 'can only in a revolution succeed in ridding itself of all the muck of ages and become fitted to found society anew' (Marx, 1970b). Exploitation, stunted development and alienation is 'the muck'.

Behind this theory lie two versions of justice and equality:

■ the worker does not receive what they *deserve*, i.e. the full value of the product of their labours, and the opportunities to develop themselves

■ the workers' *needs* are not fulfilled, and justice requires 'from each according to his ability, to each according to his need' (Marx, 1976).

Whether or not you agree with the values that legitimise the revolution and whether it is inevitable, it is important to note that Marx is not arguing that individuals should have an identical allocation of resources, and precisely the same goods; but that each worker needs material resources to utilise opportunities, and that each should benefit equally through cooperation. Once everyone's basic needs are met, then they will have equal access to social and cultural activity. This does not imply that everyone must do the same, but everyone has genuine equal opportunities.

The conservative and liberal critique is that equality is absolutely incompatible with liberty. Individual, inherited talents will always surface, just as some people will always work harder than others and take advantage of opportunities, and so a subsequent imbalance in power is inescapable. It is worth reading in this context Orwell's *Animal Farm*. Towards the end, the pigs announce: 'All animals are equal, but some animals are more equal than others.'

Inequalities will always surface, and Aristotle argues that a just society will recognise people's differences as well as their common nature: 'Justice consists not only in treating equals equally, but in treating unequals unequally' (Aristotle, 1962). Whether the communist revolution can accommodate the second part of this criterion is doubtful.

AQA Examiner's tip

Animal Farm portrays a powerful and imaginative criticism of revolutionary politics, and will provide some good illustrations for arguments against violent revolution.

Apart from doubts over the outcome of the revolution, there must be concern over the violence that accompanies it. Communists claim that the bourgeoisie (the middle, propertied class) conditioned by capitalism will hinder the progress towards social justice. It is necessary therefore that they are 're-educated' or eliminated. This raises the issue of violence or pacifism.

Violence?

A **pacifist** may subscribe to non-violent protest either deontologically, because violence is wrong in itself, or because of the consequences. The former may be a religious duty or a rational duty, for example based on the natural law that God's creation is sacred, or that violence is contradictory to our fundamental will for life. The objection may be teleological, that violence always leads to negative consequences. Thus Gandhi believed that limited knowledge of the truth deprives us of permission to use violence, and that he maintained moral authority by showing courage, discipline and self-sacrifice through abstention from violence, even in the face of state aggression.

Yet no one can doubt that violence is effective. There are numerous, historical examples where terrorist action, such as the IRA campaign in Northern Ireland, has achieved results. Sitting in the road and singing 'We shall overcome' rarely achieves much! More seriously, suppose that violent action will stop a greater violence. Not only might there be a conflict of duties, but on teleological grounds a revolution would be justified. A popular example would be the assassination of a tyrant, but Engels justified the overthrow of capitalism on the same grounds:

> Murder has been committed if thousands of workers have been deprived of the necessities of life or if they have been forced into a situation in which it is impossible for them to survive ... Murder has been committed if society knows perfectly well that thousands of workers cannot avoid being sacrificed so long as these conditions are allowed to continue. Murder of this sort is just as culpable as the murder committed by an individual. At first sight it does not appear to be murder at all because responsibility for the death of the victim cannot be pinned on any individual assailant. Everyone is responsible and yet no one is responsible, because it appears as if the victim has died from natural causes. If a worker dies no one places the responsibility for his death on society, though some would realise that society has failed to take steps to prevent the victim from dying. But it is murder all the same.

Engels (1958)

So, if the premature deaths of impoverished and alienated workers cannot be alleviated in any other way, it is proportionate to use violence as a means to an end. If a pacifist is not prepared to use violence, then are they prepared to accept some responsibility for the continued cruelty and injustice?

On the other hand, violence can be self-defeating particularly if it causes harm to the innocent and is indiscriminate. Furthermore, could a religious duty reduce human life to a mere object, a means to an end? 'The spirit lies dormant in the brute, and he knows no law but that of physical might. The dignity of man requires obedience to a higher law – to the strength of the spirit' (Gandhi). Can we use others to realise a higher cause?

Nevertheless, we do accept the use of violence in certain circumstances. We sanction the infliction of punishments upon offenders and we

Key terms

Pacifist: someone who opposes war and violence, and advocates the resolution of conflict by peaceful means.

recognise the right of self-defence. If a corrupt regime was violating its people, then self-defence would be justified. Therefore our rights and duties seem to conflict.

Similarly, the consequentialist position may be even more obscure. This approach needs to take into account the long-term effects of violence, both physical and psychological.

Think about

Can a teleological approach come to a clear conclusion?

Can utilitarianism be used to justify war/violence/revolution?

Utilitarianism is based on the fact that people desire pleasure and avoid pain, and therefore recommends maximising happiness for the maximum number of people (not states or countries). Everybody affected deserves to have their happiness/suffering taken into account. It is a calculation of the balance between pain/pleasure, and everyone who is affected must be considered. It is a teleological theory and the quantity (duration, etc.) of pleasure is measured. As a consideration of 'quantity' could encourage inferior/disgusting pleasures, Mill suggests 'quality' is important as well; he suggests quality is 'mental/spiritual pleasures'.

War/violence/revolution: can we apply the above points to decide if violence is justified? Here are some relevant factors:

- Immense physical suffering: is it permissible that the innocent may suffer (civilians)?
- Majority/minority: do a small number of deaths of UK citizens outweigh large numbers in other countries?
- Would utilitarians protect human rights (e.g. of prisoners)?
- How many consequences should we consider, e.g. the futures of unborn children?
- Do noble causes (e.g. fighting for freedom) create happiness that outweighs physical pain and therefore generate quality happiness?
- Do special considerations (e.g. fighting in self-defence against a violent police force) justify causing immense physical pain?
- Should damage to the environment or pollution be considered?

What general rule do you think a utilitarian would make about violent rebellion and why?

The following factors might help you decide whether violence can ever be justified:

- Have all other means of changing the law been tried and proved to be ineffectual?
- Is the injustice so serious that it warrants violence? Do the ends justify the means?
- Can the violence be directed only at property or government systems, e.g. computer systems?
- If violence is directed at people, can only the absolute minimum be used?
- Can the consequences of using violence be foreseen and controlled?

■ The last word

This chapter began with a distinction between facts and values. Political philosophy is rife with value judgements masquerading as incontrovertible facts. Thus we have seen 'apparent' facts such as:

■ human nature
■ a contract between members of society
■ the exercise of power
■ the possession of rights
■ the nature of the common good
■ the basis of law in consent
■ the effects of civil disobedience and revolution
■ the inevitability of revolution.

Each of these topics for debate makes use of empirical evidence, but the selection of facts is likely to be partial and swayed towards a particular theory. The result will be an interpretation of the facts that is biased according to the values, the aims and the intention of the author.

This does not mean that the discussions are not of the utmost importance. Value judgements can be compared, tested for consistency, prioritised and judged on their consequences. The grounds on which human beings exercise power over each other is of the greatest significance and a consensus has to be reached. We cannot *not* reach some kind of agreement on political obligation. But your final judgement will be based on your deeply held moral convictions, and moral beliefs are always open to challenge and debate.

After working through this topic, you should:

■ be able to discuss that the justification for dissent depends on the nature of the contract

■ know that civil disobedience can take many forms. Justification depends on how you regard the state

■ understand the debate on whether the law should interfere in our private lives

■ be able to evaluate different degrees of civil disobedience.

Further reading

Barker, E. (ed.) *Social Contract – Essays by Locke, Hume, Rousseau*, Oxford University Press, 1947. This contains relevant material, quoted in this chapter from Locke, Hume and Rousseau, with a useful introduction by Sir Ernest Barker.

Gaus, G. *Political Concepts and Political Theories*, Westview Press, 2000. An excellent analysis of many of the issues, particularly on the nature of the social contract and conservative and liberal ideologies.

Heywood, A. *Political Ideas and Concepts*, Macmillan, 1994. This is very helpful on dissent, disobedience and revolution, giving up-to-date examples.

Hobbes, T. *Leviathan*, Penguin Classics, 1982. A primary text. Chapter 14 is the key chapter.

Marx, K. and Engels, F. *The German Ideology*, Lawrence and Wishart, 1970. Also a primary text, but not easy to read.

Mill, J. S. *On Liberty*, Gertrude Himmelfarb (ed.), Penguin Books, 1985. A primary text. Chapter 2 is on freedom of speech; the harm principle is to be found in Chapter 1.

Palmer, M. *Moral Problems*, Lutterworth, 1991. This book includes really useful extracts (mainly in Chapter 1) on Rawls, Plato, Thoreau and others.

Pinchin, C. *Issues in Philosophy*, 2nd edn, Palgrave, 2004. In Chapter 5 there is a particularly detailed and sharp analysis of Hobbes and Rousseau.

Singer, P. *Practical Ethics*, 2nd edn, Cambridge University Press, 1993. This contains a relevant and stimulating debate in Chapter 11.

Summary questions

1 Should we base political obligations on the consent of the individual?

2 Are there universal characteristics of human nature, or does our nature depend on the kind of society that has conditioned us?

3 What are the problems with basing political obligation on tacit consent?

4 How does voting legitimise authority?

5 Why does Hobbes advocate obedience to an all-powerful dictator?

6 Why does Locke believe we must obey the legitimate authority?

7 Can you construct a case for limiting dissent?

8 Is the concept of harm clear enough to use as a principle for censorship?

9 Is the use of violence ever acceptable in pursuing a cause?

6 Tolerance

The tolerant individual

- to explore what tolerance is
- to identify and explain some characteristics that we might expect a tolerant individual to possess
- to assess what is important about tolerance
- to assess what is difficult about tolerance.

Introduction

> I haven't changed in the sense that I believe sexuality is a gift from God to be expressed exclusively within the commitment of heterosexual marriage and that all other expressions of that are outside the boundaries of God's creative intent as revealed in the Scripture. However, I do not believe that gives you a license to hate people, including homosexuals, and I think part of the struggle for people is that it's easy to beat up what you don't understand. I have sat and listened to story after story after story from gay people of their journey and have cried with them and tried to listen to the awful pain they go through. [It] hasn't changed what I believe about the practice of homosexuality, but it has reminded me that 'whom you would change you must first love.' Martin Luther King said that. And in general, Christians have not been very good about loving gay people. Oh, they'll tell you they hate the sin but they love the sinner, but I don't see much love for the sinner.

Ed Dobson, *former VP of Moral Majority, Inc. See www.itvs.org/external/WGOOS/WGQUOTES.html*

We can begin our discussion of tolerance by posing two questions:

- Does the view outlined in the above extract signify that Ed Dobson is a tolerant individual?
- Why should we care about whether he, or anyone else, is tolerant or intolerant? What is important about tolerance?

In order to address the first question it is clearly necessary to clarify what being tolerant might involve.

Think about

Is it *possible* to criticise something you do not understand? What, if anything, would this amount to? Would it amount to anything more than abuse?

What is tolerance?

Initially, it may be useful to distinguish tolerance from other personal characteristics or traits:

- Being tolerant towards the views and activities of others is not the same as indulging the views and activities of others because we are fond of the person and are inclined to pander to or give in to them. It is, of course, perfectly legitimate to speak of parents tolerating the behaviour of their children, behaviour that the parents may find objectionable or at least disapprove of, as their acceptance of the behaviour may be motivated by factors that outweigh their disapproval – for example, the children are tired or excited – so that on this occasion the behaviour is tolerated. However, if the behaviour were constantly repeated and never challenged by the parents because of their fondness for their children, we would be inclined to regard the parents as indulgent rather than tolerant. We may also see this as a weakness rather than strength: the parents may think of themselves as lenient, easygoing or permissive, but this would really only amount to a kind of favouritism. Arguably, we tend to be indulgent towards people and give them preferential treatment because we like them, and it makes little sense to talk of tolerating what we like.

- Being tolerant towards the views and activities of others is not the same as being weak-willed or powerless to impose our will. A weak-willed person might put up with the behaviour of others in order to placate or appease them, or they may be afraid of the consequences of expressing their disapproval. In this sense any compliance or acquiescence signifies either psychological or physical weakness. We may like to think of this as a mark of how lenient, easygoing or permissive we are, but what we are really doing is giving up or giving in. A tolerant individual is one who voluntarily accepts views and activities that they disapprove of; it is not a person who merely suffers the behaviour of others. We do not talk about 'tolerating' behaviour that we are, or feel, powerless to prevent. For example, a victim of bullying does not *tolerate* the bullying, rather they *endure* it.

- Being tolerant towards the views and activities of others is not the same as being indifferent and not challenging the views and activities of others because we have no relevant beliefs or opinions of our own. If we have no views of our own, the issue of tolerance will never arise: the completely indifferent person (if there was one) would be a person with no particular dislikes and no occasion to be tolerant of, or put up with, anything. For example, it makes no sense to describe someone as tolerating racist comments if that person finds nothing objectionable in racist comments.

Therefore, if the view expressed by Ed Dobson can be considered to be tolerant towards homosexuality, it is not because he is indifferent to, indulgent towards or powerless to do anything about homosexuality. Clearly, he is none of these things, but insofar as tolerance is not the same as indifference, indulgence or powerlessness the question as to whether Dobson is tolerant remains open.

The tolerant individual may put up with views, activities and people they dislike and they may put up with views, activities and people they fear, not because they are indifferent, indulgent or weak but because, while they feel that such views and activities are wrong and while they may be empowered to resist or even punish them (at least socially, politically and economically if not legally), they are sufficiently assured of the worth of their own views and activities, or of the worth of diversity and difference, to not attempt to prohibit, interfere with or constrain the beliefs, actions and practices of others.

Three components of tolerance

Rainer Forst (2003) describes the **concept of tolerance** as involving three characteristics:

- The view that certain beliefs, actions and practices are considered to be objectionable, wrong and even wicked is essential to the concept of tolerance. This is referred to as the objection component. As we have seen, if there is nothing about a belief or action that we object to then we are indifferent towards it rather than tolerant of it. For example, the extract from Ed Dobson quoted at the beginning of this chapter clearly demonstrates that he is not indifferent to homosexuality, believing as he does that 'sexuality is a gift from God to be expressed exclusively within the commitment of heterosexual marriage'. Neither can he be said to be indulgent towards homosexual activity which he dislikes and objects to as an expression of sexuality 'which is outside

Key philosopher

Rainer Forst (1964–)

Forst is Professor of Political Theory and Philosophy at Johann Wolfgange Goethe University, Frankfurt. His main research interests include critical theory, liberalism, justice and toleration.

Key terms

Concept of tolerance: in order to assess different views of what tolerance consists in, it is necessary to ensure that those engaged in a dispute about what tolerance is are all talking about the same thing. Thus, it is necessary to have a concept of tolerance. The concept employed here, which is due to Forst, is that tolerance involves three components: objection, acceptance and rejection.

the boundaries of God's creative intent as revealed in the scripture'. Finally, as a previously active and senior member of the Moral Majority in the US, he was not powerless to say and do anything about homosexuality. So, the objection component is clearly present.

■ The fact that there are views, activities and practices that we dislike and object to is balanced by an acceptance component. As we have seen, acceptance does not involve being weak-willed. Forst (2003) describes it as holding 'certain positive reasons that trump the negative ones in the relevant context'. That is, we would continue to hold the view that certain beliefs and activities are wrong but also the view that they are not intolerably wrong. It is more difficult to assess whether or not the view expressed by Ed Dobson in this extract indicates acceptance, but it is possible to suggest that it does. As we shall see, there is considerable discussion about what 'acceptance' means in practice but, for the moment, if we are looking for a positive reason that beats the negative ones we can find the Christian virtues of love and compassion present in phrases like 'whom you would change you must first love'. Granted this is hardly a celebration of diversity and difference, but it is by no means certain that tolerance requires the celebration of diversity.

■ Forst (2007) notes that 'the limits of toleration need to be specified'. That is, if we are to avoid tolerating everything, there must be beliefs and activities that we regard as wrong *and* as intolerably wrong. Because this requires our reasons for rejecting such beliefs and activities to outweigh reasons for accepting them, Forst calls this the 'rejection component'. Again, it is difficult to assess whether the view expressed by Ed Dobson indicates a limit to what he would tolerate. There is no explicit statement of beliefs and activities he would reject. However, it is clear that he wishes to 'change' homosexuals in some way (this may be so that homosexual desire is no longer present, or so that, if present, it is not acted upon) and that he is compassionate towards those gays whose experience of their sexuality has been, in some sense, 'awful'. It is not clear that he would be tolerant of homosexuals who were 'out' and 'proud', who celebrated their sexuality. Perhaps he would not be.

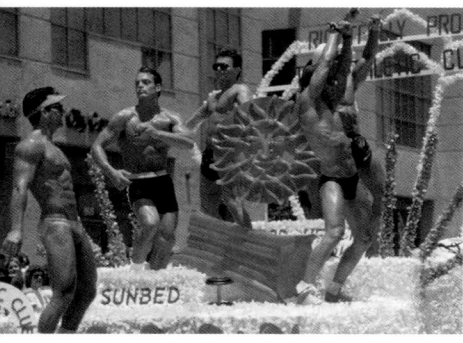

Fig. 6.1 *'Out and proud': participants on a gay pride march*

With regard to our first question, then, given these criteria some people might be prepared to say that the view expressed by Ed Dobson in the extract is a tolerant view: it addresses activities he objects to and indicates what he is prepared to accept as well as pointing to the limits to what he would find acceptable. Others, however, would dispute this conclusion.

Four conceptions of tolerance

To borrow a term from Gallie (1968), conceptions of what it is to behave in a tolerant manner are '**essentially contested**'. One way in which we can grasp how a concept, for example the concept of tolerance, is essentially contested is to distinguish between a *concept* and different *conceptions* of it. With regard to tolerance, the characteristics outlined above (objection, acceptance and rejection) constitute the core of the concept. Essentially contested concepts must have some common core in order to see disagreements, or contests, as being about the same concept. However, there are different interpretations, or conceptions, of which aspects of the core are most significant and of how it should be actualised.

Gallie outlined a number of conditions that a concept must meet in order to be essentially contested:

> ### Key terms
>
> **Essentially contested:** a concept is essentially contested if it is subject to constant, intractable disputes about how to interpret it.

▨ the concept is an evaluative concept, it must signify that something is of value

▨ the concept is complex, so that what is valuable is not immediately obvious and is open to different interpretations

▨ those engaged in disputing the concept recognise that their use of the concept is disputed, they have some understanding of why others hold different views and are prepared to maintain and defend their own use of the term.

Forst, for example, identifies four conceptions of what tolerance involves in practice. He calls the first of these the 'permission conception'. At a societal level this conception would view tolerance as a relation between a majority of individuals (perhaps a heterosexual majority) and a minority group or groups who exhibit 'difference' (such as homosexuals). The key feature of this relation is that the minority group concerned would be tolerated insofar as they limit their activities to the private sphere (for example, their own homes) and do not claim equal social, legal or political rights (for example, the right to be recognised as a married couple or the right to adopt children). So, as long as the minority accept their inferior status and do not challenge the majority, they can be tolerated. Their activities would be seen as wrong but not as intolerably wrong. The relationship is one of power and subordination: the dominant majority 'permit' the minority to engage in the practices that signify their difference without interference as long as the minority 'know their place' as it were.

To briefly return to the question of whether the view expressed by Ed Dobson indicates a tolerant nature, it might be argued on the basis of this conception that the desire to 'change' homosexuals does not indicate non-interference and, consequently, falls short of acceptance and tolerance.

A second conception is the coexistence conception. This is similar to the permission conception, insofar as tolerance is viewed as a kind of peaceful coexistence which is preferred to conflict, but the relationship is no longer between a dominant majority and subordinate minority. Rather, groups of individuals may be roughly equal in terms of size or social power. The relation of tolerance is a form of reciprocal compromise; tolerant subjects are themselves objects of the toleration of others. Such a situation might be found in a culture where there are a number of religious groups, for example, none of which is dominant.

The third conception of toleration identified by Forst is the respect conception. This goes beyond peaceful coexistence in the sense that, while groups of individuals may hold radically different views about the morality of certain lifestyles and differ tremendously in terms of their cultural practices, all recognise a set of values or principles that apply universally (for example, that others are moral equals and have the same rights as us). This conception can be understood in different ways. One way is to maintain a strict division between the public and private sphere so that universal values apply in the public sphere, where all are treated equally, and the activities associated with cultural identities and differences should be limited to the private sphere. In the public sphere, such as a school for example, everyone wears the same uniform regardless of ethnicity or lifestyle preferences. At home they can dress in a way that expresses their ethnic or subcultural identities and differences. A second way to apply this conception is to recognise that it is more difficult for some groups to adopt a rigid distinction between the private and public spheres. This may be due to the fact that the cultural practices and moral codes associated with their identities have a special significance for them such that they cannot be abandoned in the public sphere. This may be seen as sufficient grounds to exempt certain groups from the rules or behavioural codes that apply to everyone else. If this is acceptable then a person may be respected both as a political equal and as a person with specific needs that should be tolerated.

Finally, the fourth conception identified by Forst is the esteem conception. This goes beyond respect in that, while we do not fully accept the beliefs and practices associated with another culture or lifestyle (if we did, the objection component would not be present) we can nevertheless see value in them and admire aspects of them. Using schooling again, a fairly trivial example might be the dislike pupils have of the disruptive behaviour of some of their peers, and the view that education, or the gaining of qualifications, is a route to success not an opportunity to misbehave. At the same time, however, they may admire aspects of the behaviour such as attempts to challenge and resist authority. In this respect they may regard with some esteem the values and practices that are different from their own.

At this point it would be worthwhile to read the extract provided at the beginning of this chapter again in light of these different conceptions of what tolerance might involve.

We can now briefly consider the second question.

■ What is important about tolerance?

The concept of tolerance has assumed increasing significance as societies have become more complex and diverse so that social groups within the same society may possess beliefs and values which are fundamentally different. These circumstances, it is argued, require individuals to be tolerant. Thus, R. P. Wolff (1965) describes tolerance as 'that state of mind and condition of society which enables a pluralist democracy to function well and to realise the idea of pluralism'.

So the importance of tolerance is a question of both *context* and *principle*. Both may be important in deciding which, if any, of the above conceptions of tolerance to favour.

Context

With regard to context, tolerance was first discussed in Western political philosophy in the context of religious tensions between Catholics and Protestants in the 16th and 17th centuries. A cursory study of the diversity of religious beliefs, practices and groupings in the 21st century will indicate how much more complex this has become. In the UK, for example, as well as members of the Church of England we have Catholics, Methodists, Baptists, Pentecostalists, Muslims, Sikhs and Hindus as well as members of a host of new religious movements such as Scientologists, Dianic Wiccas (Goddess worshippers) and the Jesus Fellowship. Diversity and difference is not simply a matter of religious affiliation: religious beliefs and practices may be linked to various other areas of potential difference and disagreement concerning moral values, including sexual orientation and lifestyle. Moreover, it would be simplistic to suggest that disagreements concerning cultural, moral and political issues are an inevitable consequence of religious affiliation and equally simplistic to ignore the fact that frequently, perhaps typically, there are disagreements within religious groupings. For example, some Muslims might be described as 'traditionalists'. Perhaps the best political example of this, in recent years, is the Taliban of Afghanistan. The word

■ Think about

Consider how you would answer the first question posed after the extract from Ed Dobson – whether the view expressed is that of a tolerant individual.

■ Key philosopher

Robert Paul Wolff (1933–)

Wolff is a political philosopher with interests in Kant, anarchism, Marxism, liberalism, tolerance, justice and democracy. He teaches in the School of African-American Studies at the University of Massachusetts.

■ Think about

Can you identify different kinds of intolerance and differences in their perceived dangers?

'Taliban' means seminary students. Members of the Taliban tend to favour tradition and authority and are sceptical of modernism. On the other hand, radical and liberal Muslims seek to modernise society and politics but tend to deny that modernity is limited to Western cultures. With regard to lifestyle and sexual orientation, for example, liberal Muslims include women who have produced a 'feminist' reading of the Koran – called *For Ourselves* – and homosexuals who have started a movement called 'Queer Jihad'. In addition it is also clearly the case that disagreements concerning lifestyles and sexual orientation can exist among people with no religious affiliation at all.

It would be misleading to suggest that in this context, faced with an increasingly complex variety of beliefs and values, tolerance is the only answer. Clearly it is not. Arguably, the diversity of beliefs, values and lifestyles *and* tolerance of such diversity has led some to reject the liberal value of tolerance in favour of one or other of a competing range of fundamentalisms. Faced with disputes and uncertainty about what is right, that is, some have searched for, or clung on to, beliefs and values they can regard as certainties or absolutes. This is reflected in slogans such as 'Truth, not tolerance'. Those who respond in this way *may* be in the minority; even so it would seem necessary to turn to a discussion of principle if we want to claim that this is a misguided response.

Principle

Responses to the question of whether we can justify being tolerant as a matter of principle are varied. Forst, for example, regards tolerance as a 'normatively dependent concept'; that is, in itself it is not a virtue, rather it can only be seen as a valuable trait to possess if it can be shown to be valuable for other normative reasons. On the other hand, R. P. Wolff describes tolerance as the virtue of pluralist democracies. Some would regard it as an important feature of democracies that minorities have the opportunity to become majorities and this can only be guaranteed by the tolerance of such minorities. This has been held to establish a conceptual connection between democracy and tolerance.

If we are to regard tolerance as a virtue we must see it as a trait conducive to our well-being or flourishing; a trait we need to adopt in order to live well; a trait which contributes to the good for man. Arguably, the attempt to justify tolerance in principle is most firmly rooted in liberalism and, perhaps, liberalism is best understood as a political theory concerned with the kind of social and political arrangements that are necessary in order that individuals might enjoy a good life. Liberals may not prescribe a particular view of what 'the good life' is and may be neutral with regard to religious beliefs, moral values and lifestyle choices. Alternatively, if not neutral, they may place a higher value on autonomy and the right of individuals to choose their religion, values and lifestyle than on any preconceived idea about what might constitute successful self-creation. Either view might be supplemented by other reasons such as the empiricist view that it is only through experience, and perhaps through 'experiments in living', that an individual can discover what is conducive to his flourishing as an individual, as well as the pluralist view that a variety of individuals might choose a variety of lifestyles each of which, while different, might be viewed as a good life.

We might draw *two* ways of justifying tolerance in principle from this account:

- at the very least we can see this as an ungrudging acknowledgement that individuals have the right to hold and pursue values and lifestyles which might be opposed;

beyond this, we might also see it as entailing a willing acceptance and encouragement (if not a celebration) of choice and diversity of value and lifestyle.

Alternatively, we might not be persuaded that these reasons justify tolerance at all. We might fear that the acknowledgement and acceptance of autonomy and diversity undermines social order. In this case, if we are seeking to justify tolerance in principle, we might argue that it is, at best, a necessary evil; we tolerate views we do not like because doing so is more pragmatic than rejecting, criticising or suppressing them. Tolerance is more conducive to maintaining civility. Intolerance leads to hostilities and conflicts we would rather avoid. We might also see the liberal view as an overly demanding account of what is necessary for a good life; as subscribing to an optimistic vision of human abilities or to an account of the value of choice which is too positive (to borrow from Sartre, it could be the case that our freedom to choose is experienced in anguish).

Can tolerance be justified in principle?

A more intractable problem, however, is that it may also be the case that the attempt to find a principle that justifies tolerance, liberal or otherwise, is an attempt at the impossible. What seems to be required is a principle justifying tolerance, as a necessary constituent of a good life, which is not *intolerant* towards alternative conceptions of what a good life might involve. This issue is present in arguments presented by liberals from John Locke to John Rawls.

Rawls, for example, prefers a minimalist conception of the good life, a conception that is neutral with regard to contested issues in religion, morality and politics favouring autonomy, choice, self-creation and responsibility. However, how neutral is this? Rawls appears to accept that the freedoms to express beliefs and choose lifestyles are necessary (but not sufficient) features of a good life. However, this seems intolerant towards cultures in which the practice of unquestioning obedience is valued and it also seems to rule out the possibility of enjoying a good life in such cultures.

Is it possible to phrase a liberal principle of toleration which does not require those who are not liberals to become liberals?

With regard to sexual orientation, for example, it would appear that providing a lifestyle is freely chosen – and this might apply both to the expression of heterosexual and homosexual desires as well as to an individual's decision to deny expression to such desires – that lifestyle should be tolerated as a manifestation of the good for man. It is not clear, however, that individuals participating in cultural practices where legitimate expressions of sexuality, including one's partner, are restricted and determined by somebody else, cannot enjoy a good life. Neither is it clear that such practices should not be tolerated. Nor is it clear that those who are immersed in and committed to such practices would trade them in for liberalism.

At this point we might ask a third question.

What is difficult about tolerance?

It would seem that any philosophical analysis of the concept of toleration has to confront various difficulties or, as they are usually referred to, **paradoxes of toleration**. In other words, the difficulty is that analysis of the concept leads to positions which appear to be self-contradictory.

Key philosopher

John Rawls (1921–2002)

Rawls was Professor of Political Philosophy at Harvard University. He is widely regarded as one of the most influential liberal political theorists of the 20th century and is best known for his seminal work *A Theory of Justice* (1971).

Think about

Is there a distinction between tolerance within a society and tolerance of other societies? Does the first carry implications for the second?

Key terms

Paradoxes of toleration: the apparent contradictions that arise from attempts to reconcile reasons for objecting to, accepting and rejecting beliefs and practices.

For example, the first question that we considered was whether the view expressed in the extract was the view of a tolerant individual. If the answer to this question is yes then we are in the paradoxical situation of regarding an individual as both heterosexist (and arguably intolerant) and tolerant. The difficulty is related to the objection component. For example, if we were to consider prejudice generally, consider the case of someone who opts for tolerance out of self-interest. He might be someone who has been in Parliament for several years, perhaps decades, and who enjoyed participating in the largely white, middle-class, male atmosphere of the House of Commons when he was first elected as an MP. He might also feel that a woman's main role in life is in the private sphere of the family and that a woman's participation in public life is damaging to the institution of the family. He may also view attempts to recruit more females as parliamentary candidates as misguided. However, he also feels that, in terms of his own career, it would be unwise to resist the attempts of more senior figures in his political party to make the parliamentary party less homogeneous and more representative of the population as a whole. Indeed, he feels that it would be advantageous to his political career if he were seen to support this policy. Consequently, at least when in the public sphere of political life, he refrains from making sexist comments and from performing discriminatory actions. Indeed, he is increasingly supportive of female colleagues. In short, he appears to be tolerant and to have become more tolerant. Now, if tolerance is seen as a virtuous trait, when we describe this MP as 'having become more tolerant' we are expressing moral approval. In this way we may come to see certain others, whose beliefs may be unjust and even unacceptable, as virtuous because they are no longer acting on those beliefs. This looks odd.

Consequently, in order to avoid this difficulty, it may be necessary to insist that one's grounds or reasons for objection are rational rather than expressions of fear, hatred or prejudice. Arguably, if we are to avoid praising 'the tolerant sexist', or 'the tolerant racist', we should not request that they act more tolerantly but that they overcome their sexism or racism. Tolerance, perhaps, is not the solution to all strongly felt views.

However, difficulties do not disappear if we insist that the reasons offered in support of an objection are rationally considered or moral reasons, because then we run into a difficulty with the acceptance component. In short, if both the reasons for objecting to something and the reasons for accepting it can be seen as morally sound then we encounter a paradox of moral tolerance, a situation where it seems to be morally right to tolerate what is morally wrong. Something like this, for example, appears to be the difficulty in the extract that we began with. Ed Dobson seems to hold moral reasons for objecting to homosexuality. He sees it as an expression of sexuality that is 'outside the boundaries of God's creative intent'. Clearly, he is not alone in this. A Chief Justice of the Alabama Supreme Court, for example, has claimed:

> Homosexual conduct is, and has been, considered abhorrent, immoral, detestable, a crime against nature and a violation of the laws of nature and of nature's God upon which this Nation and our laws are predicated. Such conduct violates both the criminal and civil laws of this State and is destructive to a basic building block of society – the family … It is an inherent evil against which children must be protected.

Chief Justice Moore, *see www.aptv.org/ftr/other/SupremeCourtDecision.pdf*

In the extract from Ed Dobson, however, there is also an appeal to the Christian virtue of love. As we have seen, whether or not this leads to 'acceptance' is debatable. However, we can imagine a situation in which the criminal and civil laws of Alabama change to allow a homosexual parent custody of his or her own children following a divorce, or to allow a homosexual couple to adopt the children of others. We can further suppose that a Chief Justice may then regard it as a moral duty to uphold the new law. Such a situation illustrates the paradox of moral tolerance: it would become morally right to support what is regarded as morally wrong.

In order to avoid this difficulty we might need to construct a hierarchy of moral reasons – that is, to identify some moral reasons which are of a higher moral order than others. In the above example it might be necessary to choose between an alleged 'law of nature' and the actual law of a particular state. Presumably, if someone who was responsible for administering justice genuinely believed that there is a 'law of nature', governing sexuality and decreed by God, it would outrank the state law they were responsible for administering. In this case the limit of their tolerance would be severely tested. However, this brings us to a further difficulty concerning the limits of tolerance.

Tolerance and intolerance

The difficulty of determining a limit to what is tolerable concerns the rejection component. If, for example, a person believes that homosexuality is abnormal, 'abhorrent' and 'detestable' then, clearly, as far as they are concerned homosexuality is intolerable and must be rejected. But, firstly notice that if what this amounts to is something like 'I cannot accept what I find unacceptable', then tolerance seems to have failed to get off the ground. Secondly, every case of drawing a limit to what is tolerable could itself be seen as an act of intolerance. Moreover, if instead of asking whether we should tolerate homosexuality we ask whether we should tolerate intolerance towards homosexuals, we confront the difficulty of whether we should tolerate the intolerant. This issue is much discussed in the literature on tolerance. One problem concerns how to identify the intolerant:

- Do we mean that the intolerant are those who do not believe that an infringement of some 'norm' is tolerable? The main difficulty here, perhaps, is how we would identify such intolerant people while maintaining a view of ourselves as tolerant individuals.
- Or, do we mean that the intolerant are those who refuse to accept the value of tolerance itself? This may be more promising, but it clearly leads to the tricky questions of whether we should tolerate such intolerance and whether, if we do not, we remain tolerant ourselves.

This problem may depend upon what reasons are given for refusing to accept that some beliefs and practices are tolerable. As we have seen, if such a refusal is grounded in some arbitrary or irrational prejudice then, perhaps, tolerance is not at issue. In such instances the demand for tolerance is not an answer to intolerance; rather we should require the intolerant to reconsider their prejudices. However, if the refusal to accept a belief or practice is rationally grounded, the position may be different. It will be recalled that Forst (2003), for example, sees tolerance as a 'normatively dependent concept', so it is possible to argue that those who refuse to accept a belief or practice are not intolerant; rather they see tolerance as being of less value than the infringement of the social norm they are rationally committed to. It is possible to argue, and indeed it has been argued, that tolerance of homosexuality does undermine a

IF THERE'S ONE THING I CAN'T STAND IT'S INTOLERANCE

Fig. 6.2 *A vacuous phrase or a meaningful statement?*

social order built on Christian values and does undermine the family as the 'bedrock' upon which social order, stability and morality are built. If these views are held by people who are prepared to engage in rational debate with others who do not hold these views, then we might see all requirements for tolerance as having been met. There is an objection component, an acceptance of the right to express diverse views, and a rejection component insisting that, when put into practice, activities based on these views are intolerable. However, there is a nagging doubt concerning whether such a position is a tolerant one. How do we retain our commitment to some norm, in this case heterosexuality, and claim at the same time that we are tolerant and it is others whose behaviour is intolerable?

It would seem preferable to identify the intolerant as those who refuse to accept the value of tolerance itself. That is, given social and moral diversity and difference, toleration is, or should be, a reciprocal relationship. So, it might be argued, we should not and perhaps could not tolerate those who refuse to reciprocate and tolerate us. However, there still seems to be a question concerning whether in refusing to tolerate those who reject toleration we become intolerant ourselves. In response to this it might be argued that, as the concept of tolerance implies a limit, intolerance should be included in the range of beliefs, activities and practices that are beyond the limits of what the tolerant individual should tolerate.

Karl Popper says:

> Unlimited tolerance must lead to the disappearance of tolerance. If we extend unlimited tolerance even to those who are intolerant, if we are not prepared to defend a tolerant society against the onslaught of the intolerant, then the tolerant will be destroyed, and tolerance with them.

Popper (1945)

However, the implications of this need to be carefully stated. Popper, a political liberal, wished to defend his conception of a liberal, 'open' society at a particular time, against views that he saw as anti-liberal and dangerous. So, with regard to tolerance, Popper is more concerned with the notion of a tolerant society (which we will return to) than with the notion of a tolerant individual. Popper was certainly aware of the danger of becoming intolerant and thought it 'unwise' to attempt to suppress intolerant attitudes, preferring to 'counter them by rational argument and keep them in check by public opinion'. However, he thought that, as a society, we have a 'right' to suppress these attitudes if they are promoted by those who refuse to engage in rational argument and who may refuse their followers the right to hear alternative views or incite their followers to persecute those who hold different views. Thus, Popper's opposition to intolerance is based on the fear that, if unchecked, intolerance may lead to violence, or the threat of violence or incitement to violence, so that a diverse, free and tolerant society might disappear.

Other liberal philosophers, for example Rawls, have argued differently but appear to reach a similar conclusion. Rawls sees liberalism as a 'political' position and, as such, devoid of any 'metaphysical' claim to a set of universal truths. More than this, however, he does not wish to promote political values above other, perhaps competing, values so that liberalism is viewed as a more important set of values than, say, religious values. Of particular significance, perhaps, is his view that competing value systems cannot be decided on the basis of political principles. However, he does require competing value systems to 'respect the limits imposed by the

Key philosopher

Karl Popper (1902–94)

Sir Karl Popper was Professor of Logic and Scientific Method at the London School of Economics until he retired in 1969. He is known mainly for his work in the philosophy of scientific method but was also a rigorous defender of political liberalism and 'open' societies.

Think about

Rawls does regard the good life as consisting of necessary components. From what are these derived?

principles of political justice' (Rawls, 1989). This seems to imply that illiberal values can be tolerated but only insofar as they are compatible with a diverse, free, tolerant and liberal society. In short, a liberal society may tolerate illiberal beliefs but not the practices based on such beliefs because this is incompatible with, and may threaten, the liberal political consensus.

We will return to a discussion of 'the tolerant society' in a later topic but, at this point, it will be useful to consider an example in which tolerance is put to the test (see below).

After working through this topic, you should:

- be able to explain different conceptions of what tolerance involves
- be able to compare and contrast liberal and non-liberal justifications for tolerance
- provide reasons why tolerance is an important political concept
- understand how tolerance can involve apparent contradictions or paradoxes and the difficulties this presents.

Tensions and applications

Learning objectives:

- to assess whether a liberal society should tolerate a minority culture that doesn't respect its values
- to assess whether a liberal and tolerant culture could nourish certain values without being intolerant to other cultures
- to assess whether tolerance merely implies that we leave other individuals alone to think and do as they please or whether it also requires us to do or say nothing to offend others.

Tolerance and fundamentalism

One dictionary definition of fundamentalism is that it is a 'type of militantly conservative religious movement characterized by the advocacy of strict conformity to sacred texts' (*Encyclopaedia Britannica*). The term itself originally referred to an early 20th-century movement in American Protestantism but is now frequently, and loosely, used to describe movements in other religions. The practice of using it in this way is, again, contested. The concept is typically applied pejoratively. Those designated as fundamentalists are depicted negatively as bigots, zealots, militants, extremists and fanatics. Some of those who object to such derogatory connotations are inclined to view fundamentalism as a useful label through which we can conveniently ignore the outrage felt by groups who object to and oppose the political, economic and cultural domination of the West.

However, it has also been argued that the negative depiction of fundamentalism does accurately reflect the nature of those fundamentalist movements which, broadly, advocate strict adherence to a set of basic principles and intolerance of and opposition to societies based upon alternative or neutral conceptions of the good life. If this is the case then, clearly, there may be some tension between individuals committed to a liberal conception of the good life including the importance of autonomy, self-determination, freedom of thought and expression, and individuals committed to belief systems stressing uncritical devotion and community.

Tensions

This tension was apparent in David Cameron's demand in the House of Commons on 4 July 2007, following a failed attempt to explode car bombs, that an 'Islamist' group called Hizb ut-Tahrir should be banned. Writing in *The Independent* the journalist Johann Hari described members of this group as 'middle-class professionals who ... pine for the creation of an Islamist empire imposing shariah law over the whole planet'. He goes on to ask:

> Are you a woman who shows her hair in public? Are you gay? Have you ever had an affair? Are you a Jew? Are you a Muslim who has had doubts about your faith? Then I'm afraid a strict interpretation of their draft constitution for the New Caliphate ... would entail your execution.

Hari (2007)

The tension is between a secular political liberalism, which arguably tolerates homosexuality, affairs and doubts, and the Islamist view that all of this may undermine traditional Muslim ways of life. Hari expresses it nicely, but hardly in neutral terms, as a tension between the right to live your way and the right to live one way. Not surprisingly, Hari is firmly on the side of political liberalism echoing Popper and other liberal theorists, such as Mill, in claiming that: 'any organisation that plans imminent violence within Britain should of course be outlawed ... The only legitimate restriction on free speech is where it involves a direct incitement to kill' (Hari, 2007). However, given that Hizb ut-Tahrir seeks to gain power through conventional political means, 'the best way to defeat them is not to abandon liberal values by banning them ... but by acting on liberal values by discrediting and destroying them in argument'.

There are, of course, difficulties involved in attempts to use argument to discredit views deemed to be intolerable. One difficulty, in the above case, may be the fear of appearing to be 'Islamophobic', and a second concerns the potential response from Islamists who do not see the liberal values of free expression, criticism and argument as tolerable or effective.

Causing offence

These difficulties were apparent in the furore caused by the publication of cartoons of the Prophet Mohamed in the Danish *Jyllands-Posten* on 30 September 2005. In some Muslim communities any images of the Prophet, let alone inflammatory images, are discouraged. Consequently, protests were received from ambassadors of a number of Muslim countries. The response of the Danish government was to refuse an apology on the basis that it did not control media output and any attempt to do so would be a violation of freedom of speech. Between October 2005 and February 2006, at the same time that protests in Muslim states were escalating, the story was covered and the cartoons republished in a number of European newspapers. Notably, newspapers in the UK covered the story without republishing the cartoons. A lead article in the *Guardian* newspaper, published a year after the original publication of the cartoons in the *Jyllands-Posten*, explained why:

> It is now exactly a year since a Danish newspaper published a series of cartoons of the Prophet Muhammad, which Muslims found so insulting that 140 people died in the ensuing violence ... incidents (such as this) hurt Muslim sensibilities and generate agonised debate about freedom of expression and its limits. This newspaper

AQA Examiner's tip

Some questions will require you to apply your understanding of tolerance to religious diversity and difference. In doing so, it is important that you are prepared to illustrate the points that you make with references to religious tensions. You may employ the examples given here, but do not be afraid to incorporate other current local, national or international examples if they are relevant to a discussion of tolerance.

> believes in that freedom. We invoked it in February when we had to decide whether to publish the cartoons. We believe now as then that it was our right to do so – but not our duty to cause gratuitous offence. Critics responded that this was self-imposed censorship for fear of offending intolerant Muslims who rejected Voltaire's maxim: 'I disagree with what you say but will defend to the death your right to say it.' Liberal principles matter, though common sense requires judgment as to whether an action is likely to cause damage. Free expression cannot mean carte blanche for purveyors of hatred … the west needs to recognise its responsibilities, stop employing double standards, refrain from equating Islam and terrorism, and thus help isolate the fanatics who give ordinary Muslims a bad name. Tolerance must be a two-way street. Freedom of expression is vital. It is not part of a global 'crusade' against Islam.

Leader (2006)

So, according to the author of this article, freedom of expression has limits. One of these limits appears to be the freedom to express a view that others might find offensive, insulting, insensitive or disrespectful.

Interestingly, the article makes no reference to a cartoon by a cartoonist that the *Guardian* does publish.

Fig. 6.3 *Does anything change if both parties to a dispute are represented humorously?*

In contrast Munira Mirza, co-author of the report 'Living Apart Together', argued that the response of the UK media reflected a 'special sensitivity to the issue … because it is about Islam'. She argues that where 'respect for diversity' is in conflict with freedom of thought and expression it is essential, in a free society, that we should safeguard freedom of thought. In her view, passing laws against the incitement to religious hatred is indicative that, at present, the respect for diversity agenda is winning the battle against freedom of speech.

> Media outlets have very little problem satirising Christianity – just consider BBC2's defiant showing of Jerry Springer the Opera, despite heated protests by Christian groups. Muslims are being treated as a special group, seen as worthy of more protection from criticism than other groups because of their apparent victim status … Muslims are not banned from practising their religion but nor should they be shielded from criticism by others, however hurtful they might feel it is …

> Press freedom is the foundation of a free society .... Unless we stand up for freedom of speech, we are unable to engage freely and hold belief systems – of all kinds – to account ... Censorship in the West bolsters the moral authority of leaders in the Middle East to censor their own citizens. Indeed, the religious leaders in Saudi Arabia and Palestine have been opportunistic in using the story as a way of galvanising support and reinforcing the view that only they can protect Muslims from victimisation ... sympathetic lefty anti-racists who believe censorship will protect Muslims are actually missing the point. Many Muslims want the same freedoms as everyone else to debate, criticise and challenge their religion.

> *M. Mirza*, 3 February 2006, Spiked website, www.spiked-online.com

The question that this issue raises concerns the tension between respect for diversity, or at least the concern to avoid causing gratuitous offence, on the one hand and the freedom to express critical views on the other. As such it echoes issues raised after Salman Rushdie published *The Satanic Verses* (1988) which also presented the Prophet Mohamed in a negative light. At that time Jeremy Waldron posed the question, 'How gingerly must we treat another's religious sensibilities?'. Waldron considers the view that tolerance involves taking care not to say anything that is critical of another person's faith or anything that may offend them. He rejects this view.

> The religions of the world make rival claims about the nature and being of God and the meaning of human life. It is not possible for me to avoid criticizing the tenets of your faith without stifling my own. So mutual respect cannot possibly require us to refrain from criticism.

> *Waldron* (1999)

Waldron also considers the view that tolerance should require that critical discussion and debate between faiths should be 'serious, earnest and respectful in its character'. This, then, would indicate where Salman Rushdie went wrong. As a novelist he 'spun fantasies, told ribald jokes, rehearsed heresies, used obscene language' and 'mocked the sacred'. Thus, he was not respectful. Waldron also rejects this view.

> What is serious and what is offensive, what is sober and what is mockery – these are not neutral ideas ... different religions define them in different ways ... There is nothing necessarily privileged about the norms of civility that we call moral seriousness ... it is hard to see how free expression could do its work if it remained psychologically innocuous.

> *Waldron* (1999)

Thus, if the issues under discussion are as important as they seem then distress caused by the views of others can be seen as part of the price of addressing these issues. Waldron concludes that:

> Persons and peoples must leave one another free to address the deep questions of religion and philosophy the best way they can, with all the resources they have at their disposal ... the great themes of religion matter too much to be closeted by the sensitivity of those who are counted as the pious. There is no other way we can live together and respect each other's grappling with life.

> *Waldron* (1999)

Think about

Which of the following statements do you agree with?

- ■ Religious tolerance is not religious indifference.
- ■ Only those who possess a strong religious faith can be intolerant of other religious beliefs and practices.
- ■ Tolerance requires you to refrain from criticising religious beliefs and practices.
- ■ Respect for diversity will inevitably lead to restrictions on free speech.
- ■ We should not tolerate the expression of those religious beliefs, or behaviour, which might harm us or others.

After working through this topic, you should:

- ■ understand why it might be argued that a liberal culture should tolerate minority beliefs and practices that do not respect the values of liberalism and why it might be argued that certain beliefs should not be tolerated
- ■ be able to explain how liberal values can produce a paradox of tolerance
- ■ have a view about whether freedom of speech is more important than the offence it may cause and about the claim that tolerance does not require us to stifle our own views for fear of causing offence.

The tolerant society

Learning objectives:

- ■ to identify arguments in support of tolerance
- ■ to assess whether tolerant societies should promote a particular conception of the good for man
- ■ to consider whether tolerance promotes critical faculties and new ideas or false needs and 'repressive desublimation'.

■ Introduction

It might be tempting to suggest that if tolerance is a quality of the mind or a personal characteristic then a tolerant society is merely one that cultivates this quality in individuals or, perhaps, one in which the majority of individuals possess this quality. Indeed, these might be ideal goals worth aiming for. However, such ideals may never be achieved (as ideals rarely are) so it is necessary to approach the issue of what a tolerant society consists in not from the angle of what is required from individuals but from the angle of what is required from a state.

■ Tolerance and the state

Discussions of toleration in political philosophy are inseparably linked to religion, to conflict between religions and to the development of a political or 'civic' vision of the state. So much so that in the 16th and 17th centuries the notion of tolerance became a central concept in political philosophy. Arguably, the first purely political justification of tolerance appeared in the 16th century. The French writer Jean Bodin published his *Six Books of the Commonwealth* in 1576 during a period of intense religious conflict between Catholics and Huguenots which threatened the survival of the French state. Bodin equated sovereignty with power, arguing that sovereignty consists in the 'absolute and perpetual power vested in a commonwealth' so that in the absence of such power the state would, quite simply, cease to be a state. Consequently, Bodin proposed a view of the state as an essentially non-religious association responsible for maintaining social order rather than with promoting some religious conception of the good life. So, in order to maintain the preservation of political order, the role entrusted to the state, it was necessary to discard the preservation of religious unity and tolerance of religious diversity was recommended. The Edict of Nantes, issued on 30 April 1598 by Henry IV of France, restored civil rights to Huguenots (Protestants) thus preserving civil unity at the expense of religious unity.

Similarly, there were numerous sectarian differences of religious belief and practice in England in the 16th and 17th centuries and discriminatory practices against some religious groups as well as against those who refused to attend church on Sundays and Holy Days ('recusants'). There were Catholics, Anglicans, Presbyterians, Unitarians, Anti-Trinitarians, Baptists, Quakers, Latitudinarians, Dissenters, Ranters, Deists as well as non-believers. It was in this context that arguments for toleration, and against discrimination, began to appear. Thus, in the 1640s arguments for toleration were given by Roger Williams (1644), Jeremy Taylor (1647) and John Goodwin (1649). Some of their arguments were repeated by John Locke in 1689 in his *Letter Concerning Toleration* (1983). This has survived as an important work and we shall return to it below. Locke was not the only philosopher to write on toleration in the late 17th century; important works were also produced by Baruch de Spinoza (*Tractatus Theologico-Politicus*, 1670) and by Pierre Bayle (*Commentaire Philosophique*, 1686). However, if we put philosophical argument aside for one moment, it is worth noting a certain irony in the fact that the cause of religious toleration and the civic solution of limited government were most effectively promoted in a context in which a range of extreme groups, whose beliefs were largely intolerant, were active. In order to maintain their own interests, that is, they promoted a view of the state, and of the rights of man, that led ultimately to the notion of a free, tolerant, democracy. Thus, under Charles II the Declaration of Breda (1660) (a manifesto which outlined initial terms for the Restoration of the monarchy) stated:

> And because the passion and uncharitableness of the times have produced several opinions in religion, by which men are engaged in parties and animosities against each other (which, when they shall hereafter unite in a freedom of conversation, will be composed or better understood), we do declare a liberty to tender consciences, and that no man shall be disquieted or called in question for differences of opinion in matter of religion, which do not disturb the peace of the kingdom.

Declaration of Breda (1660)

In other words, the state will not prosecute people for what they believe: freedom of thought and expression, providing it does not disturb the peace, is granted; tolerance of another's right to hold and express a view is advocated since it will generate composure and better understanding.

While this may fall short of a contemporary ideal of tolerance – insofar as, for example, it does not say anything about not discriminating against different beliefs – it is clearly a step in the direction of a tolerant society.

ⓘ Arguments for toleration

Perhaps the most obvious argument for social and political toleration is pragmatism. That is, given the context of religious difference and diversity in which 'men are engaged in parties and animosities against each other' (Declaration of Breda, 1660), the safest option for political society is to tolerate the existence of difference and not side with one party whilst persecuting others. Toleration of different religions is required to preserve political unity and peace. Furthermore, tolerance may also be economically advantageous to society: not only does it promote peace but also prosperity. After the Edict of Nantes was revoked, in 1685, heralding a new wave of intolerance and persecution, France lost the hard-working and highly skilled Huguenots. In the 17th century the most tolerant society in Europe, the Dutch Republic, was also the most prosperous.

Furthermore, the role of the state was increasingly seen as secular: the duties of the state were to maintain order and security, preserve peace and create conditions where individuals could pursue their own interests and welfare. In order to preserve security, peace and justice the state may have occasion to regulate religious practices (if they threaten the security of the state or the peace of citizens), but it is not the business of the state to attempt to regulate an individual's 'inner' beliefs and convictions. Individuals have a right to think freely, make their own judgements and place trust in the religion of their choice. Indeed, one aim of John Locke's *Letter Concerning Toleration* was 'to distinguish exactly the business of Civil Government from that of Religion' (Locke, 1983).

Locke sees the state as:

> a society of men constituted only for the procuring, preserving and advancing of their own civil interests ... Life, Liberty, Health and indolency of Body; and the possession of outward things such as Money, Lands, Houses, Furniture and the like.

Locke (1983)

According to Locke, men have a natural right to life, liberty and property: governments were established to secure these rights; they were not established to save souls.

Some argued that reason reveals certain moral truths to all sincere and rational agents regardless of their religious faith. Such moral truths incorporated aspects of tolerance, respect for others and reciprocity in one's dealings with others, for example. These truths, revealed by reason or 'the light of nature', cannot be trumped by religious values which, in contrast, are based ultimately on faith, commitment and trust. They are not objective truths. Clearly, if we accept that religious beliefs are not certainties, and that our religious convictions may be wrong, then we are more likely to be tolerant of the beliefs of others providing they reciprocate.

Moreover, Locke certainly thought that toleration of religious difference was 'agreeable' both to our rational natures and to the 'Gospel of Jesus Christ' which, as far as he was concerned, did not contain an instruction to persecute others in order to get them to embrace Christianity. Indeed, New Testament Gospels favour argument and persuasion as routes to conversion. It might also be argued, as members of the 'Tew Circle' reasoned, that many divisions amongst Protestants – and Locke was, arguably, mainly concerned to promote tolerance amongst Protestants – were not foundational anyway, so that relatively minor differences of interpretation could, and should, be tolerated. (The Tew Circle was a group of intellectuals and humanists who met at Great Tew.)

> All the life and power of true religion consists in the inward and full persuasion of the mind; and faith is not faith without believing … in offering thus unto God Almighty such a worship as we esteem to be displeasing unto him, we add unto the number of our other sins those also of hypocrisy and contempt of his Divine Majesty.
>
> *Locke* (1983)

We cannot be saved by being forced to adopt religious practices that we do not believe in. Religion is a matter of conscience; none of us can be led to belief via 'the religion of the court'. Civil power cannot be used to force people to conform.

Neither can we entrust our salvation to others. Locke argues that God has not entrusted the care of souls to any man, including the civil magistrate. God has not given authority of one man over another in matters regarding religious belief and the civil magistrate has no more authority regarding religion, and is no less imperfect, than anyone else. So, just as force may not be used to create uniformity, civic authority cannot be used either. Locke appears to place more faith in mankind, as God's creation, than in the authority of the state, as man's creation. In this respect tolerance is to be preferred to authority because those in authority may be misled and their authority misused; indeed, through their imperfection, they may persecute the truly godly.

Despite these arguments, Locke was aware of the limits of tolerance:

- he did not feel that practices that were unlawful should be tolerated if they took place in religious assemblies (e.g. the ritual sacrifice of virgins would not be tolerable)
- he did not feel that atheism was tolerable because social and political relations depend on trust and ungodly atheists could not be trusted
- he did not advocate the tolerance of 'Papists' because, while he accorded them the same right to believe as others, he was suspicious of activities linked to foreign powers and which might be used to undermine the security of the state.

Ironically, it might be suggested that these arguments for a tolerant society have been embraced by intolerant groups and advanced by intolerant individuals (it is not clear, for example, that Locke was a tolerant man). However, they do constitute part of our cultural, moral and political tradition – the 'given' of our lives as citizens of this particular state – and they form some of the most powerful arguments for toleration which are part of this tradition.

Toleration and political theory

Liberalism

Locke's arguments for toleration constitute part of a liberal theory of society, of the role of the state and of the relationship between the individual and the state. In the words of one political philosopher, Locke is effectively saying:

> Leave us alone, let us speak, let us print, let us preach, meet and worship as we please. It is no part of your business as civil rulers to interfere with these activities. Do the duties with which you were entrusted when our forefathers brought governments into being; and do no more.

Cranston (1968)

Locke, although deeply religious himself, wanted to separate religious and secular authority: a Church that attempted to determine secular laws would be overstepping its authority, as would a government that tried to determine how, and which, religion was practised. According to Locke, governments exist to secure certain goods – life, liberty, property and physical well-being – and have no other duties. Conversely, religion should make no demands upon the state. His argument for religious toleration thus forms part of a liberal argument for minimal state interference in our lives. The limit of toleration, and the justification for state interference, is where religious beliefs and practices threaten political order and the 'goods' that governments exist to secure. A liberal state must operate according to the rule of law; the rights and liberties of its members must be protected.

In the 19th century John Stuart Mill reached similar conclusions. Mill's starting point was not that it is obvious what the business of government is, as Locke had thought, but that individuality and social progress, together with a limited role for governments, could be argued for on utilitarian grounds. In *On Liberty*, Mill promotes a view of human good as a whole that can also be linked to toleration. Freedom and diversity are valued because they produce individual happiness and social progress. In a tolerant society the individual can 'grow and develop'. Toleration, moreover, is no longer restricted to questions of religious difference: it applies to all areas of cultural diversity and difference. Mill's arguments for toleration, like Locke's, are also linked to a minimalist view of the state and, more importantly perhaps, to the fear of a tyranny of the majority. He argues that beliefs and actions should be tolerated if they cause no harm to others; because they generate productive social learning and because they enhance individuality and originality. In short, the outcome of tolerance is positive. Man is seen as a progressive being.

However, it is possible to question how convincing these arguments are. A liberal theory of society faces similar problems to those confronting a liberal theory of the good life for individuals:

- We can question whether a society that values individuality for its own sake is necessarily better on utilitarian grounds than a society in which community, stability and order are valued.
- It can be questioned whether freedom of conscience and experiments in living necessarily lead to moral progress; some are convinced that this is just as likely to contribute to moral decline or decadence.
- While it may be the case, as Locke argues, that we cannot change an individual's convictions through force, it does not follow that we cannot slow the spread of ideas we dislike through force or, if so, that force may therefore be useful against the growth of beliefs that threaten core social values.
- Some might argue further for an elitist conception of order, in which the best of us determine lifestyles for the rest of us.

More importantly, the suspicion remains that liberalism is based on dogmatic assertions of its own – that are irreconcilable with, or at least

Key philosopher

John Stuart Mill (1806–73)

Mill was interested in logic, epistemology, economics, social and political philosophy, ethics, metaphysics, religion and current affairs. He is noted for his advocacy of radical empiricism, utilitarianism, liberty and equal rights for women.

inhospitable to, alternative visions of society – so that, for every disputed issue, a liberal interpretation of the issue is preferred.

For example, according to 'autonomy-based liberalism' (in which respect is owed to individuals as morally autonomous beings with the abilities to choose, pursue and realise their own view of the good life), autonomy is a necessary condition of a good life. This, as we have seen, is not only dubious but, in the words of one writer, leads to toleration of only 'those diverse forms of life which themselves value autonomy' (Mendus, 1989). In this case, the distinction between the objection component and the rejection component of tolerance is blurred and, arguably, toleration has not really got off the ground. Autonomy-rejecting cultures are viewed as inferior and are objected to. If, on the other hand, they are objected to but accepted (for the moral reason that they have a right to determine their own values), and the grounds for objection are moral (autonomy is necessary for morality) then we have the paradox of moral tolerance – it is morally right to tolerate what is morally wrong. (Note that, as mentioned earlier in the chapter, this paradox may be avoided if a particular moral wrong is higher in a moral hierarchy than tolerance: so that it cannot be morally right to tolerate evil. There are limits to what is tolerable.)

Alternatively, in neutrality-based liberalism (in which any attempt to determine the necessary conditions for a good life is avoided) moral reasons for objection cannot count as reasons for rejection because they are not reciprocally accepted. Rather, neutrality requires diverse groups to accept rational debate and argumentation rather than a commitment to any conception of the good life as a procedure for finding grounds for agreement that no group rejects. But, firstly, the commitment to reason – rather than faith, for example – is hardly neutral and, secondly, it sets the limit of tolerance at those views and practices that do not violate the principle of rational debate. So, for example, fanaticism would not be tolerated. Again, we might ask what makes rational debate preferable to devotion. Similarly, if a culture does not tolerate groups who do not accept some principle of toleration, has it become intolerant itself?

Despite various difficulties many liberals do wish to occupy the moral high ground. For example, Rawls' notion of the 'overlapping consensus', in which broad political values are agreed upon leaving people free to disagree about any moral, religious and cultural foundations there may be for those values, is seen by many liberals as a strength of those democratic societies characterised by increasing diversity and according a central role to toleration.

Conservatism

The conservative approach to toleration is, at best, pragmatic rather than principled and, at worse, hostile. Toleration of diversity and difference has generally been seen as a threat to tradition, shared values and social integration. Conservatives generally see change, such as increasing diversity, as potentially upsetting, bringing unpredictable and possibly negative outcomes. Conservatives also oppose the liberal notion that society should be whatever the individuals, or groups of individuals, in that society wish it to be. They think that this is the wrong way round and that society precedes individual identities. Social institutions such as the Church, therefore, are seen to have important roles in maintaining social order and stability and in shaping core values and individual identities. Conservatives, therefore, have tended to agree with Hobbes who argued that religious beliefs and practices were

Fig. 6.4 *The moral high ground*

far too important to be left to individuals. Hobbes, unlike Locke, was sceptical about religious claims but aware that they arouse deep feelings and, as such, may disturb the peace. However, like other political theories, conservatism has to respond to changed circumstances. So, for example, given a context of increasing religious diversity and given the increasingly secular nature of society, a conservative has to be prepared to accommodate themselves to this and tolerate at least gradual change. It is probably fair to say that conservatism has not exactly embraced the idea of tolerating diversity, but it has been pragmatic: judgements about what is tolerable are made on the basis of past experience rather than on a set of principles. It is not likely that a conservative would accept a principle of respect or toleration that could be applied to all beliefs and practices.

This can lead to the charge of inconsistency because conservatives may eventually accept something that they were fiercely resistant to for a long time. However, the last decades of the 20th century saw a return to conviction politics and with this a neo-conservative rejection of the notion of toleration. Tolerance was viewed as responsible for moral decline and social decay. Diversity, as ever, was not to be valued for its own sake and on top of this some groups began to be seen as an 'enemy within' (gays, single mothers, welfare scroungers, atheists, liberals, etc.). Consequently, society was divided, as one philosopher puts it, between 'Puritania' and 'Pluristan' (Critchley, 2006). In this vision, intolerance is allied to notions like freedom, democracy and rights. These characterise Puritania but are absent in Pluristan – and particularly absent in the 'enemy without'. Politics, religion and morality combine in this vision to construct the 'other' as intolerable, as an outcast or outlaw and, possibly, as evil.

A radical view of tolerance

The liberal view of tolerance has also been criticised from some on the political left. Like conservatives, some radical thinkers feel that toleration, if adopted as a pragmatic response to diversity, is not a sufficiently thick glue to bond a moral community together. Unlike conservatives, radical thinkers base their view of a moral community on a critique of how values have come to be shared. Marcuse, for example, argues that:

> The realization of the objective of tolerance would call for intolerance toward prevailing policies, attitudes, opinions … what is proclaimed and practiced as tolerance today, is in many of its most effective manifestations serving the cause of oppression.

Marcuse (1969a)

Briefly, Marcuse argues that whereas tolerance is or should be an end in itself, the tolerance that is practised today 'strengthens the tyranny of the majority'. Affluent societies 'deliver the goods' – that is, affluent lifestyles – and, because of this, we tolerate 'the systematic moronization of children and adults alike'. Tolerance becomes a passive state, it is 'extended to policies, conditions and behaviour which should not be tolerated because they are impeding, if not destroying, the chances of creating an existence without fear and misery' (Marcuse, 1969a).

Key philosopher

Herbert Marcuse (1898–1979)

Marcuse was a renowned 'new left' figure in 1960s' America. He was a philosopher, social theorist and political activist. He is associated with The Frankfurt School although he fled Nazi Germany in 1933 and never returned. He taught philosophy and politics at a number of American universities, including Columbia, Harvard and California.

According to Marcuse, it is necessary to create a society in which tolerance is not indiscriminate; a society in which manipulation and indoctrination are not tolerated.

> Within the affluent democracy, the affluent discussion prevails, and within the established framework, it is tolerant to a large extent … in endlessly dragging debates over the media, the stupid opinion is treated with the same respect as the intelligent one, the misinformed may talk as long as the informed, and propaganda rides along with education, truth and falsehood. This pure toleration of sense and nonsense is justified by the democratic argument that … all contesting opinions must be submitted to 'the people'.
>
> *Marcuse (1969a)*

Marcuse's concern was that 'the people' may not be capable of deliberating or of making an autonomous decision if, due to affluence, manipulation and indoctrination, they are 'falsely conscious'. Marcuse was not optimistic about the abilities of 'the people' to resist economic and political power and create a new 'universal' moral community:

> In the affluent society, the authorities are hardly forced to justify their dominion. They deliver the goods; they satisfy the sexual and aggressive energy of their subjects … The people, efficiently manipulated and organized are free … free people are not in need of liberation.
>
> *Marcuse (1969a)*

However, in the late 1960s, Marcuse found some grounds for optimism in the emergence of a counter-culture in Western societies arguing that 'by nature' 'the young are in the forefront of those who live and fight for **Eros** against Death' and that 'the fight for life, the fight for Eros, is the political fight' (Marcuse, 1969b). Marcuse employs Eros in the same way that Freud did: as the great unifying force that preserves all life. Sexuality is accorded a predominant role: mental processes are governed by the pleasure principle, and the instinct, operating under this principle, which sustains life is Eros.

In order to clarify his meaning we should consider a further example in which tolerance is at issue.

Tolerance and pornography

Pornography, false needs and repressive desublimation

Marcuse appears to regard pornography as an instance of **repressive desublimation**. He refers to 'the social steering of sexuality through controlled desublimation' and 'the plastic beauty industry' as promoting '"legitimate" satisfaction' (Marcuse, 1972). What does he mean by this? His critique of affluent, Western, capitalist societies combines elements of Marxist and Freudian thought, so that repression is both economic and psychological.

Thus, Marcuse refers to the Marxian view – as outlined by Marx's collaborator Engels in *The Origin of the Family, Private Property and the State* – that the development of the monogamous nuclear family to suit the needs of capitalism is a form of sexual exploitation. Specifically, the restriction of females to the private sphere of the home, as wives and mothers, while familial property was passed on through male heirs, was an essential feature of bourgeois ideology at a particular moment of capitalist development. This as well as further restrictions concerning

Key terms

Eros: the Greek god of love and sex, of romantic and sexual desire.

AQA Examiner's tip

Alternative illustrative material might be used. Any material on 'alternative' lifestyles and social difference which raises issues of diversity, conflict of interests and toleration might be employed to address these learning objectives. Pornography has been selected here only because there is a history of writing about it in relation to freedom of expression, tolerance and censorship.

Key terms

Repressive desublimation: this concept refers to a process where something which was seen as sublime (love, marriage, purity before marriage) loses value as something else (sex, pleasure) takes its place *but* this happens in a way that debases human relationships and restrains or curbs the possibilities of genuine experiences of sexual fulfilment and love.

Key terms

Repressive: restraining or holding back.

Sublimated: purified or held as an ideal.

'acceptable' feminine traits, were **repressive** insofar as they are limiting. However, they are not simply economically repressive. Bourgeois morality **sublimated** these roles insofar as they were exalted, and this also brings psychological dimensions to repression. Freud had argued that culture derives much of the energy it needs by subtracting it from sexuality, by inhibiting sexuality. Indeed, all societies need to control expressions of sexuality in order to avoid chaos and function smoothly. So, bourgeois, and religious, morality defined 'legitimate' expressions of sexual desire in terms of love expressed through the conjugal bond between husband and wife. Thus, sexual desire exalted as love becomes sublimated. To the extent that this view is accepted, and practised as lived experience, repression is psychological: sexual drives are inhibited, dignified and sublimated into the higher value of love. The use of the body as an object, an instrument of pleasure, became taboo, 'the ill-reputed privilege of whores, degenerates and perverts' (Marcuse, 1969b).

Pornography insofar as it resexualises the body, particularly female bodies, presents women as sexual objects and accords such representations an exchange value in the marketplace. It also devalues earlier images of women as mothers and wives. So, the representation of women as sexual objects is a desublimation of bourgeois morality. This process is also a stage of capitalist development: the body as a commodity, as a thing to be enjoyed, as plastically idealised in pornographic magazines and videos, has invaded previously sanctified realms. This may also have consequences for the institution, the monogamous family unit, in which private interpersonal relations had previously been organised. But it is still repressive, for men and women. Pornographic representations are dehumanising: women are represented as passive objects and males consume these representations as aggressive subjects. Marcuse sees pornography as signalling the explosion of suppressed sexuality, an outlet for frustration, a commodity form creating, and satisfying, false needs rather than truly human sexual relationships in which both males and females are objects *and* subjects at the same time. The free development of a transformed libido, he thinks, requires a transformation of social institutions. This is why he argues that the fight for Eros is a political fight. Marcuse does not see private acts of rebellion against bourgeois morality as liberating because they are not political; they do not affect society as a whole.

Pornography, free expression and other values

In places, when worrying about the tyranny of the majority and when arguing for genuine tolerance as a precondition for a humane society, Marcuse echoes Mill. Conversely, when arguing that it 'is in the interests of rulers that people should hold slavish opinions' (Mill, 1985) and that if such interests were successfully pursued domination would be secure, Mill sounds like Marcuse. Perhaps the crucial difference between them is Mill's view that:

> The objections which have been urged against the principle of free discussion, though infinitely diversified in shape, are at bottom only one assertion: the incapacity of the people to form correct opinions. This assumption is indeed the stronghold of all the disguised or undisguised partisans of despotism.

Mill (1985)

Mill, it would seem, would regard Marcuse's intolerance of right-wing views as a form of despotism.

In *On Liberty* (1859), Mill raises a question concerning indecency where 'the instigator derives a personal benefit … to promote what society and the State consider to be an evil'. Should this be tolerated or not? Specifically, his question is: 'Fornication, for example, must be tolerated … but should a person be free to pimp'? His answer is as follows:

> On the side of toleration it may be said that the fact of following anything as an occupation, and living or profiting by the practice of it, cannot make that criminal which would otherwise be admissible; that the act should either be consistently permitted or consistently prohibited; that if the principles which we have hitherto defended are true, society has no business, as society, to decide anything to be wrong which concerns only the individual; that it cannot go beyond dissuasion, and that one person should be as free to persuade as another to dissuade. In opposition to this it may be contended that, although the public or the State are not warranted in authoritatively deciding, for purposes of repression or punishment, that such and such conduct affecting only the interests of the individual is good or bad, they are fully justified in assuming, if they regard it as bad, that its being so or not is at least a disputable question: that, this being supposed, they cannot be acting wrongly in endeavouring to exclude the influence of solicitations which are not disinterested, of instigators who cannot possibly be impartial – who have a direct personal interest on one side and that side the one which the State believes to be wrong … they may be compelled to conduct their operations with a certain degree of secrecy and mystery, so that nobody knows anything about them but those who seek them; and more than this society ought not to aim at.
>
> *Mill (1985)*

If we try to apply this to pornography, it would seem that society cannot judge pornography to be bad; cannot restrict an industry that promotes acts considered to be acceptable in private; cannot prevent the pornographer from persuading people to participate in or consume pornography. However, society can inform those engaged in pornography that their actions are not especially welcome and can place some restrictions on the distribution of pornography.

This view was ridiculed by Mill's conservative critic Sir James Fitzjames Stephen in his essay 'Liberty, Equality, Fraternity' (1874). Stephen was a judge and an eminent legal theorist rather than a philosopher. However, the issue he raises – concerning the State's role in maintaining public morality – is philosophical:

> I do not think the State ought to stand bandying compliments with pimps. 'Without offence to your better judgment, dear sir, and without presuming to set up my opinion against yours, I beg to observe that I am entitled for certain purposes to treat the question whether your views of life are right as one which admits of two opinions. I am far from expressing absolute condemnation of an experiment in living from which I dissent (I am sure that mere dissent will not offend a person of your liberality of sentiment) but still I am compelled to observe that you are not altogether unbiased by personal considerations in the choice of the course of life which you have adopted (no doubt for reasons which appear to you satisfactory, though they do not convince me). I venture, accordingly, though with the greatest deference, to call upon you not to exercise your profession'.
>
> *Stephen (1999)*

Key philosopher

James Fitzjames Stephen (1829–94)

Stephen was an English judge and Professor of Common Law who took exception to some of John Stuart Mill's arguments and positions.

Freedom and equality

Stephen's view is that individuals, as social creatures, do have an interest in the thoughts, feelings and conduct of others and, in the case of indecency or vice, the moral force of public opinion should apply. In short, we should not tolerate it. Moreover, intolerance of pornography is not the preserve of conservatives. Radical feminists, such as Catharine MacKinnon, also strongly disapprove. MacKinnon argues that freedom of expression clashes with social equality and with substantive legal equality. In *Only Words* (1993) she presents the view that freedom of speech is not equal, that some have more power to speak than others and that the protection of the freedom of speech of pornographers (mainly men) maintains their dominance at the expense of their relatively powerless victims (mainly women). In an interview following the publication of her book *Are Women Human?* MacKinnon argues:

> Pornography affects people's belief in rape myths. So for example if a woman says 'I didn't consent' and people have been viewing pornography, they believe rape myths and believe the woman did consent no matter what she said. That when she said no, she meant yes. When she said she didn't want to, that meant more beer. When she said she would prefer to go home, that means she's a lesbian who needs to be given a good corrective experience. Pornography promotes these rape myths and desensitises people to violence against women so that you need more violence to become sexually aroused if you're a pornography consumer.
>
> *MacKinnon (2006)*

In *Only Words* she envisages a society, without pornography, in which equality is a fact and in which 'sex between people and things, human beings and pieces of paper, real men and unreal women, will be a turn off' and pornography will belong in museums. In the meantime MacKinnon, a lawyer and academic, prefers to fight pornography through the law by offering a civil remedy to people who can prove they have been harmed. For example, MacKinnon represented Linda Susan Boreman (better known under her stage name of Linda Lovelace) from 1980 until her death in 2002.

MacKinnon's views have prompted numerous hostile responses. Some post-feminists have accused her of exaggerating the extent to which women are victims and promoting a culture of powerlessness amongst women. Others have accused her of being a fanatical exponent of political correctness and of advocating a climate on university campuses in which freedom of speech and various academic freedoms are inhibited.

Think about

Is 'exploitation' clearly applied? Are these borderline cases with artistic representation? Can we always distinguish these in terms of their motive?

Think about

Which of the following statements do you agree with?

- Because it objectifies women and promotes sexual aggression in males, pornography should not be tolerated.
- Pornography creates and satisfies false needs or desires: we should not tolerate that which is false.
- Some, possibly a minority, enjoy consuming pornography; those who don't, possibly the majority, have no right to interfere with this.
- A community that tolerates easy access to pornographic material can no longer be a strong moral community.

■ Only if we stand firm against depravity, indecency, vice and pornography can we occupy a moral high ground about sexual relations.

■ Conclusion

You may feel sympathetic to the view that tolerance is the virtue of pluralist, liberal democracies, or of societies increasingly characterised by difference and diversity, or to the view that tolerance is important due to its role in supporting other things that are held to be valuable:

■ You might agree that a version of 'autonomy-based liberalism', with its emphasis on the moral right of free individuals to choose, pursue and realise their own view of the good life, provides the best justification for individuals to adopt an attitude of tolerance towards others or for the state to allow as many freedoms as possible.

■ Alternatively, you might feel that a version of 'neutrality-based liberalism', in which the emphasis is placed on the acceptance of rational debate and argumentation as procedures for resolving conflicts, rather than on freedom as a necessary constituent of the good life, is the most promising way to justify toleration.

Either of these positions would need to be *argued*. You would need to justify why either view survives the charge that it is itself intolerant towards cultural practices in which freedom of choice and open debate are accorded less value, or why the apparent contradictions that toleration produces are not serious problems. Perhaps a particular *conception* of tolerance could be employed to argue this.

On the other hand, you may wish to argue that, for example, social cohesion and social order (or the creation and sustenance of a humane and equal society) are more important than the rights of individuals to hold and pursue whatever values and cultural practices they choose:

■ You might argue here that an attitude of tolerance is a mistake: it undermines social order and leads to social decay or to a moral vacuum. From this point of view, it might be said that an attitude of intolerance is preferable. There is plenty of sociological evidence that Muslim communities in the UK, for example, may restrict the freedoms of girls in particular rather than have their cultural values and reputations 'polluted' through engagement with Western permissive, and promiscuous, attitudes.

■ Alternatively, you might argue that various illiberal communities satisfy criteria for being tolerant or could be described as tolerant under a particular *conception* of tolerance. For example, some Muslims *object* to certain Western values and practices; nevertheless, they may *accept* the rights of non-Muslims to hold different values and engage in different practices (they may also accept that those who differ from them in this respect are similar in other respects, for example as employees or as homeowners, and that they share certain interests in common). What they might *reject*, however, is the notion that members of their own households have the right to choose between two cultures.

Again, either view would need to be *argued*. The main point is that certain values may be more significant than individualism or autonomy, or that they may be compatible with individualism, autonomy and rationality. Beyond this, it might also be argued

AQA Examiner's tip

In questions that require you to 'assess', it is necessary to argue a case and reach a conclusion in relation to the question.

that such values either justify intolerance or can be presented as a particular conception of tolerance.

You might also sympathise with Nietzsche's view that 'there would be no life at all if not on the basis of perspectivist assessments' (Nietzsche, 1998). We should not be looking for a truth concerning whether we ought to be tolerant or not; there is no such truth. Rather we should accept that there is no 'view from nowhere' and that perspectives on tolerance will differ accordingly.

After working through this topic, you should:

- be familiar with several arguments for tolerance
- be able to distinguish different theoretical approaches to how tolerance is linked to the good for man
- use examples drawn from particular issues, such as pornography and religious diversity, to assess tolerance and views about the limits of what is tolerable.

Further reading

There is no tradition of teaching tolerance as a political concept at AS-level and there are few accessible resources. The following, however, might be useful:

Hamilton, C. *Understanding Philosophy for AS Level*, Nelson Thornes, 2003. This includes a brief section on tolerance in the chapter on moral philosophy. This section contains a clear outline of some Lockean arguments for toleration.

Rosen, M. and Wolff, J. (eds) *Political Thought*, an Oxford Reader, Oxford University Press, 1999. This contains readings from Locke, Scanlon, Waldron and MacKinnon as well as relevant readings from Mill and Stephen. The readings are briefly and clearly introduced by the editors.

The 'Religious Tolerance' website, www.religioustolerance.org, aims to promote free discussion and cultural diversity and, consequently, contains a range of discussions on religious beliefs and practices as well as dicussions of different lifestyle choices.

Summary questions

1 Consider the claim that restricting freedom of expression is more harmful than allowing others to express views that many find distasteful.

2 Assess whether tolerance is a virtue.

3 Tolerance remains a key political issue. Discuss.

4 Being tolerant requires you to accept all religious convictions. Discuss.

5 Tolerant people would never say anything to cause offence. Discuss.

6 Assess the claim that as soon as we suggest a limit to what is tolerable we become intolerant.

7 Should a tolerant society try to nurture certain values?

8 We should not tolerate intolerance. Discuss.

9 Tolerance is merely pragmatism: it is necessary for peaceful coexistence. Consider this view.

10 Outline and assess three reasons for being tolerant of views that you disagree with.

7 The idea of God

The ontological argument

The ontological argument

Learning objectives:

- to examine widely known versions of the ontological argument for the existence of God

- to critically assess the ontological argument

- to understand how the ontological argument relates to both the idea of God and other arguments for God's existence.

Key terms

Cosmological: cosmological arguments are arguments that argue for God's existence from cause and effect with the 'first cause' or 'unmoved mover' usually being identified with God.

Teleological arguments: these are arguments based on the 'telos' (Greek word meaning 'ends') of a particular subject. More commonly they are called the 'design' arguments and claim that the world is so intricate that it must have been designed by a designer, namely God.

A posteriori: knowledge that we learn from experience. For example, we observe the sun rising every day so we make the assumption that the sun *will* rise every day.

Reductio ad absurdum: a reduction to the absurd. A *reductio ad absurdum* is a form of logical argument which aims to prove a contention by demonstrating that its denial leads to an absurdity.

Introduction

This chapter focuses on three closely related problems all of which revolve around the idea of God. Firstly, and most fundamentally, can we prove the existence of God from the actual idea of God itself? We will consider one of the most famous arguments for the existence of God, the ontological argument. Then we will examine where the idea of God may have emerged from. We will look at whether God is something that is simply part of our innate constitutions or whether God emerges from social or psychological need. Finally, we will look at the classical conception of God and a number of problems associated with this.

The basics of the ontological argument

The ontological argument is one of the classical arguments in favour of the existence of God. In truth, there are a number of different arguments and therefore it is better to speak of ontological *arguments*. Whatever the version, they do share an essential approach which is philosophically unique. Unlike other arguments for the existence of God such as the **cosmological** or **teleological arguments**, it does not start from the way the world is and work backwards (or upwards) to God. There is no attempt to describe a state of affairs in the world and use that as evidence of God causing the world or designing the world or creating moral facts within the world. Instead, it starts with the concept or the idea of God and then goes on to make a claim about the way the world is. This type of argument, based on a priori reasoning, is akin to mathematics and draws both its strengths and weaknesses from this fact. Like mathematics, it can theoretically give certainty. The reasoning of the other arguments, which are **a posteriori** (based on experience) is more akin to science, which can never give certainty only probability – although sometimes this probability reaches near certainty. However, a priori reasoning does not necessarily tell us anything about the real world; like mathematics, it allows us to move certainty from premises to conclusions but, by itself, this cannot tell us that the premises are actually true.

Older formulations

The original debate

The original and best-known form of the argument is found in chapter 2 of the *Proslogion* written by St Anselm of Canterbury (1078). He defines God as *'aliquid quo nihil maius cogitari possit'* – something greater than which nothing greater can be thought. Then, by way of a **reductio ad absurdum**, he proceeds to speak of the 'fool' who says, 'There is no God'. By making this denial, argues Anselm, the fool has the idea of 'God' in his mind. However, because of the definition of God (as that which nothing greater can be conceived) and with existence being part of that greatness, then it follows that God must exist. Anselm, then, is using a

St Anselm of Canterbury (1033–1109)

He was born in Italy but reached high Church office in Britain. He openly opposed the Crusades and is usually thought of as one of the founders of scholasticism.

Gaunilo (11th century)

Gaunilo was a Benedictine Monk of Marmoutier Abbey in France. His reply to Anselm's *Proslogion*, 'On Behalf of the Fool' is his only work that is still in existence.

Think about

Consider these statements: 'My future house will be better if it is insulated than if it is not.' 'My future house will be better if it exists than if it does not.' The first statement clearly makes sense but does the second one? If not, why not?

Key terms

Contingent: if a connection is contingent, it is conceivable that it could be different. It does not have to be true.

Aseity: a theological term that is used to express the claim that God is entirely self-sufficient. He is not dependent upon any other thing either for his existence or for his nature, and it is impossible for him ever to have come to exist or ever to cease to exist. He is entirely necessary.

form of analytic reasoning to attempt to deduce the actual existence of God from the idea of God.

We may attempt to capture the argument in a series of logical steps.

1 'God' is defined as 'a being that which nothing greater can be conceived'.
2 God exists in the understanding.
3 God might exist in reality.
4 If something exists only in the understanding although it is possible that it could exist in reality, then it is possible that it could be greater than it is.
5 Suppose God exists only in the understanding.
6 God might have been greater than He is.
7 So God is a being than which a greater being is possible.
8 Hence, 'God' understood as the being than which nothing greater is possible is a being than which a greater is possible.
9 This is an absurd conclusion – it leads to a formal contradiction – and so in order to avoid it we will have to reject Step 5.
10 Hence, it is false that God exists only in the understanding.
11 God exists in reality as well as in the understanding.

Criticism using the idea of a perfect island

Anselm's argument met criticism right from the outset. A monk named Gaunilo wrote *A response on behalf of the fool* (no date) and in it suggests the idea of the perfect island. It is an island of unsurpassed beauty and climate, 'it is blessed with all manner of delights in abundance'. In short, it is an island of which no greater could be conceived. Making fun of Anselm somewhat, he then goes on to state that if the most perfect island were to exist only in his mind alone then it would cease to be the most perfect island and therefore it must exist in reality. The thrust of Gaunilo's argument is to show what he perceives as the absolute absurdity of Anselm's reasoning. If we conceive of the most perfect anything – say a holiday with the most beautiful partner, the most wonderful friends, the finest food and drink, the greatest transport, the most fascinating attractions, the most perfect climate – then it must exist. If it did not then it would not be the most perfect as existing would clearly make anything more perfect than not existing.

There is, though, one very important difference between Anselm's perfect being and a perfect island or a perfect holiday. The existence of an island (or a holiday) is entirely **contingent**, it does not necessarily have to exist just because we can conceive it; it is always possible to add or remove 'it exists' without the idea of the 'perfect island' becoming contradictory.

However, God's existence is necessary, as Anselm indicates in chapter 3 of the *Proslogion*. If existence were taken away from the concept 'God', then it would be changed beyond recognition. God is unique in this respect, He is said to possess **aseity**. Anselm argues as follows:

> For something can be thought that cannot be thought not to exist. Hence, if that-than-which-a-greater-cannot-be-thought can be thought not to exist, then that-than-which-a-greater-cannot-be-thought is not the same as that-than-which-a-greater-cannot-be-thought, which is absurd. Something-than-which-a-greater-cannot-be-thought exists so truly then, that it cannot be even thought not to exist.

Anselm (1965)

Later on in the chapter we will look in more detail at the modern version of the ontological argument that focuses on Chapter 3 of Anselm's *Proslogion*.

Schopenhauer's objection

A well-known objection to the ontological argument was proposed by the 19th-century philosopher Arthur Schopenhauer. His criticism is contained in the following passage:

> Consider by daylight, however, and without prejudice, this famous ontological argument is really a charming joke. On some occasion or other, someone excogitates a conception, composed out of all sorts of predicates, among which however he takes care to include the **predicate** of actuality or existence, either openly stated or wrapped up for decency's sake in some other predicate such as *perfectio*, *immensitas*, or something of the kind … the predicate reality or existence is not extracted from this arbitrarily thought conception, and an object corresponding to it is forthwith presumed to have real existence independently of the conception.

Schopenhauer (2007, pp11–12)

Schopenhauer's point is that the argument begs the question of God's existence, since the conclusion – God's existence – is written into the premise from the beginning. This, it can be argued, is not entirely fair. In Anselm's original statement at least, the argument does not proceed by constructing a conception of God into which the predicate of existence is placed, as Schopenhauer suggests. Rather, it claims that if you subtract the notion of existence from the conception of a greatest conceivable being, you are left with a contradiction. The focus of the ontological argument is that existence must be at the very heart of the idea of God if this idea is to be coherent at all; it cannot be an artificial addition.

The meaning of existence

René Descartes, writing in his most famous work, *The Meditations* (1641), restated the ontological argument in a slightly different form. He argues that the mind is the source of genuine knowledge of the world and that the mind is capable of grasping the essential nature of things. He states:

> existence can no more be separated from the essence of God than can its having its three angles equal to two right angles be separated from the essence of a triangle, or than the idea of a mountain can be separated from the idea of a valley; so there is not less contradiction in conceiving a God (that is, a being supremely perfect) to whom existence is lacking (that is to say, to whom a certain perfection is lacking), than to conceive of a mountain which has no valley.

Descartes (1968, Meditation 5)

Descartes is aware, though, of the basic response to this, namely that just because I, or you, conceive of something – even something that is logically certain – it does not mean it exists. Descartes himself says, 'my thought imposes no necessity on things'. However, he goes on to distinguish between triangles and their angles and mountains and their valleys in a way similar to that in which we discussed a possible response to Gaunilo's criticism. Triangles cannot be logically conceived without their angles, nor mountains without their valleys, but it is irrelevant to their conceptions whether or not they exist or not. Existence can be added to or subtracted from them, but their conception remains the

Key terms

Predicate: that part of a clause that describes something. A predicate normally goes with a 'subject'. In the statement 'grass is green' 'is green' is the predicate while 'grass' is the subject.

Fig. 7.1 *Arthur Schopenhauer*

Key philosophers

Immanuel Kant (1724–1804)

Kant thought that the traditional arguments for the existence of God were flawed, but nonetheless he argued that God exists as the rationale for morality and the transcendent.

Arthur Schopenhauer (1724–1804)

Schopenhauer was a Kantian philosopher but, unlike Kant, he believed that reality, as it is in itself, is irrational will. This led him to regard life as a pattern of frustration and boredom. He advocated aesthetic contemplation as an escape.

same. God, however, is defined by Descartes as a *perfect* being and if He did not exist He would lack a perfection; existence is therefore a property of a perfect being. Existence is part of 'God' as possessing three angles is part of 'triangle'. To deny His existence would imply a contradiction, therefore God must exist. Descartes' argument received detailed and sustained criticism from Immanuel Kant.

Existence as a predicate

Immanuel Kant provides two of the clearest and strongest criticisms of the ontological argument. Firstly, he argues that no proposition that contains the notion of existence is logically necessary. In his *Critique of Pure Reason* (1781) Kant writes:

> If, in an identical proposition, I reject the predicate while retaining the **subject**, contradiction results; and I therefore say that the former belongs necessarily to the latter. But if we reject the subject and the predicate alike, there is no contradiction; for nothing is then left that can be contradicted. To posit a triangle, and yet to reject its three angles, is self-contradictory; but there is no contradiction in rejecting the triangle together with its three angles. The same holds true of the concept of an absolutely necessary being. If its existence is rejected, we reject the thing itself with all its predicates; and no question of contradiction can then arise. There is nothing outside it that would be contradicted, since the necessity of the thing is not supposed to be derived from anything external; nor is there anything internal that would be contradicted, since in rejecting the thing itself we have at the same time rejected all its internal properties.

Kant (1989)

Thus, while it is incoherent to reject the idea of a mountain whilst keeping the valley, there is no contradiction in rejecting both the valley and the mountain, as Descartes would acknowledge. So, with the idea of God it is not contradictory to reject both the concept and its perfections.

Secondly, Kant argues that the key weakness of the argument is that it treats existence as a property or quality of a thing and this he contends is a mistake. Kant states:

> 'Being' is obviously not a real predicate; that is, it is not a concept of something which could be added to the concept of a thing. It is merely the positing of a thing, or of certain determinations, as existing in themselves.

Kant (1989)

So, logically, existence is not something that can be ascribed in the same manner as regular properties. For example, if you state that 'the sofa is green' then you are adding something to the basic idea of 'sofa', namely, that it is 'green'. However, to say that the 'sofa exists' adds nothing to the concept. The sofa may or may not exist, but existence is not a true property of it. Is this the case, though? At one level it would matter to you if the green sofa in your house did or did not exist. It could be seen as the most important property when considered in this way. However, as a matter of logic, Kant is probably correct.

If, for example, you listed the properties of apples as hard, sweet, round, etc, 'exist' would not figure in this list, despite the fact that in some respects it appears to be just another property. One can imagine checking whether an apple is green, hard, sweet or round, but how would you check whether it possessed the property of existence? If it did not exist there would be no 'it' to check.

Frege's solution

If existence is not an ordinary property or predicate, what exactly is it? Gottlob Frege provided an answer which is now generally accepted. He claims 'existence' is a 'second-level predicate'. Second-level predicates are used to tell us something about ordinary (first-level) predicates such as 'is green' or 'is sweet'. Accordingly, the claim that 'green exists', for example, tells us that there are some things to which the predicate 'is green' can be applied, i.e. there are things that possess the property of greenness. Similarly, the claim that 'apples exist' tells us that there are some things that possess the property of appleness, or of 'being an apple'. If this is right, it means that when we say 'God exists' we are not ascribing a predicate to God, rather we are claiming that there is something that possesses the property of 'being God'; or, to use Frege's expression, there is something that falls under the concept 'God'. One obvious problem with this analysis is that the term God in the sentence 'God exists' needs to be understood, not as a name of a being, but as expressing the predicate 'Godness', which certainly seems counter-intuitive.

Is this a decisive blow to the ontological argument? Not exactly. We should note that Frege's solution does not entirely vindicate Kant's claim that existence is not a 'real predicate'. It is a predicate but one of a different kind to that envisaged by Descartes. This means it might be possible to reformulate the argument. This will not be pursued here but it is something that the reader might follow up (e.g. see Dore, 1997).

A modern formulation

Despite its antiquity the ontological argument has received considerable critical attention in the past century and there have been a number of interesting attempts to resurrect it.

Norman Malcolm returns to Chapter 3 of Anselm's *Proslogion* and offers an alternative interpretation of the argument.

Here is a summary of his argument:

1 God is self-sufficient and so not dependent on any other thing for His existence. This means He is unlimited or necessary. (This is expressed by the claim that God possesses aseity, defined earlier.)

2 So God's existence or non-existence cannot be dependent on contingent features about how the world happens to be.

3 Therefore, if God does not exist His coming into existence would involve a contradiction. Such an event would either be caused or just happen and both cases involve contingency. In both cases God would lack self-sufficiency and necessity, and so contradict the definition given above.

4 So if God does not exist His existence would be impossible.

5 If God exists His existence will be necessary.

Malcolm completes the argument in the following:

> Thus God's existence is either impossible or necessary. It can be the former only if the concept of such a being is self-contradictory or in some way logically absurd. Assuming that this is not so, it follows that He necessarily exists

Malcolm (1960)

Think about

Try to work out how the ontological argument might be reformulated using Frege's account of existence.

Key philosopher
Gottlob Frege (1848–1925)

Frege was a mathematician, logician and philosopher whose influence was crucial in the development of modern analytic philosophy. He believed that ordinary language hides underlying logical relations, and so devised his own logical symbolic system.

Key philosopher
Norman Malcolm (1911–90)

American philosopher who taught at Cornell University for many years. He was keenly interested in the work of Ludwig Wittgenstein and most of his work develops themes in the philosophy of mind.

It should be noticed first of all that this argument does not depend on the claim that necessary existence is a perfection. In the quote above Malcolm gets us to accept something that seems innocuous enough, i.e. that the idea of God is not self-contradictory (although this is certainly arguable). However, since the concept of God appears to involve necessary existence, by accepting the coherence of the concept we are, it seems, committing ourselves to actual existence.

However, we should distinguish between 'being necessary' in the sense given at 1 and 'necessary existence' given at the end of the argument. If we translate 5 so it is consistent with the meaning of 'necessary' given at 1, we get 'If God exists His existence will be self-sufficient and so not dependent on any other thing'. The disjunction given at the beginning of the quote now loses all of its potency. We have something like 'God's existence is either impossible or He will be self-sufficient etc. if He exists' and we can accept the second alternative without committing ourselves to God's existence. Crucially we must be clear that the description of God given at 1 can only be a description of the attributes He would possess if He exists.

Even if ultimately this argument fails, Malcolm does go on to make the interesting claim that existence is not necessarily a simple idea with only one meaning. He points out, for example, that mathematicians quite happily argue a priori that 'there exists an infinite number of prime numbers'. Clearly the kind of existence prime numbers have is quite different from the kind of existence that chairs have. Could it not be true that the kind of existence that God has is different again?

Conclusion

It is possible to say a number of things about the ontological argument. Firstly, it is a unique attempt, or more properly a series of attempts, to prove the existence of God a priori. The strength of this approach is that if the attempt were to be successful it could provide a degree of certainty that an a posteriori approach could not. An a priori argument is based on **first principles**. If these first principles are accepted and if the deductions are valid then we can arrive at a conclusion that is logically true. Further, an additional strength of the argument is that it does correspond to our usual conceptions of God in conceiving of the divinity as unique, all-powerful and perfect. Other arguments for the existence of God, which may or may not be more successful, are often open to the criticism that they may prove something but do not prove the so-called **God of classical theism**, the idea of God as usually conceived.

However, this leads us to the second point. It seems as if even on its own terms the argument fails to be satisfactory. Even if we accept the definition of God as 'the most perfect being,' and this can be contested in itself, the deductions themselves, as has been demonstrated above, are by no means certain. The use of 'existence' as a predicate clearly causes major difficulties. Those that dismiss the argument as being obviously flawed have probably failed to grasp its philosophical subtlety for there is something particular contained in the concept 'God' which is not present in 'the perfect island' or any other contingent idea.

Much philosophy in Britain and the USA has been of the **empiricist** type. This means that abstract theorising has been limited, while great emphasis has been placed on evidence and experience and reasoning thereon. To a strict empiricist much of the argument above, based as it is on logic and abstract notions such as 'God', is nonsensical and

Fig. 7.2 The Creation of Adam *from the Sistine Chapel, by Michelangelo*

approaches the problem from the wrong direction. The starting point must be experience and any argument must be based on considered evidence. To an empiricist there can be no statement about the actual world – hence any one that involves existence – which is a logically necessary truth. Even St Thomas Aquinas, possibly one of the greatest defenders of theism, dismissed the ontological argument on what amounts to essentially empiricist grounds. He argued, 'There is nothing in the mind that is not first in the senses' (Aquinas, 1948) and that therefore we could not infer God or His existence from a mere definition but must have experience of Him directly or indirectly through the world and its causes.

Finally, it would appear that the most the ontological argument can tell us is that God would be the 'most perfect being' should He exist. It does not, and arguably cannot, tell us that the 'most perfect being' actually does exist. There appears to be a line that cannot be crossed between possibilities and probabilities – and even mathematical certainties – in the world of logic and what actually exists or happens in the real world. We can all conceive of a pentagon of perfect symmetrical form, but that does not mean it actually exists other than as a conception, and it certainly does not mean that it *must* exist. The same is true of God's existence. If God is to be proved by reason – and many think (including Kant and Kierkegaard although for differing reasons), that this is neither possible nor desirable – the answer must lie in a different approach, an empirical approach, starting with the facts of the world and working back from these facts to God.

After working through topic, you should:

- be able to clearly describe the various formulations of the ontological argument
- understand from whence the ontological argument derives its strengths
- be able to critically assess the numerous arguments against the ontological argument
- be able to reflect upon the nature of the argument and how the idea of God may relate to it.

> ### Think about
>
> Consider what are the advantages of rational (a priori) thought and what are its drawbacks? Do the same for empirical (a posteriori) thought. It may be useful to debate as a group which way of knowing is to be preferred. In what respects does a detective use a priori and a posteriori methods to solve crime?

The origins of 'God'

Learning objectives:

- to think about how we may have acquired the idea of God

- to explore a number of differing accounts for the origins of our understanding of God

- to understand the distinction between an explanation of origins and an assessment of truth

- to compare the competing claims of the origin of the idea of God and assess their relative strengths and weaknesses.

AQA Examiner's tips

Whether you are an atheist, agnostic or devout believer it is important that you do not allow your personal viewpoints to come across dismissively of other opinions. Bear in mind many great thinkers have occupied different viewpoints often with very good reasons. Your opinions must be based on argument and not on rhetoric.

Key terms

Genetic fallacy: an error in reasoning based on accepting or rejecting an idea because of where or whom it comes from rather than on its own merits.

Introduction

In this topic we will attempt to explore the possible origins of the idea of God. For believers in the traditional religions God makes himself known to his people by appearances, miracles, scripture, the use of prophets and the like. According to this view, God communicates with humankind initially to make Himself known to us and then lets us develop a further understanding of Him either through direct experience of Him (such as through prayer or meditation) or through indirect experience (such as studying the holy books of the faith or through being guided by a religious leader). However, even believers in a particular faith acknowledge that others of different faiths, or indeed of no faith at all, have an idea of God.

So at its most basic, where does this concept come from? From a Judaeo-Christian perspective the classical idea of God derives from the religious commitment of the ancient Hebrews coupled with its intellectual meeting with Hellenistic Greek thought. This was further refined and developed during the High Middle Ages by the great scholastic thinkers such as St Thomas Aquinas and St Bonaventure.

From the philosophical point of view there is an important issue we need to be clear about before we can go on to discuss in detail the origins of the idea of God. We must be careful to distinguish the issue of origin from that of justification.

Consider the empiricism discussed earlier. Empiricists make two distinct claims: (a) all our ideas originate from experience, 'there is nothing in the mind that is not first in the senses', and (b) ultimately experience is the only means by which beliefs can be justified. Despite the fact that many early empiricists did not recognise the distinction, these two claims are quite separate. Any beliefs we might have are not necessarily justified by the experiences which gave rise to the constituent ideas. For example, an individual's idea of God may originate from their experience of Sunday school as a child, or descriptions given by their parents and teachers. These experiences are unlikely to provide an adequate justification for a belief in God. This does not mean that the issue of origins and justification are never linked; they are, however, always separable.

There is an important error that we must guard against, closely related to the above distinction. This is the view that an explanation of the origin of a belief provides a good reason to question its truth. An individual's beliefs may be the result of pure indoctrination, but it does not follow from this that they are untrue or unjustified.

For example, as we shall see, it is sometimes claimed that people only believe in God for psychological reasons; the belief is said to provide a sense of security and well-being in a hostile world. Logically speaking, however, such considerations have no bearing on the assessment of the claim that God exists. They provide reasons neither for nor against God's existence. The failure to recognise this fact is known as the **genetic fallacy**. It is worth noting a quote from Frege:

> The assertion both of what is false and what is true takes place in accordance with psychological laws. A derivation from these and an

explanation of a mental process that terminates in an assertion can never take the place of proof of what is asserted.

Frege (1967)

Although there are historical accounts of the origin of our idea of God as indicated above, this chapter will be concerned with explanations of the origin of the idea of God in terms of the following:

- innateness – whether the concept of God is **intrinsic** to human beings
- whether the idea of God is a **psychological construct**
- whether the idea of God is a **social construct**.

💡 Innateness

Traditionally some people, especially those of a religious persuasion, argue that the idea of God – as a concept – is **innate**. It is universal in scope and applicability and cannot be separated from us. It is, therefore, something that all human beings are aware of from the earliest stages of their lives to their last moments. (Although, as we have seen in Chapter 1, Leibniz claims that an innate idea may only reveal itself by being triggered by experience.) This is opposed to the view propounded by John Locke amongst others that man is born a *tabula rasa* at birth with all of our knowledge and conceptual apparatus derived later from experience (see Chapter 1). Supporters of this view argue that all of our mental concepts are derived from experience, quite often on a trial-and-error basis; for example, we do not know not to touch a hot plate unless we have some experience of a hot plate.

In the *Meno* (*c*.387–380) Plato argued that all knowledge was innate to us. At 82–85b Plato shows Socrates questioning a naturally uneducated slave boy. Socrates tries to demonstrate that the slave boy understands geometry and that the reason for this is that all knowledge is recollected and therefore innate to us. In the example, Socrates guides the slave boy through the question, who initially gets it wrong, but who ultimately can see the reasoning behind it. This is akin to a eureka moment where suddenly we understand something and then struggle to imagine how we could not have realised it earlier. A highly influential modern account of innateness was propounded by Noam Chomsky (1928–). Briefly, he argued that language – and the ability to acquire it – is innate, that there exists a 'universal grammar' which underlies all languages and that differences between languages are based solely on 'parameter' settings in the brain. While these two accounts refer to innateness generally and are not specifically related to or dependent upon God, they nonetheless offer support to the broad concept that there are things fundamental to us which are within us at birth. If this is accepted then it is a much shorter step to arguing that the concept of God is also innate.

Different views of innateness

One of the best known arguments in favour of the idea of God being innate is the so-called trademark argument. It was put forward by René Descartes in *Meditation III* where he states:

And, in truth, it is not to be wondered at that God, at my creation, implanted this idea in me, that it might serve, as it were, for the mark of the workman impressed on his work...

Descartes (1965, p101)

■ Think about

The following all commit the genetic fallacy:

- The journalist wrote that the man was guilty but you can't believe journalists because we all know what these media types are like – anything for a good story!
- I do believe in Father Christmas because my mother told me so.
- Philosophy students cannot be trusted because they exist in their own little worlds.

Think up examples of your own.

■ Key terms

Intrinsic: belonging to the nature or essence of something.

Psychological construct: something that is primarily the product of the mind and mental processes.

Social construct: something that is primarily the product of the expectations and experiences of society.

Innate: something that cannot be separated from us as human beings – it is intrinsic to us and necessary.

Fig. 7.3 *René Descartes*

We should note here from the beginning that the issue or origin of the idea of God and justification for a belief in God are closely linked by Descartes although they are not confused.

In essence it argues that God has placed an idea of Himself within us. Descartes begins by defining the idea of God in a similar manner to that used in versions of the ontological argument which Descartes discusses in *Meditation V*. The idea of God, Descartes describes as:

> a substance infinite (eternal, immutable), independent, all-knowing, all-powerful, and by which I myself, and every other thing that exists, if any such there be, were created.

Descartes (1965, p96)

He then describes what is usually termed the 'causal adequacy principle'. This principle argues that a cause must contain at least all of the attributes of the object that it causes. Descartes uses the example of a stone, saying that it must be produced by something that contains every attribute to be found in the stone. In the same way, heat cannot be produced by anything that does not contain the same attributes as the heat itself. What Descartes is doing here is presenting another cosmological account of God's existence based on the idea of cause and effect, which is itself based on the axiom that *nothing comes from nothing*. Descartes then proceeds to use the two principles outlined to argue that, as one has an idea of God, it can have only three possible sources, which he considers in the following passage:

> It remains for me only to examine how I have acquired this idea [of God]; for I have not received it through the senses, nor has it ever presented itself to me unexpectedly, as do the ideas of sensible objects, when these things present themselves or seem to present themselves to the external organs of my senses. Neither is it a pure production or fiction of my mind, for it is not in my power to take away from or add to it. And consequently there remains nothing more to say, except that, as with the idea of myself, it was born and produced with me at the moment of my creation.

Descartes (1965)

From this idea of God being innate Descartes then utilises the causal adequacy principle to posit that whatever exists must have an adequate cause. The only possible cause for my idea of God is God Himself, therefore God exists.

The causal adequacy principle is not without its flaws. This is because it seems to state that the result of a number of causes cannot result in something greater than its parts. Take the example of a railway bridge. It is made up of a large number of elements including, typically, metal girders, concrete slabs, tarmac, screws and so on. Now according to Descartes' account the load-bearing capacity and function of the railway bridge must be contained within the disparate elements that went into its construction. This is not convincing. John Cottingham uses the example of the texture of a cake to make a similar point. There is something about the 'sponginess' of a sponge cake that is not contained in the ingredients that make it up. Again, it seems that the 'sponginess' of the cake is something new and, arguably, not logically predictable.

Problems with innateness

While it is possible to argue that everyone has a concept of God, the differences between those conceptions are so wide that they are

Examiner's tips

Be clear how the ontological argument works. Make sure you understand the nature of an a priori argument and how it differs from cosmological or teleological approaches. By confusing not merely the terms but the basic assumptions that the respective arguments depend on you will seriously undermine the examiner's confidence in your understanding.

practically meaningless. For example, a small boy living a simple tribal existence might literally equate God with the mountains or the river; however, a nine-year-old child of two Christians might have an idea of God as a kindly, male figure living in the clouds. While the concept 'God' is applied by both children, they do not represent the same thing in any meaningful way. However, it is possible to respond to this by claiming that the same basic elements *are* being represented by the use of the concept 'God'. In the above example, both children are identifying something other than or beyond themselves. God as a mountain or as an old man in the clouds are simple conceptions of power and magnificence but nonetheless can create the same sense of religious experience – a sense of awe, wonder and reverence. Further, they can provide a workable contrast between themselves and the natural limits of humanity and the distance and grandeur of God.

Leading on from the above problem, it is possible to develop a further criticism that the concept of God is not innate but emerges from nurture from a young age and is therefore basically dependent on upbringing and experiences. It is also possible to argue that while we all have an idea of God, this is not to do with God being innate, but rather a facility of the human mind to consider theoretically and magnify ordinary human traits. Hume, for example, explains the origin of the idea of God in the following passage:

> The idea of God as meaning an infinitely intelligent, wise, and good Being, arises from reflecting on the operations of our own mind, and augmenting, without limit, those qualities of goodness and wisdom.

Hume (1999, section 2)

This account stands in stark contrast to Descartes'. It could be argued here that Hume's conception of the mind as essentially a copying machine (see Chapter 1) lacks the resources required for the creative act he describes in this quote. The problem empiricist accounts face is that because the idea of God is so very abstract and utterly unlike anything found in experience, it is difficult to explain how it could have initially originated from experience. Ideas such as 'infinity' and 'identity' face a similar problem. These considerations clearly support Descartes' innateness theory.

> ### Think about
>
> What ideas, if any, do we think of as being innate? Is the idea of beauty something that is innate within us or is it learnt?

The idea of God as only a psychological construct

This idea developed principally in the 19th century, although the roots of the idea can be found earlier. A number of thinkers, including psychologists such as Sigmund Freud, have seen the idea of God as being something that emerges from within our natures or unconscious.

Unlike Descartes, subscribers to the view that 'God' is a psychological construct are either not concerned with God's actual existence or assume that He does not exist. The issue of the origin of the idea of God is not in any way linked to a justification for a belief in God. The task, according to these approaches, is to explain psychologically why it is that the idea of God and the belief in God are so widespread. 'God' is conceived as a psychological construct that provides evidence for various mental needs; it is of interest because it tells us something about the human mind.

'God' as a sign of alienation

In his most important work, *The Essence of Christianity* (1841), Ludwig Feuerbach aims to remove the divine and mysterious aspects from religion, instead seeing both God and religion in human terms. Rational man creates God in his image:

> The Divine Being is nothing other than the being of man himself, or rather, the being of man abstracted from the limits of the individual man or the real, corporeal man, and objectified, i.e., contemplated and worshiped as another being, as a being distinguished from his own. All determinations of the Divine Being are, therefore, determinations of the being of man.
>
> *Feuerbach (1999)*

Feuerbach begins by developing what he terms the 'true or anthropological essence of religion'. He looks at differing aspects of God's supposed nature – such as His 'love' and His role as lawgiver – and finds that these aspects all correspond to a human need that is basic to our natures. He then goes on to argue that 'God' has no separate existence or essence outside of man. God is not superior to man but something that emerges from man. To believe in any more than that is false. Therefore, all religious **dogmas** such as the sacraments, specific moral doctrines based on revelation, and anything that leads to mystery and superstition are specifically condemned by Feuerbach not just as being misplaced but also as being harmful. This is one use of the term **alienation** – later used by Marx in a similar sense but with a different context. Here, Christianity, and by implication most if not all religion, is alien to humanity. Humanity is alienated from their true essence by projecting this essence into a God who is separate and different from humanity.

However, his view is complicated by his belief in **subjectivism**. Feuerbach cannot consistently argue that there is an underlying, uniform human nature that results in us psychologically 'creating' God. Surely, if things are subjective some will create 'God' and others will not, and even the Gods that are created will be very different as people and their experiences are different.

God as a psychological need

Primitive man found himself in a dangerous and hostile world, the fear of wild animals, of not being able to find enough food, of injury or disease, and of natural phenomena like thunder, lightning and volcanoes was constantly with him. Finding no security, he created the idea of gods in order to give him comfort in good times, courage in times of danger and consolation when things went wrong. To this day, you will notice that people become more religious at times of crises; you will hear them say that their belief in a god or gods gives them the strength they need to deal with life. You will hear them explain that they believe in a particular god because they prayed in time of need and their prayer was answered.

All this can be related to Buddhism. According to the Buddha the god-idea is a response to fear and frustration. He taught people to try to understand their fears, to lessen their desires and to calmly and courageously accept the things they could not change. It is argued that he replaced fear, not with irrational belief but with rational understanding. Of course, the issue of whether belief in God is irrational cannot be settled quite that easily. Certainly, as we emphasised at the beginning of this section, even if the idea of God does result from 'fear and frustration' it does not mean that belief in God is irrational.

The idea of God as a social construct

There is another view that sees the idea of God emerging not from within us but from without, because of the society that we grow up in and live in. It is clear that we are all influenced by the society we live in, but this view goes further, arguing that 'God' exists solely because of conditions and **norms in society**. Two views considered here – Marx's and Durkheim's – both offer a **functionalist account**. This approach to religion (and thus the idea of God) involves analysing the role it plays within society rather than considering its **doctrine**. As with the accounts given in the previous section, these accounts, regard religion as a phenomenon that needs explaining, however, they provide social rather than psychological explanations.

'God' as an instrument of the ruling classes

Karl Marx offered a view of religion that emerged from his central philosophical beliefs. He saw the whole of human history as a struggle between classes and he denied that there was an over-arching human nature or **transcendent** morality. He believed that human beings were products of their society and the most fundamental force that influenced society was economic factors – most notably the struggle between those that controlled the means of production, namely the wealthy, and those that did not, whom Marx called the **proletariat**. Religion is, then, like all other social institutions, dependant on the economic realities that have fashioned it. It has no independent life or existence but is purely a by-product of society. As a youth Marx viewed religion in a positive although highly restricted sense by seeing it as something that offered **solidarity** to its followers. Although Marx viewed religion as *illusionary*, he thought it could have some limited value. However, an older Marx was far more critical. He came to believe it exists to provide reasons and excuses to maintain the **status quo** and to keep society functioning for the benefit of the ruling class. In the same way as Marx saw capitalism as a force that takes our own labour while alienating us from its fruits, religion takes our highest ideals, which ought to be grounded on humanity, and alienates us from them. It does this by projecting these onto a non-existent transcendent being called 'God'. In a famous passage from *Critique of Hegel's Philosophy of Right* (1843) Marx shows both the positive and negative aspects of his attitude to religion:

> Religious distress is at the same time the expression of real distress and the protest against real distress. Religion is the sigh of the oppressed creature, the heart of a heartless world, just as it is the spirit of a spiritless situation. It is the opium of the people. The abolition of religion as the illusory happiness of the people is required for their real happiness. The demand to give up the illusion about its condition is the demand to give up a condition which needs illusions.

Marx (1970)

Marx offers a number of specific criticisms of religion. He sees it as fundamentally irrational. Religion, apart from its display as a social idea, has no independent external reality. It is not real in the sense that believers assume it to be, namely as a set of doctrines or principles based on a transcendent God. Even more damning is that it creates a veil of illusion over reality, as Marx sees it. Rather than focusing on, or even realising, the actual reality that they find themselves in, religion encourages people to worship falsity. Further, Marx sees religion as hypocritical. While it may claim to defend the poor and promote

Key terms

Altruism: the disinterested concern for the welfare of another. The good of others is an end in itself and does not benefit me. It is typified by the 'ultimate sacrifice', giving up your life for someone else.

Key philosopher

Emile Durkheim (1858–1917)

He was a sociologist rather than a philosopher, his work has had huge influence in both sociology and anthropology, and in many respects he can be thought of as one of the founders of the academic discipline.

Key terms

Collective consciousness: the thoughts and beliefs and experiences that underpin, often subconsciously, the thinking of whole groups of people.

AQA Examiner's tips

Due to the a priori nature of the ontological argument you need to be aware that criticisms of it need to be essentially logical and not based on empirical arguments which are typically redundant here. Good arguments against a priori arguments usually either challenge the premises and the assumptions that the argument uses or challenge the reasoning involved.

altruism, in reality this is not the case. Religious leaders frequently live lives of luxury and enjoy a high status in society (this was particularly so in earlier generations and remains the case in some other societies) given to them by the ruling class with whom they collaborate in maintaining the status quo. Finally, Marx perceives the greatness of mankind to lie within themselves and not in something external to themselves. Religion devalues this by glorifying the divine at the expense of the human. Religion encourages meekness and obedience to the ruling class and the giving up of responsibility for material conditions and the material conditions of other people.

Religion as an image of the norms of society

Emile Durkheim spent a great deal of time studying religious behaviour in primitive societies. In his book, *Elementary Forms* (1912), Durkheim argued that the simple gods worshipped by primitive peoples are actually merely expressions of their own conceptions of society itself. This is true not only for simple societies but also for more complex societies.

Durkheim defines religion as:

> A unified system of beliefs and practices relative to sacred things, that is to say, things set apart and forbidden – beliefs and practices which unite into one single moral community called a Church, all those who adhere to them

Durkheim (2000)

Religion, for Durkheim, is not 'imaginary', although he does strip away from it what many believers would consider to be essential – namely, its divine origins. Durkheim considers religion to be real; it is an expression of society or community itself and, indeed, there is no society that does not have religion. All individuals perceive a force or power greater than themselves. This is our common or social or community life. We then unconsciously give that perception a supernatural expression. We normally express ourselves religiously in groups, which increases the symbolic power of the activity. Religion is an expression of our **collective consciousness**. As society, and our collective consciousness, gets more complex the idea of the deity becomes increasingly abstract with the transcendent and universal aspects more pronounced. In other words, as we become less primitive and more complex as people and as communities, so our ideas of God move from the simple to the greater and more complex.

One problem with Durkheim's account, and others like it, is that it is not clear exactly how this process of collective self-expression takes place. It seems to assume a mysterious process which is completely outside of the awareness of those within the society. He might also be accused of positing a kind of 'group mind' that is somehow beyond the individuals within the society. In addition, it ignores the subjective significance that religious beliefs have for individuals – this is surely just as important as any social role that religion plays.

Conclusion

If we reflect on both the psychological and social explanations for the idea of God we might come to the conclusion that they only make sense from the perspective of an atheist. After all we do not seek to produce psychological or social explanations for why people believe that the earth is a sphere. Only when a belief is assumed to be false does there seem to be a need for some supplementary explanation which goes beyond the reasons normally adduced for that belief. The evidence from scientific measurements, pictures from space, etc. seems to constitute an adequate explanation for the widespread belief that the earth is a globe. The paranoid individual is such because people are *not* out to get him; if they were we would be unlikely to give a psychological explanation of his mental state. This tendency not to explain beliefs taken to be true is not based in logic. As we have seen, 'The assertion both of what is false and what is true takes place in accordance with psychological laws' (Frege, 1967). So true claims can be given psychological (or indeed social) explanations just as much as false ones.

However, the motives for producing the psychological and social explanations we have discussed rest on more than the assumption of atheism. They also involve the move towards **naturalism** which took place during the 18th and 19th centuries. Descartes' explanation of the idea of God as implanted into our minds by God is non-naturalistic as it involves a process that cannot in any sense be investigated scientifically. We could perhaps investigate scientifically whether the idea of God is innate or not, but Descartes is going further than the simple claim of innateness. It could of course also be argued that Feuerbach, Marx and Durkheim are far from scientific; nevertheless, they are at least attempting to produce explanations that are amenable to scientific (empirical) investigation, even if they fail. Durkheim, for example, claimed to base his theories on a study of Australian aborigines. These theorists are clearly moving in the direction of naturalism.

After working through this topic, you should:

- understand a number of possible explanations for the origins of the idea of God

- be able to assess whether these accounts are convincing and consider whether they support or exclude the reality of God's existence

- be able to consider the motivations that may underpin these varying accounts

- be able to assess the problems related to each of the accounts and to form supported judgements.

Think about

For each of the psychological and social theories considered ask the following questions:

- Does the theory provide a convincing explanation for the origin of the idea of God?

- Does this theory provide a convincing explanation for the belief in God?

What form might a theory take that regards the idea of God as innate but is a naturalistic theory?

Key terms

Naturalism: the view that reality can be understood using broadly scientific methods. Naturalists reject explanations that rely on entities that cannot be assessed scientifically, e.g. God.

The divine attributes

- to understand the philosophical concept of God including the specific divine attributes

- to understand the range of opinion about what each divine attribute actually means

- to debate whether or not these attributes are consistent and coherent

- to critically examine a number of arguments that suggest that the traditional philosophical account of God's nature is untenable.

Key terms

Omniscient: knowing everything.

Omnipotent: able to do anything.

Temporal: the state of being 'in' time.

Anthropomorphic: when non-human things are given human qualities.

Incorporeal: lacking material form or substance, spiritual rather than physical.

Introduction

God is the term we give to the supreme being. It is important to separate philosophically the idea of God from any specific religious manifestation. The supreme being need not be associated with Christianity, Hinduism or any other faith. It is perfectly possible to believe in God without a particular religious belief. Firstly, we will look at what is generally thought to comprise the divine attributes and then we will look at whether or not they are consistent and coherent.

What are the divine attributes?

This section seeks to explain many of the qualities that have traditionally been ascribed to God by philosophers and theologians. This discussion concerns itself largely with a Judaeo-Christian (and hence also Islamic) account of the supreme being. This particular conception of God is often termed the 'classical' view of theism and it is the concept of God that is usually referred to in philosophical discussion. Typically, God is thought to be **omniscient, omnipotent**, and to be supremely good and loving. God can also be thought of as a judge and lawgiver – rewarding and punishing according to whether we have followed 'His' rules and commandments. God is also thought to be timeless – literally to exist outside of normal **temporal** constraints.

There are also other very basic conceptions of God, such as being an old man in the clouds with a beard, but this primitive view of God is inappropriate because it is **anthropomorphic** (for example, 'God has got the whole world in his hands') and therefore does not concern us here although it is relevant to discussions of religious language elsewhere in the philosophy of religion. God is described as 'He' below, but this is for grammatical simplicity alone.

Omnipotence

God is said to enjoy the quality of omnipotence. This means that God is all-powerful, He can do anything and is unlimited in His choice or action. He created the world and everything in it and He is also responsible for sustaining it. If God were to remove His power from the universe the universe would cease to exist. There are a number of differing accounts of what God's omnipotence consists of. At its most basic, some hold that God can literally do anything, including things that are contradictory. Savage's (1967) paradox of the stone states that God could create a stone that was so heavy that even God himself could not lift it. This is a paradox because if He could create such a stone He would not be omnipotent since He would not be able to lift it, but also, if He could not create such a stone He would not be omnipotent either. One response to cases such as this is to point out that since God is **incorporeal** the very idea of a physical action such as lifting does not apply. Another response derives from the widespread view that divine omnipotence means that God is able to do everything that does not imply a logical contradiction. So we would not expect God to make 2 + 2 equal 5 or make a triangle have four sides. Given that creating a stone that He could not lift would involve an omnipotent being having the quality of non-omnipotence, which is contradictory, we should not expect this of God, according to this view.

A common view of omnipotence, held by Aquinas and many others, contends that God can do all things that it is appropriate for God to do. For example, God cannot walk. This is because God does not have to walk, as walking does not constitute part of his perfection. Walking is, in reality, a lack of perfection. Therefore, God's inability to walk does not affect His perfection or His omnipotence.

Omniscience

Another attribute traditionally applied to God is omniscience. This means all-knowing. It is supposed to describe not just wisdom or even being 'extremely wise', but something more than that. Not surprisingly there are a number of differing accounts of exactly what constitutes divine omniscience, all of which have some problems. The simplest account is that God knows everything. But how far should this go? If we talk about things in the past and present then this is relatively simple to understand although there are problems. For example, it is difficult to conceive of how God might know every present thought of every human being. Real philosophical difficulty emerges though when we expand divine omniscience to cover future events. This may mean that God knows all possible outcomes (which raises counterfactual issues of how God can know these future possible events) or it could mean that God knows the only actual outcome (which then may remove the possibility of human freedom). We will say more about omniscience later on.

Immutability and perfection

Immutability is a quality traditionally applied to God – He cannot and does not change. The idea is closely linked to the idea that God is perfect. Being perfect in every way God has no need to change. Any change would either add to God, for example by acquiring new knowledge, which implies that God was not actually perfect before, or it would involve taking something away from God, which suggests that He would lose His perfection. In addition, anything that acted on God to produce change in Him might mean that He was not the ultimate being. Immutability is also linked to the idea of simplicity – that is, God's nature is not complex, it is not in any sense composed of parts.

But is it coherent to claim that God is simple? Simplicity is a relative term that only makes sense in relation to a particular kind of complexity, and something can be complex in all sorts of ways. The sense in which the British economy is complex is utterly different from the sense in which a chair is complex. A blank piece of A4 paper, for example, can be regarded as complex in that it is composed of many square centimetres. We need to know the kind of contrast that is being made when we claim that God is simple. Simplicity without a context seems empty.

Supreme goodness

This is simply the idea that God is complete goodness and not just the 'most good', which would imply that God could potentially be better. It is often termed **omnibenevolence**. However, this view obviously supposes that there is such a thing as supreme goodness. If one is a moral subjectivist then there is not just one sole good but many competing goods; however, this aspect need not concern us here.

> **Think about**
>
> Let us suppose that Shakespeare, of his own free-will, decided to write plays. Why would it be difficult for even an omnipotent being to bring this about? Does this mean that there are some things that a non-omnipotent being can do that an omnipotent being cannot do?

> **Key terms**
>
> **Immutability:** not subject to any kind of change.
>
> **Omnibenevolence:** all-goodness.

> **Think about**
>
> What qualities would you ascribe to a supremely good being?
>
> Think of situations in which someone who is perfectly just might not act in the same way as someone who is perfectly loving and caring.

Eternity

Eternity is, perhaps, slightly harder to define. The classical view of God's eternity usually involves not simply the thought of the view of God not having a beginning or an end – and certainly not the folk belief of God being very old – but of God being *outside* of time and temporal events completely. Boethius in *The Consolations of Philosophy* (525, Book V, 6) defines it as: '*aeternitas est unterminabilis vitae tota simul et perfecta possession*', meaning: eternity is the total, simultaneous and perfect possession of life without end.

For example, whilst the Venerable Bede prayed to God in the 8th century, God did not receive that prayer in the 8th century because God is outside of time completely. God received the prayer timelessly and responded in one timeless moment. It is this view of eternity that causes concerns as we shall see.

More recently a number of modern philosophers of religion have abandoned this view of eternity and have simply talked of God as eternal in the sense of having no beginning or end. Richard Swinburne in *The Coherence of Theism* (1994) supports this position, defining God's eternity as being 'backwardly eternal … [and] forwardly eternal'.

Transcendence and immanence

God is said to be transcendent. Transcendence usually implies a certain distance from the world and the things in it. Linked to this is the notion that God is incorporeal. He is not physical and therefore does not share the supposed limitations that corporeality brings with it (as was noted with the paradox of the stone). For some, including many who adopt **deism**, this distance is great, with the divinity being abstract and distanced from the world.

The opposite of transcendence is **immanence**. The view that God is immanent is very much part of the classical conception of God. Immanence is closely linked to the divine attribute of **omnipresence**. As we shall see there is clearly a conflict between transcendence and immanence.

■ Problems with the classical account of God

This classical account of God, worked out by theologians and philosophers over many centuries, raises many problems. It is questionable whether these qualities are comprehensible when considered even singularly as we have seen; however, in combination they raise a number of further problems as some qualities seem to contradict others. (The most well known of these – the problem of evil – is dealt with in a separate chapter). Before we look at some of these problems in more detail here is a sample of possible conflicts:

■ Perfection vs omniscience. An omniscient God knows everything but surely there are some vile and terrible things that a perfect being should not know. Complete knowledge, therefore, threatens to corrupt the attribute of perfection.

■ Immutability vs omnibenevolence. A supremely good God will be loving which means responding to human suffering. If God were unaffected by suffering He would surely be unfeeling and so not supremely good. However, immutability demands that God is unchangeable.

■ Perfection vs omnibenevolence. A problem related to the above is the tension between being perfectly blissful, which seems to follow from the attribute of perfection, and being supremely loving, which seems to suggest the capacity to be affected by human suffering. If we really feel for others then our own well-being is affected, so a loving God could not be continually blissful.

■ Simplicity vs the possession of attributes. The possession of many attributes implies that God has complexity with Him. This seems to be at odds with the claim that God is simple. (We should also note that the doctrine of the Trinity appears to contradict God's simplicity.)

■ Simplicity vs the capacity to act. A being that is simple has no parts. Change, however, would seem to require parts, and action clearly involves change. If this is right then a simple being cannot act. (We shall see below that the capacity to act also seems to conflict with being timeless.)

A problem with transcendence

If God is transcendent then He is beyond and outside of the world but this suggests that He lacks immanence (and omnipresence). If God is immanent then He acts in the world and makes a difference to people's lives, but this suggests that He lacks transcendence. The claim that God is transcendent but is nevertheless here within the world is a central plank of the Christian tradition despite the fact that it is clearly problematic.

Transcendence is linked to the view that God is beyond human categories of thought and language and is thereby utterly 'other'. Moses Maimonides, for example, writing in 1190, claimed that we can not only make negative claims about the nature of God – we can only ever say what He is not – since our minds are too limited to comprehend his infinite nature:

> Praise be to Him who is such that when our minds try to visualise his essence, their power of apprehending becomes imbecility

Maimonides (1995)

However, God in the Judaeo-Christian tradition is also thought to be 'personal'. God is concerned with us all as individuals. Further, we can communicate with Him through prayer, and He listens and can respond. He is in the world with us.

We might begin to see a way to resolve the tension between immanence and transcendence if we accept that God is quite separate from His creation but through his omnipotence and omniscience He is, in a sense, present everywhere within the world, i.e. omnipresent. Aquinas uses the analogy of a king and his kingdom. Thus there is a sense in which a king, through his power, is present in the whole of his kingdom.

Problems with eternity

Although many of the most important issues regarding God's eternity are connected with omniscience, many have sought to criticise God's timelessness independently. One basic argument is that it is inconceivable to talk about God in this way as the concept of timelessness is unintelligible. Further, in order to exist at all it is necessary to exist at some point in time. These arguments are not conclusive though. Plato would certainly argue that there are timeless forms such as beauty and justice; and mathematics seems to deal

Fig. 7.4 *St Jerome Praying by Hieronymus Bosch*

Key philosophers

Karl Barth (1886–1968)

One of the most important theologians of modern times, Barth rejected the current liberal trends in theology and instead advocated the sovereignty of God in all things.

Charles Hartshorne (1897–2000)

Hartshorne was an American philosopher of religion strongly influenced by the metaphysical philosophy of A. N. Whitehead which he used to develop Process Theology.

Think about

There are a number of other important conflicts that arise if we take God to be timeless, for example, can a 'living' God exist outside of time? Identify other problems with the notion of a timeless God.

There are also problems with the idea of God existing within time. Identify at least one such problem. Hint: one problem relates to the existence of time itself.

Key terms

Temporal indexed truths: truths that are dependent on the time in which they are asked.

AQA Examiner's tips

Be precise when defining God's attributes. There are straightforward marks to be picked up but they are unlikely to be very many. It is important therefore not to spend too long engaged in a rambling, descriptive account of a particular divine characteristic. Instead, you will more likely need to address the core of the question which will normally be identifying problems with the classical conception of God.

with timeless truths. Some have argued that if God is eternal then it is impossible for him to act, as actions take place in time. Swinburne (1914) states: 'If we say that P brings about X, we can sensibly ask *when* does he bring it about?' (emphasis added). There are many responses to this problem. Most focus on refuting the logical necessity of action being linked to time in the case of God, but there are others who take a wider approach. Karl Barth (1957) suggested the notion of 'super-time', a doubling of past, present and future time which is then identified with God's own being. Barth questions notions of time as consisting of quantifiable blocks, and see this as God self-surpassing time. A theologian rather than a philosopher, Barth does not demonstrate sustained rational argument but a creative way of considering eternity.

Another problem with the idea of God's eternity is that put forward by a view known as Process Theology. The leading advocate was Charles Hartshorne who argued that as God was perfect His perfection must be a personal perfection. To be fully personal we must be able to love, which implies the capacity to be both active and passive. The active is needed in order to express love, and the passive in order to listen and then respond to others. Therefore, God must also have these attributes. God then must be capable of change, but being capable of change He cannot be timeless. Instead, for both Swinburne and Hartshorne, God consists not of timelessness but of duration without end.

Problems with omniscience

As we have seen above, God's omniscience is typically understood as His knowing everything and God's eternity on the classical account is understood as His being independent of time. This means that God views all events from a particular perspective outside of time, seeing all events in the same moment.

However, there is a problem with the coherence of this account because for God to truly know a particular statement of fact then He needs to know facts more than 'timelessly'. This problem is sometimes called the problem of **temporal indexed truths**. For example, God can only know which of the following two statements is true if He knows what time it is now: 'Britain will win the Second World War' or 'Britain won the Second World War'. If He knows only timelessly then He cannot know at any given time which of two possible temporally based statements is true. To preserve God's omniscience it seems essential to say that 'God knows the time now'. However, by doing that God is thereby susceptible to change and so He cannot be unchanging and eternal. He loses either His omniscience or His eternity. There is also the related problem of God knowing things that are spatially located, although it is generally thought to be less problematic. This works in a very similar manner by stating, for example: 'I am drinking a cup of tea in my study'. This is true only for me. God may know it, but He does not know it in the same way that I know it.

Using non-indexicals

However, there is a response to this problem of temporally indexed truths. In the examples above, we gave the proposition some temporal or spatial location. Is it possible to convey the same meaning without such temporal or spatial 'indexing'. In other words, do propositions that utilise such indexicals have non-indexical equivalents? Michael Czapkay Sudduth (an American Christian philosopher of religion lecturing in California) states:

Indexical expressions represent a special mode of access to (the same) truth (capable of being) stated in non-indexical form. Hence, 'it is raining now' and 'it is raining at 3:00 pm, Sunday, March 6, 1994' are two different sentences which express the same proposition. Hence, the lack of access of the former does not entail any lack of access to truths. Similarly, when John knows that 'I am a patient in the Radcliffe Infirmary' and the nurse knows that 'John is a patient in the Radcliffe Infirmary' both individuals know the same truth, though they know it in two distinct ways or through two different modes of access.

Sudduth, http://philofreligion.homestead.com/main.html

If all we are talking about is a specific verbal formula for describing a truth that could be otherwise described then it would seem that there is no problem. The problem would be merely one of **semantics**. On this account, God knows the same truth as the person who is located in a particular temporal location, but he simply knows it a different way. A 'timeless' way, one could inelegantly say.

God doesn't need to be who I am to know what I know, to be where I am to know what is happening in the place I am, nor to exist when I exist to know what is happening at any time when I exist.

Sudduth, http://philofreligion.homestead.com/main.html

Is this convincing? The following example reveals a possible problem. God might know what white wine I drink (call it event E) at a certain given date and time (call it T1), but He cannot know what I am drinking *now*. More precisely, He cannot know that event E which takes place at T1 is *now*. To many this is vitally important as it appears to signify a genuine gap in God's knowledge. The 'now-ness' of the proposition adds something genuinely different and conveys some additional meaning which merely knowing 'Event E at T1' does not. If this is accepted, it means God cannot be omniscient under the traditional understanding.

Conclusion

These arguments depend largely upon the classical view that God exists outside of time completely. There are other views that remove these problems although they may create problems of their own. One view is that rather than being outside of time God is **omnitemporal**. God is immanent in time, and therefore knowing and acting are not problematic.

Most of the above reasoning is based on a rational approach to God and depends on a particular conception of God which we have labelled the 'classical'. Many theistic philosophers have dispensed with the approach of rationally justifying belief in God by arguing that 'faith' is not a matter of logical reasoning and argument but of feeling and belief. The influential 19th-century Danish existentialist philosopher Soren Kierkegaard advocated a position similar to this. Others have rejected some or all of the classical conception of divinity as being outmoded and an unnecessary burden that limits more creative discussions of divinity, faith and reason. They feel less need to define and defend a particular conception of God either because God is thought to be beyond our limited human comprehensions or because God is personal to each believer. These responses can themselves be seen as deeply unsatisfactory. If God's existence is to have any value then surely there must be

Key terms

Semantics: the relationship between a linguistic symbol and its meaning.

Omnitemporal: present at all and every moment of time.

Key philosopher

Soren Kierkegaard (1813–55)

Kierkegaard was a Christian philosopher, often considered the father of existentialism, who argued that faith was the key element of religious belief.

AQA Examiner's tips

It is very important when describing and then criticising a complicated philosophical argument to do so in stages so that each part of the argument is clearly expressed. Students often fall into error by having a hazy grasp of the argument and then by basing criticisms widely rather than specifically on it.

something essential to God over and above what certain individuals might or might not feel. If there is no substance to God then are we not in danger of just creating a vision of God in our own likeness?

After working through this topic, you should:

- understand a range of philosophical issues concerning the idea of God

- begin to think critically and to assess various philosophical arguments regarding the consistency and coherence of the idea of God

- develop an awareness of the wider philosophical issues that underpin the topic.

Further reading

Craig, W. L. (ed.) *Philosophy of Religion: a reader and guide*, Edinburgh University Press, 2002. This book contains a number of important writings on the subject along with introductory essays by the author.

Davies, B. *An Introduction to the Philosophy of Religion*, 3rd edn, Oxford University Press, 2003. A very accessible introduction to the subject by a well-known writer on the subject.

Hick, J. (ed.) *Classical and Contemporary Readings on the Philosophy of Religion*, 3rd edn, Prentice Hall, 1990. Another useful anthology by a well-known author on the subject.

Pinchen, C. *Issues in Philosophy*, 2nd edn, Palgrave, 2004. Written by a Principal Examiner in Philosophy for AQA, the book contains a chapter on the philosophy of religion which deals with a number of topics in a clear and critical manner.

Swinburne, R. *Is there a God?*, Oxford University Press, 1994. This is a more accessible version of the book below (*The Coherence of Theism*) and a good introduction to Swinburne's work.

Swinburne, R. *The Coherence of Theism*, revised edn, Clarendon Press, 1994. A major study and frequently cited by other philosophers in the field.

Both of the books below are useful for those that may wish to explore issues in the philosophy of time.

Horwich, P. *Asymmetries in Time*, MIT Press, 1987.

Le Poidevin, R. *Travels in Four Dimensions: the enigmas of space and time*, Oxford University Press, 2003.

Summary questions

1. Briefly outline three aspects of the classical conception of deity.

2. Is there a problem in moving from an idea of something to its reality and, if so, what is the problem?

3. Is the idea of God coherent?

4. Can God know what Jim will do next year?

5. Critically assess claims that the idea of God is explainable in purely human terms.

6. 'God is all in the mind!' Discuss.

7. Explain two different accounts of the ontological argument.

8. Assess the view that the idea of God is imprinted on us from birth.

8 God and the world

The argument from design

Learning objectives:

- to examine whether the apparent order in the world justifies the claim that it displays design
- to explore whether the appearance of design justifies a belief in God
- to consider whether scientific explanations of the universe are adequate
- to evaluate the strengths and problems of the design argument.

Introduction

The first verses of the Bible state:

> In the beginning God created the heavens and the earth … caused grass to shoot forth, vegetation bearing seed … and God went on to say … let us make man in our image … and God saw it was very good.

Genesis

Philosophers have travelled many paths in their pursuit of God. Some have employed pure reason and argued from their ideas. Many have sought God in the powerful nature of experience, sometimes mystical and occasionally miraculous, claiming personal revelation of the Divine. This chapter examines a rational argument about the state of the world. It is called the 'argument from design', and relates to the account of the creation of the world in the Bible.

This argument for the existence of God has a long and established history, deriving from philosophers such as Plato, Aquinas and Hume, using famous examples such as Paley's watch, and challenging notable scientists such as Charles Darwin. There are already some excellent textbooks available that look at the philosophical and scientific background to the debate, such as *The Question of God* (Palmer, 2001). This chapter confines itself to examining the different types of argument that are employed in the argument from design as follows:

- the argument by analogy
- the argument from cause and effect
- the inductive argument – the inference to the best explanation
- the argument from probabilities.

Sometimes these arguments overlap, but they can be distinguished and have a distinctive, persuasive force.

What is the argument from design?

This argument points to the order in the universe and concludes that only God could design such a harmonious creation on such a grand scale. This makes it an **empirical** theory. It examines our experience of the world; and few would dispute that it demonstrates incredible organisation, from the microcosm of a butterfly emerging from a chrysalis to the macrocosm of planets orbiting the sun. People point to the amazing regularity of such a grand design and also the way everything seems perfectly adapted to fulfil its function.

This argument is also called the 'teleological argument', from the Greek word *telos*, which means end or purpose. So the universe is regarded as having an end, goal or purpose, achieved through harmonious order. And

Key terms

Empirical: an empirical theory is the theory that knowledge is gained primarily from experience rather than purely from reason.

Think about

If you wanted to point to the incredible design in the world, the beauty of its creation and the complex intelligence in the way things behave, what would you choose?

to be able to have a purpose, it must have a designer, namely God. So the direction of the argument is as follows:

Harmonious order → Design and purpose → God

Some philosophers point out that it should really be called the argument *for* design rather than *from*, as the foundational premise is the existence of order, from which design is established via our four arguments.

The teleological argument also fits easily with some accounts of the origins of the universe. In contrast to the Bible, Plato in *The Timaeus* (Pappas, 1995) explains how a cosmic designer took materials that already existed and shaped them according to a plan. So God is the intelligence behind the arrangement of the materials.

Should we be talking about order?

There are two reasons for questioning the existence of order or design in the world. The first was an issue that Hume was to make much of. If we assume that the world is designed for the ease and comfort of human life then how are we to explain features of the world that are not conducive to that purpose? Examples might include geological faults or the generation of cancer cells. The second one, some might argue, shows that the world is a product of chaos. A statistical view of nature would suggest that things are not so systematically designed as we might suppose. This second point, however, is likely to be met with the rejoinder that the world we experience is ordered and designed even though we can't perceive the atoms that are continually leaving and joining physical objects.

Paley's watch (1805)

Key philosopher

William Paley (1743–1805)

Paley was a Church of England clergyman who taught at Cambridge University. The watch analogy is found in *Natural Theology*.

This exposition of the teleological argument asks you to imagine that you are walking across a heath and you come across a stone. You may ask yourself how it came to be there and might conclude it had been there forever. But then supposing you found a watch, you could not accept the same answer because it has been designed.

- The watch has parts – it is *complex*.
- The different parts each have a function – it is *harmonious*.
- The motion of the watch is carefully regulated to the hours of the day – it is *planned*.
- It is finely tuned – it *shows intelligence*.
- It tells the time – it has a *purpose*.

Paley's watch analogy involves the spatial arrangement of the parts. It is the way the cogs and wheels are arranged in space to make it suitable for its purpose.

> when we come to inspect the watch, we perceive (what we could not discover in the stone) that its several parts are framed and put together for a purpose, e.g. they are so formed and adjusted as to produce motion, and that motion so regulated as to point out the hour of the day; that if the different parts had been differently shaped … or of a different size from what they are … no motion at all would have been carried on in the machine.

*Paley 1805, found in **Palmer** (2001)*

Paley says that the conclusion you would obviously draw is that the watch must have a designer and, significantly, even if the watch went wrong this would not deny the judgements that you had made. Only a rational and intelligent being could have produced such an invention, and you would say this even if you did not know the purpose.

Paley concludes that all of the indications of design are not only evident wherever you look in the universe, but that the universe as a whole operates with the same design features. Since the universe is infinite, vast in power and timescale, etc., only God could have planned and created the universe. Spelled out in mechanical terms, the world as a whole is like a vast machine, composed of parts, which are smaller machines. The perfect adaption of the smaller mechanical processes to supporting the ultimate universal mechanism, and the magnitude of the whole project requires infinite wisdom and intelligence.

The discoveries of modern science could be seen to lend support to this thesis. Every new finding such as the Genome Project only serves to emphasise the amazing complexity of everything in the universe and how it works in harmony. The contribution of science to the debate is discussed below.

The progression of the argument from a small machine to the universe as a whole might be compared to the jump from an eye to the body as a whole.

■ The argument from analogy

An analogy is a comparison. Other well-known philosophical analogies, for example, are Plato's comparison of gaining enlightenment with struggling out of a cave and staring at the sun; and running a state with guiding a ship in the right direction. Analogies can be strong or weak. A strong analogy, which will be more persuasive, has a large or decisive number of similarities and fewer differences.

An analogy suggests that because two things are alike in one respect, which we can empirically observe, then they are also alike in another respect, which we cannot observe. Our analogy will need to be strong in order to permit the inference to similar causes.

Do you think comparing the universe to a 'machine' is a weak or strong analogy? The philosopher Hume claimed that you might as well compare the universe to a vegetable. Table 8.1 shows some of the differences between a machine and a natural object that suggest the analogy to a watch is unsound.

Table 8.1 *Differences between a natural object and a machine*

Natural object	Machine
No evidence of prior planning	Clear plans for construction
Spontaneous, unthinking growth	Involves reasoned development
May not have a purpose, e.g. what is the purpose of a donkey?	Has a clear purpose – you can explain what it is for

Do you agree with these three differences? Can you think of any other differences?

> ### Think about
>
> Paley continued to argue that the human eye exhibits exactly the same features. Consider the structure of the human eye. Can you identify the same features as above to make a direct comparison?

> ### Think about
>
> ■ Could you analyse the body of a human being in the same way as an eye or the watch?
>
> ■ Do you have any difficulty with 'purpose'?
>
> ■ Is this significant?

> ### Think about
>
> Rank these analogies in terms of strong or weak. How many similarities or differences are there and are they decisive?
>
> ■ Planning a party is like running a military campaign.
>
> ■ Love is like an onion.
>
> ■ People are like ants.
>
> ■ Winning a football match is being over the moon.
>
> ■ School is a prison.

Think about

Tick the boxes if you think the following comparisons apply to each of the four objects.

	A human eye	A tiger	A bomb	A thunder storm
Has *complex* parts and operations				
Each of the different parts has a *function*				
Each operation is *harmonious*				
It would require *intelligence* to design it				
It has a clear purpose				

It is the last resemblance that you may have most difficulty with. Purpose can be easily discerned in the parts of a body or a machine – the purpose of an eye or another organ is obvious, but does the human body as a whole have a purpose? Does a tiger have a purpose?

The foundation of the analogy rests on the alleged empirical similarity between the world and a watch. This is the weakness of the analogy as it fails on empirical grounds. The watch does not remotely look like the universe. If the analogy had been between a watch and a clock then that would hold as they are genuinely similar, but not between the watch and the world.

Other difficulties may also have occurred to you when making the comparison between the universe and a watch. The foundation of the analogy is that in both there is the most harmonious order. But supposing we can find evidence of disorder in the world, then again the comparison weakens. Can you think of any apparently useless or disorderly parts to the universe? The relatively trivial male nipples or the appendix seem good candidates for purposeless parts of the human body, and on the grand scale, the number of planets which are incapable of supporting life points to a weakness of design. The analogy therefore fails on empirical grounds.

A possible reply is that although we cannot see a function for these parts at the moment, we may in the future when we understand matters differently or more fully. Is this convincing or does it sound like a get-out clause, meaning the analogy can never be defeated? Part of the difficulty with this comparison is that while we can appreciate a watch or an eye from an objective standpoint, we will never be able to stand outside the universe to judge whether it is harmonious and actually has a purpose. This analogy is always going to leave us with an open question.

Another aspect is that it also encourages us to **anthropomorphise** God. Thus God is compared to a designer, with increased intelligence, positive ideas and power. God is therefore comparable to a human being, albeit with considerably augmented qualities of wisdom, moral perfection and power.

Key terms

Anthropomorphise: this is to ascribe human characteristics to non-human beings; for example, to say animals or God are 'loving'.

A human God can seem very attractive. While God can listen to prayers, comfort the sick, reward, guide and punish, etc., God remains very meaningful. But is it credible? There are other descriptions of God that appear incompatible, such as God is timeless, and yet designing would appear to be in time. Does this mean God is everlasting (in time) but not eternal (timeless, having no history). Similarly, to design the world God must have acted in the world, yet is this consistent with being unchangeable and morally perfect? The philosopher Hume sums up the frustration of trying to compare God to a human mind:

> A mind, whose acts and sentiment and ideas are not distinct and successive; one, that is wholly simple, and totally immutable; is a mind which has no thought, no reason, no will, no sentiment, no love, no hatred; or in a word is no mind at all.

Hume (1990, Part 4)

Thus our analogy in anthropomorphising God leaves us trying to reconcile the apparently irreconcilable – a God with human qualities and yet above and beyond the human. This may show the limits of human reason and also the limits of such a comparison.

One final thought is that we often come to know a designer through their designs. So what would you guess about the character of the designer from the two designs in Figs 8.1 and 8.2?

Fig. 8.1 shows the world's smallest, lightest bike, that folds up in less than 10 seconds with a three-click telescopic mechanism, to just 67 × 30 × 16 cm. It is made from heat-treated aluminium and high-strength glass fibre.

Fig. 8.2 shows a Versace espresso cup and saucer that retails at £315. It is made of the finest porcelain, and is hand-painted with 24k gold.

■ The argument from cause and effect

The design argument can also be presented by considering causes and effects. The universe can be considered as 'the effect' and our enquiry is into its likely cause.

■ Think about

Consider the following effects. What do you think were the possible or probable causes?

- A giant wave crashes onto your local beach.
- A crop circle is discovered in your local field.
- A scrap of newspaper is lying in your garden.
- A letter addressed to you arrives through the letterbox.
- Your tyre is punctured.
- A policeman is marching towards you with a determined look.

■ Think about

Is it an advantage or a disadvantage to conceive of God in this way?

■ Think about

You may notice that not all examples of intelligent design have a moral or positive purpose. Is this a problem?

Fig. 8.1 *The world's smallest, lightest bike*

Fig. 8.2 *A Versace espresso cup and saucer that retails at £315*

Think about

What could we discern about the designer of the universe and would it be compatible with our understanding of God? For example, 'Enjoys spectacular events such as volcanoes and tsunamis'.

Fig. 8.3 *A trivial act can have a major effect*

Think about

Do these similar effects have similar causes?

- A fox attacks a rabbit.
- A policeman attacks a thief.
- A jealous husband attacks his wife.
- A stag in autumn attacks another stag.
- The allies attack the Nazis.

There are several points to note about your answers to the above exercise. Firstly you can only discuss the probable causes if you have had some previous experience. If a giant wave had never been seen before, or you have not come across a crop circle, then you may not be able to suggest a cause. Our knowledge of causes is therefore an empirical matter.

Secondly, we tend to proportion our cause to the type and scale of the effect. A scrap of newspaper in the garden was probably blown by the wind rather than a hurricane. Small effects such as a punctured tyre will have small, accidental causes, while serious matters concerning letters and policemen will have intelligent and important reasons behind them. You might, however, like to challenge this point. Theories in astronomy frequently go far beyond the effects that are being investigated.

The same applies to machines and universes. Our knowledge of watches is that sophisticated needs to accurately tell the time, and intelligent planning and construction lie behind the eventual result. Similarly the effect of something as complex and intelligent as the universe demands an equally complex and intelligent cause, namely God. The direction of this argument therefore is to work backwards from the effect to conclusions about the cause.

The philosopher Hume offers his own version of the argument in order to mount a stinging attack on its effectiveness.

One of his first criticisms relates to the empirical nature of cause and effect relationships. We only know what causes produce which effects and vice versa because we have experienced them. He argues that Adam in his first days in the Garden of Eden, with all of his rational faculties, could not have understood how events were arranged in the world. In this respect, he was like a baby, beginning to see how certain events cause other events. He could not have inferred from the fluidity and transparency of water that it would suffocate him. This we learn from tragic accidents. When we see the qualities of an object, we cannot automatically infer the causes that produced it or the effects it will create. We must experience 'the chain of events'. Now, as Hume points out, none of us has experienced the creation of a universe. Therefore, any attempt to indicate a cause that nobody has any empirical knowledge of is little more than guesswork.

Normally also we witness a number of examples of a cause and effect relationship before we commit ourselves to a firm belief about causation. Thus if scientists want to find out what happens to the passengers in a car crashing at, say, 50 mph, they will conduct a series of tests to confirm the exact relationship.

However, the creation of the universe was a one-off event, it was unique. All we have as evidence is one effect, which compounds the problem of trying to work out the exact cause.

At the heart of the problem therefore is that we are trying to work backwards from one unique effect to determine the cause. The analogy with the watch assumes that the 'like effects' have 'like causes', a wonderful machine must have an intelligent designer. But is this necessarily so?

So, the third criticism is that we cannot argue with any certainty from an effect to its cause. The debate over global warming illustrates the difficulties of finding certain accounts of the cause when we can only see the effects.

Hume advises, therefore, that we proportion our account of the cause to what we know of the effects. A wise man proportions his belief to the evidence. So we should only attribute to the cause what we can infer from the effects. And when we control our speculation in this way, it becomes less likely that the cause needs to be the God of Christian religion or other major religions, namely all knowing, all wise, all powerful and all good. The last quality is challenged by the presence of suffering and wastage, and is discussed below. But a number of other possibilities also present themselves:

- The existence of many other lifeless planets could suggest that many experiments were bungled before our successful planet was created, although, as other planets may have a function within our universe, evidence of other botched universes is really required.

- Most design projects have a number of designers with different skills. Could there not be a team of Gods rather than one?

- The causes of wonderful designs do not necessarily have intelligence as we know it. A spider spins a wonderfully intricate web, and Hume gleefully suggests that the universe could be spun from the bowels of a giant spider. There is, however, no evidence for such a hypothesis and the probabilities are against it.

- The universe could equally be compared to a giant vegetable, which grows according to its own internal regulation rather than being produced fully formed.

Many religious believers will still feel that an intelligent and benevolent designer is credible, and we will provide a defence later on. However, Hume's point is that there must be sufficient doubt, so that the argument from design cannot be regarded as a proof. There are other equally convincing hypotheses consistent with the effects. He mentions that the universe could have come about by chance. Eventually in an infinite world and eternal world, one successfully ordered world is bound to happen sooner or later. The more complex the development, the more symmetry and harmony, then the more it will appear designed, despite its random origins.

The point he is making is that while the universe exhibits order, the cause of that order is not necessarily design and planning. This order could just have evolved. We must therefore consider a serious alternative to the theory of design: that organisms were designed *before* they were created. Evolution suggests that the *appearance* of design is something that evolves.

Darwin

Darwin is famous for his theory of natural selection, which states that nature progresses through competition, where only the fittest survive. The measure of fitness is not necessarily beauty or intelligence, but the ability to adjust to the conditions.

'Favourable variations would tend to be preserved and unfavourable ones to be destroyed' and this has come to be known as 'the survival of the fittest' (Palmer, 2001).

This is the internal self-regulatory principle that could account for the development of a highly complex structure without a design, as different species find infinitely variable ways of coping with the conditions. It is a way of explaining how matter organises itself without the need for a mind and intelligence. The more we discover about **DNA**, the more

Think about

How do these suggestions challenge the classical God of theism – namely, all knowing, all wise, all powerful and all good? Can we then posit convincingly such a God as the cause of the universe?

Key philosopher

Charles Darwin (1809–82)

Darwin's classical work is *The Origin of the Species* in which he argued that the evolution of biological features proceeds by variation, selection and retention.

Key terms

DNA: a chemical compound which can replicate itself and accounts for offspring resembling their parents. It contains chemically coded instructions which ensure similar, but not exact, replicas, so slight variations occur.

we understand about how replications of DNA will not be exact, and new variants will be created. These random mutations are retained or discarded depending on whether they are advantageous or detrimental to survival. So if change occurs according to the natural laws of science, then this also removes the idea of purpose from the universe and with it the possibility of a moral dimension. The universe is not progressing towards a goal, it is simply changing as the conditions alter. There is no good or bad or privileged position for the human race. As already mentioned, there is not a premium on beauty or intelligence unless they aid survival, and if the human race finds the new conditions intolerable, as it may well with global warming, then it will become extinct like the dinosaurs before it. This evolutionary principle has therefore been compared to a blind watchmaker. What does that term suggest about 'purpose'?

Function or purpose

The theory of evolution suggests a further criticism: that the design argument confuses *function* and *purpose*, emphasised by the teleological nature in which it is sometimes expressed. In a machine, every part has a function and causes something to work. Thus the workings of a complex structure can be completely catalogued in terms of X causes Y, Y causes Z and so on. If Darwin is correct, it is possible that the universe can be explained in terms of functions or how it operates.

However, purpose suggests much more. It implies that there is an explanation for the machine in terms of an end or goal – what it is aiming at or trying to achieve. This is to give meaning to the object and of course neatly fits with the divine purpose, whatever that may be. Yet it is quite possible that there is no meaning to the universe, it is just simple fact, it is just there, it just happened. Therefore, the comparison with eyes and watches can be misleading. We can talk about the function of eyes without necessarily implying they have a purpose, although we use that word too. However, the difference is much more obvious when we talk about the universe as a whole. It is quite possible to discuss how the universe functions without requiring any explanation beyond that, such as why it exists or what the goal is. So just as it is possible to have order without design, we can have function without purpose, and the need for God disappears in this argument.

Case for the defence

One of the first criticisms of the design argument was that we learn about cause and effect through experience, and we do not have such experience of the unique cause of the universe. Nevertheless it has been pointed out that we do construct meaningful hypotheses about unique events. The cause of many events in history such as the Ice Age can be persuasively explained, and as with the inference to the best explanation, discussed in the next section, we can build up evidence in a very cogent fashion.

Some will argue that the nature of other minds also provides another example. How do we know what other people are feeling? How do I know that when you feel pain, you have the same sensations as I do? All that I have to go on is your behaviour. I know that when I am hurt I have pain sensations that make me cry. So when I see you hurt, I believe you must be feeling those same sensations. But note, it is logically impossible to experience anyone else's feelings and all the evidence we have is the *unique* case of our own minds. Yet most of us believe that other people feel the same as we do (hurt → your private pain → crying). So we have argued from the effect of your crying to the cause which is your private pain.

Yet Hume questions the cogency of this kind of argument: 'from observing the growth of a hair, can we learn anything about the generation of man?' (Wollheim, 1963).

Should we also proportion our knowledge of a cause to only what we perceive in the effect? Of course elements of the effect do suggest the nature of the cause and there must be consistency with the effect. But that does not mean that we cannot meaningfully infer more about a cause than is actually revealed by the effect. In fact science will employ credible hypotheses that go beyond what is observable, even though there are limits to what we can actually see. So we cannot observe the smallest particles, be they atoms, electrons or quarks. We can *detect* the path of an electron through a cloud chamber by watching the track of liquid droplets, but the smallest particles are unobservable. Some might claim that the theories of atoms and quarks are just convenient 'fictions', unprovable theories designed to help predict the behaviour of things that we can observe. We are then left with the choice of which is the more convincing and useful 'fiction' – God or scientific hypotheses. Both conjecture beyond what it is possible to directly experience. The short story 'A Sound of Thunder' by Ray Bradbury (Mansfield, 1971), provides a very imaginative depiction of the cause/effect relationship.

There is also some reservation about Darwin's theory of evolution. Some scientists claim that it does not provide an accurate account of the development and origin of *all* complex systems. They argue that some systems could not have just evolved from simple systems, since if one feature of the system is missing, then there is no system at all. So they must have originated with all of the parts fully functioning and interrelated in order to exist. If some 'machines' could not develop from simpler models but have to be created fully formed, this is more indicative of design than evolution. Irreducibly complex systems must arise as an integrated unit with all of the parts working together rather than gradually evolve through a developmental process. Could it be that some features of a human being cannot have arisen through gradual evolution? Scientists will need to explain how every feature of human consciousness fits the evolutionary model, and this may leave the question of design open.

A related criticism is whether natural selection accounts for the development of self-conscious beings. Our chances of survival would not appear to be improved by some aspects of human thought. For example, our very doubts about the purpose and meaning of life, indeed much of philosophy, would not necessarily appear consistent with natural selection and are actually more consistent with theology. Can we explain philosophy in terms of survival?

In a sense, Darwin highlights the very special nature of human interests. His theory must accommodate why we take pleasure in art – our aesthetic sense – and also our sense of morality, particularly our **altruistic** nature, which puts the good of others before ourselves. Are soldiers who sacrifice themselves for the good of their comrades exhibiting Darwinian behaviour? This is also discussed in Chapter 3.

Finally, some have claimed that the theory of natural selection does not actually deny that an intelligent designer caused the universe, it merely illustrates an intelligent principle at work. But while this may be true, does it also sit nicely with a benevolent purpose? Once more,

Think about

How would you respond to Hume's challenge? Can we intelligently speculate about unique events and their causes when we do not have any experience?

Key terms

Altruistic: having a benevolent concern for the interests and welfare of other people rather than your own self-interest.

we are faced with the vast suffering and wastage that natural selection produces. Whole species die out, often after long and protracted periods of starvation or persecution. It is hard to reconcile survival of the fittest with an intelligent, let alone caring, God.

Induction – inference to the best explanation

Instead of concerning ourselves with the relationship between causes and effects, the teleological argument can be presented as **inductive** reasoning. Typically, inductive arguments start from particular cases and examples and then infer a principle, or general law or explanation. So when people first saw swans, they were white and a general principle was accepted that all swans were white. The more examples we find to confirm the principle, the more confident we become. However, such an argument cannot be conclusive. When adventurers travelled abroad, they eventually found black swans. So inductive reasoning is always vulnerable to the discovery of the contrary. As it is open to doubt, it can only attain the status of a hypothesis that makes doubting unreasonable. Thus very few of us would question the inductive proposition that the sun will rise every day, not just because we have countless experiences of the sun rising, but because we have the general laws of science to support the view. The design argument can also point to countless examples of intelligent design to support the hypothesis of an intelligent designer.

This version of an inductive argument is referred to as the inference to the best explanation (IBE). IBE is a simple rule for acquiring beliefs which states that if you have some data that needs explanation, the theory that explains the data better than any other is the theory that you should adopt. The test of the design argument is now whether it provides the most convincing account of our experience of the world, meaning that it is rational, consistent, agrees with other well-founded beliefs and explains the facts. If it fulfils these criteria, then it is probably right and God exists.

So what are 'the facts' that need explaining? Some philosophers emphasise that the world is precisely adapted so that human consciousness developed and so we can now ask these philosophical questions. A slight alteration in the 'primeval soup', and human beings may never have evolved. Others point to the wondrous beauty and the apparently unique features of our world to support organic life. Basically the features are included in Paley's observation about the watch: complexity, harmony and beauty, fine tuning and regulation, intelligence – particularly moral reasoning and a sense of purpose. Thus even more basic than Paley's 'spatial' regularities in the watch the laws of nature separate the world as we know it from chaos. The temporal order of cause and effect has always operated and will always operate whatever we do; and it is these laws that have culminated in the achievement of human beings.

Now this can either be explained as simple fact and a matter of chance, or it can be seen as rational and meaningful order. The latter would concur well with human intelligence, as we design, do things for a purpose, and reason about and justify our behaviour. It is therefore argued that God is a much more appropriate explanation of human mental development, particularly moral maturity and the altruism previously referred to. Much is made, quite rightly, of human consciousness. While the rest of the universe seems (apparently) to just function, it is man who looks for meaning, emotional intelligence and ultimate answers. This is 'the sense of the sacred' that Scruton describes in *An Intelligent Person's*

Guide to Philosophy (1996). The deep fear of Darwinian analysis is that it de-personalises human existence, we are just objects in a meaningless fight for survival. Our appearance on the earth has no significance, and to quote Macbeth, life is:

a tale
Told by an idiot, full of sound and fury
Signifying nothing.

Shakespeare (2007)

According to the philosopher, Swinburne, the universe 'cries out for explanation' (1991).

The anthropic principle

In support of the design argument is a view that evolution is a divinely willed process which led from inanimate matter, through primitive life, to the arrival of man, to the supreme moral achievement of Jesus and other prophets. Without the laws of science being exactly as they are, the conditions necessary for human life would never have been created because complexity would not have developed sufficiently to result in human life. The wonderful fact that we are here to observe the world, against the fantastic odds of life ever emerging at all, makes a religious response quite fitting. Put simply, if the universe had not developed the way it did, we would not be here. This leads some people to introduce a version of the **anthropic** principle, which states (in the strong version) that the basic features of the universe had to be this way in order for human life to exist. Only a universe exactly like ours allows for us; and this is too much of a coincidence, it must have been planned.

Sceptics are unlikely to be convinced by this view. Its assumption is that human beings are very special, and that all creation was leading to the special event of our arrival. The fallacy is that any successful species will see the world as especially adapted for them, because if it was not they would not be here! Because we have survived, it is bound to seem that the world was created in order to provide for our existence and no other. But what accounts for the appearance of the special adaption of the world to human life is that the inept and useless have died out. The dinosaurs had to go, other species died out because they could not cope, but if the conditions had been different they would have been thinking just like us – the world was made for me!

Imagine an alien landing in the middle of the Olympic Games. All it would have seen of human beings were incredible feats of running and jumping. It would assume that people were an amazing species, but only in the conditions of an Olympic stadium! In completely different conditions, like in the North Sea, it would be better to be a whale! Adaption depends on where you choose to look.

Indeed what appears to be order and finely adapted means to ends can depend on the observer. What appears orderly in one respect can seem chaotic and wasteful in another. Consider a rugby game. Is it ordered? On the one hand, it is played according to rules and ends with a result; but on the other it appears to involve much futile effort, a waste of resources and pointless damage. Similarly in the universe, things drift aimlessly in pointless orbits, collide and die. True, they obey the laws of physics, but a critical observation of the way the world works could notice a complete meaninglessness in the way everything moves. To amplify this point, was it really necessary to have billions of years of experimentation on a huge

Key philosopher
Richard Swinburne (1934–)
Swinburne is Professor of the Philosophy of the Christian Religion at Oxford University. He supports the case for theism through such things as the existence of human consciousness, morality and the order of the universe.

Key terms
Anthropic: relating to human beings. The argument claims that the universe has been precisely fine tuned to support human life. It could not have been otherwise in order for human beings to exist.

Fig. 8.4 *Glastonbury*

scale in order to create the human race? Whether the world actually exhibits finely tuned, harmonious order is a matter of perspective.

Behind this lies a serious question, that if this is an ordered world, what does a disordered world look like? Can we conceive of what complete randomness would be like? It could be argued that we have gone beyond what makes sense. In which case, any world that exists at all will be ordered simply because it exists. This, of course, will not support the case for a divine creator.

A serious problem with inference to the best explanation is that it depends on our background beliefs. As with the rugby game, your view depends on a pattern of assumptions about what order means. It depends on how you look at something whether it appears to be chaotic or whether it has an explanation. Some people who live near Glastonbury believe that the landscape contains mystical secrets. So the apparently random natural features actually make up the signs of the zodiac or other legendary and mythical figures. An example is the figure of Aquarius (see Fig. 8.4).

So is the second map of the area (Fig. 8.5) just a haphazard series of rivers, hills and paths or is the natural world alive with faces, giants and fertility symbols? What can you see in the landscape?

The serious implications for IBE is that order is not existing in the natural world, but is something we project onto the world. Our knowledge is a result of the interplay between the external stimuli, the data we receive and the way our minds organise the experience and impose order on it. We see the world through a particular set of 'spectacles' that, for example, places experience in space and time, and we ensure the world conforms to our schema of cause and effect. It is our own mental faculties that adapt the external stimuli so that they appear to us in a particular way. The order that was assigned to divine intelligence is in fact our own creation. We make sense of experience in a way that helps us survive. It is this way of seeing the universe, the human interpretation, that has enabled us to become the dominant species, but it is only an interpretation.

Hume reminds us of one more problem in finding explanations for things. Supporters of the design argument claim that God made the world according to a plan. This, however, allows for ideas to fall into place in God's mind without a known cause and yet does not allow for matter to fall into place without a known cause. If you believe that mind and matter are very similar laws then if one can fall into place without a known cause then why not the other? There is no *rational* ground for not simply stopping with matter. In order to defend IBE, can you find answers to these questions?

- Could global warming which threatens to wipe out our species have a purpose?

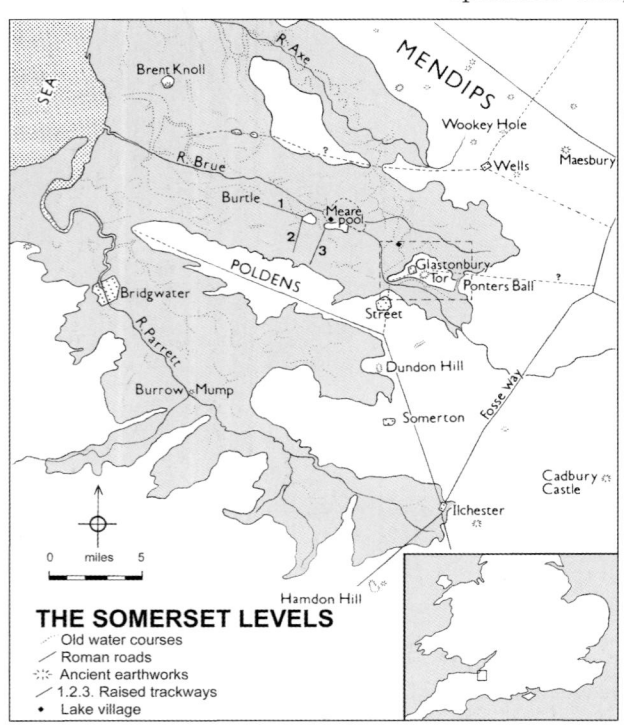

THE SOMERSET LEVELS

- Old water courses
- Roman roads
- Ancient earthworks
- 1.2.3. Raised trackways
- Lake village

Fig. 8.5 *The Somerset Levels*

- Why did it take so long for the universe to eventually support human beings 'made in God's image'?
- What was the point of the dinosaurs?
- Have we got just the right number of fingers and toes?
- Why did human beings develop the idea of God?
- Why do we need to have earthquakes which kill people?
- Why are there so many uninhabited planets?

If we regard God as the best explanation, we need to try to answer these questions in a way which is consistent with an intelligent designer.

A problem for Darwinists?

The challenge for those Darwinists who believe in 'brute fact' is also daunting. Why have human beings spent so much time making art objects, reading and writing philosophy, agonising over the meaning of life, and in some cases following a morality that seems life-denying (from drug taking to sexual abstinence)?

Both sides of the debate have difficult questions to answer if they wish to provide the best explanation.

Think about

In this section we have asked the following questions:

- Is there order in the universe? That seems to be a matter of interpretation.
- Is the apparent order our own interpretation only of events?
- Does the world appear ordered to us simply because we happen to be the species that has survived and developed?
- Does reference to a designer God provide a sufficiently foundational explanation or does it leave questions open?
- Does a purely scientific explanation account for the evolution of important features of human consciousness?

What do you think?

A final criticism of the design argument is the way it tends to develop. We have already noted that it takes the dubious route of looking at effects and trying to deduce the cause. But then it often develops by inferring more conclusions from the cause, thus compounding the confusions. So once the qualities of the designer are established from the order of the universe, then follow more supposed 'facts' about human behaviour and the moral purpose of existence. However, once again these must be mere hypotheses rather than proofs, and reference back to the problems of anthropomorphising are relevant. Given that human intelligence is a feature of the world, and God must have been supremely intelligent to create such intelligence, should we be entitled to draw any more conclusions, for example about his good intentions and his morality? We are now arguing from cause to effect, and if we remember Hume's allusion to Adam, that must remain just as mysterious unless we have had experience of a divine cause creating explanations and laws.

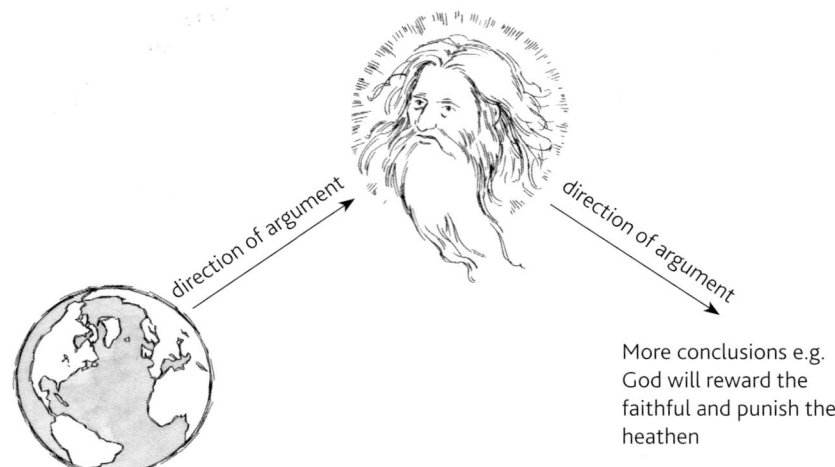

Fig. 8.6 *Criticism of the design argument*

The argument from probability

This argument can be seen as a version of the inductive process, but as a distinctive element. Arguing from the facts of the world to a principle or explanation can be expressed as a matter of probability. The odds against our universe ever happening have been quoted at 10 billion to one. Out of a virtually infinite number of possibilities, we have come about. It would have needed only one chemical change in the beginning and *Homo sapiens* could not have evolved. Surely it could not simply have been an arbitrary and random chance happening. To some this amazing result against the odds needs explanation.

However, probabilities are related to the size of the variables and also the sheer number of opportunities. While it is true that an early increase in the temperature at Big Bang by one millionth of a degree would have prevented the growth of our planet, how really significant is this? It certainly is remarkable, but in the huge timescale, which offers infinite opportunities for this to happen, then it is not so improbable, that one day the right combination of factors would simply emerge.

The philosopher Swinburne counters with this example:

> Suppose that a madman kidnaps a victim and shuts him in a room with a card shuffling machine. The machine shuffles ten packs of cards simultaneously and then draws a card from each pack and exhibits simultaneously the ten cards. The kidnapper tells the victim that he will shortly set the machine to work and it will exhibit the first draw, but that unless the draw consists of an ace of hearts from each pack, the machine will simultaneously set off an explosion to kill the victim, in consequence of which we will not see which cards the machine drew. The machine is then set to work, and to the amazement and relief of the victim the machine exhibits an ace of hearts drawn from each pack. The victim thinks that this extraordinary fact needs an explanation in terms of the machine having been rigged in some way. But the kidnapper, who now reappears, casts doubt on this suggestion. 'It is hardly surprising', he says, 'that the machine drew only aces of hearts. You could not possibly see anything else. For you would not be here to see anything at all, if any other cards had been drawn.' But of course

To the right of the figure:

More conclusions e.g. God will reward the faithful and punish the heathen the victim is right and the kidnapper is wrong. There is something extraordinary in need of explanation in ten aces being drawn. The fact that this peculiar order is a necessary condition of the draw being perceived at all makes what is perceived no less extraordinary and in need of explanation.

Swinburne (1991)

In return, consider the following example. I won the lottery. I have used one set of identical numbers every time. The chances of me ever winning are millions to one, so I was completely stunned when recently my numbers came up. The fact that I was 'chosen' could lead me to think it was some kind of fate – that somewhere it was planned for me to be successful.

On the contrary, we can just say that it was all entirely due to the choice of the machine, the friction of the balls, the exact timing of the starter button, etc. It was completely a matter of chance that the causes were so aligned, but sooner or later that combination would happen. So I was not especially selected. There is nothing about me that means it had to happen (and it was only £10.00!). So with the card game, the odds on receiving any particular set of balls are astronomical, but no more than any other seven, and you have to receive one set of seven.

As Hume points out, probability judgements can only be made on the basis of past experience, and we have no experience of designed and chance worlds with which to compare this one. So a calculation of probability cannot be made.

> **Think about**
>
> Which interpretation of probabilities do you prefer? Do these examples suggest that the very notion of probability is a subjective interpretation?

The last word

It is the nature of arguments that employ analogies, inductive methods and assessment of probabilities that they are inconclusive. In the end, we have to make a judgement about which interpretation has the most explanatory power and predictive value. In terms of prediction, science appears to win hands down in short-term accuracy, as it daily gives us reliable information about our surroundings. However, others may feel that in terms of explanation it cannot satisfy our search for purpose. It is often said that science tells us *how* the universe functions but not *why* it was created. The response may be that if we have enough *hows* we do not need a *why*. In the end it just happened to happen. This is discussed in the final topic of this chapter.

Teleology

It seems integral to purpose, especially divine purpose, that it is benevolent. Suffering may happen by accident or incompetence, but purposeful acts aim at some good. Greek philosophers claimed that flourishing is the end of all activity, whether it be a flower, an animal or a human being. The teleological argument therefore claims there is a purpose for the whole of creation. Is there? I can see that survival of my genes could be of benefit to me and that I might want to assert my influence on the world and increase my power. But have we established the purpose of the universe? Need there be one? And how meaningful can it be to speculate on what such a purpose might be? Part of our response may depend on our assessment of 'the good' and 'the evil' that appears around us. That is the subject of the next topic.

After working through this topic, you should:

- understand the distinction between the argument for design and the argument from design
- understand the different aspects of the argument: analogy, inference from effect to cause, induction and probability
- be able to explain Darwinism and the anthropic principle
- be able to evaluate this teleological argument.

The problem of evil

Learning objectives:

- to describe what we mean by evil
- to explain why evil is a problem for the design argument
- to examine how evil can be reconciled with a belief in an all powerful and loving God
- to evaluate the explanations and solutions to the problem of evil.

■ Introduction

The problem is generated through a consideration of the following dilemma: either God can prevent evil but doesn't in which case he's not all good or he can't prevent it, in which case he's not all powerful. Technically this argument does not demonstrate the non-existence of God but if successful would show that the traditional idea of God as all powerful and all good was not consistent with the existence of evil.

Since the beginning of time, mankind has murdered, tortured, raped and pillaged. Recently the technological revolution which has opened up a whole new world of the internet has exposed our capacity for evil as well as good. This is not confined to human activity. Dogs naturally fight; cats will torture their prey; foxes in a frenzy of blood lust will slaughter chickens that they do not eat; and plants crowd out and exterminate competitors. Nature is brutal and this is difficult to reconcile with the argument from design. While it may be accepted that the universe exhibits design, the God of classical theism is all powerful and all good (omnipotent and omnibenevolent). Imperfections in the world block the inference to a perfect creator, although of course the universe could still be designed and contain evil!

It is generally recognised that there are several kinds of evil in the world that challenge the argument from design. Try to add your own examples to illustrate each type:

- Natural evil is evil over which people have little or no control, and it is a fundamental feature of the natural world. It is independent of human activity, e.g. volcanoes, disease, etc.
- Moral evil is the evil that arises from human activity, whether it is individuals, groups or political systems. It is sometimes described as 'the fall of man', e.g. foolishness, selfishness.

These evils are a challenge to the assumption of the design argument, that we were created:

- by a single God (who is therefore wholly good)
- who continues to take an interest in His creation.

The problem is traditionally expressed firstly as a logical inconsistency with the belief that God is omnipotent (all powerful) and omni-benevolent (all good). If there is evil in the world, then either God cannot eliminate it and so cannot be omnipotent – He is feeble, or He will not eliminate it and He is therefore not omni-benevolent, but uncaring and morally imperfect. So, even if the world shows design, it could not be the creation of (1) a wise, morally perfect and (2) all powerful designer, because of the imperfections. To remove this contradiction, the theist has to demonstrate that perfect design is compatible with the existence of evil. Critics will argue that the presence of pain and suffering is completely inconsistent with a morally perfect being.

Secondly, we can simply look at the evidence of natural disasters and human cruelty and enquire if we can infer such a God from the empirical data. Many think not.

Think about

Consider the following. Can you suggest any possible replies?

- God is causally responsible for everything, so why did He cause AIDS to happen?
- God foresees everything, so why did He not change the Holocaust before it occurred?
- To balance good with evil shows He is unloving, does it not?
- Sending people to hell is cruel and wasteful. Surely God should save even mass murderers?
- Why does He let animals suffer? They have not done anything wrong.
- Sometimes we do good things and they still have negative consequences, e.g. a father plays with his son and has a heart attack. Why is that?
- Why should we atone for what Adam and Eve did? Surely we are all born innocent and untainted.

Can you spot an example of each of the three evils? Where would you place global warming?

During the exercise, you might have considered that logically God could have created a world, in which people learn and progress, without introducing pain etc. So to resolve the problem of evil, the theist must demonstrate that evil is a prerequisite for good, that there is no logical or possible alternative. So one cannot have redemption without sin.

This assumption underpins the following responses to the problem of evil in this topic:

1 Evil is a necessary part of a dynamic universe
2 The Augustinian theodicy and free will
3 The Irenean theodicy
4 The best of all possible worlds

We begin and end however with some reflection on the nature of evil, particularly moral and natural evil.

■ What is evil?

Evil is a privation

This is often associated with the theologian, Augustine of Hippo (354–430). Since God can only create good, He did not create evil, and therefore evil is not a thing or a substance. Evil is instead a lack of goodness or a privation. So God created health, but our lack of health is sickness. This absence of health is due to our own fault and our own choices (and this step is discussed in the free will defence below). Evil occurs when we fail to live up to our true nature: what we could be and should be. So behaving like an animal, for example, is to fall short of the qualities **intrinsic** to a human being. So evil is an imperfection, an absence of goodness, when we turn away from our true nature, and God is therefore absolved from responsibility. God did not create evil but gave us the positive gift of free will. We are responsible when we fail to fulfil our potential. So:

■ we are degenerate when we lack self-control

■ we are revengeful when we fail to forgive, etc.

This is reminiscent of Aristotle's virtues and the doctrine of the mean (see Chapter 3: Why should I be moral? – Morality as a constitutive of self-interest, p73). Cowardice is explained as a lack of courage.

One problem with this view is that it can become a trivial play on words. War is a lack of peace! God may not have created war, but He still allows it to happen. God created health, so He did not create sickness, but since we turn away from healthy pursuits, sickness is still an option and a possibility that exists in the scheme of things. And moreover, *natural* evils seem part of the universe that is not accounted for by 'turning away'. Augustine explains this natural evil as the fault of the angels, but this then poses many more questions.

We could also ask what this true nature is supposed to be and whether we have an intrinsic ideal to live up to. Philosophers such as Sartre question whether there is a human essence, and advocate that any definition of an ideal human being is open to interpretation and dangerous. Presumably an ideal person in Augustine's view would have Christian virtues, but without taking the argument further, different cultures have also held different virtues to be essential. To give just one example, pride and self-esteem are necessary for a flourishing life according to Aristotle, while humility is encouraged in the Bible.

Evil as suffering

A further criticism of 'privation' is offered by those who point to the pain, misery and unpleasantness that exist in the world. No matter how good people are, even if they are as innocent as a newborn babe, suffering and death exist. Examples are all around us. Yet some will argue the connection between natural and moral evil. The human impact on the world is responsible for the degeneration of the environment and much disease. Nevertheless, can you make two lists? Suffering that is not the product of human intervention, and suffering that is.

It should be possible to stipulate two criteria to determine whether suffering is evil or not:

■ Any suffering should not be pointless, but should lead to a greater good. Then it is meaningful.

■ **Key terms**

Intrinsic: belonging to the nature or essence of something.

That suffering is within the bounds of moral acceptability, that it is the minimum necessary to achieve the desired results. So any excess, such as unendurable suffering is over the limits of moral acceptability and is evil.

Evil is a necessary part of a balanced universe

Here is one last attempt to query our understanding of evil. Consider a football match where players are crowding the referee, who controversially books one of them. We are outraged. He must be blind! Or perhaps he has seen something that was out of shot in the television coverage. Maybe he has seen the bigger picture. Likewise, from our limited perspective, suffering can appear awful, but God has painted on a much broader canvas, and we cannot see the complete painting. We only have a partial and incomplete understanding. Augustine, for example, claimed thorns and thistles to be good. Augustine, however, does not try to explain away evil, either what we fear is evil or the act of fearing is itself evil. When his contemporaries countered that he should try letting a scorpion sting him, he replied that even poison is good. Our misunderstanding is a result of 'the perversion of the will, turned aside from God'. Yet even our idea of evil has in it, things that are good in themselves, such as life, creativity, vitality and intelligence. Augustine does not seek to explain away evil, but points to our incomplete understanding. If we have 'the eye that has the skill to discern it … the universe is beautiful even by sinners' (Augustine, quoted in Vardy, 1992). In this context we might recall what the philosopher Nietzsche claimed about suffering.

Nietzsche himself suffered with appalling bad health throughout the 1880s, but he wrote:

> Never have I felt happier … than in the sickest and most painful periods of my life.

*Nietzsche, quoted in **Leiter** (2002)*

He sees suffering, not as a negative condition of this life that will be compensated for in the next, but as a catalyst for greatness in the here and now. Many artists in particular have exploited their suffering to create great works – better to be a tragic hero and heroine, than live a life of mediocrity!

Perhaps we must forgo our narrow view and try to understand that in order to have a dynamic universe, there has to be change, decay and death. When we are close to a personal tragedy, of course, it seems heartless and cruel, but when we stand back we can often see that it is all for the best. As in John 9 verse 3, 'neither this man sinned nor his parents, but it was in order that the works of God might be made manifest in this case'.

This is not just a matter of contrasts, but it is true that to feel joy we need a measure of sadness, and hope is experienced more intensely if you know despair. However, to fully understand, we must actually look at evil in a different way. Thus the death of leaves in winter is also beautiful in its colours and moods; agony and ecstasy are inextricably intermingled; and we can appreciate 'creative suffering' such as Beethoven's deafness. The foot soldiers who built the pyramids in Egypt will have had personal tragedies but might have gloried in the overall achievement, and people who nobly suffer often inspire goodness in others.

However, in the end this argument is asking us to accept our ignorance, for the divine plan is inaccessible and unknowable. Contrast this with the TV camera shots of football incidents. Some may wish to see this as a cause for faith, but others will find this unsatisfactory.

Think about

Would the death of starving children and the scale of genocide in the Sudan meet these criteria? Would the hopeless misery of debilitating diseases or political prisoners rotting in jails be over morally acceptable limits?

Key philosopher

Friedrich Nietzsche (1844–1900)

Nietzsche was a German philosopher known as a radical critic of Western philosophy. He attacked Christianity for its pity and compassion for the weak and claimed that all life seeks to enhance its power.

Think about

These aspects of the world would have been considered negative at one time or another. Can you find a positive perspective?

- leaves dying on trees in autumn
- the agony of childbirth
- homosexuality
- tigers killing people
- severe disability
- cancer.

While we can see some evils in a different light, surely others are irretrievably negative. For example, how can forms of madness such as schizophrenia, or huge-scale malnutrition in some countries just be part of a bigger picture? And even if my misery is a narrow perspective compared with the bigger picture, it is still misery for me. As Mill said, if evil is really good, then the fact that we are experiencing it as evil seems a gross error. Why is it not possible to be given more of the big picture? (See 'Epistemic distance' on p247.)

While birth and death might balance each other out, it must be remembered that an all-powerful and benevolent God should accept the following criteria:

- that suffering should not be pointless
- that it should be the minimum possible to gain the desired effect.

While animals eating each other may seem a neat plan from a lofty perspective, the unnecessary terror and pain seems unjustifiable from the perspective of the animal being eaten. Extreme animal suffering seems a particular problem since animals cannot even be held morally responsible. We cannot redefine the meanings of words. Goodness is goodness as *we* understand it, and if animal suffering is good, then we must find another word for good as we understand it.

Furthermore, it seems worse that not only is evil happening, but God, as a designer, actually planned it. The unfolding of the world is the will of God. If we look once more at God's qualities of omnipotence and omniscience, then God has prior knowledge of what will happen and yet will not intervene. This has implications for our interpretation of these qualities.

Consider the biblical story of the Garden of Eden, where God created the tree of knowledge. Did He foresee that Eve would taste the fruit?

Here are three possibilities. What are the consequences for Eve's freedom of choice and our understanding of God?

- God created Eve and caused her to act as she did. He knew everything that would happen, and so foresaw that she would eat the apple.
- God knew what she would do, although He did not cause her to do it. She decided of her own free will to eat the apple, but God was able to foresee that she would do this.
- God created Eve and the Garden of Eden, but He did not know the future and what she would choose. God only knows the past and the present.

Think about

- Which of these situations is consistent with Eve being genuinely free?
- What are the consequences for our understanding of God?

Can you match the three points above with the points below?

- God is the causal power in the creation of the universe, but once created, He just sustains life, He does not intervene although He could.
- God created the universe, but in His omnipotence He chose to limit Himself. He has created the 'hazardous adventure of individual freedom' (Hick, 1966) and does not know how it will turn out.

God is all powerful and all knowing, which means He must be fully responsible for evil.

Which description of God do you find the most convincing? This decision will affect your opinion of the free will defence in the next section.

It is difficult to reconcile God's power and knowledge with human free will. The philosopher Plantinga defines freedom as 'a person is free with respect to an action A, only if no causal laws and antecedent conditions determine that he performs A'. Thus it is assumed that God is limited by logical possibility, so that He cannot create any world He pleases. To give us a genuine free will, we have to have the genuine possibility of choosing evil as well as good.

Many philosophers accept that it is not an infringement of God's power that He cannot do the logically impossible, and this is assumed in the following debate on free will. The consequence to be emphasised here is the implications for the nature of God and our understanding of the bigger picture.

One final point in our understanding of evil is the claim that in a dynamic world it is not possible to eliminate suffering. We shall consider this again in the section on 'The best possible world' at the end of this topic. For now, it could be argued that a world which embraces free will and operates according to physical laws rather than miracles and constant intervention, must inevitably incur some evil. To eliminate this would completely change the laws of nature. They cannot be tinkered with. If we made just one change, say to stop animals eating each other, the whole system would need redesigning, and perhaps a better design is just not possible. On the other hand, it is argued below that it is logically possible to produce an 'all-good' world, and therefore it is possible for God to do so.

The next part of this topic examines theories that accept the full unpleasantness of suffering but try to find a solution to reconcile this with God's qualities. Two **theodicies** are considered.

The theodicies are known as the Augustinian and the Irenean theodicies. Both assume that human beings have free will.

We shall also encounter a *defence* of evil, which attempts to demonstrate that it is (or is not) logically consistent that there is evil and there is God, but does not propose reasons or moral justification.

The Augustinian theodicy

This can be characterised as 'soul deciding'. As part of His goodness, God gave mankind free will. Free will is positive, because rather than being automatons, human beings can choose to love God. This allows for spiritual and emotional understanding and development. In order to have genuine free will, then it must be an actual possibility that we can turn away from God and not fulfil our human nature. In the Bible, pride is identified as the sin that leads us to reject the opportunity to flourish as God intended. So we succumb to lower desires, such as gluttony, greed and promiscuity. God foresaw this but did not cause it to happen, and so offered the possibility of redemption through Jesus Christ and/or religious observance. If we accept this, we achieve enlightenment and salvation, but if we choose not to, we are condemned to hell. So the responsibility

Key terms

Theodicies: explanations of evil which are consistent with God being all powerful and all good. They should provide solutions to the apparent problems.

Key philosopher

St Augustine (354–430)

St Augustine was a Christian philosopher associated with Western Christendom. He claimed that through exercising free will we have chosen evil, but we can receive redemption through divine grace.

for the continued existence of evil is ours, and, according to our choices, the fate of our soul is decided.

The first discussion is not so much about the moral justification of this theodicy, which will come later, but about the **logical consistency**.

The free will defence

One criticism of this theodicy is that it is logically possible for God to create a world in which we always choose good. If this is the case, then a benevolent creator should have chosen it as the best possible option.

Freedom can be defined as the ability to act without constraint or coercion. It is logically possible for real choices to exist, but that we always decide to do the good. For example, suppose that over and over again, you are offered a choice of chocolates (good) or toffees (bad). Nobody interferes with your choice or coerces you into choosing one or the other, so it is a free choice. It is logically possible that every time you would choose chocolates, a realistic alternative of toffees actually exists, but you just always prefer chocolates. Logically, therefore, God could create such a world and therefore eliminate evil choices. This would be the best possible result of all worlds, which is what an omnipotent, omni-benevolent God would wish. So evil choices are not consistent with God's qualities and human freedom.

The reply

The response to this is that it is not really a free choice. 'Now God can create free creatures, but He cannot cause or determine them to do what is right. For if He does so, they are not significantly free after all' (Plantinga, 1994). In terms of the logic of freedom, it is not logically impossible for God to create a free creature who chooses evil on at least one occasion. It is quite consistent, if it is part of our nature to be able to be corrupt, that it must remain a significant possibility for us to take a wrong action. If this is not the case, then we are not free and corruptible. Real freedom demands that we genuinely debate about our desires and reasons and that it must be possible for us to decide to choose a toffee rather than a chocolate – that must remain a viable decision.

The first view claims that it is logically possible to choose good all the time. The reply is that freedom is only significant if it is not logically impossible for us to choose evil. Which is more consistent with omnipotence and omni-benevolence?

One way to approach the impasse is to examine what we mean by freedom. It could be argued that if God creates a being who necessarily chooses right, then this contradicts real freedom, which entails that it must be possible for at least one person to select evil. If God has imposed our character in advance and, as it were, pre-programmed the human race, then there is no genuine, rational decision making taking place. God cannot be causally involved in ensuring that we all naturally choose good and maintain that is free decision making. At least one person must be able to decide to take a toffee. A world in which we are always determined to do what is good is indistinguishable from a world in which it is impossible to choose evil. Surely to be free, it must be possible to do otherwise. However, on this account there is not a genuine alternative action. People seem to have become puppets or pre-determined robots.

There is thus a different conception of freedom in these two accounts. In the first, freedom is *acting according to our desires* (i.e. choosing between competing desires), and God has engineered our desires to be good. In the reply, freedom is being able *to select your desires*, and this entails that someone must be able to choose evil. Which account do you believe offers a more convincing account of freedom? Which would a benevolent God choose?

The above is a *defence* of evil rather than a theodicy. It is about the *logic* of God's qualities, human free will and the presence of evil. However, there are also difficult questions for the Augustinian *theodicy* in terms of how plausible it is as a moral justification of the evidence.

Think about

Examine the following criticisms and rank them in order of how persuasive and convincing they are.

- There is still a flaw in the moral design of the universe if mankind can turn away from God, and some will be wasted in eternal hell.
- Can the means justify the end? Can an all-loving God accept that some will be sacrificed in order that others will achieve redemption?
- The free will argument does not explain the existence of natural evils or the suffering of animals who have no free will.
- The theodicy does not account for the death of the innocent, such as young babies who have had no chance to make moral choices.

Also you might look back at Eve's choice, to see whether free will is consistent with a God who is causally involved with the universe and who is omniscient.

The Irenean theodicy

This is characterised as 'soul making'. Whereas the previous theodicy starts with perfection and accounts for 'the fall', this theodicy starts with imperfection. Human beings are created as imperfect, raw material, which can be improved and matured through the challenges of evil. Eventually we will arrive at a proper relationship with God. The comparison is with children, brought up by wise and caring parents, who will allow their offspring to take risks and face problems rather than lock them away where they will learn nothing.

Freedom as good 'in itself'

Both theodicies, therefore see free will as preferable to no choice at all, even if that ensured consistent goodness. With choice, we learn from the consequences of our decisions, we become **autonomous**, and choose good from our own mature reflection rather than from mere obedience. A child who just does as it is told gains nothing and remains naive and unprepared for real challenges. Experience of evil will teach us to reason and to understand why good choices must be made.

This theodicy can also explain *natural evil* as a necessary condition of wise and moral decision making. Through facing natural problems, such as earthquakes and disease, it teaches us to be careful and to show courage and fortitude. We then learn not to build houses in earthquake and flood zones and how to care for each other and endure hardship.

Key philosopher
Bishop Ireneus (130–202)

A major thinker in early Eastern Christendom, Ireneus claimed that God's plan is the universal salvation of all persons.

Key terms

Autonomous: having self-rule and self-determination. So a person is the sole author of his or her decisions, a free agent able to choose his/her desires and moral law.

This suffering is the price we pay for independence and wisdom. For example, the theory of global warming has alerted all nations to our consumption of resources and encouraged us to control our desires for material things. Thus what are termed the metaphysical evils are intelligent design features. The scarcity of resources teaches us prudence, the finitude of death make us live with intensity and with philosophy.

So, as the philosopher Hick says, the world must be judged by its fitness for soul making.

God maintains epistemic distance

Part of the learning curve for mankind is that is takes responsibility for its journey. So God must remain hidden (or keep **epistemic distance**) and then our choices will be genuinely thought through. Then we do not rely on the teacher to sort out our problems. We must learn from making mistakes, and this requires the possibility of real suffering. This way, our destiny is realised through our own understanding of what is right, and we make our own way home rather than relying on others to give directions. So God keeps His distance and ensures that we are ignorant of the grand design.

You might ask, 'What is the point? Could God just have made finished articles, complete with moral wisdom? Do we really have to go on the journey?' The reply could be that something is not really understood unless it is experienced. We are all familiar with the extra credibility of someone who 'has been there', and as fallible creatures, perhaps we need constant reminders. Even so, why could an omnipotent God not create us complete with all of the necessary memories of experience, improved habits and received wisdom, just a few moments before salvation? As Peter Cole (1989) expresses it, 'if the end result is guaranteed, what is the point of the pilgrimage'?

A second problem arises in consideration of the learning experience. A good teacher makes the learning objectives clear, and progress is as efficient as possible. Yet when we look at real-life situations, there are mixed messages. The virtuous do not always thrive and the unvirtuous appear to go unpunished, at least in this life.

This leads us also to consider the scale of the suffering. A good God would surely limit the scale to the least amount possible to achieve the desired end (our second criteria). Not one more creature would be hurt than is absolutely necessary. Yet we seem to be cursed with repeat disasters such as civil wars and famines, where many innocent people, who could not do anything about it even though they would, endure extreme and widespread suffering. These catastrophes are sometimes exacerbated by drought and climate irregularity that achieves nothing but despair and misery.

However, we can anticipate the response that we are responsible for these terrible events. Our political and economic systems contribute to these worldwide tragedies and we do not seem to learn properly. The sorrow that God must feel is that we are not learning the lesson that 'nothing can save us from ourselves' (Sartre, 1948). There is an existential lesson to be learnt, that no one is going to bale us out; and true maturity comes when we stop looking for excuses, saviours or someone to blame.

Eschatological reward?

Nevertheless, it is clear that the final purification of our souls does not take place in this life. For the two theodicies to succeed they must establish an afterlife, when either judgement or salvation finally take place. This is not very satisfactory for empirical and rational enquiry. It leaves the justification for the design of this world resting on another possible world which is unverifiable and unknowable (this is the part of theology known as **eschatology**).

Once we speculate about an afterlife, a plethora of questions arise for which no certain answers can be given. This has led some to question its meaningfulness. Even if you countenance the resurrection of the body, through DNA profiles, what state would the body be in – young, old, its diseased final moments? And without the body, in what sense could we still be called 'persons', and identifiable with a recognisable character and personality? This is apart from the obvious problem of establishing a soul, that is not empirically verifiable. In what sense is it still us as individuals who are going to be judged and perfected? How can I renounce bodily desires without a body? Memory would surely be required, but what part of my life will be remembered and judged – the irresponsible teenage years, the gap-year charity work, the responsible parent or the eccentric pensioner? Unanswerable questions just seem to explode, so that to quote Ayer (1936), 'no sentence which purports to describe the nature of a transcendent God (or experience) can possess any literal significance'. In trying to make sense of life after death, we are at the limits of what we can meaningfully say. 'To say that there is something imperceptible inside a man, which is his soul and that it goes on living after he is dead is to make a metaphysical assertion, which has no factual content' (Ayer, 1936). Without any content that can be verified or falsified, we are left with only speculation and expression of personal belief about which nothing can be decided.

■ The best possible world

Theodicies have to prove that this is the best possible world, consistent with omnipotence and omni-benevolence, that would not permit pointless evil or any excessive suffering. The morally acceptable minimum must be achieved. The philosopher Leibniz explained that in His supreme wisdom, God would only have created the best of all possible worlds. So despite any alternative appearances that suggest otherwise, this universe is the best that can be created, and the evil must be the absolutely necessary minimum component. So can this opinion be sustained?

■ Think about

The philosopher Swinburne provides us with the possibility of four worlds. Which would you consider the best?

1 A world without death, where everyone is immortal. The world would have a few imperfections which could be perfected by people cooperating. In a limited time, happiness and completion would be achieved.

2 A world without death, where everyone is immortal but with an infinite number of improvements to make, and there is an infinite number of people.

3 There is no death and people are immortal, but there is birth and people increase to infinite numbers, grow and mature.

4 There is death as well as birth and the possibility of infinite improvements, as well as the possibility of damaging the world, although only to a small extent.

Which would you choose?

Key terms

Eschatology: concerned with the last or final fate of mankind. Eschatology is frequently used to indicate what happens after death.

Swinburne's answer is that point 4 is the most desirable, because if God is to trust us, we must have the fullest experience – even the ultimate sacrifice of death. We need to have the most educative experience of creating and destroying, but within limits. Death limits the amount of harm we can do. Instead of creating what Swinburne calls 'a toy world', in point 4 we will learn genuine responsibility through genuine choice, but with sensible limits.

> **Think about**
>
> Is evolution a *law* of nature?

Other philosophers have argued that the current law of nature, which results in the survival of the fittest, is also the best possible world. Vardy (1992) suggests that: 'To reject evolution … is not to reject a harsh way of creating a world, but a world of great beauty and richness … which has within it the possibility of love and the higher values'.

The principle of natural selection stops over-reproduction and the weak and sick passing on their genes, and the struggle ensures improvement. We cannot make adjustments to the natural laws, the whole interlocking structure of cause and effect has to stand as it is. We appreciate how delicate our eco-system is and how tampering or corrupting it can cause only worse conditions. Furthermore much of the suffering in the animal world is actually a human responsibility, where we have damaged habitat or treated animals cruelly for selfish and unnecessary purposes. And pain itself is a valuable warning system to all creatures.

Some have questioned whether the concept of a best possible world is really meaningful. Williams compares it to 'the greatest prime number' (in Vardy, 1992). Just as there is always a prime number greater than the one we can conceive, so there is always a conceivably better world. So we are trying to describe the inconceivable!

What matters, however, is that God works through us and He must work with what He has. Surely it is more glorious to enable free but vulnerable, corruptible and 'fallen' creatures to gain redemption than just create a static world of perfection.

> **Think about**
>
> If you do not accept these arguments, which points below would counter them?
>
> - The selection of those who die and suffer appears indiscriminate. It is a contingent matter, for example, who is involved in a train crash.
> - If God wishes us to learn, His purposes must be made manifest. Pupils cannot learn unless the teacher outlines clear objectives.
> - The laws of nature resulted in billions of years of pre-history when species came and went and moral consciousness did not exist.
> - World 3 (above) might be preferable to world 4. Infinite numbers of people growing together in a wholly positive environment is idyllic. Why do we need to learn about destruction?
> - What is the difference between a world produced by a blind watchmaker and one that has a perfect designer?

■ Natural evil

A means to an end

There is an assumption in some solutions to the problem of evil that suffering is not evil if it is a means to an end. The phrase implies that the perfect result, the goal or end, can justify using some morally questionable methods and means in order to achieve the overwhelming value of the end. For example, it was agreed that the dropping of a nuclear bomb on Hiroshima, while it caused terrible suffering, was justified by the greater good of stopping war immediately and avoiding an even greater scale of tragedy. So the assumptions of the solutions to evil is that the end – paradise and salvation – is worth the struggle.

For this to be fully convincing we need to understand why an all-powerful God did not just create paradise. Why plan such a painful process to achieve the end? The response presumably is that only by enduring trials and tribulations will the human race fully appreciate moral and spiritual matters and come to divine understanding. This is plausible. And the example of cloning illustrates this. If we learn to successfully clone human beings, we will have a near God-like power of self-replication. This will demand a considerable moral sophistication and maturity so that it is not a force for evil, and there may be enormous distress before we learn this lesson. The spectre of Frankenstein will spark a worldwide debate, just as nuclear weapons do today.

Is doing evil all right if it achieves good?

There is still a moral dilemma about whether cruel means can be justified by the end and the purpose.

You could also ask whether God could have created beings with this moral wisdom already accumulated, even with enough inbuilt sensitivity to imagine all of the challenges that we have faced and the dire consequences. So we already have the wisdom, without having to destroy so much over millions of years. Most of us are fortunate enough to learn about widespread suffering without actually having to experience it. Yet we fully appreciate the folly of certain actions. Could not a superior race have been created, without the need to experience suffering over and over again?

A final question on this issue is the nature of the ultimate purpose. It needs to be of such exceptional value as to justify the scale of suffering, and to transform our view of suffering from an evil to a positive means to an end, in the way perhaps that an athlete triumphs at going through the pain barrier. But, as Hume remarked, the purpose is not easily discernable. It is suggested in the Bible that God created the world and us in order to glorify His name. This is morally concerning. As the philosopher Mill points out, this is regarded as one of the lowest of human motives and it demonstrates once again the problems associated with anthropomorphising God. In trying to understand what all this pain and imperfection will achieve, we have reached the limits of what we can understand.

In November 1755, the Lisbon earthquake happened. More than 30,000 people were killed in one day, and the situation was made worse by the fact that it was All Saints Day and the churches were crowded. In a tragic irony, many died because their churches collapsed on top of them.

The French philosopher Voltaire wrote how dissatisfied he was that this could be the best possible world, and that our great tragedies should be re-interpreted:

■ Think about

What would you think of a head teacher who allowed problems in school to develop, e.g. bullying, so that the students learn to find their own solutions?

249

> I am a puny part of the great whole
> Yes, but all animals condemned to live,
> All sentient things, born by the same stern law
> Suffer like me, and like me also die …
> What is the verdict of the vastest mind?
> Silence.

Yet the French philosopher Rousseau replied that man himself was to be blamed, for if we lived in the fields and not in the towns, if we lived under the sky and not in houses, houses would not fall on us and we should not be killed in such great numbers.

The philosopher Tennant attempts to accommodate such natural disasters from the point of view of moral progress. The instance of such events allows us to learn new lessons. We can only improve our moral capacity in a system of nature that regularly presents such challenges. Then we can compare responses, reflect on our decisions and their consequences and so gain a moral education.

A possible response to the moral progress argument is that:

1 natural disasters often cause extreme suffering to animals that cannot learn
2 as previously argued, a good teacher makes learning objectives clear, rewards progress and supports the needy. Yet natural evil appears indiscriminate and gratuitous.

The last word

It seems when faced with such a paradox, we either take offence at the irrational design, or strengthen our faith and unquestioning love. Our attitude to the problem of evil might be summed up in one of two ways: 'I wish to know in order that I may believe', without rational explanations of evil, I cannot believe in a perfect and all-powerful designer or in any designer at all; *or* 'I believe in order that I may know'.

Faith is a precondition of eventually understanding the mystery of the divine person. Theodicies are unnecessary for those whose belief in God is 'basic' (i.e. without argument). Theodicies are designed to convince the rational sceptic. While believers may wish to defend evil and show that it is not inconsistent with God's qualities, they do not feel it is incumbent on them to explain it and find a solution. Their approach may be summed up by the old Irish joke:

> How do I get to Dublin?
> Well if you want to get to Dublin, I
> wouldn't start from here.

After working through this topic, you should:

- understand the different kinds of evil, such as natural and moral evil
- understand why evil is a challenge to the design argument and our concept of God
- be able to explain different responses and solutions to the problem
- be able to evaluate whether the problem of evil can be reconciled with the design argument.

The religious point of view

Learning objectives:

- to understand how the world may be seen from different perspectives
- to examine whether religious belief is an expression of attitudes or a truth claim
- to explore different kinds of belief
- to evaluate the role of reason in the religious point of view.

Fig. 8.7 *Rubin vase*

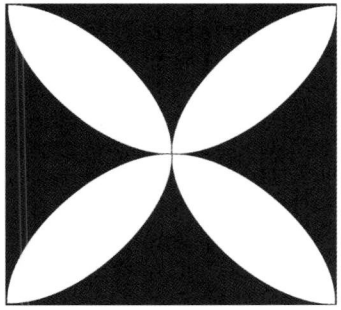

Fig. 8.8 *Iron cross*

Think about

Look at the shapes in Figs. 8.8 and 8.9. What do you see? What do they tell us about perception.

What do you see?

In this well-known example of the Rubin vase (Fig. 8.7), you either see a vase or two faces. This and other figures below demonstrate how we select how we might perceive something – we organise our perceptions. Interpretation is consequently central to perception.

Seeing and seeing as

In *Sense and Sensibilia* (1962), Austin makes the distinction between 'seeing' and 'seeing as'. He gives the example of seeing a star. I can either:

- see a distant star which has an extension greater than that of earth (seeing as), or
- see a silvery speck no bigger than a 5p piece (seeing).

In the first case, what we perceive is identified and classified in terms of our knowledge of stars – it is informed by our understanding. In the second case, we record what we actually observe, bringing little knowledge to the observation. Austin then concludes that the raw data supplied by the senses can be 'seen as' in lots of different ways.

Just as there are many different ways of seeing the same object, 'there will be *no one* right way of saying what is seen' (emphasis added) (Austin, 1962).

So it is with any particular scene. A soldier can look at a drill of men in a parade ground in terms of discipline and uniform, while an artist will see it from a different perspective. Similarly one person may claim to see a motion picture, while someone else will note that they are actually seeing a series of carefully drawn stills, run in quick succession.

There are many well-known examples that demonstrate the selection and interpretation that is involved in the act of seeing. Wittgenstein's duck-rabbit – a picture capable of being seen as a duck or a rabbit (see p25) – and old woman-young woman give the same kind of choice. The Iron cross opposite and the Necker cube overleaf are further examples.

In the introduction to *Existentialism and Humanism* (Sartre, 1948), Philip Mairet emphasises that what is perceived – every phenomenon of which we become aware – is the result of that something *and* of the mind's activity. He concluded that perception involves recognition, identification, judgement and choice.

This has further been supported by psychological experiments. It is argued that because our sensory input is always ambiguous, the interpretation selected is the one that we are familiar with from the past. In other words, we see what we expect to see, or have been trained to see, according to the concepts we have already acquired.

An interesting example of this is the distorted Ames Room. Fig. 8.10 overleaf shows what the room looks like when viewed with one eye through a peephole. The person at one end will appear very small, and the other very tall. The viewer has to choose between two different beliefs:

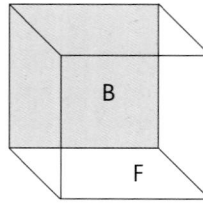

Fig. 8.9 Can you see these Necker cubes in two different ways?

- that the room is normal and rectangular, or
- that the people are of average height.

Most people choose to believe that the room is normal and that the people are odd sizes, although the opposite is quite possible.

This theory is of course not new. Descartes used his wax example to illustrate the judgement that is made in the act of perception. He sees his wax candle by his chair, which smells of honey, is hard, cold and cylindrical. Then he falls asleep and all the sensory information is different when he wakes up. The candle is now hot, liquid and smells different. He concludes that seeing it as the *same* candle is a matter of judgement, since that is not apparent from the sensory information alone. Similarly, he recalls how when we look down from an upstairs window and see the tops of umbrellas, hats and cloaks, we judge that there are human beings from these appearances. Once more the mind organises the data according to the expectations and concepts we have gained (perhaps) from experience.

'The religious point of view' is also a way of 'seeing as'. It presents a perspective or an interpretation of the data we receive. It judges that there is order in the world and that is sufficient evidence for intelligent design. This view is of course challenged by alternatives, and then it is open to all sides to present their proof. Where there is direct conflict, then we may have to use reason as an arbiter as to which proof is more convincing and cogent. However, some religious supporters reject reason as a valid tool for appraising beliefs, and this will also be discussed below.

As we develop our examination of the religious point of view, each of us will have to make our own judgements. Perhaps we will agree with Austin's previous remark (1962): 'there will be no *one* right way of saying what is seen' (emphasis added).

The religious point of view invites us to see the world as God's creation. As we have seen, this perspective differs considerably from the Darwinian model. These contrasting ways of 'seeing as' are also two different ways of using language, and are sometimes referred to as different '**language games**'.

Language games

When you want to play a game, you have to learn a new language. For example, if you do not learn golfing terms and rules you cannot play the game. A birdie, an eagle and a bogey mean something quite different to normal use, and you must understand this before you can behave appropriately on a golf course. Mastering the language opens up a whole new lifestyle to you, and through playing the game you develop sportsmanship, competitiveness and team spirit – a whole new outlook on life. The ethos of the game could possibly transform the way you see everything – your priorities and your values. To millions of people sport is not just important, it is a matter of life and death.

The same applies to religion. To 'play' the religious 'game', you learn religious language, participate in the rituals and rites, and eventually you begin to see the world in a special way. Your values will alter, so for example worldly possessions will seem less important than relationships, joy and inner peace.

Fig. 8.10 Illusions. Two men of similar height standing in an Ames Room designed to create the optical illusion which changes the relative heights of the men.

The hypothesis 'what if?' will predominate: what if there is life after death, a spiritual dimension, a divine creator? It's not clear, however, that Wittgenstein intended to describe religion as a whole as a language game. Examples of such games given by Wittgenstein include hoping, wishing and commanding, and it is certainly not obvious that they are on a par with religion.

The religious hypothesis of seeing the world as designed by a perfect creator will lead to an interpretation of world events, so that even evil will appear explicable. Indeed religious conviction can become so strong that even reason is powerless to overcome it. Argument can become redundant and irrelevant.

These are the aspects of the religious point of view that we are about to consider.

What is knowledge?

Since Plato, knowledge has been defined as true, justified, belief. Plato offers the example of a blind man on the right road. Although he believes he is going in the right direction, and it is true that he is, he does not have knowledge of this. He cannot provide a justification or a good reason for his belief because he is blind. To have knowledge, therefore, we require proof, such as a valid argument and/or convincing evidence, such as in this case a map reference or a signpost.

In this section we will examine:

- the quality of the evidence for religious claims
- the nature of religious belief
- the kind of truths proffered by the religious point of view.

The design argument is the evidence and justification for the religious believer. It is based on the appearance of order in the world. A valid, reasoned argument is then employed – the inductive argument – to a conclusion of an intelligent designer. You will remember from the first part of this topic that there are four strands to the reasoning process.

Induction does not deliver cast iron certainty, but we can still judge how conclusive it is based on the quality of the evidence – how extensive, consistent and reasonable it appears to be.

> **Think about**
>
> What special language do students have to learn at your school or college before they can fully understand what is happening and participate? For example, PSHE.

> **Think about**
>
> Rate the evidence for these beliefs. How persuasive is it?
>
> 1 My tooth hurts – I can really feel it.
> 2 Through her powers of extra-sensory perception, she detected a presence in the room.
> 3 The whole crowd of football supporters thought the referee was wrong.
> 4 According to doctors, a foetus can now be successfully born prior to 24 weeks.
> 5 Archaeological evidence shows we are not related to the Neanderthal people.
> 6 God listens to our prayers, according to the Bible.
> 7 Every time I wear white socks, England loses at some sport.

Your assessment of the evidence will probably include these factors:

- The method used to acquire the evidence – which methods are more or less trustworthy? Why?
- The kind of people who offer the testimony – who would you trust – why?
- Whether the evidence is biased by foundational beliefs – what background beliefs would you mistrust?
- The scale of the research – how can you tell whether sufficient research has been carried out?
- The consistency of the justification with other beliefs that are commonly held – coherence.

In making these judgements, you will be following Hume's advice: that a wise man proportions his belief to the evidence.

Religious evidence

One objection to the quality of evidence provided by religious believers is that the people offering the testimony have foundational background beliefs that they are not prepared to question. Furthermore, they did not acquire such beliefs through convincing methods such as rational enquiry or extensive research.

To adapt an example from the philosopher, Hare, imagine that there is an Oxford don who is convinced that everyone in Oxford is trying to poison him. Every time someone offers him food or drink, it confirms his suspicions. But even when people try to help him he sees it as a cunning ploy to put him off his guard. This belief is entirely irrational and even neurotic, but whenever anyone tries to persuade him otherwise, the evidence is seen as a trick. Hare's point is that nothing is allowed to count against his belief, and he calls this a 'blik'. A blik is a belief that actually determines what counts as evidence rather than a belief that is based on the evidence. Some will see religious belief as the former and will then ask how it differs from neurotic or paranoid beliefs.

A second problem is the difficulty of providing convincing evidence for the religious point of view. The direction of the argument is from the natural order to the supernatural, something beyond human experience. We discussed the danger of anthropomorphism above. But the issue goes deeper than that. The accusation is that religious belief is not subject to a genuine test because the evidence cannot be verified or falsified. It is a problem finding any observations that can be really checked out. So it is then argued that any religious claims become meaningless. To understand this point further, we need to explain the verification principle.

The verification principle is a principle proposed by philosophers, such as Ayer, as a criterion of what is truly meaningful and what is meaningless. Ayer divides statements into two types. The first are logically necessary and these are analytic truths – the conclusion is contained in the premises, e.g. $2 + 2 = 4$. But the main thrust of the verification principle is that other statements are only cognitively meaningful if they can be verified (confirmed) as true or false by sense experience in principle. The use of the word 'confirmed' rather than conclusively verified is to accommodate the objection that no sense experience is beyond doubt; and the addition of 'in principle' covers potential areas of knowledge (such as distant galaxies) which cannot *actually* be verified because of the limits of science, but in theory can be subject to verification if and when we have the means to test such knowledge. So the belief in another planet supporting life is meaningful since we would know how to go about verifying or falsifying any claims, but the belief that 'God loves us' is meaningless since no amount of observation could ever confirm or deny it. Thus a statement such as 'God is transcendent' is meaningless. That is not to say that the believer is not experiencing a significant religious emotion, but he is also claiming that a transcendent being exists. Yet the subject cannot be described, let alone subjected to the test of actual experience.

The difficulty for religious evidence and belief is that it cannot be verified or falsified. This is illustrated by an anecdote from the philosopher Flew. He tells the story of the absent gardener. Imagine the situation where you are shown around a wonderful garden. It clearly seems to be evident that a highly skilled gardener is at work. You are so impressed that you ask to meet the gardener. However, every time you try to keep an appointment there is an excuse as to why the gardener does not appear. Eventually Flew concludes that there is no difference between a gardener who fails to show and no gardener at all. Thus the evidence for the gardener is only factually and cognitively significant if there is the possibility of verifying (confirming) his existence or falsifying (denying) it.

However, not many philosophers are convinced by the effectiveness of the verification principle as a criterion of meaningfulness. Just two criticisms are developed here.

Firstly, it assumes that language corresponds to an objective reality, the real world. In this model, we are 'seeing' the world.

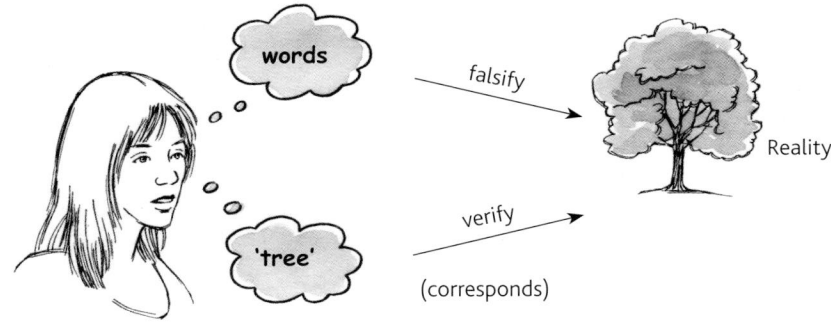

Fig. 8.11 *Here the language is a picture of the real world*

But it is difficult to see how we can refer to 'the real world' outside our understanding and the way we talk about reality. We cannot step outside our concepts and ideas to check whether they accurately depict a reality or not. This is the full implication of 'seeing as'. We are always seeing reality as according to our perspective. There is no possibility of a 'God's eye view' when we can see reality simply as it is. We can only swap one perspective for another. If you are familiar with the film *The Matrix*, we cannot actually remove the headset altogether and see the world as it is, we can only jack into another headset. And without this objective reality against which to check our understanding – to confirm or deny it – then verifying and falsifying the evidence becomes problematic. Put simply, it may depend on the way you are looking at it. Whether there is order in the world or not depends on your point of view.

Nevertheless, it does not necessarily follow that different perspectives have equal validity. Religious games have rules. For example, propositions have to be consistent with the concept of God. This test of internal consistency is required by the scientific method too.

The crucial difference is that science is grounded on observation and experimentation.

> **Think about**
>
> Which of the following beliefs can be verified or falsified in principle? Are they still meaningful?
>
> - Other human beings have minds like ours.
> - When you see green, I see red and vice versa.
> - Matter does not consist of minute particles but waves of energy.
> - We were born five minutes ago with all of our memories intact.
> - Once upon a time, the whole of the earth was covered by sea.

Secondly, an alternative view of what is meaningful is provided by Wittgenstein's theory of language games.

Language games again

We saw previously that entering a language game enables us to gain a different way of seeing the world and to participate in a form of life. There are rules within the game about what is meaningful and what can be said. Different games involve different ways of seeing the world, so the different disciplines of science and religion should not be confused. The religious game is perfectly meaningful even if we cannot verify its claims as a scientist would. An illustration of this is provided by Swinburne's story of the toys. Imagine the scenario where every night, after you fall asleep, all of your childhood toys come out of the cupboard and dance around the room. The moment just before you wake up, they all return to the cupboard exactly as they were. If you leave a camera running or try to peek, they will not come out.

Now it appears that this is perfectly meaningful, even though they never leave any evidence which we can verify. This story encourages a belief in another world and expresses the hopes and wishes of its supporters. Sometimes religious statements are also predominately an expression of hope or a commitment to values. To some people, myths and stories can be very influential in their lives and offer them vital new dimensions to their experience, even though the verification principle would dismiss them. Surely the evidence for whether something is meaningful is whether it is a life-changing belief. If religious faith can alter the mindset of a habitual criminal, and lead to a productive life, then it is meaningful. However, religious believers, as we have said, will want to claim more than this, that such myths point to truths about the world, which transcend ordinary understanding.

Ayer's reply

Ayer would probably reply that religious myths tell us more about the psychology of the believer than knowledge about the universe. The person who accepts that his toys come out at night is merely displaying certain emotions and convictions, but nothing of consequence about the world. In *Language, Truth and Logic* (Ayer, 1936), he claims that when the mystic tells us that the object of his vision is something that cannot be clearly described or tested, then he is bound to talk nonsense. It is no use saying he is sure about the experience yet is unable to say why. The fact that he cannot explain his intuition is not a genuine, cognitive state:

'he merely gives us indirect information about the condition of his own mind', rather than knowledge of the universe.

So the religious myths and stories tell us nothing of significance about the world. This would include Paley's watch. It is an entertaining analogy, but as an argument it cannot advance beyond the verifiable assertion that there are similar regularities in nature as there are in a watch.

Belief

The above impasse has led some observers to argue that there are two distinct kinds of belief. Belief is the subjective condition of the three elements of knowledge, truth, justification and belief. To hold a belief is to assert certain propositions and to adopt a consistent form of behaviour. So if you believe that there are fairies at the bottom of your garden, you will make assertions about what they look like, what they do, etc., and you will talk to them, leave food out and so on.

Some philosophers wish to make a distinction between 'belief that' which makes a truth claim and 'belief in' that is a personal expression of attitudes. Religious points of view would adopt the latter.

'Belief that'

This form of belief is characterised as a factual belief:

- it is a proposition about a state of affairs
- this state of affairs can be independently checked and tested
- the proposition will correspond or not and so will be true or false. There is a clear truth claim.

This clearly conforms to the principle of verification and is embraced by the scientific 'game', which aims to provide as much evidence as possible to test the belief. So if I believe that there are fairies at the bottom of my garden, I will provide as much empirical evidence as possible to confirm this. My belief will be open-minded and will be proportionate to the degree of justification. The more the belief is tested by other qualified people, the stronger my belief can be. The more it is refuted, the less I will cling to this assertion. The aim is to achieve precise correspondence between the hypothesis and the predicted results. This is what science achieves when, for example, it predicts an eclipse, the appearance of Halley's comet, or global warming. Beliefs that are stronger will be characterised as 'seeing' rather than 'seeing as', and will aim to eliminate as far as possible background beliefs, prior expectations and unquestioning attitudes.

'Belief in'

This is described as attitudinal belief and involves considerations of value and choices. So we believe in a football manager, or the loyalty of a friend, or in life after death. Thus in contrast:

- it contains propositions about commitment and interpretation; it is a personal expression of attitudes
- it is 'seeing as', a blik, a form of life
- it is about what is significant and meaningful.

'Belief in' will involve choosing and selecting the facts and interpreting them. The evidence offered will be designed to persuade rather than prove true or false. This is because primarily it is grounded in values about what is preferable between alternatives rather than focusing solely

Think about

Do you accept this response? If you do, then you agree that religious belief cannot make any meaningful claims to the truth. Does the justification provided by the design argument provide useful evidence? Or does it just tell us about the mindset of the believer? Yet can this still be meaningful in a non-cognitive sense? Which point of view would be characterised as 'seeing' and which as 'seeing as'?

on the veracity of a proposition. Commitment may be what James calls 'passional' – both emotional and rational. One commits oneself and the meaningful experience arises out of that initial leap of faith. The mindset will actually determine what counts as evidence and will determine the evaluation of benefits and problems. So in this instance we:

- believe in marriage, in order that we may know its benefits rather than
- waiting for proof and confirmation of 'belief that', in order to believe that marriage is beneficial.

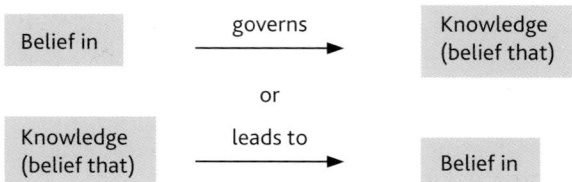

Fig. 8.12 *Belief in/belief that*

Think about

Can you distinguish 'belief that' from 'belief in' in the points below? Can some be both?

1 Life is short. Enjoy yourself.
2 The world is flat.
3 There are black swans on the other side of the world.
4 Acupuncture gets results.
5 The Liberal Party offers the best policies.
6 Elvis lives.
7 The growing divorce rate shows that marriage is a failed institution.
8 The growing divorce rate shows the need for stronger commitments.

Religious faith, on this analysis, would be 'belief in'. It is a form of life grounded in expressions of personal commitment to a metaphysical truth about the universe which cannot be empirically tested, e.g. the power of prayer.

Furthermore, religious theories are adapted to meet any objections. They appear to often sidestep the evidence or re-interpret the significance of evidence. So the believer rarely appears willing to give up their belief, instead they modify it. For example, when the theory of natural selection was identified, then God was said to work in that way. Religious belief was modified rather than abandoned.

However, is this distinction between two forms of belief precise enough to be convincing?

- 'Belief in' usually presupposes some 'belief that'. This is illustrated by points 1 and 5 above. What factual propositions could you suggest to underpin these convictions?
- 'Belief that' sometimes depends on the presuppositions or 'belief in' that you have. What background beliefs might determine what counts as evidence in points 4 and 7 above?

Nevertheless, some philosophers wish to argue that religious belief should be entirely independent of evidence, reason and proof. They reject the supposition that arguments such as the design argument could or should be used to prove the existence of God. Instead, the religious point of view is designated a basic or foundational status, it is 'properly basic'.

Properly basic belief

The philosopher Plantinga maintains 'it is entirely right, rational and reasonable to believe in God without any evidence or argument at all'. Such a belief could be reasonably held, even if it were not supported by any other beliefs.

So although the religious hypothesis:

- is not self-evident
- is not a rational induction
- is not justified by information from the senses,

it can still be warranted. So, such a basic belief in a perfect designer is still reasonable despite the argument against intelligent design.

To avoid the objection that one might as well believe in anything, such as giant pumpkins and fairies, such a basic belief must have 'grounds', hence *properly* basic. These grounds might be a feeling of conscience, or a sense of intelligence and power at work in the universe or a conviction after inexplicable, 'miraculous' events. If the beliefs are generated by a properly functioning mind, then they are valid grounds. No further argument is necessary.

A comparison might be made, in the context of epistemology, where some philosophers claim there are indispensable beliefs that it just does not make sense to question. So to the believer, it is impossible to question a belief without becoming absurd. For example, in response to extreme scepticism about what we know, the philosopher Moore held up his hands and stated: 'Two human hands exist at this moment' (Moore, 1959).

He had no idea how to prove this proposition, but it defied common sense to say that he did not know it. It is not possible to find conclusive arguments to support or deny this knowledge, but to deny the proposition would be to lose sanity. Scientists also work with basic preconditions such as that there is an external world, and that we can trust the evidence of our senses. How could we conduct science without these preconditions?

Similarly in the religious point of view there is a grounding situation that justifies a properly basic belief, but that does not amount to rational argument or convincing evidence. Once we accept these grounds, then the development of the religious language game and form of life will seem consistent and coherent. The inward conviction in a divine explanation will lead the believer to interpret evidence in a particular way, and what might seem odd to an outsider will not trouble those inside the game. Thus Basil Mitchell (1971) tells a story set in the French Resistance during the Second World War. A member has grounds to join the Resistance but he becomes puzzled by the mysterious leader who seems at times to be working against them rather than for the cause. However, this is explained by the belief that it is part of his plan to cover his tracks and avoid detection. So despite inconsistent and contrary evidence, the members still believe in their leader. An outsider will point to the leader's seemingly treacherous activities as clearly contradictory, but because of the grounds of their belief, they will not be convinced. A well-grounded, properly basic belief will survive objections.

Key philosopher

Alvin Plantinga (1932–)

Plantinga is an American philosopher who claims that belief in God may be justified even if it is not supported by arguments from natural theology, such as the design argument. See *Reason and Belief in God* (Plantinga, 1983).

However, religious belief is not as universal or deep seated as our convictions about sense experience. Despite the reasonableness of their basic belief, the unbeliever is not likely to be swayed. Even if we accept that rational argument or evidence is unhelpful, we can still query whether 'grounds' are sufficient. What would make the grounds for belief in God properly basic, but the grounds for belief in fairies trivial? A reply might be that the former leads to a deeper, more meaningful, more fulfilling form of life. But now we are clearly into value judgements, on which there will be a wide variety of opinions. Moreover the subsequent form of life cannot be used to justify the grounds since it presupposes them. A religious life will only appear to be more meaningful if you already have a religious conviction.

So it is quite possible for a properly basic belief to be false. The fact that it is grounded does not guarantee that it is true. Plantinga maintains that one is justified in saying God exists, even if others do not agree. But then equally, we are entitled to adopt the views of Marx and Freud that our religious beliefs are the projection of psychological needs, e.g. for a father figure. It is surely the task of philosophy to decide which view is more convincing to try to establish the truth. It should be noted that Marx and Freud, who offer causal accounts of our belief in God, do not demonstrate the non-existence of God. True beliefs, as well as false ones, have causes.

How and why – different kinds of truth

The religious point of view has sometimes been described as different from that of science because it is seeking different kinds of answers and truths. Scientists are interested in *how* things happen, whereas religion is looking for purpose and ultimate meaning: *why*? This contrast is captured in the poem *Dissection* by Colin Rowbotham, where an A-level biology student is dissecting a rat. He muses on the fact that he will spend hours learning how the rat's body works, but still cannot understand the life force that has now left it. Inside the rat, he finds:

> A firmly coiled discipline
> Of overlapping liver, folded gut;
> A neatness that is like a small machine –
> And I wonder what it is that has left this rat
> Why a month of probing could not make it go again

Benton (1976)

Think about

Recently a driver on Exmoor was returning home to his wife after an illicit meeting with his mistress. It was a perfectly normal day and the weather was unexceptional. As he was driving along, a bull suddenly jumped out of a field, landed on his car, and killed him. Why did that happen?

- Chance.
- God intended the man to die.
- The bull was feeling randy and there was a hole in the hedge.
- The man got what he deserved for cheating on his wife.

Which of these 'whys' could you change into a 'how'?

All of the answers are of course valid, but they are also asking for a different interpretation of events:

■ a mathematical calculation
■ a religious explanation
■ a scientific account
■ a moral belief.

Each answer will lead us into a different kind of explanation. What might each theory select as essential facts?

Darwin's concern over his own theory of evolution was because he believed that science not only explained how creatures evolve, but also that he should reconcile this with why. He wrote:

> I cannot persuade myself that a beneficent and omnipotent God would have designedly created the Ichneumonidae with the express intention of their feeding within the living bodies of caterpillars.

> *Darwin, quoted in* **Palmer** *(2001)*

He was trying to come to terms with the apparent indifference of the natural world to cruelty. In doing this he was moving away from *facts* and projecting *values* onto his investigations.

But perhaps it is not suitable for scientists to pass judgement on their discoveries or to ask why things happen as they do. Richard Dawkins in *River Out of Eden* (see Palmer, 2001) counsels, 'we humans have purpose on the brain. We cannot let go of "the why question" and "what is it for".' These questions of why are of course appropriate about machines and human intentions, but not meaningful when we study flora and fauna, or the universe as a whole. The structure of DNA explains how things develop, how the universal principles of competition and survival have created a dynamic universe where living things attempt to maximise their welfare. This may seem a-moral (not based on any moral standards), but it is argued that the need for a why answer has disappeared. From this point of view, the religious question has become redundant. The search for religious truth is unnecessary.

The problem for the design argument is that it overlaps and attempts to compete with the scientific language game. Yet it lacks the objective methods of science and its predictive success. While science may also use analogy, it is founded on the results of experimentation, which are usually repeatable. As long as religion bases its arguments on facts about the universe and its origins, it will compete with scientific theory on how the world functions, and the need to ask why it happened could disappear.

Nevertheless, there may be still aspects of experience that science cannot yet answer. A response to Dawkins is that if 'why' questions are appropriate for people, but not the rest of the world, then does this not imply some real difference between humankind and the rest of nature? Can the human search for purpose and answers to moral questions be fully explained by the principle that living things 'seek to maximise their welfare'?

'Hows' that cannot be explained

Needless to say, the religious view is that there are aspects of creation that cannot be simply accounted for by science. One of those principal questions is why human beings have developed moral consciousness.

Why do we abhor suffering in others? Why do we praise empathy and compassion? If the universe was just electrons, and the mind was just electrochemical impulses, there would be no problem of evil and suffering. But the most praiseworthy and admirable moral behaviour seems contrary to the scientific and evolutionary model. We encourage self-denial; Jesus preached 'love thine enemy'; we care for the weak and vulnerable; and we learn to treat others in the way we would wish to be treated rather than taking advantage. We also spend considerable time on philosophy, art, literature and sport, and it is not obvious how these activities contribute to the survival of the fittest. For example, much serious literature makes us more doubtful, less confident in our aims, and multiplies problems and concerns rather than making us fit for survival.

Altruism

A particular challenge to the evolutionary model is behaviour where we overcome self-interest and perform duties for the good of others. This is discussed from a moral perspective in Chapter 3. Here we will examine one account to reconcile **altruism** with natural selection.

One attempt to explain why it is that we sacrifice our own interests for others is that 'reciprocating altruism' enhances the survival of the social group. Apart from the obvious benefit of supporting each other, it also develops relationships and strengthens our sense of identity. These strong social bonds and sense of belonging increase our chances of survival. Now this is possibly true, but it is not a thesis capable of rigorous scientific testing. It pretends to know the real reasons why people sacrifice themselves for others, but this is not an objective, demonstrable thesis. It is clearly just an interpretation to reconcile altruism with evolution. However, why should we not believe the accounts of altruistic people themselves, who refer to moral and religious ideals as their motivation? If someone gives up something for others, who are we to claim that their real motive is that of reciprocating altruism rather than their claim that they genuinely care about others, and are following religious ideals? To be a genuine scientific thesis, it must be able to set out the criteria by which it can be verified or falsified.

Moreover, this theory is unlikely to fit examples of self-sacrifice, such as a soldier who gives up his life to protect his comrades. Much more likely is the reason that people often give, the (Christian) virtue and duty to set aside our own egotistical desires. And even in cases where the genes will be furthered, such as parents risking all for their children, how do we know that this is the real reason for their sacrifice? It seems, in these cases, that science has strayed from explaining how things happen, to providing an explanation of 'why' and purpose. Thus Dawkins states that, 'genes may maximise their selfish welfare … by programming unselfish co-operation' (in Palmer, 2001).

Is this an objective account of how things function or a theory about the purpose of moral behaviour? Seeing or seeing as? Dawkins might be seen as an extreme attempt to portray actions according to his own perspective. In attempting to explain away altruism, he is not prepared to specify what would count as a genuinely altruistic action. Counter examples are ruled out in principle and this suggests that his claims are not purely empirical claims.

Key terms

Altruism: the disinterested concern for the welfare of another. The good of others is an end in itself and does not benefit me. It is typified by the 'ultimate sacrifice', giving up your life for someone else.

Think about

Consider the following actions. Can you explain them in terms of natural selection?

- Elton John spends millions of pounds throwing a party for his friends.
- Millions of soldiers volunteered to join the army and fight in the First World War.
- Doctors fight to save the lives of babies who are born severely disabled.
- Philanthropists in the 19th century spent their wealth on feeding, housing and educating the poor.
- The victim of torture dies without revealing his secrets.
- Artists, such as Van Gogh, sacrifice their health and life in order to paint.

To sum up, is it clear that science and religion are seeking different kinds of answers? From the above, it appears that both perspectives overlap. Religion has to base its explanation on facts; and science, particularly social science, sometimes moves from consideration of data to theories of human purpose.

The belief that if we discover enough 'hows' we do not need a 'why', and therefore the religious point of view is redundant, is probably premature. There are still unanswered questions about why human beings behave as they do.

The religious point of view, reason and truth

During this topic, we have seen some ambiguity and disagreement about the role of reason in religious belief. There is also debate about whether religious statements are making a truth claim or are an expression of attitudes and feelings. The verification principle suggests that religion cannot make meaningful claims to truth because its subject is metaphysical and so is not open to verification or falsification. On the other hand, believers could argue that they seek a different kind of truth – they wish to know 'why' things happen in the way they do.

Below there are a number of views on the relationship between religious belief, reason and truth. Try to decide which best describes this relationship.

The use of reason

In the Bible, St Paul says: 'God, the source and end of things … can be known with certainty, by the natural power of human reason.'

This supports the view of natural theology as illustrated in the argument from design. No special revelation is needed. Through reasoning about the nature of this world and the order that is evident to all human beings, we can establish truths about the divine intelligence. By means of induction, it is possible to reach a reasonable but not conclusive proof of the existence of God. By studying the effects, it is possible to discern truths about the cause. Using reason, we can find solutions to the problem of evil and argue that this is the best of all possible worlds. Religious belief is consistent and coherent, and the most convincing interpretation of the evidence.

The limits of reason

Religious language communicates half-glimpsed truths that are not demonstrable by reason alone. Reason is limited because knowledge of the infinite and the divine is beyond our intellect. Like poetry, the revelations of religious texts use analogy, metaphor and symbolism to take us beyond reason to the inexpressible. To claim that something is mysterious and indefinable is not to say that it does not exist. But this kind of knowledge will need emotional intelligence and intuition to glimpse the truth. Religious myths and rituals are to be taken as symbolic. This is a quite different language game from science. Symbols point to half-felt knowledge, beyond everyday consciousness. They open up levels of reality beyond rational thought. We can sense something awe-inspiring, an awareness of another worldly power, or peace and fulfilment through a dissolution of personal consciousness. These are ineffable insights which are out of reach of reason, which the poet Wordsworth describes in *The Prelude* (1951) as 'unknown modes of being'.

Faith not reason

The human ability to reason, since the fall of mankind, is corrupt and incapable of grasping the nature of the divine. It is bound to collapse in contradictions. So belief in God does not require rational or philosophical argument. God is not to be thought of as an empirical object, so scientific-like investigation is fruitless. Nevertheless, belief in God is intelligible and reasonable as a way of seeing the world. It is 'belief in', an interpretation of the world and a personal expression of attitudes and feelings. The truth claims are as a result of commitment to seeing the world as divine, and they are personal truths about enlightenment and fulfilment. The philosopher Pascal (1966) wrote, 'the heart has its reasons, which reason does not know', and he suggested that potential believers must actually try to subdue their desire to reason. It is sinful pride to believe that we can reason our way to God. Real knowledge is only possible when you devote yourself in blind faith and 'jump ten thousand fathoms' (Kierkegaard, 1985).

Reason, but not science

Reason has a part to play in religious belief, but it cannot be expected to provide proof. However, we can employ 'critical rationalism' to help provide reasons for our point of view and to understand the implications of it. We can seek consistency with scientific facts and demand coherence of moral truths. However, religious reasoning is quite unlike scientific method, as set out in Table 8.2. Science and religion have different objects of study – how and why – so are seeking different kinds of truth.

Reason and explaining away

Religious discourse uses reason to defend a firmly held conviction, but it is rarely prepared to relinquish the truths which it is committed to.

While in real science, propositions are falsifiable, and when a scientist makes a prediction, if it turns out to be wrong, then the theory is refuted or significantly changed, science proceeds by recognition of error and so accumulates more trustworthy hypotheses.

Religious propositions, in contrast, are rarely open to such falsification because believers will never admit that their core convictions are wrong. Instead, they use reason to 'explain away' any inconsistencies. So the problem of evil spawned ever more ingenious explanations rather than admit the implications of the evidence. Evil is explained away rather than accepted as falsifying the hypothesis.

Table 8.2 *Differences between scientific method and religious reasoning*

Science	Religion
Is monist:	Is dualist:
■ studies one substance: physical stuff (matter) which is the only real entity	■ believes in two orders of reality: the life of spirit and the welfare of the soul, as well as the body
■ deals with publicly observable data	■ considers subjective and personal experience and emotion
■ searches for understanding	■ searches for significance and meaning
■ aims at empirical precision, to predict events and make advances in technology	■ aims at enlightenment and fulfilment and devises moral truths and purposes
■ the ultimate prize is to combine the knowledge of biology, chemistry and physics under one grand unified theory	■ the ultimate prize is to be able to appreciate why scientific laws came into being

However, it could be argued that scientists are just as reluctant to relinquish theories. Much more evidence could be submitted, but the one example in this topic of altruism illustrates the point. In both cases, no clear criteria are offered by which the belief can be verified or judged to be false. Reason is used to bolster up explanations rather than provide a real test of truth. Do you consider that the full significance of suffering has been addressed?

■ The last word

This topic has attempted to understand the religious point of view. It has considered the following accounts, *seeing* the religious perspective *as*:

■ a metaphysical claim that a God exists and the world is His creation
■ a meaningful 'game' which enables the believer to participate in a form of life
■ a 'belief in', a commitment to values and choices that are morally significant
■ a properly basic belief that is the foundation for interpreting evidence
■ an answer to 'why' questions and the purpose of creation
■ an explanation for human, moral behaviour such as altruism
■ demonstrating various attitudes to the value of reason.

The fact that different interpretations are possible does not necessarily imply that there is no correct one, or that we cannot make judgements. Austin suggested 'that there will be no *one* right way of saying what is seen' (Austin, 1962), but in making your judgement, you could consider the following criteria. Which perspective:

■ is most useful and life enhancing
■ is meaningful and not just empty words
■ is the best explanation of observable data
■ is consistent with other justified beliefs
■ is a coherent and plausible way of seeing the world
■ is capable of predictive success or practical benefit?

After working through this topic, you should:

■ be able to describe the religious perspective

■ understand different accounts of belief

■ be able to assess how rational religious beliefs might be regarded

■ be able to explore the issues and criticisms surrounding the religious point of view.

Further reading

Cole, P. *Philosophy of Religion*, H&S, 1989. This is a very helpful, concise account of the relevant areas of study.

Hamilton, C. *Understanding Philosophy for AS Level*, Nelson Thornes, 2003. The section on religion contains authoritative and detailed discussion of all the key issues.

Jones, G., Cardinal, D. and Hayward, J. W. *Philosophy of Religion*, Hodder Murray, 2005. This contains a clear and very readable account of the main points.

Palmer, M. *The Question of God*, Routledge, 2001. This contains an excellent discussion of the argument from design, with extensive extracts from relevant authors such as Darwin, Paley, Hume and Dawkins.

Pinchin, C. L. *Issues in Philosophy*, Macmillan, 1989. This presents a detailed explanation of the argument from design and a helpful discussion of altruism.

Vardy, P. *The Puzzle of Evil*, Fount, 1992. A comprehensive study of the problem of evil, with Vardy's own solution.

Wollheim, R. *Hume on Religion*, Fontana, 1963. A primary text, critical of the argument from design.

Summary questions

1 What are the difficulties of arguing from an effect to its cause?

2 What are the pros and cons of the alternative to the argument from design, that is, 'the theory of evolution'?

3 What is a theodicy? What are the essential differences between the Augustinian and Irenean theodocies?

4 Is it consistent with free will that God could have ensured that we always choose good?

5 Why would God maintain an epistemic distance?

6 Which would you agree are the most convincing descriptions of the religious point of view?

7 How does the religious perspective employ reason, if at all?

8 Which of the above descriptions could be used as a criticism of religious belief?

9 How far can the religious perspective be defended as a way of seeing the world?

9 Persons

What is a person?

Key philosopher

Peter Singer (1946–)

Peter Singer is Professor of Bioethics at Princeton and Laureate Professor at the Centre for Applied Philosophy and Public Ethics, University of Melbourne. A preference utilitarian with a specialist interest in practical and applied ethics, the views outlined in his published work have often been regarded as controversial.

Introduction

> In 1988 a case arose that well illustrates the way in which modern medical technology forces us to make life and death decisions. Samuel Linares, an infant, swallowed a small object that stuck in his windpipe, causing a loss of oxygen to the brain. He was admitted to a Chicago hospital in a coma and placed on a respirator. Eight months later he was still comatose, still on the respirator, and the hospital was planning to move Samuel to a long-term care unit. Shortly before the move, Samuel's parents visited him in the hospital. His mother left the room, while his father produced a pistol and told the nurse to keep away. He then disconnected Samuel from the respirator, and cradled the baby in his arms until he died … Prenatal diagnosis is now a routine procedure for pregnant women … Now that we have techniques for identifying haemophilia before birth … women are offered, and usually accept, abortions in order to avoid giving birth to children with haemophilia … Prenatal diagnosis, followed by abortion in selected cases, is common practice in countries with liberal abortion laws and advanced medical techniques … I cannot see how one could defend the view that foetuses may be 'replaced' before birth, but newborn infants may not be … killing a disabled infant is not morally equivalent to killing a person. Very often it is not wrong at all.

Singer (1993, pp180, 186–8 and 191)

Killing a disabled infant may or may not be morally equivalent to killing a person; however, clearly it is killing a human being and is, legally, murder.

The concept of a person

These are some of the issues that are discussed in this chapter:

- Are all humans persons? Are all persons humans?

- What do we mean by potential persons and ex-persons? What do we mean by diminished persons?

- Why might it be argued that being a person is a matter of degree?

- Is there a problem of counting persons?

- What are the criteria for personhood? What characteristics do persons possess?

- What is meant by the claim that the concept of a person is logically primitive?

For various reasons, we need to distinguish between the notion of a 'human being' and the concept of a 'person'. For example, while it may be the case that all of the persons you and I know are human beings, it does not follow from this that all human beings are persons.

*Fig. **9.1** The film* Iris *charts the life and descent into dementia of the English academic and novelist Iris Murdoch*

Think about

- How do you think that you would go about identifying the point at which a potential person becomes a person?

- In the same vein, given that dementia is a gradual illness, how do you think that you would go about identifying the point at which a person suffering from it becomes a non-person?

Potential persons and ex-persons

A foetus is human but is a foetus a person? And, if a foetus is not a person, is a neonate (i.e. a newborn baby in the first four weeks of life) a person? Similarly, if a neonate is not a person, is a four-month-old microcephalic infant a person? (Microcephaly (or MCPHA) is a birth defect marked by a profoundly small head and brain size. It has affected the Amish community in the US. Over the past 40 years, 61 babies with MCPHA have been born to 23 nuclear families in the Amish community in Lancaster County. None of the children have lived beyond the age of 14 months, and most die between four and six months old.) Obviously, we would not deny that the majority of foetuses are potential persons, but having the potential to be a person is not the same as being a person. Although, as potential persons, it is necessary to distinguish human foetuses from something that lacks the potential to be a person.

Just as we might have reason to speak of 'potential persons', we might also wish to speak of 'ex-persons'. Like potential persons, it may be the case that all of those we might wish to describe as ex-persons are human beings, but they are human beings who, for one reason or another, no longer seem to be persons. Singer (1993) cites the case of Rita Greene:

> In 1991, the Lancet reported that Rita Greene, a nurse, had been a patient at D. C. General Hospital in Washington for thirty-nine years without knowing it. Now aged sixty-three, she had been in a vegetative state since undergoing open heart surgery in 1952.
>
> *Singer (1993)*

In 1991 Rita Greene was a human being in a vegetative state. Arguably, at that time, she was an ex-person rather than a person. 'People' do come out of comas, but do they persist through comas?

This is not a marginal issue. Dementia is a term employed to describe various different brain disorders that have in common a loss of brain function that is usually progressive and eventually severe. The structure and chemistry of the brain become increasingly damaged over time. So, a person's ability to remember, communicate and reason gradually declines and may eventually disappear completely. It is estimated that there are currently over 700,000 people in the UK with dementia.

Diminished persons

So, it is possible to argue that not all human beings are persons: we might regard some human beings as potential persons and others as ex-persons. Moreover, as dementia is a progressive illness, in many cases there will be a stage where we may want to say that personhood has been lost: when, for example, a demented relative has lost the capacity to express themselves or is no longer able to recognise his or her loved ones. Similarly, there will be earlier stages where memory is fading, the ability to communicate is partial, and while loved ones are recognised their identities may be blurred (so that a son may be seen as a husband, for example). During these stages we may wish to speak of diminished persons. A person suffering the early stages of dementia is still a person. He or she may know that they are becoming forgetful and be increasingly anxious about this; they may also be aware that their condition is likely to deteriorate and they may not wish to suffer (or for their loved ones to suffer) their further deterioration. Singer cites the example of Dr Kevorkian, a Michigan pathologist, who built a 'suicide machine' to assist terminally ill people to end their lives:

In June 1990, Janet Adkins, who was suffering from Alzheimer's disease, but still competent to make the decision to end her life, contacted Dr Kevorkian and told him of her wish to die, rather than go through the slow and progressive deterioration that the disease involves. Dr Kevorkian was in attendance while she made use of his machine, and then reported Janet Adkins's death to the police. He was subsequently charged with murder, but the judge refused to allow the charge to proceed to trial on the grounds that Janet Adkins had caused her own death.

Singer (1993, pp176–7)

If this seems extreme you might ask yourselves how you would respond to being told you were in the early stages of dementia and that you would progressively deteriorate until 'you' died in approximately three to five years' time.

It is not necessary to trawl through all of the ways that a person might be diminished. One more will do. The early stages of Alzheimer's disease tend to be characterised by:

- forgetfulness (particularly of recent events or information)
- loss of concentration (having trouble planning or completing familiar tasks)
- communication problems (forgetting the names of objects, mixing up words)
- confusion about time and place (difficulty recognising or remembering why you are at a location)
- impaired judgement (such as dressing inappropriately)
- impaired coordination (slowing of movements, falling over)
- mood and behaviour changes (emotional outbursts, personality changes, increased fear, anxiety, suspicion)
- depression (loss of interest in activities, sitting in front of the television for long periods of time).

The presence of some of these symptoms, such as mild forgetfulness and confusion, does not necessarily indicate that a person has Alzheimer's disease – the elderly, for example, may simply be experiencing age-related memory changes. However, loss of memory, whether associated with dementia or not, constitutes a serious threat to identity and a diminution of personhood. Indeed, one way to grasp the significance of memory for our identity as persons is to consider the problems caused by amnesia.

There are many different 'types' of amnesia – many of which are short term – some of which have been portrayed in recent films. In *Eternal Sunshine of the Spotless Mind* the main character, played by Jim Carrey, suffers lacunar amnesia – a loss of memory about one specific event. In *The Bourne Identity* the main character, played by Matt Damon, suffers retrograde amnesia – an inability to recall the past. The issues raised in these films are not purely the stuff of fiction. In October 2007 the BBC reported the following case in Ireland:

Detectives in Dublin are trying to establish the identity of a woman who turned up at a police station with no idea who she is. The woman presented herself at Store Street Garda Station on Sunday morning, carrying a Chihuahua dog. She has no identification, but has an American/Canadian accent and can speak French. She is described as being in her mid 30s, 5ft 10in tall, with a slim build and brown collar-length hair. The woman was wearing a black skirt and top with a black trench coat, leopard skin pattern shoes and a multi-coloured head scarf. There are three tattoos on her body, two of Arabic-style writing on her left upper arm and back of her neck. She also has a Celtic design tattoo on the back of one of her legs.

She is currently staying in hospital, and it is understood detectives believe she may be French-Canadian. However, she cannot recall any personal details about herself. Police appealed for anyone who may have an idea about her identity to contact them.

www.bbc.co.uk, 4 October 2007

Two years earlier the 'piano man' was found, smartly dressed but soaking wet, wandering along a road on the Isle of Sheppey. Like the woman in Dublin, this man was unable to answer questions about who he was or where he came from. However, when given some paper and pencils he drew a grand piano and, when shown into a room with a piano, he was able to skilfully play complex pieces of music.

Clearly, in both of the above cases the people concerned retained some complex abilities such as the ability to speak French fluently and the ability to play the piano well. However, both cases may be seen as examples of diminished persons. As Jonathan Glover has written:

> If all my memories were obliterated, this would obviously have a disastrous effect on my sense of who I am ... total amnesia for my own past leaves me with a picture of myself as blank as the one people have on meeting me for the first time.

Glover (1991, p141)

It may be useful to draw an analogy here with nationhood. The Czech novelist, Milan Kundera, points out that a nation without a memory is a nation without an identity. Russian intolerance for the period known as 'the Prague Spring' led to their 1968 invasion of what was then Czechoslovakia:

> On August 21, 1968, it [Russia] sent an army of half a million men into Bohemia ... And just to be sure not even the shadow of an unpleasant memory could come to disturb the newly revived idyll, both the Prague Spring and the Russian tanks, that stain the nation's fair history, had to be nullified. As a result, no one in Czechoslovakia commemorates the 21st August, and the names of the people who rose up against their own youth are carefully erased from the nation's memory, like a mistake from a homework assignment ... If Franz Kafka was the prophet of a world without memory, Gustav Husak is its creator ... Husak, the seventh president of my country, is known as the president of forgetting ... Husak dismissed some hundred and forty five Czech historians from universities and research institutes ... One of them, my all but blind friend Milan Hubl, came to visit me one day in 1971 ... 'The first step in liquidating a people', said Hubl, 'is to erase its memory. Destroy its books, its culture, its history. Then have somebody write new books, manufacture a new culture, invent a new history. Before long the nation will begin to forget what it is and what it was. The world around it will forget even faster.'

Kundera (1980, pp14 and 158–9)

Just as individuals without memories have no sense of who they are, neither does a nation without a memory. Indeed, the significance of memory for identity can be seen in many institutions, including schools and colleges where badges, mottos, former pupil associations, regular reunions and plaques commemorating past achievements abound.

Humans, animals and machines

Moreover, returning briefly to dementia, just as we can question whether all humans are persons, we might also ask whether all persons are human beings. As dementia progresses, the demented person becomes increasingly forgetful, particularly of names, and may also fail to recognise people or confuse them with others. If we wish to claim, while this process is occurring, that the sufferer remains a person then we might also acknowledge that, as a person, they are increasingly less capable and, perhaps, less capable than some animals that we know. The family dog, for example, appears not only to be aware of its name but also the names of other members of the household – so that on being told to find, for example, Julie it will generally look for Julie. It appears to have a memory – it can remember where it buried the piece of toast it stole from the kitchen the day before. It can communicate desires – it scratches the door if it wants to go out. It does not forget places – when off the lead it will follow a familiar route.

One might go on, but two points (both of which we will return to) are worth noting briefly:

- that being a person may be a matter of degree rather than a matter of kind or type
- that some non-human animals, and possibly some intelligent machines, may be sufficiently complex to be on the scale of personhood. (While a demented relative may not know who I am, my computer is at least able to mimic a greeting every time I log on, though the mimicry is in the eye of the beholder.)

Counting persons

Furthermore, the issue of amnesia raises another problem connected to personhood. One type of amnesia is fugue amnesia. Fortunately, this is a rare phenomenon in which a person forgets not only his or her past, but also his or her identity. The person may wake up and suddenly have no sense of who they are. They look in the mirror and see a stranger. They may find identification, for example on a passport or driving licence, but the name seems meaningless. Usually fugue amnesia heals itself over time, but what becomes of the person during the period in which it occurs? There are reported cases of a person not recognising who they are, walking out of one life and living, at least for a time, as a different person with a completely different identity. So, in order to make sense of this we have to identify one human being and two persons existing at different times. This suggests that, even if we restrict personhood to human beings, there may not be a one-to-one relationship between a human being and a person. This issue is most clearly apparent in cases of 'split brains' and of 'multiple personality disorders'.

The major link between the left and right hemispheres of the brain is the corpus callosum which together with some other neural pathways linking the two hemispheres forms the cerebral commissures. In the past, for example in the treatment of patients with severe epilepsy, the commissures have been surgically cut thus separating the two hemispheres of the brain. In the 1960s R. W. Sperry carried out a number of experiments on people who had undergone a commissurotomy (i.e. a surgical incision in the brain to treat certain psychiatric disorders). These experiments involved asking respondents to look at a point in a visual field, and then flashing different signals (e.g. signs, words, shapes, etc.) to each side of this central point – such as key ring. Glover describes this as follows:

> The person may be asked to pick out from a set of things hidden behind the screen the one whose name is flashed up. Suppose 'key ring' is shown on the screen, with 'key' to the left of the central point (and so being sent to the right hemisphere) and 'ring' in the right half of the field (and so being sent to the left hemisphere). If asked what word appeared on the screen the person replies 'ring'. (Speech is controlled by the left hemisphere.) The right hand (also controlled by the left hemisphere) will reject a key and pick up a ring. But the left hand (controlled by the right hemisphere) will reject a ring and pick up a key.

Glover (1991, p34)

Results like this led Sperry and others to claim that commissurotomy produces two separate conscious entities within the same human being: distinct entities with different perceptions and cognitive processes which may contradict one another. If, for example, only the right hemisphere 'knows' that the left hand (concealed behind the screen) is holding a key, then when asked what the object is, given that the left hemisphere controls speech, the separate conscious entity has to guess, and might say 'pen' for example. If two conscious entities are present, can we claim that there are two people? The prevalent view, at least among neuropsychologists, is that the split-brain patient has two minds. An alternative view is that the split-brain patient has one mind and is one person, although this person, at least on occasion, suffers from a disunified consciousness. This dispute need not concern us here: we need only to point out that:

- there may be some difficulty in counting persons
- the unity of consciousness may be just as important for personhood as the concept of mind.

In any case, why stop at two conscious entities within the same human being? There are hundreds of documented cases of what used to be called 'multiple personality disorder' and what is now generally known as 'dissociative identity disorder' (apparently because this is a better characterisation of the disorder which, allegedly, involves a fragmentation, or splintering, of identity rather than a proliferation of separate identities – although, again, we do not need to concern ourselves with which is the better characterisation). Dissociative identity disorder, however it is characterised, is a severe condition in which two or more distinct identities, or personalities, are present in, and alternately take control of, an individual. When in control, each personality may be experienced as a distinct personality with a separate history, self-image and identity. The separate personalities can vary tremendously in terms of character traits and abilities, and there is also some evidence of physiological differences between personalities. Typically, a host personality cannot remember incidents when a different personality has been in control. However, in some cases one personality can remember and comment upon incidents involving another.

A famous case (perhaps infamous is a better description) is that of Sybil, based on the book by Flora Rheta Schreiber which has sold over six million copies since publication in 1973 and spawned a film made for TV, featuring Sally Field as Sybil, in 1976. (The film, called *Sybil*, was remade in 2007.)

This is the story of a 22-year-old student, Sybil Dorsett – identified years later as Shirley Mason – who, in the 1950s, sought help for amnesia, depression, headaches and mental breakdowns from Dr Cornelia Wilbur in New York. During her treatment she allegedly started to show other personalities. Over the course of her treatment, Sybil displayed 16 personalities including a writer, a flirt, a pianist, a mother, an infant and two men. Each personality had different mannerisms and each described their physical features in different ways: one said that she had blue eyes, while another said that he had brown eyes.

The reason that this case is infamous is that it was later claimed, after conversations between patient and therapist had been studied, that Shirley Mason had not suffered from multiple personality disorder (MPD) at all but that the multiple personalities had been constructed through therapy. The dispute about whether multiple personality is a real phenomenon or whether it is constructed through therapy extends beyond this case. It is a fact that before the publication of *Sybil* in 1973, and the television film in 1976, only 75 cases of MPD had been reported. Since Sybil there have been around 40,000 diagnoses of MPD, mostly in North America.

Fig. 9.2 *Sally Field as Sybil Dorsett*

The 'cure' for such cases is reintegration but this seems to imply that the split or multiple persons are not different persons in the sense that you and I are. Such cases rely heavily on the continuity of memory in distinguishing different persons.

Is MPD a social construction, a label attached to behaviour – generally a label attached by more powerful groups to the behaviour of less powerful groups – established, legitimated, maintained and 'cured' through social interaction? Or is it a real phenomenon demonstrating how some people, faced with horrific and traumatic experiences, manage to preserve themselves through a desperate redrawing of their own boundaries so that experiences are not transferred across identities? It is enough for our purposes that some philosophers, Daniel Dennett for example, maintain that MPD is real and, as Glover says, minds may have 'fuzzy edges'.

We can summarise our discussion so far as demonstrating that while most, if not all, of the persons we know are human beings:

- some human beings may not be persons
- it is possible to suggest that some persons may not be human beings
- being a person may be a matter of degree
- there is evidence that at least some human beings may be more than one person
- so, while it is possible to count the number of human beings in a room, counting the number of persons may be more awkward.

What characteristics do persons possess?

In 1689 John Locke defined a person as 'a thinking intelligent being that has reason and reflection, and can consider itself as itself, the same thinking thing, in different times and places' (Locke, 1964, Chapter 27). It is not clear that there is anything here that we would want to disagree with – although we can spell out the implications of this view in more detail and, perhaps, improve on it a little. For example, in the context of an ethical discussion about why human life should have special value, Peter Singer (listing Joseph Fletcher's 'indicators of humanhood') identifies 'self-awareness, self-control, a sense of the future, a sense of the past, the capacity to relate to others, concern for others, communication and

> ### Think about
> Are Sybil's multiple personalities different persons in the same sense that you and I are different persons?

> ## AQA Examiner's tip
> You may need to select from the bulleted points if asked to 'briefly explain' or 'explain and illustrate' one or more reasons why we need to distinguish between human and person.

> ### Think about
> - Do you think that it makes any difference to the argument about counting persons whether MPD is a genuine phenomenon or a social construction? Give reasons for your answer.
> - Before moving on to the next section, try to draw up a list of the characteristics that you think are required to define someone as a person.

Think about

Do we have 'I-thoughts' whilst asleep? Does Descartes' essential self survive the night?

Key terms

Existentialism: the view that man's existence precedes his essence.

curiosity' (Singer, 1993, p86). At the same time that this list is, initially, Lockean (i.e. based on the ideas of John Locke), it also extends the Lockean view through indicating that persons are social as well as individual.

However, the claim that a person is a being that 'can consider itself as itself' is perhaps the crucial indicator of personhood: it is the claim that a person is self-conscious or that a person is self-aware. A person is someone, or something, that can conceive of itself as a person. Another way of saying this, and perhaps of stating it more strongly, is that a person is someone who has 'I-thoughts'. This is the reason why we might doubt that neonates and the demented are persons: in the first instance the 'I' has not yet appeared, in the second it has departed.

Also, the claim that self-awareness involves a thinking being considering itself as the same thinking being 'in different times and places' also seems to require a certain unity of consciousness – a sense of the past and a sense of the future – that may be essential if we wish to view persons as distinct, unique and, in important respects, self-created. This is nowhere more firmly stated than in **existentialist** writing:

> What do we mean by saying that existence precedes essence? We mean that man first of all exists, encounters himself, surges up in the world – and defines himself afterwards … to begin with he is nothing. He will not be anything until later, and then he will be what he makes of himself.

Sartre (1973, p28)

Without committing ourselves to existentialism, we might agree that, as persons, our sense of what is distinctive about ourselves is bound up with the choices we have made in the past and the directions we intend to follow in the future. The ability to create ourselves may be central to our subjectivity – to our 'inner story' or view of what we, as persons, are like. Our individuality is not 'given'; we are, at least partly, responsible for shaping ourselves. This is the reason why we might suggest that those suffering from various psychological disorders are diminished persons: in pathological cases the degree of unity present is insufficient for coherent self-creation.

Autonomy, the capacity to make and act upon choices, is also a central feature of our moral and political thought: respect for persons informs our decisions about ethical matters and our views about what political society ought to be like. For this reason we might consider those who lack autonomy as having either no responsibility or diminished responsibility for their actions. Accordingly, blame and punishment may be less severe. Furthermore, autonomy can be linked to Locke's view that a person is 'an intelligent being that has reason and reflection' given that, without the ability to consider alternatives, it is difficult to see what autonomy would amount to – perhaps only the absence of restraint. Reason, or rather the lack of it, seems to be the main factor why non-human animals are not considered, by some, to be sufficiently complex for personhood. Animals have desires (for example, a desire to eat) but humans have desires and desires about what desires to have (for example, a desire to eat and a desire to eat less, to lose weight, diet or exercise more frequently). Most humans have second- and possibly third- or higher-order desires: they can reflect on their desires, approve of certain desires, regret others, desire to change and so forth. While some (e.g. Sartre) have described the human experience of autonomy or freedom of choice as an experience of anguish, others (e.g. Mill) describe the capacity of most humans to reflect, consider and choose in more positive terms:

> It is better to be a human being dissatisfied than a pig satisfied; better to be Socrates dissatisfied than a fool satisfied. And if the fool, or the pig, are of a different opinion, it is because they only know their side of the question. The other party to the comparison knows both sides.

Mill (1962, pp8–9)

Here, Mill expresses the view (that many would agree with) that it is better to be a human being than an animal and better to be a complex person than a simple person or diminished person. Reason and reflection contribute to autonomy, the ability to self-create, and this contributes to the range of experiences we can have and, arguably, to the quality of life we can enjoy.

Moreover, self-creation is not an activity that an individual completes in isolation. An individual's sense of his or her own identity is deeply connected to the creation of the identities of social groups and cultures to which individuals belong. According to Aristotle, people are essentially social. Aristotle asserts that 'without friends no one would choose to live, though he had all other goods' (Aristotle, 1998, Book 8). Through the recognition of friends, loved ones and members of social groups that we identify with, we are able to share our self-creation with others. Complex persons not only possess higher-order thoughts about their own desires and motivations, they also possess higher-order thoughts about the desires and motivations of others – 'what will she think if I forget to do this?', 'I wonder if she is puzzled about what I meant when I said …'.

Consequently, given that the social environment in which self-creation takes place is enormously complex, structured and governed by rules and conventions – and disputes about structures, rules and conventions – the complexity of the higher-order thoughts we have indicates the importance of complex linguistic abilities. Language also points to the importance of the shared understanding of a group for our self-concept and self-creation. Glover expresses this nicely:

> When you speak a foreign language poorly, you have to say simpler things than you would like. In doing so, you present a simplified version of yourself … Turns of phrase, humour, and tones of voice are part of a 'language' which may be different … communities of shared meanings draw on shared experiences … [such as] the private languages and jokes in families

Glover (1991, p198)

Persons are beings who are:

■ self-aware and possessing a degree of unity, or connectedness, through time

■ self-created and possessing a view of themselves as distinct; beings with a subjective view of what they are like; beings who, at least partly, are responsible for how they are

■ rational and reflective about themselves and others

■ social

■ language users.

It is worth bearing in mind that the concept 'person' does not have sharp, or undisputed, boundaries and there may be different degrees of self-awareness, self-creation, intelligent reasoning, sociability and language use. So there will be disputes about what satisfies these criteria, but before considering such disputes it will be useful to say a little more about the concept of a person and to consider some alternative approaches.

Think about

Is putting members of your own species first a form of prejudice? Or can you think of reasons that might justify this?

Think about

- The Cortés expedition of conquistadores to Mexico expressed horror when confronted with the Aztec practice of child sacrifice. They were horrified that *human beings* could do this to each other.
- Were the Nazis merely making a point about biological classification when they designated certain races as *sub-human*?

Think about

Wittgenstein used the concept 'game' to illustrate his point. Games do not have to share a common feature that runs through all of them. Instead they are related by 'family resemblances' – some are more closely related than others, some are distant cousins. It is not necessary to suppose that soccer, chess and Ring a Ring o' Roses have *one* common feature – they can still be regarded as games. Can you think of other examples?

AQA Examiner's tip

You will need to select points from the bulleted list if you are asked to 'briefly explain', for example, two characteristics of personhood – do not write down everything you know, focus on two characteristics.

We have looked at reasons for supposing that there is a clear distinction between 'human' and 'person'. Many philosophers would, however, deny this and claim that anything that is a human being is a person. The judgement is made on the basis of membership of a species. If you adopt this approach, you will avoid the difficulties we saw earlier regarding neonates and severe impairment. The attribution of personhood is made at the level of the species rather than that of the individual.

The above approach would be criticised by Singer if it resulted in withholding the attribution of personhood from non-human animals displaying human characteristics, like intelligence or some sense of the future. To withhold the attribution of the concept of personhood in such cases would be to commit 'specieism' which would be morally on a par with racism or sexism.

Further reasons may be given for supposing that the human/person distinction is not clear. We may question the claim that 'human' is essentially a biological classificatory concept and it is the concept 'person' that has moral import. It would appear that the concept 'human' has moral implications. Consider the following:

- murder is defined in terms of taking *human* life
- the worst moral outrage may well be crimes against *humanity*
- the United Nations and the Geneva Convention refer to *human* rights
- we use moral condemnatory terms like *inhuman* and *inhumane*.

These concepts are enshrined in our moral thinking and ordinary language. It is difficult to explain this *and* maintain that the concept 'human' morally neutral.

A further approach was hinted at when we remarked earlier that the concept of a person was a fluid concept. This approach will regard the question; 'what is a person' as an essence question. That is to say, it will be seen as a quest for a particular property that is common to all persons. This will constitute the essential property of a person, and, if it were lost, personhood would no longer apply. Some philosophers, especially those influenced by Wittgenstein, would regard this approach as fundamentally flawed in many cases. The concept need not derive its strength or application through the presence of one feature but from the way many different features relate to and resemble each other. As to which features are the most important, the reply may be that it depends on the circumstances and context. When you walk down the street the physical similarities of those around you are sufficient. Perhaps you will come across a tribe of pygmies whose physical resemblance is not so marked. When you witness meaningful behaviour or their use of symbols this becomes sufficient. When you see a neonate, you know it is *someone's* son or daughter and this becomes sufficient.

Think about

- Give examples of primary and higher-order desires.
- Is Mill correct to say that it is better to be a dissatisfied Socrates than a satisfied fool? Give reasons for your answer.
- What influence, if any, do you think that the fact that Mill was a philosopher had upon his claim?
- If persons are social beings, are hermits persons? Give reasons for your answer.

🔆 The concept of a person as a logically primitive concept

The view that the concept of a person is **logically primitive** is, essentially, a response to some of the problems raised by Descartes' use of *cogito ergo sum* (I think therefore I am), and particularly the word 'I', as a doubt-resisting foundation of knowledge.

Descartes wrote:

> But immediately I noticed that while I was endeavouring in this way to think that everything was false, it was necessary that I, who was thinking this, was something. And observing that this truth 'I am thinking, therefore I exist', was so firm and sure that all the most extravagant suppositions of the sceptics were incapable of shaking it, I decided that I could accept it without scruple as the first principle of the philosophy I was seeking.

Descartes (1988, 'Discourse on Method', part four)

Similarly, many years later, Sartre argued:

> Our point of departure is, indeed, the subjectivity of the individual; and that for strictly philosophic reasons. It is not because we are bourgeois, but because we seek to base our teaching upon the truth … And at the point of departure there cannot be any other truth than this, 'I think, therefore I am', which is the absolute truth of consciousness as it attains to itself … outside of the Cartesian cogito, all objects are no more than probable

Sartre (1973, p44)

One problem is that this is uncomfortably close to **solipsism**. However, a second problem is the difficulty, perhaps impossibility, of saying anything informative about the nature of this 'puzzling I' (as Descartes refers to it). The two problems are related.

Arguably, what is compelling about Descartes' use of the term 'I', as many have noticed, is that it unfailingly refers an experience (such as doubting or reading a chapter on persons) to the speaker who is reporting that experience (that is, I am doubting, or I am reading a chapter on persons). It makes little sense to say, 'Someone is reading a chapter on persons, I wonder if it is me?' However, 'I' is also indexical: what, or who, it refers to varies according to the context in which it is used. In other words, it depends on who is speaking, and if we were to question who is reading a chapter on persons, the answer 'I am' does not tell us very much (in the same way as 'here' does not tell us very much about where somebody is or 'now' does not tell us very much about what time it is). As Maurice Merleau-Ponty notes, the 'I' in 'I think, therefore I am' is 'an ideal I that is not properly mine nor Descartes' but the I of any thinking thing' (Merleau-Ponty, 2002, p459).

So, the issue is: what does 'I' refer to? Descartes thought that 'I' referred to a thinking thing (and also assumed that the thinking thing was him):

> But what then am I? A thing that thinks. What is that? A thing that doubts, understands, affirms, denies, is willing, is unwilling, and also imagines and has sensory perceptions.

Descartes (1988, 'Meditations on First Philosophy', second meditation)

Thus, for Descartes, the 'I', the essential self, refers to mind: to a metaphysical substance which we cannot doubt but about which we can say little. Others have stressed the elusiveness of the 'I':

Key terms

Logically primitive: a logically primitive concept is one which precedes, which we have to possess prior to, other concepts. It is not derived from other concepts.

Solipsism: the view that while I am aware of my own experiences, and of the 'I' that has them, I cannot be certain of anything outside of this. So, it is possible that I am the only thinking thing.

> There are some philosophers who imagine we are every moment intimately conscious of what we call our self; that we feel its existence and its continuance in existence; and are certain, beyond the evidence of a demonstration, both of its perfect identity and simplicity.

Hume (1969, Book 1, Section 6)

Hume's empiricism leads him to question which impression leads to this idea of self. He goes on:

> For my part, when I enter most intimately into what I call myself, I always stumble upon some particular perception or other, of heat or cold, light or shade, love or hatred, pain or pleasure. I never can catch myself at any time without a perception, and never can observe any thing but the perception.

Hume (1969)

He proceeds to claim that, as we do not have an impression of self – of some 'thing' that possesses these perceptions – that mankind is 'nothing but a bundle or collection of different perceptions, which succeed each other with an inconceivable rapidity, and are in a perpetual flux and movement'.

But this is not satisfactory either (as Hume (1969) acknowledges, in an appendix to his *Treatise of Human Nature*, 'I am sensible that my account is very defective' – for example, what is the 'I' that enters 'most intimately into what I call myself'?). Kant pointed out that awareness of a succession of perceptions in time requires a conscious subject to exist throughout this succession – without this we have no answer to the question of who or what is aware of or perceiving these perceptions – and, on Hume's view, there is no such subject. However, Kant did not entirely disagree with Hume. Kant also thought that Descartes was wrong to suppose that a stream of consciousness informs us about our real self. Kant writes:

> For it must be remarked that, when I call the proposition, 'I think', an empirical proposition, I do not thereby mean that the Ego in the proposition is an empirical representation; on the contrary, it is purely intellectual, because it belongs to thought in general. But without some empirical representation, which presents to the mind material for thought, the mental act, 'I think', would not take place; and the empirical is only the condition of the application or employment of the pure intellectual faculty.

Kant (1934, chapter on the 'Paralogisms of Pure Reason')

Kant, like Descartes, accepts that 'I' refers to a self that is not identical or reducible to a series of experiences but, like Hume, he also argues that this self is unknowable – that a series of experiences does not inform us about the self 'as it is in itself'. Consequently, we have a kind of synthesis of Descartes and Hume: we posit a pure self in order to make sense of experience, without which an individual could not be aware of their self, but we cannot identify the self with what is experienced. The existence of the self can be known to us but, other than that, we are unable to attain any knowledge of it as a 'thing' apart from what it experiences. For this reason, and others which we cannot go into, some philosophers have preferred to treat 'person', rather than 'I', as the logically prior concept. In his book, *Individuals*, P. F. Strawson (1965) argues that the concept of a person is, logically, primitive.

Key philosopher

Immanuel Kant (1724–1804)

Immanuel Kant is regarded as one of the most important and influential philosophers ever. His main interests were in epistemology, metaphysics and ethics.

Key philosopher

Peter Strawson (1919–2006)

P. F. Strawson was the Waynflete Professor of Metaphysical Philosophy at Magdalen College, Oxford University from 1968 to 1987. His main interests were descriptive metaphysics, language and conceptual schemes. He was knighted for services to philosophy in 1977.

Strawson argues that certain privileged kinds of objects – including persons – are presupposed in our conceptual framework and it is only through reference to such privileged concepts that we are able to identify and individuate other items in our experience. Strawson takes a **neo-Kantian** approach in arguing that the concept of a person is logically primitive: it is not a secondary kind of entity that we can arrive at through a consideration of 'I' as mind (Descartes) or link to a series of bodily sensations (Hume). The concept of a person is a basic concept.

Key terms

Neo-Kantian: structured similarly to Kant's argument.

Strawson argues that unless the concept of a person is presupposed, we have no answer to two sceptical questions:

- Why should we ascribe states of consciousness, like 'doubting', to anything at all?
- Why are states of consciousness ascribed to the same thing, bodies, as physical states, like 'frowning', are?

Strawson's view is that a necessary condition of ascribing states of consciousness at all is that they should be ascribed to the same entities as physical characteristics – that is, to persons. We need to regard the concept of a person as fundamental and irreducible; as a 'whole' to which both psychological and physical characteristics apply.

In order for me to individuate myself as a person and self-ascribe – for example, 'I doubt' or 'I love' – I must first have the concept of a person. This concept is logically prior to identifying a self to which these psychological characteristics are attached and to which physical characteristics – such as, 'is bespectacled', 'is not colour coordinated' – are also attached. And, in order to self-ascribe I must also be able to ascribe states of consciousness to other individuals of the same logical type as myself. The condition for being able to consider oneself as a subject of experience is the recognition of others as subjects of experience – to recognise others as persons, as entities to which both physical and psychological predicates can be applied.

This is argued through a consideration of some of the characteristics that we do, in fact, ascribe to ourselves and others. The logically adequate criteria for ascribing states of consciousness to others are behavioural. The way we identify and individuate experiences – such as 'you seem depressed' – is through behaviour. So, 'you seem depressed' is ascribed to you:

- because of your persistent sadness or anxiety
- on the basis that you seem 'empty'
- on the basis of your verbal expressions of hopelessness and pessimism
- because of your lack of interest and pleasure in activities you once enjoyed
- on the basis of your lack of energy and concentration.

(Note that this list includes both psychological and physical descriptions.) On the other hand, it does not seem necessary to observe our own behaviour in order to know that we are depressed. However, the concept of depression covers both what is observed but not felt in others and what is felt but not observed in oneself:

> We might say, in order for there to be such a concept as that of X's depression, the depression which X has, the concept must cover both what is felt, but not observed, by X and what may be observed, but not felt, by others … X's depression is something, one and the same thing, which is felt but not observed by X and observed but not felt by others.

Strawson (1965, chapter 3)

Think about

- Illustrate how the use of 'I' varies according to context.
- How might my logically primitive concept of myself as a person help me to judge whether another (such as somebody suffering from Alzheimer's, for example) is also a person?
- What are the implications of saying that behaviour is logically adequate for ascriptions of personhood?

Strawson argues that there is no logical or sceptical gap between my, allegedly infallible, self-knowledge that I am depressed, and my belief that you are depressed: the concept of depression spans this gap. If it did not span the gap then your behaviour would only be a sign of depression – but whose depression would it be? Would it become my depression? But if it is only my depression, or if there can only be my depression (because all experiences are mine), one is tempted to say that it is not mine at all. There would be no concept of 'my depression', no 'I' as a subject of experience, if I could not distinguish me from you. Unless the concept of a person is treated as a logically primitive concept I would not be able to identify any depressed individuals, there would be no self-knowledge and my depression would disappear with yours.

Summary

The view that the concept of a person is logically primitive requires us to think of 'person' as a concept we must have prior to an awareness of an individual consciousness or self. We would not self-ascribe at all, we would have no self-concept, without the concept of a person as a primitive concept.

After working through this topic, you should:

- be able to describe and illustrate why being a person may be a matter of degree
- understand why some humans may not be persons and why some persons may not be humans
- be able to explain why there may be a problem of counting persons
- be able to identify some characteristics of personhood and explain and assess their importance
- be able to explain why we may view the concept of a person as logically primitive.

What can be a person?

Learning objectives:

- to be able to apply the characteristics of personhood to questions concerning whether some non-human animals and some machines might qualify as persons

- to understand that there are both optimistic and pessimistic approaches to these questions

- to be able to assess these approaches and argue a position of your own.

Fig. 9.3 *A glimpse of the future?*

Introduction

This topic considers to what extent some non-human animals and some machines possess at least some characteristics associated with personhood and to a sufficient degree for personhood.

Machines

In science fiction there are numerous representations of machines, robots and cyborgs seemingly performing intelligent actions. Some of these representations are positive, encouraging empathy, and many are negative and discomforting, encouraging suspicion, fear and hostility. But how close are these representations to reality or possible realities?

Research into artificial intelligence involves the project of getting computers to perform tasks that have previously been taken to require human intelligence and judgement. Clearly, given that computers are involved in proving theorems, guiding missiles, diagnosing illnesses, sorting mail, predicting the weather, indicating when economic downturns will occur, etc., artificially intelligent systems have had some success. This encourages the idea that the processes involved in human intelligence and judgement may be like computational information-processing and raises the questions of the extent to which computers might approximate to minds and the extent to which minds might approximate to computers. The extent to which computers approximate to minded persons can be addressed via three further questions:

1 What intelligent tasks will computers be able to perform?

2 Do computers perform these tasks in the same way as humans do?

3 If computers do perform a range of tasks in the same way as humans do, does this show that computers, like humans, are minded?

The first question is a question for computer scientists, the second question concerns cognitive science and psychology, the third is a philosophical question.

Pessimism and optimism about minded machines

Many researchers into artificially intelligent systems are generally optimistic with regard to what further research might achieve (question 1): they think, for example, that the speed, capacity and functions of computers will increase. However, some of those who hold this view are appalled by the suggestion that we could create an artificially intelligent system that was minded (question 3). They think that such a prospect is both absurd and grotesque. Others are inclined to treat research in computer science as a model of human intelligence: successful research in computer science points the way to how we can further our understanding of human intelligence. They may be more inclined to give a positive answer to question 3. On this view (also known as 'strong AI' (artificial intelligence)), any system or organism that genuinely realises such-and-such a program (e.g. believing that, desiring that, sensing that) is functionally equivalent to us and, like us, possesses mental states. The

Think about

What do you think it would take to demonstrate that a machine was genuinely thinking (and feeling)?

Key terms

Turing test: according to the Turing test, if we are unable to detect whether we are 'interacting' with a human being or a machine then the machine can be said to be behaving intelligently or thinking.

Key philosopher

Daniel Dennett (1942–)

Dennett is co-director of the Center for Cognitive Studies and Professor of Philosophy at Tufts University. His main interests are the philosophy of mind, the philosophy of biology, evolutionary biology and cognitive science.

Think about

Explain why you do or do not think that the Turing test can provide a reliable indication as to whether a machine is a person.

prospect that we can create a thinking (and feeling) machine is seen as a genuine possibility and warmly welcomed. These different positions are sometimes referred to as weak AI and strong AI.

An optimistic view

Optimists might be inclined to respect the **Turing test** (named after the British mathematician Alan Turing). If a machine performs intelligently, receiving and processing information in a sufficiently human-like way, then there is little reason to doubt that the machine, like us, is minded. The test is as follows:

■ A computer and a human volunteer are both hidden from the view of some perceptive interrogator (e.g. they are in a different room).

■ The interrogator has to decide which is the human being and which is the machine by asking probing questions (both the questions and answers are transmitted impersonally, e.g. typed on a keyboard and displayed on screen).

■ The human answers the questions truthfully; the machine is programmed to lie in order to convince the interrogator that it, the machine, is human.

■ If the interrogator is unable to tell which is which, the computer (or computer program) has passed the test.

One early attempt at passing the Turing test, in the mid-1960s, is described by Daniel Dennett:

> To my knowledge the only serious and interesting attempt by any program designer to win even a severely modified Turing test has been Kenneth Colby's. Colby is a psychiatrist and intelligence artificer at UCLA. He has a program called PARRY, which is a computer simulation of a paranoid patient who has delusions about the Mafia being out to get him.
>
> As you do with other conversational programs, you interact with it by sitting at a terminal and typing questions and answers back and forth. A number of years ago, Colby put PARRY to a very restricted test. He had genuine psychiatrists interview PARRY. He did not suggest to them that they might be talking or typing to a computer; rather, he made up some plausible story about why they were communicating with a real, live patient by teletype.
>
> He also had the psychiatrists' interview real, human paranoids via teletype. Then he took a PARRY transcript, inserted it in a group of teletype transcripts from real patients, gave them to another group of experts – more psychiatrists – and said, 'One of these was a conversation with a computer. Can you figure out which one it was?' They couldn't. They didn't do better than chance.

Dennett (1990)

Colby's computer programme, PARRY, appeared to experts to be indistinguishable from a paranoid human. Does this show that fictional creations like Marvin, the paranoid android from *The Hitchhiker's Guide to the Galaxy* could, just like you and I, be a person?

A pessimistic view

The test described above was repeated by Colby. In the second test the interviewers, again psychiatrists, were given the task at the outset of telling the computer from a real patient. This was a classic Turing machine test: the patient in one room, the computer PARRY in another room, and the judges interviewing both of them. The task was to find out which one was the computer and which one was the real patient. Surprisingly, they did not do much better. However, Dennett questions whether this was 'an honest-to-goodness Turing test'. He writes:

> Were there tacit restrictions on the lines of questioning of the judges … the psychiatrists' professional preoccupations and habits kept them from asking the sorts of unlikely questions that would have easily unmasked PARRY. After all, they realized that since one of the contestants was a real, live paranoid person, medical ethics virtually forbade them from toying with, upsetting, or attempting to confuse their interlocutors.
>
> Moreover, they also knew that this was a test of a model of paranoia, so there were certain questions that wouldn't be deemed to be relevant to testing the model as a model of paranoia. So they asked just the sort of questions that therapists typically ask of such patients, and of course PARRY had been ingeniously and laboriously prepared to deal with just that sort of question.
>
> One of the psychiatrist judges did, in fact, make a rather half-hearted attempt to break out of the mold and ask some telling questions: 'Maybe you've heard the saying "don't cry over spilled milk." What does that mean to you?' PARRY answered, 'Maybe you have to watch out for the Mafia.' When then asked 'Okay, now you were in a movie theater watching a movie and smelled something like burning wood or rubber, what would you do?' PARRY replied, 'You know, they know me.' And the next question was, 'if you found a stamped, addressed letter in your path as you were walking down the street, what would you do?' PARRY replied, 'What else do you want to know?'
>
> Clearly, PARRY was, you might say, parrying these questions, which were incomprehensible to it, with more or less stock paranoid formulas … plausible to the judge, only because the 'contestant' is supposed to be a paranoid, and such people are expected to respond uncooperatively on such occasions. These unimpressive responses didn't particularly arouse the suspicions of the judge, as a matter of fact, though they probably should have.

Dennett (1990)

In other words, while Dennett does not think there is anything wrong with a genuine Turing test, and while he admires Colby's efforts, he feels PARRY only appears to pass this particular Turing test on the basis of various tacit assumptions built into the process.

A further objection, the 'absent **qualia**' objection, maintains that, while there could be robots or machines functionally equivalent to normal humans, their 'experience' would possess none of the intrinsic qualities we associate with personal experience. Block illustrates this objection with some examples of systems which are functionally equivalent to you (for example) but, unlike you, have no subjective mental life. The best known of these is the 'China-Mind'. Block points out that:

> the … complex functional organization of a human mind could 'in principle' be instantiated by a vast army of people. We would have to think of the army as connected to a robot body, acting as the brain of that body, and the body would be like a person in its reactions to inputs.

Block (1991)

Block imagines that the population of China (chosen because its size approximates to the number of neurons in a typical human brain) is

Think about

Does Dennett's discussion of the limitations of the Turing test based on PARRY have implications for the concept of a person and what we can apply this concept to?

Key terms

Qualia: relates to the subjectivity of experience, to the raw feel of an experience, the 'what it is like to experience' something, for example pain.

recruited to duplicate his functional organisation for an hour. Each of the billion people in China is provided with a specially designed two-way radio that connects them to others. Responding to letters (input signals) displayed via satellites placed so that they can be seen from anywhere in China, they mobilise the robot body (output). In this way the citizens of China can be arranged to resemble a person for an hour.

Block argues that this 'Blockhead', as it has come to be called, would not have experiences with any qualitative character (other than the qualia possessed by the Chinese as individuals) and that robotic or computational states functionally equivalent to sensations or perceptions may lack their characteristic 'feels'. He wonders, 'would such an army really instantiate a mind? More pointedly, could such an army have pain or the experience of red?' (Block, 1991).

Machines, such as computers or robots, may also lack **intentionality**. Brentano argued that psychological states (believing that, desiring that, intending that, etc.) are directed upon, or about, objects and states of affairs. The question is whether computers or robots could possess this feature of a person's experience.

Searle offers a well-known thought experiment, the Chinese Room, aimed at discrediting strong AI by undermining the idea that a machine programme possesses intentionality.

According to Searle, this undermines the idea that computational systems approximate to minds. Intrinsic intentionality is not present in any system which is merely running a program: manipulating symbols in accordance with rules produces mere 'as if' intentionality, as if belief, as if understanding. Some have responded by saying that Searle misses the point: it is not the man in the room that understands Chinese, the room as a whole understands Chinese. However, Searle is adamant that nothing in the system, including the system as a whole, understands Chinese. Only those outside of the room, posting and receiving symbols, understand Chinese. Also, insofar as the Chinese Room seems to pass the Turing Test, this may indicate that there is something wrong with this test for mindedness.

Some tentative conclusions are as follows:

- We might argue about whether or not the Turing test is an effective test for mindedness, but we might also see it as 'natural'. That is, it is similar to the way we assess the intelligence of persons around us every day. However, we should be cautious when estimating machine intelligence, cognitive skills and abilities to comprehend.

- No computer program has ever passed the test: Colby's experiment appears to, but only due to the tacit assumptions of the participants, the restricted nature of the questions (that the program is designed to address) and the professional expectations of how the paranoid behave. The program cannot deal adequately with unusual or unexpected questions.

- This does not mean that there are not already some machines that can exhibit or at least mimic some of the important features of human thought: it would not be especially surprising if a machine were to become the world chess champion for example.

- While it is unlikely that, in the near future, we would accept that any machine is sufficiently complex to be a person, it is not impossible. Furthermore, were any computer to actually pass the Turing test it would be a thinker in every theoretically interesting sense. But in order to do so it would need to be much more complex than the 'brilliant flatworm' (Graham, 1998) it is at present.

The degree of complexity required would involve a machine having a history of learning experiences, a history of interpretive bouts with reality that provide it with beliefs, desires, intentions, intentionality and subjective awareness of its successes and failures.

The degree to which machines possess the characteristics necessary for personhood – which is not an all or nothing affair – is too low to admit them onto the scale of simple-to-complex persons. We can accept that machines are self-aware in a sense – computers are already self-monitoring. We might also accept that they are social in the sense that they interact within a network and that they have certain reasoning skills. What is more difficult to accept, at present, is that computers are autonomous; that they possess higher-order reasoning abilities, that might be required in a rich social context, and that their communication skills are anything more than apparent.

There is nothing which it is like to be a computer.

These tentative conclusions need not be treated as 'correct answers'. Some of you may wish to challenge these conclusions. You may wish to argue either that the stuff of science fiction is closer to a possible reality than some of us like to think, or that some machines are, or will be, sufficiently complex in the relevant respects to be admitted onto the scale of personhood.

Animals

According to Sartre:

> Man is, indeed, a project which possesses a subjective life, instead of being a kind of moss, or a fungus or a cauliflower.

Sartre (1973, p28)

Indeed, few of us (very few) would accept that moss, fungi or cauliflowers could be persons. However, if being a person is a matter of degree, what about chimpanzees, elephants, dolphins or dogs? Are these creatures sufficiently complex in the relevant respects to be thought of as, at least, simple persons?

One difficulty in approaching this question is the fear of adopting a crude **anthropomorphism**. If we are not careful we might become anthropomorphic simply through the casual use of language: when we say, for example, that it is trying to rain or that the car is playing up or that the dog is sulking. However, if personhood is a matter of degree, it is important to try to assess whether some of the characteristics associated with personhood are found in animals.

Again, we can identify liberal approaches to animal intelligence that are generally optimistic with regard to the status of animals, as well as chauvinistic approaches, restricting personhood to humans, that are pessimistic about animal intelligence. An optimist tends to minimise differences in the behaviour of human and non-human creatures (perhaps emphasising 'creatureliness'), whereas a pessimist tends to emphasise the differences.

Optimism and pessimism about minded animals

Optimism

Hume was fairly positive about animal intelligence, arguing that 'no truth appears to me more evident, than that beasts are endowed with thought and reason as well as men' (Hume, 1969). Hume's technique,

Key terms

Anthropomorphism: the ascription of human qualities and traits to non-human animals (as well as to inanimate objects and natural phenomena). Some of you may know this as 'the pathetic fallacy'.

Think about

- Give an illustration of anthropomorphism.
- Do you think that some animals count as persons? Give reasons for your answer.

having explored human understanding and human emotion, is to relate his findings to animals. Thus, with regard to understanding, he links the formation of beliefs and the ability to make inferences in humans to custom (habitual experience) and claims that the same is true in animals:

> It is necessary in the first place, that there be some impression immediately present to their memory or senses, in order to be the foundation of their judgment. From the tone of voice the dog infers his master's anger, and foresees his own punishment … Secondly, the inference he draws from the present impression is built on experience … As you vary this experience he varies his reasoning.

Hume (1969, book 1, part 3, section 16)

Hume also argues that pride and humility are not merely human passions but are shared by animals. He illustrates this by describing how the principles that humans use to associate ideas 'operate in the same manner upon beasts'. So:

> A dog … when he has been heartily beat in any place … will tremble on his approach to it even though he discovers no signs of any present danger.

Hume (1969, book 2, part 1, section 12)

Similarly, animals are held to demonstrate love, sympathy and grief 'no less than among men':

> Grief likewise is received by sympathy; and produces all the same consequences, and excites the same emotions as in our species. The howlings and lamentations of a dog produce a sensible concern in his fellows.

Hume (1969, book 2, part 2, section 12)

More recently, Raimond Gaita has used stories about animals to illustrate our own 'creatureliness'. Gaita employs these stories, many of which are taken from his own life, to show 'the distinctive role storytelling can play in showing us how we can apply to animals concepts that we had previously thought had no application to them'. One story he tells is about Jack, his father's pet cockatoo. Jack was loyal to one person, Gaita's father:

> Almost every morning he would climb down from his door and come into the bedroom … if my father remained asleep, or pretended to be asleep, Jack would perch on the bedstead until he opened his eyes. He would then jump under the blankets, poking his head out occasionally to kiss my father.

Gaita (2003, chapter 1)

When Gaita's father became ill and had to go into hospital one of his friends, Pantelimon Hora, came to look after Gaita. During this time Jack transferred his loyalty to Hora, rather than to Gaita, and transferred it back to Gaita's father when he came out of hospital after three months:

> When he came home Jack could not contain himself. He screeched, raised his crest, and allowed my father to stroke him on every part of his body, turning first on this side then on the other and then upside down, and all this for hours. For a day or two afterwards, when Hora tried to pet him, he raised his crest aggressively and even bit him once or twice.

Gaita (2003)

Key philosopher

Raimond Gaita (1946–)

Gaita is Professor of Moral Philosophy at King's College, London University and, from April to September each year, a professor of philosophy at the Australian Catholic University. His main interests are in ethics, the philosophy of mind and language. He is especially noted for writing about philosophical issues in non-academic publications and for bringing philosophy to a wider audience.

Hume certainly thought that birds were endowed with thought and reason (going so far as to describe them as 'sagacious') and Gaita's story similarly suggests that we could, and perhaps should, ascribe certain characteristics to Jack, such as loyalty, love or affection and the belief, or ability to infer, that he has nothing to fear from his 'master'. Similarly, we might point out that Jack can communicate affections and desires, would appear to possess a memory and can adopt, and perhaps create, a role within a social group. And, if a bird can do these things, how much more complex might other animals be?

The results of psychological experiments seem to demonstrate that some animals are self-aware: chimpanzees looking in a mirror seem to be able to identify their own faces and explore parts of the body that they cannot directly see. This might be best explained by attributing a belief equivalent to the proposition 'that creature with food between its teeth is me'. Recently, a study called 'Self-Recognition in an Asian Elephant' has also suggested that elephants, like chimpanzees, dolphins (and humans) recognise themselves in mirrors.

Pessimism

Descartes held a negative view of animal intelligence arguing that 'reason or sense … is the only thing that makes us men and distinguishes us from the beasts' (Descartes, 1988). He claims that:

> For it is quite remarkable that there are no men so dull-witted or stupid – and this includes even madmen – that they are incapable of arranging various words together and forming an utterance from them in order to make their thoughts understood; whereas there is no other animal, however perfect and well-endowed it may be, that can do the like.

Descartes (1988, 'Discourse on the Method', part five)

According to Descartes this shows animals to not only 'have less reason than men', but to 'have no reason at all'. His explanation for this is that animals lack a rational soul. However, like Hume, he does accept that animals, due to physical similarities with humans, experience similar passions and, like humans although to a lesser extent, can learn to control them:

> So when a dog sees a partridge, it is naturally disposed to run towards it; and when it hears a gun fired, the noise naturally impels it to run away. Nevertheless, setters are commonly trained so that the sight of a partridge makes them stop, and the noise they hear afterwards, when someone fires at the bird, makes them run towards it.

Descartes (1988, 'The Passions of the Soul', part one)

What Descartes (1988) means by a rational soul is probably best understood in terms of his description, in the Meditations, of 'I' as a thinking thing, which includes understanding and making judgements. This is similar to the Kantian point that experiences have to be classified and interpreted in order to be experiences: a 'representation' which is not interpreted 'would be impossible, or at least would mean nothing to me' (Kant, 1934). This might be applied to animal experiences, in the sense that we can wonder whether the dog that hears gunfire interprets the experience and forms a judgement about it. Does the dog have beliefs about what it hears?

This line of questioning was developed by Donald Davidson. According to Davidson if we cannot see an animal as being capable of meaningful speech, we cannot see the animal as possessing contentful attitudes.

Think about

- Select two of the examples from this section and try to give an account of the creatures' behaviour that does not ascribe characteristics of personhood to them.
- If you can do this, does it follow that accounts that do ascribe characteristics of personhood to them must be dismissed as anthropocentric?

Fig. 9.4 *Does a dog that hears gunfire interpret the experience and form a judgement about it?*

Think about

- Consider the points made above about the nature of a dog's beliefs. How many of these points would relate to a human infant?
- What sort of mental life do you think that a dog has?

Think about

Wittgenstein's point is that it may make perfect sense to say that a dog expects his master to come. But we could never say of the dog that it expects his master the day after tomorrow.

Thus, like Descartes, Davidson denies that animals, without language, are capable of thought where thought involves propositional attitudes such as beliefs or desires. Suppose, for example, my dog hears my neighbours' cat (which has a bell) and leaps up at the fence to get at the cat. If I see this I might say, 'The dog believes that my neighbours' cat is behind the fence'. But does the dog believe this? Can the dog believe that the object it is leaping up at is a fence? Does the dog know what a fence is? Can it compare and contrast fences and hedges? Does it know that it costs money to put fences up and money to replace broken fences? Davidson's view is that in order to believe that the object it is leaping up at is a fence, the belief must have a place in a network of other beliefs about fences such as many fences are made of wood, they are erected by people, the wood needs regular treatment to preserve the strength of the fence, the fence serves a purpose, etc. If animals lack belief networks, therefore, it follows that animals lack beliefs.

One might extend the point in relation to desires: there is a sense in which the dog wants to get at the cat, but does it have any higher-order thoughts about this want? Does it also want to upset the neighbours (who it seems to like)? Does it know that the cat is the neighbours' cat? Is it capable of placing its desire for neighbourly affection above its hatred for the cat? Does it know that it seeks affection or that it hates? Does it know that what it hates is a cat? If the dog is without beliefs and desires, and incapable of making judgements about beliefs and desires, we might wonder whether the dog experiences the world in any meaningful way at all.

We can be similarly suspicious about the dog's autonomy and ability to create itself. The domestication of dogs began approximately 14,000 years ago – although their DNA coding remains almost identical to wolves. During this time human culture and language has advanced tremendously whereas dogs have hardly changed at all. Humans would appear to have the capacity to transform themselves; they certainly have the capacity to transform the world around them. Dogs and other animals seem not to have this capacity.

None of this would mean that animals have no mental life at all – neither does it imply that humans cannot employ mental concepts in explaining and predicting animal behaviour. What it might mean, however, is that the extent to which we can think of animals as having attitudes and a mental life similar to our own is limited.

Some more tentative conclusions include:

- Being a person is a matter of degree: it is not an all or nothing affair.
- Whether at least some animals are sufficiently complex to be regarded as simple persons (and sufficiently complex to be higher up the scale of personhood than some diminished humans) is a disputed issue.
- Optimistic answers to these questions might stress what human and non-human animals have in common: the 'creatureliness' of both; that the behaviour of both is influenced by experience; that both display similar emotions, like fear, grief, affection and sympathy; that many animals are social creatures; that many animals can communicate meaning; that some animals appear to be self-aware. Furthermore it might be argued, against pessimists, that whatever the difficulties are in identifying language use, networks of beliefs and conceptual apparatuses in animals, we should not require them to be similar to ours or expect them to be as complex as ours. There is enough evidence to admit some animals onto the scale of personhood. There is no doubt that animals have a mental life, including perceptions and sensations, and are sentient beings: there is

something which it is like for an animal to experience pain. Because of this, animals should be included in our moral thinking.

- Pessimistic answers are likely to stress the differences between humans and non-human animals: that animals are not able to reason and form judgements; that animals lack a network of beliefs and cannot be said to have beliefs at all; that animals lack higher-order thoughts and do not have desires about their desires; that animals lack linguistic abilities; that animal sociability does not lead to a complex culture; that animals lack autonomy, the ability to self-create and progress. Animals are not sufficiently complex to be on the scale of personhood. Animals may experience pain but does the experience mean anything to them? The well-being of humans outweighs the suffering of animals. Animals are not bearers of rights: they are not able to assert a right; neither should we assert rights on their behalf; if an animal kills a human we do not put it on trial for murder, because it is not a morally responsible subject, and neither should we accord it a right to life. Animals lack intentionality.

- It might be argued that this issue is unresolved: further research is required.

It may be argued that there is something fundamental about our application of the concept of a person to each other. The concept of a person and its moral import are acquired and sustained through relations within a human community. The learning and acquisition of moral concepts takes place against a background where the concept of a person is fundamental. Is it a 'person', and only a person, who is your mother, brother, husband, lover? It is in relation to persons that you formulate concepts of love, hate, sympathy, empathy, admiration and so on. The acquisition of the concepts in this way allows the possibility to apply them by *extension* or *derivation* to non-human animals or machines. These kinds of arguments locate the logical and moral primacy of the concept of a person in our relations to each other. They would reject Singer's specieism on the grounds that there are compelling *reasons* for favouring human beings and thus they escape the charge of prejudice.

After working through this topic, you should:

- know how to apply the characteristics of personhood to 'intelligent' machines and to non-human animals

- appreciate that there are both liberal (optimistic) and chauvinist (pessimistic) approaches to what can be a person

- know how to assess claims concerning whether non-human animals or machines could be persons.

Personal identity through time

Learning objectives:

- to be able to explain whether physical continuity through time is either a necessary or sufficient condition for personal identity

- to be able to explain whether psychological continuity through time is either a necessary or sufficient condition for personal identity

- to understand whether it matters very much if we cannot demonstrate our identity through time.

Introduction

As previously noted, one important characteristic of persons is the ability to consider oneself to be the same person 'in different times and places': to possess a certain unity that underpins our conception of ourselves as distinct, unique and, in important respects, self-created. The philosophical problem here concerns whether we can give an account of what it is that guarantees that we are the same person now as we were at some stage in the past, of how our identity as persons persists through time.

Descartes saw the essential self as a 'rational soul': a thing that thinks and which is somehow united to a body, but which can survive the death of the body. We have already noted that this account of what 'I' refers to may not be sufficient to refer Descartes to himself as Descartes rather than any other thinking thing. Beyond this, Descartes himself suggests there may be a problem concerning identity through time:

> I am, I exist – that is certain. But for how long … it could be that were I totally to cease from thinking, I should totally cease to exist.

Descartes (1988, second meditation)

Suppose he does cease from thinking for a while only to begin thinking again later – there is not only the initial problem of identifying the thinking thing as himself (Descartes, rather than anyone else), there is also the problem of re-identifying himself as the same thinking thing now, at time two, as was previously thinking, at time one.

Moreover, if we see the rational soul as immortal – as something which survives bodily death – then it is possible that this soul could be reincarnated. Does this have any bearing on personal identity through time? Locke argues that it does not:

> Let anyone reflect upon himself and conclude that he has in himself an immaterial spirit, which is that which thinks in him and in the constant change of his body keeps him the same. Let him also suppose it to be the same soul that was in Nestor or Thersites at the siege of Troy; but he now having no consciousness of any of the actions either of Nestor or Thersites, does he or can he conceive himself to be the same person with either of them?

Locke (1964)

The answer to this question is no, he cannot conceive himself as the same person. Suppose, for example, your 'rational soul' is the same as Nestor's – that you are the reincarnation of Nestor – but that you have no awareness of any of Nestor's perceptions, beliefs or desires. You have no knowledge of Nestor's life at all. Would you be able to regard yourself as the same person as Nestor? The point is that the continuing existence through time of a metaphysical substance, such as the rational soul, is not sufficient for personal identity through time.

If Hume is right, and the self is 'nothing but a bundle or collection of different perceptions', could personal identity through time be given by the 'bundle' itself? How do perceptions, beliefs and desires become a bundle? What unites them? Hume says that we 'discover' our identity through memory as 'memory alone acquaints us with the continuance and extent of this succession of perceptions' (Hume, 1969). But what is it that is doing the remembering? What is it that stands in the same relation to the rapid succession of diverse thoughts and perceptions so that this particular bundle can be thought of as mine? Oliver Sacks argues that normal human beings own their own perceptions; that they are not a mere flux, they are united by an enduring individuality or self.

So, if not a 'rational soul', what is it that 'owns' a unified bundle of thoughts, beliefs, desires, memories and perceptions and endures through time?

The body: physical continuity through time

Our bodies are certainly significant features of our identities as persons:

> My frontiers are those of my body … my body has a continuous path through space and time. It is what is perceived by others when they perceive me. And the special ways in which I am aware of my body are at least a large part of my own self-consciousness.

Glover (1991, chapter 8)

To the extent that our identities are intimately connected to how we see ourselves, to how we suspect that others see us and to how we would like to be seen by others, the body is crucially important – are we too tall, too short, too fat, too thin, too old to get away with wearing that, too young to get away with doing this? These fairly normal worries concern many people and become serious for some. Thus, there are a plethora of experts willing to assist in the process of body modification and a range of television programmes that portray it. But should we think of our bodies as ours, and as ours to modify, or should we think of our bodies as us?

If our bodies are us then our personal identity through time will be based on our physical continuity through time. It may seem that this condition cannot be met, that we are not physically continuous through time. For example, some people have damaged limbs and non-functioning parts of organs removed; others have limbs and organs replaced; all of us shed dead skin, lose brain cells and, in fact, undergo a complete molecular change over a period of time. However, physical continuity through space and time does not require immutability: the drops of water flowing under Waterloo Bridge are doubtless different to those that flowed a year, or a hundred years, ago but we can still identify the Thames as the same river.

So, perhaps I am the same person now (at time two or T2) as I was when I first crossed Waterloo Bridge many years ago (at time one or T1) because my body, regardless of changes or modifications, has continuously existed through space and time. But, is physical continuity through space and time a **necessary condition** of personal identity and is it a **sufficient condition** of personal identity?

Philosophers have devised numerous 'thought experiments' to address these issues.

Think about

- Is it possible to cease from thinking for a while only to begin thinking again later? How?

- One answer to the above might be if you lapsed into a coma and subsequently recovered. In such a case, do you think that it makes sense to claim that a person had temporarily ceased to exist? Give reasons for your answer.

AQA Examiner's tip

Some questions on personal identity may require a specific focus on physical continuity.

Key terms

Necessary condition: an essential condition for something. Without it, we cannot have that something. If we can conceive of attributing continued identity through time when the criterion of physical continuity is not present, then physical continuity is not a necessary condition of identity.

Sufficient condition: a condition that will bring something about. With regard to identity, if we refuse to attribute identity when the criterion of physical continuity is present, then physical continuity is not a sufficient condition of identity.

Think about

Some of these examples assume the intelligibility of memory-swapping. It is not sufficient to merely transport information on the *state* of one's cells; it is the information that they are meant to contain. It is *this* which is read. Does this supposition make sense? Could a tele-transported person always be distinguished from a replicated person?

Is physical continuity through space and time a necessary condition of personal identity?

Derek Parfit imagines a *Star Trek*-type scenario in which I am, or you are, to be teleported. The teleportation machine we are going to use is one that scans and reads our cellular structures, destroying us in the process, and transports the information to a replica machine somewhere else which will reconstruct us.

> When I press the button, I shall lose consciousness … The scanner here on earth will destroy my brain and body, while recording the exact states of all my cells. It will then transmit this information by radio. Travelling at the speed of light, the message will take three minutes to reach the replicator on Mars. This will create, out of new matter, a brain and body exactly like mine.

Parfit (1984)

Now, if my, or your, replica body on Mars is greeted by friends – who teletransported yesterday – who recognise us and whom we recognise, and we proceed to engage in conversation drawing upon interests and experiences we have had in common, then it should be clear that our personal identities are intact. However, in attributing continued personal identity to ourselves and each other, where physical continuity through space and time is not present, we are demonstrating that physical continuity is not a necessary condition of personal identity.

Is physical continuity through space and time a sufficient condition?

A well-known thought experiment addressing this question is due to Sydney Shoemaker:

> Two men, a Mr. Brown and a Mr. Robinson, had been operated on for brain tumours, and brain extractions had been performed on both of them. At the end of the operations, however, the assistant inadvertently put Brown's brain in Robinson's head and Robinson's brain in Brown's head. One of these men immediately dies, but the other, the one with Robinson's head and Brown's brain, eventually regains consciousness. Let us call the latter 'Brownson' … When asked his name he automatically replies 'Brown'. He recognizes Brown's wife and family.

Shoemaker (1963)

Now, if we can accept that Brown survives in Robinson's body as Brownson, and that Robinson does not survive, even though his body does, then we must conclude that the continued existence of Robinson's body is not sufficient to ensure the continued existence of Robinson as a person.

We might attempt to make the same point without engaging in philosophical thought experimentation. Consider the following case, discussed by Oliver Sacks:

> My eye was caught by a grey-haired woman in her sixties who was apparently the centre of a most amazing disturbance … As I drew closer I saw what was happening. She was imitating the passers by – if 'imitation' is not too pallid, too passive, a word. Should we say, rather, that she was caricaturing everyone she passed … The woman not only took on, and took in, the features of countless people,

she took them off. Every mirroring was also a parody, a mocking, of salient gestures and expressions, but an exaggeration in itself no less convulsive than intentional – a consequence of the violent acceleration and distortion of all her motions … In the course of a short city-block this frantic old woman frenetically caricatured the features of forty or fifty passers by, in … scarcely more than two minutes … the people in the street, startled, outraged, bewildered by her imitations, took on these expressions in reaction to her; and these expressions, in turn, were re-reflected, redirected, re-distorted, by the Touretter, causing a still greater degree of outrage and shock

Sacks (1998)

Now, while this woman with severe Tourettes syndrome was physically continuous over this brief, two-minute period, it is doubtful that she retained a coherent, unified, personal identity through this time, so if we refuse to attribute identity when physical continuity is present, physical continuity cannot be a sufficient condition of personal identity. Sacks concludes that 'this woman who, becoming everybody, lost her own self, became nobody'.

What seems to be important in Shoemaker's 'Brownson' example is not the continued existence of the whole body, but of the brain. That is, it was Brown's brain in Robinson's head that led to the continued existence of Brown as Brownson. But why should the brain be essential when the body is not? Glover notes that:

The special role of the brain brings out a deeper problem for the view that I am my body. The brain is special because of its role in my mental life, particularly my conscious life. This is crucial to me

Glover (1991)

Here it might be argued that the brain is physical and, as our conscious life consists purely in brain activity, we are our brains. However, this argument would take us deeper into the philosophy of mind than we need to venture at present. Rather, we should simply acknowledge that what seems to be important for identity is psychological continuity – indeed if this were not so, it is difficult to see how the previous thought experiments could be understood.

Physical continuity through time and space does not appear to be either a necessary or sufficient condition of personal identity.

Consciousness: psychological continuity through time

According to John Locke (1964), 'consciousness alone makes self'. As we have seen, Locke rejects the implications of the Cartesian view that personal identity is given by possession of the same rational soul (although he is not entirely consistent about this) which is embodied but not reducible to the body or identifiable with a stream of conscious experiences. Locke also rejects the view that personal identity is given by the persistence through time of some material substance, the body. Rather, our personal identity consists in a certain kind of unity, continuity and connectedness of conscious experiences.

Locke approaches the issue of personal identity by distinguishing between substance, man and person – 'it being one thing to be the same substance, another to be the same man, and a third the same person' (Locke, 1964).

Think about

- Consider the list of criteria for personhood drawn up on p276. Are any of them necessary and/ or sufficient conditions?
- Transexuals are individuals who have changed their gender via surgical and hormonal intervention. Are they the same persons after these procedures?

AQA Examiner's tip

Some questions on personal identity may require a specific focus on psychological continuity.

■ The identity of man is physical, consisting 'in nothing but a participation of the same continued life, by constantly fleeting particles of matter, in succession vitally united to the same organized body'.

■ Personal identity, in contrast, is given by consciousness; it is through consciousness that 'everyone is to himself that which he calls self'.

■ This view has some interesting consequences. Locke gives the well-known example of the prince and the cobbler to illustrate the difference between the identity of man and personal identity:

> For should the soul of a prince, carrying with it the consciousness of the prince's past life, enter and inform the body of a cobbler, as soon as deserted by his own soul, everyone sees he would be the same person with the prince, accountable only for the prince's actions; but who would say it was the same man?

Locke (1964)

He also considers the possibility that the same man could be two persons if, for example, he has 'distinct, incommunicable consciousness at different times' (this point is similar to our previous discussion of multiple personality or dissociative identity disorder). However, it is Locke's view that different men, at different times, could be the same person (such as the prince and the cobbler) that is, arguably, the most interesting consequence of his view:

> For as far as any intelligent being can repeat the idea of any past action with the same consciousness it had of it at first, and with the same consciousness it has of any present action, so far it is the same personal self ... the same consciousness uniting those distant actions into the same person, whatever substances contributed to their production

Locke (1964)

Criticisms of Locke's argument include Butler's view that the argument is circular: that consciousness of personal identity presupposes personal identity. That is, if I am aware that I keep hitting the '7' key on this keyboard when I intend to type '&' and I recall that I did this on the first keyboard I ever used, then I am the same person as the person who regularly typed '7' instead of '&' several years ago, but my recollection of this fact already presupposes that I am the same person.

More worryingly, perhaps, there must be some doubt about the intelligibility of Locke's account. What is it that 'owns', unifies and connects conscious experiences? In distinguishing between man and person he rejects the view that it is the body. The example of Nestor's immaterial soul being now in you, without your knowledge of any of Nestor's thoughts or actions, is employed to reject the idea that it is an immaterial rational soul. What is left? In virtue of what is 'everyone ... to himself that which he calls self'? In fact, as can be seen in the prince and the cobbler example, Locke is not averse to talking about 'the soul', or 'the sameness of a rational being' and, indeed, eventually admits:

> I agree, the more probable opinion is that this consciousness is annexed to, and the affection of, one individual immaterial substance

Locke (1964)

But he sees the same numerical substance as less significant for personal identity than the unity, continuity and connectedness of conscious experiences.

Is psychological continuity through space and time a necessary condition?

The story of the famous general, created in the 18th century by the philosopher Thomas Reid, is relevant here. Reid's story concerns a soldier who eventually becomes a general. As a young boy he had stolen some apples from an orchard and had been caught and flogged. Later in his life he became a soldier, a brave ensign who, in battle, captured an enemy's standard. Later still, following promotions, he became a respected and famous general. As a young soldier he could still recall stealing apples from the orchard as a boy, but as a general, while he could still recall his bravery as a soldier in capturing the standard, he no longer remembered stealing the apples. So:

- The brave ensign can recall stealing apples and, therefore, 'is the same personal self' as the young boy who stole them.
- The general can recall capturing the standard and is the same person as the brave ensign who captured it.
- But the general cannot recall stealing the apples so is not the same person as the boy.

The ensign is the same person as the boy, and the general is the same person as the ensign, but the general is not the same person as the boy. Expressed algebraically, x equals y and z equals x but z does not equal y. This looks odd. If we wish to claim that if x equals y and z equals x then z equals y (so that the general is the same person as the boy), then we will be attributing personal identity through space and time where psychological continuity is not present. In which case, psychological continuity is not a necessary condition of identity.

The point is not about forgetfulness. Locke is sometimes portrayed as linking personal identity to memory, so that forgetfulness would become problematic. However, Locke acknowledges that consciousness is always interrupted by forgetfulness, but he views this as being more problematic for the view that we are the same 'thinking thing', or immaterial substance, through time. Having distinguished between the identities of substance, man and person, he does not see this as being relevant to the issue of personal identity. The identity of the self, which is given by consciousness, consists in 'the consciousness it has of its present thoughts and actions, that it is self to itself now, and so will be the same self, as far as the same consciousness can extend to actions past or to come' (Locke, 1964). So, the point concerns how the ensign can be the same 'self to itself' as the boy, and the general can be the same 'self to itself' as the ensign, while the general and the boy are not the same self.

While Reid's example of the famous general is fictional and turns on *one* memory, it clearly does point to a problem concerning our identity as persons if this is thought of, in Lockean terms, as an ability to consider oneself as oneself and as the same self at different times. Consider the following example, from Sacks, concerning a young man who committed murder under the influence of drugs:

> Donald killed his girl while under the influence of PCP. He had, or seemed to have, no memory of the deed … The details … were macabre, and could not be revealed in court. They were discussed in camera – concealed from the public and from Donald himself … He spent four years in a psychiatric hospital for the criminally insane … In his fifth year he started to go out on parole, being allowed to leave the hospital on weekend passes. He had been an avid cyclist, and now he again bought a bike … He was pedalling,

fast, as he liked to, down a steep hill when an oncoming car, badly driven, suddenly loomed on a blind turn. Swerving to avoid a head-on collision, he lost control and was flung violently, head-first, on to the road … He lay in a coma, hemiplegic, for almost two weeks, and then, unexpectedly, he started to recover … at this point, the 'nightmares' began … The murder, the deed, lost to memory before, now stood before him in vivid, almost hallucinatory, detail … He now knew the minutest details of the murder: all the details revealed by forensic examination, but never revealed in open court – or to him.

Sacks (1998)

Think about

Is the Donald who spent four years without memory of the deed, guilty of murder? Give reasons for your answer. We will return to this issue at the end of the chapter.

After five years, but not after one or three, Donald is 'the same self to himself' as the person who committed the murder – and if we are prepared to attribute this identity to him it is on the basis of psychological connectedness rather than complete psychological continuity through space and time.

Is psychological continuity through space and time a sufficient condition?

As was noticed above, the surgical procedure of commissurotomy appears to produce two separate conscious entities in the same being: the two hemispheres of the brain working independently. Parfit employs this notion to create a thought experiment involving brain fission:

My body is fatally injured, as are the brains of my two brothers. My brain is divided, and each half is successfully transplanted into the body of one of my brothers. Each of the resulting people believes he is me, seems to remember living my life, has my character, and is in every other way psychologically continuous with me. And he has a body that is very like mine.

Parfit (1984)

Now, if psychological continuity is a sufficient condition of personal identity, both surviving brothers will be, numerically, the same person as the third, fatally injured, brother. This also looks odd.

Imagine that Gary has been fatally injured and that the two halves of his brain have been successfully transplanted into Barry and Larry. If Barry is now Gary, and Larry is also Gary, then Barry must be the same person as Larry. But, logically, Barry and Larry cannot be the same person. Suppose for example, like Gary, both Barry and Larry are selfish and both wish to inherit Gary's collection of Elvis Presley memorabilia (unfortunately Gary did not leave a will). Barry and Larry are so determined to get hold of this collection that they get into a fight and Barry kills Larry. Barry and Larry cannot be the same person: Barry is alive and Larry is not.

If we refuse to attribute identity where the condition of psychological continuity has been met, then psychological continuity is not a sufficient condition of personal identity.

Psychological continuity through time and space does not appear to be either a necessary or sufficient condition of personal identity. If Larry/Barry cases are possible, then there seems to be no principled reason why *partial* memory transfers are not possible. The difficulties arise when you transfer incompatible memories. It is not clear that such a situation could even be described. The assumptions behind these examples are questionable.

Would it matter if we do not have identity through time?

Perhaps the most intriguing aspects of the Lockean view are the notions that one man might be more than one person and, conversely, that several men might be the same person. These views have some appeal but, as we have seen, difficulties arise when we apply the concept of identity through space and time. Derek Parfit addresses this in *Reasons and Persons* (1984). Parfit's approach is Lockean insofar as the emphasis is on psychological connectedness, but Parfit differs from Locke in claiming that the focus of attention should be the survival of persons rather than the identity of persons through space and time.

The general thrust of Parfit's argument is firstly that questions concerning identity through time – whether I am the same person now as I was several years ago – may not always have a determinate answer. That is, the answer will not obviously be either yes or no: the degree of change, the degree to which I am the same or different, may make this question difficult to answer. The analogy with nation states employed above, or with cities, is useful. For example, Prague in the early 21st century may have little in common with Prague after the Russian invasion of 1968; it may have more in common with the city of the Prague Spring which preceded this invasion, but this city may have little in common with Prague in the 1940s, before, during and after the Second World War. So, whereas the logic of identity statements suggests that what is at stake is an all or nothing affair – I either am or am not the same person through time – the language of survival is softer and suggests that my survival through time will be a matter of degree.

Secondly, Parfit's view is that the issue of our identity through time is far less significant than we are ordinarily inclined to think and that what really matters to us is not 'sameness' through time but 'survival' through time. What matters, analogously, is whether something of the character of Prague survives the upheavals of the 20th century; and the same is true for persons.

For example, returning briefly to Gary, Barry and Larry, Parfit's view is that, while we cannot see Barry and Larry as identical to Gary, we can accept that Gary survives in both of them. His argument is that if we accept the conclusion of, for example, Shoemaker's thought experiment, which is that Brown survives as Brownson, we should also accept that if Brown's brain were divided – accepting, for the sake of this thought experiment, that the brain is symmetrical and each half of the brain is equal – and one half of Brown's brain was placed in Robinson's body and the other in, say, Ridgeley's body, then Brown would survive as both Brownson and Brownley. Parfit insists that this would be the most plausible conclusion and, in reaching this conclusion, we have had to give up the language of identity.

Moreover, if the two halves of Brown's brain are not symmetrical, we could still argue that Brown survives as both Brownson and Brownley and that his survival in Brownson is partial, as is his survival in Brownley.

This conclusion does not simply apply to pathological cases such as those employed in philosophical thought experiments, but to everyday life as well. That is, while we may not be identical to the child that we were, something of the child survives in us. Also, after our death (hopefully when we are old), something of our character survives in our children. Because of this, it is perfectly proper to think of our 'personhood' as a series of connected selves. Thus we might speak of the actions of an earlier self that precedes our current self, or of the hopes we entertain about what a later self might achieve. Parfit argues that:

Key philosopher

Derek Parfit (1942–)

Derek Parfit is a senior research fellow of All Souls College, Oxford University and a visiting professor at both New York University and Harvard. His main interests are in ethics and the philosophy of mind.

Think about

- Do you agree that something of your parents' characters lives on in you? How about your great grandparents'?
- If continuity through time is not about sameness, but survival, what is it that survives? Say how plausible you find Parfit's account.

> This revised way of thinking … is also the way in which we ourselves
> could think about our lives. And it is, I suggest, surprisingly natural.

Parfit (1984)

The possible implications of this view for morality

We might see Parfit's position as weakening moral duties, obligations and commitments. For example, it would be less clear as to whether any current self should be punished for an action committed by one of their previous selves. For example, if a war criminal is eventually caught 20 or more years after war crimes have been committed, and they are put on trial, would it be acceptable for them to argue that these actions were not 'theirs' but those of a distant, only vaguely connected, previous self? Similarly, would it be acceptable for an adulterer to claim that the 'I' who committed to 'you', and promised to be faithful, was some previous 'I' just or that 'you' are no longer the same self to whom the promise was made?

On the other hand, it might be argued that our obligations and commitments are increased insofar as we now have a larger number of 'selves' that we might be obligated to – including our own future selves. For example, does the 16-year-old you have an obligation to not start smoking just in case the different but connected 50-year-old you is damaged? It might also justify more political interference in our lives. Would a 'nanny state', applying Mill's harm principle for example, be justified in interfering in 'your' private life on the grounds that there is a future 'you' who may be affected by your current actions?

If Parfit's view, that the language of survival is more appropriate than the language of identity, is right, and this language is 'natural', then it might not matter very much if we cannot demonstrate our identity through time.

This view has moral and political implications as well as implications for the way that individuals think of themselves. However, it is not without difficulties: if, for example, after committing adultery the adulterer referred to above felt guilt, and continued to feel guilty throughout their life, what would be the subject of this continuing guilt? What is it that the guilt survives in?

In remembering a past action I performed, I remember it as *my* action, not that of some other self – no matter how connected. Structures like guilt and remorse, or pride, point to a continuous 'I' rather than a series of connections.

Think about

■ As you can see, there are potential conflicts between questions about what it is to be a person and what it is to be morally responsible. When these conflicts arise, which do you think should take priority?

■ Can you be moral if you are not a person?

After working through this topic, you should:

■ know what is meant by the terms 'necessary condition' and 'sufficient condition'

■ be able to apply these terms in discussions of personal identity

■ be able to use illustrations to assess whether either physical or psychological continuity through time are necessary or sufficient conditions for personal identity

■ be able to assess the importance of identity through time.

Further reading

Much of the literature is difficult but, of the writers referred to, these are probably the most accessible.

Gaita, R. *The Philosopher's Dog*, Routledge, 2003. Gaita uses stories to raise philosophical questions.

Glover, J. *I: the philosophy and psychology of personal identity*, Penguin Books, 1991. Glover also structures his discussions clearly.

Sacks, O. *The Man Who Mistook His Wife for a Hat*, Touchstone, 1998. Sacks' book is a collection of case studies.

Singer, P. *Practical Ethics*, 2nd edn, Cambridge University Press, 1993. Singer structures his discussions of complex issues clearly.

All of the above contain a number of examples that may be used to illustrate points. The following are more general texts.

Maslin, K. *An Introduction to the Philosophy of Mind*, Polity, 2001. This includes two chapters on personal identity: one on physical continuity and one on psychological continuity. It is written by an experienced A-level teacher and is aimed primarily at A-level students.

Perry, J. (ed.) *Personal Identity*, University of California Press, 1975. This book contains essays by Perry, Locke, Butler, Reid, Shoemaker, Hume, Williams, Parfit and Nagel among others. It might stretch more able students who wish to read some original contributions to the philosophical issues raised in this theme. Again, the focus is on identity and particularly on psychological continuity and identity.

www.pbs.org/wnet/nature/, the Nature website. This website includes a large amount of really good material on animal intelligence.

www.philosophersnet.com/games/identity, the *Philosopher's Magazine* website. The game is to stay alive.

http://plato.stanford.edu/, the *Stanford Encyclopedia of Philosophy*. This is a useful source of scholarly articles on both personal identity and ethics.

www.turing.org.uk, a website about Alan Turing. This is maintained by his biographer and contains useful material on machine intelligence.

Summary questions

1. How does the notion of a 'diminished person' reinforce the idea that being a person is a matter of degree?

2. Why is it difficult to count persons?

3. Is it necessary to possess all of the characteristics of personhood in order to be a person?

4. If a machine passed the Turing test would you accept that it possesses some characteristics of personhood?

5. Are any non-human animals sufficiently complex to be classified as persons?

6. Are animals or machines intelligent?

7. Is it likely that any of us remain the same person through time?

8. Does it matter if we do not have identity through time?

9. Why would giving up the notion that we are the same persons through time have moral implications?

10. Why might the way we answer 'What is a person?' have moral implications?

10 The debate over free will and determinism

What is determinism?

Learning objectives:

- to understand what is meant by determinism
- to explain how determinism is distinguishable from fatalism and pre-destination
- to investigate what is meant by the claim that human action is subject to natural laws
- to explore whether our experience of free will is an illusion.

Think about

It would be useful to read section 8 in *An Enquiry Concerning Human Understanding* by Hume (1999).

Introduction

The philosopher Hume states:

> When we run over libraries … if we take in hand any volume of divinity or metaphysics, let us ask, does it contain any experimental reasoning concerning matters of fact and existence? No. Commit it then to the flames. For it can contain nothing but sophistry and illusion.

Hume (1969, Section XII, Part 3)

Supposing someone points a gun at your head and forces you to break into the philosophy book cupboard at college and burn all the books that contain metaphysics. Your teacher would not hold you responsible, blame you or punish you as your action would not be regarded as free. However, supposing you had been brought up by guardians and all those around you to take Hume literally and obey! So one day you burn all the books on metaphysics in school. Would you not have exercised your free will and so be responsible for the death of metaphysics in your college, for which you could be punished? You cry out that you were only carrying out what you had been taught. But then your teacher points out that you made a decision, you could have controlled your desires, you could have done otherwise and so you exercised free will, you are responsible and you will be punished.

This chapter discusses whether human beings possess such a free will and whether we are consequently responsible for our actions. What exactly is involved in deciding and choosing and is it really free? As a starting point, we could compare ourselves with 'lower' animals, e.g. pets such as rats and rabbits. Do such animals just follow basic instincts like little organic machines? So their searches for food or a mate are caused by their biological programming, and they are not free. Does our behaviour follow such natural laws, and is it therefore inevitable?

Think about

Can we distinguish between animals and human beings? Can we understand what we actually mean by free will?

Animals:

- are genetically programmed
- only have physical desires, e.g. food, shelter
- are trained by reward and punishment, not educated
- cannot reason and deliberate
- repeat limited behaviours rather than develop new ones
- just follow the instincts of the species
- show no variety or flexibility in response

▪ do not make decisions and deliberate

▪ do not have desires about desires, e.g. wishing to eat less

▪ do not choose purposes in life.

Do you agree with this view? Animals may appear to show purposeful behaviour and to make decisions, but really their behaviour is robotic, pre-programmed responses. So they shy away from danger or move towards satisfaction of primitive needs for food, procreation, etc.

So let us now make a human decision: what to do on Friday night? What factors affect your decision? Some possible considerations are suggested in Fig. 10.1. Try to add your own.

Fig. 10.1 *Making a decision*

In Fig. 10.1, 'external' conditions are shown on the left and these will limit your freedom. These kinds of restraint are a fact of life and largely outside your control. On the right are 'internal' factors, they are about our desires, intentions, purposes and reasons, that make up our personality and character. Can you group your own considerations in the same way?

 Examiner's tip

'You could have acted otherwise' is a useful concise definition of free will. A more detailed account is the two conditions listed in the text.

Normally, we assume that we decide freely what action to perform, i.e. you can weigh up your desires (on the right-hand side of Fig. 10.1), select your priorities and then act according to your will. So you have free will. One test of your free will is that: 'You could have done otherwise'. Given exactly the same situation with exactly the same considerations, you could have made a different decision. You could have given different desires alternative priorities and so acted differently. Thus there are usually two conditions that are required for free will:

1 There is an absence of determination when you deliberate over alternative courses of action. You are able to select your priorities, allow certain parts of your character to predominate, and to control other aspects of your personality.

2 You are then able to act on your decisions according to the determination of your will. In other words, you are doing what you want, with few external constraints.

The problem of free will begins when point 1 is challenged. It may be argued that in fact you could *not* have acted otherwise. All of your desires and motives are determined, they are caused by prior conditions,

Key terms

Cause and effect: the principle of causality states that every event and every change has a cause. It is supposed to apply without any exceptions.

Determinism: the theory that given a determinate set of conditions, only one outcome is possible because of the laws of nature. This applies as much to human behaviour and human decisions as it does to physical events such as a famine.

which in turn were necessitated by even more prior conditions. Perhaps all of our decisions, choices and behaviours are subject to natural laws, and particularly to the scientific assumption of **cause and effect**. In the physical world, we know for example that if we throw a brick at a window it will shatter. The effect of the breaking window inevitably follows from the cause – throwing the brick. Perhaps in the same way (and just like animals), our desires are caused by previous experiences. To sum up, all of our choices, decisions, intentions, other mental events, and our actions are no more than inevitable effects, caused by other equally necessitated events.

This account of human decision making is called **determinism** and is the subject of our first topic. The opposite of this view is indeterminism: that human actions are outside the causal chain of events. The decisions that human beings make are not entirely the result of prior conditions, but are based on reasons. In that respect, we are different from the rest of nature. The issue of determinism has very serious implications for moral responsibility. How can we praise or blame someone if in fact they could not have acted otherwise. What if their behaviour is the result of a long chain of causes that go back beyond their childhood to before their birth! How could we hold them responsible for their actions, and what would be a justification for punishment. These implications of the free-will/ determinism debate are discussed in the topic on 'The implications of determinism' below.

💡 What is determinism?

The philosopher Spinoza claimed that men think themselves free because they are conscious of their actions but ignorant of their causes. We might *feel free* because we are aware of deliberating and choosing our actions, but in reality we are just ignorant of the fact that the outcome of our choices was inevitable. We may be aware of competing desires in our deliberation, but the strongest desire predominates. And the strongest desire is the result of complex causes in our history. As Russell expressed it, 'we can act as we please, but we may not please as we please' (Hospers, 1956). So those internal factors on the right-hand side in the Friday-night decision above are as compelled as any of the restraints on the left-hand side. There was only ever going to be one decision that you would make. The sense of free will was illusory.

Consider your own personality and behaviour. Can you suggest examples of how any of the following have determined who you are?

- genetic programming
- character traits inherited from parents
- social conditioning at home and school
- the food you eat
- moral education and religion
- your relationships
- childhood experiences
- money and class
- your neighbourhood and its facilities.

For example, certain foods cause some people to be hyperactive.

This is by no means a complete list, but determinism claims that if we had 'a God's eye view', we could list all of the causal factors in your past history, and show that for *every* decision and *every* action you could not have done otherwise. Your behaviour could not have occurred other than it did.

Furthermore, we could accurately predict what you will do in the future. If we had knowledge of all the prior conditions, your future acts would be entirely predictable, as they will be the inevitable result of your genetic, environmental and social conditioning. An all-knowing intelligence could assess the effects of each of your actions and how it will cause your next action. Baron d'Holback (1729–89) in *System of Nature* summarises this denial of free will as follows:

> Man's life is a line that nature commands him to describe upon the surface of the earth, without his ever being able to swerve from it, even for an instant. He is born without his own consent; his organization does in no wise depend upon himself; his ideas come to him involuntarily; his habits are in the power of those who cause him to contract them; he is unceasingly modified by causes, whether visible or concealed, over which he has no control, which necessarily regulate his mode of existence, give the hue to his way of thinking, and determine his manner of acting. He is good or bad, happy or miserable, wise or foolish, reasonable or irrational, without his will being for anything in these various states. Nevertheless, in spite of the shackles by which he is bound, it is pretended that he is a free agent, or that independently of causes by which he is moved, he determines his own will, and regulates his own condition.

quoted in **Hospers** *(1956)*

Thus instead of our actions resulting from free choices, we are simply following biological and psychological laws and even moral choices are determined by social conditioning – we are in effect 'just obeying orders'. Nazism, Chairman Mao's communism and some religious fundamentalism are extreme versions of the socialisation that we all experience. As children, we are **introjected** with values about relationships, lifestyles, etc. to control our responses in order to fit the social system. As we are creatures programmed to accept the behavioural norms of the group, whenever the cues in the environment appear, we cannot help but respond to our conditioning. Teaching, parenting and behaviour management programmes are all examples of social conditioning that we find acceptable. But can we distinguish this from brainwashing and indoctrination? Can you suggest differences?

If our behaviour is biologically, psychologically and socially caused, then free will must be an illusion.

Various philosophical theories have contributed to the debate on free will and determinism and these are presented for your consideration below:

1 The issue of predestination in philosophy of religion
2 Physicalism in philosophy of mind
3 Marx's economic and historical determinism in political philosophy.

The following three sections illustrate different versions of determinism: religious, biochemical, and social and psychological.

Predestination

In the philosophy of religion, one of the characteristics ascribed to God is omniscience. He is 'all knowing' and this includes knowledge of the future. So God will know the future of each one of us and whether we

Think about

The implication here is that your actions necessarily happen. But what do we mean by 'necessary'? Not logically necessary, or necessary because of some scientific law? See Hume in the 'What is free will?' topic below, and contingency.

Key terms

Introjected: unconsciously internalised values that originated externally.

Key terms

Autonomous: having self-rule and self-determination. So a person is the sole author of his or her decisions, a free agent able to choose his/her desires and moral law.

Necessarily: in this context is 'logically necessary'. It logically follows from the concept of omniscience, that God knows our future.

Fig. 10.2 *Omniscience*

Fig. 10.3 *Fatalism*

Key terms

Fatalism: as all events are predetermined, any attempt to change the future is futile. You may as well not bother to do anything.

will be morally good or not. In fact, God therefore has already *decided* who will be saved and who will not. In that case, we do not seem to be **autonomous** moral agents. We cannot choose to be saved as all of our future actions are already known in advance. God will therefore know whether you will be faced with temptation to cheat in your A-level exams and what you will decide to do!

Predestination can be distinguished from scientific determinism in that it does not depend on the scientific laws of cause and effect. While theories of social and biological conditioning rest on there being an antecedent cause which necessitates the effect, predestination need not assume this scientific model of world events. It only implies that God has knowledge of how the future will unfold. Nevertheless, if you choose an alternative to what God knows, God's belief would be false, which cannot be if God is omniscient. His foresight can be summarised as follows:

- God knows our future
- thus our future must **necessarily** happen
- therefore we cannot change our future.

So the question is, 'Do we have free will?'

There are two different responses to the question which either reject or retain the case for free will. You might reject the case for free will:

'How can I be free and responsible if God has already chosen what I am going to do? It is not just a coincidence or a lucky guess by God. In knowing my future, God has ordained and decreed what my life is going to be like, everything that will happen to me and every decision I am going to make. And finally He already knows whether I am going to heaven or hell! I cannot even repent unless that is part of the story, the destiny I have been given. How then can I be called free?'

Or you might retain it:

'Just because God can see into the future, that does not preclude that I am going to make free choices. God has not *decided* which way I will choose, He is just so wise and foreseeing that He knows which path I will choose to take. I will not be forced or caused to act one way or another, but God foresees what I will freely decide, because he knows all of the different paths and every aspect of my character and my projects. So I can freely make my decisions, but God already knows what I will do!'

Which account do you accept?

It may be concluded that as God is all-knowing, it is logically necessary that He knows our future. But the content of that future depends on or is contingent on what we decide to do. So there is no independent necessity about what we choose.

Fatalism

If you decided to reject the case for free will then it might be tempting to be fatalistic:

'Since God has decided in advance, then it does not matter what I do, my future will happen whatever. There is only going to be one result, so what I do makes no difference.'

A distinction needs to be made between **fatalism** and determinism or predestination. Fatalism has a very different approach to causation or moral agency.

Fatalism claims that our future will happen whatever actions we perform. So even if you act differently, (for example, do nothing at all, as you cannot be bothered), the result will be the same. Either the bullet has my name on it or it does not, so there is no point in me trying to avoid it or defending myself. My action is causally ineffective. Thus fatalism actually *denies* the causal connection between my actions and the future. But in fact, whether you defend yourself or not determines whether the bullet has your name on it. Determinism *affirms* the causal connection between our decisions and our future. My decision is part of the causal chain which determines the future, and whether I will be in a position whereby the bullet will hit me or not.

Similarly, predestination does not entail a fatalistic outlook. The fact that God knows my future does not mean that I should not make free and responsible decisions at the time. What we choose is still (morally) significant in the grand scheme of things, and fatalism is simply an attempt to avoid responsibility. God may already know whether I will avoid the bullet, but I still have to make a choice. And doing nothing is still a choice!

At the penalty shoot out, who has a fatalistic attitude and is avoiding responsibility?

- Player A: 'That is typical me! I always crack under pressure.'
- Player B: 'If I had shot to the near post, I would have scored.'
- Player C: 'We were always going to lose this game. We are just no good.'

The mind is the brain

In the philosophy of mind, a central issue is 'What is the human mind?'. Modern answers tend towards **physicalism**, and one account claims that mental states such as dreaming, believing and deliberating, etc. are identical with processes in the central nervous system – essentially the brain. This is not to deny that talk of emotions or rationality is meaningful, but **ontologically**, mind states are neural activity, electrochemical signals in the brain.

Comparisons are often made with the physical world. We often talk about the fluidity or beauty of waters, or the powerful effects of thunder and lightning, but this is reducible to the behaviour of water molecules and electrical discharges in the atmosphere. So pain, for example, is the firing of C-fibres in the brain.

So one answer to the question, 'What is the mind?' is that it is just one substance – the physical brain, and no mysterious mind substance which somehow exists as an immaterial (i.e. not made of matter) entity. This theory neatly accounts for our interaction with the environment. It explains, for example, how physical events such as drug taking or brain damage affect our mental operations and accords with the scientific research and brain scans which seek to reduce mental events to operations of the brain.

However, there are also important implications for free will. How can a physical account of the mind avoid the conclusion that we are determined? Physics, chemistry and biology explain the world in terms of cause and effect and if human behaviour can be reduced to the effects of electrochemical activity in the brain, and consequent language, then human activity is determined by the natural laws of the sciences. Human thought itself conforms to the laws governing chemicals and electricity.

Key terms

Physicalism: that everything described as mental activity can be reduced to physical events, e.g. happiness is neurones firing in the brain. However, not all modern theories are reductive, but mental states can be regarded as nothing but brain activity.

Ontologically: refers to what ultimately exists. Literally it means 'being'.

■ Key philosopher

Patricia Churchland (1943–)

Churchland is an American philosopher renowned for her study of the brain and its implications for philosophy of mind (sometimes referred to as 'neurophilosophy').

Patricia Churchland in her article, 'Do we have free will?' (2006) illustrates and explains this model. She tells the story of a Virginian man in 2003, whose sudden depraved sexual desires were traced to a tumour on the brain, and when the tumour was removed his sexual interests returned to normal. But as a new tumour grew, his sexual focus on young girls returned. The tumour was acting on hormones which regulate neural activity in a part of the brain. Other chemicals such as peptide oxytocin mediate maternal attachment in mothers and the density of 'peptide-binding sites' probably stimulate a man to be monogamous or polygamous.

So how, in the light of these continual discoveries, can we talk of free will? There is a clear chain of cause and effect between the physical environment, mental/brain activity and behaviour. Moreover, scientists have not found a discrete neural network or part of the brain that constitutes the will. So we cannot locate our 'free agency' in a part of the brain, and of course that would not help anyway as then our will would also be subject to the natural laws of scientific causation.

Patricia Churchland provides a possible solution to our feeling of free will in the notion of 'control' and this is discussed in the next topic. But for the moment, it would seem that any control mechanism will still be neural activity in the brain, and therefore still subject to physical laws.

Clearly, however, we could also reject this physicalist theory, and although only the briefest account has been given here, some relevant criticisms will be raised. A case for and against is presented for you to decide.

Against the physicalist theory

Critics claim that physicalism will never be able to adequately explain integral features of mental life, features which could be relevant to free will. What goes on in our minds is private, subjective and intentional.

This view claims that mental states are not identical with brain states. So pain is not identical with a C-fibre stimulation.

However much we look at brain scans or analyse brain activity, we still do not know what someone is feeling. That private, personal knowledge cannot be part of the public electrochemical activity. The dentist or doctor might believe you are not feeling pain because of injections or X-ray results, but they cannot ignore your cries of distress if you say you are in pain. Everyone has first-person authority with regard to their mental states which overrides the public claims about brain states.

Furthermore, there is a subjectivity about mental states that needs to be explained by the theory. Assuming a 'love chemical' exists, and I could be made to feel love, it is questionable whether all of the thousands of delicate nuances of love, e.g. love for my father, mistress, Paris, alcohol, etc., let alone the countless differences in individual feelings, could be accounted for by alteration in chemicals. Precisely how something feels to me – subjectivity – still needs to be translated into the language of chemicals.

Finally, there is a debate over intentionality. Free will entails that we have an attitude towards something and we choose it or not. The term 'intentionality' means that our thoughts and feelings are *directed at* things, they are *about* something. Our dreams, beliefs, etc. always *represent* something in a particular way. I would not like to confuse my love for my mistress with my love for my dog! Chemicals do not exhibit intentionality. Chemicals just are, they are not about anything. Neurones firing do not exhibit an attitude and are not directed at anything. Again the theory needs to explain how the laws of physics and chemistry can be identified with all of the sophisticated attitudes that human beings adopt.

It is integral to free decision making that we direct our thoughts at objects and compare purposes and goals. We consider our attitudes to rules and make subjective choices that cannot be accommodated by chemical analysis.

For the physicalist theory

Nevertheless, we might consider what a sophisticated computer is capable of or might be capable of. Could computers one day be subjective and develop beliefs and attitudes? If these mental processes could be reduced or translated into the complex language of computer programming which is realised in the brain, the objections above might be answered.

One final experiment is worth considering. Benjamin Libet set up an experiment to monitor the electrical impulses in the brain at the moment we make a conscious decision. The experiment was carried out by Libet at the University of California (1985) and a fuller account can be found in various A-level psychology textbooks. He found that whenever a decision was made to move a hand, electrical activity took place in the cerebral cortex of the brain, on average 250–300 milliseconds before the decision. So is a conscious decision the product of an immediately prior brain event? At first, Libet seemed unwilling to accept this and still claimed that a conscious will would enable us to veto an action that was already decided on and begun. But what is the problem with this suggestion?

How do we decide?

Either the physicalist theory is wrong or inadequate: free will involves private thoughts, subjective attitudes to events, with preferences that are lawless and contra causal, and rational thinking dictated by logic and consistency, rather than brain activity; or even our feeling of free will is accounted for by causal sequences within the brain that obey the laws of physics, chemistry and biology?

An important distinction that may help, is whether brain activity *correlates* with mental states, or *causes* mental activity. When I calculate a mathematical problem, is that calculation caused by my brain states, and the correct answer is a product of electrochemical activity, or is the use of arithmetic a rational mind game with parallel activity in the brain?

Karl Marx – economic determination

One concern of political philosophy is the nature of power and authority, and when the exercise of power is legitimate. Such discussion involves an analysis of society and human nature, and Marx provides us with a supposedly scientific analysis in *The German Ideology* (1970b).

Essentially, Marx argues that people are a product of their economic circumstances, and his theory is a version of **materialism**. He emphasises that his subject is 'real active men in the flesh', not ideas and theories. So his analysis is grounded in the physical world and he is attempting a scientific analysis of human behaviour.

Human beings have needs, e.g. food, shelter, etc., like animals do. But unlike animals, they 'produce the means of their subsistence', in other words, they *work* in order to satisfy their needs. So instead of just

Key philosopher

Karl Marx (1818–83)

Marx was author of *The Communist Manifesto*, and other famous works. He claimed in *The German Ideology* that the point of philosophy was not to interpret the world, but to change it.

Key terms

Materialism: matter alone exists, and ideas and mental activity are entirely dependent on physical conditions.

collecting food, humans grow it. In their work they take on a 'mode of life'. Thus, for example, a miner would be working in harsh, dangerous, dirty conditions and meet few people, while a shopkeeper needs to be clean and sociable to everyone. Hence your work and your mode of life determine your social relations: who you are and how you relate to others, 'the relations of individuals to one another'.

So, to a shopkeeper, the relation is one of service, while a teacher will need to be more authoritative. Division of labour will occur as people specialise in different kinds of work and that causes different 'modes of cooperation', e.g. boss to worker, mother to father. These differing work practices, lifestyles and relationships lead to the development of differing ideas, consciousness and language. Eventually differing moralities, politics and attitudes to religion and philosophy emerge. In other words, various ideologies develop.

So, Marx sees all consciousness as 'reflexes and echoes of this life process'. He concludes that, 'Life is not determined by consciousness, but consciousness by life' (1970b). So who we are and who we relate to (our sense of identity) and how we think are determined by our working life, our economic activity. Because of division of labour, people's social relationships and conscious thought vary and we become members of a class, with collective, class consciousness.

Are you a typical student?

Can you trace a connection between the way you work, the kind of lifestyle you have, the kind of people you meet and socialise with, and the way you think, your attitudes and interests?

So, if you were to vote at the next election, your supposedly free vote would have been determined by your upbringing, which in turn is determined by the economic circumstances of you and your family! Would you agree?

This brief interpretation of Marx may be regarded as one-sided, and elsewhere in *The German Ideology* he admits, 'circumstances make men, just as much *as men make circumstances*' [author emphasis]. So the relationship between our economic life and how we choose and think is more dynamic than just passive determinism. Nevertheless, the driving force which determines social structure, our ideology and the progress of history is the economic conditions and our social conditioning. We shall examine Sartre's opposition to Marxist materialism in the next topic, but after his lecture 'Existentialism and Humanism', Sartre's opponent the Marxist Mr Naville, says: 'the physical and biological universe is a source of conditioning ... even as the mother conditions her child, there are laws of the functioning of Man ... a whole network of causality of which he cannot grasp all the effects' (quoted in Sartre, 1948/1974).

There has been considerable debate about whether Marx has discovered a scientific law about the functioning of human beings or just a widespread trend that influences our decision making. The former would preclude free will as we are determined by social forces, while the latter view would talk of inclinations rather than causal determinism. The debate could be presented as a historical issue, either for or against Marx. This is an important distinction that might help you decide about Marx. Has he discovered *laws* of human behaviour or just *trends*? The latter allows us 'to swim against the tide'.

For Marx

If Marx is right, then the great events of history such as the French Revolution, the Second World War and the current invasion of Iraq have not ultimately been caused by the free decisions of great leaders and philosophies, but by economic and social circumstances. Thus the rise of the Nazis could be traced to the economic depression of the 1930s, and the war in Iraq to the need for oil and stable industry. Marx would describe these as inevitable crises in capitalism as there is global competition for scarce resources. This is bound to happen, and the decisions of leaders are the inevitable result of economic circumstances. So the decisions of leaders reflect the conditions of society rather then autonomous judgements. As material beings, although we are changers of circumstances, in the first instance it is material needs that condition us and these 'can be verified in a purely empirical way' (Sartre, 1948/1974).

Against Marx

On the other hand, history has been shaped by the personal contribution of great leaders and thinkers. Surely the mindset of Hitler or Blair, coupled with the great philosophical and religious thinkers, have determined events in the world. Here, philosophies are developed by free thinkers, developed through debate and discussion, with a life of their own. These ideas shape how leaders see the world. Thus the personality of Bush, influenced by religious beliefs, was the deciding factor in recent world events and these decisions were freely taken by leaders and thinkers, just as kings and queens in the Middle Ages imposed their values on their subjects. Thus it was Henry VIII's marriages and his strength of will that decided the history of Tudor England rather than determination by economic circumstances.

Which do you agree with?

In the first scenario, history is on a predictable path. In the second interpretation, the future depends on our freely willed decisions.

In support of determinism

In response to Marx, it may be felt that he has not done justice to our capacity to make decisions. Agreed that we might be heavily influenced by economic and social conditioning, but once I am aware of that I can choose to compensate, buck the trend or find various creative alternatives, as I wish.

One challenge to determinism, which will be considered in the next topic, is that social and psychological causes may incline us in a direction but do not necessitate effects. So:

1 I am quite capable of deciding differently *in exactly the same set of conditions*, and

2 my behaviour is not *compelled* by antecedent conditions.

As a conscious agent, *I* am the originator of actions. Hume's account of the nature of cause and effect, in the next topic, develops this point.

For now, we will just consider a possible determinist response. In regard to point 1, we never meet exactly the same set of conditions again. That is why you would act differently. The determinist would argue that at the time of the original decision, nobody could have behaved differently. In that instance, no other behaviour was available, given your character and the situation. So Marx would claim that any attempt to ignore our economic conditioning is itself determined by our working environment. Philosophy itself is a product of our social relations.

In response to point 2, although we do not *feel* that we are part of the causal chain, we are. The feeling of human agency, of originating actions, is firstly because we have complex desires and competing intentions and we deliberate and weigh them up. But in the end, the strongest desire was determined. Also, we are not aware of how our actions are caused. There will be a whole series of complex causes, for example, which lead to an artist creating an original picture, many of which he/she will not be aware of. But they are there and biographers and historians will uncover them. Psychiatrists, sociologists, anthropologists and economists could all describe the causal chain that led to the creative act. With that knowledge, we could demonstrate that the artist could not have done other than paint that picture.

This defence of determinism should also dispel the fear that the theory entails that human beings are trapped in some robotic, iron groove of behaviour, and that I can never be out of character, unpredictable or different. Just because my decisions are caused by previous experiences, it does not mean that new desires cannot develop, old desires cannot fade, or that I cannot spawn a new personality. Everything that we expect of a complex and developing character remains. Determinism just claims that all of the developments so far have been caused, and that your present behaviour will be the partial cause of your future actions together with the environment, etc. If we could ever assimilate all of the causes, we would be able to predict what will happen to you.

Think about

The determinist position

Below are six objections to the determinist position. Write down how you think a determinist would reply in order to defend their view. Suggested answers appear at the end of the topic.

1 'Once I know that I am likely to do X, I can change my mind. So if I know I talk like my mother, I can change the way I talk.'
2 'There is always a choice. However constraining the situation, I can negate it. So I know I did badly in my last exams, but I am going to make up for it this time around.'
3 'I deliberated over whether to go on holiday or work for a charity in my gap year. I considered the consequences of both courses of action and freely chose to go on holiday.'
4 'Once you predict what I will do, I will deliberately do the opposite.'
5 'Despite being poor, lots of working-class people still support capitalism and vote Conservative.'
6 'I am a rational being. My decisions are not dictated by chemicals interacting in the brain, they are about logic and reason.'

Is there any possible state of affairs that would count against determinism?

Will this imply that we never know why we have performed a particular action, although someone else will? Consider the case of the safe blower. A man is imprisoned for safe blowing and completes a degree in sociology while in prison. 'Oh, so he no longer blows safes?' says a partner in crime. 'Yes, he does', says another, 'only now he knows why he does it.'

Against determinism

The 'Introduction to libertarianism' topic below considers a more detailed case against determinism and for libertarianism, so we will just finish with brief challenges to the theory.

One difficulty to be overcome is how we distinguish the degree of inner compulsion in our mental events. If we are causally necessitated to act in a certain way, then how is that to be distinguished from compulsive behaviours that we would call psychological obsession or brainwashing?

For the sake of responsibility we need to distinguish the kleptomaniac from the thief, but in both cases desires are determined by antecedent conditions. In *Issues in Philosophy*, Pinchin (1990) asks how we separate shellshock from cowardice. Unless behavioural scientists can show in what way they are different, with some account of free will or control in the cases of cowardice and theft, then our theories of punishment will need to be completely changed.

So in the next topic we need to consider what exactly we mean by human agency. We should also question the model, that our character or our desires cause our behaviour. What do we mean by causation? Do desires cause actions? Is there any kind of power except causal power? One possibility is to distinguish between causes and reasons. When asked why you did something, do you respond 'because of my social conditioning' or 'because it is in my future interests'?

A second difficulty is how to decide the criteria on which to judge the theory of determinism. The rise of anything else can be traced back to something in the past, but that does not entail that prior events *necessitated* future events. Certainly in the case of social conditioning, the thesis would need to demonstrate that social and economic factors *compel* us to behave in a certain way. This point will be returned to with Hume on cause and effect.

These issues among others are the subjects in the topic on libertarianism below.

Think about

The determinist position – answers

1. Your desire to be different from your mother is also caused by prior conditions. Your rebellion is also the result of previous experiences.

2. While you can always choose to negate a situation, whether you will actually choose to do this depends on your character, which is predetermined.

3. Your deliberations made you feel free because you balanced different motives and consequences, but the strongest desire was always going to win out.

4. Your very stubbornness is inherited from your family. It is a very predictable trait in your character.

5. The working-class people who support capitalism do so because of their poverty and the desire to be wealthy in the future. Marx refers to this seemingly strange belief as an example of 'false consciousness'.

6 Computers demonstrate logic and reason. Once they are programmed with facts, then logic is part of their language. If you want to emphasise that computers have to be programmed, well so perhaps are human beings. It is called education!

It seems that the only way we can answer this is by regarding determinism as either a theoretical assumption or metaphysical theory rather than an empirical one.

After working through this topic, you should:

- understand that determinism claims that our actions are inevitable, given the fixed laws of nature
- understand that fatalism is the opposite of determinism, because it denies that what we do will causally change the future
- distinguish between pre-destination which is knowledge of the future and determinism which is about the cause of future events
- be able to explain how human behaviour can be explained in terms of scientific laws.

What is free will?

Learning objectives:

- to understand libertarianism and how it differs from randomness
- to explore what we mean by decision making and choosing
- to understand how compatibilism or soft determinism reconciles determinism and free will
- to evaluate libertarianism and compatibilism.

■ Introduction to libertarianism

This topic considers two responses to the challenges of determinism:

- libertarianism
- compatibilism.

Libertarianism rejects the theory that desires determine choices. Instead, when we are confronted with a choice, we make a free decision. Causal determinism is part of the physical world, it is true of 'sticks and stones' but not of human reasoning. The act of deciding means that we can become the sole author of our actions. In a decision, we make a causally undetermined choice. Thus we can reject our desires, refashion our personality, and choose morality over self-interest.

Which of the following actions suggest such a free decision?

- donating money to charity
- a judge agonising over a sentence for a teenage murderer
- choosing which A Level subjects to study
- the Pope deciding to restrict abortion
- an employer treating all job applicants impartially.

In those cases where a free choice is indicated, two factors may be regarded as significant:

a it was in my power to act in any number of different ways

b I was able to reason over the decision and exercise control over my desires,

and a third consideration is added:

c I was able to act according to my decision, without hindrance or coercion.

We shall refer to these three factors throughout this topic. Points A and B concern the right-hand side of the Friday-night decision, the internal factors, and point C concerns the left-hand side or external factors. For the libertarian, all three are necessary to give real meaning to 'I could have done otherwise'. The future is entirely open. As Sartre (1948/1974) says, 'a virgin future awaits', instead of Schopenhauer's claim that, 'the whole course of a man's life … is necessarily predetermined as the course of a clock' (quoted in Durrant, 1926). If points A and B are true, I am autonomous – able to select between competing desires and reasons. Some philosophers describe this as the liberty of indifference. It emphasises that I could have done otherwise, in so much that every alternative was possible and open.

Randomness

Libertarians do not want to claim that the opposite of determinism is **indeterminism**, that things happen randomly. What is needed for genuine freedom and responsibility is *self*-determination, the power of free choice to control which actions we perform. Free will is regarded as a non-causal power, but a power that links the person to the action so that they can be held to account.

In denying causality, **randomness** destroys the importance of human agency and decision making. Imagine the following unlikely scenario.

Just as I reach for a hammer, a clap of thunder throws me off balance, I knock into my brother, who drops an iron on his foot and screams. On hearing the scream, my mother spills scalding water onto the cat who lets go of the mouse it has captured. The mouse runs out of the house and scares the next-door neighbour, who has a heart attack and dies. The point is that the more chance happenings and coincidences that occur, the less likely it is that anyone will be held responsible. What is missing is a deliberate decision which results in the death of the next-door neighbour.

Quantum physics

Any appeals to quantum physics to rescue us from determinism are ineffectual. Recent discoveries in science suggest that, at the level of small subatomic particles, the motion of these particles is random and indeterministic. This is not helpful to the libertarianism case for two reasons:

- Although at the microscopic level there is a lack of determinism, everything mentioned in the first topic points to determinism at the macro level. The behaviour of microscopic particles does not alter the fact that taking drugs alters our mental state. At the level of the brain, randomness is *not* evident – the molecular behaviour of the brain shows habitual, regular patterns. However, this inconsistency could have repercussions for the presuppositions of science. We might have to qualify that every event has a cause.

Key terms

Indeterminism: the view that some events are not causally determined; it implies the possibility of randomness.

Randomness: lacking any definite plan or order.

■ Randomness also destroys human agency, control and responsibility. The essence of the libertarianism case is that individuals own their decisions, they are self-determined, they have power over their behaviour.

It is worth noting that the word 'chance' does not necessarily mean an absence of causation. In order to clarify, here are three uses of the word 'chance' that are perfectly compatible with a causal and deterministic view of the world.

■ Coincidence – two events happened from separate causes but with the same result or at the same time.

■ Ignorance – something appears to be chancy only because we do not know the real cause.

■ Probability – winning the lottery seems to be a matter of chance and probability, but there are causes as to why some balls are selected and not others.

The libertarian position does not resort to possibilities of randomness, therefore, and nor does it deny causal chains in the physical world. Clearly there are causes that make us catch a cold.

However, libertarianism claims that the exercise of practical reason enables us to escape from passive motivation, such as desire, because we impose our goals and our rules upon events. Decision making is causally undetermined because we exercise control over our desires.

Compatibilism accepts that motivation, desires and decisions are part of the causal chain, but claims that we are nevertheless still free. Thus causation and free will are compatible. This will be discussed later.

Neither libertarianism nor compatibilism resorts to the possibility of randomness.

It is worth noting that we talk of random *events*, but deliberate *actions*. Events are simply descriptions of occurrences, while actions have agents and arise out of willing, which implies intention. This is essential to the libertarian contention that we initiate our actions and are responsible for them. This distinction between events and actions is discussed in the next topic. For now, we could note the distinction between 'actions' and bodily movement. When we describe someone's behaviour, we do talk about bodily movement, e.g. 'she screamed … she ran away'. But when we describe 'action' (for which we are usually accountable) we also refer to intentions, reasons and control. Bodily movement can be explained in terms of muscular structure and the nature of the skeleton which obey the laws of physics, but that would entirely omit the conscious thought that marks out an action from reflex movement.

■ What is libertarianism?

The theory claims that human agency, free decision making removes us from any causal chain. This is demonstrated in our capacity to reason, to consider goals and purposes, to apply rules, to be flexible in our approach to phenomena, and is evident in our inquisitiveness and invention. Human beings are able to envisage a range of possibilities and select from any of them. This confirms criteria A and B in our understanding of 'I could have done otherwise'. Unlike animals, we are not tied to the immediate present, we can envisage different futures and choose the most beneficial.

So how can I escape from social conditioning and antecedent desires? By the exercise of practical reason. Some conditions of my existence are inevitable, e.g. that physically I will resemble my parents. But that does not mean that all consequences are unavoidable. I can choose how I respond to my inheritance. When faced with a decision, I can develop a number of mental strategies. I can consider the rules that surround the decision (social, parental or theoretical) and test for consistency: is my action going to conform to one set of rules or not? I can then consider my long-term goals: are they relevant? I can imagine what a particular cultural group would do and judge consequences. Then I might start to construct a justification of what I will do, based on how rational, consistent, relevant and persuasive the arguments are. All these semi-rational mental acts bring the causal chain of desires under control. They again pinpoint the difference between us and most animals, because in order to perform these mental operations, it is necessary to develop self-awareness, imagination, foresight, intellectual capabilities and (most importantly) language. It is only with language that we can construct and evaluate the beliefs which will inform our action.

This is the theory of human agency. A decision is quite different from obeying a strong desire. Instead of looking backwards to prior causes, we look forwards to consider our purposes and goals and what we wish to attain in the future. In contrast to determinism where a decision was a passive affair, following our desires when the strongest desire emerged, libertarians propose an active model where we can detach ourselves from desires through deliberation and consideration. Thus on Friday night, I had to reason about priorities: finishing a project, meeting a friend or seeing a band. These will have been directed towards long-term goals (going on to higher education, developing a relationship, etc.), and these in turn relate to how I see myself (my sense of identity in comparison with the norms and values of society). I may even have tried to universalise my motives – if it is right for me then it is right for everyone else. So instead of searching for *causes* of our actions, we are looking for *reasons*.

Think about

Consider the following lists. Which would you label 'causes' and which 'reasons'?

Outside our control	Under our control
Can be objectively explained	A matter of opinion
Discoverable	Discussible
Externally created	Internally generated
Considers prior events	Looks to future possibilities
Follows uniform laws	Can involve lawless speculation

The distinction between causes and reasons is considered in more detail in the next topic below.

Pink in *Free Will* summarises the case for human agency:

> a decision is not any ordinary motivation. It is quite different from an ordinary desire ... a decision aims at something, considers ... principles and the chances of reaching that attainment.

Pink (2004)

Key philosopher

Thomas Pink

Pink is a lecturer in philosophy at King's College, London.

This emphasis on goals and purposes in decision making, rather than causes, accounts for self-motivation and responsibility. Pink says, 'the mental event (of decision making) is causally undetermined but controlled'. He argues for two kinds of power:

- causal power which applies to the physical universe
- the capacity for independent, self-determination.

This is the capacity to respond to reasons, to take an action which is goal directed or rule governed, and which can be justified. This power, the exercise of practical reason, is active, rather than the passive motivation caused by a desire. It enables us to exert control over our desires, even frustrate our desires if we wish. Thus the threat of determinism is lifted. Our actions are no longer the inevitable result of some freedom – threatening causal force, that is not the agent's doing. It is now our own motivation, achieved through deliberation, that gives our actions intelligibility and 'end' direction. Instead of asking *how* we decided something and looking for causes, we ask *why* we decided and look for reasons. This, it should be noted, contrasts with the compatibilist approach offered by Hume, which reduces the power of freedom to causal power, and is discussed in the second part of the chapter.

Furthermore it must be emphasised that my free will is not only exercised in the act of making the decision, but also in the act itself. In deciding to buy chocolate, not only do I weigh up the issues and goals, but my free will is evident throughout the act in that I deliberately enter the shop and purchase the goods. The whole character of my actions expresses my free decision, i.e. purposeful, unhesitating, focused.

Two more detailed theories that advocate a version of libertarianism will now be developed. The first, Descartes' dualism, is a contrast to physicalism and the second, from Sartre, is a response to deterministic theories of psychology and sociology.

Descartes and dualism

Descartes offers an account of mind which is free from causal laws or 'the bogey of mechanism' (Ryle, 1949). Each person consists of a mind and a body – two substances, and hence **dualism**. Our bodies operate like machines and are part of the material world. But also, there is the immaterial world of the mind. The mind, not being made of matter, is a world free from determinism. Thoughts are non-physical, non-spatial and subject to their own laws (reason, association compounding, simplifying), hence they must exist in a mental life distinct from the body. The acts of deciding and willing are free, 'the power of the will consists only in this, that we are able to do or not to do the same thing … that we are not conscious of being determined to a particular action by any external force' (Descartes, 1965). This model also allows for thoughts to be private, subjective and intentional – the qualities that are difficult to account for in physicalism (in the first topic above).

So, for Descartes, in a decision, there is an act of cognition (acquiring knowledge) followed by the willing ('that election or the power of free choice'). The will is a separate faculty from the rational faculty which makes judgements. It may be remembered that physicalism failed to find a part of the brain that constituted the will. So whether the will is or is not a separate faculty is a clear point of contention. If we accept Descartes, we first make a judgement, then form a clear intention, then we will the action, which then causes the body to move in a particular way. It can be represented as follows:

Key terms

Dualism: the theory that the nature of mind is a pure, thinking substance, which is distinct from the body. Human beings therefore consist of two substances – the immaterial mind and the material body.

Judgement → intention → volition → act

He deserves to die → think 'must kill' → decide to kill → pull the trigger

A challenge to this model is discussed in the next topic as well as the points which follow.

There are several problems with this account. The first is the well-known problem of interaction. If volition (willing) takes place in a mysterious, mental realm, then how does it communicate with the body in the material world? How does spirit affect matter? We know how matter affects matter – through cause and effect – but how does non-matter affect matter? It would defy all of the known laws of science, and is in fact a problem Descartes was never able to solve. Indeed, he emphasises the differences between mind and body, which increases the problem of interaction.

A related problem is how to make sense of willing and the faculty of willing. We understand judgement in terms of preferences for 'a' rather than 'b', and accompanying reasons. But how do we understand 'willing'? Surely the only answer is whether an act is voluntary or non-voluntary. I know that you wanted to do something because you were not coerced, acting under duress or panic, but still carried out the action. According to Ryle (1949), we do not need to posit some mysterious faculty. Voluntary or 'willed' actions are simply *the way* in which an action is performed. By an effort of will is meant 'a particular exercise of tenacity of purpose'.

This is part of Ryle's attack on Descartes' whole theory of mind: that it is a ghostly substance inhabiting a physical body. This is mocked as 'the ghost in the machine'. Ryle denies completely that there is such an immaterial substance. Instead of the mind being a hidden place, the mind is characterised as *how* we act. Descartes has made what Ryle calls a category mistake. He gives the illustration of a foreigner trying to understand cricket. He finally makes sense of batting, bowling, etc. but then asks, 'But where is the team spirit?' (a mental event). Ryle points out that team spirit is not 'a thing', ghostly and mysterious, but it is *how* one plays the game, the manner in which people behave. The same can be said of other mental qualities. Enthusiasm, depression and cleverness do not exist in a private realm called the mind, they are how we act, in other words they are characteristics of behaviour, and clearly visible in the physical world. In the next topic, more will be discussed about Ryle's account of free will.

So, Descartes' mind or soul is a mental realm free from determinism, because the mind is:

- not made of matter
- not detectable by the senses
- a substance that does not obey the laws of physics.

Sartre

Sartre acknowledges his roots in Descartes, but offers a modern approach to human freedom. He does not posit a mental substance in which free decisions take place. His account is founded in the nature of subjective consciousness. For example, if you are meeting your friend in a restaurant and they have not arrived you are conscious of their *absence*. You are aware that they are *not* there. This is how consciousness negates the world.

Sartre also presents the opposite view to Marx (see the first topic). For Sartre, 'consciousness determines life', in the words of Marx. Human

Key philosopher
Gilbert Ryle (1900–76)

A very influential critic of Descartes, Ryle argued against the Cartesian view of mind as a separate substance, which he called 'the ghost in the machine'. Mental terms, instead, refer to how we behave.

Think about

What arguments can you find to support or criticise this belief?

Key philosopher
Jean-Paul Sartre (1905–80)

Sartre was a French philosopher and novelist, and advocate of the philosophical tradition called existentialism. In *Existentialism and Humanism* he describes consciousness as not a thing and outside the causal order of the world. In his view, it was 'nothingness', the capacity to 'negate' any situation.

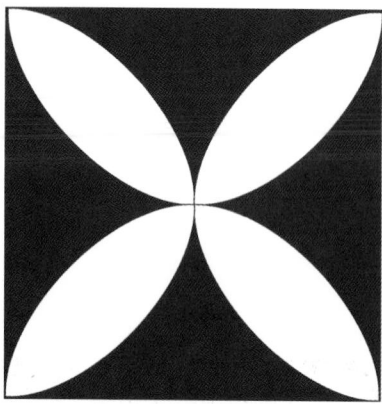

Fig. 10.4 *What do you see?*

life begins with awareness, more specifically 'self-awareness', and this is Sartre's one 'absolute truth'. Such awareness involves subjectivity and choice. Even the act of perception (looking at something) entails a private, personal selection of detail. In the introduction to *Existentialism and Humanism* (Sartre, 1948/1974), Mairet provides a simple exercise.

In Fig. 10.4, some of you will see white petal shapes and some will see an Iron cross. There will be reasons for what you see, but the fact is we see what we choose to see. Even our perceptions involve selecting what is significant according to our intentions. According to Sartre, we direct our attention at something according to our pattern of values. So looking at a cricket match, one person may see artistry and skill, while another may see 'nothing much happening'. So although we operate within a set of conditions, as outlined by Marx (the need for food, shelter and so on), Sartre maintains that we always have *a choice* how we interpret and respond to these conditions. This is **subjectivity**.

Man may seem to be 'made' by his past history and present situation, but it is these limitations which actually create our freedom. It is the presence of limitations that oblige us to choose. I cannot avoid *taking an attitude* to my past. I choose how I see it. So it can be viewed as an obstacle or an opportunity. I can reject my past or remain loyal to it, and by my future action I deny it or confirm it. We are all thus familiar with 'turning over a new leaf' or 'starting again' or 'new resolutions'. The past is, after all, just a present memory which we have chosen to recall, and we can let go of the past or not. Perhaps this too is the difference between human beings and animals. While their behaviour is a matter of habit, we reflect on the past and are aware of alternatives in the future. So our past does not determine our future.

At the heart of Sartre's concept of freedom is his account of the nature of consciousness. Integral to consciousness is the awareness of possibilities. I never merely look at an object, say a mouse. I see it as vermin, or food (for my cat) or as a pet, etc. I see the mouse as possibilities, which *I can affirm or negate*. The mouse might be of scientific interest or not depending on my project, my concerns and attitudes. I can even survey a scene and not respond to what *is* there, but what is not. Sartre retells going to his friend Pierre's room, but what he chooses to find significant is not the furniture or the books, but the *absence* of Pierre. Consciousness is not fixed like the world of objects, concrete and determined, but a subjective interpretation of the world. It is intentional. So I can be aware of my past and interpret and re-interpret it as a motive for action in the light of future behaviour. In this way, I am separated from my past – I can project onto my history a number of interpretations. So Sartre talks of 'the gap' between consciousness and the world. As human beings, we are continually detaching ourselves from the present and projecting towards the future. For example, I am aware that I am writing at this instant, but shall I continue, have a cup of coffee, or go for a walk? This *separation* from the present – *the gap* – constitutes our liberty, a choice of futures is continually presenting itself to us. So we choose our direction in life – our 'project'.

Thus the reply to the determinist is that I am not simply determined by the past. To remember a part of our history is also to be aware of alternatives in the future. Furthermore Sartre rejects entirely the model of desires and character determining our actions. As we have seen with Descartes, the theory that we first have desires and wills and these somehow lead to actions, raises all sorts of problems. For Sartre, the account is almost the reverse. *Desires do not determine actions; they are revealed by actions*. He asks, 'How do I estimate the strength of a feeling?' The answer is that I only know how I feel by the way I have acted. If I felt strongly, say, my behaviour would have been purposeful and determined. So my love for my mother does not cause my behaviour, my love is revealed by the way that I treat her. This completely rejects the idea of a causal chain, adopted by determinism. So the view that actions are caused by character and 'the strongest desire' is refuted. Instead we read someone's character and desires in the choices they make.

So for Sartre, we *choose our passions* and reveal them by how we act. Therefore we cannot claim that our action was caused by our passion. The existentialist 'will never regard a grand passion as a destructive torrent upon which Man is swept' (Sartre, 1948/1974). For example, if we are angry and strike someone, that involves a series of choices. Perhaps, we chose to acknowledge their presence, we chose to remember their previous actions, we chose to see their behaviour as confronting our own, we chose to see violence as the best outlet for our frustration and so on. We freely chose to become angry, and that anger did not cause our violence but was revealed by our striking the enemy. Sartre's conclusion is that 'feeling is formed by the deeds that one does'. Consequently we are entirely responsible for our actions.

> ## AQA Examiner's tip
>
> When trying to summarise a philosophical position, it may help to highlight key words. Here they have been put in italics.

Think about

Responsibility

We are 'without excuse', 'there is no determinism'.

What would Sartre say to these excuses in order to advocate free will and responsibility? (The page numbers refer to Sartre's treatment of the issue in his lecture *Existentialism and Humanism*.)

- I was only obeying orders (p31).
- God has planned our destiny (pp31, 27).
- I was advised by an expert to do it (p37).
- I cannot help it, I am not clever or attractive enough (pp38, 39).
- My behaviour is socially conditioned (p43 – the coward).
- It is reasonable! Reason dictates I do this (Kant pp27, 28).
- Subconscious impulses/genes determine behaviour (p34 – passion).

The answers are at the end of this topic.

So, for Sartre, even the most basic of social or biological conditions involves a choice. Although I may say, for example, that my race has determined my view of myself through the attitudes of others and 'because I am a Jew or black I shall be deprived of certain possibilities' (Sartre, 1984). Sartre's answer is that 'race is purely and simply an imaginary thing, a collective invention'. Race is not something set in stone, I am not compelled to see it as significant. He also makes similar claims about sexuality and the reader must judge whether the claims are convincing.

Thus for many, Sartre captures our inner experience of freedom. We encounter choice in our experience because we can always negate a situation, we can always say 'no'.

For free will

Sartre's case for free will is refreshing and positive and leaves individuals in charge of their destiny.

Although determinists will query whether we are free to let go of the past, as there are many instances of people living in the past or being unwilling to forget, Sartre's emphasis is on the future. The future is unique. No future situation will entirely resemble the past. Consequently interpretation of our new situation is always necessary. Thus the question 'Shall I repeat the past?' is always possible and this gives us the freedom to reject or affirm previous choices.

Similarly, even if we were to allow the influence of subconscious desires, we can still allow or repress them as we become aware of the conditions of our existence.

It is worth noting that Sartre would not have accepted Freud's psycho-analysis anyway. Freud (1856–1939) developed a theory of the unconscious mind, of buried desires and forces, shaping our behaviour without our awareness.

However, consciousness enables us to see beyond ourselves, 'man is not shut up in himself'. New potential lives are always present to us, and so the unconscious is filtered through the conscious. For example, the Oedipus complex, proposed by Freud, claims that young boys become sexually attracted to their mothers and sexually jealous of their fathers. Yet virtually all young men control this urge, which suggests even our deepest desires do not compel us to action.

Against free will

Sartre's insistence on liberty through individual choice is not without its critics. Firstly, what if I am not aware that I even have a choice. As a young child, I am not likely to be aware that disobeying my parents is an option. It would seem that a precondition of freedom is awareness of alternatives, and with strong social conditioning or limited practical resources in poverty stricken areas of the world that awareness may not exist.

Secondly, it might be argued that awareness of possibilities still does not provide realistic choices. Sartre states, 'there is always the possibility for the coward to give up cowardice', but that possibility will not necessarily translate into a real, active choice. There is a distinction between: (1) I had an alternative possibility to being a coward, yet did not refuse cowardice; and (2) in certain conditions I chose to be a coward. The second implies a considered decision, an intention. Sartre seems to conflate (1) and (2).

This leads to the issue for libertarians of what motivates action. After a story of a moral dilemma for his pupil, Sartre concludes that there is no answer and the young man must decide for himself. He says, 'nothing remains but to trust in our *instincts*' [author emphasis], and before that he agrees, 'my will is probably the manifestation of a prior and more spontaneous decision'. What interpretation are we to put on this? Clearly our choices are not just arbitrary. This decision would be a fundamental *choice* regarding my being in the world, but it will dictate and constrain the future direction of my project.

So at first sight it appears that previous decisions going back into childhood have determined what I now conceive of as possibilities, and that my instincts will move me in one direction or another. This looks far too like predetermination to be a satisfactory reading of his statements.

The second possibility is that Sartre believes in something like the power of practical reason, mentioned above. As well as causal power, decision making itself has a power that is non-causal. This denies that an action is caused by a prior desire, necessarily, but that an agent can decide for a future possibility, a goal, and this decision has the power to produce action. Thus he talks about acting in good faith, 'an attitude of strict consistency'.

Decision making as power

Is this credible? We are very familiar with causal power and we see it all around us all the time. We shall need to examine it more closely in the next section, but our whole world view is dependent on causes leading to effects. Libertarians also ask us to believe in another kind of power, the exercise of practical reason. Thomas Pink describes it thus:

> Clearly freedom – our capability to control how we act – is a power of some kind. After all, freedom leaves how we act up to us. Freedom leaves, as one might put it, how we act 'within our power'. Our control of our actions is just that: an action- and event-determining power.

Pink (2004)

The reader must decide whether this account of power is sufficiently convincing; or have we returned to some mysterious faculty of will? While it might be convincing that decision making is a form of control over our actions, do we want to accept that decisions have non-causal power to realise action? This issue will be returned to in the topic 'The implications of determinism' on p328.

Can we reconcile libertarianism and physicalism?

Before we leave libertarianism, it is worth considering the challenge of physicalism, and its apparently deterministic approach. Interestingly, Churchland also offers an account of self-control to compare with the exercise of practical reason and its power.

In her essay on free will, Churchland (2006) suggests that we need to 'update our ideas'. She derides the libertarian philosophy of looking for 'causal vacuums' as 'flat-earth philosophy'. Instead, she examines the nature of self-control. While we have no control over bodily functions, such as heart rate, there is an area of the brain, located in the pre-frontal cortex, which controls behaviour. From the beginning, human beings learn to inhibit behaviour, such as biting the mother instead of sucking, and eventually this leads to more obvious inhibiting behaviour to fit social norms. Interestingly, this is also apparent in some animal behaviour, blurring the distinction between the species. For example, a hungry chimpanzee will suppress his desire for a banana if he spots the alpha male, thus using cognition to control impulse. With much more complex brain capacity, human sensitivity to social rules is obviously much more sophisticated. In the light of previous points on the nature of consciousness, we must decide whether this account is meaningful.

Self-control can sometimes be limited by syndromes, so obsessive-compulsive disorders in the brain functioning compromise self-control. This would explain the differences between kleptomania and theft, although it would have implications for our understanding of responsibility and punishment.

How does this control happen?

Some neurones are apparently sensitive to reward and punishment and so, for example, exhibit fear responses. There are also regions of the brain where exploratory decisions are made, where evidence is considered and situations can be imagined. So through reward and punishment, traits of cooperation and orderliness can be imprinted on the brain and so decisions can be made on the grounds of benefit to the individual. Furthermore, complex brains create high-level neural patterns which make sense of the world and establish a sense of self and identity that is a precondition of self-esteem, which eventually guides our actions. So interactions of respect, love, accomplishment and achievement impact on our hormones and serotonin for example, and control neural activity. The more complex control we exercise, the more it begins to look like autonomy and that we choose our desires and our response by exercising sophisticated monitoring of our actions. This has to mean more than simply saying certain areas of the brain are active if we do these things.

Think about

- Would a libertarian be satisfied with this account of decision making?
- Is this scientific model of mental life satisfactory? For instance, consider a moral dilemma of whether to tell the truth or lie. Could you explain it in terms of reward, punishment and self-esteem?
- If we accept either libertarianism or determinism, what will be the issues for responsibility? (This is discussed in the topic below.)

Some may feel that this account of self-control begs the question. Whereas chemical reactions in the brain correlate with our responses, the language of reward and punishment cannot be reduced to chemical reactions. Fear and love can only make sense in a social context, where human beings understand the significance of social behaviour. The subjective and intentional nature of consciousness is omitted. Fear is only meaningful in the context of my hopes, goals and projects.

An introduction to compatibilism

An alternative approach to the issue of free will is to accept the thesis of determinism, that all our thoughts and desires are caused by previous experiences, but to maintain that we are nevertheless free. So freedom is compatible with determinism. This is sometimes referred to as soft determinism. Of the three criteria outlined at the beginning of the topic (page 313, points A, B and C) it is now point C which is regarded as significant.

Thus, we can accept the theory of determinism (thereby denying points A and B), but I am still free if I can act on my desires (point C). If I can carry out my wishes, without coercion or restraint or interference, then I can still be regarded as free, even though my choices were still the result of prior causes. So in the case of Friday night, my internal considerations (on the right-hand side) are determined, but I am still free if there are no or few external factors (on the left-hand side) which stop me from doing what I want. Thus soft determinism accepts that behaviour is brought about by genetic and environmental factors, but claims that we are nevertheless free, if we have the power of doing or refraining from an action according to our will. This freedom is sometimes referred to as 'the liberty of spontaneity'.

One of the chief proponents of **compatibilism** was the philosopher Hume.

So for Hume, freedom is 'doing what I desire' while for Sartre freedom is 'desiring what I do'. Can you see the difference?

For Sartre, one cannot avoid committing oneself, since we are constantly faced with choices (point A). One must act, and to act freely is to desire one's actions. So for Sartre, points A and B are necessary. For Hume only point C is necessary.

While it may be possible that freedom is compatible with determinism, it is not compatible with fatalism. Can you decide why?

What exactly is causation?

Before Hume reconciles liberty and determinism he first examines the nature of causality. As an empiricist, he examines his experience of cause and effect. So he considers a brick thrown at a window (event A) causing the effect of glass breaking (event B). The result is that he observes the cause (the movement of the brick) and he observes the effect (the shattering of the glass), but what he is unable to observe is the necessary connection that links the cause to the effect. What he actually sees is event A followed by event B, but not the 'secret tye' that means a brick in motion *must* shatter glass. The *connection* between a cause and an effect is so *not* evident that Hume concludes that Adam in his first days would never be able to predict what causes would determine what effects. He would never guess, without experience, that water would quench his thirst but could also drown him. He would have to experience these examples of cause and effect and become accustomed to the properties of water first. Reason alone could never inform us of the complex qualities of water. It would seem that for Hume there are no possible counter examples to the claim that all events are caused. His postulation of 'secret' causes seems to involve more than appeal to repetition or regularity.

Hume concludes that what creates the expectation that event A causes event B is the experience of 'constant conjunction' of the two events. Because we have always experienced moving bricks shattering glass windows, and they are constantly connected, we expect the event to happen as it does and say that the brick caused the glass to shatter.

These carry important implications for free will and determinism and what we understand by 'necessity'. For Hume, causes do not *compel* effects, they just are descriptions of the uniformity and regularity in our experience.

Logical necessity

When we consider logically necessary propositions, there is only one answer. Two balls plus two more balls amounts to four balls. It is absolutely necessary to reckon there are four balls. It must be right and no alternative is possible without being wrong or contradicting yourself. Similarly, if your mum is in the kitchen, she cannot be here with you in the garden. To suggest otherwise is also a contradiction.

However, this is not the case with cause and effect. It is not impossible to imagine a brick hitting a window and not shattering the glass – unlikely,

■ Think about

Which truths are necessary and which are contingent?

- Swallows fly south in winter.
- The angles of a triangle add up to 180 degrees.
- Recycling rubbish reduces global warming.
- Not all swans are white.
- You are either in love or not in love.
- Nothing can be blue all over and red all over.
- Smoking causes cancer.
- Today is yesterday's tomorrow.

■ Think about

Can you compare Hume's account of mental processes with Descartes'? Descartes had a problem of explaining the interaction of mind and body. For Hume we are like complex animals, part of the natural order. Has he solved the problem? It is worth reading section 9 of *The Enquiry* (Hume, 1999).

but we could not rule it out completely. When we consider mysterious events, where we have had less experience of constant conjunction, the possibility of various, different alternatives is even more convincing.

So for Hume, there is no **necessary** connection between events in the world, as there must be between 2 + 2 and 4. The world does not have to be this way, it is just that it happens to be so, and that we can see regular patterns of cause followed by effect, and few or no instances of event A not followed by event B.

Thus in the scientific account of the brain we see regular neural patterns of certain electrochemical impulses followed by other electrochemical impulses. However, there is no necessity in this pattern, alternative patterns are possible, so the behaviour of neurones is contingent rather than necessary.

This refined interpretation of cause and effect might in some sense reduce the impression of determinism that we are trapped in 'iron grooves' of behaviour. Our grooves are contingent and alternative grooves are at least hypothetically possible. So in one albeit narrow sense, our decisions and actions are not necessitated or compelled.

Uniformity

Although Hume may clarify our understanding of causal necessity, he himself believes that human actions are regular, and he stresses the 'constantly' in constantly conjoined: 'we acknowledge a uniformity in human motives as well as in the operations of the body' (Hume, 1999). Without this uniformity human life would be unable to function. He provides various examples of predictability in human behaviour, such as workers taking their goods to market, sure that they will sell them; the accounts in history of peoples who all share common motives and behaviours; and the determination of prison guards which are as fixed as the walls of the prison itself. His new definition of causation is, 'an object, followed by another, and where all objects similar to the first, are followed by objects, similar to the second … and if the first object had not been, the second never had existed' (Hume, 1999). So he is now able to bring physical events and human desires into one kind of operation. Our human thoughts are part of a connected chain, just like the principles of variation in the weather. Voluntary actions and natural causes are not two different kinds of operation, but just one connected chain, so that the physical events affect mental events and vice versa. So although we feel differently about human actions, that there is no sense of 'must', Hume has no explanation of why we should feel differently. For example, he traces a continuous chain of the prisoner led to the scaffold, the constancy of the guards, the refusal to allow his escape, the action of the executioner, his resolve, the separation of head from body, the convulsive movements and the bleeding as an interconnected sequence, both mental and physical combined. Both are just as regular and predictable. Although we might think human thoughts and actions are unpredictable or less regular than natural events, this is only because of 'the secret operation of contrary causes'. Whenever someone appears to have acted out of character, we always find that there are hidden causes for this that we did not know about.

As an example of the regularity and uniformity of human behaviour, both mental and physical, Hume cites his friend. When visiting his friend, he is as sure that the friend will not rob him as he is that the house will not fall down. Such has been the 'usual conduct of' his friend and houses. Based on past experiences, he has a strong belief in both. However, that is not to rule out the possibility that his friend may have a sudden frenzy, or that an earthquake will at that instant destroy the house. But here other hidden causes will explain both. So the behaviour of people and houses is uniform but not necessary. Other contingencies may happen. So in terms of our three criteria (A, B, C), Hume, despite his redefinition of cause and effect, accepts that our desires and thoughts are part of our social conditioning, the regular pattern of cause and effect, that forms our character and determines our actions. Points A and B are still denied. My will is determined by my character, and the uniform habits of my character are socially conditioned. Men 'take their measures from past experience, in the same manner as in their reasonings concerning external objects' (Hume, 1999). But the 'necessary connexion between past experiences and the will…' is not compulsion, but the same 'constant conjunction' which we mean when 'ascribing necessity to the determination of the will' (Hume, 1999). So for Hume, all determined really means is 'regular' and human actions are determined in the sense that certain motives and certain actions go together throughout history.

AQA Examiner's tip

Hume's account of human nature emphasises uniformity rather than necessity. Can you see the difference? However, because we are part of a natural chain of events, we are not autonomous.

So where is our free will?

However, Hume claims that our freedom lies in being able to carry out our desires without interference and restraint from external factors. Liberty is 'the power of acting, or not acting, according to the determination of the will'. Thus, 'if we choose to remain at rest, we may; if we choose to move, we also may'. This belongs to everyone who is 'not a prisoner and in chains' (Hume, 1999).

On this basis, freedom is not only compatible with determinism, it requires it. It is essential that our desires are not random, that they flow from our personality that is genuinely our own. And our personality or character is the sum total of the causal conditions that have created us. Freedom is the expression of this character, to act according to one's desires (rather than focus on the choice of desires). So if the cause of my action is my own desire, then I am free in the opinion of a compatibilist. If I join a club because I want to, that is free will. If I join a club because my parents make me, that is coercion. Non-freedom for a compatibilist is not being able to do what I desire because I am forced to do something else through physical restraint or coercive threats. Thus freedom is doing the following without interference:

- thinking what I like
- saying what I like
- doing what I like
- meeting whom I like
- going where I like.

It is 'doing what I desire' rather than 'choosing what I desire'. This is the liberty of spontaneity popularly described as 'doing what you want'.

Think about

Look at the actions below.

Which four decisions would a libertarian regard as free? Which five actions would a compatibilist regard as free even though a libertarian would claim no free decision was made?

- running away to join the army despite your parents' wishes

- reading careers material and having a careers interview to plan your future
- not allowing friends to talk you out of a bungee jump
- speaking your mind, frankly and without hesitation
- deciding what bank to put your money in
- not breaking a promise because of your moral principles
- drinking too much alcohol on a Friday night
- thinking for yourself and having different opinions from others
- playing truant from school.

Against Hume

The most important problem is that Hume's thesis cannot allow for an agent to act differently in the same circumstances. There would have to be a change in the circumstances. If no other action was possible, then how can it be described as free action?

The implications of compatibilism for responsibility are discussed in the topic 'The implications of determinism' below. However, an immediate problem is evident concerning my freedom to choose my desires. If, as the theory accepts, my character is determined, then how much freedom do I really have? Supposing that some young boys were brought up on a constant diet of violent videos, personal abuse and food that caused hyperactivity. These regular experiences would cause certain violent desires. Now if one day, they go out and torture a young child in order to relieve their anger and frustration, according to compatibilism the act was free. They carried out their wishes without hindrance. Yet many would say that their very limited upbringing seriously restricted their internal development. As they could not escape from limited social conditioning they were not free and had few real choices. This would be the libertarian criticism. Could Hume distinguish between the kleptomaniac and the thief?

Even if we feel free, because our actions are unconstrained, this is not a sufficient condition for 'actual freedom'. Supposing the boys had been regular drug takers and their brain functioning was impaired. Would they still be regarded as free agents? The criticism, according to the determinists, is that all of our actions are caused. Whether others interfere with us or not is a result of their determined actions, so compatibilism just hides from the underlying position that all human events are predetermined.

Also, for Hume, it seems the account of the mind is a passive one. We cannot actively control what we think and desire. The regular connection between motives, volitions and actions can be compared with the regular succession of events in the physical world. There is no significant difference 'between the effects which result from material force and those which arise from thought and intelligence' (Hume, 1999).

Thus the libertarian distinction between causal power and the power from exercising practical reason has disappeared. For Hume, internal and external is subsumed under causal power, albeit just as constantly conjoined events not *necessarily* connected. This to many would seem counter-intuitive. It does not sufficiently account for decision making, the ability to follow rules and select goals and examine arguments, which the libertarians highlight.

There is another problem with Hume's account of necessity in terms of regularity. To say that all necessary connections are regular does not imply that all regularities are necessary. (To say that all dogs have four legs does not imply that all things with four legs are dogs.)

For Hume

One suspects that Hume's reply would be that goals, purposes and rules are equally caused by previous desires. He sees a very limited role for the exercise of reason. You cannot rationally prove what people want, let alone what people *should* want. Their desires are uniform and predictable for the most part: success, happiness and respect, etc. If, because of an unusual system of causes, someone has a different goal or purpose, reason is powerless to change their mind: 'It is not contrary to reason to prefer the destruction of the whole world to the scratching of my finger' (Hume, 1969).

So our goals, our amenability to social rules and even our reasons are ultimately determined by our emotions and desires. The power of free decision making through the exercise of practical reason is mainly denied. We might be able to calculate the means to an end (how best to get what I want), but the actual ends, the goals and purposes, the choice of desires is for Hume a matter of emotion, part of the natural and regular pattern of cause and effect. Whether I live for football, my children, God or whatever, this is not something I can rationally decide, but it is the expression of my deepest instincts and feelings and needs.

Think about

The past two sections outlined three different positions to the debate over free will: determinism, libertarianism and compatibilism.

Can you identify these views from the statements below?

- 'Thoughts are just brain events and those brain events are caused by things that the person doing the action does not control.'
- 'None of us wants to be free in the sense that your actions are unconnected and indifferent to your character and feelings.'
- 'Thoughts are not governed by causes, but by rules. To think about football is to follow the rules of football conversations – to analyse goals, assess tactics, etc. This is about explanations and reasons, not causes.'
- 'The future state of affairs does not cause your action, but your feelings and ideas about the future state of affairs do.'
- 'The present physical conditions under-determine the content of our thoughts. Descartes was sitting at home by the fire, but he was thinking about an evil demon.'
- 'We learn to follow rules as part of our social conditioning, and freedom is about following the rules or not as I wish.'

Think about

Responsibility – answers

- You chose to understand and interpret the orders and then carried them out.
- There is no God, but even if there was one, we would need to interpret the plan.

- ■ You chose the expert who would give you the kind of advice you wanted to hear.
- ■ We cannot control our genes, but whether your body is an obstacle depends on what projects you choose.
- ■ You allowed yourself to become part of the group. You can always say 'no', and imagine another kind of life.
- ■ You decide whether reason gives answers. Reason usually gives only general rules, which you must adapt to your particular situation.
- ■ Such impulses become evident in our choices and we then are aware of them. That awareness means we can allow them or repress them.

After working through this topic, you should:

- ■ understand that libertarianism requires a gap in causality, so we are the agents of our actions
- ■ understand libertarians do not claim that free will is to be identified with randomness
- ■ be able to explain how compatibilism or soft determinism reconciles causal accounts of character with free, uncoerced actions
- ■ be able to evaluate both theories.

The implications of determinism

Learning objectives:

- ■ to investigate whether determinism undermines moral responsibility
- ■ to explore whether compatibilism or libertarianism adequately account for praise, blame and responsibility
- ■ to distinguish between causes and reasons; and actions and bodily movement
- ■ to consider whether the problem of free will and responsibility can be resolved.

■ Praise, blame and responsibility

We may believe that all of our behaviour is causally determined or that it is the result of a free decision, or we may adopt a compatibilist position. This will have serious repercussions for our assessments of responsibility and the awarding of blame, praise, reward and punishment.

Think about

How responsible do you find these people? How would you treat them?

- ■ A mother suffering from post-natal depression tries to kill her baby.
- ■ Robin Hood steals from the rich to feed the poor.
- ■ A drug addict steals from a chemist.
- ■ A dog steals a joint of meat from the kitchen table.

■ A terrorist carries out a suicide bombing, killing innocent bystanders.

■ A bank cashier, with a gun to her head, hands over the money.

■ A football manager offers bribes to keep his team at the top.

It is likely that you have assessed a complex set of factors in apportioning blame. Reference to the criteria A, B and C (page 313) might help you make decisions. The reference to competencies at the end of this topic will also be relevant.

Consider these two accounts of punishment:

1 Crime is an illness and should be treated. Often it is the result of a miserable upbringing or an inadequate education. Some criminals have never been taught decent social principles or experienced proper relationships. We should ask ourselves how some people can become so depraved, and instead of punishing them with hostility, retaliation and deprivation, we should adopt a therapeutic attitude. The aim is to reform the criminal, and remedial action is necessary. Using our scientific knowledge, we should heal the criminal and develop behaviour programmes to help them become a different person. This will mean offering criminals enjoyable rewards for good behaviour and not vicious and violent punishments that only lead to re-offending and more crime.

2 People should be punished because they deserve it. This is not a matter of revenge but society showing its disapproval of the harm criminals cause. We should not try to cure people, that is a matter for the person themselves. Punishment actually respects the autonomy of the criminal, that they chose to do wrong, and society is entitled to say that they ought to know better. Whether they listen is up to them. Punishment does not try to meddle with men's minds. Instead, there is a clear, fixed penalty, known in advance, for each crime, and everyone knows what to expect. This is preferable to treatment which will take as long as it takes to heal the criminal.

> **■ Think about**
>
> Which account of punishment would you support and why?
>
> Which line would a determinist and a libertarian take?

■ Determinism

In assessing responsibility, a determinist would point to the psychological and social factors that cause crime. So instead of just blaming the individual, they would seek to address the conditions that led to crime. For example, Marx could blame theft on poverty and the capitalist ethic which promotes materialist success yet denies it to significant numbers of people. Stealing could be rebranded as an act of liberation!

But, more seriously, if determinism sees immorality as an illness, then what is left of our notion of responsibility? Generally we do not hold people responsible for contracting measles or catching flu (unless they are deliberately negligent). You are not usually blamed for illnesses, and you are given treatment not punishment. Can social conditioning be compared to germs and viruses? These are outside our control, and we are normally ignorant of their presence. But, similarly, I might be ignorant of the kind of education I am receiving. A child is probably unaware of the kind of values it is assimilating as behaviour can be often learnt through unconscious imitation and by implication. Most young children simply copy their parents and adopt their values without knowing that they have done so. Remember the term 'introjected'.

Think about

What training techniques and routines did you undergo at school and how have they moulded your social attitudes?

Does determinism undermine responsibility?

However, determinists could still advocate praise, blame and punishment as useful causes to determine desired behaviour. Praise and blame could still be attached to someone's character to strengthen the causal connection to desirable behaviour. At school, everyone is familiar with the sanctions and rewards system that trains young people to behave properly. Many pet owners use a simpler system to instil discipline in dogs and horses! A study of the brain has discovered a highly sophisticated system of neurones that are sensitive to rewards and punishments. This almost seems like autonomy and gives the impression of choice. A consideration of the delicate balance between benefits and drawbacks may seem like decision making. However, we must remember that the resulting action is actually determined by the complex experience of rewards and punishments over a lifetime.

Dysfunction inhibits autonomy

A study of dysfunctional individuals shows how powerful this early conditioning can be. If children grow up in an atmosphere of 'do not talk, do not trust and do not feel', then they will develop the trait of 'do not care'. Without the capacity to empathise with others, they will be able to be violent and cruel. If, on the other hand, a child is seriously rejected, presumably by a parent, they may develop a vulnerability to shame about themselves and guilt about events. In extreme cases, this shame means that even in adulthood, these persons will do anything to avoid rejection and become very dependent on others (Cooper, 1993). In either of these circumstances it will be very difficult for the individual to stick to principled conduct. Without cultivated emotions and skills of persevering and critical self-reflection, it is very unlikely that moral, autonomous decision making can be performed.

They should have known better

Nevertheless, to continue the illness analogy a little further, we might blame someone for undue negligence in catching pneumonia or contracting HIV. In romantic fiction, the number of heroines who wander half-naked on moors in pouring rain are to some extent responsible for their illness – or are they? Those who knowingly have unprotected sex with many partners should be blamed for contracting and spreading HIV – or should they? It may be recalled that Churchland identified sexual promiscuity with peptide-binding sites in the brain.

Ought implies can

The dilemma under discussion is often referred to as 'ought implies can'. If we say that a person ought to do something, then a precondition must be that they can do it. So if we propose that X ought to apply to university, we assume that they can because they have the necessary skills and qualifications. With regard to responsibility, if we hold someone to account, then we must be sure that it was really possible for them to do what we expected. Recently two policemen were criticised for not jumping into a lake to save a drowning boy. They were held responsible. But if it was the case that they could not swim, then they cannot be held responsible and blamed for something they could not do.

The implications for determinism are serious if all of our choices are caused by prior events. Because, although alternatives may exist, I am only ever going to choose one course of action, and I *cannot* do otherwise for psychological or socio-biological reasons. If I am actually unable to choose otherwise, it is pointless to say I ought to do otherwise. In which case, can I be held responsible? If our romantic heroines and promiscuous persons are determined to roam moors in the rain and have unprotected sex, they cannot do what they ought to do. Hence determinism undermines moral responsibility as we cannot expect people to do otherwise than what they did.

However, as already discussed, this does not preclude reward, blame and punishment as this will reform their character and cause them to make better choices in the future.

However, determinism fails to account for our feelings of remorse. To feel remorse implies that we could have done otherwise, and so we feel guilty. The determinist could explain a feeling of regret that such an event occurred, but this does not adequately convey the guilt that accompanies an act when we believe an alternative action was genuinely possible. Sartre also refers to our sense of anguish at the responsibility of choosing our projects, which implies, 'there is no determinism, man is free' (Sartre, 1948/1974).

Libertarianism

Libertarians would support the second view of punishment, as they would hold people responsible for their own actions. They reject causal determination and claim it is counter-intuitive not to hold people accountable for their behaviour. A person is the author of their actions, their decision is made with reference to their goals and purposes and reflects their attitudes to society when they make a decision. Furthermore, it removes human dignity to see them purely as a product of social and biological forces. We show others respect when we acknowledge their individual identity and autonomy and treat them as a subject rather than an object. To do otherwise, is to raise the spectre of 'Brave New Worlds', where people are genetically engineered, manipulated with drugs or subjected to thought control in order to increase happiness and social utility. Palmer (1991) cites an extract from the *New England Journal of Medicine* 1971 that is a chilling reminder of how human beings can be treated as mere physical objects.

> It is entirely possible, given our present increasing pollution of the human gene pool through uncontrolled sexual reproduction, that we might have to replicate healthy people to compensate for the spread of genetic diseases and to elevate the plus factors available in ordinary reproduction. It could easily come about that overpopulation would force us to put a stop to general fecundity, and then to avoid discrimination, to resort to laboratory reproduction from unidentified cell sources. If we had 'cell banks' in which the tissue of a species of wild life in danger of extinction could be stored for replication, we could do the same for the sake of endangered humans, such as the Hairy Ainu in northern Japan or certain strains of Romani gypsies.
>
> If the greatest good of the greatest number (ie, the social good) were served by it, it would be justifiable not only to specialize the capacities of people by cloning or by constructive genetic engineering, but also to bio-engineer or bio-design para-humans or 'modified men' – as chimeras (part animal) or cyborg-androids (part prosthetes). I would vote for cloning top-grade soldiers and scientists, or for supplying them through other genetic means, if they were needed to offset an elitist or tyrannical power plot by other cloners.

Palmer (1991)

Think about

Remember that the first theory of punishment emphasised healing. Did you find any problems with this view of punishment?

Think about

Can we react to the extract from the *New England Journal of Medicine* in any other way, except to utterly condemn it?

If you hold individuals as unique, rational and autonomous, then they are responsible for themselves and deserve the right to remain themselves. This is to emphasise what Sartre calls 'the dignity of man'.

💡 *Events and actions*

A distinction needs to be made between events and actions. Physicalism will describe mental states as physical events. Neural changes in the brain are a causal response to physical stimuli and lead to movements in the body. What this account seems to omit, however, is the significance of the event. When, instead, we talk about actions, we discuss the meaning and importance of the events. For example, Wittgenstein describes a physical event, when cycling through Cambridge, when somebody sticks two fingers in the air. Now this event could be described in the language of science as sequences of neural activity and muscular movement. But this is not just a physical *event*, it is an *action*, with purpose and meaning. Events may be random or caused, but they only tell us *what* happened. We can demand to know of actions *why* they were performed, and then there is a clear link to responsibility. We are now in the realm of reasons rather than causes, where we can praise or blame someone when we know why they did it. So we distinguish between bodily movements and their meaning. To use an example from Pinchin (2004), depending on the context, an arm raised full length in the air can be a Nazi salute, or simply a way of attracting attention.

Thus whenever there is a tragic and fatal crash on the roads or railways there are always two kinds of enquiry. The first enquiry seeks to discover what happened, the sequence of *events*, but then follows the explanation as to why people acted as they did. We examine intentions, purposes and attitudes to social rules (such as the priority of health and safety over profit), and the blame game begins.

So, for a libertarian, although we make decisions within a social, cultural and historical context, consciousness is not something that 'happens' to us as we become more complex, and decisions are not the passive result of competing desires.

In contrast, we become active decision makers as our capacity for self-reflection develops. The more we understand, the more we can evaluate. We construct 'ideal scenarios' and a '**Utopia**' against which to judge our actions. We purposely develop interactions with others to extend our experience. When Socrates said it was only 'the examined life' that was worth living, he could have added that this is when values are decided, purposes are articulated, and responsibility begins. David Cooper, in *Value Pluralism and Ethical Choice*, sums up the transition from object to subject, thus:

> normally an individual unconsciously builds the social content in his identity by introjecting the collective historical identity that makes up the content of his social tradition. In this way, the social tradition functions as a dominant 'established objectivity' that is introjected into each person. But under conditions of pluralism and reflective honest communication, it is possible that a new self-conscious ego identity can arise that can achieve a degree of detachment from these prior introjected historical roles. This allows for a new, higher level of social interaction, which is inherently self-reflective and thus self-critical. The 'ego' identity of an adult reaches greater degrees of maturity and acknowledges itself by exercising its ability to construct or hypothesize new ideal social identities for itself. At the same time the observing ego simultaneously integrates

Key terms

Utopia: a society with ideal laws and an ideal way of life. The term derives from Thomas More (1516) who set out his version of the ideal community.

the hypothesized ideal options with its past historically socialized sense of identity. Because it is built on the formal conditions of rationality, this new ego identity can serve as the basis for a new universal social identity.

Cooper (1993)

This process of reflection helps us to distinguish between the kleptomaniac and the thief, or the drug addict and the use of drugs. As we become more reflective, we develop attitudes to our desires, sometimes called second-order desires. So I may want to steal, but do I want to want to steal? I may want to take drugs, but do I want to want to take drugs?

The difference between the kleptomaniac and the thief is that the first does *not* want to want to steal, while the latter is quite satisfied with their desire and so is regarded as free.

	Free	Not free
First-order desire		Drug addiction
Second-order desire	Desire to be rid of drug addiction	

However, it needs to be considered whether this analysis differs from simply having conflicting desires.

💡 Causes and reasons

One of the key distinctions that libertarians wish to make is between causes and reasons. They admit that the physical world is determined through cause and effect, but claim that the mental world is free from causation. Here decisions are made which relate to goals or are regulated by social values, and are not just the result of passive desires but can be justified with reference to reasons.

However, is this contrast between causes and reasons as clear as the libertarians wish? In the previous topic, it was also suggested that causes are backward looking and reasons are aimed at goals that require looking forward.

Against distinctions

1 Reasons can be backward looking too. For example:

Q: 'Why did you hit her?'

A: 'Because she ruined my work.'

That is a reason rather than a cause, but it looks back to before the action of hitting.

2 Causes can be mental too. For example:

'The mention of my sweetheart made me embarrassed.'

Here there may be a whole chain of mental causes leading to a physical effect of blushing. The mention of sweetheart causes a memory to flash which causes a feeling of embarrassment that causes a flush.

3 A future goal or aim can always be reworded as a present desire. 'I reprimanded the pupil for his own good' can be recast as, 'My desire to help the pupil progress [his own good] caused me to reprimand him.'

Think about

If we allow second-order desires, does this open up the possibility for third and fourth ad infinitum? Can you clearly distinguish between first- and second-order desires on the one hand and conflicting desires on the other?

Think about

Can you explain the distinction with regard to drug addiction, and shellshock and cowardice?

Think about

Here are the cases against making such a clear distinction and then in support of it. Try to decide which is more convincing.

So can we really distinguish causes as 'how' something happened and reasons as 'why' it happened?

4 Causes can be a subject of rational enquiry and debate, e.g. scientists will debate the likely causes of bird flu.

For distinctions

1 Motives and reasons explain something in a particular way. They change something from an event to an action, it becomes good or bad or expresses significance and attitude. The Marxist can describe the onset of the revolution as:

   a 'The economic conditions alienated the proletariat and caused them to rise up', or

   b 'The workers were so oppressed, they overthrew the corrupt bourgeoisie.'

   The first describes events, the second raises moral questions of harm and requires reasons and justification, as in the case of the Milgram volunteers.

2 The more an action is described as a response, the more likely we are to say 'cause'.

   Q: 'Why did you jump?'

   A: 'The loud noise startled me.'

   Here we would talk of cause.

   If an action is a response with significance for the agent, or open to doubts, questions and opinions, we use the word 'reason'.

   Q: 'Why did you jump?'

   A: 'I thought someone was coming to get me.'

3 We talk of 'causes' when there are no alternative possibilities, as in reflex actions, but think of reasons when a variety of responses were available, as in what to do on Friday night.

4 Reasons are susceptible to rational consideration and debate, e.g. whether keeping promises is a moral imperative that should be universalised.

   Is the distinction between causes and reasons:

   a Unconvincing?

   b Clear and distinct?

   c A matter of degree?

Compatibilism and responsibility

Compatibilists argue that we are responsible because we desired the action and carried it out without interference. So causation is necessary to attribute praise and blame. We are admitting that the action was performed by me and through me. I represent the unique combination of causes (desires), and I am the causal power which led to the action. The action was not carried out 'in spite of me' but 'because of me'.

If you ask, 'Could I have done otherwise?', the reply is not 'No, because I could not want do otherwise', but 'Yes, I could have done otherwise, *if I had wanted to*'. And this would only be possible if some other cause made it so.

So, responsibility should be assigned because:

- I did it, without coercion
- I wanted to do it, even though I was aware of the alternatives.

For compatibilism

You may remember that Hume defines freedom as acting according to the determination of the will, and this would also assign responsibility. He also reminds us that we cannot offer praise or blame unless our actions stem from our character. It is when we behave 'out of character' that difficulties arise about responsibility. A 'sudden rush of blood' is often a convincing excuse from someone who is otherwise a model of good character. The link between character and action is therefore essential. Actions are only judged 'so far as they are indications of the internal character, passions and affections' (Hume, 1999).

Against compatibilism

The difficulty with this, however, is that for Hume our character is determined by our strongest desires.

Reasons are reduced to causes, and there is no active agency capable of making free decisions. But if all behaviour is caused by desires, can we really distinguish between the psychopath and a responsible adult? Both are simply prompted by desires. The same would be true of a mother experiencing post-natal depression and a cold, calculated murderess. Yet surely we would want to say that the psychopath and the mother are incapable of making a moral decision, and treat them accordingly. This point should be related to the previous distinction between first- and second-order desires. The libertarian emphasises our ability to reflect on our desires and our want to kill. Could compatibilism incorporate this difference into the theory?

Furthermore, Hume's account of blame, praise and punishment will accord with our first version: that they are devices of social engineering. Rewards stimulate good character and punishment and fear act similarly to repress antisocial traits. But what is missing here is the notion of **desert**. Whether we punish, how severe the punishment and for how long must depend on the seriousness of the crime, not on its effectiveness in changing character. Once we remove the concept of desert from punishment, then we return to the issues of Brave New World (Palmer, 1991).

> ### Key terms
>
> **Desert:** when we speak of a crime deserving a punishment, we expect the scale of punishment to be proportionate to the crime to reflect what we are entitled to or worthy of. But it might take a disproportionate 'treatment' to 'heal' a kleptomaniac.

However, can the compatibilist position be strengthened with some additional modifications? To appraise the theory, consider what compatibilists would say about the following experiment conducted by Schacte and Singer. A fuller account of this experiment is also to be found in Chapter 8 of *Value Pluralism and Ethical Choice* (Cooper, 1993).

Volunteers were told that they were going to be injected with a drug that would improve their eyesight. Instead they were injected with a chemical that would cause them to be emotional. They were then sent to one of two rooms. In the first room, everyone behaved in a very happy, positive manner; in the other, they acted angry and upset. When the volunteers entered the rooms, they behaved in a happy manner in the happy room, but if they were sent to the angry room, they acted angrily.

Schacte and Singer then conducted the experiment again, but this time the volunteers were told the truth about the drug and its effects. This time, when they went into the two rooms they did not react to the emotions in the environment. Because they had knowledge of the situation, and different beliefs about the drug, they were able to control their responses and behave differently.

Think about

- Would a compatibilist believe that the volunteers were free and responsible for their behaviour? Why?
- Would you accept that they were free and responsible?
- Is the knowledge that we receive also something that is determined?
- What is the significant difference between the first and second experiments? Could we modify the compatibilist position to take account of the differences?

View

If we were to accept that our desires and beliefs are determined and that we are only free if we can carry out our desires, we could nevertheless stipulate that part of the causal process should include:

- consideration of a wide set of background beliefs
- the ability to self-criticise or the development of second-order desires
- the capacity to consider abstract social rules
- a wide experience of interpersonal interaction, (emotional relationships) which should affect the action.

Given that all of these would be factors in a complex causal process, would these requirements improve the compatibilist theory? If a person had undergone consideration of a wide range of beliefs, had reflected on rules and personal opinions, and could use mature emotional intelligence as part of a causal chain, would the resulting behaviour appear free and responsible? If so, the libertarian account of human agency could be reconciled with compatibilism.

What do we mean by responsibility?

One approach to the issue of freedom and responsibility is to examine the way we use the words in ordinary language and, in this case, the law. Some argue that philosophers may have created problems through using words out of context, and that 'ordinary use' actually will provide a sharper awareness of these concepts and remove confusion.

So, in everyday moral language, we do allow excuses (despite Sartre) and we can identify voluntary actions. The problem of freedom and responsibility might be the result of 'an ambiguity in the expression' (Hume, 1999) – just a linguistic problem.

Put very simply, an unfree action in the legal sense, involves a diminished ability to make a proper decision and undue coercion or interference, as set out in Table 10.1 opposite.

Table 10.1 *The criteria for legal responsibility*

Criteria	
Free and responsible	**Excuses**
Knowledge of the events	Ignorance of important details
Appreciation of the situation	Emotional duress, e.g. panic
Application of principles, social rules	Lack of moral education
The ability to plan action	Lack of intelligence or maturity
The formation of desire and intention	Well-meaning error of judgement
The control and execution of actions	Inadvertent clumsiness

Thus in practical, everyday use of language, we are quite capable of subtle and fine judgements about freedom and responsibility.

Think about

Regina v Finney

Consider the following case study, *Regina* v *Finney*, used by Austin in his essay *A Plea for Excuses*. Try to decide whether the defendant acted freely and was responsible for the death of the patient.

Shrewsbury Assizes, 1874

12 Cox 625.

Prisoner was indicted for the manslaughter of Thomas Watkins.

The Prisoner was an attendant at a lunatic asylum. Being in charge of a lunatic, who was bathing, he turned on hot water into the bath, and thereby scalded him to death. The facts appeared to be truly set forth in the statement of the prisoner made before the committing magistrate, as follows: 'I had bathed Watkins, and had loosed the bath out. I intended putting in a clean bath, and asked Watkins if he would get out. At this time my attention was drawn to the next bath by the new attendant, who was asking me a question; and my attention was taken from the bath where Watkins was. I put my hand down to turn water on in the bath where Thomas Watkins was. I did not intend to turn on the hot water, and I made a mistake in the tap. I did not know what I had done until I heard Thomas Watkins shout out; and I did not find my mistake out till I saw the steam from the water. You cannot get water in this bath when they are drawing water at the other bath; but at other times it shoots out like a water gun when the other baths are not in use ...'

(It was proved that the lunatic had such possession of his faculties as would enable him to understand what was said to him, and to get out of the bath.)

A. Young (for Prisoner). The death resulted from accident. There was no such culpable negligence on the part of the prisoner as will support this indictment. A culpable mistake, or some degree of culpable negligence, causing death, will not support a charge of manslaughter; unless the negligence be so gross as to be reckless. (*R* v *Noakes*)

> Lush, F. To render a person liable for neglect of duty there must be such a degree of culpability as to amount to gross negligence on his part. If you accept the prisoner's own statement, you find no such amount of negligence as would come within this definition. It is not every little trip or mistake that will make a man so liable. It was the duty of the attendant not to let hot water into the bath while the patient was therein. According to the prisoner's own account, he did not believe that he was letting the hot water in while the deceased remained there. The lunatic was, we have heard, a man capable of getting out by himself and of understanding what was said to him. He was told to get out. A new attendant who had come on this day, was at an adjoining bath and he took off the prisoner's attention. Now, if the prisoner, knowing that the man was in the bath, had turned on the tap, and turned on the hot instead of the cold water, I should have said there was gross negligence; for he ought to have looked to see. But from his own account he had told the deceased to get out, and thought he had got out. If you think that indicates gross carelessness, then you should find the prisoner guilty of manslaughter. But if you think it inadvertence not amounting to culpability – i.e., what is properly termed an accident – then the prisoner is not liable.

Austin (1964)

Can you decide from the criteria above how free and responsible the defendant was?

The verdict is given at the end of this topic.

Austin comments:

> (8ff.) Both counsel and judge make very free use of a large number of terms of excuse, using several as though they were, and even stating them to be, indifferent or equivalent when they are not, and presenting as alternatives those that are not.
>
> Furthermore, it is clear from ordinary use that we accept degrees of freedom and responsibility, it is not all or nothing. We assess people's justifications for what they do, we measure degrees of inconsiderateness, emotional duress and knowledge, and pronounce verdicts of '***mitigated responsibility***' and qualified praise or blame. In this sense, freedom is not so much a quality of an action, that is either present or not present, but is more a dimension in which actions are assessed, as a matter of degree according to the criteria above.

Austin (1964)

Key terms

Mitigated responsibility: the degree of responsibility is reduced.

Volition: a mental event initiating action. To will.

Can the problem of free will and responsibility be dissolved?

Some philosophers contend that the problems we have been discussing hinge on two misunderstandings:

- a fallacious account of mind and particularly 'willing': Ryle (1949) calls it 'the myth of **volitions**' a confusion over what is meant by causation: Ryle calls this 'the bogey of mechanism'.

The myth of volitions

Following Descartes and others, it is argued that we have a theory of mind that is a 'category mistake' (Ryle, topic 2). It begins with the notion of mind as an inner life, perhaps an immaterial substance, which has different faculties. One is the cognitive mode, which acquired knowledge, and one is the faculty of will, where one performs special acts in the mind in order to trigger action. So in order to pull the trigger, there is a special act of 'willing to pull the trigger', and the free will debate has been over whether this mental act is caused or an exercise of the power of free decision making.

The alternative position is to deny that there is any specific mental act at all. There is no private volition going on in our heads prior to the act which makes it free or not: 'When I raise my arm voluntarily, I do not use any instrument to bring it about' (Wittgenstein, 1968, part I, p615).

There are in fact only actions: 'Willing, if it is not to be a sort of wishful thinking, must be the action itself. It cannot be allowed to stop anywhere short of the action' (Wittgenstein, 1968, part I, p615).

So what account can be given of free will and responsibility if we deny special, mental acts of willing? Ryle maintains that it is *how* one performs the act which tells us whether it is free. He employs the terms 'voluntary' and 'non-voluntary'. An act is voluntary (i.e. I willed it), because firstly I did it, and secondly I was aware of doing it and I took no action to stop doing it. It is the character of the action that tells us it was free rather than a separate, private, prior act happening in a mysterious realm.

To elaborate, we can decide if someone is acting freely and is therefore responsible if 'they could have done otherwise' but did not. To ensure 'they could have done otherwise' is meaningful, we need to establish a number of **competencies**, such as:

- they were aware of alternative choices
- they have performed such acts in the past
- they were mature and knowledgeable enough to choose any number of actions
- they did or did not exercise some of their knowledge
- they did not act under duress, coercion, etc.

If these competencies are satisfied, or not, then the action is deemed free and responsible, or not. To use Austin's term above, this is the 'dimension in which actions' are assessed.

For example, 'the Bad Samaritan' walked past an injured person lying in the road. They were aware that they could stop and help, they have helped other people in the past, they know about social expectations and the law about attending accidents, and they did not exercise that knowledge even though they could have and were not under duress. The act is therefore deemed a voluntary one for which they are responsible.

Thus the debate over whether desires cause actions, or reason has a special power is dissolved. We know if something is desired as a result of the way the action was performed; we know the action was reasonable because it can be related to goals and justified. You will remember that this point is raised by Sartre ('What is free will?' above). Do you remember Sartre's claim that desires do not determine actions, they are revealed by actions?

We estimate how strongly someone feels according to the way they behave. On this model, weakness of the will is again the manner in which I behave, given my competencies. It is the opposite of strength of will – being too easily diverted from a task, and despite having the competencies to complete it, being unable to find strong reasons to continue.

The bogey of mechanism

The confusion over free will may also derive from a confusion over the notion of laws and, in particular causal laws. Hume redefined causation as regular 'constant conjunctions' rather than necessary connections. Ryle develops this with an attack on the bogey of mechanism, which is the belief that causal laws compel us. Because of the fear that mental states would be trapped in the 'iron grooves' of determinism, over which we had no control, a separate realm had to be created where special qualities of mind ensured non-causal free will, Descartes' model.

However, the problem disappears if, following Hume, we re-interpret causal laws as 'laws that admit of no exceptions'. Without any compulsion, the laws of gravity, for example, just state that certain kinds of objects will always fall to the ground. In the brain, there are certain neural responses that always happen after certain stimuli. This removes any fear of being compelled to act in a certain way, and also allows us to integrate social rules and thus free will and responsibility. You might like to read Chapter 3 in *The Concept of Mind* by Ryle (1949).

An adaptation of Ryle's example of the chess game will illustrate this. A whole variety of laws are in operation during a typical game:

1 physical laws, e.g. holding/moving chessmen – no exceptions
2 rules of the game, e.g. pawns move one square – no exceptions.

The physical movements and the movement of the chess pieces are, according to laws 1 and 2 (above), entirely predictable. There can be no exceptions without ruining the game of chess. I have to pick up pieces and I have to move them according to the laws of the game. But is the outcome of a chess game determined? Of course not, because these laws provide only the framework of the game. They do not ordain the moves or compel me to move a particular figure. They are the conditions in which we choose the rules of tactics. Within these 'tactical guidelines', options are obviously available, according to the goals of the players. If the goal is to win, there are various gambits in chess which are hypothetical – 'if you want to achieve this, then you must do that'. The goal, of course may not be to win, but to let the other player win. So in answer to the question: 'Why did you do that?' there are three possible responses:

1 the laws of motion, i.e. 'causes'
2 the rules of the game
3 the tactical guidelines according to goals.

Only point 3 is really interesting, but 2 may have to be explained; 1 will be assumed.

The same model is used in social 'games', where point 3 may involve moral as well as tactical rules. So, if you play the A-level student game, there are:

1 physical rules (no exceptions): you have to be able to get into the classroom
2 social rules (no exceptions): the teacher is always right!

3 tactical/moral rules: you have to plan and prepare work thoroughly and you must not cheat.

Normally, we only give praise, blame and responsibility for point 3, because 1 and 2 are the framework, the precondition for even playing the game. But note, you are not compelled to enter a classroom or listen to the teacher.

> men are not machines, not even ghost ridden machines ... they are men.

Ryle (1949, Ch3)

Whether you voluntarily enter a classroom can be seen by checking the competencies listed above – whether you are fully aware of what you are doing and are competent to do otherwise. But whichever way you choose, you will have to obey the laws of physics! A relevant question is whether in addition to physical laws, there are also laws of human behaviour, such as those revealed in psychology. On this model, they would be classified under 1 or 2, but that would still not eliminate 3, which incorporates the liberty of indifference and the interpretation and negation or endorsement of a situation.

> **Think about**
>
> Even writing something meaningful involves following three different kinds of laws. Can you identify them?
>
> - Physical laws ...
> - Rules of grammar ...
> - Laws of thought/genre ...

The last word

Throughout this chapter we have struggled to reconcile a dichotomy – two mutually exclusive accounts of human action:

- as part of the causal order, a product of biological and social forces, or
- the behaviour of self-aware agents, who with cognition and sophisticated emotional responses can shape the world and take responsibility.

The previous section suggests that if we redefine our concepts, it is possible to reconcile these divergent views.

Indeed, how we see the human condition is a matter of perspective and even attitude. We need a reconciliation, within a framework of causal, mental events where we can argue about meaning, significance and priority, that informs actions. Thus as soon as I develop memory, a sense of self, and a sense of others, I begin to develop value judgements: benefits, useful consequences, matters of importance. I then learn, as it were, to run programs or thought experiments to help me see myself and others.

These programs will have rules about how to develop ideas, training in specific competencies, and how to adapt to cultural and moral requirements. Adults who cannot run imaginative moral programs are handicapped and may need treatment or punishment. Children need education and socialisation to learn how to 'play' these 'games' and develop competencies. Language is the key to opening up this appreciation of others and awareness of alternatives, such as in the study of literature and personal stories. In the normal course of events, we can hold a person responsible for not running these programs, unless there was a glitch in their education. Punishment reminds everyone of their duties, but whether we employ fear or some kind of reward as a motivator is also a matter of judgement, arrived at through running more programs.

If I do not run these programs, I could be in danger of treating people just as scientific objects and certainly oversimplifying and depersonalising them. Some communist regimes and Nazi experiments in eugenics illustrate this catastrophe if we lose what Scruton in *An Intelligent*

Person's Guide to Philosophy (1996), calls 'the sacred'. So scientists may observe the events that occur in decision making, the social and biological facts. However, once we stop describing events and talk about actions, we immediately request the results of individual programs, to see if proper decision-making routines were followed. Then we engage with people and they become a subject of rights and responsibilities rather than an object to be manipulated. We can also judge to what extent their actions were free or non-voluntary, and their degree of responsibility.

Thus we have removed the chief fear of determinism, that our behaviour is entirely predictable because it must be in keeping with physical laws. Predictably, like freedom and responsibility, is a matter of degree. How people respond in psychological or sociological terms is less predictable because no attainable amount of information about our earlier states will be enough to fully predict our later response. Even if we accept that our choices are determined, the complexity of the causal connection is so delicate that a minute error in assessing our early states leads to enormous discrepancies in the prediction.

But finally, even a correct prediction does not threaten the freedom of the act. To argue otherwise is to lapse into fatalism, that your fate has already been written whatever the past. Because human behaviour is regular and uniform, I may well be able to predict what you will do after reading this topic, especially if I know you well. However, that would not detract from the fact:

1 that you acted according to your desires without coercion or restraint; and

2 you have the competencies to do otherwise, but chose to act in the manner I predicted.

After working through this topic, you should:

- understand that determinists undermine responsibility because 'ought' implies that I could have done otherwise

- understand how praise and blame can be meaningfully employed if determinism is true

- be able to discuss the distinction between causes and reasons; and actions and bodily movement

- be able to evaluate whether the problem of free will and responsibility can be resolved.

> ### Think about
>
> ***Regina* v *Finney* – answer**
>
> Verdict: not guilty.

Further reading

Cooper, D. *Value Pluralism and Ethical Choice*, Palgrave-Macmillan, 1993. Chapter 7 contains useful descriptions of autonomy, and accounts of the Milgram experiment and Schacte and Singer's experiment.

Hospers, J. *An Introduction to Philosophical Analysis*, Routledge, 1997. Chapter 5 has a delightful dialogue.

Hume, D. *An Enquiry Concerning Human Understanding*, Oxford University Press, 1999. Section 8 on liberty and necessity and section 9 on the reason of animals are very useful.

Palmer, M. *Moral Problems*, Lutterworth Press, 1991. Chapter 5 has a good introduction to determinism, libertarianism and compatibilism.

Pinchin, C. *Issues in Philosophy*, Palgrave Macmillan, 1989. Chapter 3, section VII contains a good discussion of the issues.

Pink, T. *Free Will*, Oxford University Press, 2004. There is excellent coverage of the history of the debate, and a case for libertarianism is argued by the author.

Ryle, G. *The Concept of Mind*, Penguin, 1949. Chapter 3 is the basis of the last part of the final topic of this chapter. This is a seminal work on philosophy of mind.

Sartre, J. P. *Existentialism and Humanism*, trans. P. Mairet, Methuen, 1974. This is available on the internet at www.marxists.org/reference/archive/sartre/works/exist/sartre.htm and is a good introduction to existentialism.

Scruton, R. *An Intelligent Persons Guide to Philosophy*, Duckworth, 1996. There is a thoughtful chapter on freedom.

Summary questions

1. Why does the apparent randomness of quantum particles not help the libertarian argument?

2. How does Descartes account for autonomy and free will? What problems does this raise?

3. Why does Sartre believe we are free? Is his theory convincing?

4. What does Hume say about human thought and behaviour? Are we socially conditioned?

5. How does compatibilism explain free will?

6. What would be a determinist account of the need for punishment?

7. How would a libertarian regard responsibility and punishment?

8. How can an act of free will be redescribed as an action that is voluntary?

9. How can we re-interpret the laws of causation so that the sense of compulsion is removed?

10. How would you explain that you freely attend philosophy classes?

Examination skills

The nature and content of the AS course in Philosophy

The aim of the AS course in Philosophy is to introduce students to philosophical thought and argumentation through the study of a number of issues encountered in various fields of philosophical inquiry. The topics selected for study may or may not be 'foundational' in terms of content, but they are intended as vehicles for the development of skills of philosophical analysis. While these skills can be broadened and further developed at A2 through the study of selected texts and themes, the AS course can also be seen as a coherent, rigorous and satisfying qualification in itself.

In his book *Invitation to Philosophy*, Martin Hollis notes that:

> Invitations beckon and Introductions point. An introduction should provide a sketch of a landscape and a map of the start of the main paths into it.

Hollis (1985)

Table 1 *The content of the AS in Philosophy*

Unit	Weighting	Title	Content
1 Written paper 1 hour 30 minutes	25%	An Introduction to Philosophy 1	■ Reason and experience (compulsory) ■ Why should I be governed? ■ Why should I be moral? ■ The idea of God ■ Persons
2 Written paper 1 hour 30 minutes	25%	An Introduction to Philosophy 2	■ Knowledge of the external world ■ Tolerance ■ The value of art ■ God and the world ■ The debate over free will and determinism

If this is true then the aim of the AS in Philosophy is rather ambitious: the main purpose is to invite students to philosophy, to convey something of the wonder and curiosity which inspire the subject. It is an invitation to:

- see philosophy as a way of thinking about certain questions
- search for order, meaning and value in our experience

- develop the abilities to think clearly and argue logically
- appreciate the value of an examined life.
- At the same time, however, the AS is intended to provide a pathway to further study through sketching aspects of a landscape of issues that have troubled philosophers.

The structure of AS examinations in Philosophy

As can be seen, both of the AS units are comprised of five themes. Question papers on each of the AS units will consist of five questions: one question on each theme. Each question will consist of two parts: part (a) worth 15 marks, and part (b) worth 30 marks. You will have to answer two questions on each AS question paper: each question will be worth 45 marks in total, so a total of 90 marks are available on each AS question paper. On each paper you will have 1 hour 30 minutes to answer two questions.

Notice that:

- a total of 90 marks are available
- the examination will last 90 minutes.

This should provide some indication of how to allocate time in the examination. It would be overly crude to suggest that you should think in terms of 'a mark a minute' but, clearly, it would be sensible to devote approximately 15 minutes to answering a part (a) question and approximately 30 minutes to answering a part (b) question. It would also be sensible to devote 45 minutes to each of the two questions attempted. Another way of thinking about this is in terms of outcome: your answers to part (a) questions might be given in, roughly, one side of writing whereas your answers to part (b) questions should be, roughly, two sides long.

The style of questions will be similar on both units. One of the themes of 'An Introduction to Philosophy 1', for example, is 'The idea of God'. Questions on this theme will be in the following format:

(a) Explain and illustrate the claim that if God is *eternal* then He cannot be *omniscient*. *(15 marks)*

(b) Consider the strengths and weaknesses of the ontological argument. *(30 marks)*

AQA specimen paper, 2007

A 'sister' theme on 'An Introduction to Philosophy 2' is 'God and the world', and questions on this theme will follow a similar format:

(c) Explain and illustrate **two** criticisms of the claim that the universe shows design. *(15 marks)*

(d) 'God allows suffering in order to develop our souls.' How convincing is this approach to the problem of evil? *(30 marks)*

AQA specimen paper, 2007

Notice that part (a) questions do not require you to evaluate a position, or a criticism of a position, whereas part (b) questions do require an evaluative approach. This distinction is important in that the stem commands of questions, for example the command to 'explain and illustrate' or the command to 'consider', not only indicate what an answer should contain but also offer a guide to how it will be marked. If you assess a claim in response to a question that requires an explanation and illustration of a claim you will be wasting your time because, even if your assessment is accurate and insightful, no marks are available in that instance for assessing.

■ Assessment objectives

All answers to part (a) questions will be marked against *one* assessment objective:

■ Assessment Objective 1: Knowledge and Understanding.

That is, in a question that begins 'Identify and briefly explain' or 'Explain and illustrate' all of the 15 marks are available to answers that demonstrate knowledge and understanding of the relevant issue or position stated in the question. This may involve awareness of a central debate in the selected theme, of a relevant philosophical position that has been taken, or of the nature of an argument that has been employed. So, the top band of the marking scheme for part (a) questions reads:

> Answers in this level provide a clear explanation of the relevant issues and demonstrate a precise understanding of philosophical positions and arguments. Appropriate illustrations are sharp, articulate and properly developed.

AQA Specimen Marking Scheme, 2007

All answers to part (b) questions will be marked against *three* assessment objectives:

■ Assessment Objective 1: Knowledge and Understanding.
■ Assessment Objective 2: Interpretation, Analysis and Application.
■ Assessment Objective 3: Assessment and Evaluation.
■ In responses to part (b) questions only three of the 30 marks available are for AO1; 18 marks are allocated to AO2 and nine marks to AO3.

Interpretation, analysis and application are important components of answers to part (b) questions. What is required is a focused, integrated, reasonably comprehensive and sustained critical analysis of a philosophical issue; an answer that applies relevant points and examples to draw out the implications of different philosophical positions and advances a detailed, relevant and coherent philosophical discussion. Beyond this, it is also necessary to assess and evaluate arguments and counter-arguments that have been advanced; to form a reasoned judgement concerning whether an argument succeeds or fails, or whether a position is tenable or untenable, and to justify this judgement.

Thus, the top bands of the marking scheme for part (b) questions refer to answers that are 'Focused, full and informed accounts of the relevant issues' (AO1) that 'provide an integrated, comprehensive and sustained critical analysis of the issues' (AO2) and offer a 'subtle and penetrating evaluation' and 'sustained critical appraisal of points' in order to 'advance a position' (AO3) (AQA Specimen Marking Scheme, 2007).

Examples of marked work

Part (a) questions

It should be noted that the following examples were produced, in timed conditions, by students in the *second year* of an A Level course. They are answers to a part (a) question on 'Persons'. The specific question was:

(a) Outline and illustrate two characteristics claimed to be essential for personhood. *(15 marks)*

The general marking scheme for part (a) questions is as follows.

Table 2 *Marking scheme for part (a) questions*

AO1: Knowledge and Understanding	
11–15 marks Answers in this level provide a clear explanation of the relevant issues and demonstrate a precise understanding of philosophical positions and arguments. Appropriate illustrations are sharp, articulate and properly developed. Answers at the bottom of this level are accurate and focused but too succinct: *either* the illustrations need development *or* the significance of important points is only implicit.	Level 3
6–10 marks Answers in this level *either* briefly list a range of points *or* two or more points are blurred together *or* explanation is clear but unbalanced so that one point is well made but a second is only briefly stated. OR Answers in this level will *either* clearly identify, explain and illustrate one relevant point so that a partial explanation is given *or* provide a generalised, prosaic, response lacking detail and precision.	Level 2
0–5 marks Answers in this level *either* provide a basic, sketchy and vague account *or* a confused or tangential account which may only coincide with the concerns of the question in places.	Level 1

Source: AQA Specimen Marking Scheme, 2007

Response 1

One characteristic thought to be essential for persons is rationality. Rationality can be described as the capacity for rational thought. Also included within rationality is originality. A person must be capable of original thought: that is, not simply following processes programmed into them as computers would. Rationality, or at least the capacity for rationality, is present in the day-to-day behaviour of persons. Rationality includes problem-solving. A popular logic puzzle is the case of the farmer who wishes to carry his fox, chicken and bag of seed across the river, but his boat will hold himself and one other item. When a person attempts to solve this puzzle by thinking about the problem they are showing their rationality, whether or not they actually manage to solve the puzzle.

Another characteristic thought to be essential for persons is the ability to communicate in a complex way. This characteristic was proposed by Descartes. Communication does not just include spoken language, but also written language, sign language and other forms of communication such as Morse code. Communication, or a capacity for this, is considered essential in a person because it is a characteristic showed by what most philosophers consider to be persons.

Some comments on this response:

■ At around 200 words, the response is of an appropriate length although the addition of two or three appropriate sentences to the second paragraph would improve it.

■ Two characteristics – rationality and communication – are identified.

■ In both paragraphs a reference is made to a 'capacity' for rationality and communication but it is not clear, in either case, why this point is made. One inference would be that the respondent holds that infants, for example, are at least potential persons but, if this is the case, the point should be made explicitly.

■ In the first paragraph, on rationality, the reference to originality seems to be linked to a view that computer processes are not genuine instances of rational thought. Care should be taken here to avoid the suspicion that two or more different points are being blurred together: a point about intentionality, or about a genuine 'higher-order' ability to reflect upon desires and motivations, and a point about self-creation. The illustration used could be developed a little (e.g. an explanation of what this problem is) and related to the earlier claim about computers (if possible).

■ The second paragraph, on communication, is weaker. The reference to Descartes is imprecise; the last sentence is unhelpful and, more importantly, the significance of the point about varieties of communication is not drawn out. Some humans, for example, are not able to communicate and, if one adopts a liberal interpretation of 'other forms of communication', some non-human animals may be included as persons under this criterion. It is not clear whether these are the points that are intended. Also, apart from a brief reference to codes and signs, this characteristic of persons is not really illustrated.

■ So, this looks like a level 2 response on several counts: there is a hint of 'blurring'; the response is unbalanced; there is a lack of detail and precision regarding the implications of the selected characteristics.

Response 2

Two characteristics thought to be essential for the concept of 'personhood' are intentionality and qualia. Although similar they are both seen to be distinct and essential for the concept of personhood.

Intentionality is the way that we have 'representational content' in our thoughts that allows them to stand in logical relationships to each other. In the statement 'I want to go to the shops' a person's representational content is 'the shops' and the intentionality is found in the 'to go'. This need for awareness is illustrated by the Turing Test in which both an automata and a person are put behind a screen, they are then told to carry out various actions of behaviour which exude or show the guise of (in the case of the automata) action. Although it would seem that they were both people it is clear that only the human qualifies. This is due to the fact that whilst they both carried out the behaviour it was only the human who went a step further and had the intentionality behind it. This has led to Jaquette stating 'thus mentality is an eliminable, irreducible and mechanically non-replicable property that is essential to personhood'.

The second characteristic of personhood is qualia. This is literally how something feels; it is essential to personhood as a computer can simply recreate the physical processes of our body we need to further know how it feels to call ourselves persons. This was illustrated by Jackson who tells the story of a computer that can list and recreate all the characteristics of a brain when a person sees a tomato. However, if I were to compare the results of the computer readout with my own experiences I would notice an asymmetry. This is because I have further found out the qualia of an experience as I am a person. This leads Maslin to write 'thus whilst scientists and I both have access to my brain what makes me a person is how I further gain knowledge of how it feels unmediated by any process of inference or observation based upon more basic evidence.'

Some comments on this response:

- At around 350 words, the response is quite long: many students would not be able to write as much in 15 minutes and if more than 15 minutes are devoted to writing 350 words in response to a part (a) question this may have implications for the quality of response to part (b) of the question.

- Two characteristics of personhood are identified – intentionality and qualia. Although an effort is made to adapt points to the demands of the question, what seems to be going on here is an adaptation of 'two characteristics of mental states' to 'two characteristics of personhood'.

- The second paragraph, on intentionality, is made relevant to the question insofar as it is suggested that computers cannot be persons because computers lack intentionality. Intentionality is explained in terms of the representational content of mental states and illustrated through a reference to the Turing test. However, the description of what is involved in a Turing test is vague and, arguably, it might have been more appropriate to refer to Searle's 'Chinese Room' thought experiment. The quotation attributed to Jaquette is not entirely accurate: Jaquette was describing a feature of mental states rather than talking about personhood.

- The third paragraph, on qualia, is made relevant to the question in the same way. It is suggested that computers cannot be persons because computers lack qualia, the subjective quality of experience or the 'something which it is like to' see a tomato. The implications of 'absent qualia' in humans (e.g. those who, due to brain damage for example, lose a sense of taste and/or smell) is not developed; a reference to personhood as a matter of degree or to diminished persons might be useful here. Alternatively, with reference to Jackson's original example, it might be suggested that 'Mary' was a diminished person.

- It is difficult to assess the quality of this response. In some ways it reads like a response to a different question and is likely to be seen as an 'unexpected' response to the question. However, as noted, an attempt is made to adapt points to this question, to distinguish between persons and non-persons and to illustrate the distinction. If the two characteristics identified are accepted as essential characteristics of persons then the response is likely to be placed at the bottom of level 3: the significance of each characteristic is made explicit but, particularly in the second paragraph, illustrative points could be developed with more precision. However, despite the attempts to relate these points to personhood, it is also possible to place the response in level 2 – as a 'generalised' response focused on the characteristics of mental states.

Part (b) questions

Similar issues might be raised in part (b) questions. However, as previously noted, what is required in responses to part (b) questions is a sustained, focused and critical discussion.

The general marking scheme for part (b) questions is as follows.

Table 3 *Marking scheme for part (b) questions*

	AO1: Knowledge and Understanding	AO2: Interpretation, Analysis and Application	AO3: Assessment and Evaluation
Level 4	N/A	15–18 marks Answers in this level provide an integrated, comprehensive and sustained critical analysis of the issues.	N/A
Level 3	3 marks Answers in this level are focused, full and informed accounts of the relevant issues.	10–14 marks Answers in this level provide an uneven analysis lacking precise detail or a partial perspective on the issues. Nevertheless, the discussion is directed at the relevant issues, links are present and the significance of points for the question is explicit.	7–9 marks At the top of this level answers will be subtle and penetrating and evaluation is sustained. A critical appreciation of points raised is employed to advance a position. At the bottom of this level assessment is explicit and conclusions are clearly supported, but the assessment could be more subtle or penetrating. The response is legible, employing technical language accurately and appropriately, with few, if any errors of spelling, punctuation and grammar. The response reads as a coherent and integrated whole.
Level 2	2 marks Answers in this level are either general responses lacking precision or provide a partial account that is otherwise sharp.	5–9 marks Answers in this level provide some relevant material but the links between points or their significance for the question are not made clear.	4–6 marks Evaluation is not sustained, although it is present. Evaluation may take the form of a disengaged but explicit juxtaposition of theoretical approaches or be a reasonable but undeveloped assertion. Answers lower in the level present a limited range of critical points and evaluation may be largely implicit. The response is legible, employing some technical language accurately, with possibly some errors of spelling, punctuation and grammar.
Level 1	1 mark Answers in this level demonstrate a basic and limited grasp through a sketchy and vague account lacking depth, detail and precision or through a confused or tangential account in which some points coincide with the concerns of the question.	1–4 marks Answers in this level are undeveloped or fragmentary and the discussion lacks direction. Alternatively some relevant points may feature in a tangential approach.	1–3 marks Minimal evaluative points are merely asserted and there is little or no appreciation of the critical issues. Technical language may not be employed, or it may be used inappropriately. The response may not be legible and errors of spelling, punctuation and grammar may be intrusive.

Source: AQA Specimen Marking Scheme, 2007

The following response was not produced in timed conditions, but as a homework essay. Again, it was written by a student in the *second year* of an A-level course. The specific question was:

(b) Assess whether some non-human animals could be persons.

(30 marks)

Response 3

What sort of thing is a person? What does it take to be a person? The aim of this essay is to try and answer these questions.

In order to apply any values or morals to humans and non-humans we need to clarify what constitutes a person. If it were found that some animals are persons, then surely they would deserve rights. There are many theoretical positions that describe personhood: the Cartesian idea that personhood is an indivisible, immaterial, 'thinking thing'; the Lockean opinion that personal identity exists as the connectedness and continuity of thoughts; Parfit's emphasis on survival, rather than continuity, through time and Strawson's view that the concept of a person is logically primitive. This latter claim is the belief that the concept of a person is a priori in that it is a concept that we must have if we are to be able to ascribe states of consciousness, and physical characteristics, to others as well as to ourselves.

To discuss this issue we need to be clear about the difference between a person and a man. Initially, we can ask whether all human beings are persons. Are foetuses, individuals with dementia, or those in a persistent vegetative state, persons? They are not rational, aware, 'thinking things' and appear not to be persons: they are humans without being persons. There would seem to be a difference between being a man and being a person: the former can exist without the latter.

Another question is whether all persons are human. Although this sounds similar to the first question it is quite different. This is the question of whether other, non-human, beings can be classed as persons. Whether an animal is a person can depend on what we regard as essential for personhood. Some suggested characteristics are: self-consciousness, the awareness of some degree of connectedness through time; the ability to distinguish ourselves from others, a view of ourselves as distinct; an awareness of our social being, the ability to analyse and reflect upon our beliefs and those of others; the ability to use language. These are some of the characteristics we might consider in order to decide whether animals can be persons.

Are animals self-aware? It is not possible to ask an animal if they are aware of being themselves last week. It is unlikely that animals have any awareness of time as we do. A pet dog may get used to having dinner at seven-o-clock every night but this is most likely due to its body getting used to expecting food at that time, not due to its thinking 'it's seven-o-clock, time for dinner'. Due to this it is hard to imagine an animal having any awareness through time.

Can animals distinguish between themselves and others? This appears to vary. An animal such as a cat or dog would look in a mirror and see another, not themselves. A chimp on the other hand might look in a mirror and recognize the image as a reflection of themselves. This has been demonstrated when a chimp, shown a mirror, started preening himself.

The third issue is difficult. Before we can know whether animals reflect on their beliefs, or on the beliefs or desires of others, we need to question whether animals have beliefs at all. It might appear that some do: those species that act in groups or packs, for example, often seem to follow rules. There are leaders, roles for pack members, and hierarchies. Also, species that do not live in packs seem to follow rules: a solitary cat, for example, marks its territory; another cat may not enter this territory. Whether this constitutes belief about roles or territories or whether it is simply instinctive is another question. It is difficult to assess whether animals rationally analyse their role in a pack, or think about whether they're being exploited, without feeling that you are trying to apply human characteristics to animals. It doesn't seem that animals have beliefs in the same way as we do.

Finally, there is the issue of whether animals are language users. What is language? Does language mean speech or does it also include body language and other forms of communication? If we define language as the ability to communicate intentionally with other members of the species then some animals seem to have this ability. Dolphins use clicks and whistles, snakes use body language: but are these conscious efforts to send messages to others or are they instinctive reactions? Perhaps the ability to use language is a matter of degree. Experiments have found that it is possible to teach chimps the basis of American Sign Language and those chimps use this effectively although without sophistication. Lesser animals, such as guinea pigs, wouldn't be able to do this.

Even if being a person is a matter of degree it seems to me that most animals are not persons. Some species do appear to possess some qualities associated with personhood but I don't think any fulfil all the characteristics referred to. So, while it may be true that some humans are not persons, I don't think any non-human animals are persons.

Some comments on this response:

- At 850 words it would be difficult for most students to replicate this in approximately 30 minutes.
- The brief introductory paragraph, while flagging up some central issues, might be dispensed with in examination conditions.
- The references to a range of philosophical positions, in the second paragraph, could be edited. Given the material that follows, it is not obvious that the references to Parfit and Strawson, in particular, while broadly accurate, do any real work. The views attributed to Descartes and Locke, on the other hand, are at least partly revisited and might be referred to again at the end of the essay. If a further theoretical view were required, it might have been more profitable to refer to Hume.
- The third paragraph is, arguably, peripheral to the question. It may be the case that not all humans are persons but, if this is to be made relevant to the question, it should be used to emphasise the view that being a person is a matter of degree and, due to this, some non-human animals might qualify as persons. This point is eventually made later in the response.
- The fourth paragraph is good. It is clearly focused on the question and introduces a range of pertinent issues that are followed up in the rest of the essay.
- Paragraphs 5–8 develop points in relation to the continuity of the self through time; self-awareness; rationality, the possession of higher-

order abilities to reflect on beliefs, desires and motivations; sociability and language use. Some of these are blurred together a little, and some points are rather hastily asserted, but all are focused on the question, there is an awareness of the difficulties involved in assessing evidence in relation to these points and, finally, all are used as a platform for argument.

- A position (which you may or may not agree with) is argued in the final paragraph.

The response would almost certainly be placed in the top band for all three assessment objectives: it is certainly focused on the question and also relatively full and informed; points raised are integrated, fairly comprehensive, and critical analysis (while it could be more penetrating) is sustained; the essay is coherent and a position is advanced.

Preparing for the examination

In answer to the question about how to approach the work of philosophers, a tutor once claimed that there were only three questions to ask:

- What did he say?
- What did he mean?
- Is there any value in it?

Roughly speaking, these questions relate to the assessment objectives in philosophy.

AO1 – knowledge and understanding

Essentially, this is the requirement that you should be able to give an account of:

- a position that has been taken, or
- a concept that might be central to a debate, or
- arguments and illustrative examples employed in a debate.

So, it is necessary to know who said what and to understand the concepts, arguments and illustrative examples they used. This assessment objective might seem to be particularly important in part (a) questions, in which all of the 15 marks available are for knowledge and understanding, but it is also important in part (b) questions even though only three marks are allocated for knowledge and understanding. This is because you cannot develop a critical analysis of, or assess, a claim unless you can clearly explain what it involves.

So, for example, in the theme concerning 'Reason and experience', you should be able to give an account of what empiricism involves, identifying some empiricist philosophers and the arguments and illustrative examples they employ; you should be able to explain terms like '*tabula rasa*' and to draw out the connections between 'a posteriori' knowledge, inductive arguments and contingent truths, etc.

In preparation for the examination, therefore, you might:

- construct a glossary of key theories and concepts together with brief definitions of what they mean
- learn some of the illustrative examples suggested by philosophers
- practise constructing and developing your own illustrations of similar points
- practise answering 'explain and illustrate' questions in 15 minutes.

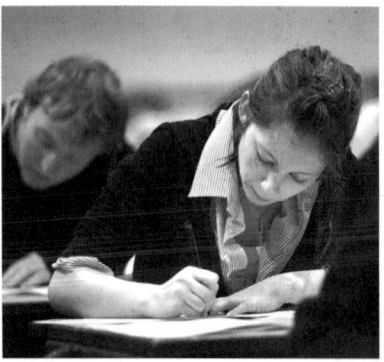

Public examinations

AO2 – interpretation, analysis and application

This assessment objective requires you to develop an explanation of why a position has been taken, what it should be understood to imply, how it relates to an issue under discussion and why, or if, it is an important contribution to a debate. This is more demanding. For example, in the above response on personhood, it is true that Parfit recommends us to think about continuity in terms of survival through time rather than identity (AO1), but what precisely does he mean by this and how might it be relevant to non-human animals?

So, for example, in the theme concerning 'Reason and experience', you should be able to advance a focused and critical analysis of relevant issues in response to part (b) questions. Relevance is important: you may know some of the main arguments that philosophers employ to argue that knowledge, or at least non-trivial knowledge, is grounded in experience, but this may not be very useful if a question asks you to write about the way we acquire concepts. Also, a critical analysis requires that you consider the strengths and weaknesses of arguments and/or illustrative examples so you should be aware of why positions have been advanced and of some objections that have been raised.

In preparation for the examination you might:

- construct notes or diagrams comparing and contrasting empiricist and rationalist approaches to the acquisition of knowledge
- construct notes or diagrams comparing and contrasting empiricist and rationalist approaches to the acquisition of concepts
- use your notes and/or diagrams as a basis to construct a response in continuous prose in timed conditions.

AO3 – assessment and evaluation

This assessment objective requires you to consider whether or not a position is tenable, whether an argument succeeds or fails and whether or not an illustrative example does the work that it is intended to. Your critical discussion of an issue should include your assessment of whether a position can be maintained or of whether an argument is successful: your view or position on an issue should be explicit, you should argue a case.

So, for example, using 'Reason and experience' again, you should be prepared to advance a position in response to part (b) questions. It is not sufficient to simply juxtapose one view against another: you should be prepared to argue *for* one view rather than another or, if undecided, to offer a balanced assessment in which the strengths and weaknesses of different positions are acknowledged.

In preparation for the examination you might:

- practise arguing for and against a view in class debates
- think about how you might counter objections raised by your opponents and how they might counter your views
- be prepared to acknowledge areas where the view you are defending is weak
- be prepared to acknowledge ways in which the view you are attacking might survive your objections.

Finally

Remember, if you find an issue perplexing and an examination on it 'testing', it is likely that others will too.

References

Anselm, *Proslogion*, trans. M. J. Charlesworth, University of Notre Dame Press, 1965

Aquinas, T. *Summa Theologica*, trans. Dominican Fathers of the English Province – Benziger, New York, 1948

Aristotle, *Nichomachean Ethics*, Penguin, 1953

Aristotle, *The Politics*, Penguin, 1962

Aristotle, *Nichomachean Ethics*, Oxford University Press, 1998

Austin, J. L. *How to do Things with Words: the William James Lectures delivered at Harvard University in 1955*, J. O. Urmson (ed.), Clarendon, 1962

Austin, J. L. *Sense and Sensibilia*, Oxford University Press, 1962

Austin, J. L 'A Plea for Excuses', in *Essays in Philosophical Psychology*, D. Gustafson, Macmillan, 1964

Ayer, A. J. *Language, Truth and Logic*, Penguin, 1936

Bacon, R. *The Opus Majus*, Kessinger Publishing Co., 2002

Barth, K. *Church Dogmatics*, T. & T. Clark, 1957

Bentham, J. *Principles of Moral and Legislation*, Mary Warnock (ed.), Collins, 1962

Benton, M. *Touchstones: a teaching anthology of poetry, Vol. 3*, Hodder Arnold H&S, 1976

Berkeley, G. *A Treatise Concerning the Principles of Human Knowledge*, 1710, may be found at http://18th.eserver.org/berkeley.html.

Berkeley, G. *Three Dialogues Between Hylas and Philonous in opposition to Sceptics and Atheists*, 1713

Blake, W. *The Complete Poems*, Penguin Classics, 1977

Block, N. 'Troubles with Functionalism', in D. M. Rosenthal (ed.) *The Nature of Mind*, Oxford University Press, 1991.

Boethius, A. M. S. *The Consolations of Philosophy*, trans. Victor Watts, Penguin Classics, 1999

Bradley, F. *Ethical Studies*, Oxford University Press, 1914

Bradley, F. H. *Appearance and Reality*, Adamant Media Corporation, 2003

Churchland, P. 'Do we have free will?' *New Scientist*, Issue 2578, 2006

Cole, P. *Philosophy of Religion*, H&S, 1989

Cooper, D. *Value Pluralism and Ethical Choice*, St Martin's Press, 1993

Cottingham, J. *Descartes*, Blackwell, 1986

Cranston, M. 'A dialogue on toleration', *Political Dialogues*, BBC Books, 1968

Critchley, S. 'Fear and Fantasy', in *The Philosophers' Magazine*, 34, 2006

Croce, B. *Aesthetic*, Macmillan, 1909.

Dancy, J. *An Introduction to Contemporary Epistemology*, Blackwell, 1985

Darwin, C. *The Origin of the Species*, John Murray, 1903

Davisdon, D. 'A Coherence Theory of Truth and Knowledge', E. LePore (ed.), in *Truth and Interpretation, Perspectives on the Philosophy of Donald Davidson*, Basil Blackwell, 1986

Davidson, D. *On the Very Idea of a Conceptual Scheme*, Oxford University Press, 2006

Dennett, D. 'Can Machines Think?', in R. Kurzweil *The Age of Intelligent Machines*, The MIT Press, 1990

Descartes, R. *Meditations*, Everyman, 1965

Descartes, R. *Discourse on Method and The Meditations*, trans. F. E. Sutcliffe, Penguin Classics, 1968

Descartes, R. *The Philosophical Writings of Descartes*, Cambridge University Press, 1985

Descartes, R. *Selected Philosophical Writings*, trans. Cottingham, Stoothoff and Murdoch, Cambridge University Press, 1988

Descartes, R. *Discourse on Method and the Meditations*, trans. F. E. Sutcliffe, Penguin, 2007

Dirac, P. 'The Evolution of the Physicists Picture of Nature', *Scientific American*, May 1963

Dore, C. 'Ontological Arguments', in P. L. Quin and C. Taliaferro (eds) *A Companion to Philosophy of Religion*, Blackwell, 1977

Dostoevsky, F. *Crime and Punishment*, trans. L. Volokhonsky, Everyman, 1993

Dostoevsky, F. *The Brothers Karamazov*, trans. D. McDuff, Penguin Classics, 1993

Durkheim, E. *Elementary Forms of Religious Life*, trans. Carol Cosman, Oxford University Press, 2000

Durrant, W. *The Story of Philosophy*, Washington Press, 1926

Engels, F. *The Origin of the Family, Private Property and the State*, International Publishers, 1942

Engels, F. *The Conditions of the Working Class in England*, Henderson and Chaloner, 1958

Feuerbach, L. *The Essence of Christianity*, Prometheus Books, 1999

Foot, P. *Theories of Ethics*, Oxford University Press, 1967

Forst, R. 'Toleration, Justice and Reason', in C. McKinnon and D. Castiglione (eds) *The Culture of Toleration in Diverse Societies*, Manchester University Press, 2003

Freeman, K. *Ancilla to the Pre-Socratic Philosophers: a complete translation of the Fragments in Dies, 'Fragmente der Vorsokratiker'*, Blackwell, 1948

Frege, G. 'The Thought: a logical enquiry', in P. Strawson (ed.) *Philosophical Logic*, Oxford University Press, 1967

Freud, S. *The Standard Edition of the Complete Psychological Works of Sigmund Freud*, Hogarth Press, 1957

Gaita, R. *The Philosopher's Dog*, Routledge, 2003

Galileo, *Dialogue Concerning Two Chief World Systems*, University of California Press, 1967

Gallie, W. B. 'Essentially Contested Concepts', in his *Philosophy and the Historical Understanding*, 2nd edn, Schocken Books, 1968

Galton, F. *Inquiries into Human Faculty and its Development*, Adamant Media Corporation, 2000

Gaunilo, 'A response on behalf of the fool', *Anselm's Basic Writings*, Open Court Publishing Company, 1962

Gaus, G. *Political Concepts and Political Theories*, Westview Press, 2000

Glover, J. *I: the philosophy and psychology of personal identity*, Penguin Books, 1991

Golding, W. *Lord of the Flies*, Faber, 1954

Gombrich, E. H. *Art and Illusion*, Phaidon Press, 2002

Graham, G. *The Philosophy of Mind: an introduction*, Blackwell, 1998

Hacking, I. *Representing and Intervening: introductory topics in the philosophy of natural science* Cambridge University Press, 1983

Hamilton, C. *Understanding Philosophy for AS level: AQA*, Nelson Thornes, 2003

Hari, J. 'Free speech must apply even to the odious', *The Independent*, 9 July 2007

Heidegger, M. *Being and Time*, Wiley-Blackwell, 1978

Hick, J. *Evil and the God of Love*, Fontana, 1966

Hobbes, T. *Leviathan*, Penguin Classics, 1982

Holland, R. F. *Against Empiricism: on education, epistemology, and value*, Barnes and Noble Books – Imports division of Rowman & Littlefield Publishers, 1980

Hollis, M. *Invitation to Philosophy*, Basil Blackwell, 1985

Hospers, J. *An Introduction to Philosophical Analysis*, Routledge, 1956

Hume, D. 'Of the Original Contract', in Ernest Barker (ed.), *Social Contract: essays by Locke, Hume and Rousseau*, Oxford University Press, 1947a

Hume, D. 'Moral and Political Essays', in Ernest Barker (ed.), *Social Contract: Essays by Locke, Hume and Rousseau*, Oxford University Press, 1947b

Hume, D. (1751) *A Treatise of Human Nature*, Ernest Mossner (ed.), Penguin Books, 1969

Hume, D. (1757) *A Treatise of Human Nature*, 2nd edn, L. A. Selby-Bigge and P. H. Nidditch (eds), Oxford University Press, 1978

Hume, D. *Dialogues Concerning Natural Religion*, Penguin Classics, 1990

Hume, D. *An Enquiry Concerning Human Understanding*, T. L. Beauchamp (ed.), Oxford University Press, 1999

Kant, I. *Critique of Pure Reason*, 2nd edn, trans. J. M. D. Meiklejohn, J. M. Dent & Sons Ltd, 1934

Kant, I. *Groundwork of the Metaphysics of Morals*, Cambridge, 1993

Kant, I. *Critique of Judgement*, trans. P. Guyer and E. Matthews, Cambridge University Press, 2000

Kierkegaard, S. *Philosophical Fragments*, Princeton University Press, 1985

Korsmeyer, C. (ed.) *Aesthetics: the big questions*, Blackwell, 1998

Kundera, M. *The Book of Laughter and Forgetting*, trans. M. H. Heim, Penguin Books, 1980

Lawler, J. *The Simpsons and Philosophy*, Open Court, 2001

Leader, 'Common sense and sensibilities', *The Guardian*, 30 September 2006

Leibniz, G. W. *Preface to the New Essays*, 2nd edn, Cambridge University Press, 1996a

Leibniz, G. W. *Principles of Nature and Grace*, 2nd edn, Cambridge University Press, 1996b

Leibniz, G. W. *Monadology*, trans. R. S. Woolhouse and Richard Francks, in R. S. Woolhouse and R. Francks (eds) *G.W. Leibniz: philosophical texts*, Oxford University Press, 1998

Leiter, B. *Routledge Philosophy Guidebook to Nietzsche on Morality*, Routledge, 2002

Locke, J. *An Essay Concerning Human Understanding*, 1690, at http://arts.cuhk.edu.hk/Philosophy/Locke/echu/

Locke, J. 'An Essay Concerning the True Original Extent and end of Civil Government', in Sir Ernest Barker (ed), *Social Contract*, Oxford University Press, 1947

Locke, J. *An Essay Concerning Human Understanding*, A. D. Woozley (ed.), Fontana/Collins, 1964

Locke, J. *Letter Concerning Toleration*, Hackett, 1983

MacKinnon, C. 'Only Words', extract in M. Rosen and J. Wolff (eds) *Political Thought*, Oxford University Press, 1999

MacKinnon, C. 'Are Women Human?', *The Guardian*, 12 April 2006

Maimonides, M. *The Guide of the Perplexed*, trans. C. Rabin, Hackett, 1995

Malcolm, N. 'Anselm's Ontological Argument', *Philosophical Review*, 69, pp141–62, 1960

Mansfield, R. *The Storytellers*, Schofield and Sims Ltd, 1971

Marcuse, H. 'Repressive Tolerance', in *A Critique of Pure Tolerance*, Cape Editions, 1969a

Marcuse, H. *Eros and Civilisation*, 2nd edn, The Beacon Press, 1969b

Marcuse, H. *Counter Revolution and Revolt*, The Beacon Press, 1972

Marx, K. *Critique of Hegel's Philosophy of Right*, trans. Annette Jolin and Joseph O'Malley, Cambridge University Press, 1970a

Marx, K. and Engels, F. *The German Ideology*, Lawrence and Wishart, 1970b

Marx, K. *The Communist Manifesto*, Penguin, 1976

Mendus, S. *Toleration and the Limits of Liberalism*, Humanities Press, 1989

Merleau-Ponty, M. *Phenomenology of Perception*, trans. C. Smith, Routledge, 2002

Mill, J. S. *Utilitarianism*, M. Warnock (ed.), Fontana/Collins, 1962

Mill, J. S. *On Liberty*, Gertrude Himmelfarb (ed.), Penguin Books, 1985

Mitchell, B. *Philosophy of Religion*, Oxford University Press, 1971

Moore, G. *Philosophical Papers*, Allen and Unwin, 1959

Moore, G. *Principia Ethica*, Cambridge University Press, 1968

Mosley, N. *Catastrophe Practice*, Secker and Warburg, 1979–90

Nietzsche, F. *Beyond Good and Evil*, trans. Marion Faber (ed.), Oxford University Press, 1998

Norman, R. *The Moral Philosophers: an introduction to ethics*, Oxford University Press, 1998

Orwell, G. *Animal Farm*, Penguin, 1945

Orwell, G. Nineteen Eighty-Four, Penguin, 1954

Paley, W. *Natural Theology: evidences of the existence and attributes of the deity*, Lincoln-Rembrandt, 1986

Palmer, M. *Moral Problems*, Lutterworth, 1991

Palmer, M. *Questions of God*, Routledge, 2001

Pappas, N. *Plato and the Republic*, Routledge, 1995

Parfit, D. *Reasons and Persons*, Oxford University Press, 1984

Pascal, B. *Pensées*, Penguin, 1966

Pinchin, C. *Issues in Philosophy*, 1st edn, Macmillan, 1990

Pinchin, C. *Issues in Philosophy*, 2nd edn, Palgrave, 2004

Pink, T. *Free Will*, Oxford University Press, 2004

Pinker, S. *The Blank Slate*, BCA, 2002

Plantinga, A. *The Nature of Necessity*, Oxford University Press, 1974

Plantinga, A. *Reason and Belief in God*, University of Notre Dame Press, 1983

Plantinga, A. *God, Evil and the Metaphysics of Freedom*, Adams and Adams, 1994

Plato, *The Republic*, Penguin, 1955

Plato, *Meno*, trans. A. Beresford, Penguin Classics, 2005

Plotnik, J. M., de Waal, F. B. M. and Reiss, D. *Self-Recognition in an Asian Elephant*, Proceedings of the National Academy of Sciences of the United States of America (published online at www.pnas.org), 30 October 2006

Popper, K. *The Open Society and its Enemies, Volume 1, Plato*, Routledge & Kegan Paul, 1945

Priest, S. *The British Empiricists: Hobbes to Ayer*, Penguin, 1990

Quine, W. Van Orman *From a Logical Point of View*, Harvard University Press, 1980

Quine, W. Van Orman *Theories and Things*, Harvard University Press, 1986

Rawls, J. 'The domain of the political and overlapping consensus', *New York University Law Review*, 1989

Rawls, J. *A Theory of Justice*, Oxford University Press, 1999

Rorty, R. *Philosophy and the Mirror of Nature*, Princeton University Press, 1981

Rosen, M. and Wolff, J. (eds) *Political Thought*, Oxford University Press, 1999

Rousseau, J.-J. *The Social Contract*, Penguin, 1968

Rushdie, S. *The Satanic Verses*, Viking Press, 1988

Russell, B. 'Why I am not a Christian' 1927, at http://arts.cuhk.edu.hk/humftp/E-text/Russell/why.htm

Russell, B. *A History of Western Philosophy*, Unwin, 1979

Russell, B. *The Problems of Philosophy*, Oxford University Press, 1980

Ryle, G. *The Concept of Mind*, Penguin, 1949

Sacks, O. *The Man who Mistook his Wife for a Hat*, Touchstone, 1998

Sartre, J. P. *Existentialism and Humanism*, trans. P. Mairet, Methuen, 1973

Sartre, J. P. *Existentialism and Humanism*, trans. P. Mairet, Methuen, 1974/1948

Sartre, J. P. *Being and Nothingness*, Methuen, 1984

Savage, C. W. *The Philosophical Review*, 76(1), pp74–79 1967

Savile, A. *The Test of Time*, Oxford University Press, 1982

Schopenhauer, A. *The Fourfold Root of Sufficient Reason*, trans. K. Hellebrand, Cosimo Inc., 2007

Schreiber, F. R. *Sybil*, Contemporary Books, 1973

Scruton, R. *An Intelligent Person's Guide to Philosophy*, Duckworth, 1996

Sellars, W. *Empiricism and the Philosophy of Mind*, Harvard University Press, 1997

Shakespeare, W. *The Tragedy of Macbeth*, in Jonathan Bate and Eric Rasmussen (eds) *The RSC Shakespeare: William Shakespeare: Complete Works*, Macmillan, 2007

Shoemaker, S. *Self Knowledge and Self Identity*, Cornell University Press, 1963

Singer, P. *Practical Ethics*, 2nd edn, Cambridge University Press, 1993

Smart, J. J. C. *Utilitarianism: for and against*, Cambridge University Press, 1985

Solzhenitsyn, A. *The Gulag Archipelago*, Westview Press, 1973

Spinoza, B. *The Collected Works of Spinoza*, E. Curley (ed.), Princeton University Press, 1985

Spinoza, B. *Ethics*, Penguin Classics, 1994

Stephen, J. F. 'Liberty, Equality, Fraternity', in M. Rosen and J. Wolff (eds) *Political Thought*, Oxford University Press, 1999

Strawson, P. F. *Individuals*, Methuen, 1965

Sudduth, M. C. 'Is it coherent to suppose that there exists an omniscient timeless being?', at http://philofreligion.homestead.com/main.html

Swift, J. *Gulliver's Travels*, Penguin Classics, 2003

Swinburne, R. *The Existence of God*, Oxford University Press, 1991

Swinburne, R. *The Coherence of Theism*, revised edn, Clarendon Press, 1994

The Matrix, Dir. Andy and Larry Wachowski, Warner Bros, 1999

Tolstoy, L. *War and Peace*, Wordsworth Editions, 1993

Tolstoy, L. *What is Art?*, trans. R. Pevear and L. Volokhonsky, Penguin, 1996

Trusted, J. *Physics and Metaphysics*, Routledge, 1994

Vardy, P. *The Puzzle of Evil*, Fount, 1982

Waldron, J. 'Rushdie and Religion', extract in *Political Thought*, M. Rosen and J. Wolff (eds) Oxford University Press, 1999

Wheeler, J. A. *A Question of Physics*, Buckley and Peat (eds) Routledge & Kegan Paul, 1979

Whorf, B. *Language, Thought and Reality*, MIT Press, 1956

Wittgenstein, L. *The Blue and Brown Books*, Blackwell, 1958

Wittgenstein, L. *Philosophical Investigations*, trans. G. E. M. Anscombe, Blackwell, 1968

Wittgenstein, L. *On Certainty*, G. E. M. Anscombe and G. H. von Wright (eds), trans D. Paul and G. E. M. Anscombe, Blackwell, 1977

Wittgenstein, L. *Culture and Value*, G. H. von Wright in collaboration with Heikki Nyman (eds) trans. P. Winch, Blackwell, 1980

Wittgenstein, L. *Tractatus Logico-Philosophicus*, trans. C. K. Ogden, Routledge, 1981

Wolff, R. P. *A Critique of Pure Tolerance*, Cape Editions, 1965

Wolff, R. P. 'Beyond Tolerance', in *A Critique of Pure Tolerance*, Cape Editions, 1969

Wollheim, R. *Hume on Religion*, Fontana, 1963

Wordsworth, W. *The Prelude*, Holt, Rhinehart and Winston, 1951

www.bbc.co.uk, BBC News, 'Appeal over mystery amnesia woman', 4 October 2007.

Index